THE

LIFE AND EPISTLES

OF

ST. PAUL.

VOL. I.

LIFE AND EPISTLES

OF

ST. PAUL.

BY

THOMAS LEWIN, ESQ., M.A., F.S.A.,

OF TRINITY COLLEGE, OXFORD, AND OF LINCOLN'S INN, BARRISTER-AT-LAW;
AUTHOR OF 'TREATISE ON TRUSTS,' 'FASTI SACRI,' 'SIEGE OF JERUSALEM,' AND 'CÆSAR'S INVASION.'

VOL. I.

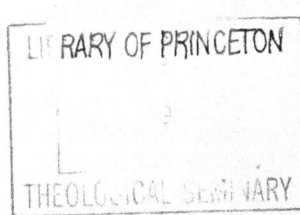

NEW YORK:
SCRIBNER, WELFORD AND ARMSTRONG.
1875.

[*The right of translation is reserved.*]

Windham Press is committed to bringing the lost cultural heritage of ages past into the 21st century through high-quality reproductions of original, classic printed works at affordable prices.

This book has been carefully crafted to utilize the original images of antique books rather than error-prone OCR text. This also preserves the work of the original typesetters of these classics, unknown craftsmen who laid out the text, often by hand, of each and every page you will read. Their subtle art involving judgment and interaction with the text is in many ways superior and more human than the mechanical methods utilized today, and gave each book a unique, hand-crafted feel in its text that connected the reader organically to the art of bindery and book-making.

We think these benefits are worth the occasional imperfection resulting from the age of these books at the time of scanning, and their vintage feel provides a connection to the past that goes beyond the mere words of the text.

As bibliophiles, we are always seeking perfection in our work, so please notify us of any errors in this book by emailing us at corrections@windhampress.com. Our team is motivated to correct errors quickly so future customers are better served. Our mission is to raise the bar of quality for reprinted works by a focus on detail and quality over mass production. To peruse our catalog of carefully curated classic works, please visit our online store at www.windhampress.com.

PREFACE.

The history of the following Work (which has engaged the author's attention more or less for upwards of forty years) is briefly this. During my college life a friend presented me with Greswell's 'Harmony of the Gospels,' and accompanying dissertations. I perused the latter with great interest, and found in them a storehouse of learning as regards the life of St. Paul, but in so loose and disjointed a shape that much further labour was required for moulding the scattered fragments into a consecutive narrative. However, I undertook the task, little dreaming upon how wide a sea I was embarking—what a labyrinth I was seeking to thread—into what ramifications the subject would branch out. I forthwith began collecting materials, and after a long interval I put pen to paper. It was a labour of love, but proceeded slowly. I could not say, "*nulla dies sine lineâ*," or even "*nullus annus sine lineâ*," for other occupations, intervening, diverted and distracted my attention; but the design was never wholly absent from my mind, and my ideas meanwhile were assuming shape. At length the end was attained, and I submitted the manuscript to an eminent firm for publication, when, to my great surprise, I was informed that they were already pledged to bring out a precisely similar work, and under precisely the same title—"The Life and Epistles of St. Paul."*

The Preface to the first edition of my Work bears date the 10th of April, 1851 —more than twenty-three years ago! There has thus been ample time for reviewing my labours, and during the interim my leisure hours have, in a great measure, been devoted to the improvement of my early efforts. I have made numerous corrections, and have also introduced much additional matter, but have endeavoured to make the

---

* I need scarcely say that reference is here made to the 'Life and Epistles of St. Paul,' by Messrs. Conybeare and Howson, which was published in numbers, the first number appearing when my own work was about half printed, and my own work appearing in its entirety when theirs had advanced about half-way.

current run still in the old channel. I have aimed at swelling the stream of the narrative without diverting it. Many errors have been expunged, and hiatuses supplied, but faults and failings still abound, and would do so were another quarter of a century to be expended upon aspiring after that perfection which is visible to the mind's eye, but can never be attained—

> "That like the circle bounding earth and skies
> Allures from far, and as I follow flies."

Time, the monitor, warns me that "the day is far spent and the night is at hand;" and I have, therefore, resolved once more on publication.

The part of the Work upon which the greatest pains have been bestowed is the chronology. When the first edition was issued, though I had applied myself with some diligence to the investigation, I was far from having sounded the depths of so abstruse a subject. No sooner, therefore, had I launched the 'Life and Epistles,' than I turned my attention with all the care and ability I could command to the adjustment of the dates. The result, after many years of study, was 'Fasti Sacri,'[1] a series of chronological tables from B.C. 70 to A.D. 70, comprising all the leading events in sacred and profane history, and supported by extracts from the original authorities, and accompanied with dissertations on the topics of greatest interest. The 'Life of St. Paul' and 'Fasti Sacri' must indeed be regarded as twin works so interlaced together, as by their very nature to be inseparable.

The First Edition was almost destitute of illustrations, and now it may be thought that I have fallen into the opposite extreme, as the Engravings, great and small, exceed 370. This profusion was not from a wish to give buoyancy to my labours by the aid of embellishment, but from a sincere desire to place the subject before the reader in as graphic and vivid a form as possible. Pictures drawn from the ideal world, though proceeding from the hands of the greatest masters, were passed over, but the pages abound with views of places and actual scenery as well as with maps, plans, and coins.

Such a multitude of illustrations could not have been inserted had I not met with the utmost liberality from both publishers and authors. I cannot attempt to enumerate the names of all to whom I am indebted in this respect; but there are some to whom I am bound to make special acknowledgment. To John Murray, of Albemarle Street, I cannot express myself too strongly. On applying to him for permission to copy some of the woodcuts in his Illustrated New Testament, edited by

---

[1] 'Fasti Sacri, a Key to the Chronology of the New Testament.' By Thomas Lewin, Esq., &c. Sold by George Bell & Sons, York Street, Covent Garden.

Messrs. Churton and Jones, he not only acceded to my request but forwarded electrotypes of such plates as I desired, and repudiated the idea of remuneration for the expense incurred in the process. To "The London Publishing Company," and to Mr. Brand, their representative, of Paternoster Row, I am greatly beholden for the leave kindly given me of selecting several views from Carne's 'Syria and Palestine' —a work deservedly popular, and presenting beautiful specimens of steel-engraving, which can be but feebly imitated by the best-executed woodcuts. To Richard Bentley, of New Burlington Street, and to Messrs. Chapman and Hall, of Piccadilly, I am also indebted for the use of illustrations in books of travel published under their auspices.

I have met with no less liberality and kindness from authors. To the Rev. C. W. King, of Trinity College, Cambridge, in particular, I should be very ungrateful not to tender my warmest thanks for permitting me to take electrotypes of numerous gems in his exhaustive work on 'Antique Gems.' To the Rev. J. L. Porter, the author of 'Five Years in Damascus,' I am obliged for being allowed to copy his plan of Damascus. I much regret that Sir F. Madden and John Yonge Akerman are no longer living to accept my gratitude for similar favours received at their hands.

From the authorities of the coin department of the British Museum I have experienced the utmost courtesy, and my thanks are due especially to Mr. Barclay V. Head, author of "The Chronological Sequence of the Coins of Syracuse," who undertook and carefully executed the task of selecting for me the most appropriate and best-preserved specimens.

Amongst private friends who have contributed their aid, I am under obligation to Mrs. Mountain for two views copied from her sketch-book, and to Lieutenant Chisholm-Batten, R.N., for assisting me in the plan of Ephesus.

Some of the illustrations have been obtained from rude sketches made in the course of my own travels; for I may here mention that at different times I have visited many of the principal scenes of the Apostle's ministry, as Jerusalem, Jaffa, Acre, Rhodes, Ephesus, Troas, Mitylene, Athens, Cenchrea, Corinth, Malta, Puteoli, and Rome. Where I did not bring away sketches I have been enabled to judge from local knowledge of the fidelity of views derived from other sources.

The Epistles have been inserted at length, under the impression that, read in their proper places chronologically, and in connection with the circumstances under which they were penned, they would be better understood, and thus convey to the reader a force which, without reference to the occasion of inditing them, might have escaped notice. They have been translated as literally as possible, and the deviations from the Authorized Version, which are not numerous, have arisen partly from an improvement of the original text by the labours of modern critics, and partly from the fact that many of the words employed by the translators have since fallen into disuse or lost their meaning, and it may be added with deference, that in some few cases the sense of the original had not, according to the best scholars, been correctly apprehended. The Notes to the Epistles are brief, and seldom either critical or doctrinal, but calculated rather to assist the narrative historically.

I now bid farewell to a work which, however it may be received by the public, has been an agreeable and instructive companion to myself for the greater part of my life.

Let me conclude with the words of our great, if not our greatest poet,—words little called for by his genius, but highly applicable to my own shortcomings:—

"What is writ is writ:
Would it were worthier!"

6, QUEEN'S GATE PLACE,
October 2nd, 1874.

CONTENTS OF VOL. I.

CHAPTER I.
The Birth and Education of Saul 1

CHAPTER II.
Sketch of Jewish History from the Death of Herod the Great to the Martyrdom of Stephen .. 16

CHAPTER III.
The Rise and Progress of Christianity to the Martyrdom of Stephen 28

CHAPTER IV.
The State of the Jews in Heathen Countries—The Conversion of Saul on his Way to Damascus 43

CHAPTER V.
Retirement of Saul into Arabia—An Account of Damascus—Saul returns to Damascus, and begins to preach the Gospel—The Jews plot against his life, and he escapes to Jerusalem and thence to Tarsus 55

CHAPTER VI.
The Call of the Gentiles—The Gospel is preached to the Greeks at Antioch—Account of Antioch—Barnabas sent thither—He brings Saul from Tarsus 81

CHAPTER VII.
The History of Judea from the Martyrdom of Stephen to the Death of Caligula A.D. 41—Barnabas and Saul take up Alms from the Church of Antioch to the Church of Jerusalem 98

CHAPTER VIII.
Saul, now called Paul, makes his First Circuit in company with Barnabas and Mark—He visits Cyprus, Pamphylia, Pisidia, and Lycaonia 113

CHAPTER IX.
The Council at Jerusalem on the Question whether the Law of Moses should be observed by the Gentiles 156

CHAPTER X.

Paul's Second Circuit—He visits Cilicia, Lycaonia, Pisidia, Phrygia, and Galatia—Paul's supposed Blindness .. 164

CHAPTER XI.

Paul carries the Gospel into Europe—He preaches at Philippi, Thessalonica, and Berœa .. 197

CHAPTER XII.

Paul at Athens—Corinth—Ephesus—Jerusalem .. 240

CHAPTER XIII.

Paul rebukes Peter at Antioch—He commences his Third Circuit, and visits Galatia, Phrygia, and Ephesus—Writes the Epistle to the Galatians, and the First Epistle to the Corinthians—The Riot of Demetrius .. 308

ILLUSTRATIONS INSERTED IN TEXT OF VOL. I.

FIG.				PAGE
1. Coin of Herod the Great	Engraved by	R. B. Utting		16
2. Coin of Herod Archelaus		R. B. Utting		16
3. Coin of Herod Antipas		R. B. Utting		17
4. Coin of Herod Philip		R. B. Utting		17
5. View of Cæsarea Philippi	Drawn by	Percival Skelton		18
6. Portrait of Augustus	Engraved by	R. B. Utting		18
7. Portrait of Livia, the wife of Augustus		R. B. Utting		18
8. Coin of Judea, struck in the time of Marcus Ambivius		R. B. Utting		21
9. Coin of Judea, struck in the time of Annius Rufus		R. B. Utting		21
10. Portrait of Mæcenas		R. B. Utting		21
11. Coin of Tiberius, the tribute money shown to our Lord		R. B. Utting		22
12. Coin of Judea, struck by Valerius Gratus		R. B. Utting		23
13. Coin of Judea, struck under Pontius Pilate		R. B. Utting		23
14. View of the traditional scene of the martyrdom of Stephen	Drawn by	W. Simpson		39
15. A Shekel	Engraved by	R. B. Utting		43
16. A Half-Shekel		R. B. Utting		43
17. A Didrachm of Ephesus		R. B. Utting		44
18. A Tetradrachm of Antioch, the coin taken from the fish's mouth		R. B. Utting		44
19. Front face of Julius Cæsar		R. B. Utting		45
20. Profile of Julius Cæsar		R. B. Utting		45
21. Roman Aureus, with the head of Julius Cæsar		R. B. Utting		45
22. Coin of Damascus		R. B. Utting		48
23. View of Bostra	Drawn by	Harden S. Melville		58
24. Coin of Antioch under Flaccus	Engraved by	R. B. Utting		61
25. Coin of Zenon, or Zenodorus		R. B. Utting		61
26. Sketch of the Site of Abila	Drawn by	T. P. Collings		62
27. Coin of Abilene	Engraved by	R. B. Utting		62
28. Coin (much defaced) of Aretas		R. B. Utting		67
29. Plan of Damascus	Drawn by	T. P. Collings		69
30. Elevation of East Gate of Damascus		T. P. Collings		70
31. View of Straight Street		T. P. Collings		70
32. Coin of Cæsarea-on-Sea	Engraved by	R. B. Utting		76
33. Contemporary portrait of Cicero		R. B. Utting		78
34. Chart of the Coast of Tarsus	Drawn by	T. P. Collings		78
35. Coin of Tarsus (Metropolis)	Engraved by	R. B. Utting		79
36. Falls of the Cydnus	Drawn by	Thos. Sulman		80
37. Coin of Tarsus (Free City)	Engraved by	R. B. Utting		84
38. View of Gaza	Drawn by	Harden S. Melville		84
39. Coin of Joppa	Engraved by	R. B. Utting		85
40. Plan of Jaffa	Drawn by	T. P. Collings		85
41. View of Jaffa		Percival Skelton		86
42. Exterior of the traditional house of Simon the Tanner		T. P. Collings		87
43. Interior of the traditional house of Simon the Tanner		Wm. Simpson		88
44. Plan of the city of Antioch of Syria		T. P. Collings		92
45. Coin of P. Quinctil. Varus, Prefect of Syria	Engraved by	R. B. Utting		94
46. Coin of L. Volusius Saturninus, Prefect of Syria		R. B. Utting		95

b 2

xii   ILLUSTRATIONS.

FIG.			PAGE
47. Coin of Agrippa I.	Engraved by	R. B. Utting	98
48. Coin of Drusus	"	R. B. Utting	99
49. Coin of Antonia	"	R. B. Utting	101
50. Coin of Caligula	"	R. B. Utting	102
51. Coin of Herod of Chalcis	"	R. B. Utting	105
52. Coin of Claudius relating to the great famine	"	R. B. Utting	108
53. The Mausoleum of Queen Helena (commonly called the Tombs of the Kings)	Drawn by	Thos. Sulman	109
54. The Entrance to the Tombs of Queen Helena, illustrating the *rolling stone* of the Holy Sepulchre	"	Thos. Sulman	109
55. Coin of Claudius, in commemoration of the conquest of Britain	Engraved by	R. B. Utting	110
56. Road from Antioch to Seleucia	Drawn by	T. P. Collings	116
57. Coin of Seleucia	Engraved by	R. B. Utting	116
58. Section of hill on the north of Seleucia	Drawn by	T. P. Collings	117
59. View of tunnel and cutting (the great culvert) at Seleucia	"	T. H. Wilson	117
60. Plan of the ancient ports of Seleucia	"	T. P. Collings	118
61. Plan of the ruins of Salamis	"	T. P. Collings	121
62. Coin of Salamis	Engraved by	R. B. Utting	121
63. Coast between Paphos (now Baffa) and Old Paphos (Palaio Papho)	Drawn by	T. P. Collings	122
64. Temple of Paphian Venus restored	"	T. P. Collings	123
65. Plan of the ruins of the Temple	"	T. P. Collings	124
66. Coin representing the Temple of Venus	Engraved by	R. B. Utting	124
67. Coin of Cyprus under a Proconsul	"	R. B. Utting	125
68. Coin of Amyntas, King of Galatia	"	R. B. Utting	134
69. View of Perga	(From J. Murray's Illustrated N. T.)		134
70. Coin of Perga	"	R. B. Utting	135
71. Plan of Antioch of Pisidia	Drawn by	T. P. Collings	137
72. Coin of Antioch of Pisidia	"	T. P. Collings	137
73. Coin of Iconium	Engraved by	R. B. Utting	144
74. Lycaonian soldier, from the bas-relief of an ancient tomb in Lycaonia	Drawn by	Harden S. Melville	146
75. Representation of Jupiter and Mercury	"	T. P. Collings	149
76. Medal representing the ceremony of a pagan sacrifice	"	T. P. Collings	150
77. Coin of Archelaus, King of Cappadocia	Engraved by	R. B. Utting	153
78. Coin of Antiochus IV., King of Commagene	"	R. B. Utting	153
79. View of the port of Attalia	Drawn by	H. A. Ogg	154
80. Plan of the port and city of Attalia	"	T. P. Collings	155
81. Coin of Attalia	"	T. P. Collings	155
82. Plan of the ruins of Pessinus, capital of the Tolistobogii	"	T. P. Collings	181
83. Coin of Pessinus	Engraved by	R. B. Utting	181
84. View of Sebaste or Ancyra, now Angora, capital of the Tectosages	Drawn by	J. C. Reed	183
85. Coin of Sebaste or Ancyra	Engraved by	R. B. Utting	183
86. Front of the Temple of Roma and Augustus at Ancyra	Drawn by	Thos. Sulman	184
87. Specimen of inscription in the Temple of Roma and Augustus at Ancyra	"	T. P. Collings	185
88. Coin of Tavium, capital of the Trocmi	"	T. P. Collings	185
89. Plan of the remains of Alexandria Troas	"	T. P. Collings	193
90. Coin of Alexandria Troas	Engraved by	R. B. Utting	193
91. View of port of Alexandria Troas, from the land side	(From J. Murray's Illustrated N. T.)		194
92. View of Alexandria Troas, from the sea	Drawn by	Thos. Sulman	199
93. Chart of Island of Samothrace	"	T. P. Collings	200
94. Coin of Samothrace	Engraved by	R. B. Utting	200
95. View westward from the foreshore of the Troad, to show that the plain of Troy was visible from Samothrace, as represented by Homer	Drawn by	Wm. Simpson	200
96. Coin of Macedonia Prima	Engraved by	R. B. Utting	202

ILLUSTRATIONS.

FIG.			PAGE
97. Coin of Macedonia Secunda	Engraved by	R. B. Utting	203
98. Coin of Macedonia Quarta	,,	R. B. Utting	203
99. Coin of Neapolis	Drawn by	T. P. Collings	204
100. View of the road by which Paul started from Neapolis over Mount Pangæus for Philippi	,,	J. C. Reed	205
101. The tomb of Vibius on the road to Philippi	,,	Thos. Sulman	206
102. Coin of Philippi	Engraved by	R. B. Utting	207
103. Gem with portraits of Octavius and Antony and Lepidus (the Triumvirate)	,,	R. B. Utting	207
104. Coin with portrait of Brutus	,,	R. B. Utting	208
105. Coin of Cassius	Drawn by	T. P. Collings	208
106. Plan of Philippi	,,	T. P. Collings	208
107. View of Thyatira, the birthplace of Lydia	,,	H. R. Robertson	213
108. Coin of Thyatira	Engraved by	R. B. Utting	214
109. Coin of Brutus, with lictors	Drawn by	T. P. Collings	217
110. Ruins in the market-place of Philippi, where Paul was scourged	,,	Thos. Sulman	219
111. Coin of Amphipolis	,,	T. P. Collings	223
112. Map of part of Macedonia from Philippi to Berœa	,,	T. P. Collings	223
113. Coin of Thessalonica	Engraved by	R. B. Utting	225
114. Triumphal arch across the main street at Thessalonica, erected in honour of the victory of Octavius and Antony over Brutus and Cassius at Philippi	Drawn by	Thos. Sulman	226
115. Plan of Thessalonica	,,	T. P. Collings	227
116. View of Thessalonica	(From J. Murray's Illustrated N. T.)		227
117. The church in which, according to tradition, Paul preached at Thessalonica	Drawn by	Thos. Sulman	231
118. A clepsydra or water-clock	Engraved by	R. B. Utting	233
119. Coin of Berœa	,,	R. B. Utting	235
120. View of Athens from the entrance to Port Piræus	Drawn by	Wm. Simpson	238
121. Plan of Ports and Long Walls of Athens	,,	T. P. Collings	242
122. Plan of Athens	,,	T. P. Collings	243
123. A Philosopher studying a roll of papyrus before a gnomon, or sun-dial	Engraved by	R. B. Utting	246
124. View of Temple of Theseus	Drawn by	T. P. Collings	247
125. View of Athens from the south, from a point near the Monument of Philopappus	,,	Percival Skelton	248
126. Gate of the Agora, or market on the north of the Acropolis	,,	T. H. Wilson	249
127. Temple of the Winds, or Clock Tower	,,	T. P. Collings	251
128. View of site of the court of Areopagus where Paul stood	,,	Thos. Sulman	253
129. Plan of the Acropolis	,,	T. P. Collings	255
130. Coin of Athens, showing Propylæa, and Temple and Image of Minerva	Engraved by	R. B. Utting	255
131. Remains of the Parthenon, or Temple of Minerva	Drawn by	T. P. Collings	255
132. Portrait of Epicurus, Founder of the Sect of Epicureans	Engraved by	R. B. Utting	259
133. Portrait of Zeno, Founder of the Sect of the Stoics	Drawn by	T. P. Collings	259
134. Portrait of Aratus the Cilician Poet, Author of the Phænomena, quoted by St. Paul	,,	T. P. Collings	266
135. Portraits of Socrates and Plato	Engraved by	R. B. Utting	267
136. Plan of the Isthmus of Corinth	Drawn by	T. P. Collings	270
137. Coin of Corinth	,,	T. P. Collings	271
138. Portrait of Lais	,,	T. P. Collings	272
139. Tomb of Lais	,,	T. P. Collings	272
140. Doric Temple at Corinth	,,	Percival Skelton	273
141. Representation of a tragic poet dictating to an amanuensis	,,	T. P. Collings	287
142. Plan of the port of Cenchrea	,,	T. P. Collings	299
143. Coin of Corinth, with representation of the port of Cenchrea	,,	T. P. Collings	300
144. View of the Cilician Gates, the pass over Mount Taurus from Cilicia into Cappadocia	,,	H. A. Ogg	311

ILLUSTRATIONS.

FIG.				PAGE
145. Coin of Ephesus inscribed with name of town-clerk	Drawn by	T. P. Collings	..	316
146. Another Coin of Ephesus inscribed with name of town-clerk	Engraved by	R. B. Utting	..	317
147. Coin of Laodicea, inscribed with title of Asiarch	Drawn by	T. P. Collings	..	318
148. Coin of Hypæpa, inscribed with title of Asiarch	Engraved by	R. B. Utting	..	318
149. Plan of Ephesus	Drawn by	T. P. Collings	..	320
150. Coin of Ephesus, with Temple of Diana	,,	T. P. Collings	..	321
151. Coin of Ephesus, with temple and river		T. P. Collings	..	321
152. Plan of Temple of Diana of Ephesus according to Falkener		T. P. Collings	..	322
153. Plan according to J. Fergusson	,,	T. P. Collings	,,	322
154. Plan according to Leake		T. P. Collings	..	322
155. Coin of Ephesus representing the Temple of Diana with eight columns in front	,,	T. P. Collings	..	323
156. Alabaster image of Diana of Ephesus in the Museum of Naples		T. P. Collings	..	325
157. Coin of Claudius with image of Diana of Ephesus	Engraved by	R. B. Utting	..	326
158. View of the great theatre at Ephesus in its present state	Drawn by	H. R. Robertson	..	328
159. Ground-plan of the great theatre at Ephesus		T. P. Collings	..	328
160. View of the remains of the stadium at Ephesus	,,	Percival Skelton	..	329
161. Ground-plan of the stadium at Ephesus		T. P. Collings	..	329
162. Coin representing a beast fight		T. P. Collings	..	330
163. Aureus of Augustus	Engraved by	R. B. Utting	..	336
164. Denarius of Tiberius		R. B. Utting	..	336
165. As of Antioch		R. B. Utting	..	336
166. A Χαλκοῦν		R. B. Utting	..	337
167. Plan of Hierapolis	Drawn by	T. P. Collings	..	356
168. Coin of Hierapolis	Engraved by	R. B. Utting	..	356
169. Remains of the Plutonium at Hierapolis	Drawn by	H. A. Ogg	..	357
170. Coin of Laodicea	Engraved by	R. B. Utting	..	358
171. Three coins of Colossæ, showing three different modes of spelling the name	,,	R. B. Utting	..	358
172. View of Chonas	Drawn by	Percival Skelton	..	360
173. Mode of threshing by oxen in the East	,,	R. H. Moore	..	387
174. Mode of ploughing in the East		R. H. Moore	..	387
175. Medallion of Laodicea with presentation of prizes at games	Engraved by	R. B. Utting	..	388
176. Wrestlers, from an ancient vase	Drawn by	T. P. Collings	..	389
177. Coin of Nero with macellum or market	,,	T. P. Collings	..	390
178. Figure of a trumpeter		T. P. Collings	..	397
179. Coin of Ephesus inscribed Νεωκόρων	Engraved by	R. B. Utting	..	411
180. Coin showing two meanings of word Νεωκόρος	,,	R. B. Utting	..	411
181. Coin inscribed Δ Νεωκόρος (4th time Νεωκόρος)	,,	R. B. Utting	..	411
182. An ædicula, or miniature shrine, of Cybele, in illustration of the silver shrines of Diana of Ephesus	Drawn by	T. P. Collings	..	414

LARGER ILLUSTRATIONS IN VOL. I.

			TO FACE PAGE
Portrait of St. Paul (*Frontispiece*)	Drawn by	T. P. Collings	
View of Tiberias, before the earthquake	,,	G. Freudismacher	16
View of Tiberias, after the earthquake	,,	G. Freudismacher	16
View of scene of St. Paul's conversion	,,	Wm. Simpson	48
View of Petra	,,	Perceval Skelton	66
Plan of Petra	,,	T. P. Collings	66
View of Damascus	,,	Perceval Skelton	68
View of Eastern Gate of Damascus	,,	Perceval Skelton	72
View of wall of Damascus where St. Paul escaped	,,	J. Watkins	72
View of Tarsus	,,	Thos. Salmon	78
View of Joppa from the South	(From J. Murray's Illustrated N. T.)		90
View of Antioch of Syria	,,	Perceval Skelton	92
View of Eastern Gate of Seleucia of Pieria	,,	H. A. Ogg	118
View of port of Seleucia	,,	H. A. Ogg	118
View of ruin at Salamis	,,	W. H. Prior	126
View of Old Paphos	,,	W. H. Prior	126
View of New Paphos	,,	W. H. Prior	126
View of Antioch of Pisidia	,,	J. C. Reed	136
View of Iconium	,,	Perceval Skelton	144
View of Lystra, showing the churches	,,	W. H. Prior	148
View of Lystra, showing the mountains	,,	W. H. Prior	148
View of Neapolis	,,	J. C. Reed	204
View of Philippi	,,	Thos. Salmon	208
View of Amphipolis	,,	Thos. Salmon	222
View of Cenchrea from the north	,,	Perceval Skelton	298
View of Cenchrea from the south	,,	Perceval Skelton	298
View of Ephesus from the west	,,	Wm. Simpson	302
Capital of Column of Temple of Diana at Ephesus	,,	T. P. Collings	324
Sculptured Drum of Column	,,	T. P. Collings	324
Base of Column	,,	T. P. Collings	324
View of Laodicea	,,	Thos. Salmon	360
View of Hierapolis	,,	Thos. Salmon	360

MAPS AND PLANS IN VOL. I.

Map of Palestine and Syria	Lithographed by	E. Weller	60
Map of Cyprus	,,	E. Weller	120
Map of St. Paul's first circuit in Asia Minor	,,	E. Weller	130
Plan of Perga	,,	E. Weller	134
Map of Asia Minor according to its nationalities	,,	E. Weller	164
Chart of Plain of Ephesus	,,	E. Weller	248

ILLUSTRATIONS IN ADDENDA.

			PAGE
Plan of Temple of Ephesus as discovered by J. T. Wood	Drawn by	T. P. Collings	xix
Specimen of an Ephesian spell or charm	,,	T. P. Collings	xx
Greek drachma, equivalent to a Roman denarius	Engraved by	R. B. Utting	xx
Portrait of Menander, the comic poet quoted by St. Paul	Drawn by	T. P. Collings	xx
Coin of Ephesus inscribed Δις Νεωκόρων	,,	T. P. Collings	xx

N.B.—The woodcuts, both those inserted in the text and the larger illustrations, have (with the exception of the coins engraved by R. B. Utting) been executed under the superintendence of H. N. Woods, to whom the author is obliged for the care and pains taken by him.

CORRIGENDA AND ADDENDA TO VOL. I.

P. 35, in 15th line from the bottom.

For "Feast of Pentecost, *March* 19, A.D. 37," read "Feast of Pentecost, *May 9th*, A.D. 37;" and a few lines after for "the fourth day of his stay, and, therefore, about the *22nd of March*," read "the fourth day of his stay, and, therefore, about the *22nd of May*." Unless these corrections be made, there will be some confusion in the reader's mind as to the dates. At p. 26 the dates are correctly given.

P. 152, note 8.

In this pedigree James, Bishop of Jerusalem, is referred to as "author of the *Epistles*," for which should be read "author of the *Epistle*."

P. 226, note 91.

The passage here referred to applies not to *Thessalonica* (as supposed in the note), but to Proconsular *Asia*, and shows that the Proconsul was attended with ὑπατικαὶ ῥάβδοι, i.e., the same number of lictors as the consuls were at Rome, viz., twelve. The passage *intended* to be cited was the one which immediately preceded the above, and is as follows: ἐξ 'Ρωμαίων ὑπείκουσι ("Ελληνες) ῥάβδοις· τοσαῦται δὲ Μακεδόνες. Jos. Bell. ii. 16, 4. As Macedonia was not like Asia a *Consular*, but only a *Prætorian* province, the Proconsul was attended by six lictors only, as here stated by Josephus.

P. 271, note 111.

Achaia was at this time a *Prætorian* province, i.e., governed by one who had been a Prætor merely, and, therefore, the Prefect of Achaia was attended by only six lictors: ἐξ 'Ρωμαίων ὑπείκουσι (οἱ "Ελληνες) ῥάβδοις. Jos. Bell. ii. 16, 4.

P. 279, note 158.

It is here stated that St. Paul styles himself an apostle in all his Epistles except those to the *Thessalonians* and *Hebrews*, but to these exceptions should be added also the Epistle to the *Philippians*, in which St. Paul does not style himself an apostle apparently because the Epistle was rather a letter *inter amicos*, than an apostolical development of Christian doctrine.

P. 314, note 24.

To the authority here cited should be added the following: Τί δὲ αἱ πεντακόσιαι τῆς 'Ασίας πόλεις; οὐχὶ δίχα φρουρᾶς ἕνα προσκυνοῦσιν ἡγεμόνα καὶ τὰς ὑπατικὰς ῥάβδους. Jos. Bell. ii. 16, 4. It appears incidentally from the above passage that in Proconsular Asia from its peaceful character no *military* force was maintained, and, therefore, the statement in the text about the *Legates* under "the Proconsul of Asia" should have been applied to the provinces generally, with the exception of Asia. Indeed, the words "*of Asia*" crept into the text *per incuriam*.

P. 322.

At the page referred to are given three plans of the Temple of Diana of Ephesus, one by E. Falkener, another by J. Fergusson, and another by Colonel Leake. In the 'Athenæum' of 20th of July, 1874, No. 439, will be found a plan of the Temple, corrected from the latest explorations by J. T. Wood. It differs little from the conjectural plan of J. Fergusson.

The platform on which the Temple stood was ascended by fourteen steps (being four steps more than those of the sixth Temple, which had only ten steps. Philo de Septem Mirac. Mir. vi.). The circuit round the lowest of the fourteen steps was 239 ft. 4½ in. in breadth, by 425 ft. 2¾ in. in length, and thus not very materially differing from the measurements of Pliny, who assigns 220 feet to the breadth and 425 feet to the length. Plin. N. H. xxxvi. 21.

The circuit of the colonnade at the top of the steps was 163 ft. 9½ in. in breadth by 342 ft. 6½ in. in length.

The ambiguous language of Pliny left it open to doubt whether the columns supporting the Temple were 100, or 120, or 128, and J. T. Wood decides in favour of the 100 columns, which he arranges as in the subjoined plan.

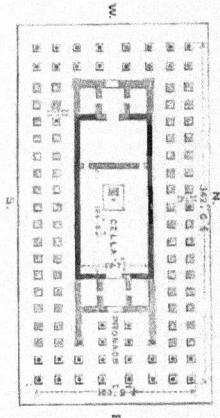

The thirty-six columns stated by Pliny to have been sculptured round the drums or bases are placed by J. T. Wood thus,—sixteen in two rows of eight each in front, and sixteen in two rows of eight each at the back, and the remaining four in the Pronaos or vestibule. These thirty-six columns are distinguished on the above plan by the dark shading. The existence of the walls coloured dark is considered as certain. The other walls are conjectural. Two columns found in situ at the sides are also coloured dark.

P. 334.

In the description of Ephesus allusion is made to the spells or charms in common use for the purposes of magic, and called Ἐφέσια γράμματα. I was not aware at the time that any specimen of the black art had sur-

vived, but I have since met with one in the French work now in course of publication, "Dictionnaire des Antiquités," and it is here presented to the reader. The original is preserved in the museum at Syracuse. It is not of metal, but in terra cotta. The date, to judge from the style of the letters, must have preceded the Christian Era. The figure in the centre is unquestionably that of Diana of Ephesus, but the inscription cannot, and was never intended to be understood. Here and there, however, there is just a glimmering of sense. Thus, in the first line, may be read something like Ἀρτεμ Φαοσ Ιερον, "Holy light of Diana," and the last letters are Αρχ, the abbreviation of Ἀρχιερεύς, or high priest. It must have been brought from Ephesus to Syracuse by some devoted worshipper of the great goddess, and used perhaps as an amulet to secure the wearer against the assaults of demons or evil spirits.

P. 336.

Reference is here made to the coinage commonly current in the days of the Apostle, and it will be seen that the Greek drachma, formerly 9¾d., was at this time of the same weight with, and was equivalent to the Roman denarius, viz. 8½d., so that in Roman writers drachmæ were called denarii, and in Greek writers denarii were called drachmæ. The following is a specimen of the Greek drachma coined in the reign of the Emperor Nero, and which should have been inserted in its proper place, but was accidentally omitted.

Obv. Νερωνος Καισαρος (of Nero Cæsar).—Rev. Δραχμη (a drachma). From a coin in the British Museum.

P. 401.

The well-known iambic, Φθείρουσιν ἤθη χρήσθ' ὁμιλίαι κακαί, "Evil communications corrupt good manners," is cited by St. Paul from the comedy of 'Thais' by Menander, and the following portrait of Menander, as handed down from the ancients, should have appeared in the body of the work.

Head of Menander, the comic poet cited by St. Paul. From Bellorius.

P. 411.

We have at this page exhibited three coins of Ephesus, one inscribed Νεωκορος simply, another inscribed τρις (thrice) Νεωκορος, and another inscribed Δ (fourth time) Νεωκορος. We now subjoin a coin inscribed Δις (twice) Νεωκορος.

Coin of Ephesus from the Pembroke collection.

THE LIFE AND EPISTLES OF ST. PAUL.

CHAPTER I.

The Birth and Education of Saul.

I.	II.
In Cydnus' clear but chilly wave	Where Tarsus, girt with greenest trees,
His weary limbs was wont to lave	Her image fair reflected sees
Great Philip's greater son—	In that fast-flowing stream—
By Egypt's queen, on Cydnus' tide,	In childhood's hour was wont to stray,
The Roman, proof 'gainst all beside,	Poring upon the classic lay,
By beauty's smile was won.	Or lost in heavenly dream—
But now, I ween, in Christian lays	He who should carry far and wide
Hath Cydnus earned a holier praise.	The banner of the Crucified.
	Anon.

It might naturally be supposed, that before the capture of Jerusalem by Titus (A.D. 70),[1] which of course led to a general dispersion of the Jews, a people so distinguished by their peculiarities from the rest of mankind would seldom stray beyond the limits of their own native Judæa. The fact, however, was far otherwise. The tribes were, from the first, of a wandering spirit, and addicted to commerce; and besides this, the tyranny of their domestic princes, and the encouragement given them abroad by Alexander the Great and his successors, and subsequently the severities exercised against them under the oppression of a foreign yoke, conspired to scatter them amongst all the nations of the earth. Scarcely was there a capital, not only within the precincts of the Roman Empire, but even over the known world, in which the descendants of Abraham were not jealously watched, as formidable for their numbers and wealth. In most cities of consequence they had their synagogues, in others their proseuchæ or oratories. In many—as in Alexandria, Antioch, and Damascus—they acquired the privilege of living under the jurisdiction of their own chief magistrate, called generally ethnarch, and sometimes alabarch or archon.[2] No wonder, therefore,

---

[1] See Fasti Sacri, p. 360, No. 2154.

[2] ἐν γοῦν Αἰγύπτῳ κατοικία τῶν Ἰουδαίων ἐστὶν ἀποδεδειγμένη· χωρὶς καὶ τῆς τῶν Ἀλεξανδρέων πόλεως ἀφώρισται μέγα μέρος τῷ ἔθνει τούτῳ. καθίσταται δὲ καὶ ἐθνάρχης αὐτῶν, ὃς διοικεῖ τε τὸ ἔθνος καὶ διαιτᾷ κρίσεις, καὶ συμβολαίων ἐπιμελεῖται, καὶ προσταγμάτων, ὡς ἂν πολιτείας ἄρχων αὐτοτελοῦς. Jos. Ant. xiv. 7, 2, quoting Strabo. So Claudius recites, in his edict to the Alexandrians, that τελευτήσαντος τοῦ Ἰουδαίων ἐθνάρχου, τὸν σεβαστὸν μὴ κεκωλυκέναι ἐθνάρχας γίνεσθαι, βουλόμενον ὑποτετάχθαι ἑκάστους ἐμμένοντας τοῖς ἰδίοις ἔθεσι καὶ

when we read that at the dawn of the Christian era, Tarsus, which was "no mean city" (being, indeed, the metropolis of Cilicia, and not far distant from Judæa), numbered amongst its citizens a multitude of Jews. Amongst them was the father of Saul, a Jew of the tribe of Benjamin.[3] From his residence in a Gentile city, where Greek was the spoken language, he was an Hellenist; but he was at the same time a Hebrew of the Hebrews,[4] or (in other words) could trace his descent in the direct line from Abraham, and had not been ingrafted amongst the people of God as a proselyte. A tradition is mentioned by Jerome, that the parents of Saul were residing at Gischala, an inconsiderable city of Galilee, and that on its capture by the Romans they migrated, with Saul their child, to Tarsus.[5] But the statement that Saul was a native of Gischala is contradicted by his own express testimony, for he tells us that he was born at Tarsus;[6] nor is there any occasion upon which, after the commencement of the Christian era, Gischala could have been taken hostilely by the Romans. If there be any foundation at all for the rumour, it can only amount to this—that Saul's ancestors had, at some time or other, been settled at Gischala, and had thence removed to Tarsus.

From the excellent education which the sire bestowed on his son, and the noble principles instilled into him, we cannot doubt that the father of Saul was a person of gentle extraction, and accustomed to move in the very highest grade of society. He was certainly a Roman citizen (for his son was freeborn),[7] though we know not how so important a privilege was originally acquired.

One hypothesis, too hastily advanced, is, that all Tarsians were Romans, but for this there is not the slightest foundation. The capital of Cilicia was a free city,[8] and

---

μὴ παραβαίνειν ἀναγκαζομένους τὴν πάτριον θρησκείαν. Jos. Ant. xix. 5, 2. So in Sardis, the Roman proprætor writes to the "magistrates and senate and people of Sardis" as follows: Ἰουδαῖοι πολῖται ἡμέτεροι προσελθόντες μοι ἐπέδειξαν ἑαυτοῖς σύνοδον ἔχειν ἰδίαν κατὰ τοὺς πατρίους νόμους ἀπ' ἀρχῆς, καὶ τόπον ἴδιον, ἐν ᾧ τά τε πράγματα καὶ τὰς πρὸς ἀλλήλους ἀντιλογίας κρίνουσι, τοῦτό τε αἰτησαμένοις ἵνα ἐξῇ αὐτοῖς ποιεῖν, τηρῆσαι καὶ ἐπιτρέψαι ἔκρινα. Jos. Ant. xiv. 10, 17. Even after the destruction of Jerusalem by Titus, the Jews, so long as they paid the poll-tax of the didrachm into the Roman exchequer, were allowed to live under their own laws; and the ethnarch, by the tacit allowance of the Emperor, had jurisdiction even to the extent of capital punishment. Thus: καὶ νῦν γοῦν Ῥωμαίων βασιλευόντων καὶ Ἰουδαίων τὰ δίδραχμον αὐτοῖς τελούντων, ὅσα, συγχωροῦντος Καίσαρος, ὁ ἐθνάρχης παρ' αὐτοῖς δύναται ὡς μηδὲν διαφέρειν βασιλεύοντος τοῦ ἔθνους, ἴσμεν οἱ πεπειραμένοι. γίνεται δὲ καὶ κριτήρια λεληθότως κατὰ τὸν νόμον, καὶ καταδικάζονταί τινες τὴν ἐπὶ τῷ θανάτῳ, οὔτε μετὰ τῆς πάντη εἰς τοῦτο παρρησίας, οὔτε μετὰ τοῦ λανθάνειν τὸν βασιλεύοντα. Origen, Epist. ad Africanum, s. 14. The ethnarch of Alexandria had the local name of alabarch: see Jos. Ant. xviii. 6, 3; xviii. 8, 1; xix. 5, 1; xx. 7, 3; and in Antioch he was called archon. Jos. Bell. vii. 3, 3.

[3] Philip. iii. 5; Rom. xi. 1.
[4] Philip. iii. 5.
[5] Paulus .... de tribu Benjamin et oppido Judææ Gischalis fuit, quo a Romanis capto cum parentibus suis Tarsum Ciliciæ commigravit. Hieron. Vir. Illust. c. 5. And again: Talem fabulam accepimus. Aiunt parentes Apostoli Pauli de Gischalis regione fuisse Judææ, et eos, cum tota provincia Romanâ vastaretur manu, et dispergerentur in orbe Judæi, in Tarsum urbem Ciliciæ fuisse translatos; parentum conditionem adolescentulum Paulum secutum. Hieron. Comment. in Epist. ad Philem. vv. 23, 24.
[6] Acts xxii. 3.
[7] Acts xxii. 28.
[8] Plin. N. H. v. 22.

THE BIRTH AND EDUCATION OF SAUL.

as such was exempt from a Roman garrison, and governed by its own laws, and enjoyed an immunity from public taxes—a privilege procured to them by the influence of Athenodorus, the Stoic philosopher of Tarsus, and private tutor to Augustus;[9] but this was the limit, and nowhere is it hinted that a Tarsian could, as such, claim the citizenship of Rome. In later years, indeed, this honour was sometimes conferred on a township, or even a whole people,[10] and many natives of Tarsus (as Athenodorus, the tutor of Augustus; and Nestor the Academic, the tutor of Marcellus, Augustus's nephew; and Nestor the Stoic, the tutor of Tiberius)[11] were possessed of influence at the Imperial Court, and might even have solicited a grant of the citizenship in favour of their countrymen; but such an assumption rests on conjecture only, and is contradicted by the fact that Lysias, the captain of Fort Antonia, although already informed that Saul was a *Tarsian*, yet inquired further, "Tell me, art thou a *Roman?*" and expressed surprise at receiving an answer in the affirmative.[12]

Another theory is, that the father of Saul had at one period of his life been the slave of some powerful Roman, and was afterwards manumitted with the solemnity of the *vindicta*, which conferred on the freedman the *civitas* or freedom of Rome; and the misfortunes of Tarsus may be thought to lend some countenance to the idea. In the civil wars, between Octavius and Antony on the one side, and Brutus and Cassius on the other, Tarsus, which had espoused the cause of the two former, was obliged on a luckless day (B.C. 43) to open its gates to the army of the victorious Cassius. Most of the inhabitants were on this occasion sold into servitude, to raise the enormous fine which the conqueror exacted.[13] The vast slave-market of Rome was supplied from the coasts of Asia Minor through Delos;[14] and the father of Saul, then a youth, may have become the property of some wealthy Roman, and may subsequently, by his own good conduct, or the compassion of his master, have acquired his freedom. At all events, when the cause of Octavius and Antony eventually triumphed on the plains of Philippi, the Tarsians (who, for their attachment to the party now (B.C. 42) the victors, had been reduced to bondage) were, by a general edict, declared entitled to their liberty;[15] and the slaves thus liberated may, with their freedom, have received the citizenship of Rome, the ordinary accompaniment of manumission, and in this instance a suitable reward for their former sufferings.[16] From the question in the First Epistle

---

[9] ὃς καὶ διδάσκαλος ἐγένετο Καίσαρος σεβαστοῦ θεοῦ, ἐφ' οὗ ἡ Ταρσέων πόλις καὶ φόρων ἐκουφίσθη. Lucian, Macrob. 21.

[10] Senec. Ἀποκολ.; Tac. Ann. iii. 40; xi. 23; Suet. Octav. 47; Tac. Hist. i. 8 and 78.

[11] Ἀθηνόδωρος Σάνδωνος, Ταρσεὺς, Στωϊκὸς, ὃς καὶ διδάσκαλος ἐγένετο Καίσαρος σεβαστοῦ θεοῦ, ἐφ' οὗ ἡ Ταρσέων πόλις καὶ φόρων ἐκουφίσθη, ἔζω καὶ ὀγδοήκοντα ἔτη βιοὺς ἐτελεύτησεν ἐν τῇ πατρίδι, καὶ τιμὰς ὁ Ταρσέων δῆμος αὐτῷ κατ' ἔτος ἕκαστον ἀπονέμει ὡς ἥρωι. Νέστωρ δὲ Στωϊκὸς ἀπὸ Ταρσοῦ διδάσκαλος Καίσαρος Τιβερίου ἔτη δύο καὶ ἐνενήκοντα. Lucian, Macrob. 21.

[12] Acts xxi. 39; xxii. 27.

[13] App. Bell. Civ. iv. 64.

[14] Strab. xiv. 5 (tom. iii. p. 220, Tauchnitz).

[15] App. Bell. Civ. v. 7.

[16] If the father of Saul was a freedman, it would tend to explain the part which Saul took in the stoning of Stephen, for the persecution arose from the libertini (or freedmen) and men of Cilicia. Acts vi. 9. Saul, as a native of

to the Corinthians, "Am I not *free?*"[17] and from the subsequent remark, "Though I be *free* from all men, yet have I made myself a slave to all,"[18] one is disposed to ask whether the writer had not been taunted with his father's slavery. The coincidence, however, must be purely accidental.

Others have supposed that an affluent fortune enabled the father of Saul to purchase the Roman franchise, which was certainly at one time the subject of traffic.[19] And had he lived in the days of Claudius, who was extravagant in the distribution of the Roman citizenship, the conjecture (as Saul's family was of high rank) would be plausible. But Saul's father flourished under Augustus, who made a great favour of conferring the Roman franchise, and cannot be supposed to have sold it for money. However, Mark Antony was less scrupulous, and could lend himself for a bribe to any act, however unconstitutional. But, even then, the objection arises, how the father of Saul, who presents himself before us as a man of high honour and right feeling, could condescend to employ means so irregular for the attainment of the privilege.

Perhaps the most feasible of all hypotheses is, that the Roman franchise was conferred on the father, or some ancestor, of Saul as a reward for distinguished services to the Roman State: not, indeed, for military prowess in the field, as a rigid Jew could not conscientiously enlist in the Roman army, but for some exertion of his personal influence in favour of Octavius and Antony, in their struggle against Brutus and Cassius. No city was more deeply involved in the political intrigues of the day, or saw greater vicissitudes in consequence, than Tarsus; and the father, or ancestor, of Saul, as a wealthy burgess, may have been fortunate enough to side with the party which eventually triumphed, and may then have reaped the reward of his zeal, and perhaps also of his sufferings, by receiving the diploma of the Roman citizenship.

In whatever previous adventures the father of Saul had been engaged, it is certain that a few years after the commencement of the Christian era, he was quietly settled in the once more flourishing town of Tarsus; and here was born to him Saul, the subject of our narrative, as we learn from himself, "I am verily a man which am a Jew, born at Tarsus, a city of Cilicia."[20] The exact date of his birth is uncertain,

---

Tarsus, was certainly from Cilicia; and if his father was libertus, Saul himself would be a libertinus, or son of a libertus. This, however, assumes that Luke, by libertini, means freedmen, which is disputed. See the discussion of this in a subsequent page.

[17] 1 Cor. ix. 1.

[18] 1 Cor. ix. 19.

[19] Acts xxii. 28; Dion, lx. 17. The facility of acquiring the citizenship of Rome varied according to the temper of the Emperor. Augustus was jealous of extending the privilege. Dion, lvi. 33; Suet. Octav. 40. So was Caligula; and even where the Roman freedom was granted to a *nata and his issue*, he would not allow the freedom to descend beyond the *son*. Suet. Calig. 38; and see Philo, Leg. ad Caium, c. 36. But Claudius was profuse (Dion, lx. 17; Senec. Ἀποκολ.), while he made the *false* assumption of the citizenship a capital offence. Suet. Claud. 25. Nero bestowed the honour on the most frivolous grounds. Suet. Nero, 12. The franchise was granted by letters patent called a diploma. Suet. Calig. 38; Nero, 12.

[20] Acts xxii. 3. If only to show how far the malice of inveterate enemies can extend, we must here make a passing allusion to one of the fictions formerly current against Saul. The calumny was spread by the Jews that he was no true Israelite, but a Gentile, born of a Greek

THE BIRTH AND EDUCATION OF SAUL.

but we may place it about A.D. 2.³¹ On the eighth day (the customary time) the child was circumcised by the name of Saul, an appellation which, ever since the days of the son of Cis, the king of Israel, had been fondly cherished as reflecting lustre on

father and Greek mother; that he went up from Tarsus to Jerusalem to push his fortunes, and there fell in love with the High Priest's daughter; that in order to win her hand he became a proselyte, and submitted to circumcision; that the lady rejected his addresses; and that, in spite, he then became a renegade, and employed all his talents to the subversion of Judaism by the establishment of Christianity. ἐξ Ἑλλήνων δὲ αὐτὸν ὑποτίθενται, λαβόντες τὴν πρόφασιν ἐκ τοῦ τόπου διὰ τὸ φιλαληθὲς ὑπ' αὐτοῦ ῥηθὲν ὅτι Ταρσεύς εἰμι, οὐκ ἀσήμου πόλεως πολίτης. εἶτα φάσκουσιν αὐτὸν εἶναι Ἕλληνα καὶ Ἑλληνίδος μητρὸς καὶ Ἕλληνος πατρὸς παῖδα, ἀναβεβηκέναι δὲ εἰς Ἱερουσαλὴμ καὶ χρόνον ἐκεῖ μεμενηκέναι, ἐπιτεθυμηκέναι δὲ θυγατρὶ τοῦ ἱερέως πρὸς γάμον ἀγαγέσθαι, καὶ τούτου ἕνεκα προσήλυτον γενέσθαι καὶ περιτμηθῆναι, εἶτα μὴ λαβόντα τὴν κόρην ὠργίσθαι καὶ κατὰ ἐπιτομῆς γεγραφέναι καὶ κατὰ τοῦ Σαββάτου καὶ νομοθεσίας. Epiphan. adv. Hæres. lib. i. tom. ii. c. 16.

³¹ Philo the Jew, on the authority of Hippocrates, the famous physician, divides the ages of man as follows:—

Child (παιδίον)	up to	.	7 years.
Boy (παῖς)	„	.	14 „
Youth (μειράκιον)	„	.	21 „
Young man (νεανίσκος)	„	.	28 „
Man (ἀνήρ)	„	.	49 „
Elder (πρεσβύτης)	„	.	56 „
Old man (γέρων)	from that time forward.

Philo de Mund. Opif. s. 36. At the stoning of Stephen (A.D. 37), Paul was νεανίας (Acts vii. 58), i.e. according to the above scale, between twenty-one and twenty-eight; and in A.D. 62 he was πρεσβύτης (Philem. 9), i.e. between forty-nine and fifty-six; and if he was (say) fifty-three (πρεσβύτης) in A.D. 62, he would be twenty-eight (νεανίας) in A.D. 37, and his birth would therefore be in A.D. 9. However, Philo's distribution of the several ages is highly artificial, and traceable to his love for the number 7, and was never adopted in ordinary language.

The force of the terms νεανίας and πρεσβύτης must necessarily be regulated by the ideal division of life in the writer's mind. One man may contemplate two classes only, viz. the young and the old, and then youth and age have the widest possible latitude. Another may be thinking of four stages—as 1, The child; 2, The young man; 3, The elder; 4, The old man—and then the meaning of each must be proportionally curtailed. That νεανίας had a vague signification, is evident from numerous instances. Thus, Herod the Great was about seventy when he died in B.C. 4 (Jos. Bell. i. 33, 1; Fasti Sacri, p. 137, No. 925), so that in B.C. 40 he would be thirty-four; and yet Josephus calls him and his elder brother at that time νεανίσκοι. Ant. xiv. 13, 1 and 3. Again, Agrippa I., King of Judæa, is addressed, in the year A.D. 36, as νεανίας. Jos. Ant. xviii. 6, 7. But he died A.D. 44, at the age of fifty-four (Ant. xix. 8, 2), and therefore in A.D. 36 was forty-six years old. Again, Agesilaus is said to have been made king ἔτι μὲν νέος ὤν. Xen. Ages. c. 1. But at that time he was forty-three years old. Plut. Ages. c. 40. So Cicero speaks of Mark Antony, in B.C. 49, as "adolescens" (Cic. Philipp. ii. 21); but Antony died in B.C. 30, of the age of fifty-three at the least (Plut. Ant. c. 86), so that in B.C. 49 he must have been thirty-four at the least. Again, Paul speaks of Timothy, in A.D. 64, as still νέος for μηδείς σου τῆς νεότητος καταφρονείτω. 1 Tim. iv. 12. But Timothy was adopted by Paul as his companion in A.D. 49 (Fasti Sacri, p. 290, No. 1738), at which time Timothy could not have been less than twenty; so that in A.D. 64 he would be thirty-five, and perhaps more. Wordsworth (Acts vii. 58) further suggests that David is called by Josephus νεανίσκος when he fought with Goliath (Jos. Ant. vi. 9, 5), and that "David was then thirty years of age;" but Wordsworth cites no authority for this, though I presume he relies upon Kuinoel, who states (Acts vii. 57) that David was "fere triginta annos natus." However, David could not have been nearly thirty, for, according to Josephus, David at his death was seventy years old (Ant. vii. 15, 2), and he reigned forty years (ibid.), and was therefore king at the age of thirty; and if so, he must have fought with Goliath long before that age. From the instances we have adduced (and they could be multiplied), it is clear that the term νεανίας is ambiguous, and to be interpreted according to circumstances. Favorinus, indeed, defines νεανίσκος as one ἀπ' ἐτῶν εἰκοσιπέντε ἕως ἐτῶν τριακοντατεσσάρων, ἢ τεσσαράκοντα ἴσως (Favorinus, cited by Kuinoel, Acts vii. 57), which gives a range from twenty-three to forty-one. Now, as Paul, at the martyr-

the tribe of Benjamin. It was usual amongst the Hellenists to carry two names —one for use amongst their own countrymen, and the other amongst the heathen.[22] Saul was not only an Hellenist, but he was also a Roman citizen, and therefore, *à fortiori*, would assume two names; and thus, while he was circumcised as Saul, the name most honoured in the tribe of Benjamin,[23] he was also called Paul, a favourite name amongst the Cilicians,[24] and the nearest approach in sound to the Hebrew appellation.[25] He was, perhaps, an only *son*, but there was certainly a *sister*, who afterwards married and settled at Jerusalem, and was the mother of a family; at least, she had one son, who, under very trying circumstances, was of material assistance to his uncle, and perhaps was the means of saving his life.[26] What other relatives Paul had, we have no grounds even for conjecture. In the Epistle to the Romans he speaks of his kinsmen, Andronicus and Junias;[27] and again, of his kinsman, Herodion;[28] but, unquestionably, in these instances he means his fellow-countrymen only, and not his own particular relations.[29]

We pass from the birth to the education of Saul. Tarsus was one of the three

---

dom of Stephen, was himself a member of the Sanhedrim (to which there was no admission before the age of thirty), and as he had then influence enough with the High Priest and Sanhedrim to be intrusted by them with an important mission to Damascus, Paul at that period must have been upwards of thirty. Again, Paul, in A.D. 62, pleads his advanced age as entitling him on that account to the favourable consideration of Philemon, calling himself πρεσβύτης (Philem. 9); and though Schrader argues that this is merely a title which Paul bore in the Christian community, viz. Signor (Schrader, Der Apostel Paulus, vol. i. p. 40), the word πρεσβύτης cannot in reason be rendered otherwise than as aged; and if so, we must suppose Paul at that time to have been not less than sixty. This view is confirmed by the Apostle's own language in the First Epistle to Timothy and the Epistle to Titus. In the latter he admonishes Titus as to the duties of πρεσβύται and πρεσβύτιδες (Tit. ii. 1), and then passes on to the νεώτεροι (Tit. ii. 6); and in the First Epistle to Timothy he draws the like line between the "widows indeed" (by which he means the πρεσβύτιδες), 1 Tim. v. 3, and the χῆραι νεώτεραι, v. 11; and he defines the "widows indeed," or πρεσβύτιδες, as those who had *completed sixty years*, v. 9. Paul's idea, therefore, of a πρεσβύτης must have been one who had reached the age of sixty; and if he was himself sixty in A.D. 62, he must have been thirty-five in A.D. 37, and was born about A.D. 2. The foregoing remarks assume πρεσβύτης in Philemon to be the true reading, but the word may have been πρεσβευτής (see note, post, on Philemon 9).

[22] Schrader, Der Apost. Paul. vol. ii. p. 15.

[23] Saul, in Hebrew, is שָׁאוּל, "the desired one," and some think he was so called as being the eldest born.

[24] Renan's St. Paul, p. 19, citing Pape, Wört. der Griech. Eigennamen, 2nd ed. p. 1150.

[25] Others think that Paul was so called from his diminutive proportions, Paulus in Latin signifying little; others, that he took the name after his conversion, as a mark of humility, being "the least of the apostles" (1 Cor. xv. 9); others, because his original name of Saul was odious to the Christians, on account of his former persecution of them; others, that Paul is, in fact, the same name as Saul, and is merely the form into which a Roman or Greek would convert the name of Saul, just as Jesus was called Jason and Dosthai Dositheus, &c.; others, that Saul took the name of Paul out of compliment to Sergius Paulus, his first great convert—the least probable of all the suppositions.

[26] Acts xxiii. 16.

[27] Ἀνδρόνικον καὶ Ἰουνίαν τοὺς συγγενεῖς μου. Rom. xvi. 7.

[28] Ἡρωδίωνα τὸν συγγενῆ μου. Rom. xvi. 11.

[29] This is evident from the way in which Paul had before used the same word συγγενεῖς. Thus, ὑπὲρ τῶν ἀδελφῶν μου, τῶν συγγενῶν μου κατὰ σάρκα (viz. the Jewish nation). Rom. ix. 3.

great universities of the Pagan world, and Strabo ranks it even above Athens and Alexandria;[30] though such a compliment may have been paid to it, not so much from its own intrinsic merits, as out of deference to the Imperial Family of Rome, who selected the tutors for their children from the literati of Tarsus. One singular feature distinguished this from the other universities—viz. while Athens and Alexandria were the resort of all the world, and swarmed with foreigners, at Tarsus there was little influx of strangers; but the natives themselves laid up a store of learning at home, and then carried it abroad, and more particularly to Rome, and there became the instructors of the rising generation. At Tarsus were the fairest opportunities of imbibing all the secular learning of the age. But Saul was the son of parents who, as Jews, would be averse to heathen literature,[31] and who felt themselves contaminated by coming into contact with Greeks, and Saul therefore could not be allowed to frequent the polluted haunts of Pagan academies. The numerous Jews, however, who resided there would, as well as the Greeks, have their own scholastic seminaries, under the auspices of the most eminent Rabbis; and Saul would be sent as a day-scholar to some Jewish doctor, with whom he would first be taught the elements of reading and writing, and at the age of five would be instructed in the Law and Traditions.[32] We can readily picture to ourselves the religious training to which Saul was subjected at home under the paternal roof. The mother had inherited from her ancestors a strong devotional feeling,[33] and the father had attached himself to the Pharisees, the most rigid of all the Jewish sects.[34] Saul therefore, like Timothy,[35] would, from his earliest infancy, be educated in a spirit of piety.

It was at Tarsus that Saul and Barnabas must have become acquainted with each other. Barnabas, like Saul, was of gentle lineage; at least, he inherited landed property, which, on becoming a Christian, he generously surrendered into the hands of the Church.[36] He was a Cypriot by birth,[37] and therefore was born within seventy miles from the famous University of Tarsus; and, under such circumstances, he would naturally be sent thither for his education, and would there meet with the congenial spirit of Saul. The two seem to have pursued very parallel courses, for we afterwards again find them together, far away from their native homes, at Jerusalem; and it

---

[30] Strabo, xiv. 5 (vol. iii. p. 228, Tauchnitz).

[31] Dumæ filius, qui ex R. Israelis sorore genitus erat, interrogavit avunculum, "Nunc mihi, qui universam legem didici, fas est sapientiæ Græcæ studere?" Tunc ei inculcavit avunculus dictum (Jos. i. 8), "Ne discedito liber iste legis ex ore tuo, sed studio ejus incumbe interdiu ac noctu. Age, igitur, reputa tecum quænam sit illa hora, quæ nec ad diem nec ad noctem pertineat, quam si inveneris, licebit tibi sapientiæ Græcæ operam navare." Menachoth, fol. 99 b; and see the other passages cited, Kuinoel on Acts ii. 4.

[32] R. Jehuda filius Themæ sic statuit. Puer quinque annorum ad studium Scripturæ sanctæ adplicari debet. Pirke Aboth, v. 21, cited Schoettgen, Horæ Hebr. vol. i. p. 89. Cum puer fari incipit, pater ejus cum eo confabulari debet linguâ sanctâ et docere eum legem. R. Salomon on Deut. ii. 19, cited ib.

[33] See 2 Tim. i. 3.

[34] Acts xxiii. 6; xxvi. 5; Philip. iii. 5.

[35] 2 Tim. iii. 15.

[36] ὑπάρχοντος αὐτῷ ἀγροῦ. Acts iv. 37.

[37] Κύπριος τῷ γένει. Acts iv. 36.

was this early familiarity between them that led Barnabas, when Saul, on his conversion, was repulsed by the Christians of the capital, to take him by the hand, and guarantee his good faith to the Apostles;[28] and again, when Saul was obliged to retire from Jerusalem to Tarsus, we find Barnabas setting off thither to seek out Saul, and bring him to Antioch;[29] and we all know how they united their labours in the cause of Christianity at Antioch, and afterwards started together on their first great circuit for the conversion of the heathen.

To Saul's sojourn at Tarsus we may also, perhaps, ascribe his intimacy with the family of Timothy. Saul had evidently, for years before his adoption of Timothy, been acquainted with Eunice, his mother, and Lois his grandmother;[40] and as Timothy was resident at Lystra, and there was frequent intercourse between that city and Tarsus (for both were situate on the high road from the East to Ephesus, and the doors of Jews were always open to their fellow-countrymen), we can well imagine that mutual visits may have been frequently interchanged between the two families.

It was a common proverb amongst the children of Abraham, that "He who taught not his son a trade taught him to be a thief."[41] And accordingly the young Saul, notwithstanding his station in life, and though destined for a learned profession, was instructed, in these his earliest days, in the art of tentmaking.[42] No manual occupation

---

[21] Acts ix. 27.
[29] Acts xi. 25.
[40] 2 Tim. i. 5.
[41] "It is incumbent on the father to circumcise his son, to redeem him, to teach him the Law, and to teach him some occupation. Rabbi Judah saith, 'Whosoever teacheth not his son to do some work, is as if he taught him robbery.' Rabbi Meir saith, 'Let a man always endeavour to teach his son an honest art,' &c. Tosapht in Kiddush, c. 1, and Kiddush, c. iv. hal. 2." Lightfoot on Mark vi. 3. "Rabbin Gamaliel saith, 'He that hath a trade in his hands, to what is he like? He is like to a vineyard that is fenced.' Tosapht in Kiddush, per. 1. So some of the great wise men of Israel had been cutters of wood (Maim. in Talm., Torah, per. 1); and, not to instance in any others (as might be done in divers), Rabban Jochanan, Ben Zaccai, that was at this instant vice-president of the Sanhedrim, was a merchant four years, and then he fell to study the Law. Juchosin, fol. 21." Lightfoot on Acts xviii. vol. i. p. 205. "Rabbi Johanan was called Sandelar, or the Shoemaker." Lightfoot, vol. i. p. 612. "Rabbi Juda, the great cabbalist, bare the name and trade of Hhajat, a shoemaker or tailor." Lightfoot, vol. i. p. 790. "Rabbi Jose was brought up a tanner or leather-dresser; Rabbi Judas, a baker; Rabbi Johanan, a shoemaker; Asinæus and Anilæus, who seem to have been Jews of condition in Babylon, were put out by their mother to learn the art of weaving. Jos. Ant. xviii. 9, 1." Biscoe on the Acts, c. vii. s. 3. Rabbi Isaac also was a carpenter, and Rabbi Simeon, a clothier. Schoettgen's Horæ Heb. vol. ii. p. 898, and vol. i. p. 244. So, in the New Testament, Simon was a tanner, Aquila a tentmaker, and our Lord himself was a carpenter (Mark vi. 3), and the Apostles were fishermen.

[42] He was a σκηνοποιός (Acts xviii. 3); and that he was a tentmaker is confirmed by the fact that Aquila and his wife Priscilla also exercised this calling. ἦσαν γὰρ σκηνοποιοὶ τὴν τέχνην. Acts xviii. 3. The trade, therefore, must have been one, like that of tentmaking, in which a female could take part. It was no disgrace for a man to pursue such an occupation, as even the highborn Anilæus and Asinæus were weavers (Jos. Ant. xviii. 9, 1, as mentioned ante, note [41]). Michaelis thought that σκηνοποιός meant an instrument-maker or mechanician, and the passage cited for this view is from Julius Pollux. τοὺς δὲ μηχανοποιοὺς καὶ σκηνοποιοὺς ἡ παλαιὰ κωμῳδία ὠνόμαζε. Pollux, vii. 189. But Michaelis has mistaken the sense, for Pollux here refers to the machinery used in a theatre, and it is very unlikely that

was more in vogue at Tarsus. The material of which tents were then commonly made was the *cilicium*, so called from Cilicia, the country noted for the manufacture. It was a species of cloth obtained by spinning and weaving the long and beautiful hair supplied by the goats of that province.[43] However, the skins of animals were also employed, as they still are, for the like purpose; and this is the reason why Chrysostom sometimes designates Saul as σκηνορράφος,[44] a tent-stitcher, and sometimes as σκυτοτόμος,[45] a leather-cutter. The father of Saul, in apprenticing him to a mechanic, little dreamed that his son, for the last twenty-nine years of his life, would (with occasional intermission during imprisonment, or when supported by some voluntary contributions from his followers) be labouring night and day with his own hands to procure the common necessaries of life.[46]

It was probably at this time fondly anticipated, that the precocious abilities exhibited by the young Saul might, if properly cultivated, raise him, sooner or later, to the highest political eminence. He was therefore destined to be a scribe, or lawyer;[47] that is, he was to be an expounder of the Jewish Law and Traditions, and to plead in the Jewish courts. But to fit him for this purpose, it was necessary that he should be sent from the School of Tarsus to the University of Jerusalem, to be there initiated into the higher mysteries of his own peculiar religion. He tells us that he was "brought up"[48] at Jerusalem "from his youth from the very first;"[49] and we may therefore conclude that he arrived there at an early age, perhaps at about ten, when a Jewish lad was supposed to be qualified for the study of the Mishna.[50] Saul adds that he was taught "*at the feet*"[51] of his master, in allusion to the custom of boys sitting at the feet of the Rabbi;[52] and this also shows that Saul, as he *sat* under Gamaliel, was still but a stripling.[53] As Saul passed the next quarter of a century at the Jewish capital, and his sister married and settled there, we may hazard the conjecture that the whole family also removed with him from Tarsus to Jerusalem.

Saul should have been apprenticed to a craft of that description. Besides, how could Saul, who after his conversion was half-blind, have practised a calling which required an acute sight? He could work at the coarse trade of a tentmaker, but how could he have been equal to the requirements of scientific art? Others suggest that Paul was a worker in leather, or a saddler; and others that he was a weaver. For the different meanings assigned to σκηνοποιός, see Kuinoel, Acts xviii. 3.

[43] αἰγῶν δὲ αἱ τρίχες καὶ δοραὶ, συμφυόμεναί τε καὶ συρραπτόμεναι, φορηταὶ γεγόνασιν ὁδοιπόροις οἰκίαι, καὶ μάλιστα τοῖς ἐν στρατείαις. Philo de Victimis, 836. So Suidas: Κιλίκιον τράγος· ὁ δουλ. τοιοῦτοι γὰρ ἐν Κιλικίᾳ γίνονται τράγοι, ὅθεν καὶ τὰ ἐκ τῶν τριχῶν συντιθέμενα Κιλίκια καλοῦνται. Scenitæ a tabernaculis cognominati, quæ *Ciliciis* metantur, ubi libuit. Plin. N. H. vi. 32. In Cilicia villo tonsili (capræ) vestiuntur. Plin. N. H. viii. 76.

[44] Chrysostom on 2 Tim. c. ii.; Homil. 4, s. 3.

[45] Ibid.

[46] 1 Cor. ix. 12; ix. 6; 1 Thess. ii. 9; 2 Thess. iii. 8.

[47] The νομικός of Matt. xxii. 35 and Luke x. 25 is called by Mark γραμματεύς, xii. 28.

[48] ἀνατεθραμμένος. Acts xxii. 3.

[49] ἀπὸ νεότητος—ἀπ' ἀρχῆς. Acts xxvi. 4.

[50] Pirke Aboth, v. 21. See Winer's Bibl. Realw. vol. ii. p. 251.

[51] Acts xxii. 3.

[52] Pirke Aboth, i. 4, cited Schoettgen's Horæ Hebr. vol. i. p. 477.

[53] According to others, the pupils were instructed standing, and not sitting, until after the death of Gamaliel. See Rosenmuller's note on Acts xxii. 3.

There were at this time in the Holy City two rival schools for the training of Jewish youth—viz. the school of Hillel, and the school of Shammai. Hillel is called "Pollio" by Josephus, and Shammai is called by him "Sameas." They had flourished as learned doctors of the Law at the capture of Jerusalem by Herod, B.C. 37.[54] In the school founded by Hillel, the Traditions, as well as the Law, were taught; while in the other, instituted by Shammai, the disciple of Hillel, the religious creed was confined within the narrowest limits, the Law only being admitted, and even that so construed as not to embrace the principle of a future state. Of these two colleges, the former was patronised by the sect of the Pharisees, and the latter by that of the Sadducees. Hillel was succeeded by his son Simeon, who is reported to have been the same Simeon that took the infant Jesus in his arms in the Temple.[55] On the death of Simeon, the chair was filled by his son, the celebrated Gamaliel.[56] This Rabbi was the most eminent of all the Jewish doctors, being distinguished above his contemporaries, not only by his profound knowledge of the Jewish Law, but also by an intimate acquaintance with general literature. He was, besides, a man of liberal and enlightened views, and was in the highest credit with the people for his amiable and inoffensive manners. As Saul was a Pharisee, and the son of a Pharisee, he was naturally placed under the auspices of Gamaliel. Here Barnabas was again his fellow-student,[57] and the intimacy commenced at Tarsus was now ripened at Jerusalem, as they sat together as scholars at the feet of Gamaliel. Saul must also, at the same time, have become familiar with the two sons of Gamaliel, Jesus and Simon, of whom the former was afterwards elevated to the dignity of the high-priesthood, and both of whom were probably present at the trial of Saul for heresy, many years after, before the Sanhedrim.

Saul now rapidly advanced in the study of the Law—that is, of the Jewish Scriptures and Traditions—or (as he expresses it himself) he was "taught according to the perfect manner of the Law of the fathers."[58] That he was intimately conversant with Holy Writ, is attested by the readiness of his quotations, and the felicity of their application. We may also trace in his writings the peculiar system adopted in the schools of Jerusalem for the instruction of the students. Questions were propounded, and then debated by the disputants, in the form of dialogue; arguments were

---

[54] See Prideaux's Connections, part ii. book 8.
[55] Luke ii. 25.
[56] The several successions, from Hillel to the destruction of Jerusalem, are thus given:—

Rabbi Hillel.
|
Rabban Simeon I. son of Hillel.
|
Rabban Gamaliel I. son of Simeon.
|
Rabban Simeon II. son of Gamaliel.
|
Rabban Jochanan Ben Zaccai.
|
Rabban Gamaliel II. son of Jobneh.
|
Rabban Simeon III. son of Gamaliel II.
|
Rabbi Judah Hakkadosh, son of Simeon III.
|
Rabban Gamaliel III. son of Judah.

The Rabbans above named were the only doctors upon whom the high title of Rabban was bestowed. See Lightfoot, vol. i. p. 2008.
[57] Menochius, cited Poli Synop. Acts ix. 27.
[58] πεπαιδευμένος κατὰ ἀκρίβειαν τοῦ πατρῴου νόμου. Acts xxii. 3.

urged, and objections were suddenly interposed and answered. This will account for the abrupt style so familiar to the reader: "What advantage then hath the Jew? or what profit is there of circumcision?"[59] "What then? are we better than they?"[60] "What shall we then say that Abraham, our father as pertaining to the flesh, hath found?"[61] "What shall we say then? Shall we continue in sin, that grace may abound?"[62] "What then? shall we sin, because we are not under the Law, but under grace?"[63] "What shall we say then? Is there unrighteousness with God?"[64] and examples of the like kind might be multiplied without end. We also discover in his writings occasional allusion to the traditions of the fathers, to which the learned doctors of the school of Hillel attached so much importance. Thus, we are startled by the mention of Jannes and Jambres, the names of the Egyptian sorcerers who withstood Moses.[65] In other places we are reminded of the mystical and hidden meanings to which the Jewish divines had recourse in their interpretation of Scripture. For instance, Hagar and Sarah, the bondwoman and the freewoman, are, in an allegory, made to signify the servitude of the Law and the liberty of the Gospel.[66] We must remark, however, that the strength of Saul's mind enabled him to avoid the puerile conceits and idle fancies by which the Jewish commentaries were disfigured and rendered ridiculous.

Saul, both as a scribe and a Roman citizen, would necessarily devote some portion of his time to the study of *foreign* Law, and more particularly that of Rome. It excites no surprise, therefore, that at Philippi he should extort from the Roman Duumviri, or Prætors, a confession that they had broken the law under which they lived;[67] or that he should have cautioned the officer about to put him to the torture, that, as a Roman citizen, he was exempt from the rack;[68] or that he should have pleaded his own cause before Felix and Festus, and as a Roman citizen have exercised the right of appeal to the Emperor, and then have made his own defence before the highest tribunals at Rome.[69]

Saul, as a native of Tarsus, must have spoken Greek from childhood; but it must have been while studying at Jerusalem that he acquired his knowledge of Grecian literature. He had quitted Tarsus at too early an age to have made much progress in the world of letters. But in the Jewish capital, as his faculties developed themselves, he could not have remained insensible to the flights of fancy and streams of eloquence which have captivated each succeeding generation for now nearly three thousand years. His master Gamaliel, too, the most enlightened man of his day, and familiar with heathen learning, would encourage a taste so congenial to his own. Saul, however, may afterwards have extended his knowledge of the Greek writers by his constant intercourse with Gentiles. It is certain that he imbibed and retained

---

[59] Rom. iii. 1.
[60] Rom. iii. 9.
[61] Rom. iv. 1.
[62] Rom. vi. 1.
[63] Rom. vi. 15.
[64] Rom. ix. 14.
[65] 2 Tim. iii. 8.
[66] Gal. iv. 21.
[67] Acts xvi. 37.
[68] Acts xxii. 25.
[69] 2 Tim. iv. 16.

a keen relish for the beauties of the Greek poets and dramatists. Thus we shall find him, in his address to the Athenians, appealing to the Cilician bard Aratus:—

> τοῦ γὰρ καὶ γένος ἐσμέν
> For we are also his offspring.[70]

And he rebukes the Cretans from the mouth of their own poet Epimenides:—

> Κρῆτες ἀεὶ ψεῦσται, κακὰ θηρία, γαστέρες ἀργαί.
> The Cretans
> Are always liars, evil beasts, slow bellies.[71]

To the refined Corinthians he cites from 'Thais,' one of the comedies of the elegant Menander:[72]—

> φθείρουσιν ἤθη χρήσθ' ὁμιλίαι κακαί.
> Evil communications corrupt good manners.[73]

And had the Grecian literature descended to us less mutilated by time, we might identify other quotations from the popular poets of the day.[74] That Saul had an intimate acquaintance with the Greek writings of his countryman Philo, is manifest from the close proximity of the language of the Apostle to that of the Alexandrian philosopher. The thoughts and phrases, more particularly in the Epistle to the Hebrews, are identical. Indeed, the contemplative turn of Saul's mind would lead him naturally to study the philosophy of the Greeks generally. At Athens he encountered the Stoics and Epicureans, and they would hardly have condescended to discuss such high matters with him, had he not been capable of doing battle with them upon their own ground. He must, therefore, have been familiar with the doctrines of both schools, and his religious cast of thought would incline him to the Stoics rather than the Epicureans. Thus, in his address to the Areopagus, we find him echoing the noblest sentiments of the Stoic philosophy. We can also thus account

---

[70] Acts xvii. 28.
[71] Titus i. 12.
[72] But, according to others, from a lost play of Euripides.
[73] 1 Cor. xv. 33.
[74] In the Epistle to the Hebrews (xii. 13) we have the hexameter:—

> καὶ τροχιὰς ὀρθὰς ποιήσατε τοῖς ποσὶν ὑμῶν,
> And make the pathways straight before your feet.

But though the passage is certainly a citation, the rhythm is probably accidental. The prose of all writers falls occasionally into verse. It has often been remarked that Tacitus begins his Annals with a hexameter:

> Urbem Romam a principio reges habuere.

And in the Epistles we have several instances of the kind:

εἰ ἄλλοις οὐκ εἰμὶ ἀπόστολος, ἀλλά γε ὑμῖν.
1 Cor. ix. 2.

πᾶσα δόσις ἀγαθὴ καὶ πᾶν δώρημα τέλειον.
James i. 17.

Χριστοῦ, στέλλεσθαι ὑμᾶς ἀπὸ παντὸς ἀδελφοῦ.
2 Thess. iii. 6.

τοὺς ἐχθροὺς ὑπὸ τοὺς πόδας αὐτοῦ. ἔσχατος ἐχθρὸς
1 Cor. xv. 25.

κριτής γὰρ ἐγὼ τούτων οὐ βούλομαι εἶναι.
Acts xviii. 15.

εἰ ἀρνούμεθα, κἀκεῖνος ἀρνήσεται ἡμᾶς.
2 Tim. ii. 12.

And others might be adduced.

As the English reader may not be familiar with the classic metres, we subjoin a Latin hexameter, with a well-known English translation, which is also a hexameter, and corresponds exactly with the original:—

> Quid faciam? moriar? sic Amyntas credit Amyntam?
> What shall I do? shall I die? shall Amyntas murder Amyntas?

for the great resemblance between the language of Saul and that of Seneca, a Stoic philosopher. The explanation commonly offered is, that Saul became acquainted at Corinth with Gallio, the brother of Seneca, and, as a prisoner, was confided to the care of Burrhus, the captain of the Prætorians, and the friend of Seneca; and that he thus became intimate with Seneca himself, and that each borrowed the thoughts of the other. But the truer solution is, that both had studied the learning of the same school of philosophy, and that the minds of both were deeply tinged with the colour of their early lucubrations.

The education of Saul, under the auspices of Gamaliel, continued for many years; and when the term of his tirocinium was complete, there was scarcely his equal in Jerusalem, for knowledge of the Law and for general erudition. The moral character of the man, also, was not a whit behind, for it was marked by a stern rectitude of conduct and steady adherence to principle. From this period to the time of his first appearance upon the stage of public life, we have no history of his career, but he was doubtless advancing rapidly upon the road to distinction. We may assume, as a matter of course, that he took the degree of Rab, the first step to honour amongst his countrymen; and that he afterwards became a Rabbi, the second step amongst the learned doctors. The diploma of Rabbi, conferred by the University of Jerusalem, was of the greatest service to Saul in his subsequent labours; for it enabled him to address his countrymen in the synagogues abroad, and to command, from his rank, their respectful attention. The grade of Rabbi was, it has been thought, denoted by some external badge, and, according to Lightfoot, by the breadth of the phylacteries;[75] and if so, it would account for the readiness with which Saul was everywhere received amongst his countrymen, until the peculiarity of his doctrines provoked antagonism.[76] The climax, the title of Rabban, was conferred on such only as Gamaliel, who commanded veneration by their patriarchal age.

Saul combined in himself all the qualities that indicated future greatness. Of vigorous natural abilities, and recommended by the highest accomplishments, eloquent in speech, resolute in action, and withal of unimpeachable character, how could such a man fail to climb high on the ladder of ambition? We may conjecture that he had even patronage to support him, for Gamaliel, a Pharisee, would take a natural pride in introducing so promising a disciple of his own sect to the notice of the leading characters. That Saul began to feel himself lifted above the ordinary level of mankind to a giddy pre-eminence, we may infer from his own acknowledgment. "I profited," he says, "in the Jews' religion above many my equals in mine own nation."[77]

---

[75] See Biscoe on the Acts, c. 7.
[76] That Saul was ordained a Rabbi is assumed by the learned Selden as beyond question. Presbyteratus autem dignitatem ab Gamaliele accepisse Paulum, antequam Christo nomen dederat, non videtur omnino dubitandum. Selden de Synhed. vii. 7, 7, p. 1369; and see i. 14, p. 1099. And Vitringa adds, that this is implied by his mission from the Sanhedrim to Damascus. See Biscoe on the Acts, c. 7.
[77] Galat. i. 14.

In A.D. 37, when he would be thirty-five,[78] if not before, he became a member of the Sanhedrim;[79] and as this body consisted but of three classes—viz. Priests, Elders, and Scribes—Saul must have been admitted as a Scribe. Being of the tribe of Benjamin, he could not be a Priest, and from his youthful age he could scarcely have been an Elder. With a burning zeal for the Mosaic dispensation, which he had studied so successfully, he was ready at a moment's call to stand forth as its champion. An opportunity presented itself, from the growth of the antagonistic sect of the Nazarenes; and he undertook, first by argument, and, if necessary, by more violent measures, to suppress the rising heresy. But before we advert to this (the first circumstance in the life of Saul of which we have any detailed account) we must pause for a moment to sketch the political state of Judæa.

---

[78] For the age of Paul, see ante, p. 5.
[79] That he had a vote in the Council, and gave it against Stephen, the protomartyr, is stated by himself, Acts xxvi. 10; and see Selden de Synhed. pp. 1099, 1360.

THE FAMILY OF THE CÆSARS.

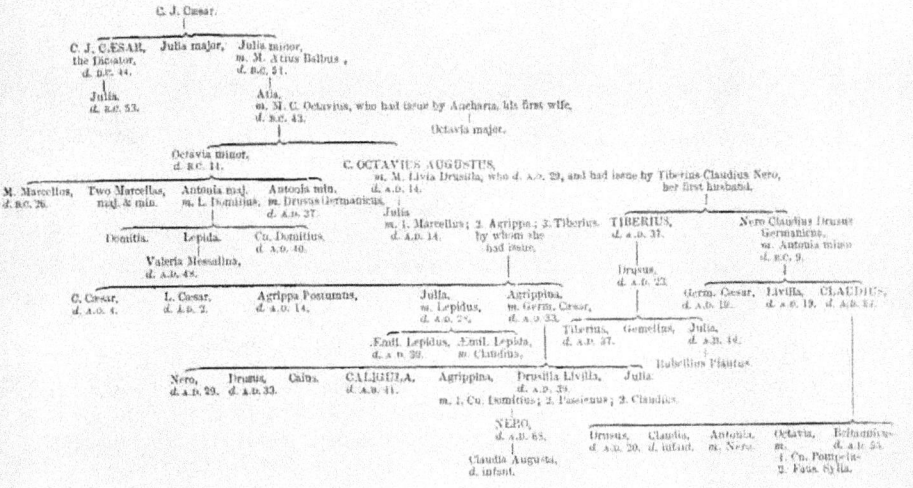

THE FAMILY OF THE HERODS.

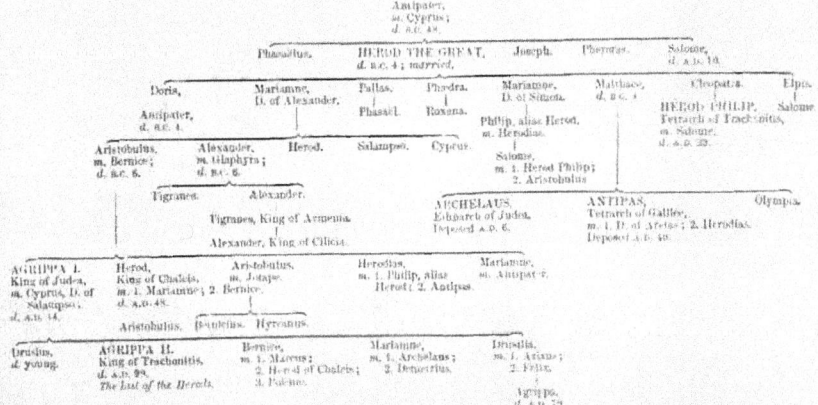

CHAPTER II.

Sketch of Jewish History from the Death of Herod the Great to the Martyrdom of Stephen.

> Judæa now, and all the promised land,
> Reduced a province under Roman yoke,
> Obeys Tiberius; nor is always ruled
> With temperate sway. Oft have they violated
> The Temple, oft the Law, with foul affronts,
> Abominations rather, as did once
> Antiochus.
>
> *Paradise Regained*, book iii.

HEROD THE GREAT (fig. 1) died on 1st April, B.C. 4,[1] when, by the award of Augustus, confirming in the main the will of the late King, his dominions were distributed amongst his three sons—Archelaus, Antipas (called in Scripture and Josephus, Herod), and Philip—and Salome, the sister of Herod the Great. To Archelaus (fig. 2) were

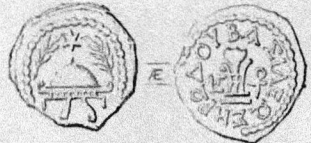 

Fig. 1.—*Coin of Herod the Great. From J. Y. Akerman's Numismatic Illustrations of the New Testament.*

Obv. A helmet with cheek-pieces, and above it a star, which is remarkable, as the birth of Christ was preceded by a star.

Rev. Ἡρώδου Βασιλέως (of Herod the King), and the legend L Γ, or third year of his reign (B.C. 38), and the monogram P, i.e. πεντηκοστή, or the value of 2 γραμμοί. See Sir F. Madden's Jewish Coinage, p. 295.

The coin is brass, or rather bronze; brass being a compound of copper and zinc, whereas the ancient coins are a compound, not of copper and zinc, but of copper and tin.

Fig. 2.—*Coin of Archelaus. From the British Museum.*

Obv. Ἡρώδου (of Herod), with bunch of grapes.

Rev. Ἐθνάρχου (of the Ethnarch), with helmet.

Archelaus succeeded, B.C. 4, to the greater part of the dominions of Herod the Great; but Augustus denied him the title of King, and styled him Ethnarch, as on the coin. As Archelaus was deposed A.D. 6, the coin must have been struck some time between B.C. 4 and A.D. 6.

assigned Judæa, Idumæa, and Samaria, with the title of *Ethnarch*. By the will of his father, Archelaus was to have reigned as *King*; but as he had been already guilty of some excesses before the award was made, Augustus, for the present, would not accord to

---

[1] See Fasti Sacri, p. 125, No. 915; p. 127, No. 924.—The reader should be apprised that B.C. 4 means, not four years before the actual birth of Christ, but four years before the received commencement of the Christian era. At the first introduction of the era by Dionysius Exiguus, in the sixth century, a palpable mistake (now of too ancient standing to be corrected) was made as to the time of our Saviour's birth. It ought to have been placed several years earlier. See Fasti Sacri, p. 115, No. 869.

him that distinction, but gave him the title of Ethnarch, with a promise that, should he conduct himself worthily in his government, he should afterwards be invested with the higher honour. The rest of the kingdom of Herod was divided into two tetrarchies. To Antipas, or Herod (fig. 3), was given the tetrarchy of Galilee and Peræa,[2] and he fixed his capital at Tiberias, on the Lake of Gennesaret, so called after his great patron, the Emperor Tiberius. It was under his jurisdiction that our Saviour resided, first at Nazareth, and afterwards at Capernaum, both cities of Galilee; and therefore it was that Pontius Pilate, when he heard that he was a Galilean, sent him to Herod. To Philip (fig. 4) was assigned the tetrarchy of Trachonitis, Auranitis,

Fig. 3.—*Coin of Herod Antipas. From Sir F. Madden's Jewish Coinage.*

Obv. Ηρωδου Τετραρχου (of Herod the Tetrarch), with a palm-branch and the legend L. AΓ, or 33, which places it in A.D. 29, the year in which our Lord opened his ministry.
Rev. Τιβεριας (Tiberias), the capital of the Tetrarchy. Herod Antipas was Tetrarch of Galilee during the whole of our Lord's ministry.

Fig. 4.—*Coin of Herod Philip. From Sir F. Madden.*

Obv. Τιβεριος Σεβαστος Καισαρ (Tiberius Augustus Cæsar).
Rev. Φιλιππου Τετ. (of Philip the Tetrarch), with the legend L. AZ, or 37, equivalent to A.D. 33, and therefore struck by Philip in the year of our Lord's Crucifixion.

Batanæa, and part of what was called the House of Zenon, or Zenodorus,[3] the capital of his tetrarchy being Cæsarea Philippi, so called in honour of the Cæsars (fig. 5). For Salome provision was made by the gift of the cities of Jamnia, Azotus, and Phasaëlis, with a royal residence at Ascalon.[4]

Archelaus, though exhorted to moderation by Augustus, could not forget old feuds, but exercised such severities against the Jews, Idumæans, and Samaritans, that at length, in the tenth year of his reign, or A.D. 6,[5] his subjects sent a deputation to Rome, to appeal against his enormities. The Emperor could not condescend to hold communication by letter with a petty subordinate prince, but at once commanded the Secretary for Jewish Affairs to sail for Judæa and bring Archelaus before him. The Ethnarch was arrested at the celebration of a feast, hurried to Rome, banished to Spain, and his property was confiscated.[6] Judæa, Idumæa, and Samaria now became Roman dependencies—and, as such, were burdened with taxes, including a poll-tax and a land-tax—and were annexed to the province of Syria.

In the time of Augustus (fig. 6) (B.C. 27)[7] the various subject provinces had been divided between the Emperor and the Senate; and Syria, to which Judæa was now

---

[2] Peræa was the country along the east of the Jordan, and extended from Machærus on the south to Pella on the north. Jos. Bell. iii. 3, 3.

[3] For the boundaries of Philip's tetrarchy, which was peopled by a mixed race of Jews and Syrians, see Jos. Bell. iii. 3, 5.

[4] Jos. Ant. xvii. 11, 4; Bell. ii. 6, 3.

[5] See Fasti Sacri, p. 146, No. 1011.

[6] Jos. Bell. ii. 7, 3; Ant. xvii. 13, 2.

[7] See Fasti Sacri, p. 79, No. 666.

attached, was one of those allotted to the Emperor, and as such was governed by a Prefect, called a *Proprætor*, who was always of consular dignity,[a] with three *Legates*, or

Fig. 5.—*Cæsarea Philippi. From a photograph of the Palestine Exploration.*

Fig. 6.—*Portrait of Augustus. From C. W. King's Antique Gems.*

Fig. 7.—*Portrait of Livia, the wife of Augustus. From C. W. King's Antique Gems.*

military commanders, under him, and a *Procurator*, who collected and managed the revenue.[b] Though Judæa thus became an appendage to Syria, yet, from the turbulent

---

[a] ἐς τὸ ἔπειτα ἐγένοντο Συρίας στρατηγοὶ τῶν τὰ ἐπώνυμα ἀρξάντων ἐν ἄστει. Appian. Syr. 51.

[b] Thus, when C. Sentius Saturninus (B.C. 6) was prefect, his three sons were his legates.

nature of the Jews, and from the distance of the country from Antioch, the capital of Syria, the Emperor thought it advisable to appoint a separate officer to administer the affairs of Judæa, subject to the control of the Syrian Prefect. At the same time, therefore, that Publius Sulpicius Quirinus, or Cyrenius, was made Proprætor of Syria, Coponius, a man of the equestrian order, was sent, by the title of *Procurator*, to be governor of Judæa under him. This sub-prefect had the power of life and death,[10] and also exercised the prerogative of appointing and deposing at pleasure the High Priest of the nation—and, in short, was (in the absence of his Syrian superior at Antioch) the absolute and despotic ruler of the country. The settlement of the constitution of Judæa, in its relation to the Imperial Government, was entrusted to Cyrenius, who is therefore designated by Josephus as Δικαιοδότης, or the Lawgiver.[11] For the purpose of assessing the tribute to Rome, a census was instituted throughout the province of all the valuable property of the inhabitants, and it was the execution of this order that called forth the violent faction of Judas of Galilee. "Under Coponius," says Josephus, "a certain *Galilean*,[12] Judas by name, incited the people to revolt, reproaching them for submitting to *pay tribute* to the Romans, and, not content with *God*, enduring also to have *men* for their masters."[13] And with this agrees the statement of Gamaliel to the Sanhedrim, "After this man rose up Judas *of Galilee*, in the days of the taxing, and drew away much people after him;"[14] where by "the taxing" is undoubtedly meant the census in the time of Cyrenius, Prefect of Syria, and Coponius, Procurator of Judæa. It is worthy of remark that Luke, in speaking of the census at the birth of our Saviour, very properly guards the reader against confounding the two censuses, by observing that "This was the *first* taxing when Cyrenius was governor of Syria"[15]—not, as it has been translated in the Vulgate, "This taxing was *first made* when Cyrenius was governor of Syria."[16] The two

---

Jos. Ant. xvi. 11, 3. (In the Wars two only are mentioned, Jos. Bell. i. 27, 3.) Volumnius was his procurator, ὁ ἐπίτροπος. Jos. Bell. i. 27, 2. So Spain (except Bætica) was in like manner a consular province of the Emperor, and had a proprætor, three legates, and a procurator. Strabo, iii. 4; and see Fasti Sacri, p. 145, No. 1009.

[10] Κωπώνιός τε αὐτῷ συγκαταπέμπεται, ἡγησόμενος Ἰουδαίων τῇ ἐπὶ πᾶσι ἐξουσίᾳ. Jos. Ant. xviii. 1, 1. μέχρι τοῦ κτείνειν λαβὼν παρὰ τοῦ Καίσαρος ἐξουσίαν. Jos. Bell. ii. 8, 1.

[11] Jos. Ant. xviii. 1.

[12] Observe that Josephus here calls Judas a *Galilean*, as he is also described in Antiq. v. 37; but, had it not been for this incidental mention of the circumstance by Josephus, the accuracy of Luke would have been questioned, as Josephus elsewhere speaks of Judas as a *Gaulonite*. Ant. xviii. 1, 1. See Blunt's Scriptural Coincidences.

[13] Jos. Bell. ii. 8, 1.

[14] Acts v. 37.

[15] αὕτη ἡ ἀπογραφὴ πρώτη ἐγένετο ἡγεμονεύοντος τῆς Συρίας Κυρηνίου. Luke ii. 2.

[16] It is very doubtful what is the true interpretation, and various hypotheses have been suggested. The following may be selected as the most plausible:—

1. The passage may be rendered, "This was the *first* taxing when Cyrenius was governor of Syria;" that is, Cyrenius was governor of Syria twice, viz. in B.C. 4 (see Fasti Sacri, p. 132, No. 955), and again in A.D. 6 (see Fasti Sacri, p. 146, No. 1012); and the taxing at the birth of our Lord was that which was commenced, indeed, in the lifetime of Herod, but was not completed until after his death, in B.C. 4, when Cyrenius was governor of Syria for the first time. This was the first taxing of Cyrenius, as distinguished from the second taxing of Cyrenius, begun in A.D. 6,

censuses were, in fact, wholly distinct. The former was a census of *persons* and *property*, not necessarily for taxation, but perhaps for ascertaining the population and resources of the Roman Empire; while that under Cyrenius, or his deputy Coponius,

and completed in A.D. 7, when Cyrenius was governor of Syria for the second time. Luke does not say that Christ was *born* when Cyrenius was governor of Syria (which he was not), but only that the birth was in the course of the census which had been ordered by Augustus about that time. ἐν ἐκείναις ταῖς ἡμέραις. Luke ii. 1. The vagueness of the latter expression is compatible with the hypothesis, that the edict was issued some time before, and according to Tertullian the census was going on so early as in the time of Saturninus, who was displaced in B.C. 6. Tertull. adv. Marcion. iv. 19. The census might last one, two, three, or more years, and therefore might continue under several prefects—as under Saturninus, Varus, and Cyrenius—but would be called by the name of the prefect under whom it was completed, viz. Cyrenius. The previous delay of bringing the census to a conclusion might have been one of the reasons for appointing Cyrenius, who was known to be a thorough man of business. In A.D. 6, on the expulsion of Archelaus, he was employed to make the second census of Judæa, and this mission may have been resolved upon from his success in carrying out the first census on the death of Herod.

This view, if I mistake not, is confirmed by a passage in Justin Martyr. Justin was born within the first century after Christ, and was a native of Judæa; and being one of the most learned men of his day, he must have known, if any one did, the true year of the birth of Christ. The passage as it stands is corrupt, for it makes Justin say that Christ was born "during the census under Cyrenius, the *first* Procurator of Judæa"—i.e. when Cyrenius was sent to Syria, on the expulsion of Archelaus, in A.D. 6. But Justin could not have meant this, for he speaks elsewhere of the nativity as in the time of Herod the Great. Dialog. cum Tryphon. p. 105. The confusion has arisen from the clerical error of a single letter, viz. from writing ν for ρ. For πρῶτον should be read πρότερον, and then the passage would run thus: "During the census under Cyrenius, when he was Procurator of Judæa *the first time*." ἐπὶ Κυρηνίου τοῦ ἡμετέρου ἐν Ἰουδαίᾳ πρότερον γενομένου ἐπιτρόπου. Apol. i. 34.

2. The passage may be rendered, "This the first taxing came to pass (or was *completed*) when Cyrenius was governor of Syria," A.D. 6-7. In other words, there were two taxings—one on the expulsion of Archelaus in A.D. 6, when Judæa became a Roman province; and the other in A.D. 44, on the death of Agrippa, when Judæa again became a Roman province—and the taxing at the birth of our Lord was the first of those two. It was a long time about, and had been commenced in the lifetime of Herod, when Augustus, in an angry moment, threatened to treat him as a subject. Jos. Ant. xvi. 9, 1-3. But afterwards, when Augustus was reconciled to Herod, the taxing was dropped until after the expulsion of Archelaus, when it was again resumed in the time of Cyrenius, A.D. 6. It is observable that Gamaliel speaks, in A.D. 34, of "*the* taxing," τῆς ἀπογραφῆς (Acts v. 37), as if at that time there had been only one; but *Luke*, who wrote about A.D. 56, speaks of the taxing at the birth of our Lord as the *first*. At the time when Gamaliel was speaking there had been only one; but on the death of Agrippa, in A.D. 44, and therefore before the date of Luke's Gospel, there had been a second taxing—viz. on the death of Agrippa.

3. The passage may be rendered, "This was the first taxing of Cyrenius, governor of Syria;" i.e. the taxing at the birth of our Lord was conducted by Cyrenius, who was then a special commissioner for the purpose, and *was afterwards governor of Syria*. This was his first taxing, as distinguished from his second, in A.D. 6-7. But this interpretation does violence to the language, for ἡγεμονεύοντος, the present participle, implies that Cyrenius was governor at the time of the census referred to. Nor is there sufficient evidence that Cyrenius was present in the East a little before the death of Herod.

4. The passage may be rendered, "This taxing was *before* the time of Cyrenius, governor of Syria." There having been two taxings prior to the date of Luke's Gospel—viz. one in the lifetime of Herod, and therefore under his direction, and the other after his death, in A.D. 6, under the direction of Cyrenius—it was necessary to distinguish the two, and therefore Luke speaks of the one in question as that which preceded the prefecture of Cyrenius. The use of πρῶτος in the sense of πρότερος is supported by authority. Thus, ὅτι πρῶτός μου

HEROD THE GREAT TO THE MARTYRDOM OF STEPHEN.

was a census of *persons* and *property* for fiscal purposes.[17] Coponius, the first Procurator of Judæa, was succeeded by Marcus Ambivius (fig. 8) A.D. 9,[18] and the latter by

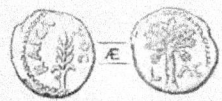

Fig. 8.—*Coin of Judæa, struck in the time of Marcus Ambivius.*

Obv. Καισαρος (Cæsar's).—Rev. A palm with bunches of dates, and the legend L. M, or [illegible] the 'Anni Augusti' from 1 Jan, B.C. 27, which would place it in A.D. 9, under M. Ambivius. See Sir F. Madden's Jewish Coinage, p. 137.

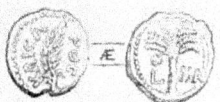

Fig. 9.—*Coin of Judæa, struck in the time of Annius Rufus. From Sir F. Madden.*

Obv. Καισαρος (Cæsar's).—Rev. A palm with bunch of dates, and the legend L. MA, or 41, equivalent to A.D. 14, and therefore struck in Judæa under the Procuratorship of Annius Rufus.

Fig. 10.—*Portrait of Barabbas. From a gem by Apollonius, whose name appears in small Greek letters cut on the gem itself. From C. W. King's Antique Gems.*

Annius Rufus[19] A.D. 12 (fig. 9).[20] These, the three first governors of Judæa, were sent by Augustus, whose general policy appears to have been, on the advice of his

ἦν, "for he was before me," John i. 15, 30; ἐμέ πρῶτον ὑμῶν μεμίσηκεν, "(The world) hated me before you," John xv. 18. And some add, τῇ δὲ πρώτῃ τῶν Ἀζύμων, Matt. xxvi. 17; and καὶ τῇ πρώτῃ ἡμέρᾳ τῶν Ἀζύμων, Mark xiv. 12. But as to this, see Fasti Sacri, p. xxxii.

5. It is not improbable that the text itself is corrupt. A slight alteration would make all smooth—viz. by substituting πρὸ ἐ ἔτη for πρώτη. It can hardly be denied that the letters πρὸ ἐ ἔτη could easily run into πρώτη, more particularly in MSS., where the words were not divided, but followed each other without a break. The passage would then stand, αὔτη ἡ ἀπογραφὴ πρὸ ἐ ἔτη ἐγένετο ἡγεμονεύοντος, &c. "This taxing was ten years before Cyrenius was governor of Syria," in A.D. 6-7. This would place the birth of Christ in B.C. 5, which would be a probable date, as Herod died on the 1st of April, in B.C. 4. As Luke is very particular in mentioning the fifteenth year of Tiberius as the year in which John Baptist began his public ministry, and as John's ministry was followed six months after by that of Christ himself (Luke iii. 1, 21), it would *à priori* be expected that Luke should insert some accurate note of time as to the *birth* of our Lord. If He was born in B.C. 5, He would be thirty-three in A.D. 29, in which year He certainly began His ministry; but Luke speaks of Him as then of about thirty, ὡσεὶ ἐτῶν τριάκοντα (Luke iii. 23), and here again (for no satisfactory exposition of the text as it stands has ever been given) it is likely that Luke wrote τριῶν τριάκοντα, or thirty-three, and that, the reduplication escaping notice, one τρία has been accidentally omitted in transcription, so that the text now reads, not thirty-three, but thirty.

Upon the whole, we regard the first of these several interpretations as the most natural and simple.

It is remarkable that Josephus records *one* census only, and I venture to offer the following explanation. The hypothesis originally propounded by Zumpt, that Cyrenius was twice governor of Syria—first in B.C. 4, on the death of

[17] The second census, in A.D. 6, was unquestionably ἀποτίμησις, or a census of property, as well as of persons, for in the time of our Lord the Jews paid a *poll-tax*, Matt. xxii. 20; Mark xii. 16; Luke xx. 24. The census at the birth of our Lord is described by Luke as the *first* census, which seems to imply that it was of the same character as the second—i.e. a census of property and persons; but during the reigns of Herod and his successor Archelaus, no tax was actually imposed by the Romans.

[18] See Fasti Sacri, p. 150, No. 1033.

[19] Jos. Ant. xviii. 2, 2.

[20] See Fasti Sacri, p. 155, No. 1047.

prime councillor Mæcenas (fig. 10), to continue his prefects in office between three and five years.[21] Coponius and Marcus Ambivius retained their posts about three years each, and Annius Rufus had been about the same time in authority when Augustus died. This event occurred on 19th August, A.D. 14, after he had reigned fifty-seven years and a half, and in the seventy-seventh year of his age.[22]

Augustus was succeeded by Tiberius (fig. 11), the son of Livia (fig. 7) the wife of Augustus, and adopted son of Augustus himself. The luxurious and lethargic habits

Fig. 11.—*Coin of Tiberius.* From J. Y. Akerman.

Obv. Portrait of Tiberius with the legend Ti. Cæsar Divi Aug. F. Augustus (Tiberius Cæsar Augustus, son of Divus Augustus).
Rev. Female figure with the legend Pontif. Maxim.
This coin is the silver denarius of the Romans, the common currency of Judæa, and remarkably illustrates the question of our Lord to those who demanded of him the Temple tax: "Whose is this image (or portrait) and superscription? And they said unto him, Cæsar's." Matt. xx. 20; Mark xii. 15; Luke xx. 24.

of Tiberius led him to adopt a line of policy wholly at variance with that of his predecessor. The governors of provinces were now but seldom changed, in order that the imperial repose might not be disturbed by the solicitations and intrigues that necessarily attended every new appointment. The reason assigned by the Emperor himself was of a more plausible character. "Once upon a time," he said, "a wounded man lay by the roadside, and a swarm of flies settled upon his sores. A traveller, who happened to be passing, had compassion upon the sufferer, and drew near to brush away the annoyance. 'Hold,' said the poor fellow, 'you know not what you are about. These flies have just surfeited themselves, and cause me but little inconvenience; but should you drive them away, a new swarm, with a fresh appetite, will descend upon me, and

Herod, and again in A.D. 6, on the expulsion of Archelaus—is now generally admitted. But this fact, which so long lay hid from the modern critics, escaped the notice of Josephus altogether. Why else does he date events as occurring ἐπὶ Κυρηνίου (Bell. ii. 17, 8; Ant. xx. 5, 2), "in the time of Cyrenius," and nothing more said, as if there were only one prefecture of Cyrenius? The materials from which he drew his history evidently stopped at the death of Herod, so that from that period to the expulsion of Archelaus, in A.D. 6, there is a chasm in his narrative. The consequence is, that as each census was under Cyrenius—the first when he was governor in B.C. 4, and the latter when he was governor in A.D. 6—Josephus confounds the two together. Thus, he tells us that the census passed off peaceably (Ant. xviii. 1, 1), which was true only of the first census in B.C. 4; and then records the outbreak under Judas of Galilee (ibid.), which was true only of the second census in A.D. 6. But what almost conclusively shows that Josephus failed to distinguish the two censuses, is the statement, in express words, that at the census under Cyrenius, "Joazar, the son of Boethus," was High Priest, and exhorted the people to submission. Now, at the *second* census under Cyrenius, in A.D. 6, Jesus, son of Sieh, was High Priest. Ant. xvii. 13, 1. But at the *first* census, in B.C. 4, Joazar, the son of Boethus, actually was High Priest. Ant. xvii. 6, 4; xvii. 13, 1; see Fasti Sacri, p. 348, No. 2060. Josephus therefore, in this instance at least, has blended the two censuses into one.

[21] See Dion, liii. 28.　　[22] See Fasti Sacri, p. 157, No. 1053.

HEROD THE GREAT TO THE MARTYRDOM OF STEPHEN.

exhaust the little blood the others have left.' And so," continued the Emperor, "should I send a succession of governors, my subjects would be pillaged without mercy; but if the same Prefect be continued for a number of years, he will plunder eagerly enough at first, but when he has filled his coffers, his rapacity will lose its edge."[23] It is certain (whatever were his motives) that during his whole reign, which lasted twenty-two years, the Emperor made but one change in the Procuratorship of Judæa. His first appointment was Valerius Gratus (fig. 12) in A.D. 15,[24] during whose Prefecture the high-priesthood was conferred on Joseph, better known by his surname of Caiaphas.[25]

Fig. 12.—*Coin of Judæa, struck by Valerius Gratus. From Sir F. Madden.*
Obv. IOVΛIA (Julia, the mother of Tiberius).—Rev. Ear of corn with the legend L. B, or second year of the reign of Tiberius, equivalent to A.D. 15, and therefore struck under Valerius Gratus. It will be observed that on the death of Augustus the type of the coins of Judæa changes from that under Augustus. See ante, p. 21.

He was the son-in-law of Ananus, called in Scripture Annas,[26] and they were on such intimate terms together, that they were regarded by the people as exercising the high-priesthood jointly. "Annas and Caiaphas" (says Luke) "being the high priests;"[27] and when our Saviour was betrayed, they "led Him away" (says John) "to Annas first, for he was father-in-law to Caiaphas, which was the high priest that same year."[28]

Valerius Gratus had governed Judæa eleven years, when, in A.D. 26, he was displaced to make room for Pontius Pilate (fig. 13), in the seventh year of whose Prefecture the

Fig. 13.—*A Coin of Judæa struck under Pontius Pilate. From Sir F. Madden.*
Obv. ΤιΒεριου Καισαρος (of Tiberius Cæsar) with the legend, L. ιϛ, or 16, equivalent to A.D. 29, and therefore struck in the year when our Lord opened His ministry, during the prefecture of Pontius Pilate.
Rev. Ιουλια Καισαρος (Julia [mother] of Cæsar), with three ears of corn tied together.
This coin may be the quadrans, or farthing, containing two λεπτα, or mites. Matt. x. 29. The λεπτον is explained as *half a quadrans*, so that the mite was probably not generally current, and not so well known as the quadrans.

ministry of our Saviour was closed by the Crucifixion. He was betrayed on Thursday, April 2nd, A.D. 33,[29] and was led that night to the house of the High Priest, where a close council of the rulers of the Jews was assembled. The Sanhedrim could sit only during the day. As soon, therefore, as the light broke, the great national assembly, the Sanhedrim, was called together, and our Saviour was arraigned before them.[30] The question was put, "Art thou the Messiah?" and when He confessed that He was

---

[23] Jos. Ant. xviii. 6, 5.
[24] See Fasti Sacri, p. 160, No. 1073.
[25] Jos. Ant. xviii. 2, 2.
[26] John xviii. 13.
[27] Luke iii. 2.
[28] John xviii. 13.
[29] See Fasti Sacri, p. 233, No. 1441.
[30] Luke xxii. 66; Matt. xxvii. 1; Mark xv. 1.

the Son of God, was pronounced guilty of blasphemy, which, by the Jewish Law, was punishable with stoning. But the Sadducees were desirous, if possible, of escaping the obloquy of their own coldblooded proceedings. It was proposed, therefore, that Jesus should be carried before Pontius Pilate, with a demand that He should be crucified. This Pilate refused, unless Jesus were proved guilty of some offence against the Roman Law; when the Jewish rulers shifted their ground, and pressed the charge that Jesus had arrogated to himself the title of "King of the Jews," and was thus guilty of treason against Cæsar. The governor—fearing, if he should release Jesus, that he should be accused by the Jews to the jealous and suspicious Tiberius, then Emperor—at length gave way to the clamours of the multitude, and pronounced sentence of death. At nine o'clock[31] on Friday morning, the 3rd of April, A.D. 33, the Saviour was nailed to the cross; at three in the afternoon He expired; and, according to the usual practice in the East, was buried the same day.[32]

Saul at this time (A.D. 33) was about thirty-one, and had been twenty-one years a resident at Jerusalem; and one is curious to know whether he was in any way implicated in the proceedings against our blessed Saviour. We should imagine not. The Crucifixion was the act of the Sadducee faction, and Saul was a Pharisee. We are not even certain that Saul ever beheld our Saviour, though they must often have been in the Jewish capital together. In 2nd Corinthians we certainly meet with the passage, "Though *we have known Christ after the flesh*, yet now henceforth know we Him no more;"[33] but the writer often uses "we" for the Christian society, without the least reference to himself personally. Again, in 1st Corinthians, he asks plainly, "Have I not *seen* Jesus Christ our Lord?"[34] But the meaning is, "Did I not behold Him after His resurrection?"—viz. at the time of Saul's own conversion on the road to Damascus. In the Epistle to the Hebrews, on the other hand, we read : "How shall *we* escape, if we neglect so great salvation; which at the first began to be spoken by the Lord, and was confirmed unto *us* by *them that heard Him?*"[35]—which leads us to infer that the writer had not heard Jesus himself; but here, as before, Paul uses the pronoun "we" in the sense of the Christians of the day, without any personal regard to himself. All is conjecture, but we should rather conclude that Saul had never been in the presence of our Saviour while He was yet on earth.

Not long after the Crucifixion (viz. at the close of A.D. 33) died Philip, the

---

[31] This was the usual hour of crucifixion. τελευταία καὶ ἔφεδρος τιμωρία σταυρὸς ἦν ... τὰ μὲν γὰρ πρῶτα τῶν θεαμάτων ἄχρι τρίτης ὥρας ἢ τετάρτης ἐξ ἑωθινοῦ ταῦτα ἦν—Ἰουδαῖοι μαστιγούμενοι, κρεμάμενοι, τροχιζόμενοι, καταδικαζόμενοι, διὰ μέσης τῆς ὀρχήστρας ἀπαγόμενοι τὴν ἐπὶ θανάτῳ. Philo in Flaccum, ss. 9, 10. The third hour (Roman time) would not be nine o'clock exactly, as the Romans did not begin their day from 6 A.M., but from sunrise, and ended it at sunset, and divided the interval between the two into twelve hours; so that in summer the hours would be longer, and in winter shorter, than our own. The Roman hours would thus agree in length with our own at the equinoxes only; but, as the Crucifixion was very nearly at the equinox, there would be no great difference.

[32] Jos. Bell. iv. 5, 2.   [34] 1 Cor. ix. 1.
[33] 2 Cor. v. 16.   [35] Heb. ii. 3.

Tetrarch of Trachonitis;[36] so that Antipas, or Herod, the Tetrarch of Galilee, was now the only son of Herod the Great who still survived. Philip had constantly resided amongst his subjects, and ruled them with great moderation. It is told of him, that whenever he walked abroad a throne was carried about with him; and if there were any complaints for the royal ear, the throne was fixed, the Tetrarch took his seat, the litigant parties were heard, and judgment given. On the death of Philip, the province of Trachonitis was incorporated into the Roman dominions, and was annexed to the prefecture of Syria.[37]

At the expiration of something more than three years from the date of the Crucifixion (viz. in the latter part of A.D. 36), the violent and despotic administration of Pontius Pilate was brought to a sudden and abrupt determination. A Samaritan impostor had persuaded great multitudes of his countrymen to meet him in arms on Mount Gerizim,[38] under the pretext that he would discover to them certain sacred treasures which had been buried there by Moses. The wary and unscrupulous Pilate, suspecting that the religious motive was merely the cover for some deep-laid political conspiracy, poured horse and foot upon the assembled multitude just as they were about to ascend the mountain, slew some, took others prisoners, and dispersed the rest. The chiefs of the Samaritan nation resented this aggression, and sent a deputation to Vitellius (then governor of Syria, to whom the Procurator of Judæa was amenable), and accused Pilate of the indiscriminate and merciless massacre. Vitellius—whom Josephus represents as a mild and amiable character, and as anxious to promote the interests of all within his province—conceiving that an unjustifiable outrage had been committed by Pilate, at once ordered him to Rome, to answer the accusation before Tiberius in person, and appointed Marcellus, a friend of his own, to undertake the temporary administration of Judæa.[39] Soon after, in the spring of A.D. 37, Vitellius proceeded to Judæa himself; and at the Feast of the Passover (which this year was celebrated on 19th March), he paid a visit to Jerusalem, when, being enthusiastically received, he further conciliated the goodwill of the people by the grant of certain immunities. Caiaphas, who had been High Priest for twenty years, and had enjoyed and abused the favour of Pilate, was deposed for his excesses by Vitellius; and the high-priesthood was conferred on Jonathan, one of the sons of Annas, and brother-in-law of Caiaphas.[40] Vitellius then took the road to

---

[36] See Fasti Sacri, p. 240, No. 1154.

[37] Jos. Ant. xviii. 4, 6.

[38] The holy mountain of the Samaritans, and of which the woman of Samaria said, "Our fathers worshipped in this mountain." John iv. 20. And so Josephus speaks of it as ὁ ἁγιώτατος τε αὐτοῖς ὀρῶν ἐπείληπται. Jos. Ant. xviii. 4, 1.

[39] See Fasti Sacri, p. 247, No. 1493. Josephus states (Ant. xviii. 4, 2) that Marcellus was sent by Vitellius to take charge of Judæa. But I doubt whether this Marcellus be not confounded with the Marullus who was sent out for the like purpose by Caligula (Jos. Ant. xviii. 6, 10); and if so, then the Jews, on the deposal of Pilate, would be left, until the arrival of Marullus, without a Roman governor at all. But if Marcellus was sent by Vitellius, he was not appointed by the Emperor, and would be armed only with very inadequate powers.

[40] Fasti Sacri, p. 248, No. 1495; p. 249, No. 1496.

Antioch; but while he was on the way, a despatch from Tiberius occasioned him to enter Judæa a second time. Herod Antipas, the Tetrarch of Galilee, and the only surviving son of Herod the Great, had given offence to Aretas, King of Arabia Petræa, who was also a feudatory of the Roman empire; and a war breaking out between them, the general of Herod Antipas suffered a total defeat.[41] "By many of the Jews," says Josephus, "it was thought that Herod's army had been destroyed by Divine Providence, as a just punishment for the death of John the Baptist. For this John, whom Herod had put to death, was a good man, and had taught the Jews to practise virtue, and to exercise justice one towards another, and piety towards God, and so to be baptized; for baptism would then be pleasing to God, if they used it, not as a purification from sins, but as a purgation of the body when the soul had been cleansed by holiness; and many converts flocking in (for they were not a little moved by his preaching), Herod, fearing lest such unbounded influence (for they were ready to do anything at his word) might lead to some civil disturbance, thought it better to anticipate the danger by putting him to death, rather than suffer a commotion to break out, and then to repent. So John, having incurred the suspicion of Herod, was sent a prisoner to the Castle of Machærus, and was there put to death."[42] Herod, finding himself worsted in the conflict, wrote to Tiberius, imploring the aid of the Roman power. Tiberius, indignant that Aretas, who owed allegiance to Rome, should have dared to take the field without the Emperor's leave, would have vented his wrath upon Aretas forthwith; but it so happened, that at this particular juncture the Roman forces in Syria had enough upon their hands in watching the aggressive policy of Parthia.[43] The Imperial vengeance, therefore, was somewhat delayed; but Tiberius never forgot an insult, and no sooner was peace made with Parthia, in A.D. 36, and intelligence thereof carried to Rome, than Tiberius commanded Vitellius to march his army against the offender, and bring him alive or dead.[44] No sooner was the mandate received by Vitellius, on his way to Antioch, in A.D. 37, than he hastily collected a body of troops, and set forward on his march for Petra. He was now at Acre, and about to pass through Judæa, when the men of authority amongst the Jews prayed that the army might be led another way, as it was contrary to their law that any images (and the military standards displayed the head of Cæsar) should be admitted within their borders. Vitellius, without hesitation, obliged the Jews, and sending forward the army by a different route, went himself, with Herod Antipas and a few friends, to Jerusalem, to offer sacrifice to Jehovah at the Feast of Pentecost, which was celebrated this year on the 9th of May. The three first days of his sojourn in the capital were marked by no other event than the transfer of the high-priesthood from Jonathan, the son of Annas, to his brother Theophilus. The fourth

---

[41] Jos. Ant. xviii. 5, 1.
[42] Jos. Ant. xviii. 5, 2. This passage, though it differs in some particulars, confirms in the main the account given by the Evangelist. Mark vi. 17.
[43] See Fasti Sacri, p. 226, No. 1414.
[44] Jos. Ant. xviii. 5, 1.

day (the 12th of May) brought the astounding intelligence that Tiberius, the Roman Emperor, had died on the 16th of the preceding March, the transmission of the news from Rome to Jerusalem having occupied about two months. Vitellius immediately caused the Jews to take the oath of allegiance to Caligula, the new Emperor, and, having received an affront from Herod Antipas, he pleaded the want of authority to continue the war against Aretas until he received further orders, and so dispersed his army to their quarters, and returned himself to Antioch.[45]

The posture of affairs in Jerusalem was now extremely peculiar. Pilate, the Procurator, had been deposed and sent to Rome at the latter end of the preceding year. Vitellius, who as Prefect of Syria had a general superintending power over the province, had returned to the seat of government at Antioch. Tiberius, whom, from his jealous and revengeful temper, the nation would not have dared, except under some urgent necessity, to provoke, was no longer their master. Never did a more favorable crisis present itself to the Jews of slighting the Roman authority, and gratifying their national vanity by at least some show of independence. The power of life and death without the fiat of the Roman Procurator had been taken from the native judicature;[46] and as this deprivation had ever been most galling to the Jewish pride, it was easy to foresee, that if there existed in the State a body of men peculiarly obnoxious to the chief rulers, but whom, from their innocent lives in the estimation of the unprejudiced Romans, there had been no means hitherto of capitally punishing, the present opportunity would be greedily snatched of wreaking upon them the long-smothered national vengeance. Such a scene of bloodshed now actually occurred, and it is on this occasion that we meet for the first time with the name of Saul.

---

[45] Jos. Ant. xviii. 5, 3; see Fasti Sacri, p. 249, No. 1495.   [46] Jos. Ant. xx. 9, 1.

CHAPTER III.

The Rise and Progress of Christianity to the Martyrdom of Stephen.

> The Spirit,
> Poured first on His Apostles (whom He sends
> To evangelize the nations), then on all
> Baptized, shall them with wondrous gifts endue,
> To speak all tongues and do all miracles,
> As did their Lord before them. Thus they win
> Great numbers of each nation to receive
> With joy the tidings brought from heaven.
>
> Paradise Lost, book xii.

THE Jews were at this period (A.D. 37) divided into the two leading sects of Sadducees and Pharisees—the former few in number, but rich, luxurious, and proud; the latter not so commanding from the influence of wealth, as in high credit with the people, from an affectation of superior sanctity and zeal for the Mosaic ritual. The honours of the State had for many years past been enjoyed almost exclusively by the Sadducees, not to say by a single family of the Sadducees—viz. by Ananus, or Annas, and his five sons (Eleazar, Jonathan, Theophilus, Matthias, and Ananus), and his son-in-law Joseph, or Caiaphas. Annas himself had been in the possession of the high-priesthood for a lengthened period, and all his five sons were at different times advanced to the same dignity.[1] As for Joseph, or Caiaphas, he had been elevated to that post, in A.D. 17, by Gratus, and continued in the office for a period of twenty years, when he was displaced by Vitellius, who appointed to the high-priesthood, first Jonathan, a son of Annas, and then Theophilus, another son of Annas.

It is observed by Josephus, that the Sadducees in general were of a cruel and implacable disposition, never sparing their enemies from any aversion to bloodshed;[2] and this remark may have been elicited from the historian by the severities in particular of the family of Annas against the society of Christians, or (as they were then called) the Nazarenes. In A.D. 33, Caiaphas, then High Priest, and his father-in-law Annas, with their partisans, had used all their influence with Pilate to extort from him the death-warrant of our Saviour. The sympathies of the Pharisees were no doubt enlisted in the same cause, as the new religion was accused of aiming directly at the overthrow of the Jewish ceremonial, to which the Pharisees were

---

[1] See the dates in Fasti Sacri, p. 348, No. 2060.   [2] Ant. xx. 9, 1; Bell. ii. 8, 14.

bigoted; but the more bitter and rancorous hatred was on the part of the Sadducees, of whose creed the fundamental tenet was denial of the resurrection of the dead. It was hoped that by the ignominious crucifixion of Christ Himself, His followers would be suppressed; and for some time this object was apparently attained. During the fifty days between the Passover and the Pentecost of A.D. 33 there was no preaching of the obnoxious principle of the resurrection, no appeal to the people by the display of supernatural powers; but when Pentecost was come, and Parthians and Medes and Elamites, and strangers from every nation under heaven, were gathered to the Jewish capital for the celebration of the feast, the Holy Spirit descended upon the Apostles; and by the miraculous gift of tongues, and the preaching of Peter, no less than three thousand proselytes were added to the Church in one day. The attention of the Sadducees was now once more called into action against the sect, and no long time elapsed before they exerted themselves with violence to check its growth.

In the autumn of A.D. 33 a man who had been a cripple from his birth, lay at the Eastern or Beautiful gate of the Temple,[3] to solicit alms; and as Peter and John were ascending the steps to pray at the ninth hour, or 3 o'clock P.M., one of the stated times of worship,[4] Peter was enabled, by the Divine power, to work an instantaneous cure. At the report of the miracle, the people ran together from all sides, and collected about Peter and John under the eastern colonnade, called Solomon's Porch, when Peter preached to them, and made five thousand converts. While he was yet speaking, the Sadducees, "being grieved that they taught the people, and preached through Jesus the resurrection from the dead,"[5] laid hands on them, and, as it was now evening, put them in hold until the next day. On the morrow the Sadducee faction (described by Luke as "Annas the High Priest,[6] and Caiaphas, and John, and Alexander,

---

[3] The *outer* Temple, to which the Gentiles were admitted, and which served very much as a market, was a square of 600 feet. Within this area was the Temple proper, or *Inner* Temple, accessible only to Jews. According to Josephus, the *Inner* Temple had *ten* gates—four on the north, four on the south, one on the east—leading from the outer Temple into the court of the women, which was part of the Inner Temple; and another opposite to it, leading from the court of the women into the court of the Israelites, the more sacred part of the Inner Temple. All the gates, but the eastern one leading from the outer Temple into the court of the women, were gilt or plated; but this eastern gate was of Corinthian brass, and far exceeded the rest in proportions and general magnificence, and was called the Beautiful gate. It was, indeed, the grand entrance to the Temple (Jos. Bell. v. 5, 3; vi. 3, 8), and the poor and the crippled here solicited charity from those ascending to the court of the women, the part of the Temple open to the Jewish public for ordinary prayer and religious exercises.

Solomon's Porch, in which the Apostles and the people after the performance of the miracle were congregated, was just opposite to, and only a few yards from, the Beautiful or Corinthian gate, and formed the eastern cloister of the OUTER Temple. See Fasti Sacri, p. 240, No. 1452, and the author's Siege of Jerusalem by Titus.

[4] δὶς τῆς ἡμέρας, πρωΐ τε καὶ περὶ τὴν ἐνάτην ὥραν. Jos. Ant. xiv. 4, 3.

[5] Acts iv. 2.

[6] Caiaphas was really the High Priest, but Annas, his father-in-law, had been High Priest, and still retained the title, as all ex-High Priests did; and from his authority over his son-in-law, he was commonly thought to be High Priest jointly with Caiaphas.

and as many as were of the kindred of the High Priest"[7]) called the Sanhedrim together, and set Peter and John in the midst; and the lame man, on whom the miracle had been wrought, was produced. When the Council saw the boldness of Peter and John, they were amazed; for were they not two of the followers of Jesus, those timorous disciples, who, on His arrest, had taken to flight? Whence, then, this change? Whence, also, the ability with which they defended themselves, for were they not "unlearned and ignorant men"? They could not understand or account for it; but the miracle was a fact which, in the presence of the man himself, could not be denied; and they let them go, but at the same time commanded them not to preach any more in the name of Jesus. Notwithstanding this injunction, the Apostles, obeying God rather than man, continued with such unabated zeal to publish the Christian doctrine, and by the finger of God to work such signs and wonders, that great multitudes of disciples were daily added to the number of the faithful. At first, the Sadducees watched the rapid growth of the Gospel in moody silence; but finding that, if they would eradicate the Nazarene heresy, they must resolve on some bold and decisive stroke, they determined on arresting the Apostles in a body, and bringing them before the Sanhedrim, in the hope of recording against them a judicial sentence.[8] The Apostles, they argued, were the organized ringleaders of the sect, and could they be removed, their followers would soon fall away. Besides, the Apostles were the mouthpiece of the Nazarenes; and by their preaching that Jesus was the Christ, Caiaphas and his Sadducee adherents, who had put Him to death, were held up to the detestation of the people. "Then the High Priest rose up, and all they that were with him (which is the sect of the Sadducees), and were filled with indignation, and laid their hands on the Apostles, and put them in the common prison."[9] And the next day, when they were brought before the Sanhedrim, the High Priest (Caiaphas, or his vicar Annas) asked them, saying, "Did not we strictly command you that ye should not teach in this name? and, behold, ye have filled Jerusalem with your doctrine, and intend to bring this man's blood upon us."[10] And when Peter boldly maintained the resurrection, the Sadducees were for putting them to death; but the Pharisees, who advocated the doctrine of a future state, and were of a less violent temper,[11] would not listen to so extreme a course; but by their leader, Gamaliel, were the advocates of moderation, "lest haply they should be found to fight even against God."[12] The body of the Sanhedrim were obliged to yield to this recommendation,

---

[7] ἐγένετο δὲ ἐπὶ τὴν αὔριον συναχθῆναι αὐτῶν τοὺς ἄρχοντας καὶ πρεσβυτέρους καὶ γραμματεῖς εἰς Ἱερουσαλὴμ, καὶ Ἄνναν τὸν ἀρχιερέα καὶ Καϊάφαν καὶ Ἰωάννην καὶ Ἀλέξανδρον, καὶ ὅσοι ἦσαν ἐκ γένους ἀρχιερατικοῦ. Acts iv. 5. From the words ἐγένετο συναχθῆναι εἰς Ἱερουσαλὴμ, Bauer well remarks, that not only the members resident in the city were assembled, but that on so important an occasion even those who resided at a distance were summoned up to the capital.

[8] "When they heard that, they were cut to the heart, and took counsel to kill them." Acts v. 33.

[9] Acts v. 17, 18.
[10] Acts v. 28.
[11] See Jos. Ant. xiii. 10, 6.
[12] Acts v. 39.

and having beaten the Apostles, and again commanded them not to speak in the name of Jesus, they once more let them go. All this occurred in A.D. 34, within twelve months, or thereabouts, from the Crucifixion.[13]

The Sadducees were now completely foiled; and, having sustained so signal a defeat, they dared not indulge their persecuting spirit for the present, but fostered it in secret, to give it vent, with redoubled violence, at the first convenient opportunity. Their attention, also, was accidentally turned into another channel by the increasing tyranny of Pilate, and particularly by one despotic act, which more immediately concerned the Sadducees, of which sect was Caiaphas the High Priest, and who in that character had the charge of the Temple, and of the sacred treasure devoted to its use. Every Jew contributed annually to the support of the Temple a poll-tax of two drachmas (about seventeen pence), and this was collected not only from the native Jews, but, with the sanction of the Roman Government, from the Jews of the Dispersion in all quarters of the globe.[14] The fund accumulated at Jerusalem from these sources was called the "Corban," or Offering. This Pilate had sacrilegiously seized upon, and converted to a profane though not useless purpose, by expending it on an aqueduct for supplying Jerusalem with water.[15] Another aggression of Pilate was, the dedication of some shields in the Temple in honour of Tiberius. The upshot of these concurring circumstances was, that toward the close of the administration of Pilate, Christianity was, in a great degree, relieved from the pressure of Sadducee persecution. The disciples, consequently, began to multiply rapidly, and a great number of the priests even came over to the faith.[16]

Not the least prominent of the Christian teachers at this time, both from his zeal in the cause and the torrent of his eloquence and the miraculous powers which he displayed, was Stephen, a Hellenist. Seven deacons (or ministers) had lately been appointed by the Church, to assist the Apostles in the discharge of their eleemosynary duties, which had become very onerous from the multitudes of converts. Stephen had been elected one of these deacons. His success as a preacher soon provoked the wrath of the Hellenistic Jews, and the first Christian martyrdom was the result. The death of Stephen, the forerunner, in many respects, of Saul himself, forms an important epoch in the history of the Church. The twelve Apostles, while they believed in Christ as the Messiah, had continued rigid observers of the Law of Moses, and were, perhaps, at first, under the impression that the Gentiles, in order to become Christians, must pass through the door of Judaism. Stephen was the appointed instrument for opening the enlarged view that Christianity, as purely spiritual, was independent of the Ceremonial Law, and that the time would come when the Temple of Jerusalem would, with its formal sacrifices, cease to be the great centre of worship. This was no more than what our Lord Himself had foretold to the woman of Samaria—viz. that "neither in Samaria, nor in Jerusalem, but in spirit and in truth," should God be worshipped.[17] The Apostles had preached the resurrection from the dead, which had irritated the *Sadducees*; but the development of the Christian scheme by Stephen, that the Temple-worship would have an end, gave the direst offence to the *Pharisees* also, and more particularly to the Hellenists, who were taunted by their brethren as having propagated the new doctrine by the mouth of Stephen, one of their number.

Before we come to the indictment itself against Stephen, we must premise a few remarks upon the Jewish Constitution. From the answer of the Jews to Pilate, "It is not lawful for us to put any man to death,"[18] it has been not uncommonly supposed, that the power of life and death had been taken absolutely from the Jews; but if so,

---

of their own sons, and yet I, the Son of God, am required to pay a tax for supporting the house of God!" The piece of money taken from the fish's mouth was στατήρ, a stater or tetra-drachm, i.e. four drachmas (Matt. xvii. 27)—viz. a didrachm for our Lord Himself, and another didrachm for Peter: "That take, and give unto them *for me and thee*." Ibid.

[15] Jos. Bell. ii. 9, 4; Ant. xviii. 3, 2.
[16] We may form some estimate as to the number of the Jewish priests, from the fact that 4289 came up from Babylon (Ezra ii. 36-39), and they must have been much increased in the time of the Apostles. Alford.
[17] John iv. 21.
[18] John xviii. 31.

what becomes of our Lord's prophecy by what death He should die?—viz. by crucifixion at the hands of the Romans, and not by stoning at the hands of the Jews; for if only Romans could put a man to death, crucifixion would, of course, be the capital punishment. But the meaning of the passage, "It is not lawful for us to put any man to death," is: "The Feast of the Passover is now celebrating, and we (the Jews) cannot by our law put any man to death during the festival"—just as, at a subsequent Passover, Agrippa arrested Peter and cast him into prison, but could not put him to death until after the feast.[19] If the Jews could not try for capital offences, how could Pilate say to them, "Take ye him, and judge him according to your law?"[20] The only restriction on the power of the Sanhedrim was, that while they could try for capital offences, they could not execute the sentence without the fiat of the Roman Procurator. In the case of our Saviour, Pilate offered to give the Jews his fiat; but this they declined, as their object was to divert the odium of the execution from themselves, by alleging that it was a Roman proceeding. Many years after this, Annas, the High Priest, and the Sanhedrim, tried James the Just, and stoned him, *without* any permission from the Procurator, and for this illegal act Annas was deposed from his office.[21]

The political state of Jerusalem at the time of the outbreak against Stephen invited an outrage. Pilate, who had pillaged the Jews, and had practised every cruelty against them, had, as we have seen, been ordered to Rome for his iniquities, so that Judæa, for the present, was without a Roman governor. Vitellius, indeed, the Prefect of Syria, had sent his friend Marcellus to preserve the peace in Judæa, in the absence of a Procurator; but Marcellus was ἐπιμελητὴς or curator[22] only, and his powers were very limited. Such was the posture of affairs in the spring of A.D. 37, when "certain of the synagogue, which is called the synagogue of the Libertines,"[23] and Cyrenians, and

---

[19] Acts xii. 4; and see, on this subject, Fasti Sacri, p. 234, No. 1441.

[20] John xviii. 31.

[21] οὐκ ἐξὸν ἦν Ἀνάνῳ χωρὶς τῆς ἐκείνου (Procuratoris) γνώμης καθίσαι συνέδριον. Jos. Ant. xx. 9, 1. In proof of the judicial character of the Sanhedrim, it may be remarked that Lysias, as representing the Procurator, summoned the Sanhedrim to try Paul, Acts xxii. 30; and so Festus offered to Paul a trial by the Sanhedrim, in the presence of the Procurator, Acts xxv. 9; who was judge as well as ruler, and accordingly Paul describes Felix as κριτήν. Acts xxiv. 10.

[22] Jos. Ant. xviii. 4, 2.

[23] It has been questioned whether these Libertines were Libertini, "Jewish freedmen," or the inhabitants of Libertina, a city of Africa to the west of Cyrene. The Jewish freedmen were extremely numerous, more particularly at Rome. Thus, Tacitus speaks of 10,000 Jews "Libertini generis," Ann. ii. 85; and Philo refers to numerous Jews who were freedmen: Ῥωμαῖοι δὲ ἦσαν οἱ πλείους ἀπελευθερωθέντες, Leg. ad Caium, c. 23; and great multitudes of these freedmen must have attended the public festivals at Jerusalem. On the other hand, as the Libertines are coupled with the Alexandrians and Cyrenians, both of Africa, the presumption would be that the Libertines were also of Africa; and we know that there was a city Libertina, near to Carthage (Λιβερτίνα ὄνομα ἔθνους, Suidas), and Victor is mentioned in one of the Fathers as Bishop of Libertina: see Barnes' Comment., Acts vi. 9. The obscurity of this town of Libertina would account for Luke's expression, τῆς λεγομένης Λιβερτίνων, "which is *called* the synagogue of the Libertines," as if the name of Libertines were not well known. Some have hazarded the conjecture, but without the least ground for it, that the word Λιβερτίνων is corrupt, and that we should

Alexandrians,[24] and of them of Cilicia, and of Asia,"[25] determined to put down Stephen, and amongst these zealots was the youthful Saul. Since his tirocinium under Gamaliel, he had been constantly residing at Jerusalem, and had watched the rise of the Nazarenes with feelings of indignation. The warmth of his heart drew a veil before his understanding, and, an ardent champion for the law of his fathers, he could not for a moment suppose that the humble Jesus was the long-promised Messiah. Impostors under that title were daily springing up, and not uncommonly professing supernatural powers in evidence of their pretended mission; but one after another they had sunk into obscurity, or been violently cut off, and their followers dispersed. It might reasonably have been anticipated, that by the crucifixion of Jesus, the religion He published would also come to an end; but when it appeared that the Nazarenes still maintained themselves as a sect, and even, as it was said, aimed at superseding the Law of Moses, Saul, "being more exceedingly zealous of the traditions

---

read Λιβυστίνων, or people of Libya. See Stephanus Byzant. art. Λίβυς.

[24] In Cyrene, the capital of Cyrenaica, one-fourth part of the population was Jewish: τέτταρες δὲ ἦσαν ἐν τῇ πόλει τῶν Κυρηναίων, ἥ τε τῶν πολιτῶν καὶ ἡ τῶν γεωργῶν, τρίτη δὲ τῶν μετοίκων, καὶ τετάρτη τῶν Ἰουδαίων. Jos. Ant. xiv. 7, 2; and see xvi. 6, 1; contr. Apion. ii. 4; Dion. lxviii. 32; Philo in Flacc. c. 6. In Alexandria two-fifth parts of the city were Jewish. Philo, Leg. in Flaccum, c. 8; and see Jos. Ant. xiv. 7, 2; xiv. 10, 1; xix. 5, 2; Bell. ii. 18, 7. The cause of so considerable a Jewish population in these countries was, that Alexander and his successors had allowed them equal privileges with the Greeks.

[25] ἀνέστησαν δέ τινες τῶν ἐκ τῆς συναγωγῆς τῆς λεγομένης Λιβερτίνων καὶ Κυρηναίων καὶ Ἀλεξανδρέων καὶ τῶν ἀπὸ Κιλικίας καὶ Ἀσίας. Acts vi. 8. The construction of this passage has been the subject of long and learned discussion.

Some think that the men of *five* different synagogues (viz. 1, of the Libertines; 2, of the Cyrenians; 3, of the Alexandrians; 4, of them of Cilicia; and 5, of them of Asia) are here referred to. But we can scarcely suppose that the opponents of Stephen were so numerous as to be drawn from so many as five synagogues. Besides, the omission of the article τῶν before Κυρηναίων καὶ Ἀλεξανδρέων, militates against this view.

Others suppose that *two* synagogues only are intended—viz. 1, that of the synagogue of the Libertines, Cyrenians, and Alexandrians; and 2, that of the Cilicians and men of Asia. The only objection to this hypothesis is, that Luke, in that case, would probably have repeated the words τῆς συναγωγῆς before τῶν ἀπὸ Κιλικίας, and have written καὶ τῆς συναγωγῆς τῶν ἀπὸ Κιλικίας καὶ Ἀσίας.

Another opinion is, that the words τῆς συναγωγῆς run through the whole sentence, and that all the parties alluded to belonged to *one* and the same synagogue; and as regards grammatical construction, this suggestion is free from objection. But, on the other hand, it seems unlikely that five different peoples, from such distinct quarters as Africa and Asia, should have combined together for this purpose. The fact that there were 460 or 480 synagogues supported by strangers in Jerusalem (see Meyer, Acts vi. 9; Lightfoot, i. 363; ii. 664, and 35) would rather tend to the inference that large numbers were not congregated together in any one.

The more natural interpretation of the passage in question is, to consider the sentence as divided into two branches, each commencing with the article τῶν as the note of division; and it is observable that, as if to point to this view, the article is not prefixed to other words where we should expect to find it, as before Λιβερτίνων, and Κυρηναίων, and Ἀλεξανδρέων. Luke therefore designates the conspirators against the life of Stephen as composed of two classes: 1, τῶν ἐκ τῆς συναγωγῆς, &c.— those of the synagogue of the Libertines, Cyrenians, and Alexandrians; and 2, τῶν ἀπὸ Κιλικίας, &c.— the men of Cilicia and Asia. Amongst those from Cilicia, Saul was the most active; and amongst those from Asia were the zealots, who afterwards sought the life of Saul himself, when he had adopted the views of Stephen. Acts xxii. 27.

of his fathers,"[26] and "thinking with himself that he ought to do many things contrary to the name of Jesus of Nazareth,"[27] entered heart and hand upon, as he thought, the righteous design of eradicating the impious heresy. "I did it," he says himself, "ignorantly in unbelief."[28]

The opponents of Stephen (including Saul) appear, in the first place, to have challenged him to a public discussion, for they "disputed with him;"[29] and Saul, whose argumentative powers were well known, was perhaps the champion on behalf of the Hellenists. Stephen was too much for his antagonists, and they could not resist the wisdom with which he spake.[30] But in the course of the controversy, the freedom with which Stephen broached the broad doctrine that the Spiritual Law of Christ was to take the place of the Ceremonial Law of Moses, and that the Temple-worship was to cease *in toto*, shocked the consciences of his audience, and laid him open to the charge of impiety.

Defeated in argument, the cabal next concerted how they might procure a legal conviction on the ground of blasphemy. Witnesses were not wanting, who could testify to words which, in the opinion of bigoted Jews, would amount to blasphemy, and by the Law of Moses the sentence for such a crime was death by stoning. There had hitherto been this obstacle to a capital punishment, that it could not be carried out without the fiat of the Roman governor; but now, by a strange coincidence, the Procuratorship was vacant. Marcellus was present, as curator, but he could not exercise a prerogative which belonged only to a Prefect regularly appointed by the Emperor. Some probably advised caution, and that, as there was no Procurator, there could be no execution; but the bolder part insisted that, as the Procuratorship was vacant, the consent of the governor was impossible, and therefore to be dispensed with.

During this hostile attitude of the two parties, arrived the Feast of Pentecost, March 19, A.D. 37. Vitellius, who was *en route* with his army for Petra against Aretas, was at Jerusalem, and during his sojourn he would keep the peace, in the absence of a Procurator, amongst the assembled multitudes. But on the fourth day of his stay, and therefore about the 22nd of March, came the news, like a thunderbolt, that the gloomy and suspicious Tiberius, of whom the world stood in awe, was no more. The whole face of things was changed in a moment. Vitellius abandoned his campaign against Petra, dispersed his army to their quarters, and returned to Antioch. The Jews were not only without a Procurator, but were released also from the presence of the Syrian Prefect. The fear of Tiberius was no longer before their eyes, and the successor on the throne of the Cæsars was a novice, who would be slow to take an affront at the very commencement of his reign.

The enemies of Stephen now started forward with the charge, that the Law of

---

[26] Galat. i. 14; Acts xxii. 3.
[27] Acts xxvi. 9.
[28] 1 Tim. i. 13.
[29] συζητοῦντες τῷ Στεφάνῳ. Acts vi. 9.
[30] Acts vii. 10.

Moses was in danger by the doctrines broached by Stephen, and Jerusalem was thrown into a ferment.[31] Pressure was thus brought to bear upon the authorities, not unwilling, perhaps, to be thus moved, and Stephen was arrested and brought before the Sanhedrim.[32] "They came upon him, and caught him, and brought him before the Council."[33]

The Sanhedrim (commonly called "The Seventy") consisted of seventy-two members —viz. the heads of the twenty-four courses of Priests, and twenty-four Elders, and twenty-four Scribes. In the times of Jewish independence, Gazith, an apartment in the Temple, had been their wonted place of meeting; but the Romans had since prohibited their assembling in Gazith, for as no Gentile might pass the sacred precincts, a conclave where the Romans could not watch their proceedings was considered dangerous. The present time, however, was one of anarchy, and in Gazith the Sanhedrim met. The accused was now arraigned before them of blasphemy, upon the two counts, that he had proclaimed the coming destruction of the *Temple*, and the abolition of the *Mosaic policy*. The indictment being read, witnesses[34] were

---

[31] συνεκίνησαν τὸν λαόν. Acts vi. 12.

[32] Acts vi. 13.

[33] To the suddenness of his arrest may be ascribed the several inaccuracies in the speech of Stephen—such as the error in the quotation by Stephen from Amos, "Beyond Babylon" (Acts vii. 43), instead of "Beyond Damascus" (Amos v. 27); and the statement that *Jacob* and the Patriarchs were buried at Sychem, in the sepulchre purchased by Abraham from the sons of Hamor (Acts vii. 16); whereas Jacob was buried at Machpelah (Gen. l. 13), and the field at Sychem was purchased of the sons of Hamor, not by Abraham, but by Jacob. Gen. xxxiii. 19. There are several circumstances mentioned in Stephen's address which are not found in Scripture, but may be traced to the traditions then received amongst the Jews: e.g. 1. That Abraham departed into Canaan *after* the death of his father Terah (Acts vii. 4), which is supported by Philo (De Migrat. Abraham, s. 32), but contradicts the account of Genesis; for Terah was 70 years old when he begat Abraham (Gen. xi. 26), and Abraham was 75 years old when he left Haran (Gen. xii. 4), and Terah therefore at that time was 145 years old. But he lived 205 years (Gen. xi. 32) and therefore died at an interval of 60 years after Abraham's departure into Canaan.—2. That the household of Jacob who came into Egypt were 75 souls (Acts vii. 14); whereas, in Genesis (xlvi. 27), they are stated to be 70, and Philo speaks of both numbers, viz. 70 and 75. De Migrat. Abraham, p. 419.—3. That "Moses was instructed in all the wisdom of the Egyptians." (Acts vii. 22), a fact derived only from tradition. Philo, Vit. Moys. p. 606.—4. That God appeared to Moses at the burning bush when he was forty years old (Acts vii. 23, 30), whereas the Old Testament (Exod. ii. 11) does not mention the exact age. (See, upon this subject, Humphry on the Acts.)

[34] Those who gave their testimony are called *false* witnesses (μάρτυρας ψευδεῖς, Acts vi. 13); but in the same sense as false witnesses rose up against our Lord (Mark xiv. 56, 57); that is, the words sworn to may have been really spoken, but their sense was perverted by the witnesses, and put in a false light, so as to give a colour which did not properly belong to them. So Luke uses also the word ὑπέβαλον (Acts vi. 11), translated "suborned;" but it means no more than that the accusers brought forward witnesses, to support a charge which was substantially unfounded. The account which has been delivered to us proceeds from the Christian standpoint; but though Christians knew that the charge was unfounded, according to the sense in which Stephen's words were spoken by him, we must not infer that the accusers resorted to perjury to procure a verdict. In one sense the whole trial was a mockery, and the witnesses were mock-witnesses; for the Jews could not by law proceed to capital punishment without the fiat of the Roman Procurator, and at this season, as we have stated, the Procuratorship was vacant.

examined to prove the charge, and the sum of their testimony was: "This man ceaseth not to speak blasphemous words against *this Holy Place*,[35] and the Law: for we have heard him say, that this Jesus of Nazareth shall destroy *this Place*, and shall change the customs which Moses delivered us."[36] Stephen stood alone, without an advocate to aid him in his defence. But he was undismayed—nay, the consciousness of his high calling, as a martyr to the truth, lighted up his countenance with such a radiance, that they "beheld his face as it were the face of an angel."[37] The High Priest (Theophilus, the Sadducee, one of the sons of Annas) then put the question, "Are these things so?"—or, in the corresponding language of our own law, "Guilty, or not guilty?" The protomartyr replied to the charges made against him, with the address of the advocate and the boldness of the martyr.[38] He denied not the facts, for the Saviour Himself had foretold the impending downfall of the Temple, and had also glanced at the abolition of the Ceremonial Law, by declaring that the time should come when men should worship the Father, neither at Jerusalem, nor at Samaria, but in spirit and in truth. The defence of the martyr was, that language of this kind amounted not to blasphemy; for, first, as to the overthrow of the Law, he showed, by a brief outline of the Jewish history, that Moses, the very person who by revelation had introduced it, had expressly forewarned them of its future absorption in another and more perfect dispensation: "A prophet shall the Lord your God raise up unto you of your brethren, like unto me; *him shall ye hear:*" and then, by pressing upon their notice how their fathers had rejected Moses, and been punished for their rebellious spirit by a long captivity in Babylon, he led them to infer what penalties (which have since been inflicted) might await them for their rejection of the Messiah. He next cleared himself from the charge of blasphemy in predicting the destruction of the Temple—that originally their fathers had worshipped in spirit; then the Tabernacle had been erected in the wilderness; and, lastly, Solomon had built the Temple. What blasphemy was it to say, that a structure which had not long been might one day cease to be? Neither Tabernacle, nor Temple, was the keystone of religion, for "the Most High dwelleth not in temples made with hands; as saith the prophet, Heaven is my throne, and earth is my footstool; what house will ye build me? saith the Lord." He concluded by charging his auditors with the true ground of their accusation against him, namely, their own wicked and persecuting spirit: "Ye stiffnecked, and uncircumcised in heart and ears, ye do always

---

[34] Stephen, therefore, was tried in the Temple, which the Romans would not have allowed. It was, thus, a time of anarchy.

[35] Acts vi. 14.

[37] Acts vi. 15.

[38] It is not clear in what language the address was delivered. The natural supposition would be, that in a conclave of Hebrews he would speak Hebrew; but the history of the Jews given by Stephen is evidently drawn by him, not from the Hebrew, but from the Septuagint. The probability, therefore, is that Stephen, being an Hellenist (i.e. born out of Judaea) spoke his native tongue, which was Greek. This language was universally understood, and was allowed to be used even at Rome, in trials before the Senate. See Tac. Ann. ii. 32; Dion, lvii. 15; Fasti Sacri, p. 162, No. 1081.

resist the Holy Ghost: as your fathers did, so do ye. Which of the prophets have not your fathers persecuted? and they have slain them which shewed before of the coming of the Just One, of whom ye have been now the betrayers and murderers." During the delivery of this address, Saul sat on the Pharisee bench. He had, perhaps, taken no insignificant part in the trial itself, and excessive must have been the anxiety with which he watched the whole proceeding. Not a word of the protomartyr would escape his attention, and he must have writhed under its cutting rebukes. The whole Council, indeed, was agitated by tumultuous passion at the audacity of Stephen in maintaining the impious heresy; and when the last biting words of the orator pierced their guilty consciences, they rose up *en masse*, and Saul amongst the foremost, in a state of frenzy. They gnashed on him with their teeth; and when Stephen, blessed with a beatific vision, exclaimed, "I see the heavens opened, and the Son of Man standing[39] on the right hand of God," their fury was redoubled, and, stopping their ears, they drowned his voice by their cries, and the voice of Saul was amongst the loudest.[40] The sentence of death was carried by acclamation. By the Law of Moses, a blasphemer was to be stoned,[41] but outside the walls of the camp or city;[42] and the witnesses against him were required to cast the first stone.[43] The zealots of the Sanhedrim now forced Stephen out of the Temple, and carried him out of the nearest gate; the witnesses stripped off their clothes, and gave them in charge to the young Pharisee, Saul; and they stoned Stephen under the very walls of the Temple, calling upon his Saviour, and saying, "Lord, lay not this sin to their charge" (fig. 14). That an active part was taken by Saul in the martyrdom of Stephen we learn from his own testimony; for he tells us that he both voted for the condemnation, and presided at the execution. "I persecuted this way," he says, "unto the *death*;"[44] and again: "Many of the saints did I shut up in prison, having received authority from the chief priests; and when they were *put to death*, I *gave my voice* [or vote] *against them*;"[45] and that Stephen, the principal or only sufferer, is here alluded to cannot be doubted. The statement also of Luke, that the witnesses laid down their clothes[46] "at a young man's feet, whose name was Saul,"[47] is confirmed by himself, for "when" (he writes) "the blood of thy martyr Stephen was shed, I also was

---

[39] Why not sitting? Because Christ had risen in the vision, as if to receive his approaching servant. Meyer.

[40] Acts xxvi. 10. Saul, as a member of the Sanhedrim, had heard the defence of Stephen, and would naturally take a note of it; and as Luke, according to an ancient tradition, wrote under the supervision of Paul, it is likely that Saul gave his note of the protomartyr's discourse to Luke, who introduced it into the Acts of the Apostles.

[41] Levit. xxiv. 16.

[42] Levit. xxiv. 14.
[43] Deut. xvii. 7.
[44] Acts xxii. 4.
[45] ἀναιρουμένων τε αὐτῶν, κατήνεγκα ψῆφον. Acts xxvi. 10.
[46] They disencumbered themselves of their loose garments, that they might be better able to handle and throw the stones.
[47] The Greek word νεανίας, a young man (Acts vii. 58), does not imply so youthful an age as the English reader might suppose; see note, ante, p. 5.

standing by, and consenting unto his death, and kept the raiment of them that slew him."[48]

The martyrdom of Stephen was the commencement of a bitter persecution.[49] The ardent Saul, still thinking he was doing God service, rushed headlong upon his mad career; and the Sanhedrim, where the bloodthirsty counsels of the Sadducees were now dominant, armed him with all the powers of the law for the suppression of the noxious sect, by scourging, and imprisonment, and excommunication, though *capital*

Fig. 14.—*The traditional scene of the martyrdom of Stephen in the valley of Jehoshaphat. The spectator is standing in the Valley of Jehoshaphat, below St. Stephen's Gate, and is looking south. From a Daguerreotype.*

punishment may not have been again inflicted. Indeed, the martyrdom of Stephen had been an act of treason against the Roman government; and though one such offence might escape with impunity, the repetition of it would necessarily draw down the Roman vengeance upon their heads. Besides, it was hoped that the ordinary pains and penalties which the Roman constitution permitted would be weapons sharp and sure enough to eradicate every fibre of the growing heresy, and these were enforced with rigour. The disciples of Jesus were hunted for throughout the city— were followed even into their private houses;[50] and if they were courageous enough to avow their faith, they were dragged before the synagogue, and were scourged until

---

[48] Acts xxii. 20.
[49] ἐν ἐκείνῃ τῇ ἡμέρᾳ, &c. Acts viii. 1. This may mean, either on that very day, or (as in Matt. xiii. 1), at that time indefinitely.
[50] Acts viii. 3.

they renounced it by blaspheming the name of Christ.[51] If stripes did not break their spirit, they had to pass through the ordeal of a lingering imprisonment.[52] So implacable was the animosity with which the young zealot waged war against the Nazarenes, that even women lost the privilege of their sex, and were cast into a dungeon.[53] "At that time," says the writer of the Acts, "there was a great persecution against the Church which was at Jerusalem. As for Saul, he made havoc of the Church, entering into every house, and haling men and *women* committed them to prison."[54]

He who hurls a stone against Heaven must expect it to fall upon his own pate, and the cruelties that Saul now practised against others were, at no distant time, to recoil upon himself. He, too, was to be stoned—he, too, was to be scourged—he, too, was to be imprisoned—and he, too, was to attest the sincerity of his faith by the seal of martyrdom. But whatever were the corporeal sufferings he endured, perhaps, when at last his mental blindness was removed, he felt no bitterer pang than from the workings of his own conscience. Throughout his writings there is an unceasing recurrence to the violent scenes of his youth. "I am the least of the Apostles," he says, "that am not meet to be called an Apostle, because I *persecuted* the Church of God."[55] "Beyond measure I *persecuted* the Church, and *wasted* it."[56] "I was before a blasphemer, and *a persecutor*, and injurious: but I obtained mercy, because I did it in unbelief."[57] And again, when pleading to his countrymen from the stairs of Fort Antonia, he began: "I *persecuted* this way unto the death, binding and delivering into prisons both men and women."[58] And in his defence before King Agrippa, the same reflection still rankled in his mind: "I verily thought with myself, that I ought to do many things contrary to the name of Jesus of Nazareth, which thing I also did in Jerusalem: and many of the saints did I shut up in prison, having received authority from the chief priests; and when they were put to death, I gave my voice against them. And I punished them oft in every synagogue, and compelled them to blaspheme."[59] Even the very words and phrases of Stephen, to which he had listened so earnestly, appear to have been written upon his memory in letters of flame, so that he was haunted by them, involuntarily, to the last day of his life. Does Stephen say, "The Most High dwelleth not in temples made with hands"?[60]—the Apostle also tells the Athenians, that "The Lord of heaven and earth dwelleth not in temples made with hands."[61] Does Stephen speak of "the circumcision of the heart?"[62]—the Apostle uses the same figurative language to the Romans.[63] Are the dying words of the protomartyr, "Lord, lay not this sin to their charge"?[64]—almost the last supplication of the Apostle was, "I pray God that it may not be laid to their charge."[65]

---

[51] Acts xxii. 19; xxvi. 11; 1 Tim. i. 13.
[52] Acts xxii. 4, 5; xxvi. 10.
[53] Acts viii. 3; xxii. 4.
[54] Acts viii. 1, 3.
[55] 1 Cor. xv. 9.
[56] Gal. i. 13.
[57] 1 Tim. i. 13.
[58] Acts xxii. 4.
[59] Acts xxvi. 9–11.
[60] Acts vii. 48.
[61] Acts xvii. 24.
[62] Acts vii. 51.
[63] Rom. ii. 29.
[64] Acts vii. 60.
[65] 2 Tim. iv. 16. See further, upon this subject, Humphry upon the Acts.

TO THE MARTYRDOM OF STEPHEN. [A.D. 37]

The persecution in Jerusalem was assuaged only when fuel was wanting to feed the fire. The Christians were apparently subdued. Many, it is to be feared, were weak enough, in the hour of trial, to bend before the storm, and renounce their faith; but the far greater part, finding their lives and property[66] in jeopardy, abandoned their homes, and sought a refuge in more genial climes. The twelve Apostles alone remained at their post, protected by the shield of Heaven from the violence of their enemies.

The line pursued for the extermination of the heresy became, in fact, the very means of its further propagation; for the disciples that were dispersed abroad carried along with them their fondly-cherished faith, and the Church of Christ was driven out of Jerusalem to embrace in successive circles the surrounding regions. In particular, we have an account of the labours of Philip, one of the seven deacons, in a city of Samaria,[67] probably Sychar, where the Saviour himself had preached a few years before, and had foretold to His disciples an abundant harvest:[68]

> Duris ut ilex tonsa bipennibus
> Nigræ feraci frondis in Algido,
> Per damna, per cædes, ab ipso
> Ducit opes animumque ferro.
>
> Hor. Od. iv. 4, 57.

> In shady Algidus the woodman's stroke
> Lops the fair branches of the sturdy oak;
> The sturdy oak, unconquered by his blows,
> Draws life and vigour, and more proudly grows.

We may imagine the rage and disappointment of the Sanhedrim, and their agent Saul,[69] when they found that, instead of nipping the plant in the bud at Jerusalem, they had only scattered the seeds to fructify in a more productive soil. What was to be done? The enthusiastic Pharisee was not lightly to be baffled, and rather than his victims should escape him, he determined to follow them, not only into the environs of Jerusalem, but even unto strange cities. There was no more inviting field for the display of the champion's prowess than the lordly Damascus. The population of the Jews alone in this the most ancient city of the world amounted to about fifty thousand,[70] and Christianity was said to have struck its roots there,[71] and it would be a notable

---

[66] "For ye had compassion on those in bonds, and took joyfully the spoiling of your goods, knowing in yourselves that ye have in heaven a better and an enduring substance." Heb. x. 34.

[67] Acts viii. 5.

[68] John iv. 5.

[69] He is described as ἔτι ἐμπνέων ἀπειλῆς καὶ φόνου, Acts ix. 1; and, according to Meyer, this means not breathing *out* threats and murder, but ἐμπνέων, drawing *in* with his breath threats and murder. But this is too great a refinement, and the text means only breathing out as we now use the expression.

[70] The men capable of bearing arms were 10,000. Jos. Bell. ii. 20, 2; and see vii. 8, 7.

[71] As there was constant communication between Jerusalem and Damascus, the seeds of Christianity may either have been already sown there before the outbreak against Stephen, or they may have been carried thither by the fugitives. Meyer.

VOL. I.

triumph could he extirpate the heresy from that capital, as he had purged Jerusalem. But how was a Jewish envoy to exercise authority in a Syrian city, at the distance of a week's journey? The answer to the question involves much curious matter, and leads to the inquiry, what was the condition of the children of Abraham in their dispersion amongst the heathen?[72]

---

[72] As to the date of St. Stephen's martyrdom, see the author's Fasti Sacri, pp. lxvii. and 251, No. 1510.

CHAPTER IV.

The State of the Jews in Heathen Countries—The Conversion of Saul on his Way to Damascus.

I.

Who yonder rides from Salem's gate,
With scornful eye and lordly state,
As bent on distant prey?
Horsemen and footmen in his train,
He courses down to Jordan's plain,
And northward leads the way,
By Basan's hill and Hauran's sand,
To Trachon's wild and savage land.

II.

The noonday sun is towering high,
No summer cloud obscures the sky,
But all is bright and clear.
And yonder doth Damascus rise,
Amid the waste a Paradise,
The pilgrim's heart to cheer.
Up, Nazarene! arise and fly!
The desolator Saul is nigh!

Anon.

However remote their domicile from Judæa, all Jews acknowledged Jerusalem as the capital of their nation.[1] In other cities they had synagogues for prayer and praise; but the Levitical priesthood at Jerusalem was their only hierarchy, and on Mount Moriah alone could sacrifices be offered. The Jews of every place were therefore contributors to the support of the national worship, by forwarding annually to the Holy City the poll-tax of the half-shekel (figs. 15 and 16), or didrachm (figs. 17 and 18) (about seven-

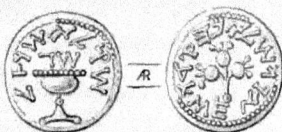

Fig. 15.—*A Shekel. From the British Museum.*

Fig. 16.—*A Half-shekel. From the British Museum.*
This was the Temple tax paid by every Jew.

teen pence), and freewill offerings proportioned to their means.[2] So in other places they had their local councils of twenty-three, for the determination of questions amongst themselves;[3] but the authority of the High Priest and Sanhedrim at Jerusalem was supreme, and to them appeals were carried up, and from them mandates were received.

---

[1] μητρόπολιν μὲν τὴν Ἱερόπολιν ἡγούμενοι, καθ᾽ ἣν ἵδρυται ὁ τοῦ ὑψίστου Θεοῦ νεὼς ὅσιος. Philo in Flac. 7; Leg. ad Caium, 36.

[2] ἀπαρχὰς ἃς ἕκαστος αὐτῶν ἐκ τῆς ἰδίας προαιρέσεως εὐσεβείας ἕνεκα τῆς πρὸς τὸ θεῖον ἀνακομιδῆς συμπορευομένους ποιεῖν ἀνεμποδίστως. Jos. Ant. xvi. 6, 7. See ante, p. 31.

[3] Ἰουδαῖοι, πολῖται ἡμέτεροι, προσελθόντες μοι ἐπέδειξαν ἑαυτοῖς σύνοδον ἔχειν ἰδίαν κατὰ τοὺς πατρίους νόμους ἀπ᾽ ἀρχῆς. καὶ τόπον ἴδιον, ἐν ᾧ τά τε πράγματα, καὶ τὰς πρὸς ἀλλήλους ἀντιλογίας κρίνουσι, Jos. Ant. xiv. 10, 17. In Alexandria the Jews had a Sanhedrim, apparently of seventy-two, by the special grant of Augustus. Philo in Flac. s. 10.

If a Jew disputed these fundamental principles he was excommunicated and ceased to be recognised as one of God's people.

But how did the Romans regard this *imperium in imperio?* They, who jealously watched every germ of political power, and prohibited public meetings, and allowed no collection of tribute but by their own tax-gatherer—how could they look on with indifference while their subjects held a conclave every Sabbath, and at stated festivals met in vast bodies and from time to time gathered treasure, to be transmitted to a turbulent

Fig. 17.—*A Didrachm of Ephesus.* From the British Museum.

Obv. Head of Diana.
Rev. Front of a stag, the emblem of Diana, and the letters Εφ (Ephesus). The drachma current at this period was equivalent to the Roman denarius, which was worth eightpence halfpenny. The value of the didrachm therefore was seventeen pence.

Fig. 18.—*A Tetradrachm of Antioch.* From the British Museum.

Obv. Head of Augustus, with the legend Καισαρος Σεβαστου (of Cæsar Augustus).
Rev. Personification of Antioch, with the legend Αντιοχεων Μητροπολεως (of Antioch Metropolis).
The tetradrachm was the highest silvercoin struck, and was also called a "stater," and was equivalent to a shekel. The Temple tax paid by every Jew was half a shekel, that is, a didrachm, or two drachms; and the tetradrachm, or stater, represented the Temple tax of two persons. This was the coin found in the fish's mouth: see *ante*, p. 31, note 34. Matt. xvii. 24.

and rebellious city? The Hebrew sojourners, too, were so unpopular in most quarters, that malicious reports would be spread, and every effort made to excite suspicion, by a misrepresentation or misconstruction of innocent proceedings. To the credit of the Romans be it spoken, that with true generosity of mind they never themselves, at least up to this period, disturbed the Jews in the exercise of their religion, and often threw around them the shield of protection against the prejudices of less enlightened nations.

The great benefactor of the Hebrew race was the illustrious Julius Cæsar (figs. 19-21). As his decrees were the foundation of all their privileges, we shall briefly state their substance.

The first was issued in favour of Hyrcanus, the High Priest [B.C. 47], who had rendered him valuable assistance in the Alexandrine war. The edict, after reciting the services of the High Priest, and confirming him and his children in the office, proceeds thus: "*I command that Hyrcanus and his children do retain all the rights of the High Priest, whether established by law or accorded by courtesy; and if hereafter any question arise touching the Jewish polity, I desire that the determination thereof be referred to him.*"[4] By the first part of this declaration, the High Priest obtained a legal recognition of his privileges—not only those claimed by him in Judæa, but also such as were allowed him by courtesy in foreign countries. The latter clause, too,

---

[4] ὅσα τε κατὰ τοὺς ἰδίους αὐτῶν νόμους ἐστὶν ἀρχιερατικὰ ἢ φιλάνθρωπα, ταῦτα κελεύω κατέχειν αὐτὸν καὶ τὰ τέκνα αὐτοῦ. ἂν δὲ μεταξὺ γένηταί τις ζήτησις περὶ τῆς Ἰουδαίων ἀγωγῆς, ἀρέσκει μοι κρίσιν γίνεσθαι παρ' αὐτοῖς. Jos. Ant. xiv. 10, 2. In some copies the last words are παρ' αὐτοῖς— viz. with Hyrcanus and his children, which seems the better reading.

was not less important, for it gave the High Priest a jurisdiction, as regards the Jewish law, over his own countrymen wherever the difference arose.

The next decree of Cæsar was another grant to Hyrcanus and his children, or (as we should say) "to him and his heirs," and ordained "that the High Priest and Ethnarch should be the *patron of all Jews that were aggrieved*."[5] This was a concession of no little practical consequence. The most beneficent laws would be utterly worthless if their provisions could be broken with impunity. Now, however, that the relation of patron and clients was established between the High Priest and the Jews of all countries, if any one suffered wrong the High Priest had authority to make a

Fig. 19.—*Front face of Julius Cæsar. From C. W. King's Antique Gems.*

This portrait is on sard, from the hand of Dioscorides, a contemporary engraver. The name of Dioscorides is in small Greek letters, beautifully cut on the gem itself.

The portrait is hard-featured and unflattering, but faithful.

Fig. 20.—*Profile of Julius Cæsar. From C. W. King's Antique Gems.*

Fig. 21.—*Roman Aureus, showing the profile of Julius Cæsar. From the British Museum.*

The head-gear is that of Cæsar, as Pontifex Maximus.

formal complaint, either to the Proconsul or to the Emperor, and the High Priest's ambassadors were to have free passage for the purpose. This privilege was on several occasions exercised with a most salutary effect.

The third edict of Cæsar related chiefly to the revenues of the High Priest, and enacted, amongst other things, that the Jews should be exempt from tribute "every seventh year, which they call the Sabbatic year, when they neither gather fruits from trees nor sow"[6]—a proof of what has been doubted by some, that the Sabbatic year still continued to be observed. It then declares, "that the ancient relative rights, either by law or courtesy, of the Jews and the High Priests towards each other should be maintained, whatever had been given them by any *decree* of the People and Senate."[7] What were the *decrees* here alluded to we know not, unless they were the edicts of Cæsar already mentioned, and which, though emanating from himself, were the decrees of the People and Senate in point of form.[8] Lastly, it conferred on

---

[5] καὶ ὁ ἀρχιερεὺς αὐτὸς καὶ ἐθνάρχης τῶν Ἰουδαίων προϊστῆται τῶν ἀδικουμένων. Jos. Ant. xiv. 10, 3.

[6] χωρὶς τοῦ ἑβδόμου ἔτους, ὃν Σαββατικὸν ἐνιαυτὸν προσαγορεύουσιν, ἐπειδὴ ἐν αὐτῷ μήτε ἀπὸ τῶν δένδρων καρπὸν λαμβάνουσι μήτε σπείρουσι. Jos. Ant. xiv. 10, 6.

[7] μένειν δὲ καὶ τὰ ἀπ' ἀρχῆς δίκαια, ὅσα πρὸς ἀλλήλους Ἰουδαίοις καὶ τοῖς ἀρχιερεῦσι καὶ τοῖς ἱερεῦσιν ἦν, τά τε φιλάνθρωπα, ὅσα τοῦ τε δήμου ψηφισαμένου καὶ τῆς συγκλήτου ἔσχον. Jos. Ant. xiv. 10, 6.

[8] However the Roman People may have made decrees before the date of this edict. See Jos. Ant. xiv. 10, 22, and xiv. 8, 5.

Hyrcanus the privilege of preferring a petition to the Senate at any time, and an answer to his petition was to be returned within ten days.

The fourth edict of Cæsar, though sufficiently brief, was of a very comprehensive character. It was issued in consequence of a decree published by the inhabitants of Parium, a city of Mysia, whereby Jews were prohibited from meeting in their synagogues, or collecting their tribute for the Temple. After reciting to that effect, it proceeded: "Now *I forbid that any such decrees be passed against those who are our friends and allies, or that they be hindered from living according to their own laws, or from contributing money for their feasts, or other sacred purposes,* seeing that they have this liberty in Rome itself. Putting down all other assemblages, I permit *these men only* to meet together and comport themselves according to the customs of their fathers and their own laws."[9] This virtually gave complete toleration to the religion of the Jews in every place, and made it illegal for any one to interfere with their customs, even as regarded their public meetings and collections of tribute, the two matters which had the most suspicious appearance. The Jews were so attached to Cæsar, for these generous sentiments in their favour, that on his death they are said to have wailed around his tomb for nights together.[10]

On the assassination of Cæsar [B.C. 44], the Senate for a moment resumed their republican powers; and Hyrcanus was alarmed lest the concessions of Cæsar, which had never been entered on the Senate Roll in the Treasury, might fall to the ground. He therefore despatched an embassy to Rome, and as all parties in that disastrous period were desirous of conciliating him, Publius Dolabella and Mark Antony, the Consuls, moved that the edicts of Cæsar should be confirmed; and the Senate decreed, that "whatever had been ordained by Cæsar, with the sanction of the Senate, concerning the Jews, but of which no record had been lodged in the Treasury, it should be as moved by Publius Dolabella and Mark Antony, the Consuls."[11]

The civil wars ended in placing Augustus on the throne [B.C. 31], and he was noble-minded enough to establish the Jews in the possession of all their privileges. The edict which he issued ran thus: "Whereas the nation of the Jews, and the High Priest Hyrcanus, have prov'd themselves loyal to the Roman People, not only at the present juncture, but also in the time of my father, Cæsar the Emperor, be it enacted by me and my Council, with the sanction of the Roman People, *that the Jews do use their own customs according to the law of their fathers, as they used them in the time of Hyrcanus, the High Priest of the Most High God.*"[12] And the decree then pro-

---

[9] ἐμοὶ τοίνυν οὐκ ἀρέσκει κατὰ τῶν ἡμετέρων φίλων καὶ συμμάχων τοιαῦτα γίνεσθαι ψηφίσματα, καὶ κωλύεσθαι αὐτοὺς ζῆν κατὰ τὰ αὐτῶν ἔθη, καὶ χρήματα εἰς σύνδειπνα καὶ τὰ ἱερὰ εἰσφέρειν, τοῦτο ποιεῖν αὐτῶν μηδὲ ἐν Ῥώμῃ κεκωλυμένων... ὁμοίως δὲ καὶ ἐγὼ τοῖς ἄλλοις θιάσους κωλύων, τούτους μόνους ἐπιτρέπω κατὰ τὰ πάτρια ἔθη καὶ νόμιμα συνάγεσθαί τε καὶ ἱστᾶσθαι. Jos. Ant. xiv. 10, 8. Some for ἱστᾶσθαι read ἑστιᾶσθαι, 'to feast.'

[10] Suet. Jul. Cæs. 84.

[11] περὶ ὧν δόγματι συγκλήτου Γάιος Καῖσαρ ὑπὲρ Ἰουδαίων ἔκρινε, καὶ εἰς τὸ ταμεῖον οὐκ ἔφθασεν ἀνενεχθῆναι, περὶ τούτων ἀρέσκει ἡμῖν γενέσθαι ὡς καὶ Ποπλίῳ Δολαβέλλᾳ καὶ Μάρκῳ Ἀντωνίῳ τοῖς ὑπάτοις ἔδοξεν. Jos. Ant. xiv. 10, 10.

[12] ἔδοξέ μοι καὶ τῷ ἐμῷ συμβουλίῳ μετὰ ὁρκω-

vides, expressly and particularly, that the Jews might forward their contributions to the Temple, and should not be obliged to attend courts of justice on the Sabbath; and that if any man were guilty of theft of their sacred books or treasures, he should be deemed sacrilegious, and his goods be forfeited to the Exchequer.

Tiberius, the successor of Augustus [A.D. 14], though he did not repeal the laws in their favour, yet, because the Jews would not offer him divine honours, was inclined to persecute them; and Caligula [A.D. 37], for the like reason, disregarded their privileges, and from time to time let their enemies loose upon them. However, on his death, the mild and liberal Claudius issued a decree to Alexandria and Syria [A.D. 41], and a similar one to the world at large, that the Jews should be reinstated in all their rights as they had enjoyed them before the days of Caligula.[13]

The rescripts of the Emperors, which we have recited, were, of course, binding upon all within the limits of the Roman Empire; but as the principal cities were still allowed to govern themselves municipally, by their councils of senators and assemblies of the people, many of them, in exercise of this affected independence, passed resolutions in conformity with the imperial edicts. Thus Ephesus,[14] Sardis,[15] Halicarnassus,[16] and Delos,[17] on disputes arising with the Jews, promulgated laws in their favour. Occasionally a city—as Parium,[18] Tralles,[19] and Miletus[20]—was refractory, and, notwithstanding the ordinances from Rome, obstructed the Jews in the practice of their religion; but when this was the case, the High Priest, as patron of all Jews that were aggrieved, despatched an embassy of complaint to the Roman governor, when the Jews were redressed, and the mischief-makers called to account. Sometimes, also, the imperial edicts were themselves of uncertain application; but the Roman authorities ever gave to them the most liberal interpretation. Thus, at Ephesus[21] and Delos,[22] when it was agitated whether the Jews were entitled to exemption from serving in the army—the Jews asserting their liberty of conscience, and that by their law they could not march on Sabbath-days, and could not touch any unclean meats—Hyrcanus, as High Priest and Patron of the Jews, sent an embassy on the subject to Dolabella, the consul, then in Asia, and the claim to exemption was allowed.

We may collect, as the summary of what has been said, that the Jews of the Dispersion, like oil sprinkled upon a waste of waters, were in daily contact with heathen society without commingling. They had their own religion and their own laws, their own places of worship and their own courts. Their eyes were ever turned towards Jerusalem, and their allegiance to the High Priest was testified, not only by the

---

μοσιάς, γνώμη δήμου Ῥωμαίων, τοὺς Ἰουδαίους χρῆσθαι τοῖς ἰδίοις θεσμοῖς κατὰ τὸν πάτριον αὐτῶν νόμον, καθὼς ἐχρῶντο ἐπὶ Ὑρκανοῦ ἀρχιερέως Θεοῦ ὑψίστου. Jos. Ant. xvi. 6, 2.

[13] Jos. Ant. xix. 5, 2 and 3.
[14] Jos. Ant. xiv. 10, 25.
[15] Jos. Ant. xiv. 10, 24.
[16] Jos. Ant. xiv. 10, 23.
[17] Jos. Ant. xiv. 10, 14.
[18] Jos. Ant. xiv. 10, 8.
[19] Jos. Ant. xiv. 10, 20.
[20] Jos. Ant. xiv. 10, 21.
[21] Jos. Ant. xiv. 10, 12, and 13.
[22] Jos. Ant. xiv. 10, 14.

annual remittance to him of a contribution towards the Temple service, but by making him the referee of all their local disputes. Thus, the High Priest and Elders of the Holy City exercised the same sort of spiritual supremacy over the synagogues of the adjacent countries, as the pope and cardinals have since assumed over the churches in communion with Rome. They promulgated edicts, and had a jurisdiction over their own people to the extent of excommunication, scourging, and imprisonment. When they had occasion to put forth this authority, they despatched ambassadors, called apostles, with mandatory letters to the local synagogues.[22]

Saul, therefore, the persecutor, having resolved [A.D. 37] on transferring the scene of his mistaken zeal from Jerusalem to Damascus, had, as a preliminary step, to obtain written credentials from the authorities of the Jewish capital to the rulers of the provincial synagogues. Theophilus, the Sadducee, the son of Annas, was still High Priest, and to him Saul applied[24] for letters of inquisition to Damascus (fig. 22), "that

Fig. 22.—Coin of Damascus. From the British Museum.
Obv. Head of Nero. Rev. The legend ΔΑΜΑΣΚΗΝΩΝ (of the Damascenes)

if he found any of that way, whether they were men or women, he might bring them bound unto Jerusalem,"[25] to answer before the Council.[26] A conclave of Elders was assembled, and as the Sadducee faction at this time prevailed, the High Priest and Sanhedrim readily granted the desired commission.[27]

It was about midsummer A.D. 37, and not very long after the martyrdom of Stephen at the preceding Feast of Pentecost,[28] that Saul, the inquisitor, the apostle or envoy of the Jewish hierarchy at Jerusalem, himself on horseback,[29] and his followers, some mounted,[30] and some on foot,[31] like a caravan at the present day, set forth upon

---

[22] See note on Acts ix. 31, by George Townsend.

[23] προσελθὼν τῷ ἀρχιερεῖ. Acts ix. 1.

[24] Acts ix. 14, 21.

[25] "Unto the Chief Priests," ἐπὶ τοὺς ἀρχιερεῖς. Acts xi. 21.

[26] Acts ix. 14; xxvi. 10, 12.

[27] See Fasti Sacri, p. 262, No. 1511. It was not immediately after the martyrdom of Stephen, for Luke, after relating that event, and before proceeding to the mission of Saul to Damascus, interposes the ministry of Philip in Samaria. Acts viii. 5.

[28] "I fell unto the groun l," ἔπεσον εἰς τὸ ἔδαφος.

Acts xxii. 7. "And he fell to the earth," πεσὼν ἐπὶ τὴν γῆν. Acts ix. 4.

[30] "And when all (viz. all that were on horseback) were fallen to the earth," πάντων δὲ καταπεσόντων ἡμῶν εἰς τὴν γῆν. Acts xxvi. 14. If, however, the word "all" is to be taken literally, then the words εἱστήκεισαν ἐννεοί, in the next note, must mean, that "when they had fallen from their horses, and had got upon their feet, they stood amazed."

[31] "And the men which journeyed with him (viz. on foot) stood speechless," οἱ δὲ ἄνδρες οἱ συνοδεύοντες αὐτῷ εἱστήκεισαν ἐννεοί. Acts ix. 7.

CHAP. IV.]   CONVERSION OF SAUL ON HIS WAY TO DAMASCUS.   [A.D. 37]   49

their mission. The distance of Damascus from Jerusalem was about 120 miles, or nearly a week's journey. The sun of their last day's pilgrimage had risen, and at noon (at which time travelling in the East becomes oppressive) they were drawing near to the city.[32] They had arrived at Caucabe ("the place of the Star"), and the domes and turrets of the capital, with its beautiful scenery, were full in sight. Saul, perhaps, in the exultation of the moment, was fondly picturing to himself the triumph he should accomplish against the enemies of his faith, when at once the Apostle of the Jews was thrown to the ground, and rose up the Apostle of Jesus Christ!

Hear the simple narrative, as he himself related it to King Agrippa.[33] "At mid-

---

[32] "He came near Damascus." ἤγγιζεν τῇ Δαμασκῷ. Acts ix. 3. ἐγγίζοντι τῇ Δαμασκῷ. Acts xxii. 6. A modern traveller (Elliott) thus describes the place of the conversion: "Scarcely a quarter of an hour's walk (from the gate on the south), on the highroad to Jerusalem, are remains of an ancient *pons*, whose reputed sanctity has caused it to be surrounded with Armenian tombs. This, as is affirmed, is the exact spot where 'a light from heaven shone round about' the zealous Pharisee." Elliott's Travels, vol. ii. p. 292.

Wilson places the scene at a quarter of a mile from the East Gate, or Bab Shurky (Travels, vol. ii. p. 152); but Elliott and Wilson must mean the same place. It will be found marked in the plan of Damascus by Porter.

However, Porter himself, who must be listened to with respect, propounds a different theory. "A tradition," he says, "as old as the time of the Crusades, locates the 'holy place' about ten miles south-west of the city, near a village called Kaukab. In the spring of 1858 I made a pilgrimage to it .... From a sombre olive-grove I emerged on the open plain, and soon found the line of the ancient road—the road along which Paul must have come. It crosses a low ridge, which separates the valleys of the Abana and Pharpar. There appeared to me to be much probability in the tradition. At this spot the traveller from the south obtains his first view of Damascus. On gaining it, Paul saw before him the city to which he was bound. His fiery zeal would naturally be inflamed by the sight, and anew he would there 'breathe out threatenings and slaughter against the disciples of the Lord.' Would it not seem that that was the time when his proud spirit was humbled, and when the passions of the fanatic were quenched for ever, by the flood of Divine grace? 'As he journeyed he came *near* to Damascus, and suddenly there shined round about him a light from heaven.'"—Porter's Giant Cities of Bashan, p. 350. Porter does not here mention his authority for the statement, that in the time of the Crusades the traditional scene of the conversion was ten miles from Damascus; but in his Five Years in Damascus (vol. i. p. 43) he quotes, De Vitry, Gesta Dei per Francos, p. 1073. However, the passage referred to in De Vitry does not bear this out, but rather the contrary, for De Vitry writes: "*Juxta* prædictam civitatem in loco, qui hodie dicitur Melgissopher, apparuit Dominus Saulo, cum appropinquaret Damasco, dicens ei 'Saule, Saule, quid me persequeris?'" The place, therefore, was *near* Damascus, and not ten miles from it. Willibald, who visited the spot A.D. 721–727, places it two miles from Damascus (Early Travels in Palestine, p. 16), which is too far, but agrees better with the present tradition than with that referred to by Porter.

There are three distinct routes from Jerusalem to Damascus:—1. The direct one, which, quitting Jerusalem by the Damascus gate on the north, follows the Roman road through Sychem and Scythopolis, and then crosses the Jordan south of the Lake of Tiberias, and thence to Gadara.—2. Another route joins the road from Egypt along the coast, and crosses the Jordan to the north of the Lake of Tiberias. 3. Another passes through Jericho, and crosses the Jordan to Heshbon, and meets the caravan track from Petra to Damascus, through Bostra. Caucabe, according to Porter, is on the direct route (No. 1), at the spot above described by him. See Porter's Damascus, vol. i. p. 43; Jac. de Vitr. Hist. Jerus. in Gesta Dei per Francos, 1073; D'Arvieux, Mémoires, tom. ii. p. 457.

[33] There are three different accounts given by Luke of the circumstances attending Paul's conversion: one in the narrative of Luke him-

VOL. I.   H

day, O king, I saw in the way a light from heaven, above the brightness of the sun, shining round about me and them which journeyed with me. And when we were all fallen to the earth, I heard a voice speaking unto me, and saying in the Hebrew self, another in the address of Paul from the stairs of Fort Antonia, and another in his defence before King Agrippa; and between these several accounts there have been discovered certain slight variations, which have opened a door to cavil. The supposed discrepancies are these:

Luke.	Paul to the Jews.	Paul to Agrippa.
1. His companions *stood* amazed, εἱστήκεισαν ἐννεοί. Acts ix. 7.	.. .. ..	1. When we had all *fallen to the ground*, πάντων καταπεσόντων ἡμῶν εἰς τὴν γῆν. Acts xxvi. 14.
2. Hearing the voice, ἀκούοντες τῆς φωνῆς. Acts ix. 7.	2. "They heard not the voice of him that spake to me," τὴν φωνὴν οὐκ ἤκουσαν τοῦ λαλοῦντός μοι. Acts xxii. 9.	.. .. ..
3. Seeing no one, μηδένα θεωροῦντες. Acts ix. 7.	3. Seeing the *light*, τὸ μὲν φῶς ἐθεάσαντο. Acts xxii. 9.	.. .. ..

1. The first difficulty may be met thus: It does not follow that by *all* are meant the whole caravan, literally, but all that were on horseback. The explanation of the apparent contradiction would then be—"All those who were mounted fell to the earth, and all that were on foot stood in amaze." But assuming the two expressions, καταπεσόντων and εἱστήκεισαν, to apply to the same persons, where is the difficulty? *All* at first were struck down by the light; but, though Paul lay blind until commanded to rise, the rest would at once start to their feet, and would stand in amaze.

2. The second objection arises from not observing the difference of expression. Paul's companions heard τῆς φωνῆς, "the sound or noise," but not (as did Paul), τὴν φωνὴν τοῦ λαλοῦντος, "the voice of the speaker." Thus, when the voice came to Jesus, "I have both glorified thee, and will glorify thee again" (John xii. 29) some, who only heard the sound, said it thundered, while others, who distinguished the words, said "an angel spake to him." So, in the Rabbinical writings are frequent instances of one person hearing the words spoken, and of others hearing the sound only. Thus, "R. Jose Galilæus ait in tribus locis Mosen Deo locutum esse, ut Aaron (quantumvis adstans) non exaudiverit." Siphra, fol. 2, 4, edit. Venet. ex versione Danzii; and see the other citations given by Schoettgen, Horæ Hebr. vol. i. p. 415. But, further, the objection assumes that the voice, or φωνή, in ἀκούοντες τῆς φωνῆς, Acts ix. 7, must be the same voice, or φωνή, as that referred to just before, ἤκουσε τὴν φωνήν. Acts ix. 4. But there are two φωναὶ expressed or implied: one, that which accompanied the light, περιήστραψεν, Acts ix. 3 (as the rushing mighty wind in the descent of the Holy Ghost on the Day of Pentecost, Acts ii. 3); and the other, the voice of the speaker. The word ἤκουσε, applied to Paul, governs the *accusative* φωνήν; but ἀκούοντες, applied to his companions, governs the *genitive*, τῆς φωνῆς; so that Luke means that Paul heard the distinct words, but the rest the sound only. This is very natural, if, as is likely, the followers were at some distance behind Paul. It is also possible, that as Jesus addressed Saul in Hebrew, such of Saul's companions as were within hearing were Hellenists, like Paul himself; but did not, like him, understand Hebrew. It is well known that in the synagogues out of Judæa, the Scriptures were interpreted, word for word, from the Hebrew into Greek, that the congregation might understand what was read. It is well observed by Wordsworth (Acts ix. 7), that "our Lord made a distinction between Saul and his fellow-travellers in regard to both senses, i.e. of *eye*, and of *ear*. *Saul saw Jesus; they* only saw the light of his appearance. *He* heard, and understood, the *words* of his voice; *they* only heard its *sound*."

3. There is here no inconsistency, even in appearance. They "saw the *light*," but they "did not" (as did Paul) "see any *person*." Had the narrative of Luke given the word μηδέν, (nothing), instead of μηδένα (no one), there would then have been a discrepancy.

As all these statements are contained in the Acts, it is obvious that Luke saw no discrepancy between them, or that he was too honest to suppress them.

tongue,[34] 'Saul, Saul, why persecutest thou me? It is hard for thee to kick against the pricks.'[35] And I said, 'Who art thou, Lord?'[36] And he said, 'I am Jesus, whom thou persecutest. But rise, and stand upon thy feet: for I have appeared unto thee for this purpose, to make thee a minister and a witness, both of these things which thou hast seen, and of those things in the which I will appear unto thee: delivering thee from the people, and from the Gentiles, unto whom now I send thee: to open their eyes, that they may turn them from darkness to light, and from the power of Satan unto God, that they may receive forgiveness of sins, and inheritance among them which are sanctified by faith that is in me."[37] And in his defence from the stairs of Fort Antonia, he adds: "And they that were with me saw indeed the light, and were afraid; but they heard not the voice of him that spake to me. And I said, 'What shall I do, Lord?' And the Lord said unto me, 'Arise, and go into Damascus; and there it shall be told thee of all things which are appointed for thee to do.' And when I could not see for the glory of that light, being led by the hand of them that were with me, I came into Damascus."[38]

"The men," it is said, "which journeyed with him stood speechless, hearing a voice, but *seeing no man*."[39] They beheld the light, and heard the sound; but they neither saw Christ, nor distinguished his words. But Saul was to be an *Apostle*, and it was required of an Apostle that he should have seen Christ; and he did see Christ at this the time of his conversion—viz. in the heavenly light that shone round about Saul before he fell to the ground. Thus, Saul asks, "*Who* art thou?" and the answer is, "I am Jesus." And again, those who journeyed with him "saw no man;" which implies that Saul did see some one. And again: "I have *appeared* unto thee for this purpose," said the Lord, "to make thee a minister and a witness, both of these things which thou hast *seen*, and of those things in the which *I will appear unto*

---

[34] The voice was in Hebrew; but if so, how, it may be said, could the speaker have referred to the Greek proverb, "It is hard for thee to kick against the pricks"? But the force of the proverb lies, not in any form of words peculiar to the Greek language, but in the idea expressed, and therefore it had the same piquancy in Hebrew or Latin as in the Greek; and it will be seen from the citations (note [35], infra) that the saying was as current amongst the Romans as amongst the Greeks; and if so, why not equally so amongst the Jews? If it was a proverb in Greek and Latin, why not also in Hebrew?

[35] An allusion to the ox kicking against the goad. This was a proverbial expression. Thus:

θέλοις' ἂν αὐτῷ μᾶλλον ἢ θυμούμενος
πρὸς κέντρα λακτίζοιμι, θνητὸς ὢν θεῷ.
Eurip. Bacc. 794.

πρὸς κέντρα μὴ λάκτιζε, μὴ πταίσας μογῇς.
Æschyl. Agam. 1624.

ποτὶ κέντρον δὲ λακτίζεμεν τελέθει ὀλισθηρὸς οἶμος.
Pind. Pyth. ii. 173.

Nam quæ inscitia adversum stimulum calces!
Terent. Phorm. act i. sc. 2, l. 27.

Si stimulos pugnis cædis, manibus plus dolet.
Plaut. Truc. act iv. scene 2.

Ne contra acumina calcitrans
Amm. Marc. xviii. 8. 3

And see Wetstein, Acts xxvi. 14, and Kuinoel Acts ix. 5, 6.

[36] The Greek word is Κύριε, which may mean either 'Sir' or 'Lord;' but I have translated it 'Lord,' rather than 'Sir' as Saul, though not acquainted with the features of Christ, and therefore ignorant of the speaker's personality; yet could not mistake the Divine character of the speaker, and would therefore address him as 'Lord.'

[37] Acts xxvi. 13–18.
[38] Acts xxii. 9–11.
[39] Acts ix. 7.

thee; delivering thee from the people (the Jews), and from the Gentiles, unto whom (viz. both Jews and Gentiles) I now send thee," or, now appoint thee an Apostle.[40] "The Lord, even Jesus, that *appeared* unto thee in the way as thou camest, hath sent me."[41] "The God of our fathers hath chosen thee, that thou shouldest know his will, and *see that Just One*, and shouldest hear the voice of his mouth: for thou shalt be his witness unto all men of what thou hast *seen* and heard."[42] And it was afterwards related to the Apostles how Saul "had *seen* the Lord in the way."[43] In the First Epistle to the Corinthians, more than once reference is made to the fact of Christ's actual appearance as the foundation of his Apostleship. "Am I not an apostle?" he says: "am I not free? have I not *seen* Jesus Christ our Lord;"[44] and again: "He was seen of James; then of all the Apostles. And last of all he was *seen* of me also, as of one born out of due time."[45] It would be needless to show that these passages allude to the period of his conversion, for there is no other occasion to which they could be referred. All other appearances to the Apostle were visions or raptures.[46] When the Apostle, indeed, was at Jerusalem, "*the Lord stood by him*, and said, Be of good cheer, Paul;"[47] but, not to contend that this was also a vision, it was of a subsequent date to the Epistle to the Corinthians, in which the fact of his having seen Christ is mentioned.

It has been already remarked, that Saul had probably not seen Christ while upon earth, and therefore it was, that when an appearance was now vouchsafed to him, he knew Him not, but said, in his ignorance, "Who art thou, Lord?" What must have been the shock to his feelings at the reply of the heavenly person—"I am Jesus, whom thou persecutest!" Then for the first time the awful truth flashed upon him, that he had been fighting against God. It is said, that "he trembled and was astonished;" for never till that moment had the possibility occurred to him, that He whom he had blasphemed should be the Son of God. Conscience-stricken, and humbled to the dust, he imploringly asked, "Lord, what wilt thou have me to do?" But not then was the moment for a bewildered mind to admit the sober light of the Gospel; the answer to his question was, "Arise, and go into the city, and it shall be told thee what thou must do." It was said by Christ, "Whosoever shall not receive the kingdom of God as a little child, shall in nowise enter therein;"[48] and, "Except a man be born again, he cannot see the kingdom of God."[49] And the prostrate Saul at the

---

[40] νῦν σε ἀποστέλλω. Acts xxvi. 16, 17.
[41] Acts ix. 17.
[42] Acts xxii. 14, 15.
[43] Acts ix. 27.
[44] 1 Cor. ix. 1.
[45] 1 Cor. xv. 7, 8.—As all the other appearances of Christ, here enumerated, were real presences, we must conclude that the appearance to Paul himself was also a real presence.
[46] "Then spake the Lord to Paul in the night by a *vision*, 'Be not afraid, but speak, and hold not thy peace.'" Acts xviii. 9. "And it came to pass, that, when I was come again to Jerusalem, even while I prayed in the Temple, I was in a *trance*," &c. Acts xxii. 17. See also 2 Cor. xii. 2, 3.
[47] Acts xxiii. 11.
[48] Mark x. 15; Luke xviii. 17.
[49] John iii. 2

present moment was dead, indeed, to Judaism, in which he had grown to manhood, but alive in Christ, to whom he was now born again as a little child.

Blind as yet both bodily and spiritually, and unable to guide his steps without compassionate assistance, Saul arose from the earth, and they "led him by the hand into Damascus," and took him to the street called Straight, to the house of one Judas.[50] For three days (which, by the Hebrew mode of reckoning, means the day of conversion, the following day, and the day after till the coming of Ananias) he was without sight, and did neither eat nor drink.[51] While the visible world was shut out, and his body worn down by continual abstinence, how busy must have been his thoughts within!—what the bitterness of his spirit at the retrospect of the past! He sought relief where alone it could be found—he prayed.[52] "Knock, and it shall be opened," and the third day his earnest supplication was heard.

There was dwelling at Damascus a certain disciple, named Ananias,[53] one of the refugees, perhaps, from Jerusalem, whom Saul had come to arrest as a renegade. Ananias knew the object of Saul's mission; and the followers of the Jewish envoy, not yet understanding the change that had been wrought, had proudly published through the city the threatened extermination of the heresy.[54] The Lord appeared to Ananias in a vision, and "said unto him: 'Arise, and go into the street which is called Straight, and enquire in the house of Judas for one called Saul, of Tarsus: for, behold, he prayeth, and hath seen in a vision a man named Ananias coming in, and putting his hand on him, that he might receive his sight.' Then Ananias answered, 'Lord, I have heard by many of this man, how much evil he hath done to thy saints at Jerusalem:

---

[50] Straight Street is thus described by Porter: 'The old city, the nucleus of Damascus, is oval in shape, and surrounded by a wall, the foundations of which are Roman, if not earlier, and the upper part a patchwork of all subsequent ages. Its greatest diameter is marked by the Straight Street, which is an English mile in length. At its east end is *Bab Shurky*, "the East Gate," a fine Roman portal, having a central and two side arches. The central and southern arches have been walled up for more than eight centuries, and the northern now forms the only entrance to the city . . . In the Roman age, and down to the time of the Mahommedan conquest (A.D. 634), a noble street ran in a straight line from the gate westward through the city. It was divided by Corinthian colonnades into three avenues opposite to the three portals. A modern street runs in the line of the old one, but it is narrow and irregular. Though many of the columns remain, they are mostly hidden by the houses and shops . . . This is 'the street called Straight,' along which Paul was led by the hand, and in which was the house of Judas, where he lodged." Porter's Giant Cities of Bashan, p. 349. The traditional house of Judas lies on the south side of the street, at a little distance to the east of the *western* gate. See the plan, fig. 34, infra.

[51] οὐκ ἔφαγεν οὐδὲ ἔπιεν, Acts ix. 9; which may be either taken literally, or that he refrained only from his usual meals.

[52] "Behold, he prayeth." Acts ix. 11.

[53] A Hebrew name, signifying "Pleasing to God," from חן, gratiosus fuit, and יה, contracted from יהוה. Kuinoel; Acts ix. 10. Mention is made by Josephus, at this very time, of an Ananias, a Jewish merchant, who was instrumental to the conversion of Helena, Queen of Adriabene. Ant. xx. 23. But the name was a common one, and we have no reason to assume that the two persons were identical.

[54] The German writers have discussed the question, whether Ananias had any previous acquaintance, personally, with Saul; but nothing in the narrative leads to such an inference, and Acts ix. 13 assumes the contrary. See Kuinoel on Acts ix. 10.

and here he hath authority from the chief priests to bind all that call on thy name.'[55] But the Lord said unto him, 'Go thy way: for he is a chosen vessel unto me, to bear my name before the Gentiles,[56] and kings,[57] and the children of Israel: for I will shew him how great things he must suffer for my name's sake.' And Ananias went his way, and entered into the house; and putting his hands on him, said, 'Brother Saul, the Lord, even Jesus, that appeared unto thee in the way as thou camest, hath sent me, that thou mightest receive thy sight, and be filled with the Holy Ghost.' And immediately there fell from his eyes as it had been scales:[58] and he received sight forthwith,[59] and arose, and was baptized. And when he had received meat, he was strengthened."[60]

Thus did Saul the persecutor become Saul the soldier of the Cross. He had been *called* to the Apostleship by Christ himself, at the time of the heavenly vision; and the *investiture* (for it must be regarded as all one transaction) was now completed by Ananias, by baptism and the laying-on of hands, and the communication of the Holy Spirit Henceforth the indomitable zeal, which had been heretofore displayed (with what vain efforts!) to the destruction of the faith, was to be exerted for its propagation. The scales had fallen from his intellectual sight, and his life, from this time till the day when he laid his head upon the block, was to be one unbroken series of toil and suffering, of contempt of the world and defiance of danger, of struggles, through good report and evil report, to the crown of everlasting glory.

---

[55] The object of Saul's mission had been kept secret at Jerusalem, but on his conversion his fellow-travellers divulged it.

[56] The word 'Gentiles' is put first, as the mission of Paul was primarily to the Gentiles, and secondarily to the Jews.

[57] As before King Agrippa (Acts xxv. 23); and probably Nero, not to mention the governors of provinces, the representatives of the Emperor, as Sergius Paulus, the Proconsul of Cyprus (Acts xiii. 12), and Felix (Acts xxiv. 10), and Festus (Acts xxvi. 1), Procurators of Judæa.

[58] ὡσεὶ λεπίδες, Acts ix. 18; and the word ὡσεὶ has led some to suppose that nothing like scales fell actually from the eyes, but only that the effect was the same as if it had been so. But, from the position of the word λεπίδες, the natural meaning is, that what fell from his eyes resembled scales.

[59] Some of the German critics urge, that the restoration of Paul's sight was a natural effect of the imposition of the cold hand of Ananias Can absurdity be carried further?

[60] Acts ix. 11-19.

CHAPTER V.

Saul retires into Arabia—An Account of Damascus—Saul returns to Damascus, and begins to preach the Gospel—The Jews plot against his life, and he escapes to Jerusalem.

> Damascus! daughter of Abana's stream,
> How beauteous still are thy enchanting bowers!
> Thy gardens, that with fruits unnumbered teem,
> The perfumes that exhale from loveliest flowers!
> Thy native charms defy the gliding hours;
> But marred, alas! the work that man hath made.
> Where now the busy mart, the street called Straight?
> The arch of triumph? and the colonnade
> That linked the eastern to the western gate?
> Havoc hath revelled here, and all lies desolate!
>
> Anon.

SAUL was a new creature. He must have felt as if suddenly dropped from one world into another, to commence a new existence, at variance with every preconceived notion, and the reverse of his whole previous career. His mind must have been stunned by the mighty revelation which had been vouchsafed him, and must have required rest and repose to regain its wonted equilibrium. His Divine Master, before entering upon his ministry, had fasted forty days in the wilderness; and Saul now withdrew himself for a season from Damascus, and took refuge in Arabia.[1] To

---

[1] Arabia, as now familiarly known, is the great peninsula between the Red Sea and the Persian Gulf; but in the Apostolic age it included the broad tract to the south of Damascus, between Jordan on the west, and the desert on the east. Ἰορδάνης, ποταμὸς διαιρῶν τὴν Ἰουδαίαν τῆς Ἀραβίας, Euseb. Onom. Ἰορδάνης; and so Jos. Bell. i. 4, 3; Ant. xii. 4, 11. Arabia comprised Philadelphia (Euseb. Onom. Ἀμμάν), and Gerasa (Ib. Ἀργόβ), and Edrei (Ib. Ἐδραεί), and Astaroth (Ib. Καρναείμ), and Canatha (Ib. Κανάθ; Stephan. Byz. Κάναθα), and Bostra, the metropolis (Βόστρα, ἡ νῦν μητρόπολις τῆς Ἀραβίας. Euseb. Onom. Βοσώρ). (Fig. 23.)

All these cities lie either within or on the borders of the great plain between Gaulanitis and Peræa on the west, and Trachonitis on the east; and it would seem as if Eusebius considered this tract to be properly Arabia, more particularly as he calls Bostra the metropolis of it, for Bostra could scarcely pass as the metropolis of the whole country to the east of the Jordan.

The name given to this part by Josephus is Auranitis, which is altogether omitted by Eusebius, and which is well accounted for, if Eusebius means Auranitis under the name of Arabia. Auranitis was, in fact, for a short time, part of the Arabian kingdom of Petra, for Zenon sold it to the Arabians; but it was taken from them by Augustus, and given to Herod. Jos. Ant. xv. 10, 1.

However, the Arabic population extended far beyond the Plain of Auranitis, for the Trachonites of the Ledja, on the east, were Arabs, οἱ Τραχωνῖται Ἄραβες, Ptol. v. 15, 26; as were the Trachonites of the mountains immediately east of Damascus, τῶν Ἀραβίων ὀρῶν τῶν ὑπὲρ τῆς Δαμασκηνῆς, Strabo, xvi. 2, 16 (p. 363, Tauchnitz); and

what part in particular he repaired has been much disputed, and cannot be satisfactorily ascertained. Arabia, in a large sense, lay all round Damascus, and it is likely that Saul, who intended shortly to return, would not retire to any considerable distance. He may have sought privacy in the neighbouring kingdom of Iturea Libani, which lay to the west;[1] or he may have travelled northward to the dominions of Sampsigeramus, King of Emesa (now Hems), who was connected by marriage with the royal family of Judæa;[2] or he may have journeyed to Auranitis (now Hauran), to the south-east, and commonly called Arabia.[3] The natives of this part are described as of a peaceful character, and more settled habits; some tending their flocks on the mountains, and others supporting themselves by the manufacture of tents from the goat's-hair of the country.[4] Such a scene would be congenial to the tone of Saul's mind, and here, if necessary, he might maintain himself, by the labour of his hands,

---

Arabians were found on the Antilibanus (τὰ μὲν γὰρ ὀρεινὰ ἔχουσι πάντα Ἰτουραῖοί τε καὶ Ἄραβες, Strabo, xvi. 2 (p. 364, Tauchnitz); Ἰτουραίων τῶν Ἀράβων, Dion, lix. 12; ἐπὶ Ἀραβίας στέλλεται εἰς τὸν Ἀντιλίβανον καλούμενον, Arrian, lib. ii. c. 20); and even as far north as Apamæa, πᾶσα ἡ πρὸς

Fig. 23.—View of Bostra. From Laborde.

νότον τοῖς Ἀπαμεῦσιν ἀνδρῶν Σκηνιτῶν τὰ πλέον, &c. Strabo, xvi. 2 (p. 360, Tauchnitz). But they do not seem to have formed any considerable element in Gaulanitis, where Syriac was spoken. See infra, p. 63.

[2] This was reckoned part of Arabia, and in A.D. 38, Socinus was appointed king of it by Caligula. Dion, lix. 12. See Fasti Sacri, p. 256, No. 1533.

[3] Jos. Ant. xviii 5, 4; and see xix. 8, 1.—Strabo says, of the Arabians who bordered on the Syrians: Ἀεὶ δ' οἱ πλησιαίτεροι τοῖς Σύροις ἡμερώτεροι καὶ ἧττον Ἄραβες καὶ Σκηνῖται, ἡγεμονίας ἔχοντες συντεταγμένας μᾶλλον, καθάπερ ἡ Σαμψικεράμου Ἀρέθουσα, καὶ ἡ Γαμβάρου, καὶ ἡ Θέμελλα, καὶ ἄλλαι τοιαῦται. Strabo, xvi. 2 (vol. iii. p. 360, Tauchnitz). See Fasti Sacri, p. 90, No. 727; p. 271, No. 1624.

[4] See ante, p. 55, note f.

[5] Burckhardt's 'Notes on the Bedouins,' p. 38.

in the art of tentmaking.⁶ Others, again, suggest that he retreated into the part of Trachonitis now called the Ledja, the general asylum of the persecuted,⁷ and where he would find a refuge in those old deserted mansions, so well described by a modern traveller.⁸ Some have even ventured the hypothesis that Saul, while in this sanctuary, opened his mission and planted a church there, and certainly a church in the earliest ages existed in this part, and flourished for centuries; but it is too much to say that it was founded by the Apostle;⁹ for he tells us that immediately on his conversion (A.D. 37) he held no communion with man, but with God only; (he "conferred not with flesh and blood;"¹⁰) and again, that he first entered upon his mission at Damascus, "I shewed *first* unto them of Damascus."¹¹ Others (as J. B. Lightfoot)¹² think that Paul travelled as far south as Mount Sinai, in Arabia proper; but this is highly improbable, for why, in that case, should he have returned again to Damascus, when Jerusalem lay in his way, and was so much nearer? All is uncertain; but we should imagine that Saul took up his abode either in Auranitis or Trachonitis.

In the solitudes of Arabia, Saul meditated in secret upon the great change that had been wrought in him, and he prayed fervently in the spirit for strength to enter upon his high mission. There it was that he received from heaven the revelations of the Gospel, that should fit him for his task. We know that he derived not his knowledge from any human instruction. "I certify you, brethren," he writes to the Galatians, "that the Gospel which was preached of me is not after man; for I neither received it of man, *neither was I taught it*, but by the *revelation* of Jesus Christ."¹³ And to the Corinthians: "*I received of the Lord* that which I also delivered unto you."¹⁴ And to the Ephesians: "If ye have heard of the dispensation of the grace of God, which is given me to you-ward: how that by *revelation* he made known unto me the mystery."¹⁵ And from the way in which he speaks of his Gospel to the Galatians, it would seem that these heavenly communications were made to him directly after his conversion while in Arabia, for he says: "But when it pleased God, who separated me from my mother's womb, and called me by his grace, to reveal his Son in me, that I might preach him among the heathen; *immediately* (εὐθέως)¹⁶ *I conferred not with flesh and blood*, neither went I

---

⁶ That the tents of the nomadic Arabians were made of *cilicia*—i.e. the coarse cloths manufactured from goat's-hair, whether of Cilicia or other parts — we learn from Pliny: Nomades inde infestatoresque Chaldæorum Scenitæ . . . . a tabernaculis cognominati, quæ ciliciis mutantur, ubi libuit. Plin. N. H. vi. 32.
⁷ Porter's Bashan, p. 92.
⁸ Ibid.
⁹ Ibid. p. 16.
¹⁰ Galat. i. 16.
¹¹ Acts xxvi. 20.
¹² Epist. to Galatians, p. 87.

¹³ Galat. i. 11, 12.
¹⁴ 1 Cor. xv. 3.
¹⁵ Eph. iii. 2, 3.
¹⁶ If the narrative of Luke stood alone, we should suppose that Saul preached *immediately* after his conversion in the synagogues of Damascus, καὶ εὐθέως ἐν ταῖς συναγωγαῖς ἐκήρυσσε, Acts ix. 20; but the testimony of Paul himself, in his own case, would be decisive, even if Luke contradicted him. But in the Acts the word εὐθέως is not appended to the conversion, but to the statement that Paul was many days with the disciples in Damascus, viz. (as appears from

up to Jerusalem to them which were Apostles before me,[17] but *I went away into Arabia.*"[18]

While the Apostle is in Arabia, putting on the whole armour of Christ, to prepare for the day of battle, let us take advantage of the pause to sketch the state of Damascus, to which he speedily returned. Of all existing cities, Damascus is the most ancient. It was already famous in the days of the patriarch Abraham, whose servant Eliezer was of Damascus.[19] Indeed, according to Nicolaus Damascenus, 'Abraham for a brief time was King of Damascus[20]—a tradition, however, which must be ascribed to the partiality of the writer, a native of the city, and who converted a temporary sojourn of Abraham *en route* from Haran to Canaan, into a permanent residence. The cause of this precocious prosperity was the fertility of the soil from the never-failing streams of the Abana (now the Barrada), which, issuing from Mount Libanus on the west, was conducted in a thousand rills through the gardens and orchards, and finally discharged itself into Lake Ateibeh, a few miles to the east.[21]

---

the testimony of Paul), after his return from Arabia.

[17] From the expression, "who were Apostles before me," we may collect that Paul regarded himself as an Apostle at the time of writing.

[18] Gal. i. 15-17.

[19] Gen. xv. 2.

[20] Jos. Ant. i. 7, 2.

[21] On the eastern side of Damascus, and on the western border of Lake Ateibeh, is the little village of Harran, and Dr. Beke maintains that this is the true Haran to which Abraham migrated from Ur of the Chaldees. The prevailing opinion is that the Haran of Abraham is that called by the Greeks Κάρραι, and by the Romans Carræ, on the River Belilk (the ancient Bilichus), which flows into the Euphrates from the east—a scene famous for the utter rout of the army of Crassus by the Parthians, in the year B.C. 53.

According to the *Authorised Version*, Haran was certainly not near Damascus, but in Mesopotamia; for Terah and his sons Abraham and Nahor and grandson Lot, quitted Ur of the Chaldees for Haran, Gen. xi. 31; Jos. Ant. i. 6, 5; and Terah died there, Gen. xi. 32. But Abraham and Lot passed on to Canaan, while Nahor remained at Haran, which was thenceforth called the city of Nahor. Now, this city of Nahor is expressly placed in *Mesopotamia*, Gen. xxiv. 10.

However, the word Mesopotamia, in the Authorised Version, is not found in the original *Hebrew*, which gives "Aram Naharaim," or "Syria of the two rivers;" and it is contended by Dr. Beke that the two rivers referred to are the Abana (or Barrada), which flows through Damascus, and the Pharpar (or Awaj), which runs from Mount Hermon, eastward, some miles to the south of Damascus. The phrase "Aram Naharaim" occurs several times in the Old Testament: as in Deut. xxiii. 4, 1 Chron. xix. 6, Judges iii. 8, 10, as well as in Gen. xxiv. 10. And the expression has always been assumed to be the Hebrew rendering of the Greek word Mesopotamia, or the Mid-river country, and this view harmonizes better with the context. Thus, Chushan-rishathaim was king of Aram Naharaim (Judges iii. 8); and we can hardly suppose that he was king of the tract only between the Abana and Pharpar, or he would have been called King of Damascus. Probably, while the whole region between the Euphrates and the Tigris was sometimes called Chaldæa, and sometimes Aram Naharaim, the subordinate parts were distinguished from each other by names of their own, viz. the southern as Chaldæa, and the northern as Aram Naharaim (Mesopotamian Syria), or, as it is sometimes called, Padan Aram (Champagne Syria, Simon's Heb. Dict.; Gen. xxviii. 2, 5).

Aram, or Syria, in its widest sense, extended to both sides of the Euphrates (1 Chron. xix. 16), and was distributed into various provinces—as, besides Aram Naharaim, or Padan Aram, we meet with Aram Maachah, Aram Zobah, &c. 1 Chron. xix. 6, &c.

The argument most relied upon for placing Haran on Lake Ateibeh, near Damascus, is a

The fortunes of Damascus, as portrayed in the historical books of the Old Testament, need not be here repeated, and we pass on to the time when the Roman influence first overshadowed the East. When Pompey, after having subdued Pontus and

passage cited by Josephus from Nicolaus Damascenus, and which runs as follows:—"Abraham reigned over Damascus, having come there as an immigrant from the land above Babylon called Chaldæa. But after no long time, having risen up with his people from this land also, he and his followers (who had multiplied) migrated to what was then called Canaan, and now Judæa. And to this day in Damascené the name of Abraham is held in honour, and a village is pointed out called 'Abraham's dwelling-place.'" Jos. Antiq. i. 7, 2. Here, it is said, we have the testimony of Nicolaus to the fact that Abraham lived in the immediate neighbourhood of Damascus; and as we know that Abraham sojourned at Haran, and as we find a Harran at Damascus, we must conclude that Harran at Damascus and Haran are identical. But does this consequence legitimately follow? Nicolaus tells us that Abraham was not long at Damascus, but sojourned there for a time only, and then passed on to Canaan. Evidently, therefore, Abraham was not moving from Ur of the Chaldees to Haran, but from Haran to Canaan; and as Haran on the Bilik lay north of Damascus, Abraham would, by the ordinary road, take Damascus on his way, and would naturally rest there to refresh his people. The passage speaks of Abraham as ruling in Damascus, when he was an *immigrant from the land of the Chaldees* on his way to Canaan; and this would be just the case if the short sojourn at Damascus was *en route* from Haran on the Bilik to the land of promise.

The advocates of Harran, near Damascus, appeal also to the language of the protomartyr Stephen: "The God of glory," he begins, "appeared unto our father Abraham, when he was in Mesopotamia, before he dwelt in Charran . . . Then came he (Abraham) *out of the land of the Chaldæans*, and dwelt in Charran." Acts vii. 2, 4. Hence it is urged that if he went out of Chaldæa to Haran, and Mesopotamia was Chaldæa, Haran was not in Mesopotamia, and therefore can only be Harran, near Damascus. But the answer is, that although, occasionally, all Mesopotamia was called Chaldæa, yet, unquestionably, Chaldæa was sometimes distinguished from it, as we shall see presently in the language of Josephus. There is, therefore, no inconsistency in Stephen saying that Abraham, when he departed from

Ur of the Chaldees, settled in Charran; for Charran, though in Mesopotamia, was not a Chaldee but a Syrian city. Bethuel, for instance, the son of Nahor, who resided there, is called "the Syrian" (Gen. xxviii. 5), and Laban himself spoke Syrian, as distinct from the Hebrew of Jacob. Gen. xxxi. 47.

The theory, that Haran is at Damascus, is contradicted by the general voice of antiquity. It can scarcely be denied that Philo and Josephus, the two most learned Jews of their day, had far better opportunities than any modern critic of determining the true site of Haran, and both of them place it in Mesopotamia. Thus Jacob, on his journey from Canaan to Padan-aram, in which was Haran (Gen. xxviii. 2), is said by Philo to have gone to *Mesopotamia* (vol. i. p. 553, De Profugis, c. 9); and Balaam, who was of Aram Naharaim (the same as Padan-aram) is described as coming from *Mesopotamia* (vol. i. p. 414; De Confus. Ling. c. 15, vol. ii. p. 122; De Vitâ Moysis, c. 18).

The language of Josephus deserves particular attention, for he tells us that Abraham and his two brothers, Nahor and Haran, all dwelt in Ur of the Chaldees: ἐν πόλει Οὐρῇ λεγομένῃ τῶν Χαλδαίων (Ant. i. 6, 5), and that on the death of Haran, the whole tribe moved to Haran of Mesopotamia: εἰς Χαρρὰν τῆς Μεσοποταμίας (ibid.); and that afterwards Abraham and his nephew Lot, the son of Haran, left *Chaldæa* (meaning Mesopotamia) for Canaan, and that he did so in consequence of some difference between him and the *Chaldees* and the *other Mesopotamites*: Χαλδαίων τε καὶ τῶν ἄλλων Μεσοποταμιτῶν. Ant. i. 7, 1. Here we have Josephus not only placing Haran in Mesopotamia, but using the word Chaldæa in the two senses before referred to: viz. first in a general way, as identical with Mesopotamia; and then as a particular part, distinct from the rest of Mesopotamia.

The early Fathers followed in the same track. Eusebius, for instance, the great authority on sacred geography, places Haran in Mesopotamia. Euseb. Onomasticon.

So far as Scripture itself affords any light, it leans in the same direction. Thus, when Jacob fled from Laban at Haran, "he passed over the river," Gen. xxxi. 21; and when "the river" simply, without any adjunct, is mentioned by the

Armenia, descended into Syria (B.C. 64), Damascus was under the sway of Ptolemy, son of Mennæus, King of Chalcis, a city then of some importance, but now a ruin, situate north-west of Damascus, in the celebrated valley between Libanus and Antilibanus.[22] Ptolemy was a heartless tyrant, and ruled with a rod of iron. His dominions apparently comprised, besides Chalcis itself, Abilené, Damascené, Paneas, Ituræa, Trachonitis, Gaulanitis, Batanea, and Auranitis.[23] One bloody act will stamp

Jews the Euphrates is always understood. Jacob, therefore, was escaping from Mesopotamia, on the other side of the Euphrates. It is further said that Laban did not hear of Jacob's flight until the third day, and that he overtook Jacob, after seven days' journey, at Mount Gilead (Gen. xxxi. 22, 23), and this was somewhere north of the River Jabbok; for Jacob, *after* the meeting between him and Laban, "passed over the ford of Jabbok" (Gen. xxxii. 22), and came to Succoth (Gen. xxxiii. 17). Assuming Haran to have been at Damascus, the distance from it to the Jabbok would be about eighty miles, at the utmost. Jacob and his flocks and herds, therefore, if they started from Damascus, travelled eighty miles in ten days, i.e. at the rate only of eight miles a day, which seems too little, as Jacob was making all haste. Laban also, though he "so hotly pursued" Jacob (Gen. xxxi. 36), travelled eighty miles only in seven days, i.e. at the rate only of eleven and a half miles a day; and so slow a progress is opposed to all probability. What the rate of travelling really was it is hard to determine, from the uncertainty of the terminus *a quo* and the terminus *ad quem*. Haran in Mesopotamia was itself about fifty miles from the Euphrates, but, apparently, the ten days' journey of Jacob is not to be measured from Haran itself, but from the Euphrates; for as long as Jacob's flocks and herds were to the east of the Euphrates, their remoteness from Haran would naturally be ascribed to the convenience of pasturage, and as Jacob concealed his flight he would encourage this idea; and that such was really the case may be inferred from the fact, that Laban at Haran did not hear of the flight until the third day—that is, the news from the Euphrates to Haran was transmitted at the rate of twenty or twenty-five miles a day. The language, also, of Genesis implies that the flight commenced from the Euphrates, for it is said, "he fled with all that he had, and he rose up and passed over *the river*." Gen. xxxi. 21.

The terminus *ad quem*, or place of meeting between Jacob and Laban, was Mount Gilead (Gen. xxxi. 23), which was so called from the stones set up there in testimony of the compact between them, viz. Gal-eed, or "The witnesses' heap." Gen. xxxi. 47. In subsequent ages the name of Gilead was extended to the whole range of mountains on the east of the Jordan, from the southern termination of Antilibanus to the River Arnon, for we read that "the Lord showed Moses all the land of Gilead unto Dan," Deut. xxxiv. 1; and see Judges xx. 1; Joshua xxii. 9. As Gilead, therefore, is used in this indefinite sense, it is impossible to collect, from the name only, where the encounter between Jacob and Laban occurred; and our only means of approximating to the truth will be to take the Euphrates as the starting-point, and consider the probable rate of travelling of the flocks and herds. In England, as I am informed, sheep may be driven from fifteen to twenty miles a day, and oxen twenty miles a day; but as with Jacob there were "flocks and herds with young" (Gen. xxxiii. 13), we cannot, though Jacob would make all haste, and would begin his journey at a time of year when the flocks and herds were most capable of fatigue, allow more than twelve miles a day, which, for the whole ten days, would make 120 miles from the Euphrates. But Laban must have started in pursuit from Haran itself, which was fifty miles to the east of the Euphrates; these fifty miles, added to the 120 miles of Jacob, would make a journey for Laban of 170 miles. As this distance was accomplished by him in seven days, Laban must have travelled at the rate of about twenty-five miles a day, which answers to the usual average of a day's journey in the East. We should surmise, therefore, that Mount Gilead was about 170 miles from Haran, and 120 from the Euphrates, in the direction of a line drawn from Haran to Succoth, where we afterwards find Jacob. But what was the very spot in particular it is impossible to say.

[22] See Fasti Sacri, p. 8, No. 68.

[23] We may take this opportunity of defining

his character: he assassinated his own son Philippion, that he might himself marry his daughter-in-law.[24] The rich burgesses of Damascus were the constant victims of his avarice, and they made several vain attempts to free themselves from his yoke.

the limits of some of the countries, the boundaries of which are not generally known and not always easy to be ascertained:—

Abilene was the country about Abila. This town lay eighteen miles north-west of Damascus, and was on the River Barrada. Pococke found the ruins, and a stone bearing the inscription, "Lysanias, Tetrarch of Abilene." The natives connected the spot with the death of Abel, the name of Abila having become unintelligible, and at last corrupted. Pocock's Travels in the East, vol. ii. p. 116. See a sketch of the site of Abila in the next page, with a coin of the country.

Chalcis was the petty kingdom of Herod, the brother of Agrippa I. The city is now in ruins, and the site is called Anjar. Chalcis stood on the slope of the watershed, or saddleback, which lies between Libanus and Antilibanus, a little to the north of the road from Damascus to Beyrout, about as far from Abila as Abila was from Damascus, and in the same line. The walls were nearly square, with eight or nine towers on each side; the shorter sides (the north and south) measuring about 335 yards—the longer (the east and west) about a quarter of a mile. Robinson's Bib. Res. (1852), p. 496.

Tyre.—The city itself needs no comment, but the borders of its territory are not so familiar. They reached southward to Carmel (Jos. Bell. iii. 3, 1), and eastward to Ituræa, in Herod Philip's Tetrarchy; for Galilee, which lay west of Ituræa, was bounded on the north by the possessions of Tyre—τὰ προσήκοντα δὲ αὐτῆς Τύρῳ τε καὶ τῇ Τυρίων χώρᾳ περατοῦται. Jos. Bell. iii. 3, 1. The Tyrian region, therefore, almost touched Cæsarea Philippi; so that our Lord, on reaching Cæsarea Philippi, would naturally pass on into the populous borders of Tyre, between Libanus and Antilibanus. Mark vii. 24; Matt. xv. 21.

Sidon.—The territory of Sidon, also, extended a great way eastward, and reached as far as the limits of Damascus; for in A.D. 33 the Sidonians and Damascenes had a dispute about their boundary-line before Flaccus, Prefect of Syria (fig. 24). Jos. Ant. xviii. 6, 3. See Fasti Sacri, p. 228, No. 1424. Our Lord, therefore, after traversing the territory of Tyre, would come upon that of Sidon. Mark vii. 24; Matt. xv. 21.

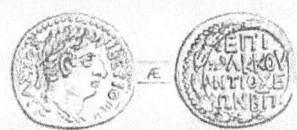

Fig. 24.—*Coin of Sidon under Flaccus. From the British Museum.*

Obv. Σιδῶνος Τιβέριος (Tiberius Augustus).
Rev. Ἐπὶ Φλάκκου Λεγάτου (of the Sidonians under Flaccus) with the legend BΠ, or 82 of the era of Antioch, and therefore struck some time between 1st Nov. A.D. 33—A.D. 34. The year A.D. 33 was the year of the Crucifixion, and the whole of our Lord's ministry was during the prefecture of Flaccus.

Paneas was the district about Cæsarea Philippi, of which city the ancient name was Panium.

Ulatha (Οὐλάθα).—This retains its ancient name, Ard-el-Hulêh, from the Lake Hulêh, called by Josephus "Samachonitis." Jos. Ant. v. 5, 1. Ulatha and Paneas, together, formed what was called Ζήνωνος οἶκος, the House of Zenon, or Zenonwick (fig. 25)—so named perhaps from its being

Fig. 25.—*A Coin of Zenon, or Zenodorus. From Pellerin.*

Obv. Head of Zenon, with the legend, "Zenodorus, Tetrarch and High Priest."
Rev. Head of Augustus, with the legend, ΣΕ ΚΑΙ (Σεβαστὸς Καῖσαρ).

continued to him for his residence, when he was stripped of his other possessions. The position of Ulatha, connected as it is with Paneas, is certainly known, and throws a light on the western limit of Trachonitis; for Josephus tells us that Ulatha, or the country about Lake Hulêh, lay between Galilee on the west, and Trachonitis on the east: Καίσαρ δὲ καὶ τὴν τούτου (Zenonis) μοῖραν οὐκ ὀλίγην οὖσαν Ἡρώδῃ δίδωσιν, ἣ μεταξὺ τοῦ Τραχωνος καὶ τῆς Γαλιλαίας ἦν, Οὐλάθαν καὶ Πανιάδα καὶ τὴν πέριξ χώραν, Ant. xv. 10, 3; and again he

---

[24] Jos. Bell. i. 9, 2; Ant. xiv. 7, 4.

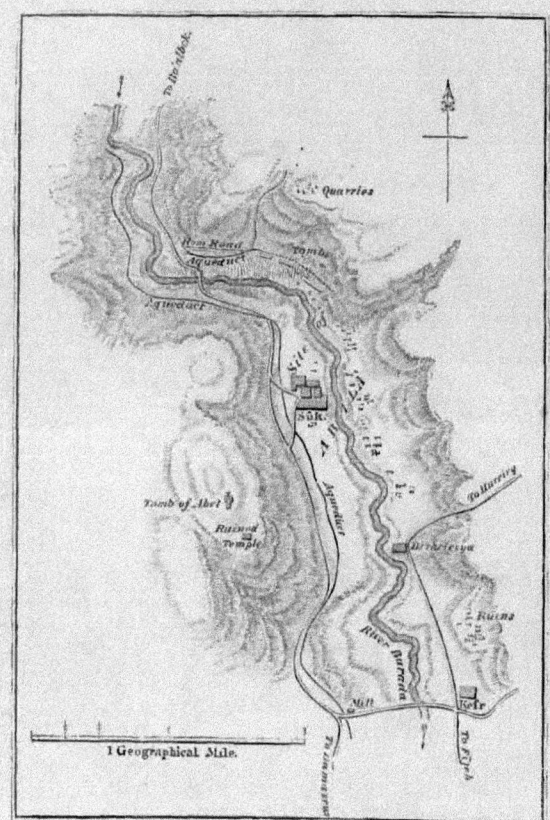

Fig. 26.—*A sketch of the Site of Abila. From J. L. Porter's Damascus.*

Fig. 27.—*A Coin of Abilene (from Bible Dictionary). From the British Museum.*

At one time (B.C. 80) they invited Aretas,[25] King of Arabia, to expel the oppressor, and offered the crown of Cœlesyria as a reward for the service; but the scheme proved abortive, and Ptolemy continued his exactions.[26] On another occasion (about B.C. 70),

repeats the same thing in the words, τὴν μεταξὺ Τράχωνος καὶ τῆς Γαλιλαίας γῆν ἅπασαν (Γλάθα), Bell. i. 20, 4; and he implies as much in another passage, where, in describing the small Lake Phiala, to the east of Panium, he writes that it was fifteen miles from Cæsarea Philippi, on the road to Trachonitis, on the right of the road, and not far from it: ἡ δέ ἐστιν ὁδεύοντι εἰς τὴν Τραχωνῖτιν ἀπὸ σταδίων ἑκατὸν εἴκοσι Καισαρείας, τῆς ὁδοῦ κατὰ δέξιον μέρος, οὐκ ἄποθεν, Bell. iii. 10, 7. Either therefore Trachonitis proper extended as far west as Ulatha, or (which is more probable) Josephus under the general term of Trachonitis means to include Ituræa. See 'Ituræa,' infra.

Trachonitis.—The word 'Trachonitis' is the Greek translation of Argob, the Hebrew name for the same country, Deut. iii. 4, 13; 1 Kings iv. 13. Strabo mentions the two Τράχωνες. ὑπέρκεινται δ' αὐτῆς (Damascus) δύο λεγόμενοι Τράχωνες, Strabo, xvi. 2. And the two Trachons are distinctly marked, one of them being the Ledja, to the south-east of Damascus, and the other the Safa, due east of Damascus. They are both of them volcanic, pear-like in shape, and two or three days' journey in breadth, and are strata of basalt, which has been poured from the bowels of the earth in a liquid state over the natural limestone of the country. See Burton and Blake's Unexplored Syria. The capital of the Ledja was Phænesus, now Missema, at the northern end of the Ledja, where Burckhardt found the inscription: Ἰσθλιος Σατουρνῖνος Φαησίοις Μητροκωμίᾳ τοῦ Τράχωνος, Χαίρειν. Burckhardt's Syria, p. 117; Boeckh's Corp. Inscript. iv. 551. Trachonitis, comprising the two Trachons, extended south to Jebel Haurân, ὑπὸ τὰ Ἀλσάδαμον ὄρος (Haurân) οἱ Τραχωνῖται Ἄραβες. Ptol. v. 15, 26. The most southern city known of the Ledja was Canatha, or Kenath, now Kunawât, Κανάθ ἐν Τραχωνίτιδι πλησίον Βοστρῶν. Euseb. Onom.

Auranitis, or the Haurân, took its name from Jebel Haurân, at the southern end of Trachonitis, and comprised not only Jebel Haurân itself, but also the extensive plain that swept round Jebel Haurân on the west side, and spread itself northward until it joined the Plain of Ituræa, or Jedour. Auranitis, therefore, lay between Trachonitis on the east, and Batanæa (of which we shall have to speak more particularly) on the west.

Gaulanitis, now Jaulan, and the Golan of the Old Testament (Deut. iv. 43; Josh. xx 8; xxi. 27; 1 Chron. vi. 71), lay on the east side of the Lake of Gennesaret. The southern limit was Gamala, near Hippos, where it joined Decapolis (Jos. Bell. ii. 20, 6), and went northward not only to Julias, or Bethsaida, described as a city of Gaulanitis (Jos. Bell. ii. 9, 1), but also to the southern end of Antilibanus, i.e. to Mount Hish. Jos. Ant. viii. 2, 3; and see Bell. iv. 1, 1. On the east, Gaulanitis was partly bounded by Batanæa (see the article 'Batanæa,' infra). The population of Gaulanitis spoke Syriac. Jos. Bell. iv. 1, 5.

Decapolis is best described by Eusebius (art. Δεκάπολις in the Onomasticon) as "the part lying on the other side of Jordan, about Hippos, and Pella, and Gadara;" so that Hippos, which lay near the south-east end of the Lake of Gennesaret, may be considered as the northern limit, and Pella, where it joined Peræa, the southern limit, and Gadara, which bordered on Batanæa, the western limit. Eusebius omits Scythopolis, as it lay on the western side of Jordan; but unquestionably Scythopolis formed part of the district called Decapolis, and was not comprehended within the province of Judæa. Decapolis, as the name implies, had originally consisted of ten cities, but apparently others were afterwards admitted into the league, though the name of Decapolis for the whole was still retained. Ptolemy ascribes to Decapolis no less than eighteen cities, and those who speak only of ten differ from one another as to the particulars. Those which most likely composed the original union were the four already mentioned—viz. Hippos, Pella, Gadara, and Scythopolis—with six others at considerable distances: viz. Philadelphia, Gerasa, Dium, Raphana, Capitolias, and Canatha, all to the east of Jordan (see Winer's Biblisch. Realw. Decapolis). Hippos, Gadara, Pella, and Scythopolis were the central towns, and their territories joined each other. See Jos. Vit. p. 9. Scythopolis, on the west of the

---

[25] Not the Aretas in the time of Paul.

[26] Jos. Bell. i. 4, 8; Ant. xiii. 16, 3.

they induced Alexandra, the Queen of Judæa, to send her son Aristobulus with an army to their assistance; but the lucky star of Ptolemy again prevailed, and the Damascenes were left to their fate.[27] On the approach of Pompey (B.C. 63), Ptolemy

Jordan, was the capital of all Decapolis, ἡ δέ ἐστι μεγίστη τῆς Δεκαπόλεως, Jos. Bell. iii. 9, 7; but of the cities on the east side, Gadara was the principal, Γάδαρα μητρόπολιν τῆς περαίας — not Περαίας, which lay south of Pella—Jos. Bell. iv. 7, 3.

What was the bond of union between these cities, some of which were separated from each other by intervening countries (see Plin. N. H. v, 16) has been a difficulty, but is capable of explanation. The key to the mystery is, that all the ten cities were either *Greek* or *Syrine*, and not Jewish. Jos. Ant. xiv. 4, 4; Bell. ii. 18, 1; Ant. xiii. 15, 4; Ant. xvii. 11, 4; Jos. Vit. 65. In the flourishing times of the Maccabees, the Jews brought them all under their yoke. Jos. Ant. xiii. 15, 4. But when Pompey conquered the East, he detached them from the princes of Judæa, and permitted them to live under their own laws, and annexed them to the province of Syria. ὡς πάσας τοῖς γνησίοις ἀποδοὺς πολίταις κατέταξεν εἰς τὴν Συριακὴν ἐπαρχίαν. Jos. Bell. i. 7, 7; Ant. xiv. 4, 4. Being thus set free by Pompey, but surrounded on all sides by the bigoted Jewish nation, they entered into a defensive alliance for mutual protection, and called themselves the Ten United States, or Decapolis. This, however, did not save them, for, on the outbreak of the Jewish war, the first act of the Jews was to plunder Scythopolis, Gadara, Hippos, Pella, Philadelphia, and Gerasa. Jos. Bell. ii. 18, 1-3.

Herod was at one time in such high favour with Augustus, that the Emperor made over to him Gadara and Hippos, with some other cities. Jos. Ant. xv. 7, 3. But on the death of Herod they were excepted from the dominions of Archelaus, and again attached to the province of Syria. Γάδαρα καὶ Ἵππος Ἑλληνίδες εἰσὶ πόλεις, ἃς ἀπορρήξας αὐτοῦ τῆς διοικήσεως Συρίας προσθήκην ποιεῖται. Jos. Ant. xvii. 11, 4; Bell. ii. 6, 3.

Scythopolis was afterwards given by the Roman Emperor to Agrippa II. Σκυθοπόλεως . . . τῆς ὑπηκόου βασιλείας (viz. Agrippa II.). Jos. Vit. 65; the reason probably being, that Scythopolis, as situate on the west side of Jordan, contained an unusually strong Jewish element. See Bell. ii.

18, 3. But, with this exception, all Decapolis (including Hippos, Gadara, and Pella) remained annexed to Syria, and never belonged either to Herod Antipas or Herod Philip, or to the kingdom of Agrippa I., or of his son Agrippa II., who succeeded to the Tetrarchy of Herod Philip. Josephus writes, that on the outbreak of the Jewish war, the Jews, in revenge for cruelties against themselves, made a furious onset upon Hippos, Gadara, Pella, and Scythopolis, which last, though subject to Agrippa II., was not within the limits of his kingdom (Jos. Bell. ii. 18, 1), and then proceeds—συνιέστη δὲ καὶ κατὰ τὴν Ἀγρίππα βασιλείαν ἐπιβουλὴ κατὰ Ἰουδαίων (Bell. ii. 18, 6). The cities, therefore, of which he had been speaking—viz. Hippos, Gadara, and Pella—were not within his kingdom, though they bordered upon it. The line of demarcation was between Hippos and Gamala, for Hippos was in Decapolis, while Gamala was in Gaulanitis, which belonged to Agrippa. Jos. Bell. ii. 20, 6.

Peræa.—This was a tract to the east of the Jordan, and the limits are well defined. It extended northward as far as Pella, where it bordered on Decapolis; and southward as far as Machærus, where it bordered on Arabia Petræa; and eastward as far as Philadelphia and Gerasa, where it bordered on Arabia. Jos. Bell. iii. 3, 3.

Ituræa.—This still retains the ancient name, with little variation, being called Jedour, derived, it is said, from the patriarch Jetur, or Ittur, 1 Chron. i. 31; and the Septuagint, in 1 Chron. v. 19, reads Ἰτουραίων. See Smith's Geogr. Dict. Ituræa was the plain between Jebel Hish on the west, and the Ledja on the east, and ran up into the mountainous region of Hermon and Antilibanus. The extent of Ituræa southward is not definitively fixed; but Burckhardt makes it reach along the Hadji, or Arabian caravan road, as far as Kusem or Nowa—the latter about 100 miles south of Damascus. It will be seen from the article 'Trachonitis' (supra), that Josephus assigns the north and east and west sides of the plain of Ituræa to Trachonitis; but he must here be speaking of Trachonitis in a large sense as including Ituræa, for according

---

[27] πρόφασις δ' ἦν Πτολεμαῖος ἀεὶ θλίβων τὴν πόλιν, Jos. Bell. i. 5, 3; ὃς (Ptolemy Mennæi) βαρὺς ἦν τῇ πόλει γείτων, Ant. xiii. 16, 3.

HISTORY OF DAMASCUS. [A.D. 37]

at once felt himself unequal to the conflict; but the storm which he could not resist with the sword, he dexterously contrived to evade by gold. He purchased immunity from the conqueror, at the price of a thousand talents;[20] and Damascus,

to Strabo, the Ituræans were not confined to the plain, but were dispersed over the mountains on the north and west; for he writes: Χαλκὶς, ἡ ὑπὸ τῷ Πτολεμαίῳ τῷ Μενναίου τῷ τῶν Μαρσύων κατέχοντι, καὶ τῶν Ἰτουραίων ὀρεινήν; and again: τὰ μὲν οὖν ὀρεινὰ ἔχουσι πάντα Ἰτουραῖοί τε καὶ Ἄραβες. Strabo, xvi. 2 (pp. 360, 364, Tauchnitz); and see Dion, lix. 12; Tac. Ann. xiii. 7; Plin. N. H. v. 19. As Strabo thus distinguishes the Ituræans from the Arabs, we may remark, by the way, that the Ituræans must have spoken, not Arabic, but Syriac.

Batanæa.—The position of this tract has been much disputed, some placing it (incorrectly, as we think) at and about a town called, at the present day, Ard-el-Bathanyeh, four miles to the north of Hit, in the neighbourhood of Jebel Hauran; whereas it ought to be identified with the modern Bottein, on the right and left banks of the Hieromax. The term Batanæa had both a large and also a limited sense. In the large sense it was equivalent to the ancient Bashan: Βασάν αὕτη Βασανῖτις, ἡ νῦν καλουμένη Βαταναία (Euseb. Onom. Βασάν), and extended from the southern end of Mount Hermon on the north to the River Jabbok on the south (Jos. Ant. iv. 5, 3), and from the Jordan on the west to the great desert on the east. Indeed, Bathan (or Batanæa) is only the Aramaic form of Bashan, and first became current after the return from Babylon. Winer's Bibl. Realw. 'Basan.' This extensive tract was afterwards broken up into various toparchies—i.e. shires or counties—as Gaulanitis, Auranitis, Trachonitis, Peræa, and Batanæa proper. The last lay next to Gaulanitis, and bordered it on the east; and is now represented by the modern Bottein, and thus retains its ancient name. Josephus (who never uses the word 'Batanæa' in the large sense, but calls Bashan 'Gilead') writes that Moses founded or enlarged Βόστρα μὲν ἐπὶ τοῖς ὅροις τῆς Ἀραβίας . . . καὶ Γαυλανᾶν ἐν τῇ Βαταναιάδι. Ant. iv. 7, 4. Here Gaulana itself, from which Gaulanitis took its name, is placed in Batanæa. How then could Batanæa have been to the east of the Ledja, far away from Gaulanitis? Besides, Bostra is placed " on the borders of Arabia " (ἐπὶ ταῖς ὅροις τῆς Ἀραβίας), and therefore Gaulana, in Batanæa, could not

have been still farther in that direction. But, farther, the pilgrims from Babylon to Jerusalem being constantly plundered by the Trachonites on the way, Herod determined to protect the pilgrims against these marauders, by erecting a fortress between Trachonitis and Jerusalem: ἔγνω Ἰουδαίοις κτίσαι ἐν μέσῳ. Jos. Ant. xvii. 2, 1. He therefore built a castle in the toparchy of Batanæa, which bordered upon Trachonitis: ἐν τοπαρχίᾳ τῇ λεγομένῃ Βαταναίᾳ. ὁρίζετα δὲ αὕτη Τραχωνίτιδι (ibid.). Batanæa, therefore, must have been on the line of route from Babylon to Jerusalem, and to the west of Trachonitis, or it could not have been *between* the Trachonites and Judæa. Bathanyeh, on the contrary, was on the east of Trachonitis. Again, Herod committed this outwork to one Zamaris, a Jewish adventurer, who had come from Babylon at the head of 500 mounted bowmen; and to secure his faithful services, Herod made him a grant of land in the same toparchy of Batanæa. Now it appears that this grant of land was not at Bathanyeh, but in Bottein next to Gaulanitis, for Zamaris was succeeded by his son Jacimus, and Jacimus by his son Philip; and at the outbreak of the Jewish war, Philip made his escape from Jerusalem, and reached his *own country*, on the borders of *Gamala*: καὶ παραγενόμενος εἴς τινα τῶν ἑαυτοῦ κωμῶν κατὰ τοὺς ὅρους Γάμαλα. Jos. Vit. c. 11. And again, Agrippa orders Philip to take a force from *Gamala*, and by their aid to restore his Babylonians to Batanæa: κελεύει . . . εἰς Γάμαλα τὸ φρούριον πορευθῆναι . . . καὶ τοὺς Βαβυλωνίους εἰς τὴν Βαταναίαν πάλιν ἀποκαταστήσοντα. Jos. Vit. 36. Batanæa, therefore, in which Philip's grant of land was situate, must have been in the vicinity of Gamala, that is, at Bottein, and not at Bathanyeh, which was far distant to the east.

Eusebius enables us to identify Batanæa by giving the names of its towns and hamlets: Καρναίᾳ Ἀσταρὼθ ἐστι νῦν κώμη μεγίστη τῆς Ἀραβίας, ἥτις ἐστὶν ἡ Βαταναία λεγομένη, ἐπέκεινα τοῦ Ἰορδάνου. Euseb. Onom. And again: 'Ασταρώθ' πόλις ἀρχαία τοῦ Ὢγ, . . . ἡ γέγονε φυλῆς Μανασσῆ. συμβέβηκε δὲ ἐν τῇ Βαταναίᾳ Ἀδραὰ πόλις τῆς Ἀραβίας ὡς ἀπὸ σημείων ἕξ· ἡ δὲ Ἀδραὰ τῆς Βόστρης διέστηκε σημείοις κε'. Euseb.

---

[20] Jos. Ant. xiv. 3, 2.

which had opened its gates to Pompey's lieutenants, Metellus and Lollius,[29] was again left a prey to the ravages of the freebooter.

In B.C. 40, Ptolemy Mennæi died, and his son, Lysanias I., succeeded to his dominions.[30] The eastern parts of the Roman Empire were at this time subject to the wayward rule of Mark Antony. His passion for Cleopatra is well known: the hero of a hundred fights was led a submissive captive by the silken cords of love. No one more fascinating than the Queen of Egypt, and no one stained with darker crimes. In her ambitious career she had taken off a brother by poison, and had dragged a sister to death from the sanctuary of Diana.[31] Avarice, the offspring of extravagance, had taken possession of her breast; and as she accompanied Mark Antony on his Parthian expedition (B.C. 36), she fixed her longing eyes on the domain of Lysanias I., King of Chalcis. He was accused of intriguing with the enemy, and was led to execution, and his dominions, comprising nearly all Cœlesyria, were bestowed on Cleopatra.[32] Antony pursued his march against the enemy, while his paramour, with female vanity, paraded her state amongst her new subjects of Damascus.[33]

The battle of Actium (B.C. 31) dispersed the fond dreams of love, and Antony and Cleopatra, who had been so reckless of the lives of others, were reduced to the

---

Onomast. And again: καὶ εἰσιν εἰς ἔτι νῦν δύο κῶμαι ἐπὶ τῆς Βαταναίας (τῆς καὶ Βατολούας) ἀλλήλων διεστῶσαι σημείοις θ΄ μεταξὺ Ἀδαρῶν καὶ Ἀβίλης πόλεως. Euseb. Onomast. Ἀσταρὼθ Καρναείμ. Here we have enumerated as cities of Batanæa —Adraa (now Edrei), Astaroth (described as six miles from Edrei, viz. to the west, and now Mezareib), and Adara, and Abila (not that in Abilene)—all in the immediate neighbourhood of Gaulanitis, and lying to the east or south of it, and all situate in or near Bottin, but far away from Bathanyeh.

The only argument adduced in favour of placing Batanæa to the east of the Ledja, is a passage in Ptolemy: Βαταναίας χώρας, ἧς ἀπὸ ἀνατολῶν ἡ Σακκαία, καὶ ταύτης ὑπὸ τὸ Ἀλσίδαμον ὄρος οἱ Τραχωνῖται Ἄραβες. Ptol. v. 15, 26. Now, four miles to the east of Bathanyeh is a town called Shuka (Porter's Bashan, p. 36), and it is said that Shuka is identical with Σακκαία, and therefore that Βαταναία χώρα must be Bathanyeh. But how can this be? For the Trachonites are placed by Ptolemy in Saccæa, and Saccæa is said by him to lie to the east of Batanæa, and therefore the Trachonites also must be to the east of it. But if Batanæa be identical with Bathanyeh, the Trachonites would lie to the *west* of Batanæa.

Rightly interpreted, Ptolemy gives the true positions. "Of the Batanæan country (to the east of which is Saccæa, and of the latter are the Trachonite Arabs under Mount Alcidamus), are the following cities" (naming them). Thus Ptolemy places Batanæa to the west of Saccæa, which he defines as comprising such part of Trachonitis as lay at the foot of Mount Alcidamus, a correct description of Shuka.

We agree with Winer, however, that Ptolemy is so inaccurate in his details, that to extract any system of geography from them is hopeless. Winer's Bibl. Theol. 'Trachonitis.' At all events, his authority cannot weigh for a moment against that of Josephus, in respect of a country to which Ptolemy was a stranger, and with which Josephus must have been perfectly familiar.

Since these observations were written, the author has met with I. G. Wetzstein's Reisebericht über Hauran und die Trachonen, from which it appears that the so-called Bathanyeh is a mere village named Btêne, with a strip of land six hours long by two broad, and without any interesting remains, and not, in that writer's opinion, having anything to do with the ancient Batanæa. See p. 85 of the work referred to.

[29] Jos. Ant. xiv. 2, 3; Bell. i. 6, 2.

[30] Jos. Ant. xiv. 13, 3; Dion, xlix. 32; Fasti Sacri, p. 51, No. 439.

[31] Appian, B. C. v. 9; Dion, xlviii. 24. See Fasti Sacri, p. 49, No. 432.

[32] Jos. Ant. xv. 4, 1, and xv. 3, 8. See Fasti Sacri, p. 63, No. 537.

[33] Jos. Ant. xv. 4, 2.

sad necessity of laying violent hands upon their own. The subject provinces of the East now lay at the mercy of Augustus, and in the distribution of his new dominions the conqueror thus disposed of the kingdom of Chalcis: Ituræa, Trachonitis, Gaulanitis, Batanæa, Auranitis, and Paneas were farmed out to Zenon, or Zenodorus, a wealthy capitalist; Abilené was now, or not long after, allotted to Lysanias II. (with the title of Tetrarch)—the son or grandson of Lysanias I., who had been so unjustly put to death by Mark Antony; and Chalcis itself was annexed to the prefecture of Syria.[34]

Damascus, like the commercial cities of Tyre and Sidon,[35] had at this time influence enough, through its opulent burgesses, to obtain the privilege of a self-governing municipality,[36] subject of course to the supervision of the Syrian Prefect. During the gentle sway of Lysanias II. over the highlands in the immediate vicinity of Damascus we hear little of the Damascenes. Once only (in A.D. 33) do we find them litigating with the Sidonians before Flaccus, the Prefect of Syria, as to their respective boundaries.[37]

About A.D. 32,[38] a quarrel arose between Herod Antipas, Tetrarch of Galilee, and Aretas, King of Arabia Petræa (fig. 28), who had succeeded to the kingdom of Petra

Fig. 28.—Coin (much defaced) of Aretas. From the British Museum.
Obv. Portrait of Aretas.—Rev. Βασιλεως Αρετου Φιλελληνος (of King Aretas, lover of Greeks).

on the death of Obodas.[39] The daughter of Aretas had married Herod Antipas; but when Herod repudiated her for Herodias, his brother Herod Philip's wife,[40] the King of Petra naturally resented the affront. A dispute about their boundaries followed, and eventually they came to open war. The general of Antipas was defeated in a pitched battle, and in the spring of A.D. 37, Tiberius took up the quarrel of Antipas, and declared hostilities against the Arabian prince.[41] It is a common opinion, that as Damascus lay on the outskirts of Syria, and naturally belonged to Arabia, to which it had been originally attached,[42] and to which it was always favor-

---

[34] See Fasti Sacri, p. 63, No. 537.
[35] Jos. Ant. xv. 4, 1.
[36] The common notion that Damascus was included in Abilené is untenable. Abila, in comparison with Damascus, was but a small town, and on the other side of Antilibanus. The Δαμασκηνοί, like the Tyrians and Sidonians, are always spoken of as an independent community. See Jos. Ant. xviii. 6, 3; Bell. ii. 20, 2. And Pliny distinguishes Damascus from Abilené. Plin. N.H. v. 16.
[37] Jos. Ant. xviii. 6, 3; Fasti Sacri, p. 228, No. 1424.
[38] See Fasti Sacri, p. 225, No. 1414.
[39] Fasti Sacri, p. 111, No. 846.
[40] Herod Philip must be distinguished from Philip the Tetrarch of Trachonitis.
[41] Fasti Sacri, p. 225, No. 1414.
[42] Δαμασκεὺς τῆς Ἀραβικῆς γῆς ἦν καί ἔστιν, εἰ καὶ νῦν προσνενέμηται τῇ Συροφοινίκῃ. Justin. cont. Tryph. s. 78. Damascus Arabiæ retro deputabatur, antequam transcripta esset in Syrophœnicen, ex distinctione Syriarum. Tertullian adv. Marcion. iii. 13. See Wetst. in 2 Cor. xi. 32.

ably disposed,[43] Aretas now seized upon Damascus by force, and annexed it to Arabia Petræa. But this cannot be, for how could Aretas, a petty prince, have dared to take up arms against the Emperor of Rome?—or, if he dared, how must he not have been instantly crushed? Another solution offers itself as much more probable. No sooner had Tiberius, the great patron of Herod Antipas, directed Vitellius, his general, to bring Aretas to account, than Tiberius himself died (on the 16th of March, A.D. 37), being succeeded by Caligula, the personal enemy of Herod Antipas, and the friend of Agrippa. Caligula, on his accession, made a new distribution of the provinces of the East;[44] and as there was great intimacy between Agrippa and the Damascenes, whose case Agrippa had formerly argued before Flaccus, the Prefect of Syria,[45] it is natural, and may be assumed, that the Damascenes, by the influence of Agrippa at court, obtained the Emperor's fiat that Damascus, at its own request, should be made over to the King of Petra. Damascus remained an appanage of Petra from this time, during the reigns of Caligula and Claudius, for we cannot otherwise account for the remarkable fact, that the coins of Damascus have the heads of the Emperors Augustus and Tiberius, but not the head of any Emperor from the death of Tiberius until the time of Nero, when the head of the Emperor reappears.[46] This shows that during the reigns of Caligula and Claudius, Damascus was detached from the Roman province of Syria, and annexed to some independent prince. There cannot be a doubt, that at the commencement of the reign of Caligula, Aretas, by whatever means he attained this dignity, was in the peaceful possession of Damascus. As a new sovereign he was anxious to gain popularity with all classes of his subjects, and in particular exhibited a conciliatory demeanour towards the Greeks and Jews, who formed no small part of the population. Aretas describes himself on his coins as Φιλέλλην, or Lover of Greeks (fig. 28);[47] and as regards the Jews, he accorded to them all the privileges which they were allowed in cities where they were most favoured. Not only were they allowed the free exercise of their religion, but they were permitted, as at Antioch and Alexandria, to govern their own community by their own peculiar laws; and the local chief of their nation, or Ethnarch, had authority to arrest and punish any delinquent amongst his own people.

Such was the political state of Damascus at the time of Saul's conversion. With respect to its localities, the picture must be so familiar to the reader that a few words will suffice. Damascus was a walled town,[48] and was of an oblong shape, lying east and west (fig. 29). It was skirted, at a little distance on the north-west, by the range of Antilibanus, and on the other sides was surrounded by an extensive plain,

---

[43] Jos. Ant. xiii. 15, 2.
[44] See Fasti Sacri, p. 256, No. 1533.
[45] Jos. Ant. xviii. 6, 3. See Fasti Sacri, p. 228, No. 1424.
[46] Eckhel, vol. iii. p. 330.
[47] Eckhel, vol. iii. p. 330.

[48] It had at one time been encompassed by a double wall, and on the north, along the bank of the river, by a treble wall. Traces of the walls still remain, but the outer wall on the east has been removed, and the moat drained and partly filled up. Porter's Damascus, vol. i. pp. 46, 52.

CHAP. V.] HISTORY OF DAMASCUS. [A.D. 37] 69

which stretched away towards the east. The River Barrada (the ancient Abana) issued from the ravines of the mountains, and as it flowed along the northern wall of the town, was distributed through the city, and created by its healing waters a Garden of Eden amidst an arid desert. The main thoroughfare was Straight Street, so called from its running in a direct line from the eastern to the western gate. It is now known as Sultany or Queen Street, and is a mile long. In the Apostolic age, it was a hundred feet wide, and divided by Corinthian colonnades into three avenues

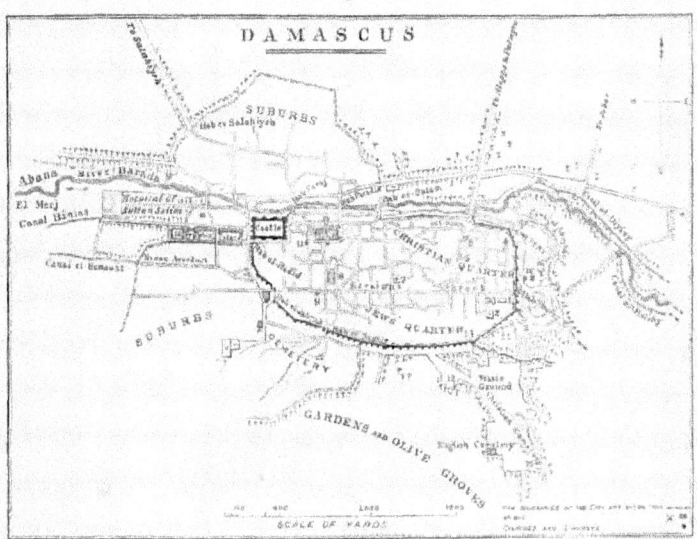

Fig. 29.—Plan of Damascus. From J. L. Porter's Damascus.

1. Armenian Convent.
2. Greek Catholic Church.
3. Syrian Church.
4. House of Ananias.
5. Lazarist Convent.
6. Latin Convent.
7. Greek Church.
8. Khan Assad Pasha.
9. House of Judas.
10. British Consulate.
11. Custom House.
12. Tomb of Sidy Bilal.
13. Tomb of St. George.
14. Bab Kisan, where Paul was let down from the Wall.
15. Scene of Paul's Conversion.
16. Leper Hospital (House of Naaman?)

—one, the central and broadest, being intended for carriages and equestrians, and the two side-pavements for foot-passengers (fig. 30). Halfway along the street was a fine Roman triumphal arch, and at each end of the street were the gates of the city, in three compartments, corresponding to the three roadways. Remains of the colonnades and gates may still be traced, but time has destroyed every vestige of their original magnificence. At present the street, instead of the lordly proportions which once called forth the stranger's admiration, has been contracted by successive encroachments into a narrow passage, more resembling a bylane than the principal avenue of a noble city (fig. 31). At a little distance from the west gate, and on the right as you enter, is still shown the house of Judas. It is a grotto or cellar considerably under the general surface. Farther along, and near the eastern gate, you turn up a narrow lane to the left, i.e. to the north, when you come to the house of Ananias, which is also a grotto.[49]

Fig. 30.—*Elevation of the East Gate of Damascus. From J. L. Porter's Damascus.*

Fig. 31.—*The spectator is here standing just without the more northern of the two side arches of the triple gate and is looking down Straight Street as it is now seen. From J. L. Porter's Damascus.*

We now resume the personal history of the Apostle (A.D. 37). From the expression used by him, "I went into Arabia, and returned again unto Damascus,"[50] we

---

[49] See Porter's Damascus; Rae Wilson's Travels, &c. A modern traveller (1838) gives the following account of the house of Ananias: "A descent of fourteen steps leads to two nearly square apartments, in one of which is an altarpiece, representing the saint (Ananias) laying his hand on Saul, who is decked out in Roman armour, becoming a persecutor of the church.

[50] Gal. i. 17.

may infer that his absence was not of long continuance; and this is the more probable, from the circumstance that his sojourn in Arabia has not even been mentioned in the Acts, which would scarcely have been the case had it occupied a material part of his life. Indeed, as his return to Jerusalem was in the third year current from his conversion, and as he spent a considerable time in Damascus,[51] no great space can be allowed for his stay in Arabia. It is certain that he did not preach in Arabia.[52] So soon then as, from religious exercises and Divine assistance, he was ready for the conflict, and probably at the end of a few weeks or at all events months, he returned to Damascus, and " was with the disciples " (to whom he had ready access by the intervention of Ananias) " certain days."[53]

We have seen that the commission given to him was to publish the Gospel both to *Jews* and *Gentiles*; but the keys of the kingdom of heaven (or the privilege of opening the Gospel to the Gentiles) were held by Peter, who had not yet received his Master's command to unlock the door for the admission of the heathen by the call of Cornelius. At present, therefore, the errand of Saul was to the *Jews*; and great was their amazement when Saul, the persecutor, entered for the first time into one of the synagogues of Damascus, and argued with irresistible force that the crucified Jesus was the Christ, the Messiah! They could scarcely believe their eyes and ears, and said, " Is not this he that destroyed them which called on this name in Jerusalem, and came hither for that intent, that he might bring them bound unto the chief priests?"[54]

But the Jews were soon actuated by other and more hostile feelings, as Saul increased in strength more and more, and brought conviction home to the minds of his hearers, that Jesus was indeed the Christ. The details of events at Damascus have not been recorded; but from the analogy of history, we may readily suppose what were the measures resorted to by Saul's bigoted countrymen to counteract the innovations

In the other the guide showed a blocked-up 'kalah' or praying-place." Elliott's Travels, vol. ii. p. 291. Local traditions are in general to be little trusted; but Damascus, we must remember, though the most ancient city in the world, was never destroyed, and therefore its features have probably suffered little alteration. The tradition so far agrees with Scripture, that the veritable house of Ananias was certainly not in *Straight Street*; for " The Lord said unto Ananias, 'Arise, and go into the street which is called *Straight*.'" Acts ix. 11. As the residence of Ananias is thus not placed expressly in some other street than Straight, but is left to inference only, the tradition carries the greater weight, as the ignorant populace would not have been sufficiently well informed to adapt the locality to a fact not expressed, but only implied. The circumstance that both the house of Judas and the house of Ananias are now grottoes, is rather an argument in favour of their genuineness, as the area of all old cities is constantly rising from the accumulation of rubbish.

[51] He was with the disciples in Damascus *certain days* (ἡμέρας τινάς) before he preached. Acts ix. 19. Then *many days* (ἡμέραι ἱκαναί) were accomplished before the plot against his life. Acts ix. 23. The force of the Scriptural expression, " many days," is very vague, but in one passage it is equivalent to three years. Thus, in 1 Kings ii. 38, 39: " Shimei dwelt in Jerusalem *many days*; and it came to pass at the end of *three years*," &c.

[52] " I was not disobedient unto the heavenly vision, but showed *first* unto them of Damascus," &c. Acts xxvi. 19.

[53] Acts ix. 19.

[54] Acts ix. 21.

upon their religion, which the prowess of the great Apostle was gradually accomplishing. At first his enemies attempted to meet him in argument; but when they found themselves unable to resist the spirit by which he spake, they sought to repel the advancing tide by opposing every barrier that the policy of a blinded fanaticism could supply. They excommunicated him, and put him out of the synagogue;[55] and when that weapon was wielded in vain, they attempted, perhaps, to break his high spirit by whipping and scourging and imprisonment. Part of the fearful catalogue that he afterwards enumerated to the Corinthians may have been enacted at Damascus: "In stripes above measure, in prisons more frequent, in deaths oft. Of the Jews *five times received I forty stripes save one*; thrice was I beaten with rods."[56] Still converts were made; and the Jews, plainly perceiving that the edifice of the Mosaic policy must soon crumble to dust before the violent onset of their dauntless antagonist, determined, as the last effort of expiring ignorance, to compass his death. What a parallel to the persecution of the martyr Stephen! *Then*, Saul was on the side of the world, directing the passions of the multitude, and brandishing the arm of the law against the defenceless victim: *now*, he was himself the object of popular fury, and stood at bay against the pitiless attack of his former associates. The mad assault upon Stephen had been veiled under the thin semblance of law, and, as if to complete the picture, it would seem that legal formalities were to cloak the premeditated martyrdom of Saul.

It was in the third year current[57] from the conversion of Saul, and therefore in A.D. 39,[58] that the Jews held a council[59] to put him to death. The present posture of affairs at Damascus offered a favorable opportunity. Had the city been subject to Roman jurisdiction, the Jews could not, without the fiat of the Procurator or Prefect, have deprived any man of life. But Aretas, to whose kingdom of Petra Damascus now belonged, was less careful of the public liberties; and in order to conciliate the Jews, he had invested their council and chief officer, called the Ethnarch, with supreme power over their own people.[60] A capital charge was therefore made against Saul, and the Ethnarch, as the representative of the Jewish nation, issued a warrant for his apprehension.[61]

---

[55] See John ix. 22; xii. 42.
[56] 2 Cor. xi. 23–25.
[57] Such is the force of the expression, ἔπειτα μετὰ ἔτη τρία. Gal. i. 18.
[58] See Fasti Sacri, p. 264, No. 1581.
[59] συνεβουλεύσαντο. Acts ix. 23.
[60] It has been assumed in the text, and there can be little doubt, that ὁ ἐθνάρχης of 2 Cor. xi. 32 was the *Jewish* chief magistrate. This was the common designation for such an officer (see p. 1), and the expression ὁ ἐθνάρχης ἐφρούρει τὴν πόλιν, 2 Cor. xi. 32, corresponds to the words οἱ Ἰουδαῖοι παρετήρουν τὰς πύλας, Acts ix. 23, 24. It should be mentioned, however, that some are of opinion, that ὁ ἐθνάρχης means the prime minister or procurator of the King of Petra, for that the civil government of the kingdom of Petra was conducted, not so much by the King himself, as by his procurator; and that although the ordinary title of procurator was ἐπίτροπος, yet that ἐθνάρχης and ἐπίτροπος were sometimes used as convertible terms—as in the case of Asander, who governed the Bosporus under Pharnaces, and who is called by Lucian (Macrob. 17) ἐθνάρχης, but by Dion (xlii. 46) ἐπίτροπος. See Anger, p. 173; Wieseler's Chronol. Apostol. p. 142.

[61] πιάσαι με θέλων. 2 Cor. xi. 32.

The gates of Damascus were watched by the Jews, night and day, to prevent his escape. Saul, as inflexible in the defence of the Gospel, as before through ignorance he had been furious against it, was willing, we cannot doubt, to lay down his life for his creed; but Providence had destined him for many a long year to stand forth as the great champion of the church, and to carry its standard triumphantly into far remoter regions. The plot against his life was divulged, and the disciples "took him" (or, laid a gentle constraint upon him), and at midnight, when the eye of caution was sealed in sleep, "let him down by the wall" (through the window of one of the houses built upon or against the wall), "in a basket."[62] He, who a short time before had come, in the blaze of noonday, and proudly mounted at the head of a goodly company, to scourge and imprison the Christian renegades—he it was, who now, himself a Christian, was fain, by the aid of a few faithful friends, to steal away from his enemies under cover of the darkness. Yet, had Saul been asked at that moment, he would unhesitatingly have replied, "I am not ashamed, for I know whom I have believed."[63]

Saul pursued his solitary journey, under the shades of night, towards the land of his fathers. His commission to the Gentiles was still in suspense, as the door had not yet been thrown open to the world at large. Obliged to fly from Damascus, he was anxious to press the tidings of salvation upon the attention of his countrymen in his native land, and more particularly in the great capital, the Holy City, where he might reasonably expect that the knowledge of his previous history, coupled with his sudden conversion, would produce an extraordinary sensation. Now that his own blindness had been purged away, the veil that was upon the hearts of the children of Abraham was a source to him of the keenest pain. He writes on one occasion: "I say the truth in Christ, I lie not (my conscience also bearing me witness in the Holy Ghost), that I have great heaviness and continual sorrow in my heart; for I could wish that myself were accursed from Christ for my brethren, my kinsmen according to the flesh;"[64] and when, at length, salvation was also proclaimed to the Gentiles,

---

[62] Acts ix. 25; 2 Cor. xi. 32. The words of Luke are "through the wall," διὰ τοῦ τείχους (Acts ix. 25), which are explained by Paul himself to mean "through a window through the wall," διὰ θυρίδος διὰ τοῦ τείχους. 2 Cor. xi. 33—i.e. through the window of a house built against or upon the city wall, and forming part of the city wall. The word for a *basket* in Luke is σπυρίς, Acts ix. 25, and in 2 Cor. xi. 33 it is σαργάνη. They both signify the same thing, viz. a wicker or flag basket for carrying provisions. Thus, the fragments when the 4000 were fed, were collected in σπυρίδας, Matt. xv. 37; Mark viii. 8, 20; and see Hesych., who defines σπυρίς as a corn-basket, τὸ τῶν πυρῶν ἄγγος, and Suidas, who defines σαργάνη as a flag-basket, πλέγμα τι ἐκ σχοινίου. These baskets were occasionally of large size, as here; and Paul, as we collect from other sources, was of little stature. However, our great dramatist, in the Merry Wives of Windsor, presents to us a basket capable of holding a person of portly dimensions.

As to the traditional place of the escape over the wall, we read in a modern traveller: "Passing out of a gate facing the south, our attention was directed to a blocked-up square in an old part of the wall of the city, just over a gate similarly built up. Here, we were told, was the window from which the persecuted persecutor was 'let down by the wall in a basket.'" Elliott's Travels, vol. ii. p. 262.

[63] 2 Tim. i. 12.   [64] Rom. ix. 1–3.

the first earnest appeal of the Apostle was always made to his own countrymen, and only on their rejection of the Gospel to the more docile heathen. What mischances befel him on his route, or what privations he endured, we have no account in the brief narrative of the Acts; but, alone and unbefriended as he travelled, he not improbably experienced many hardships, and in taking a retrospect of his life on a future occasion, he may have referred to this period when he wrote: "In journeyings often, in perils of waters, in perils of robbers, ... in perils in the wilderness, ... in weariness and painfulness, in watchings often, in hunger and thirst, in fastings often, in cold and nakedness."[65]

Though his prime object was to reach Jerusalem, it is likely that he was occupied upon the road through Galilee and Judæa in evangelizing the cities through which he passed. The Feast of Tabernacles this year (A.D. 39) was on the 21st of September; and as he entered Jerusalem only a few days before it, and he had left Damascus on a sudden, without reference to the Jewish festival, there was, perhaps, a convenient interval which he might thus profitably employ. That at some time or other he did preach through the land of Israel is evident from his address to King Agrippa: "Whereupon, O King Agrippa, I was not disobedient unto the heavenly vision; but shewed first unto them of Damascus, and at Jerusalem, and *throughout all the coasts of Judæa*, and then to the Gentiles, that they should repent and turn to God, and do works meet for repentance."[66]

At the close of his journey, what must have been his feelings as the pinnacles of the Temple appeared in sight! Three years before, he had left Jerusalem as the Apostle of the Sanhedrim, to eradicate the Christian heresy; and now he was returning, stripped of all worldly grandeur, and supported only by the hand of Providence, to propagate the very doctrine of the Cross which he had before persecuted.

He entered Jerusalem, and, conceiving that the rumour of his conversion had gone before, "he essayed to join himself to the disciples; but they were all afraid of him, and believed not that he was a disciple."[67] Intelligence at that day, from the difficulty of communication, was very slowly and imperfectly transmitted; and as the Sanhedrim would keep the conversion of Saul as quiet as possible, and as the Christians of Jerusalem generally, except the Apostles, had been dispersed abroad on the martyrdom of Stephen, the brethren still to be found at the capital may have heard some vague rumours only of Saul's conversion, and the details may not have reached them in such an authenticated form as to win their belief to so strange a story. The report that Saul, the bitter persecutor, was become the zealous preacher of the faith, was so wild and extraordinary, that it could not be easily credited. The aim of Saul, as he writes himself, was to have an interview with Peter,[68] who was regarded as the chief of the Apostles, and with whom Saul was

---

[65] 2 Cor. xi. 26, 27. [66] Acts xxvi. 19, 20. [67] Acts ix. 26. [68] ἱστορῆσαι Πέτρον. Gal. i. 18.

anxious to confer on the subject of the Christian ministry. Saul was fortunate enough to meet with Barnabas (rightly called Barnabas, or "the Son of Consolation," from his truly amiable disposition), who in youthful days had been his schoolfellow at Tarsus, and had since sat with him at the feet of Gamaliel at Jerusalem. To him Saul recounted the wonderful event which had befallen him on his mission to Damascus, and thereupon "Barnabas took him and brought him to the Apostles" (Peter and James, the Lord's brother, the rest being absent or otherwise occupied),[o] "and declared unto them how Saul had seen the Lord in the way, and that he had spoken to him, and how he had preached boldly at Damascus in the name of Jesus."[70] Upon this introduction, he was at once admitted into the closest intimacy, and Peter—who, as a married man, had, we may suppose, the readiest means of affording entertainment—received him as an inmate into his house, where he "abode fifteen days."[71]

The highborn and accomplished Saul was now the guest of Simon, the poor fisherman of Bethsaida! During the short period that Saul remained in Jerusalem, he conformed himself, as was his practice, to the observance of the Jewish Law, and prayed daily in the Temple.[72] But he had also the work of an evangelist to perform, for "it was woe to him if he preached not the Gospel!"[73] and he therefore again began his labours in the ample vineyard of the Jewish capital. It was the Feast of Tabernacles, and Jerusalem was filled with strangers from the remotest regions—"Parthians, and Medes, and Elamites, and the dwellers in Mesopotamia, and in Judæa, and Cappadocia, in Pontus, and Asia, Phrygia, and Pamphylia, in Egypt, and in the parts of Libya about Cyrene, and strangers of Rome, Jews and Proselytes."[74] To this promiscuous multitude, called Hellenists, or Jews of the Dispersion, Saul now addressed himself. The circumstance of his being an Hellenist himself, and a man of known literary attainments, was a sufficient reason for the selection of this field for his exertions. "He spake boldly in the name of the Lord Jesus, and disputed against the Grecians."[75]

But the rancour of his enemies, and the ways of Providence, which had designed for him a very different arena, brought this fair commencement of his ministry at Jerusalem to an abrupt determination. "It came to pass," he tells us, "that, when I was come again to Jerusalem, even while I prayed in the Temple, I was in a trance; and saw him saying unto me, 'Make haste, and get thee quickly out of Jerusalem, for they will not receive thy testimony concerning me.' And I said, 'Lord, they know that I imprisoned and beat in every synagogue them that believed on thee; and when the blood of thy martyr Stephen was shed, I also was standing by, and consenting unto his death, and kept the raiment of them that slew him!'"[76] Surely, he argued, they who witnessed my zeal in the defence of the Law of Moses, and saw the violence with

---

[o] Gal. i. 19. [70] Acts ix. 27. [74] Acts xxii. 17. [75] Acts ix. 29.
[71] ἐπέμεινα πρὸς αὐτὸν ἡμέρας δεκαπέντε. Gal. i. 18. [73] 1 Cor. ix. 16. [76] Acts xxii. 17–29.
[72] Acts ii. 9, 10.

which I persecuted the Nazarenes, when they behold me the fearless champion of the Name I once blasphemed—they must believe that so great and inexplicable a change can only have resulted from some miraculous interposition! "Nay but, O man, who art thou that repliest against God?"[17] The answer to the expostulation was, "Depart: for I will send thee far hence unto the *Gentiles*."[18]

At the very time of the vision, a plot, though yet unknown to Saul, was forming amongst his enemies to take away his life. He had been only fifteen days in Jerusalem, but his ministry had already been attended with such surprising success, that the unbelieving Jews saw plainly that they must rid themselves of the young zealot, or succumb before the power with which he promulgated the faith. It was a repetition of the scene which had passed three years before at the martyrdom of Stephen, except that the *persecutor* then was, by the mysterious workings of

Fig. 32.—*Coin of Cæsarea-on-Sea.* From *Académie des Inscript.* vol. xxvi. p. 446, ed. 1759.

Ob. Νερων Σεβαστος Καισαρ (Nero Augustus Cæsar).—Rev. The goddess Astarte, holding in her hand a bust of Nero, with the legend Καισαρια η προς Σεβαστω λιμενι (Cæsarea on Port Sebastus), and the legend, L. 15, or fourteenth year of the reign of Nero, and therefore struck some time between October 13, A.D. 67, and October 13, A.D. 68. This coin confirms the statement of Josephus that the harbour constructed by Herod at Cæsarea was called Port Sebastus, or Augustus. See Antiq. xvii. 5, 1.

Providence, to be the *victim* now. The brethren, however, had secret information of the plot, and snatched him from the toils of his enemies by hurrying him away to Cæsarea (fig. 32),[19] the city built by Herod the Great, just beyond the borders of Judæa, on the coast of Phœnicia,[20] and at that time the principal seat of the Roman

---

[17] Rom. ix. 20.
[18] Acts xxii. 21.
[19] Acts ix. 30. Olshausen thinks that Cæsarea Philippi is meant, as Paul tells us that after his conversion he preached through *Syria and Cilicia*, Galat. i. 21. But Cæsarea, without any addition, would naturally mean Cæsarea-on-Sea, and so Luke always designates Cæsarea-on-Sea. If, therefore, Luke had meant Cæsarea Philippi, he would have distinguished it from Cæsarea simply. Besides, Cæsarea Philippi was half as far again from Jerusalem and across the country, while to Cæsarea-on-Sea was a two days' journey only from Jerusalem by a main road, with all the appliances for rapid movement. Not only so, but the object no doubt was (as afterwards in the flight from Berœa, Acts xvii. 14), to reach the sea, whence Paul might proceed either by land or water, as circumstances permitted. The word κατήγαγον also, "they conducted him *down*," (Acts ix. 30), implies a journey from the uplands to the seashore, ἄνω always meaning an advance landward, and κάτω seaward.

Schrader thinks that Paul went direct to Tarsus, and that in the passage "I came into the regions of *Syria* and Cilicia," (Galat. i. 21), Syria is placed before Cilicia, *either* because Paul had just been speaking of Jerusalem, and regarded that as the centre, so that Syria occurred first to his thoughts; or else that the labours of the Apostle in Syria, though subsequent in time, were of more importance than those in Cilicia,

[20] κεῖται μὲν γὰρ ἡ πόλις ἐν τῇ Φοινίκῃ. Jos. Ant. xv. 9, 6.

power. It is in allusion, perhaps, to this flight from Jerusalem that the Apostle thus speaks of the Jews: "Who both killed the Lord Jesus and their own prophets, and have *driven us out*;"¹ and that Clement, in his Epistle to the Corinthians, describes Saul as one who had been "driven into exile."²

From Cæsarea the disciples sent him forth to Tarsus, his native place.³ It does not appear by what route he arrived there, whether by sea or land. On the one hand, as Cæsarea was a port, and Tarsus was not far from the coast, the natural conjecture would be that Saul embarked on board of some ship. On the other hand, he tells us himself, that after quitting Jerusalem he "came into the regions of *Syria* and *Cilicia*;"⁴ and this leads us to infer that he took the road along the shore, the beaten track for travellers to the north. We also trace his ministry in the same direction, viz. at Tyre, where he had disciples,⁵ and Sidon, where he had friends.⁶ The expression that they "sent him forth" (ἐξέπεμψαν) to Tarsus, without saying that he reached it, is remarkable; and we should surmise the fact to be, that they saw him safely on board, but that in the course of the voyage he suffered one of those three shipwrecks to which he alludes in the Second Epistle to the Corinthians,⁷ and that, after escaping to land, he thenceforth pursued the route through Syria and Cilicia to his native city. This would reconcile both accounts, and throw a light upon the passage in the Epistle. To Tarsus the Apostle came, and as he now made a long sojourn there, we shall give some account of Cilicia, and Tarsus its capital.

---

and therefore claimed precedence. Der Apost. Paulus, vol. i. p. 59. But the hypothesis does not recommend itself.

¹ ἡμᾶς ἐκδιωξάντων. 1 Thess. ii. 15.

² φυγαδευθείς, Clem. Ep. ad Cor. v.; but the only remnant of the word is δευθείς, and some would read παιδευθείς, and others μαθδευθείς.

³ Some identify Tarsus with Tarshish, and think that, as Jonah escaped from Joppa to Tarsus, so Paul sailed from Cæsarea to Tarsus. But the hypothesis is untenable. Besides Tarsus of Cilicia, there were evidently, according to the Old Testament, two cities or countries called Tarshish—one on the extreme east, for which the merchantmen started from Ezion-geber, in the Red Sea, 1 Kings ix. 26, xxii. 48; 2 Chron. ix. 21, xx. 36; and were three years on the voyage, and brought back gold and silver, ivory, apes, and peacocks, 2 Chron. ix. 21; and the other in the extreme west, bringing back silver, iron, tin, and lead. Ezek. xxvii. 12. The latter Tarshish is supposed, with some reason, to have been Tartessus in Spain, which was a colony of the Phœnicians, Arrian, xvi. 2; and it is well known that the Phœnicians engrossed the trade with Britain, where iron, tin, and lead abounded.

Tartessus, besides being the emporium for the products of Spain, was the Phœnician depot for the exports from Britain. Indeed, the island called "Albion" by the Celts from its white cliffs, was known amongst the Phœnicians, from its inexhaustible lead-mines, as ברת־אנך Barathanak (*ager plumbi*), almost identical in sound with the oldest Greek form of the name of the island, viz. Βρεταννική. ברה (*ager*) would in composition become, by the general rule, ברת; and the accent in Hebrew, the reverse of our own, falls, not on the first, but on the last syllable, and thus Barátli-anák and Britanniké would approximate. The Phœnician name of Barath-anak (the land of tin) was adopted by the Greeks under the form of Britanniké, and was translated by the word "Cassiterides," or the Tin Islands. Herod. iii. 115. Quia plumbo abundant, uno omnes nomine Cassiteridas appellant. Mela, iii. 6.

⁴ Galat. i. 21.

⁵ The expression τοὺς μαθητάς (Acts xxi. 2) implies a previous acquaintance.

⁶ Julius gave him leave to see his *friends*. Acts xxvii. 3.

⁷ 2 Cor. xi. 25.

In the time of the Republic, Cilicia was a province of great extent, and included Cilicia proper, all Phrygia to the east of Laodicea, and also Lycia, Pamphylia, and Pisidia, and the island of Cyprus. It obtained the greater celebrity in history from having fallen to the lot of the unrivalled orator M. T. Cicero (fig. 33), who governed it

Fig. 33.—A contemporary portrait of Cicero, from a gem in antique paste given in C. W. King's Antique Gems. On the side are the initials M. T. C. for Marcus Tullius Cicero.

for his year (B.C. 51) with great *éclat*. Under the Empire, the province of Cilicia was confined within its natural limits, and formed an Imperial province, governed by a Proprætor nominated by the Emperor, in subordination to the Præfect of Syria.[28] In A.D. 37, Caligula appointed Antiochus to the kingdom of Commagene, and gave him

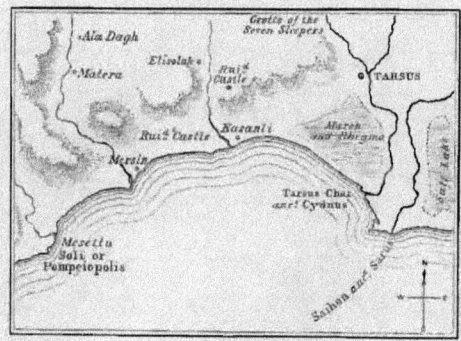

Fig. 34.—Map of the Coast of Tarsus. From Admiralty Chart and Laves and Penates.

the western part of Cilicia, being the greater portion of Cilicia Trachea;[29] while the fertile parts of Cilicia, lying towards the east, and called Cilicia Campestris, in which Tarsus was situate, were still retained by the Emperor in his own hands. In A.D. 39, the fickle Emperor deposed Antiochus, and Cilicia Trachea was reunited to the Roman province of Cilicia,[30] and was under the government of an Imperial officer, who resided at Tarsus, the capital of the province, but subject to the Proprætor of Syria.

Tarsus[31] stood in the centre of a spacious and fertile plain, four hours, or twelve

---

[28] See Fasti Sacri, p. 23, No. 191; p. 88, No. 712; p. 132, No. 955.
[29] Fasti Sacri, p. 250, No. 1505.
[30] See Fasti Sacri, p. 271, No. 1622.
[31] For the various etymologies of the word, see Stephan. Byzant.

miles, from the sea, which lies to the south, and about the same distance from the range of Taurus on the north.[32] It is said to have been founded by Sardanapalus, but was afterwards colonized by the Argives, under the auspices of Triptolemus, in the course of his wanderings in search of Io.[33] Saul, who was born at Tarsus, speaks of it modestly as "no mean city;"[34] but in fact it was the most important of all the cities of Cilicia,[35] and the acknowledged metropolis.[36] The inscriptions Ταρσεων Μητροπολεως and Ταρσου Μητροπολεως, and the like, appear on many of its coins (fig. 35).[37] The

Fig. 35.—Coin of Tarsus. From the British Museum.
Obv. Head of Adrian, and legend, αυτ. και. θι. Τρα. παρ. ω. θε. υια νι. Τραι. Αδριανος Σε.
Rev. Ταρσεων Μητροπολεως (of the Tarsians the metropolis).

city was anciently of great extent, and occupied both sides of the River Cydnus (fig. 36),[38] and, from its consisting of two distinct wings divided by the Cydnus, took the plural form of Ταρσοὶ, 'the wings.' At the mouth of the river, the waters spread themselves into a lake, which by artificial means had been converted into docks, and formed the port of Tarsus.[39] Amongst the localities of the city, may be mentioned the Forum, where Mark Antony was sitting on his tribunal, when the giddy populace left the Triumvir alone, to gaze at the gorgeous galley of Cleopatra, as it sailed up the Cydnus;[100] and on the banks of the river was a stadium, for the celebration of public games,[101] and also a gymnasium, the scene of philosophic

---

[32] Neale's Asia Minor, vol. ii. p. 264; Capt. Beaufort's Karamania, p. 271.

[33] Stephan. Byzant.; Strabo, xiv. 5 (p. 228, Tauchnitz).

[34] Acts xxi. 39.

[35] Ταρσὸν μεγίστην τῶν ἐν Κιλικίᾳ πόλεων. Diod. xiv. 20. ἐπισημοτάτη πόλις Κιλικίας. Stephan. Byzant.

[36] Ταρσὸς μητρόπολις. Hieros. Ταρσὸς γάρ παρ' αὐτοῖς (the Cilicians) τῶν πολεων ἡ ἀξιολογωτάτη καλεῖται, μητρόπολις οὖσα. Jos. Ant. i. 6, 1. Cilicia . . . matrem urbium habet Tarsum. Solinus, xxxviii.

[37] Eckhel, iii. 71. The letters A M K are of frequent occurrence on the coins of Tarsus, and the meaning is Πρώτη Μητρόπολις Κιλικίας. See a paper upon the subject in Académie des Inscript. vol. xxxi. p. 278.

[38] διαρρεῖ δ' αὐτὴν μέσην ὁ Κύδνος. Strabo, xiv. 5 (p. 228, Tauchnitz). Hanc urbem interseat Cydnus amnis. Solinus, c. 38. Cydnus Tarsum, liberam urbem, procul a mari secans. Plin. N. H. vi. 22. ταύτην διαρρεῖ ποταμὸς Κύδνος μέσος. Stephan. Byzant. Mediam (Tarsum) Cydnus amnis intersuit. Quint. Curtius, iii. 5. Captus fluminis amoenitate per mediam urbem influentis. Justin. xi. 8. Κύδνος τε σκολιοῖο μέσην διὰ Ταρσὸν ἱέντος. Dionys. Perieg. l. 868; and see a passage from Libanius, cited Wesseling, Itiner. 579. After these citations, there can be no doubt, however improbable it may now appear, that the Cydnus once flowed through the middle of the city. Either, therefore, the city has dwindled to almost nothing, or the Cydnus has shifted its channel, as the present Tersoos is at some distance from the river.

[39] ἐστιν ἐπίνειον ἡ λίμνη τῆς Ταρσοῦ. Strabo, xiv. 5 (p. 227, Tauchnitz). See plan, p. 78.

[100] Plut. Ant. 26.

[101] ἐπὶ Λουκίου Ἐντροπίου τοῦ λαμπροτάτου ἡγεμόνος ἡμῶν ἐπληρώθη ἡ περιφέρεια τοῦ σταδίου. Inscription at Tarsus, Boeckh, 4437.

discussion amongst the aged, and of athletic exercises amongst the youth of the city.[102]

In the civil wars that followed upon the assassination of the first Cæsar, Tarsus was unfortunate. Like most other cities, it had two parties, one of which favoured Brutus and Cassius, and the other Octavius and Antony. Cassius was the first to present himself at their gates, when they received him with open arms, and publicly crowned him. Shortly afterwards arrived Dolabella, the partisan of Octavius and

Fig. 36.—Falls of the Cydnus. From Laborde.

Antony, when, with a levity for which they were distinguished, they received him with the highest honours, and shouted for Octavius and Antony. For this vacillation they paid dearly. Cassius, having defeated Dolabella, marched upon Tarsus, and laid on it a fine of 1500 talents, or about £365,625. Cassius himself retired, but left a force to exact the penalty. In order to raise so enormous a sum, the public property was first exhausted, and then the sacred plate used in the service of the gods; but as the amount still fell short of the mark, their hard masters proceeded to a sale of the citizens themselves—first the young of both sexes, then the old, and lastly those of prime age. However, before these cruelties were brought to a conclusion, Cassius returned to Tarsus, and, pitying so much misery, remitted the remainder of the tribute.[103]

---

[102] Strabo, xiv. 5.   [103] App. B. C. iv. 64.

HISTORY OF TARSUS. [A.D. 39]

After the defeat of Brutus and Cassius, at the battle of Philippi, Antony made the Tarsians some compensation for their sufferings by declaring their city free, and granting them immunity from all taxes (fig. 37).[104] He also issued a proclamation,

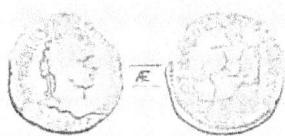

Fig. 37.—Coin of Tarsus. From Akerman.
Obv. Head of the Emperor, with the legend Αυτ. Κ. Μ. Αυρ. Σευηρος Αντωνεινος (M. Aur. Severus Antoninus Imp. Cæs.) Rev. Κοινοβουλιον Ελευθ. Ταρσου (Parliament of Free Tarsus).

that such Tarsians as had been sold into slavery should be set at liberty.[105] The father of Saul may have been amongst the number.

The Tarsians, having now regained their independence, governed themselves by their own laws, their constitution consisting of a court of Aldermen (γερουσία), and a Common Council (βουλή),[106] and the People (δῆμος).[107] The three estates together appear to have formed the κοινοβούλιον, or Parliament.[108] Soon after the battle of Philippi they fell under the sway of an artful demagogue. Boethus, a bad citizen and no better poet,[109] was advanced to the highest post; and, as he had written a fulsome epic on the battle of Philippi, he was supported by the countenance of Mark Antony. His administration of public affairs was stamped with infamy, but he contrived, by his subtle flatteries, to escape the punishment he deserved. At length, after the overthrow of Antony by Augustus, in the battle of Actium (B.C. 31), Athenodorus, the celebrated *Stoic* philosopher, who was a native of Tarsus, and who had been tutor to Augustus, returned to his own country, and seeing the disorders into which the city had fallen, and being backed by the authority of his patron Augustus, procured the expulsion of Boethus and his adherents. Athenodorus at this time was well-stricken in years,[110] and could not have been less than sixty; and as he lived to the age of eighty-two, his death would fall about B.C. 9. During

---

[104] Cydnus Tarsum, *liberam* urbem, procul a mari secans. Plin. N. H. v. 22. And see the coin with the inscription 'Ελευθέρας Ταρσού (fig. 37).

[105] App. B. C. v. 7.

[106] Answering perhaps to the γερουσία and επίκλητος at Ephesus. Strabo, xiv. 1 (p. 174, Tauchnitz).

[107] Eckhel, vol. iii. p. 73, citing Dion Chrysostom.

[108] But there are coins of Tarsus Ταρσού Μητρ. των Κιλικων Ισαυρια Καππ. Λυκαονιο, and others Κοινος των τριων Επαρχιων; and some have referred the κοινοβούλιον to the joint council of these three provinces. See Eckhel, vol. iii. p. 74, for the coins referred to.

[109] κακός μέν ποιητής, κακός δέ πολίτου. Strabo, xiv. 5. The only specimen we have of his poetry is the following epigram in the Greek Anthology, ix. 218:

εἰ τηλοῦ Δοιάντος ἐς ἱερὸν ἤλθες Ὀλύμπου,
ουκουφων ὑγροὶ ουκ ποτε καὶ Ξοάνων ὁ
δίος ὁ τεκόντος Ηράκλης ὡγήσατο κεινω,
ουδὲ κατὰ πρατέσσι τίθεα νουθερόλων,
τοτε μεν εν ξενοι Δαῖς δε δατὸ συγγενικ Ηρη,
Εδώνιοι Λεωνίη, Βακχαρ᾽ ἔρα δ᾽ ἔσεσθε.

[110] γηραιος, Strabo, xiv. 5 (p. 229, Tauchnitz).

this period he directed the counsels of the city with eminent success, and on his death divine honours were paid to him, as a Hero.[111]

On the demise of Athenodorus, Nestor, the *Academic* philosopher, who had been tutor to Marcellus, the son of Octavia, the sister of Augustus, assumed the reins of administration; and while, on the one hand, he maintained his influence at the Court of Rome, he acquired, by the skill of his government, no little popularity amongst his own countrymen.[112] When Saul now returned to his native city, in A.D. 39, Nestor probably was no longer living,[113] and we know not who was his successor. Perhaps he was not followed by any one of paramount authority, but public affairs may have been conducted, in the ordinary manner, by the Court of Aldermen, Common Council, and People.

We have already had occasion to mention that Tarsus was at this time a famous university. It was, indeed, a model school, from which was continually issuing a stream of professors in all the branches of knowledge. Rome, in particular, was full of them. Athenodorus the Stoic, Nestor the Academic, and Nestor the Stoic, had been tutors—the first to Octavius, the second to his nephew Marcellus,[114] and the last to Tiberius.[115] Athenodorus also superintended the education of the young Claudius, who afterwards became Emperor.[116] To this connection between Tarsus and the Imperial family we may, perhaps, in part ascribe the facility with which Saul, at a subsequent period, gained a footing at Rome, even within the precincts of the Palace.

Such was Tarsus, to which Saul now returned, after an absence of about twenty years.[117]

---

[111] Lucian, Macrob. 21.

[112] Strabo, xiv. 5.

[113] He seems to have been dead when Strabo wrote, about A.D. 20. Strabo, xiv. 5 (p. 230, Tauchnitz). Indeed, this must have been the case, if he was tutor to Marcellus, who died, in his twentieth year, B.C. 23. Vell. Paterc. ii. 93 see Fasti Sacri, p. 86, No. 702.

[114] Strabo, xiv. 5.

[115] Lucian, Macrob. 21.

[116] Suet. Claud. iv.

[117] Tarsus is still called Tersoos. The name has a vitality which has hitherto baffled all attempts to annihilate it. It was once called, for a time, Crania, and then Antioch, Stephan. Byzant.; but the appellation of Tarsus again became dominant, and has ever since prevailed. The present city is said to contain about 30,000 inhabitants, and stands at about a mile to the west of the Cydnus; but the remains of a theatre covered with bushes, between the town and the river, show that the modern Tersoos represents but a small portion of the ancient metropolis. The present town is about a mile in length, and has two gates—one on the south-west, and the other on the north-east. The inhabitants have the character of being quiet and well-disposed. Irby and Mangles; Capt. Beaufort's Karamania, p. 271.

Kinneir approached Tarsus from the east, and crossed the Cydnus by a bridge of three arches; and after travelling half a mile due west among gardens, entered a mean and dirty suburb and a succession of filthy streets, so narrow that two horsemen could scarcely pass abreast. He spent a week at Tarsus, and employed his mornings and evenings (for the sun during the day was too powerful to admit of his going abroad) in wandering about the town and its environs; but he could discover no inscription, or monument of beauty or art. The houses seldom exceed one storey, and are flat-roofed. The sea is not visible from the site. The Cydnus is about forty yards wide, and the water, which is clear and limpid, flows with a winding course to the south. A number of small canals are cut from the river to Tarsus, for the purposes of irrigation. Kinneir, p. 121, &c.

Saul, actuated by patriotic feelings, had essayed to preach the doctrines of salvation in Jerusalem, the mother-city of all Jews; but, having failed in the attempt, he now earnestly addressed himself to the publication of the Gospel amongst the relatives and friends whom he had left in Tarsus, his native city. To the Hellenists, or Jews of the Dispersion, there is no doubt that Saul, while at Tarsus, was actively employed in publishing the new dispensation. This, indeed, we may collect from his own words, for, in referring to his sojourn in Syria and Cilicia, he speaks of himself as fully occupied in the ministry. "I was unknown," he says, "by face unto the churches of *Judæa* which were in Christ; but they *heard only*, That he which persecuted us in times past *now preacheth the faith* which once he destroyed."[118] On the subject of Saul's labours at Tarsus, we may also call in aid the language of the Acts in speaking of one of the Apostle's journeys a few years after, where it is said that "he went through Syria and Cilicia *confirming* the churches;"[119] for, as Saul was one who did not build on another's foundation, these churches must have been previously planted by himself. Making Tarsus his headquarters, he enlarged the sphere of his labours by sowing the seeds of the Gospel throughout the whole province of Cilicia; but while he was thus employed, an event occurred which called him away to a new and wider field.

[118] Gal. i. 22-24.   [119] Acts xv. 41; and see Acts xv. 23.

CHAPTER VI.

The Call of the Gentiles—The Gospel is preached to the Greeks at Antioch—Account of Antioch—Barnabas sent thither—He brings Saul from Tarsus.

> Unheard by all but angel ears
> The good Cornelius knelt alone,
> Nor dream'd his prayers and tears
> Would help a world undone.
> Christian Year.

ORIGINALLY, *Jews* only were admitted to the Gospel; but on the dispersion of the Christians from Jerusalem, by the persecution under Saul, the Gospel was carried by Philip the deacon amongst the *Samaritans*;[1] and not long after the Ethiopian

Fig. 38.—Gaza. From Vandevelde.

eunuch, who was neither a Jew nor a Samaritan, but a *Proselyte*, was converted by the same evangelist, at or near Gaza (fig. 38), on the road from Jerusalem to Ethiopia.[2]

---

[1] Acts viii. 5. [2] Acts viii. 27.

CHAP. VI.] CALL OF THE GENTILES. [A.D. 40]

The next and final step, which we are about to describe, was to throw open the gates of salvation to the *Heathen*.

On Saul's departure from Jerusalem to Tarsus, there had ensued a momentary calm. Not that the Jewish hierarchs had any less jealousy or less hatred of the Christian community, but their whole attention was engrossed, for the time, by the attempt of Caligula to erect a statue of himself in the Holy of Holies at Jerusalem. The cry for persecution was hushed, and the churches of Judæa, Galilee, and Samaria, being left at peace, grew and were multiplied. In the spring of A.D. 40, Peter, the great

Fig. 39.—*A Coin of Joppa. From Pellerin.*
Obv. Head of Astarte.—Rev. Figure of Neptune, and the legend IOΠΠ (Joppa).

Apostle of the Circumcision, as Saul was to be of the Uncircumcision, availed himself of the opportunity to make the circuit of the churches; and after visiting the other districts, he came at last to Joppa (fig. 39), or Jaffa (fig. 40), the ancient port of Jerusalem,

Fig. 40.—*Plan of Jaffa. From Admiralty Chart.*

to the north-west of the Jewish capital (fig. 41), and took up his lodging with one Simon a tanner. The keys of the kingdom of heaven, or the privilege of unlocking

---

* See Fasti Sacri, p. 264, No. 1584.

the door of the Christian dispensation, had been committed to his keeping, and the time had now arrived when the prerogative was to be exercised. There was at Cæsarea, the seat of the Roman power, a cohort of soldiers, called the Italian Cohort;[1]

Fig. 41.—*View of Jaffa. From Admiralty Chart.*

and one of the centurions was Cornelius, a Roman, as is evident from the name, and who, though a Gentile and uncircumcised, was a worshipper of the one true

---

[1] ἐκ σπείρης τῆς καλουμένης Ἰταλικῆς, Acts x. 1. The word σπεῖρα is used by ancient writers in two very different senses: one as applied to the Roman army, and the other as applied to the auxiliary forces. The *legion* (λεγεών, or τάγμα) consisted of ten cohorts, or σπεῖραι, the commanders of which were called χιλίαρχοι (see John xviii. 12); and each cohort contained six centuries or companies, of which the commanders were called centurions, or ἑκατόνταρχαι. Luke could scarcely have meant that Cornelius commanded a century of one of these fifteen cohorts, as otherwise, while designating the name of the cohort as the Italian, he could scarcely have failed to specify the name of the *legion*. The regiments of *auxiliaries* were never called legions (a term exclusively appropriated to the Roman army), but were called cohorts, σπεῖραι. See the legions (τάγματα) of the Romans, and the cohorts (or σπεῖραι) of auxiliaries, distinguished by Josephus, Bell. iii. 4, 2; Ant. xix. 9, 2. There were usually five of these auxiliary cohorts stationed at Cæsarea (Jos. Bell. iii. 4, 2; Ant. xix. 9, 2), and each had its distinctive appellation. Thus there was the Augustan cohort (Acts xxvii. 1), and, as here, the Italian cohort, &c. Why this particular cohort was so designated it is not difficult to divine. The auxiliary force at Cæsarea was recruited almost entirely from the province: τὸ γὰρ πλέον τῆς ἐκεῖ (at Cæsarea) δυνάμεως ἐκ Συρίας ἦν

God, and enjoyed a high reputation for sanctity, and was respected for his numerous charities.[5] The narrative of his call is so minute, and yet so simple, that we shall give it in the words of the sacred historian:[6]—

Fig. 42.—*Exterior of the traditional house of Simon the Tanner. From a photograph of the Palestine Exploration.*
The open space is the little courtyard at the rear of the house, between the house and the wall overlooking the sea. The spectator has his back to the sea and is looking eastward. The well from which St. Peter is said to have baptized is sunk into the ground on the right.

"He [Cornelius] saw in a vision evidently about the ninth hour of the day [3 P.M.] an angel of God coming in to him, and saying unto him, 'Cornelius.' And when he

κατειλεγμένον. Jos. Bell. ii. 13, 7. But *this* cohort was supposed to be levied from Italy. I say supposed, for it contained but few Italians, and therefore Luke states, guardedly, not that it *was* the Italian cohort, but that it was *called* the Italian cohort. The officers, however, would no doubt be all Romans. Mention is made in an ancient inscription of a cohort of this name in Syria: Cohors militum Italicorum voluntaria, quae est in Syria. Gruter, p. 434, 1.

The Roman legions are sometimes, by misnomer, also called σπεῖραι, and hence no little confusion, which is increased by the fact that, as the legions multiplied, there was not only the First simply, but the First Auxiliary, τὰ πρώτον ἐπικουρικόν, Dion. lv. 24; and the First Italian, ibid.; Tac. Hist. i. 59, 64; ii. 100; iii. 22. But this First Italian was not raised until the time of Nero, and therefore could not be the σπεῖρα Ἰταλικῆ of Luke. Acts x. 1. ὅτι γὰρ Νέρων τὸ πρῶτόν τε καὶ Ἰταλικὸν ἀνομαζόμενον, καὶ ἐν τῇ κάτω Μυσίᾳ χειμάζον, καὶ ὁ Γαλβας τό τε πρῶτον τὸ ἐπικουρικόν, τό ἐν τῇ Παννονίᾳ τῇ κάτω, καὶ τὸ ἕβδομον τὸ ἐν Ἱσπανίᾳ συνέταξαν. Dion. lv. 24. See Wetstein on Acts x. 1; Meyer, Apostg. p. 196; Biscoe and Humphry on the Acts, &c.

[7] It has been much questioned whether he was merely a devout heathen, or so far a Jew that

[5] The Author attempted to tell it in his own language, but he found that nothing could be added to, or taken from, the account of Luke without impairing its force.

looked on him, he was afraid, and said, 'What is it, Lord?' And he said unto him, 'Thy prayers and thine alms are come up for a memorial before God. And now send men to Joppa,[7] and call for one Simon, whose surname is Peter: he lodgeth with one

Fig. 43.—*Interior of the traditional house of Simon the Tanner. From a sketch by W. Simpson.*

Simon a tanner,[8] whose house is by the sea side [figs. 42 and 43]: he shall tell thee what thou oughtest to do.' And when the angel which spake unto Cornelius was departed,

he was a Proselyte of the Gate, i.e. uncircumcised, but holding the seven precepts of Noah. The expressions εὐσεβὴς καὶ φοβούμενος τὸν θεόν (Acts x. 2), if they stood alone, would tend to show that he was a Proselyte; but the passages x. 28, 34, xi. 1, 18, xv. 7, tend to a contrary conclusion. The Gospel had been thrown open to Proselytes of Righteousness, or circumcised Proselytes, by the conversion of the Ethiopian eunuch, Acts viii. 26: and now, by the conversion of Cornelius, the heathen generally were admitted. See Meyer, Apostg. p. 196. The members of the church from this time may be thus distributed:—

CHRISTIANS.

Circumcised. | Uncircumcised.

1. Ἑβραῖοι, or Jews of Palestine, who spoke Hebrew.
2. Ἑλληνισταί, or, Jews of the Dispersion, who spoke Greek.
3. Proselytes of Righteousness, as the Ethiopian eunuch.

Proselytes of the Gate.   Heathen generally.

The seven precepts of Noah to be observed by Proselytes of the Gate were so called as said to have been revealed to Noah. See Talm. de Bab. Sanhedrin, 56 b. These seven were:—1. To abstain from idolatry; 2. From blasphemy; 3. From murder; 4. From adultery; 5. From theft; 6. To institute judges to maintain the laws; and 7. Not to eat flesh cut from the animal while alive. Jennings' Jewish Ant. book i. c. 3. But, according to Maimonides (De Regibus, c. 9), the six first were given to Adam, and the seventh only to Noah.

[7] This was thirty miles from Cæsarea.

[8] The trade of a tanner was so ill-reputed amongst the Jews, that if a tanner married without disclosing his occupation, it was, according to the Rabbins, a ground for divorce. *Hæc sunt vitia quæ quis aperire cogitur, si habet ulcus, &c.*

he called two of his household servants, and a devout soldier of them that waited on him continually; and when he had declared all these things unto them, he sent them to Joppa. On the morrow, as they went on their journey, and drew nigh unto the city, Peter went up upon the housetop[9] to pray about the sixth hour [11 to 12 A.M.]; and he became very hungry, and would have eaten: but while they made ready, he fell into a trance, and saw heaven opened, and a certain vessel descending unto him, as it had been a great sheet tied at the four corners and let down to the earth; wherein were all manner of fourfooted beasts,[10] and creeping things, and fowls of the air. And there came a voice to him, 'Rise, Peter; kill, and eat.' But Peter said, 'Not so, Lord; for I have never eaten anything that is common or unclean.' And the voice spake unto him again the second time, 'What God hath cleansed, that call not thou common.' This was done thrice: and the vessel was received up again into heaven. Now while Peter doubted in himself what this vision which he had seen should mean, behold, the men which were sent from Cornelius had made enquiry for Simon's house, and stood before the gate, and called, and asked whether Simon, which was surnamed Peter, were lodged there. While Peter thought on the vision, the Spirit said unto him, 'Behold, three men seek thee. Arise therefore, and get thee down, and go with them, doubting nothing; for I have sent them.' Then Peter went down to the men,[11] and said, 'Behold, I am he whom ye seek; what is the cause wherefore ye are come?' And they said, 'Cornelius, a centurion, a just man, and one that feareth God, and of good report among all the nation of the Jews, was warned from God by an holy angel to send for thee into his house, and to hear words of thee.' Then called he them in, and lodged them. And on the morrow Peter rose up[12] and went away with them, and certain brethren from Joppa accompanied him. And on the morrow they entered into Cæsarea. And Cornelius was waiting for them, and had called together his kinsmen and near friends. And as Peter was coming in, Cornelius met him, and fell down at his feet, and worshipped him. But Peter took him up, saying, 'Stand up; I myself also am a man.' And as he talked with him, he went in, and found many

---

et βυρσεύς. Ketuvoth, fol. 77, 1. And if a man died, his widow was not bound to marry the brother, if he was a tanner. Contigit Sidone de coriario ut moreretur, cujus frater itidem erat βυρσεύς. Dixerunt sapientes mulierem posse nuptias fratris illius detrectare. Ibidem in Mischna, cited Schoettgen's Horæ Hebr. vol. i. p.447. The house now shown as Simon's is within the town, at the south-west corner, and overlooks the sea. It has a small court at the back on the west, where is a well, from which it is said converts were baptized. According to the Mischna (Sanenh. 11, 9), Cadavera et sepulchra separant et coriarium quinquaginta cubitos a civitate. Meyer, Apostg. 199; so that the tannery itself would be *without* the city, but the house in which Simon dwelt might very well have been separate from the tanyard.

[9] The roofs of the houses in this part were then, as now, flat, and were used for the purposes of prayer and religious exercises.

[10] Griesbach, Lachmann, Tischendorf, and Alford agree that the words καὶ τὰ θηρία ("and wild beasts") are to be rejected.

[11] Griesbach, Scholtz, Lachmann, Tischendorf, and Alford reject the words τοὺς ἀπεσταλμένους ἀπὸ τοῦ Κορνηλίου πρὸς αὐτόν—" which were sent unto him from Cornelius."

[12] Griesbach, Scholtz, Lachmann, Tischendorf, and Alford read ἀναστὰς after ὁ Πέτρος.

that were come together. And he said unto them, 'Ye know how that it is an unlawful thing for a man that is a Jew to keep company with, or come unto, one of another nation; but God hath shewed me that I should not call any man common or unclean. Therefore also came I unto you without gainsaying, as soon as I was sent for; I ask therefore for what intent ye have sent for me?' And Cornelius said, 'Four days ago[13] I was fasting until this hour; and at the ninth hour I was praying in my house, and, behold, a man stood before me in bright clothing, and said, 'Cornelius, thy prayer is heard, and thine alms are had in remembrance in the sight of God. Send, therefore, to Joppa, and call hither Simon, whose surname is Peter; he is lodged in the house of one Simon, a tanner, by the sea side; who, when he cometh, shall speak unto thee.' Immediately therefore I sent to thee, and thou hast well done that thou art come. Now therefore are we all here present before God, to hear all things that are commanded thee of God.' Then Peter opened his mouth, and said, 'Of a truth, I perceive that God is no respecter of persons; but in every nation he that feareth him, and worketh righteousness, is accepted with him. The word which God sent unto the children of Israel, preaching peace by Jesus Christ: (he is Lord of all:) that word, I say, ye know, which was published throughout all Judæa, and began from Galilee, after the baptism which John preached; how God anointed Jesus of Nazareth with the Holy Ghost and with power: who went about doing good, and healing all that were oppressed by the devil; for God was with him. And we are witnesses of all things which he did, both in the land of the Jews, and in Jerusalem; whom they slew and hanged on a tree. Him God raised up the third day, and gave that he should be shewed openly, not to all the people, but unto witnesses chosen before of God, even unto us, who did eat and drink with him after he rose from the dead. And he commanded us to preach unto the people, and to testify that it is he which was ordained of God to be the Judge of quick and dead. To him give all the Prophets witness, that through his name whosoever believeth in him shall receive remission of sins.' While Peter was yet speaking these words, the Holy Ghost fell on all them which heard the word. And they of the Circumcision which believed were astonished, as many as came with Peter, because that on the Gentiles also was poured out the gift of the Holy Ghost; for they heard them speak with tongues, and magnify God. Then answered Peter, 'Can any man forbid water, that these should not be baptized, which have received the Holy Ghost as well as we?' And he commanded them to be baptized in the name of the Lord."[14]

---

[13] ἀπὸ τετάρτης ἡμέρας, Acts x. 30 — i.e. the fourth day before, inclusive. Thus Cornelius was praying at the ninth hour, or 2 to 3 P.M., on a certain day at Cæsarea, Acts x. 30; and immediately afterwards and the same day Cornelius sent messengers to Joppa, who arrived there on the morrow (the second day) at the sixth hour, 11–12 A.M.—τῇ ἐπαύριον... περὶ ὥραν ἕκτην. Acts x. 9. Peter entertained them that day, and the next day (the third) went with them to Joppa, τῇ ἐπαύριον, Acts x. 23; and the day after, being the fourth, had the interview with Cornelius, τῇ ἐπαύριον. Acts x. 24. Blunt reckons this amongst the 'Undesigned Coincidences.' See that work, p. 316.

[14] Acts x. 3–48.

The fact of Peter's holding communion with Gentiles, made, of course, no small stir at Jerusalem; and on the Apostle's return, the Hebrew disciples, who were zealous observers of the Law, and knew not by what authority Peter had acted, but heard only that he had been the associate of the unclean, cited him before them to answer the charge—"Thou wentest in to men uncircumcised, and didst eat with them." But Peter rehearsed the matter from the beginning, and concluded by saying: "'Forasmuch, then, as God gave them the like gift as he did unto us who believed on the Lord Jesus Christ, what was I, that I could withstand God?' When they heard these things, they held their peace, and glorified God, saying, 'Then hath God also to the Gentiles granted repentance unto life.'"[15]

No sooner was the admission of the Gentiles thus proclaimed, than the preachers of the Gospel addressed themselves earnestly to the great work of their conversion. On the death of Stephen, and the consequent dispersion of the disciples, the tidings of the Gospel had been carried into the neighbouring province of Samaria; and, not long after, Christianity had spread itself through Phœnicia, Cyprus, and Syria. The call of Cornelius having now heralded the admission of the Gentiles, some Jewish converts, natives of Cyprus and Cyrene (countries where the vernacular tongue was Greek), entered into Antioch, and opened their ministry amongst the Greeks,[16] or Gentile inhabitants.

Antioch was founded (B.C. 300) by Seleucus Nicator, and was named after his father Antiochus (fig. 44).[17] It had been the capital of the kingdom of the Seleucidæ, and contained their royal palace;[18] and was now the third city of the Roman Empire, Alexandria being the second.[19] It was situate sixteen miles and a half from the sea by road, or forty-one miles along the windings of the navigable river; and being seated on the northern slope of Mount Silpius, it looked down upon the Orontes, which flowed to the west along the vale beneath, on the north of the town, and was about 125 feet broad. The distance between the river and the crest of the mountain at the back of the town on the south was from one to two miles. The city was between four and five miles long, from east to west, and was encompassed by walls fifty feet high and fifteen feet thick, which were carried, at a prodigious expense, across ravines and over the ridge of the mountain on the south. The remains of them astonish the traveller, even at the present day, notwithstanding the ravages of time, assisted by the havoc of war.[20] Within the outer wall were contained four wards,

---

[15] Acts xi. 1 et seq.

[16] The reading of Ἕλληνας for Ἑλληνιστάς (Acts xi. 20) has been adopted, as supported by ancient MSS., and the testimony of Eusebius (ii. 3), and approved by Griesbach, Scholtz, Lachmann, Tischendorf, and Alford.

[17] It is still called Antakieh. The population is variously stated at from 4000 to 10,000. The city occupies but a small portion of the ancient area. The Christians have no church there, but Aleppo Gate is called, after St. Paul, 'Bab Boulous.' Smith's Geograph. Dict.

[18] Strabo, xvi. 2 (p. 355, Tauchnitz); 1 Maccab. iii. 37, and vii. 2.

[19] Jos. Bell. iii. 2, 4; Strabo, xvi. 2 (p. 355, Tauchnitz).

[20] The walls, now in ruins, are supposed to be those of Justinian, but they may be taken to represent the older walls.

each enclosed by a wall of its own. The ward to the north-west was the original city, founded by Seleucus Nicator. It lay on the plain along the banks of the Orontes. To the north-east of this was built the new city of Seleucus Callinicus. It

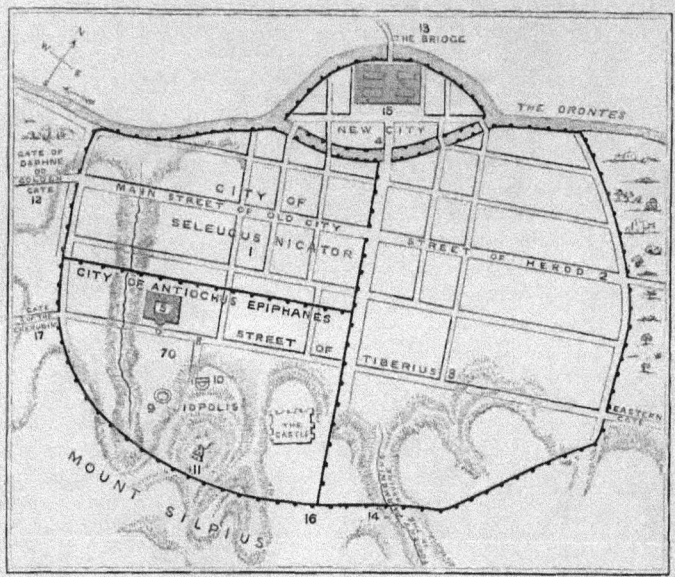

Fig. 14.—A Map of the city of Antioch of Syria, grounded on that of C. O. Müller.

(1) City of Seleucus Nicator. It was founded ἐν τῇ πεδιάδι τοῦ αὐλῶνος κατέναντι τοῦ ὄρους πλησίον τοῦ Δράκοντος ποταμοῦ τοῦ μετακληθέντος Ὀρόντου, ὅπου ἦν ἡ κώμη ἡ καλουμένη Βωττία, ἀντικρὺς τῆς Ἰωπόλεως. And a sacrifice was offered κατὰ μέσον τῆς πόλεως καὶ τοῦ ποταμοῦ, and a statue to the genius of the city was erected ὑπεράνω τοῦ ποταμοῦ. Malala, lib. viii.; and see lib. x.

(2) The Street of Herod was, according to Malala, outside the old city of Seleucus Nicator. ὁ δὲ Ἡρώδης βασιλεὺς τῶν Ἰουδαίων πρὸς τιμὴν αὐτοῦ (Augustus) ἐποίησε καὶ τὴν ὁδοστρωσίαν τὴν ἔξω τῆς πόλεως Ἀντιοχείας τῆς μεγάλης (ἦν γὰρ δύσβατος), στρώσας αὐτὴν λευκοῖς πλάκαις. Malala, lib. ix. But Josephus says it intersected the city, and reached two miles and a half. Bell. i. 21, 11; Ant. xvi. 5, 3. As the city, in the time of Josephus, extended four miles and a half in length, Herod probably continued the main street of the old city through the new city to the east. ὧν ἡ πόλις ἓξ καὶ τριάκοντα σταδίων ἐστὶν τὸ μῆκος, καὶ στοὰς ἑκατέρωθεν πεποιήκασιν. Dion Chrysost. Or. xlvii.

(3) The Street of Tiberius. This also was outside the old city of Seleucus Nicator, and was πρὸς τῷ ὄρει, viz. against the mountain, or to the south. ἔκτισεν ἔξω τῆς πόλεως ἐμβόλους δύο μεγάλους πρὸς τῷ ὄρει τῷ λεγομένῳ Σιλπίῳ, ἔχοντας διαστήματα μιλίων δ' ὑπορόφους καὶ πανευπρεπεῖς, &c. Malala, lib. x.

(4) The New City, built by Seleucus Callinicus. Strabo, xvi. 2. It stood on an island. τὴν δὲ νέαν πόλιν ἡ νῆσος, ἣν καὶ τοῦ ποταμοῦ σχίσις ἐποίησεν, ὑπεδέξατο (Libanius, Orat. xi. Antiochie.), and contained the Palace: αὐτὰ δὲ τὰ βασίλεια κατείληφε μὲν τῆς νήσου τοσοῦτον ὥστε εἰς τέταρτον μέρος τῆς ὅλης τελεῖν. Ibid.

(5) The Forum.

had the river on the north, and a branch of the stream was carried round it (artificially) on the south. On the island thus formed[24] was situate the royal palace, with a bridge on the north leading into the suburb beyond the Orontes. On the south of the city of Seleucus Nicator was the third region added by Seleucus Epiphanes, and called Epiphania. In this were situate the Forum, the Theatre and Amphitheatre, and most of the principal buildings. From Mount Silpius, on the south, there frowned over this part of the city a gigantic bust, called Charonium, or Charon's Head, carved, in vast proportions, from the native rock, and wearing a crown. To the east of the city of Seleucus Nicator and of Epiphania was situate the fourth ward, which had gradually extended itself along the open space, as the influx of new inhabitants demanded accommodation. Five miles to the south-west was a suburb, one of the most lovely spots on the face of the earth—the celebrated Daphne, where was the Temple of Apollo and Diana, embosomed in a grove of myrtles and cypresses ten miles in circumference. The Antiochians every year made a triumphal procession thither, with all the pomp and pageantry of a garish superstition.[22]

(6) The Senate House, βουλευτήριον. It stood next the Forum, and in the reign of Tiberius was burnt down, with part of the Forum. καύσας τὰ πλέον μέρος τῆς ἀγορᾶς καὶ τὸ βουλευτήριον. Malala, lib. x. It was built by Antiochus Epiphanes. ἔκτισε πρῶτον ἐν Ἀντιοχείᾳ τῇ μεγάλῃ ἔξω τῆς πόλεως (the city of Seleucus Nicator) τὸ λεγόμενον βουλευτήριον, εἰς τὰ ἐκεῖσε συνάγεσθαι πάντας τοὺς συγκλητικοὺς αὐτοῦ μετὰ τῶν πολειτευομένων καὶ τῆς πόλεως πάντων τῶν κτητόρων, καὶ βουλεύεσθαί τε δεῖ γίνεσθαι περὶ τῶν ἀνακυπτόντων καὶ τότε ἀναφέρειν ἐπὶ αὐτὸν τὰ συμφέροντα. Malala, lib. viii.

(7) The Pantheon. This was in the Upper City, and was probably one of the temples erected by Epiphanes. Julius Cæsar repaired it. ἔκτισε δὲ ἐκεῖ ἄνω καὶ μονάχιον [lego, μοναμάχιον] καὶ θέατρον. ἀνανέωσε δὲ καὶ τὸ Πάνθεον, μέλλοντα συμπίπτειν ἀνεγείρας τὸν βωμόν. Malala, lib. ix.

(8) Singon Street, where Paul preached. κηρύξαντα ἐκεῖ πρῶτον τὸν λόγον ἐν τῇ ῥύμῃ τῇ πλησίον τοῦ Πανθέου τῇ καλουμένῃ τοῦ Σίγγωνος. Malala, lib. 10.

(9) The Amphitheatre.

(10) The Theatre.

(11) The Charonium, or Giant's Head. ἐπὶ δὲ τῆς αὐτοῦ (Antiochus Epiphanes) βασιλείας λοιμοῦ γενομένου, καὶ πολλῶν διαφθαρέντων τῆς πόλεως, Λήϊός τις τελεστὴς ἐκέλευσε πέτραν ἐκ τοῦ ὄρους τοῦ ὑπεράνω τῆς πόλεως γλυφῆναι, ἔχουσαν προσωπεῖον μέγα πάνυ ἐστεμμένον, προσίχον ἐπὶ τὴν πόλιν καὶ τὸν αὐλῶνα· ὅπερ προσωπεῖον καλοῦσιν ἕως τοῦ νῦν οἱ Ἀντιοχεῖς Χαρώνιον. Malala, lib. viii.

(12) The Gate of Daphne, or Golden Gate. It was near the river. ἄγραν τῆς πόλεως καλλίσταν τε καὶ πολυοικότατον ἐν δεξιᾷ χωροῦντι πρὸς Δάφνην παρ' αὐτὸν τὸν ποταμόν. Libanius, Oratio ii. pro Rhetor. ὁ δὲ αὐτὸς Θεοδόσιος ἐχρύσωσε καὶ τῆς Δαφνητικῆς πόρτας δύο θύρας τὰς χαλκᾶς. . . . καλεῖται ἕως ἄρτι χρυσέα πύρτα. Malala, lib. xiv.

(13) The Bridge. Βορράθεν μὲν Ὀρόντης ὁ ποταμὸς παραρρεῖ τὰ βασίλεια. ἐκ δὲ μεσημβρίας στοὰ μεγίστη διώροφος τῷ τῆς πόλεως ἐπῳκοδόμηται περιβόλῳ, πυργοὺς ὑψηλοῖς ἑκατέρωθεν ἔχουσα. μεταξὺ δὲ τῶν τε βασιλείων καὶ τοῦ ποταμοῦ λεωφόρος ἐστίν. ὑποδεχομένη τοῖς διὰ τῶν τῇδε πυλῶν ἐκ τοῦ ἄστεος ἐξιοῦσας καὶ εἰς τοὺς προαστείους ἀγροὺς παραπέμπουσα. Theodoret, Eccl. Hist. iv. 26, cited Müller's Antiq. Antioch. p. 52.

(14) A ravine in Mount Silpius.

(15) The Palace.

(16) The Middle Gate, surmounted by a wolf suckling Romulus and Remus. μέσην πύλην πλησίον τοῦ ἱεροῦ τοῦ Ἄρεως, ὅπου ὁ Παρμένιος ὁ χείμαρρος κατέρχεται ἔγγιστα τοῦ νυνὶ λεγομένου Μακέλλου. Malala, lib. xi.

(17) The Gate, afterwards known as the Gate of the Cherubim, from Titus erecting over it the cherubim taken from the Ark in the Temple at Jerusalem. Malala, lib. x. Antoninus Pius began the paving of the Street of Tiberius from this gate. Malala, lib. xi.

[21] The island is no longer traceable.   [22] Strabo, xvi. 2 (p. 355, Tauchnitz).

Of the dense population which swarmed in the streets of Antioch, the Jews formed no inconsiderable proportion. Alexander the Great had regarded them with favour, and as Judæa lay between the rival kingdoms of the Seleucidæ of Syria and the Ptolemies of Egypt, they were courted by both; and at Antioch, as at Alexandria, the Jews possessed an equality of franchise with the Greeks themselves.[23] It is almost unnecessary to add, that they had numerous synagogues,[24] one of which was pre-eminent above the rest, and adorned with offerings of brass taken from the Temple of Jerusalem. Antiochus Epiphanes had committed the sacrilege, and afterwards presented the spoils to his Jewish subjects at Antioch.[25] The Jews there were under the government of their own chief magistrate, called the Archon, corresponding to the Ethnarch at Alexandria and Damascus; and doubtless they had also, as at Alexandria, a Council of Seventy-two, or of some smaller number, answering to the Sanhedrim of Jerusalem.[26] Before the Archon and the Council were determined all questions of their law, with an appeal to the High Priest at Jerusalem.[27] Possessed of such high privileges, the Jews of Antioch were continually receiving an accession of strength, by the number of Proselytes who joined them.[28] Amongst others, we read in the New Testament of Nicolas, a Proselyte of Antioch;[29] but if, as is supposed, he was the

Fig. 45.—Coin of P. Quinctilius Varus, Prefect of Syria. From the British Museum.

Obs. Head of Jupiter.—Rev. Female figure of Antioch, with the legend, Αντιοχεων επι Ουαρου (of the Antiochians under Varus), and the date ΕΚ, or 25 of the Actian era, answering to the year from the 2nd of September B.C. 7, to the 2nd of September B.C. 6.
Varus was Prefect of Syria from Midsummer B.C. 6 to Midsummer B.C. 4 (see Fasti Sacri, p. 117, No. 873), and the coin was therefore struck some time between Midsummer and the 2nd of September B.C. 6, and probably on his accession to office. He was afterwards in command in Gaul, and was cut off with two legions by the Germans in A.D. 9. See Fasti Sacri, p. 180, No. 1031.

founder of the Gnostic sect of the Nicolaitans, it had been better for Christendom had he remained a Pagan.

When the kingdom of the Seleucidæ bowed under the yoke of the Romans, Antioch was peculiarly favoured, and was declared a free city;[30] that is, was exempt from the public tribute (which in Syria was, *inter alia*, a property-tax of one per cent.),[31] and, though subject to the supreme control of the Syrian Prefect (fig. 45), was allowed the privilege of governing itself by its own municipal laws. Pagan Antioch

---

[23] Jos. Ant. xii. 3, 1; Bell. vii. 3, 3.
[24] In A.D. 39, in an affray between two factions of the city, the synagogues were burnt. Malala, lib. x.; Fasti Sacri, p. 263, No. 1579.
[25] Jos. Bell. vii. 3, 3.
[26] Philo in Flac. s. 10.
[27] Jos. Bell. vii. 3, 3.

[28] Jos. Bell. vii. 3, 3.
[29] Acts vi. 5.
[30] Plin. N. H. v. 18; Malala, lib. ix.; and ancient coins bear the inscription, Αντιοχεων μητροπολεως αυτονομου. Eckhel, iii. p. 271.
[31] ἔστι δὲ καὶ Σύροις καὶ Κίλιξιν ἐτήσιος, ἑκατοστὴ τοῦ τιμήματος ἑκάστῳ. Appian, Syr. cap. 50.

had a Senate, which consisted of about two hundred,[32] and an Assembly of the People.[33] The Senate occupied the Council-room[34] in Epiphania; but the Assembly, as at Ephesus, met in the Theatre, which served by turns as a conclave of legislators, a scene of amusement, and a place of execution of criminals.[35]

The Romans continued to the Jews the possession of their civil rights,[36] and in Antioch, up to the destruction of Jerusalem, Jews and Gentiles fraternized together on a footing of equality. Herod the Great made a handsome acknowledgment to the Antiochians of their goodwill towards his countrymen; for the main street, that ran east and west through the town, he paved for two miles and a half, at his own expense, with handsome flagstones, and erected on each side a magnificent colonnade, in which foot-passengers might in all weathers walk under shelter.[37] The Jews of Antioch, while they lived on this friendly footing with their fellow-citizens, lost none of their patriotism towards the mother-country, for no Hellenists distinguished themselves more by the richness and splendour of the offerings which they forwarded to the Temple.[38] Such was Antioch, which was destined soon to be the metropolis of Gentile Christendom.

As the heralds of Christianity from Cyprus and Cyrene entered Antioch (fig. 46),

Fig. 46.—*Coin of L. Volusius Saturninus, Prefect of Syria. From the British Museum.*

Obv. Head of Jupiter.—*Rev. επι Σατορνινου Ουολο.* (under Volusius Saturninus), with the legend ΕΛ, or 35 of the Actian era, answering to the year from the 2nd of September A.D. 4, to the 2nd of September A.D. 5. This Saturninus was the immediate predecessor of P. Sulpicius Quirinus or Cyrenius, under whom was the famous taxing.

what a busy scene must have presented itself to their thoughtful gaze! Here the Prefect of Syria, girt with the sword, the emblem of supreme power, with his legates and procurator, and council or board of advice, selected from the noblest blood of Rome, held his court in the palace where the Seleucidæ had reigned. The marketplace was teeming with swarthy Syrians and quickwitted Greeks, and with the children of Abraham, ever distinguishable by their marked physiognomy. Here and there were observed troops of legionary soldiers, the conquerors of the world. The languages that greeted the ear were as diverse as the costumes that met the eye. Syriac and Hebrew, Greek and Latin, were heard in succession. Greek however pre-

---

[31] Julianus Misopog. cited Müller's Antiq. Antioch. p. 30. The constitution of Antioch was probably like that of Seleucia, which Tacitus has thus expressed: Trecenti, opibus aut sapientia delecti, ut senatus: sua populo vis. Tac. Ann. vi. 42.

[32] Jos. Bell. vii. 3, 3.
[34] βουλευτήριον.
[35] Jos. Bell. vii. 3, 3.
[36] Jos. Ant. xii. 3, 1.
[37] Jos. Ant. xvi. 5, 3.
[38] Jos. Bell. vii. 3, 3.

dominated, and formed the ordinary vehicle of communication between such discordant materials.

A wide field was opened to the Christian missionaries, and they began with vigour to publish the glad tidings of the Gospel for the first time to the benighted heathen. The efforts of the evangelists were crowned with such success, and such numbers were in a short time converted to the faith, that the church of Jerusalem, hearing of the extraordinary progress of the Gospel in so capital a city, commissioned Barnabas[39] to proceed thither, both to settle the church on a sound foundation, and also, by his presence, to encourage further exertion. The arrival of an Apostle, next in dignity to the Twelve, had a proportionate effect; and Barnabas, finding the vineyard too extensive for his own unaided exertions, determined on calling in Saul, his school-fellow, for his co-operation in the work.

It was in the spring of A.D. 43,[40] or just ten years after the Crucifixion, that Barnabas proceeded to Tarsus, found Saul, and brought him to Antioch. Here commenced the joint labours of these two holy men, who, from this time forward, continued for many years to devote their energies, at the hazard of their lives, to the propagation of the Gospel. The very place in which they prosecuted their ministry at Antioch has been recorded by John of Antioch, commonly called Malala, or the Orator, who lived at the close of the sixth century. In general, tradition is of little value; but, in this instance, a native of Antioch, who quotes Domninus, an antiquary of a much earlier age, is entitled to some respect. According to Malala, Paul and Barnabas preached in Singon Street, near the Pantheon, in the south-western part of the city, called Epiphania. No spot could have been fixed upon more suitable for their purpose, as it was in one of the most populous districts, and in the immediate neighbourhood of the Forum.[41] The Gentile church at Antioch now grew so rapidly, under the auspices of Paul and Barnabas, that a new designation of the believers became necessary. While Christianity was preached to the Jews only, the followers of the Cross were known amongst their countrymen as Galileans or Nazarenes, and by the heathen were reckoned merely as Jews, without being distinguished by any more specific name; but when the church comprised Gentiles as well as Jews, another description was called for; and as the first great impression was made on the heathen world at Antioch, "the disciples were called 'Christians' first at Antioch."[42] The etymon of the term 'Christian' is of course Greek, from the word Χριστὸς, Anointed, or the Messiah. But the termination may be regarded as Latin, and the explanation is,

---

[39] Barnabas was a native of Cyprus, Acts iv. 36; and Christianity was first preached to the Gentiles at Antioch by men of Cyprus, Acts xi. 20; and Barnabas was probably selected for the mission because his fellow-countrymen, and perhaps his friends or relatives, had initiated the Gospel amongst the Gentiles at Antioch.

[40] For it was a whole year before Saul and Barnabas went up to Jerusalem with the contributions at the Passover of A.D. 44. Acts xi. 26; see Fasti Sacri, p. 278, No. 1665.

[41] κηρύξαντα ἐκεῖ πρῶτον τὸν λόγον ἐν τῇ ῥύμῃ τῇ πλησίον τοῦ Πανθέου τῇ καλουμένῃ τοῦ Σίγγωνος. Malala, lib. x.

[42] Acts xi. 26.

that the Romans, who made Antioch their headquarters in the East, taking the word Χριστός to be the real name of the Founder of the society, adopted the Greek word, and Latinised the form of it.[43]

Barnabas and Saul had laboured jointly at Antioch about a year, when an event occurred which strongly exhibited the implicit faith of the early disciples in the Divine origin of their religion. Certain teachers had come down from Jerusalem to Antioch, and amongst them one Agabus,[44] who had the gift of prophecy. This man foretold, under the influence of the Spirit, that Judæa was about to be visited by a famine. It had long been the practice for the Jews of the Dispersion, when Jerusalem and Judæa (the Holy City and Holy Land) were in distress, to forward alms for the relief of their brethren; and on the present occasion, in the spring of A.D. 44,[45] the converts of Antioch, both Jews and Gentiles, made a collection proportionate to their means, and sent it to the Elders of Jerusalem by the hands of Barnabas and Saul.

---

[43] The termination '-anus' is peculiarly Latin. Thus, Diocletianus . . . donec imperium sumeret, Diocles appellatus, ubi orbis Romani potentiam cepit, Graium nomen in Romanum morem convertit. A. Victor, Epit. 39. So Stephanus Byzant. in Ἀρπία. συνήθης γὰρ Ἰταλῶν ὁ τύπος διὰ τοῦ ανος; and again in Ὀστία. τὸ ἐθνικὸν Ὀστιανός . . . συνήθης γὰρ ὁ τύπος τοῖς Ἰταλοῖς. Accordingly, we hear of Cæsariani, Pompeiani, Ciceroniani, Sertoriani, Cassiani, Brutiani, Galbiani, Othoniani, Vitelliani, Flaviani, &c. See Wetstein's note on Matt. xxii. 17.

[44] Probably from עגב, 'to love,'—not from חגב, 'a grasshopper.' See Meyer, Apostg. p. 217.

[45] See the subject discussed, Fasti Sacri, c. x. p. lxix.

CHAPTER VII.

The History of Judæa from the Martyrdom of Stephen to the Death of Caligula in A.D. 41—Barnabas and Saul take up Alms from the Church of Antioch to the Church of Jerusalem.

> The theatre is thronged. The orb of day
> Sheds its bright radiance from a cloudless sky.
> The monarch on his throne, in proud array,
> Glistens with silver—dazzles every eye,
> And drinks the fulsome draughts of flattery.
> "A god! a god!" they shout; "behold a god!"
> He swells with pride, and apes the Deity.
> Up, Nemesis, with thy avenging rod!
> She smites, and down he sinks, a livid, lifeless clod!
>
> Anon.

BEFORE we follow Saul and Barnabas from Antioch to Jerusalem, we must take up the political history of the Jews for the last few years.

It will be recollected that the martyrdom of Stephen occurred at the Feast of Pentecost, A.D. 37. Pilate had been deposed, and no successor appointed; and Vitellius having, on the unexpected intelligence of the demise of Tiberius, returned to Antioch,

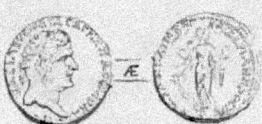

Fig. 47.—Obv. Βασιλευς μεγας Αγριππας Φιλοκαισαρ (Agrippa the great King, Lover-of-Cæsar). Rev. Καισαρεια η προς τω Σεβαστω Λιμεν (Cæsarea on Port Sebastus). From Akerman.

The assumption of the title 'great' agrees with the vanity of this king as recorded in Acts xii. 21, and the coin was struck at Cæsarea-on-Sea, the scene of his death, when smitten by the hand of God. The reference to Port Sebastus is also remarkable as confirming the statement of Josephus that the port formed by Herod the Great was called Sebastus or Augustus. Ant. xvii. 5, 1.

the multitudes congregated at Jerusalem found themselves left to their own passions without any controlling power, and seized on the opportunity of enacting that bloody tragedy. Caligula succeeded to the imperial purple; and amongst the first acts of his reign, he sent Maryllus to take charge of Judæa, by the title of Hipparch, or Master of the Horse.[1]

---

[1] Ἱππάρχην ἐπὶ τῆς Ἰουδαίας ἐκπέμπει Μάρυλλον. Jos. Ant. xviii. 6, 10.

Herod Philip, Tetrarch of Trachonitis, had died four years before, viz. in A.D. 33,[2] and his dominions had been annexed to the province of Syria; but now Caligula, on becoming Emperor, bestowed on Agrippa the title of King, and gave him the province of Trachonitis, which had been subject to his uncle, Herod Philip (fig. 47).

The fortunes of this Agrippa are so singular, and his life from this period occupies so conspicuous a portion of the Jewish history, that we may be excused for sketching an outline of his story.

He was born B.C. 11,[3] and was the son of Aristobulus, one of the sons of Herod the Great; and married Cyprus, the granddaughter of the Tyrant. In the reign of Tiberius he had resided at Rome, where he contracted an intimacy with Drusus (fig. 48), the

Fig. 48.—*Coin of Drusus. From the British Museum.*
Obs. Head of Drusus with the legend Drusus Cæsar Ti. Aug. F. Divi Aug. N.—Rev. Pontif. Tribun. Pot. st. Iter.

Emperor's son, by whom he was led into extravagances that he could little afford. In A.D. 23 Drusus died, and, as was supposed at the time, from intemperance; and Tiberius, under the impression that Drusus had fallen a victim to his vices, affected to show no signs of grief. But on the discovery, in A.D. 31, that the death of Drusus had been procured by poison, secretly administered by the instrumentality of the designing Sejanus, the Emperor became furious, and everyone that reminded him of his loss incurred his displeasure. Agrippa, amongst others, was banished from the Emperor's sight, that his presence might not recall the painful bereavement.

Broken in fortune, and discountenanced at court, Agrippa set sail for Judæa, and, on his arrival, shut himself up in a lonely castle in Idumæa. Here he meditated laying violent hands on himself; but his wife, Cyprus, the good angel that accompanied his wanderings, discovered his intentions, and diverted him from his purpose; and wrote to his sister Herodias, who had lately become the wife of Herod Antipas, Tetrarch of Galilee, to supplicate her good offices on behalf of Agrippa. The appeal was successful, and Antipas sent for him to his court; and in A.D. 32, and therefore during the ministry of our Lord, made him ædile of the town of Tiberias, and allowed him a small salary. This state of dependence was of no long continuance, for Antipas and Agrippa meeting at a feast at Tyre, and growing warm over their

---

[2] See Fasti Sacri, p. 240, No. 1454.   [3] Fasti Sacri, p. 103, No. 800.

cups, Antipas reproached Agrippa with the meanness of his circumstances; and the latter, resenting the affront, betook himself to Flaccus, then Prefect of Syria, with whom he had formerly been on a footing of intimacy at Rome.

Flaccus received him very graciously, and made Antioch his asylum. But his evil genius still pursued him. It happened that Aristobulus, a brother of Agrippa, who, for many years before, had been at variance with him, was also at this time a refugee with Flaccus; and Agrippa having been weak enough, on a certain occasion, to accept a promise of largess from the Damascenes if he would aid their cause with Flaccus, Aristobulus, whose favour was engaged on the other side, accused Agrippa to Flaccus of the secret understanding; and the fact being proved, Agrippa was obliged to seek another shelter.

What became of him for the next two or three years is not recorded; but in A.D. 36,[4] not seeing any prospect of bettering his fortunes in Judæa, he resolved on returning to Italy. The difficulty was how to raise the means. However, Marsyas, his freedman, prevailed on one who had formerly been the freedman of Bernice, Agrippa's mother, to lend Agrippa 20,000 Attic drachms, or £800, upon his bond, at a discount of $12\frac{1}{2}$ per cent. Upon receipt of the money, Agrippa went to the port of Anthedon, where he found a ship about to sail; and was on the point of embarking, when Herennius Capito, the Emperor's procurator at Jamnia, sent a detachment of soldiers, and arrested him for a debt of 300,000 drachms, or £12,000, due from him at Rome to the Imperial Treasury. Agrippa, having no subterfuge, made a show of submission; but at night he escaped from his guard, and got on board, and reached Alexandria. Here he applied to Alexander, the Alabarch or Governor of the Jews, to lend him 200,000 drachms, or £8,000. This the Alabarch refused; but the amiable and affectionate character of Cyprus, Agrippa's wife, so won upon him, that he said he would lend it to her, though not to Agrippa. The Alabarch advanced five talents, or £1200, at once; but, knowing the extravagant habits of Agrippa, and that whatever sum was put into his hands would soon be squandered, he undertook to pay the rest on his arrival in Italy.

On landing at Puteoli (the usual place of disembarkation), Agrippa addressed a letter to Tiberius (who was then at Capreæ), announcing his arrival, and begging permission to wait upon him. The Emperor returned an obliging answer, and commanded his presence at Capreæ; but the very day after this courteous reply, a letter reached the Emperor from Herennius Capito, that Agrippa was a debtor to the Treasury in 300,000 drachms, and that he was a runaway to avoid the payment. Upon this Tiberius was much displeased, and ordered Agrippa to keep out of his sight until he discharged the debt. Agrippa, as his only resource, appealed to Antonia the mother of Claudius (afterwards Emperor), to accommodate him with the money. Antonia (fig. 49) had been an intimate friend of Agrippa's mother Bernice, and from

---

[4] See Fasti Sacri, p. 245, No. 1482.

respect to her memory, Antonia advanced the sum.[5] Agrippa discharged his debt to the state, and this obstacle removed, Tiberius again received him into favour.

Fig. 49.—*Coin of Antonia. From the British Museum.*
Obv. Antonia Augusta.—Rev. Ti. Claudius Cæsar Aug. P. M. Tr. P. Imp.

As Caligula (the son of Germanicus, and Antonia's grandson) was very near to the throne, and in high credit with the people from his late father's virtues, Agrippa was very assiduous in paying court to him; and having prevailed upon one of Tiberius's freedmen, a Samaritan by birth, to lend him a million drachms, or £40,000, he was thus enabled to pay off his debt to Antonia, and also to support the expense of maintaining his friendly footing with Caligula. One day, as he and Caligula were in Agrippa's carriage together, the discourse turned on Tiberius; and Agrippa, on the impulse of the moment, prayed to God that Tiberius might soon be removed to make way for Caligula, one every way more worthy! This pious ejaculation was overheard by Eutychus, the coachman, who at the time took no notice of it, but treasured it up in his memory, to be used at a convenient occasion. Not long after, Eutychus was detected in purloining some of Agrippa's clothes; and on being carried before a magistrate and placed at the bar, he said that he had a secret communication to make to Tiberius, that intimately concerned his safety. Upon this Eutychus was sent in custody to Capreæ; but, from the dilatory habits of the Emperor, the hearing was postponed from time to time, and perhaps the matter would have gone to sleep, had not Agrippa himself, who could not believe that any serious charge was to be made, pressed it upon the Emperor's attention. At length Eutychus was called in, and interrogated as to what he had to communicate, when he charged Agrippa with the conversation in the carriage, not without considerable exaggeration of his own, to give it greater importance. The jealous temper of Tiberius immediately took fire, and he ordered Agrippa, in his purple robes as he was, to be put in fetters and carried to prison.

For six months he was in confinement, when one morning Marsyas, his freedman, came running in with the news, which he communicated in the Hebrew tongue, "The Lion is dead!"[6] The centurion who had the custody of Agrippa, and had become his

---

[5] The intimacy between Bernice and the Imperial family at Rome is incidentally confirmed by Strabo: Καῖσαρ δὲ καὶ τοὺς υἱοὺς ἐτίμησε τοῦ Ἡρώδου καὶ τὴν ἀδελφὴν Σαλώμην καὶ τὴν ταύτης θυγατέρα Βερενίκην. Strabo, xvi. 2 (p. 380, Tauchnitz).

[6] This remarkably illustrates the Apostle's allusion to the Emperor Nero, in 2 Tim. iv. 17. "I was delivered out of the mouth of the lion."

friend as well as jailer, was no sooner apprised of the event than he loosed him from his bonds, and prepared a banquet in his honour. While they were carousing with no little hilarity at the demise of the tyrant, a message arrived that the rumour was false, and that Tiberius was certainly alive. In a moment the tables were turned, and the centurion, thinking that Agrippa had imposed upon him, and afraid of losing his head for having released his prisoner, thrust him rudely from the couch and ordered him into bonds, and treated him with increased severity. So passed the night.

The next morning confirmed the first intelligence, that Tiberius was indeed no more; and then a letter arrived from Caligula, that Agrippa should be removed from the prison to his own house. A few days after, and so soon as decency permitted, Caligula sent for Agrippa to the palace, and put a purple robe upon him, and a crown upon his head, and proclaimed him King of the tetrarchy of Herod Philip.[7] This occurred about the 1st of April, A.D. 37 (fig. 50).[8]

Fig. 50.—*Coin of Caligula. From the British Museum.*
Obv. C. Cæsar Aug. Germanicus Pont M. Tr. Pot.—Rev. Agrippina, Drusilla, Julia, his three sisters.

The remainder of that year, and great part of the following, Agrippa continued at Rome, basking in the sunshine of royalty, and joining, no doubt, in all the gaieties of that queen of cities.

About the middle of A.D. 38,[9] Agrippa expressed a wish to visit his newly-acquired dominions, under the plea of arranging the many weighty matters that required the presence of the Sovereign; and Caligula, on his promise of an early return, gave him permission to depart. Agrippa set sail, and taking advantage of the Etesian winds (which annually commence in July), pursued the route by Alexandria. His arrival in Trachonitis, invested with all the trappings of kingly power, created, as may be supposed, no little stir, not only amongst his own subjects, but throughout Galilee and Judæa. The person who should have been the first to congratulate him on his prosperous fortunes, was the one to whom his success occasioned the greatest pain. Herodias, his sister, the wife of Herod Antipas, Tetrarch of Galilee, could not, without

---

[7] The above account is taken from Jos. Ant. xviii. 6.

[8] See Fasti Sacri, p. 270, No. 1503.

[9] δευτέρῳ ἔτει τῆς Γαΐου Καίσαρος ἡγεμονίας. Jos. Ant. xviii. 6, 11.

feelings of the keenest jealousy, behold the insignia of royalty upon the man who so short a time before had been a runaway from his creditors, and had lived as a pensioner on her husband's bounty. It was Antipas the *Tetrarch*, but Agrippa the *King!* The reflection was too galling to allow her a moment's peace, and she persecuted her husband with daily importunity, until he consented, with much reluctance, to commit the tetrarchy to the care of others, and to set sail for Rome, in the vain hope, by paying court to the Emperor, of improving his fortunes, and acquiring, like Agrippa, the grand object of ambition—the kingly title.

After great preparation, in order to present themselves before the Emperor with suitable magnificence, Antipas and his wife, in A.D. 39, commenced their ill-fated voyage. Their plan had not been conducted with such secresy as to escape the penetration of Agrippa. Knowing the hostile feelings entertained by them, and foreseeing the mischief they might do him, should they be left to plead their cause at Rome without a voice in opposition, they had no sooner started, than Agrippa sent Fortunatus, one of his freedmen, to Italy, with rich presents to the Emperor, and a letter of accusation against Antipas.

Fortunatus followed so fast upon the track of Antipas, that he reached Puteoli just after him; and the Tetrarch having proceeded thence to Baiæ, on the other side of the bay, where the Emperor was then staying, Fortunatus pursued him, and arrived at the very moment when Antipas was in the act of making his suit to Caligula. Fortunatus stood forth, and presented the letter of Agrippa; and the Emperor, having perused the contents, adjourned the hearing until Agrippa should appear in person. The following year (A.D. 40) Agrippa joined Caligula in Gaul, when both parties pleaded before the Emperor in person; and the charge was brought by Agrippa, that Antipas had conspired with the King of Parthia against the Roman government, and had collected a store of arms, sufficient for the equipment of 70,000 men. The Emperor demanded of Antipas, sternly, whether he had made any such preparations; and Antipas not being able to contradict it, Caligula inferred the truth of the whole accusation, deprived Antipas of his tetrarchy, and banished both him and his wife to Lyons in France, or, as another and better account has it, into Spain.[10] The tetrarchy of Antipas was now conferred on Agrippa, as a reward for his services in the detection of the supposed plot.

While the trial of Herod Antipas was still pending, Caligula, so partial to Agrippa personally, meditated a fatal blow against the Jewish nation. It was in the third year of his reign that he was impious enough to proclaim himself a deity, and exacted from his servile subjects the worship paid to the gods. The Jews alone refused obstinately, either to erect statues to the Emperor, or to swear by his name; and the blasphemous and bloodthirsty tyrant vowed, at whatever expense, to erect a statue of himself in the very Holy of Holies in the Temple at Jerusalem. Vitellius, the

---

[10] See, upon this subject, Fasti Sacri, p. 260, No. 1501; p. 265, No. 1592.

Prefect of Syria, who had ever shown a friendly spirit towards the Jews, was recalled;[11] and Petronius, his successor, was commanded to enter Judæa with an army, and execute the commission.

The Prefect, having collected his troops, marched, in the spring of A.D. 40, to the borders of Judæa. The peril was imminent. The Jews were utterly hopeless of contending successfully against the legions of Rome; but they convinced Petronius, from the reckless manner in which they offered to throw away their lives, that the Imperial edict could only be accomplished by depopulating the country. Petronius was touched, and he generously risked his own safety to prevent the massacre of an unoffending people. He returned with his army to Antioch, and thence wrote to Caligula, and represented in strong colours how the erection of the statue would be attended with the most disastrous consequences, by leading to the revolt of the whole nation.

In the meantime Agrippa, who was in high favour at court, had, by a dexterous use of his influence, not without danger to himself, obtained from Caligula a remission of the edict against the Jews; and a despatch was on its road to the East, that if the statue were not already erected, the order should not be enforced. No sooner, however, had the messenger departed, than Caligula received from Petronius the letter communicating the obstinacy of the Jews in resisting the Imperial commands. The Emperor was enraged at the insolence of the Prefect in having dared to disobey his orders, and wrote to him that, as he had become the hireling of the Jews, he must prepare for death. A few days after this, on the 24th of January, A.D. 41, Caligula was assassinated; and as the sentence of condemnation against Petronius travelled slowly, and the news that the world was rid of a monster spread with a lightning rapidity, the Syrian Prefect did not read his death-warrant until he had learnt that its force was spent.

Agrippa, in the various vicissitudes of his fortunes, had acquired a thorough knowledge of mankind, and consummate address and courtly manners—qualities which, as he happened to be now at Rome, he turned to good account. The capital having been thrown into great confusion by the blow which had been struck—the Senate on the one hand, struggling to regain their liberty, and Claudius, on the other, endeavouring, by the intrigues of his friends, to secure the Imperial purple to himself—Agrippa, who was secretly attached to Claudius (from the intimacy which had subsisted between Bernice, the mother of Agrippa, and Antonia, the mother of Claudius), stepped forth to negotiate between the two parties, and managed matters with such adroitness, that in a short time the Senate found it necessary to yield to the pressure upon them; and Claudius, without much opposition, was elevated to the throne. Services so important were acknowledged with a princely generosity. Agrippa had been invested by Caligula, first with the tetrarchy of Philip, and three years after

---

[11] See Fasti Sacri, p. 260, No. 1554.

FORTUNES OF HEROD AGRIPPA. [A.D. 44.]

with the tetrarchy of Herod Antipas. He now received, at the hands of Claudius, the remaining dominions of Herod the Great—viz. Judæa and Samaria. The Imperial gratitude extended itself even to Agrippa's relatives; for Herod, the brother of Agrippa, was, at the same time, made King of Chalcis (fig. 51), a principality of Cœlesyria, to the north-west of Damascus.[12] Agrippa thought it prudent to remain at Rome until

Fig. 51.—Coin of Herod of Chalcis. From Sir F. Madden.
Obv. A cornucopia with tie-leg and Basca (ΗΡΩΔ) of King Herod.—*Rev.* An eagle.

his benefactor was firmly established in power; but in A.D. 42, being anxious to display his splendour in the newly-acquired kingdom, he set sail for Syria. On his arrival he went up to Jerusalem, and exercised the royal prerogative by deposing Theophilus, the High Priest, and appointing Simon (called Cantheras) in his place; and shortly afterwards, not being pleased with Simon, he substituted Matthias, and again displaced him to make room for Elioneus.[13] Agrippa now fixed his permanent abode at Jerusalem, but occasionally resided at Cæsarea, the seat of the Roman government.

Such was the posture of affairs when Saul and Barnabas arrived at Jerusalem with the contribution of the church of Antioch for the relief of the poor Hebrews who had embraced Christianity. Whether Paul and Barnabas travelled by sea or land from Antioch to Judæa is not recorded, but probably (as on a later occasion) by land, in which case they would naturally confirm the various churches that lay on their route.

They reached Jerusalem at the Feast of the Passover, A.D. 44, and found the disciples in the greatest dismay, from a heavy blow just struck against the church by Agrippa.

Through all the chequered scenes of his life, amid all his extravagance and dissipation, Agrippa had ever carried with him an ardent attachment to the observance of the Mosaic Law. No one more regular in offering sacrifice in the Temple, no one more jealous of any inroad upon the ceremonials of religion.[14] Need it be said that he was a bitter enemy to the sect which propagated a faith subversive, as he thought, of all that was most holy? Full of these Jewish prejudices, he had, just before the Passover, gratified his hatred of the new religion by the execution of James, the brother of John; and as this severity was regarded by the Jews as a laudable instance of the King's attachment to the Law, he thought to improve his credit by making a victim of Peter also, the great Apostle of the Circumcision. "When," says Luke, "he [Agrippa] had apprehended him [Peter], he put him in prison, and delivered him to four quaternions of soldiers[15] to keep him, intending after the Passover to bring him

---

[12] See Fasti Sacri, p. 271, Nos. 1619–21.
[13] Jos. Ant. xix. 6, 2; xix. 6, 4; xix. 8, 1.
[14] See Biscoe on the Acts, c. 2.

[15] The Romans divided the night and the day, each into four watches. In quatuor partes ad clepsydram sunt divisæ vigiliæ, ut non amplius

forth to the people."[16] The Jewish law forbade putting any one to death during the festival,[17] and the execution, therefore, was deferred until the Holy Week should be concluded. In the meantime "prayer was made without ceasing of the church unto God for him."[18] One of the houses where prayer was made, was that of Mary, the mother of Mark the Evangelist; and as Saul and Barnabas were together, and as Barnabas was the cousin of Mark,[19] we cannot doubt that Saul and Barnabas, who would naturally join in the prayers of the church, were amongst the persons assembled in the house of Mary. "Peter," continues Luke, "was sleeping between two soldiers,[20] bound with two chains; and the keepers before the door kept the prison. And, behold, the angel of the Lord came upon him, and a light shined in the prison; and he smote Peter on the side, and raised him up, saying, 'Arise up quickly;' and his chains fell off from his hands. And the angel said unto him, 'Gird thyself, and bind on thy sandals;' and so he did. And he saith unto him, 'Cast thy garment about thee, and follow me.' And he went out, and followed him; and wist not that it was true which was done by the angel, but thought he saw a vision. When they were past the first and the second ward, they came unto the iron gate that leadeth unto the city, which opened to them of its own accord: and they went out and passed on through one street; and forthwith the angel departed from him. And when Peter was come to himself, he said, 'Now I know of a surety that the Lord hath sent his angel, and hath delivered me out of the hand of Herod, and from all the expectation of the people of the Jews.' And when he had considered the thing, he came to the house of Mary, the mother of John, whose surname was Mark; where many were gathered together praying. And as Peter knocked at the door of the gate, a damsel came to hearken, named Rhoda.[21] And when she knew Peter's voice, she opened not the gate for gladness, but ran in, and

---

quam tribus horis nocturnis necesse sit vigilare. Veget, R. M. iii. 8. Diem quadripartito, sed et noctem similiter, dividebant, idque consuetudo testatur militaris, ubi dicitur vigilia prima, item secunda et tertia et quarta. Censorinus, de Die Nat. c. 23. And four soldiers were assigned to each watch, τὸ δὲ φυλάκειόν ἐστι ἐκ τεττάρων ἀνδρῶν. Polyb. vi. 31. Hence the watch itself was called a τετράδιον or quaternion. Philo in Flaccum, s. 13, p. 981. As Peter was delivered to four quaternions, he was kept by sixteen in all—viz. by four at a time, for each of the four watches of the day and night. Agrippa, though a Jew, was strongly imbued with Roman customs, and here adopts the Roman mode of custody. So Agrippa put James to death, not in the Jewish fashion by stoning, but in the Roman fashion, by the sword (μαχαίρᾳ), or decapitation. Acts xii. 2.

[16] Acts xii. 4.

[17] So the Jews said to Pilate, "It is not lawful for us to put any man to death," viz. during the feast. John xviii. 31; and see Matt. xxvi. 5. In the following passage, therefore, "durante feste" must be understood, when the feast itself was over, but before the dispersion of the people: Non interficiunt aliquem neque in synedrio cujuscumque urbis neque in synedrio Jafnensi, sed adducunt illum ad synedrium magnum Hierosolymitanum, eumque usque ad solennem aliquam festivitatem adservant, et tunc *durante festo* interficiunt. Sanhedrin, fol. 89, 1, cited Schoettgen's Horæ Hebr. vol. ii. p. 224.

[18] Acts xii. 5.

[19] Coloss. iv. 10 (where see note).

[20] Peter was chained by the wrist to two soldiers of the quaternion, while the other two kept guard at the door.

[21] Though Luke writes that Rhoda "hearkened" only, the monks do (or did) show at Jerusalem the very window through which Rhoda looked and saw Peter. Maundrell's Travels, p. 98, 6th ed.

told how Peter stood before the gate. And they said unto her, 'Thou art mad;' but she constantly affirmed that it was even so. Then said they, 'It is his angel.'[22] But Peter continued knocking; and when they had opened the door, and saw him, they were astonished. But he, beckoning unto them with the hand to hold their peace, declared unto them how the Lord had brought him out of the prison. And he said, 'Go, show these things unto James, and to the brethren.' And he departed, and went into another place."[23]

The reason why the disciples were directed to show these things to James was, that the James here referred to, the half-brother of our Lord,[24] was the head of the church at Jerusalem, or (as we should now designate him) the Bishop. The Antiochian collection, for the relief of the poor Hebrews, had been sent, by the hands of Saul and Barnabas, to the *presbyters* (or *priests*) of the church of Jerusalem;[25] and *deacons* had been appointed in the church long before,[26] so that we have, at this early period, the three orders in the church—viz. bishop, priests, and deacons. The constitution of the Christian community had already acquired the settled form which it has ever since retained.

The distribution of the Antiochian bounty, as an office that would necessarily be of some duration, was probably committed to the care of the Hebrew church; but the principles upon which the relief should be given, may have been settled in communication with Barnabas and Saul. It would seem that the famine was just commencing—or, indeed, had already commenced; for, shortly after the arrival of Barnabas and Saul, an embassy of the Tyrians and Sidonians came to Agrippa, "because their country was nourished by the king's country,"[27] which implies the prevalence of a scarcity. Josephus places the great famine in the time of Cuspius Fadus and Tiberius Alexander[28]—that is, during the period from A.D. 44, when Cuspius Fadus was appointed, to A.D. 48, when Tiberius Alexander, his successor, was superseded.[29] Luke, therefore, is perfectly correct in his statement that the famine "came to pass in the days of Claudius Cæsar" (Acts xi. 28), for the prefectures of both Cuspius Fadus and Alexander were during his reign (fig. 52).

The Jewish historian relates a circumstance so illustrative of the contribution sent from Antioch to Judæa, that we cannot forbear inserting it. Izates, King of the neighbouring country of Adiabene, and his mother Helena, the Queen Dowager (figs. 53 and 54), had lately become proselytes to the Jewish religion. Helena, after seeing her son firmly seated on the throne, fixed her residence at Jerusalem for the purposes

---

[22] The Jews believed that on a person's death, his guardian angel occasionally appeared in his likeness. The Jews therefore meant by a person's angel, what we should now call his ghost.
[23] Acts xii. 6 to 17.
[24] See Fasti Sacri, p. 181, No. 1198.
[25] Acts xi. 30.
[26] Acts xi. 5.
[27] Acts xii. 20.
[28] ἐπὶ τούτοις δὴ καὶ τὸν μέγαν λιμὸν κατὰ τὴν Ἰουδαίαν συνέβη γενέσθαι. Jos. Ant. xx. 5, 2.
[29] See Fasti Sacri, p. 281, No. 1679; p. 287, No. 1719.

of worship. "Now her coming," says Josephus, "was of infinite service to the people of Jerusalem: for a famine about that time oppressing the city, and many dying of want. Queen Helena sent some of her servants to Alexandria, with money to buy a great quantity of corn, and others of them to Cyprus to bring a cargo of dried figs; and as soon as they were come back, bringing the provisions, she distributed food to those

Fig. 34.—*A coin of Claudius relating to the famine. From Pembroke collection.*
Obv. TI. Claudius Cæsar Aug. with a bushel measure.—Rev. Same legend, with a pair of scales.

that were distressed, and so left a most excellent memorial behind her of this benefaction towards our whole nation; and her son Izates also, when he was informed of the famine, forwarded large sums of money to the principal men in Jerusalem." [30]

It was during the sojourn of Paul at Jerusalem, at this period, that the revelation was made to him which is referred to in the Second Epistle to the Corinthians. "I know a man in Christ" (he writes) "about fourteen years ago (whether in the body I cannot tell, or whether out of the body I cannot tell: God knoweth); such an one caught up to the third heaven. And I know such a man (whether in the body, or out of the body, I cannot tell: God knoweth), how that he was caught up into Paradise and heard unspeakable words, which it is not lawful for man to utter." [31] This was written by the Apostle in A.D. 57; [32] and as "fourteen years ago" means, in Greek phraseology, the fourteenth year current before the date of the Epistle, [33] the occurrence must be referred to A.D. 44.

Barnabas and Saul, having completed their ministry at the Jewish capital, bade farewell to the Hebrew church, and taking with them Mark, the son of Mary and cousin of Barnabas, returned to Antioch. [34]

At the conclusion of the Feast of the Passover, Agrippa also quitted Jerusalem and went down to Cæsarea, to celebrate certain games there in honour of Claudius, [35]

---

[30] Jos. Ant. xx. 2, 5; see Fasti Sacri, p. 272, No. 1629.

[31] 2 Cor. xii. 2–4.

[32] See Fasti Sacri, p. 310, No. 1811.

[33] The expression is πρὸ ἐτῶν δεκατεσσάρων, 2 Cor. xii. 2; and Josephus uses the similar expression, πρὸ τεσσάρων ἐτῶν τοῦ πολέμου (Bell. vi. 5, 3), in the same sense, for the fourth year current before the war. See Fasti Sacri, p. 328,

No. 1933; and see ante, p. 90, note [b].

[34] Acts xii. 25, 12.

[35] εἰς τὴν Καίσαρος τιμὴν ὑπὲρ τῆς ἐκείνου σωτηρίας, Jos. Ant. xix. 8, 2. Wieseler (Chronol. Apostol. 132) argues that these games could not be for the safe return of Claudius from Britain, as he prohibited all games for his safety, and cites the passage from Dion: τοῖς τε στρατηγοῖς τοὺς ἀγῶνας τοὺς ὁπλομαχικοὺς ἀπηγόρευσε,

Fig. 33.—*The Mausoleum of Queen Helena, commonly called the Tombs of the Kings. From Cassas.*

This engraving represents the vestibule only of the tombs, the entrance into the tombs themselves being within the vestibule, on the left hand.

Fig. 34.—*The Entrance into the Tombs of Queen Helena. From the Author's Siege of Jerusalem by Titus.*

This engraving represents the entrance into the tombs themselves, on the left side of the vestibule, as you enter it. As the mausoleum must have been constructed a few years only after the crucifixion, it affords a most remarkable illustration of the sepulchre of our Lord. The entrance to the Tombs of Helena is square, or rather quadrangular, and is closed by a circular stone, like a millstone, not placed horizontally, but on end or upright, and rolling backwards and forwards in a groove. When rolled backwards, or to the left, the entrance to the sepulchre is laid open, and which rolled forwards, or to the right, it is closed. So Joseph of Arimathea, who was "a rich man," laid the body of our Lord "in his own new tomb, which he had hewn out in the rock, and *rolled a great stone to the door of the sepulchre.*" (Matt. xxvii. 55; Mark xv. 46); and the women "said among themselves, who shall roll us away the stone from the door of the sepulchre? And when they looked, they saw that the stone was rolled away, for it was very great." Mark xvi. 3; Luke xxiv. 2.

This festival possesses so much interest, from its connection with our own country, that we may be excused for stating the occasion of it. In A.D. 42,[36] for the first time since Julius Cæsar, the Romans, under Aulus Plautius, invaded Britain. It creates a smile to read that the legions were with difficulty prevailed upon to cross the ocean, as Britain lay beyond the limits of the habitable world. By the summer of A.D. 43, Plautius had defeated Caractacus, and slain Togodumnus, the two sons of Cunobelin, the late King of the Trinobantes, the most powerful people of the island; and Camulodunum, or Colchester, their capital, lay at his mercy. The intelligence was conveyed

Fig. 65.—*A coin of Claudius, in commemoration of the Conquest of Britain. From the British Museum.* Obv. Head of Claudius with the legend Ti. Claudius Cæsar Aug. P. M. Tr. P. Imp.—Rev. A triumphal arch with the legend De Britannis (over the Britons).

to Claudius, and, eager to wear the laurels which his general had won, he sailed from Ostia to Marseilles, traversed Gaul to Boulogne, crossed into Britain, and joined the army of Plautius on the banks of the Thames.[37] The Emperor ostensibly assumed the command, drove the enemy before him, and took Colchester. He was only sixteen days in Britain, when he returned to Italy to celebrate his triumph. He reached Rome the beginning of A.D. 44,[38] and nothing proves more clearly how formidable were our ancestors, than the rejoicings at Rome, and throughout the Empire, on the result of the campaign. To have visited so remote and barbarous a country was an enterprise in itself; but to have won a victory there, and sacked the capital, was a feat of arms almost unparalleled. Claudius was repeatedly saluted 'Imperator;' he was called 'Britannicus;' the same name was conferred on his son; the Palace was sur-

καὶ εἰ δή τις ἄλλος αὐτοὺς ὁπουδήποτε ἐπιτελοίη, ἀλλὰ μή τί γε ὡς καὶ ὑπὲρ ἑαυτοῦ σωτηρίας γεγονμένων σφῶν ἢ γράφεσθαι ἢ καὶ λέγεσθαι ἐκέλευσε. Dion, lx. 5. But this edict was directed against the abuse, practised in the provinces, of *exacting* contributions from the population, under *pretence* of doing honour to the Emperor; and it will be observed that the passage cited does not prohibit the celebration of games for the Emperor's safety, but only the celebration of them under the pretext (μή τί γε ὡς) of their being out of respect to the Emperor. Wieseler thinks that the games in question were those founded by Herod the Great, on his completion of the city of Cæsarea, and which were quinquennial, or, more precisely, at intervals of four years complete. See Fasti Sacri, p. 103, No. 805. But, as Cæsarea was dedicated in B.C. 10, it is evident that these games would not fall in the year A.D. 44, which was certainly the year of Agrippa's death. Besides, they could not without violence to the language be said to be celebrated ὑπὲρ τῆς ἐκείνου σωτηρίας. Others think that Agrippa was celebrating the birthday of Claudius on the 1st of August. But this would be too long after the Passover; and not only so, but the celebration of the Emperor's birthday was expressly forbidden by Claudius, Dion, lx. 5; and had Josephus meant this, he would have used the word γενέθλια, and not the expression, ὑπὲρ τῆς ἐκείνου σωτηρίας.

[36] Fasti Sacri, p. 274, No. 1641.
[37] Fasti Sacri, p. 277, No. 1659.
[38] Fasti Sacri, p. 279, No. 1667.

mounted by a naval crown; an arch was erected at Rome on the spot whence he had commenced his journey; and another at Boulogne, from which he had sailed (fig. 55). A triumphal procession was conducted with the utmost splendour, and his wife, Messalina, accompanied the pageant in a gorgeous *carpentum*, or state-carriage, especially decreed to her on the occasion. To commemorate the event, an annual festival was instituted at Rome, and, in the present year, chariot-races, beast-fights, athletic exercises, and war-dances were exhibited, and (which was unusual) in two theatres at once.[39] The fulsome adulation of the provinces was not wanting, and the glorious return of the Emperor was celebrated with little less magnificence in the theatre at Cæsarea. Agrippa, who had received such benefits from the Emperor, was not likely to lose an opportunity of testifying his joy at his patron's successes, and he repaired to Cæsarea, to increase the splendour of the scene by his royal presence. The appalling manner in which he was there smitten by the hand of death, has been recorded both by St. Luke and by Josephus.

It is a remarkable feature in the New Testament, that, stirring as the times then were, and violently as the whole Jewish nation was agitated, the sacred historians, having no concern with temporal matters, scarcely make any, even the least accidental, mention of passing events. The death, however, of Agrippa furnished such an instructive lesson that it has been made an exception. "He went down" (says Luke) "to Cæsarea, and there abode. And Herod was highly displeased with them of Tyre and Sidon:[40] but they came with one accord to him, and, having made Blastus, the king's chamberlain, their friend, desired peace, because their country was nourished by the king's country. And upon *a set day* Herod, arrayed in royal apparel, sat upon his throne, and made an oration unto them. And *the people gave a shout*, saying. 'It is the voice of a god, and not of a man.' And immediately the angel of the Lord smote him, because he gave not God the glory; and he was eaten of worms, and gave up the ghost."[41] It will be observed that in this brief narrative the writer of the Acts does not expressly mention any games, though the "set day" and the assembled people indicate the occasion of some festival.

We shall now give the relation of the learned and courtly Josephus, and the simple narrative of Luke will not lose by the comparison:—"When Agrippa had reigned three years over *all Judæa*,[42] he came to the city of Cæsarea, which was formerly called Strato's Tower, and there exhibited shows in honour of Cæsar, knowing it to be a festival for his safety; and a great multitude of the principal persons, and

---

[39] Dion, lx. 19 to 23; Suet. Claud. 17.

[40] It has been disputed whether Herod was or not at open war with them. But the negative may be safely assumed, as any declaration of war would be high treason against Rome. The apprehension of the Tyrians and Sidonians was that Herod would stop the usual exportations from Judæa to Tyre and Sidon. See Meyer, Apostg. p. 227. These exportations produced a considerable revenue. Jos. Ant. xiv. 6.

[41] Acts xii. 20 to 23.

[42] Agrippa received the addition of Judæa to his dominions in A.D. 41, soon after the accession of Claudius. See Fasti Sacri, p. 271, No. 1619.

such as were of dignity through the province, were assembled at it. And on the second day of the shows he put on a robe made wholly of silver, and of a contexture truly wonderful, and came into the theatre early in the morning, at which time the silver, being illuminated by the early rays of the sun, shone out after a surprising manner, and was so resplendent as to inspire an awe into all that gazed upon him; and presently his flatterers cried out, from one place and another (though not for his good), that he was a god, saying, 'Be thou propitious to us, for although we have hitherto reverenced thee only as a man, yet henceforth we hail thee as more than mortal!' The King neither rebuked them, nor rejected their impious flattery. But as he presently afterwards looked up, he saw an owl sitting on a rope over his head, and immediately understood that this bird was the messenger of ill tidings, as it had once been the harbinger of good tidings,[43] and fell into the deepest sorrow. A severe pain also arose in his bowels, beginning in a most violent manner. He therefore looked upon his friends, and said: 'I, whom you call a god, am commanded forthwith to depart this life, Providence thus rebuking the lying words you have uttered, and I, who was by you called immortal, am now led away to death. But I must submit to my fate as it pleases God, for we have had our day, and have lived in no little splendour.' As he said this, he was excruciated by the intensity of the pain. So he was carried hastily into the palace, and the rumour went abroad everywhere that he must certainly die in a little time. But the multitude presently sat in sackcloth with their wives and children, after the manner of their country, beseeching God for the King's recovery, and all was full of mourning and lamentation. And the King, being laid in a high chamber, and looking down on the people prostrate on the ground, could not himself forbear weeping. And having continued in agony for five days, from the pain in his bowels, he departed this life."[44]

---

[43] Allusion is here made to the appearance of an owl to Agrippa when he was imprisoned at Rome. Jos. Ant. xviii. 6, 7.
[44] Jos. Ant. xix. 8, 2.

CHAPTER VIII.

Paul makes his First Circuit in company with Barnabas and Mark—He visits Cyprus, Pamphylia, Pisidia, and Lycaonia.

> The healing fount that in Ezekiel's dream [1]
> Forth issued from the Temple's sacred sill—
> Behold it now no more a slender rill,
> But far and wide an overflowing stream,
> That doth each heathen land with hope and gladness fill.
>
> Anon.

WE now (A.D. 45) approach an eventful period in the life of Saul—the special mission of the Apostle to the idolatrous Gentiles. He had already preached to the Jews at Damascus, and Jerusalem, and Tarsus, and to the Greeks at Antioch. He was next to enlarge the sphere of his labours by making the circuit of the neighbouring countries.

Antioch was at this time the metropolis of the Gentile churches, and there were assembled there some of the most eminent teachers [2] of the Christian society. Such were Barnabas, whose other name was Joses, or Joseph (for it is the same word), and called Barnabas, or the Son of Exhortation, or Consolation, from his powers of preaching, or from the benevolence of his character; [3] Lucius of Cyrene (thought by many to be Luke the Evangelist [4]); Manaen, or Manahem, who had been a foster-

---

[1] Ezekiel xlvii. 1.

[2] Saul and Barnabas at this time are referred to as "prophets (or preachers) and teachers," προφῆται καὶ διδάσκαλοι. Acts xiii. 1. But from this time, viz. after the ordination of them by the Antiochian church, they are called by Luke Apostles. Acts xiv. 4, 14.

[3] The words υἱὸς παρακλήσεως will bear either sense. He had a power of preaching, as evidenced by his successful circuits, though he was not to be compared with Paul, who was the chief speaker, Acts xiv. 12; and his charitable disposition was shown by the surrender of his patrimony in Cyprus to the church. Acts iv. 36.

[4] That Luke was the same person as Lucius is a notion as old as Origen, who observes: "Some say Lucius is Luke the Evangelist, who wrote the Gospel, forasmuch as names are wont to be pronounced, sometimes according to the native form, and sometimes according to the Greek or Roman termination." Sed et Lucium quidam ipsum perhibent esse Lucam qui Evangelium scripsit, pro eo quod solent nomina interdum secundum patriam declinationem, interdum Græcam Romanamque proferri. Comm. in Rom. lib. x. s. 39 (which remains only in a Latin version). In favour of this view, it may be suggested that *Lucius* was one of Paul's colleagues at Antioch; and if so, we should naturally find him in Paul's company elsewhere: and accordingly we meet with Lucius, if he was Luke, as Paul's coadjutor at Philippi, and the very language in which Luke speaks of himself, rather implies that they had been fellow-labourers in Christ's vineyard long before: "*We* sat down (at Philippi), and spake unto the women." Acts xvi. 13. Again, Luke was with Paul at Corinth when he wrote the Epistle to the Romans; and we can scarcely suppose, that amongst the numerous salutations sent by Paul in that Epistle, the name of Luke

VOL. I.

brother of Herod Antipas;[5] Symeon, surnamed Niger;[6] and Saul.[7] In the year A.D. 45,[8] as these men were discharging the duties of their sacred office, and observing a

would not appear; but this would be the case, unless the Lucius of Rom. xvi. 21 be identical with Luke. It may be added that Luke was a physician, and that Lucius was a Cyrenian (Acts xiii. 1), and we know that Cyrene was a country famous for the medical skill of its inhabitants. πρῶτοι μὲν Κροτωνιῆται ἰητροὶ ἐλέγοντο ἀνὰ τὴν Ἑλλάδα εἶναι, δεύτεροι δὲ Κυρηναῖοι. Herod. iii. 131. However, there are arguments at least equally strong on the other side. Thus, 1. Λουκᾶς is the contraction of Λουκᾶνος, or Lucanus (a common name, as instanced in Lucan the poet), but cannot by any analogy be the abbreviation of Lucius.—2. If Lucius was Luke, the writer of the Acts, he would either, in the catalogue of the worthies of Antioch, have omitted his own name altogether, or have placed it modestly the last, and not have written "Barnabas, and Simeon that was called Niger, and *Lucius of Cyrene*, and Manaen, which had been brought up with Herod the Tetrarch, and Saul." Acts xiii. 1.—3. Luke, according to the Fathers, was a *native* of Antioch, whereas Lucius was a *native* of Cyrene; but the residence of Luke may have been mistaken by the Fathers for the place of his nativity.—4. Luke was a *Gentile*, for in writing to the Colossians, Paul sends a salutation from Aristarchus, and Mark, and Jesus surnamed Justus, "who are of the Circumcision," Colos. iv. 11; and then subjoins a salutation from Epaphras and Luke, who are thus distinguished from the brethren of the Circumcision. Colos, iv. 12-14. But Lucius appears to have been a *Jew*; for of the five prophets and teachers of Antioch enumerated in the Acts, Barnabas, Simeon, Manaen, and Saul were certainly Jews, and therefore, probably, Lucius also, who came from Cyrene, where the Jews abounded. Lucius being of Cyrene, was no doubt one of the Cyrenians who, *before the conversion of Cornelius*, were dispersed from Jerusalem and came to Antioch, and must therefore have been Jews; and if so, Lucius must have been a Jew. Again, "Timotheus my workfellow, and Lucius, and Jason, and Sosipater, my *kinsmen*, salute you," Rom. xvi. 21; and by his kinsmen the Apostle means Israelites like himself. Lucius, therefore, is here classed with those who were Israelites.

[5] Μαναὴν Ἡρώδου τοῦ Τετράρχου σύντροφος. Acts xiii. 1. The name in Hebrew is מְנַחֵם, translated by the Septuagint Μαναὴμ (2 Kings xv. 14, 16), and by Josephus Μανάημος (Ant. xv. 10, 5). But as the Greeks never ended a word properly with the letter μ, Luke, euphoniæ gratiâ, writes, by a slight change of sound, Μαναὴν. See Kuinoel on Acts xiii. 1.

This Manahem was no doubt of the family of old Manahem the Essene, who, when Herod was a lad, patted him on the back and said, "Mark, boy! you will live to be a king." When Herod was really exalted to that rank, he remembered the prophecy, and held Manahem, and for his sake the Essenes generally, in the highest honour; no wonder, then, that we find one of the stock of Manahem brought up with a member of the Herodian family. Jos. Ant. xv. 10, 5.

It has been questioned, but without much reason, which of the Herods was the foster-brother of the Manahem of Luke. Some think that it was Agrippa I., King of Judæa, who died A.D. 44. See Fasti Sacri, p. 280, No. 1678. But this Agrippa was *King*, and is so called by Luke himself (Ἡρώδης ὁ βασιλεύς, Acts xii. 1), and therefore could not be identical with the Herod described emphatically by Luke as the *Tetrarch*. Others suggest that it was Agrippa II., the son of Agrippa I.; but this could not be, for Agrippa II., at the death of his father, was only seventeen years old (Jos. Ant. xix. 9, 1), and in A.D. 45 (when Luke refers to Manahem as one of the heads of the church of Antioch) would be only eighteen; and Manahem, if he was the foster-brother of Agrippa II., would be of about the same age, i.e. about eighteen only, when he was a distinguished preacher, which would be absurd. Besides, Agrippa II. was never Tetrarch, but in A.D. 49 was made *King* of Chalcis (Ant. xx. 75, 2; Bell. ii. 12, 1), and in A.D. 53, *King* of Philip's

[6] To distinguish him from Simon Peter and Simon the Canaanite.

[7] These five, according to Meyer (Apostg. p. 234), constituted not a portion but the whole of the staff at Antioch devoted to teaching. But probably these five are singled out from the rest, as taking an active part in the event that follows —viz. the ordination for the mission of the two at the hands of the other three.

[8] See Fasti Sacri, p. 284, No. 1695.

fast, the Holy Spirit said, by the mouth of some prophet, "Separate me Barnabas and Saul for the work whereunto I have called them." Accordingly a day of solemn observance was appointed, and after fasting and prayer, Barnabas and Saul were ordained for the purpose; not that Barnabas and Saul were now for the first time called to the *ministry*, for they had been already engaged in it many years; but they were now directed to resign the church of Antioch to the care of others, and go forth themselves as ambassadors to the Gentiles. It is said that "when they had laid their hands on them, they sent them away," and we may reasonably suppose that the rite of ordination was administered by Symeon, Lucius, and Manaen; for it has ever been the practice of the Christian church, in conformity with an ancient custom amongst the Jews, to ordain to the episcopate by the hands of three other bishops.

Our Saviour had sent forth the Apostles two and two[a] for the conversion of the

---

tetrarchy (Ant. xx. 7, 1; Bell. ii. 12, 8), and accordingly, Luke designates him as king. Ἀγρίππας ὁ βασιλεύς, Acts xxv. 13; xxvi. 26, 27, 30. Others suppose the Herod in question to be Herod of Chalcis, the brother of Agrippa I.; but he also was never Tetrarch, but was *King* of Chalcis. Jos. Ant. xix. 5, 1; Bell. ii. 11, 5.

The Herod meant by Luke, and called by him *Herod the Tetrarch*, is unquestionably Herod Antipas, son of Herod the Great and Tetrarch of Galilee. Luke, in another place, expressly designates him as "Herod the Tetrarch," Ἡρώδης ὁ Τετράρχης (Luke ix. 7), and we cannot doubt that the same person is intended by Luke under this title in both references. It has been objected, indeed, that Archelaus and Antipas, the two sons of Herod by Malthace, were educated together at Rome: Ἀρχέλαος δὴ καὶ Ἀντίπας ἐπὶ Ῥώμης παρά τινι ἰδιώτῃ τροφὰς εἶχον (Jos. Ant. xvii. 1, 3), and that had Manahem been educated with them, Luke would have distinguished him as the foster-brother of Archelaus and Antipas, or of Archelaus only, as the elder brother, and not of Antipas only. But to this it may be answered, that in A.D. 45, when the mention of Manahem occurs, Archelaus had been ejected from Judæa for about forty years, viz. in A.D. 6 (Jos. Ant. xvii. 13, 2; Jos. Bell. ii. 7, 3), and perhaps was no longer living, so that his very name was almost forgotten; while Herod Antipas, on the contrary, was Tetrarch during the whole period of our Lord's ministry, and was deposed only in A.D. 40 (see Fasti Sacri, p. 265, No. 1592)—so that in A.D. 45 his reign was still fresh in every one's recollection.

Assuming that Manahem was the foster-brother of Herod Antipas, it may be asked, was this Manahem the *son* or *grandson* of Manahem the Essene? Archelaus and Antipas were recalled by Herod from Rome, where they had been educated, in B.C. 5, and Archelaus, the elder brother, is spoken of at that time as μειράκιον (Jos. Bell. i. 31, 1); and, according to Philo, μειράκιον was from twenty-one to twenty-eight (see ante, p. 5, note [a]). Archelaus then was, in B.C. 5, somewhere between those two extremes, say twenty-five; and as Antipas was a year or two younger, he may have been about twenty-three, and if so, was born about B.C. 28. Now, Manahem the Essene was a person of high reputation, and regarded as a prophet when Herod was a boy (Jos. Ant. xv. 10, 5)—that is, Manahem was at least forty, when Herod was about ten years old, but Herod was sixty-nine in B.C. 4, σχεδὸν ἐτῶν ἑβδομήκοντα (Jos. Bell. i. 33, 1), and therefore Herod was ten years old in B.C. 65. If Manahem, then, was forty when Herod was ten years old, he was forty in B.C. 65, and in B.C. 28, when the Manahem of Luke was born, he was seventy-seven; and we can hardly suppose that Manahem the Essene, when at the age of seventy-seven, had a son born to him. The Manahem of Luke must therefore have been, not the son, but the grandson, of Manahem the Essene.

[a] Mark vi. 7. So Peter and John were sent by the church of Jerusalem to Samaria. Acts viii. 14. So, when Paul and Barnabas separated, Paul and Silas went together, and Barnabas and Mark went together. So Titus and Trophimus were afterwards sent by Paul to the church of Corinth, &c.

Jews, and now Saul and Barnabas received the first joint commission for the conversion of both Jews and Gentiles.

Cilicia, the native country of Saul, had long since heard the tidings of the Gospel, from the mouth of Saul himself, while residing at Tarsus. The Apostles therefore determined on commencing their labours in another quarter, viz. in Cyprus, the birthplace of Barnabas. Thitherward they directed their course, and took, no doubt, the ordinary route (fig. 56), crossing the Orontes to the north by the bridge at Antioch,

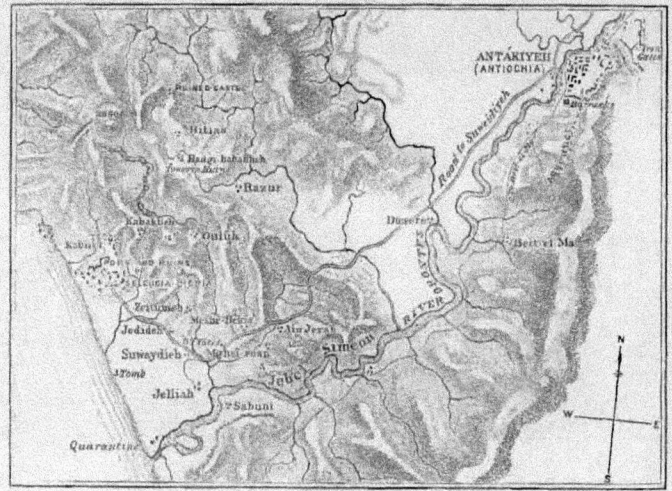

Fig. 56.—*Road from Antioch to Seleucia. From Admiralty Chart.*

and then passing down the right bank of the river till they neared the sea, and then diverging a few miles to the right to the town of Seleucia.

Fig. 57.—*Coin of Seleucia. From the British Museum.*
Obv. Female head turreted.—*Rev.* Σελευκεων της Ιερας και Αυτονομου (of Seleucia the sacred and independent).

This seaport lay at the distance of about sixteen miles by land from Antioch, and five miles to the north of the mouth of the Orontes. It was built on the slope of Mount

CHAP. VIII.]   ST. PAUL'S FIRST CIRCUIT.   [A.D. 45]   117

Coryphæus, the precipitous heights of which, overhanging the town on the east, were excavated into sepulchres, which still remain. The most remarkable feature of the place was, and still is, a deep channel, running generally from east to west

Fig. 58.—Section of hill on the north of Seleucia. From Allen's Dead Sea.

a, the eastern or upper tunnel; b, the first or most eastern open cutting; c, the western or lower tunnel; d, the western or lower open cutting; e, the stairs down to the cutting; f, the bridge across the cutting; g, the position of the spectator in the annexed view (fig. 59).

Fig. 59.—View of tunnel and cutting (the great culvert) at Seleucia. From W. H. Bartlett's Pictures of our Lord and his Apostles.
The spectator is supposed to be standing at the point g in fig. 58, and is looking down the culvert westwards.

along the north of the town (fig. 58). At the eastern end, on the highest ground, is a reservoir or basin, formed by a dam or wall thrown across a valley, for collecting a head of water. Then follows a square tunnel, the principal one, 290 feet long, 22 feet wide, and 24 feet high (fig. 59); then a hollow way, 204 feet long, and 22 feet wide, with a narrow staircase on the south side, which terminates at 14 feet from the bottom; then a second tunnel, 102 feet long; then another hollow way, 1065 feet long. Here the hollow way sweeps round to the south for 910 feet, when it terminates abruptly 30 feet above the level of the sea, and is at the end 30 feet high, and 17 feet wide. This extraordinary excavation, when the city was flourishing, served to collect and pour down the mountain-torrents into the inner port, in order to scour the port itself, and the lock by which it communicated with the sea.[10] The general features of the port may still be traced (fig. 60). The outer basin was formed by two moles projecting westward

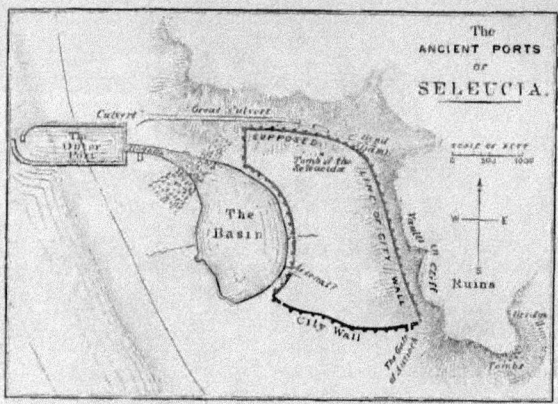

Fig. 60.—*This sketch is grounded partly on Pococke and partly on the outline in Allen's Dead Sea.*

into the sea, and about 240 paces apart, but so that the southern arm overlapped the northern, and the narrow entrance for vessels lay between them. It was from one of these piers that Paul must have embarked for Cyprus. The area of the outer basin was about four acres. From the outer basin a lock, 200 yards long by 50 yards wide, conducted into the inner basin, which was retort-shaped, and covered an area of about

---

[10] The account of Polybius is as follows:—
ὄρος ὑπόκειται παμμέγεθες, ὃ καλοῦσι Κορυφαῖον. . . . ἐν τοῖς πρὸς μεσημβρίαν αὐτοῦ κλίμασι τὴν Σελεύκειαν συμβαίνει κεῖσθαι, διεζευγμένην φάραγγι κοίλῃ καὶ δυσβάτῳ, καθήκουσαν μὲν καὶ περικλωμένην ὡς ἐπὶ θαλάσσῃ, κατὰ δὲ τὰ πλεῖστα μέρη κρημνοῖς καὶ πέτραις ἀπορρῶξι περιεχομένην· ὑπὸ δὲ τὴν ἐπὶ θαλάσσῃ αὐτῆς νεύουσαν πλευρὰν ἐν τοῖς ἐπιπέδοις τά τ' ἐμπόρια καὶ τὸ προάστειον κεῖται, διαφερόντως τετειχισμένον. παραπλησίως δὲ καὶ τὸ σύμπαν τῆς πόλεως κύτον τείχεσι πολυτελέσιν ἠσφάλιστοι, κεκόσμηται δὲ καὶ ναοῖς καὶ τοῖς τῶν οἰκοδομημάτων κατασκευαῖς ἐκπρεπῶς. πρόσβασιν δὲ μίαν ἔχει κατὰ τὴν ὑπὸ θαλάσσης πλευρὰν κλιμακωτὴν καὶ χειροποίητον κλίμαξι καὶ σκαλώμασι πυκνοῖς καὶ συνεχέσι διειλημμένην. Polyb. v. 59.

forty-seven acres, and therefore was as large as the export and import basins of our East and West India Docks put together.[11] The port is now choked with sand and mud, but it is said that the masonry is still in such perfect preservation, that the soil could be removed, and the works restored, so as to make the harbour again available for shipping, at a very moderate cost.[12] Seleucia was a free city—that is, was exempt from the Roman imposts, and was governed by its own municipal laws.[13] It was surrounded by a strong wall, which, however, included neither the port on the west nor the culvert on the north.

Colonel Chesney gives the following description of Seleucia:—

"The masonry of the once magnificent port of Seleucia is in so good a state, that it merely requires trifling repairs in some places, and to be cleared out, which might be done for about £31,000, and partially for £10,000. On the south side of the entrance there is a very substantial jetty, formed of large blocks of stone secured by iron cramps. It runs north-west for seventy yards to the sea, and it may still be traced, curving more to the north under water, and overlapping the northern jetty, which is in a more ruinous state, but appears to have taken the direction of west by south-west, forming a kind of basin, with a narrow entrance tolerably well protected, and altogether suited for the Roman galleys. The ancient floodgates are about fifty yards east of the south pier. The passage for the galleys is cut through the solid rock, on which are the remains of a defensive tower on each side. Apartments below, with the remains of staircases to the top of each, are sufficiently distinct, as well as the places where the gates had been suspended between the towers.

"Immediately on passing the gateway, the passage widens to about 100 yards; it takes the direction of south-east by east, between two solid walls of masonry, for 350 yards, to the entrance of the great basin, which is now closed by a garden-wall. The port, or basin, is an irregular oval, of about 450 yards in length by 350 in width at the southern extremity, and rather more than 200 at the northern. The surrounding wall is formed of large cut stones solidly put together, and now rising only about seven feet above the mud, which, during the lapse of ages, has gradually accumulated so as to cover, probably, about eight feet above the original level. The exterior of the basin is about one-third of a mile from the sea; the interior is close to the foot of the hill.

"On the south-east side of the walls is the Gate of Antioch, adorned with pilasters, and defended by towers. This entrance must have been very handsome. Near it, and parallel to the walls, are the remains of a double row of columns. The space

---

[11] Allen's Dead Sea, vol. ii. p. 212.
[12] It may be questioned whether the port existed, in the time of the Apostles, exactly as described above; as various improvements were made from time to time, particularly in the reign of Constantine. See Müller's Antiquities of Antioch, p. 12, note 8.
[13] Plin. N. H. v. 18.

within the walls of the town and suburbs, which have a circumference altogether of about four miles, is filled with the ruins of houses."[14]

The island of Cyprus, for which Barnabas and Saul were bound, lies about 100 miles to the south-west of Seleucia. It is sixty miles in breadth from north to south, and about 150 in length from east to west.[15] In the Apostolic age the inhabitants in general were Greeks, but vast numbers of Jews were interspersed,[16] which is the less surprising, when we consider that Herod the Great had for many years enjoyed the monopoly of the copper-mines there—keeping half the proceeds for his own use and paying a royalty of the other half to Augustus.[17] The large Jewish population to be found there may have been one reason why the envoys of Christ, who were charged to offer the tidings of salvation first "to the lost sheep of the House of Israel," were induced to select Cyprus for opening their commission. The two principal cities were Salamis at the eastern, and Paphos at the western end,[18] but there were also fifteen other towns of considerable note.[19]

Salamis stood at the mouth, on the north side, of the River Pedæus, still called the Pedæa (fig. 61). The port was apparently formed by art, and had a narrow entrance,[20] and is now nearly filled up. The site of Salamis (fig. 62) can at present be traced only by broken cisterns, fragments of columns, and the foundations of ancient buildings. About four miles to the south of the river arose by degrees the city of Famagusta, the capital of the island under the sway of the Venetians. The growth of the new town, in close proximity to Salamis, drained away the lifeblood from the mother-city, till the latter became a desolation. The remains of Salamis are now called Eski Famagusta, or Old Famagusta.[21]

Paphos, at the other end of the island, still retains its ancient name, with a slight variation, being called Baffa (fig. 63). It stood on the banks of a running stream,[22] and was about seven miles and a half[23] to the north-west of Old Paphos. It had a convenient port, protected by piers built out into the sea; but which now, from the neglect of ages, has become shallow and unsafe. The great goddess of the island was Venus, hence called Cypria; and of all the luxurious bowers devoted to her worship, Paphos was the chief. Here stood the most famous of her temples, and the priesthood attached to it was one of the richest appointments at the disposal of the Roman

---

[14] Geographical Society, vol. viii. p. 230; and see Chesney's Expedition to the Euphrates, and Allen's Dead Sea.

[15] For the ancient estimates, see Plin. N. H. v. 35.

[16] Philo, Leg. ad Caium, p. 36.

[17] Jos. Ant. xvi. 4, 5.

[18] Mela.

[19] Oppida in eâ, xv. Plin. N. H. v. 35.

[20] ἔγκυρτος τοῦ λιμένος στενὸν τὸν ἔκπλουν. Diod. Sic. xx. 50.

[21] Pococke, vol. ii. p. 214.

[22] See Eurip. Bacch. 400 :

ἱκοίμαν ποτὶ Κύπρον,
νᾶσον τᾶς Ἀφροδίτας,
ἐν ᾇ θελξίφρονες νέμονται θνατοῖσιν Ἔρωτες,
Πάφον θ' ἃν ἑκατόστομοι
βαρβάρου ποταμοῦ ῥοαὶ
καρπίζουσιν ἀνόμβροι.

[23] διέχει δὲ πεζῇ σταδίους ἑξήκοντα τῆς Παλαιπάφου. Strabo, xiv. 6 (p. 244, Tauchnitz).

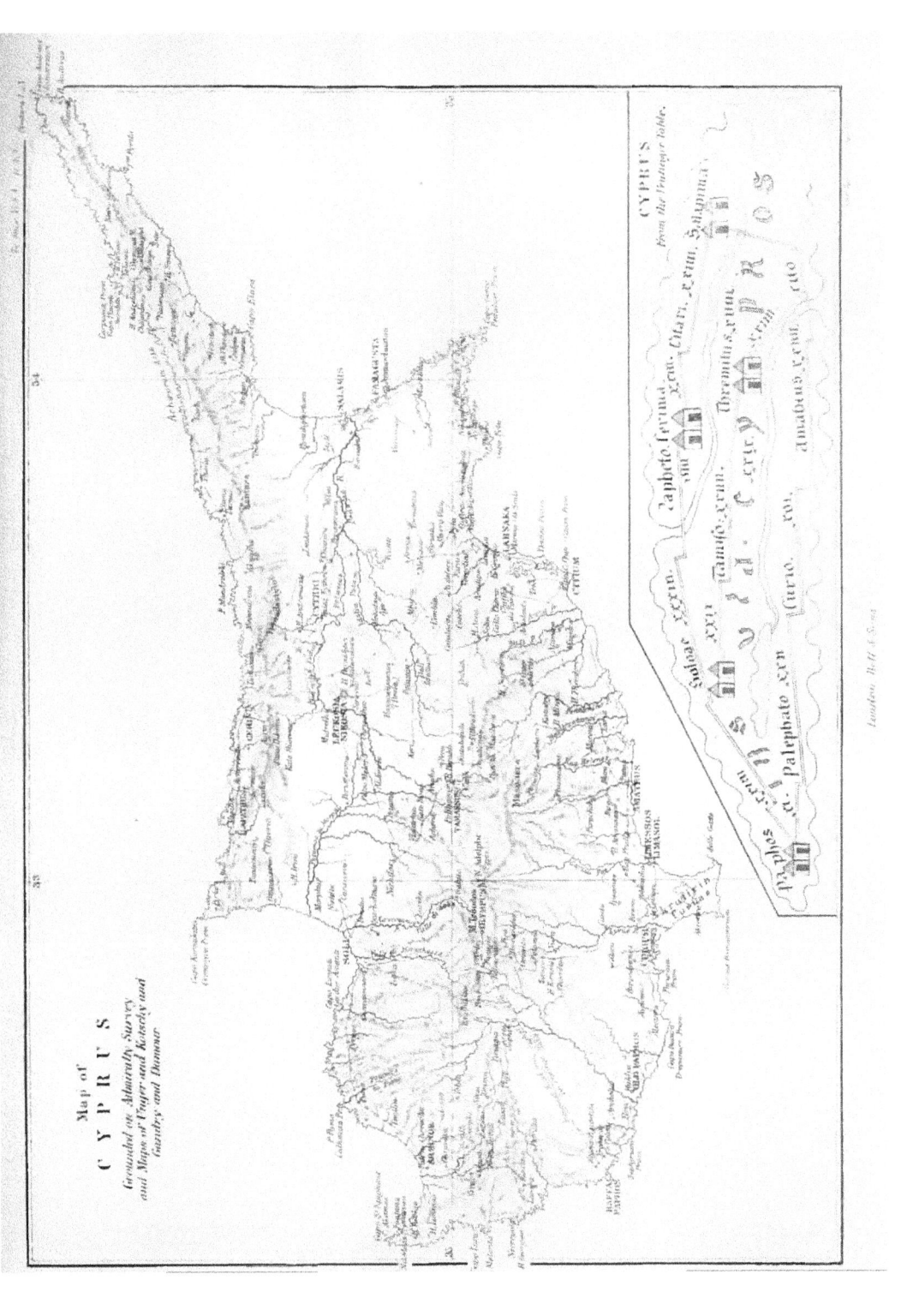

Emperors.[24] The country around teemed with abundant vegetation, and the air itself was soft and balmy; and the goddess, perhaps, owed her birth, not, according to the

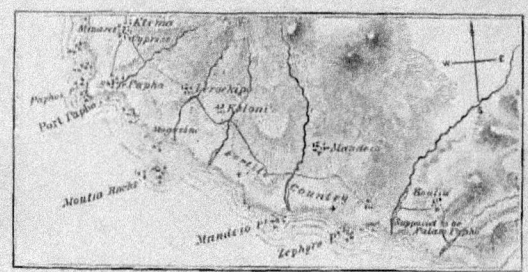

Fig. 63.—Coast between Paphos (now Baffa) and Old Paphos (Palaio Papho). From Admiralty Chart.

fable, to the cool waters of the sea, but rather to the warmth of the climate that glowed upon land. What poet has not sung of the Paphian Venus?—

> ἡ δ' ἄρα Κύπρον ἵκανε φιλομμειδὴς Ἀφροδίτη
> ἐς Πάφον, ἔνθα δέ οἱ τέμενος βωμός τε θυήεις.
> Odyss. θ. 362.

> Ipsa Paphum sublimis abit, sedesque revisit
> Læta suas, ubi templum illi, centumque Sabæo
> Ture calent aræ, sertisque recentibus halant.
> Æneid, i. 419.

> The goddess spake, and vanished to the skies,
> Well pleased again to seek her Paphian bowers;
> Where temples and a hundred altars rise,
> Teeming with incense, crowned with fairest flowers.

The reader must not picture to himself an exquisitely-finished statue of the goddess, like the Venus de' Medici, commanding the admiration of all that gaze upon its transcendent beauty. Not so. The worship of the Paphian Venus was derived by the Cypriots from the Phœnicians, and by them from the Assyrians,[25] and was stamped with the character of the remotest antiquity. The only visible object of adoration was a white block of uncertain material, and resembling in shape a cone, with the upper part truncated (fig. 64).[26] The altars also did not, as with the other gods, reek with the blood of victims; but the flame of the sacred fire never ceased, and the fumes of frankincense pervaded the air.[27] Once in every year the population, of both sexes,

---

[24] Plut. Cato Min. 35.
[25] Pausan. Attica, i. 14, 6.
[26] Παφίοις ἡ μὲν Ἀφροδίτη τὰς τιμὰς ἔχει, τὸ δὲ ἄγαλμα οὐκ ἂν εἰκάσαις ἄλλῳ τῳ ἢ πυραμίδι λευκῇ, ἡ δὲ ὕλη ἀγνοεῖται. Maxim. Tyr. 38. Simulacrum deæ, non effigie humana, continuus orbis latiore initio tenuem in ambitum, metæ modo, exsurgens. Tac. Hist. ii. 3.
[27] Sanguinem aræ obfundere vetitum, precibus et igne puro altaria adolentur. Tac. Hist. ii. 3.

Fig. 84.—*Temple of Venus as restored. From D. F. Münter and G. H. Helcek's Temple of Paphos. Copenhagen, 1824.*

The image of the goddess is here represented as a cone ending in a point, but it is said that the summit was truncated. The doves at the two opposite angles of the roof are not intended for real doves, but figures carved in stone or wood. The semicircular court in front was where the sacred doves were fed, as may be collected from the coin on the next page. In the middle of the court is the altar on which the incense was burnt. The above sketch must be regarded only as giving a general idea of the shrine.

streamed in from all parts of the island to Paphos; and a grand triumphal procession, like the Panathenæa at Athens, moved thence, in honour of the goddess, to Old Paphos, the spot where her worship had been at first cultivated (figs. 65 and 66).[25]

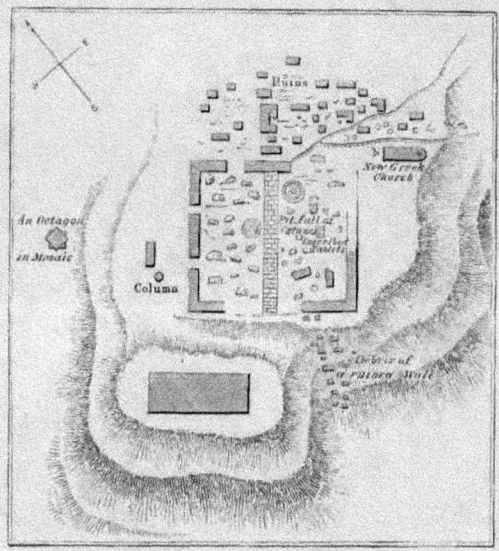

Fig. 65.—*Ruins of the Temple. From Münter and Belsch.*

The peribolus of the temple was the square area within the four walls in the centre of the engraving. The peribolus was divided by a wall running from north to south, and the shrine was in the compartment to the east.

Fig. 66.—*Coin representing the Temple of Venus. From Münter and Belsch.*

In the centre of the coin is the rude image of the goddess with two doves—the sacred birds—hovering about her. Two sculptured figures of doves are seen also on the roofs of the two wings of the Temple. In front of the Temple is a semi-circular open court paved and with its gates thrown open, and within the court is another dove.

Cyprus, like the rest of the world, was under the dominion of the Romans, and the Governor at this time was Sergius Paulus. It redounds greatly to the credit of

[25] πανηγυρίζουσι διὰ τῆς ὁδοῦ ταύτης κατ᾿ ἔτος ἐπὶ τὴν Παλαίπαφον, ἄνδρες ὁμοῦ γυναιξίν, ἐκ τῶν ἄλλων πόλεων συνιόντες. Strabo, xiv. 6 (p. 214, Tauchnitz).

the writer of the Acts, that, incidentally, minute circumstances are mentioned, which are apparently unimportant, and attract no observation; but which, when submitted to the microscopic examination of the critic, are found to be so accurately expressed, that the most careful contemporary historian could not have used language more appropriate. Thus, Sergius Paulus is styled, by Luke, the Deputy of the country, or, more properly, the Proconsul,[29] and the justness of the term is very striking. In

Fig. 67.—*Coin of Cyprus. From Akerman.*

Obv. Laureated head of Claudius, with the legend Ti. Claudius Cæsar Aug.—Rev. Κυπριων επι Κομινιου Προκλου Ανθυπατου. The name of Proclus is partly obliterated, but the whole name appears in other specimens. As the coin was struck in the reign of Claudius, the date of it must be some time between A.D. 41 and A.D. 54, and therefore only a little before or a little after the Apostle's visit.

the time of Augustus (B.C. 27), the various provinces of the Empire were, by arrangement, divided between the Emperor and the Senate.[30] Those most in need of a military force were, from policy, retained by the Emperor for himself, and were under the rule of Prefects appointed by him, called Propraetors.[31] The countries of a more peaceful character were assigned to the Senate, and the officers from time to time nominated by them were called Proconsuls. Cyprus had at first been allotted to the Emperor, and was an Imperial province; but, before Luke wrote, the Emperor and the Senate had made an exchange—the former assuming to himself Dalmatia, which had belonged to the Senate, and renouncing in the Senate's favour the province of Gallia Narbonensis, and also *the island of Cyprus*, which thus became *Proconsular*.[32] The exactness of the writer of the Acts, in this respect, is attested by an ancient coin of Cyprus, struck in the reign of Claudius, when Cominius Proclus, who is thought to have succeeded Sergius Paulus, was Proconsul. On the obverse of it are the head and name of Claudius, and on the reverse is the inscription, Κυπριων Επι Κομινιου Προκλου Ανθυπατου.—" Of the Cyprians. Under Cominius Proclus, Proconsul "[33] (fig. 67).

We now return to Saul and Barnabas, whom we left on their voyage from Seleucia. They landed at Salamis, being the nearest convenient port for them; and here they found a multitude of Jews, and many, perhaps, known personally, if not to Saul, at least to Barnabas, their fellow-countryman. They may also have occasionally met with a Christian convert, for upon the dispersion of the brethren from Jerusalem, consequent on the martyrdom of Stephen, some of the fugitives had

[29] ἀνθύπατος. Acts xiii. 7.
[30] See Fasti Sacri, p. 79, No. 666.
[31] ἀντιστράτηγοι.
[32] Dion, liii. 12; Fasti Sacri, p. 79, No. 666.
[33] See Eckhel, iii. 84; Mondl's Thesaur. Numis. p. 106.

travelled to Cyprus, but "preaching the Word to none but unto the Jews only,"[34] as the Gentiles had not then been called. The two Apostles still regarded the ancient people of God as entitled, preferentially, to the first communication of the Gospel; and therefore, though on a special mission for the conversion of the Gentiles, they first opened their ministry at Salamis, in the Jewish synagogues.

It is added by the historian, "and they had also John to their minister."[35] We know not precisely what were the functions to which this John, better known as Mark the Evangelist, obliged himself by undertaking the office; but we may suppose that, for the decent discharge of their duties, the two Apostles would necessarily require the attendance of some faithful friend. The same Greek word is employed by Luke on one occasion in his Gospel, and the use of it there may assist us in attaching to it some more definite signification. When our Saviour, in the synagogue at Nazareth, had read a passage from the prophet Isaiah, he closed the book and gave it to the minister,[36] so that the officer here meant was apparently the clerk of the synagogue. It is likely that the services of Mark were of a varied description, and that he sometimes assisted in religious ceremonies, and was sometimes the secretary and amanuensis of the Apostles, and particularly of Saul. Perhaps one employment, as occasion presented itself, was the celebration of the rite of baptism; for the Apostles themselves, being so unremittingly engaged in expounding the doctrines of the Gospel, could not conveniently find time for baptizing, but delegated to others, duly authorized for the purpose, the onerous duty of formally admitting the multitudes of converts into the pale of the Church. Such a practice may also have been adopted, in order that the disciple might not suppose himself the liegeman of the Apostle who baptized him, rather than of Christ in whose name he was baptized. To the Corinthians the Apostle writes: "I thank God that I baptized none of you, but Crispus and Gaius; *lest any should say that I had baptized in mine own name.* And I baptized also the household of Stephanas. Besides, I know not whether I baptized any other, for Christ sent me not to baptize, but to preach the Gospel."[37] The value of Mark's services (so readily volunteered, and afterwards so mysteriously withdrawn at Perga) cannot be questioned. After a lapse of more than twenty years, Saul, a prisoner at Rome, with almost his last words wrote to Timothy: "Take Mark, and bring him with thee, for he is profitable to me for the ministry."[38]

At Salamis, in particular, the Jews abounded,[39] and Paul and Barnabas preached

---

[34] Acts xi. 19.
[35] Acts xiii. 5.
[36] τῷ ὑπηρέτῃ. Luke iv. 20.
[37] 1 Cor. i. 14 to 17.
[38] 2 Tim. iv. 11.
[39] This is evident from the several synagogues in the place. Acts xiii. 5. The vast multitude of the Jews in Cyprus, generally, is attested by ancient writers, as by Jos. Antiq. xiii. 10, 4, and xvii. 12, 2, and Philo, Leg. ad Caium, s. 36. In the insurrection of the Jews against the Gentile inhabitants, in the reign of Hadrian, they massacred 240,000 of their enemies. Milman's Hist. of the Jews, vol. iii. p. 112. One cause of this multitude of Jews in Cyprus was, that the famous copper-mines of the island had been granted as to one moiety, and leased as to the other moiety, by Augustus to Herod the Great, and Herod would

for some time in their synagogues, but with what success does not appear, unless, as Mark is mentioned on this occasion to have been their minister, we may presume that there were numerous converts to be baptized. Taking leave of Salamis, they bent their steps to the west, publishing the Gospel up and down, as they went, throughout the *whole* of the island.[40] At length they came to Paphos,[41] the capital, and the residence of Sergius Paulus, the Roman Proconsul, and distant about 100 miles from Salamis.

There resided at the court of the Proconsul at that time a Jewish impostor, by the name of Bar-jesus, whose surname was Elymas, or "the magician," the word Elymas in Arabic signifying a cunning man, as we trace our term wizard from wise-ard.[42] The Proconsul is described by Luke as an intelligent person[43]—in short, one of the *savans* of the day; and it is a strong confirmation of the accuracy of the description, that we find Pliny the Elder citing Sergius Paulus more than once as an authority on questions of natural philosophy.[44] The same inquiring turn of mind that distinguished the Proconsul was transmitted to his posterity, for Galen speaks of a son (or grandson) of the same name in the most flattering terms: "Sergius Paulus, a man of the first stamp in all things, both in word and deed, as regards philosophy."[45] It follows, of course, that the Proconsul did not blindly acquiesce in the gross idolatries of the heathen superstition. He had probably listened, not without advantage, to the discourses even of Elymas, who, though a false teacher, and making a trade of religion, and practising on the credulity of the people by the knavish profession of supernatural powers, had yet communicated to the accomplished Roman many wholesome truths touching the nature and attributes of the Deity. At all events, Elymas was in high credit with the Proconsul. But the same thirst after knowledge which had led to the advancement of Elymas, now induced the governor to send for Barnabas and Saul.[46] If so much light had been derived from the Jewish religion, what might not be expected from Christianity, which,

---

naturally depute the working of the mines to his own countrymen. Jos. Antiq. xvi. 4, 5.

[40] The Textus Receptus has merely the words τὴν νῆσον (Acts xiii. 6); but Griesbach, Schultz, Lachmann, Tischendorf, and Alford all read ὅλην τὴν νῆσον.

[41] By Paphos must be understood New Paphos.

[42] The word in Arabic is Alimon, or Elim, and in the plural, Oulèma. See Meyer's Apostg. p. 236; Kuinoel, Acts xiii. 8. The name of Elymas may also be derived from the Hebrew עֲלוּמָה (*magus*). In fact, Arabic and Hebrew are cognate languages. See Rosenmüller on Acts xiii. 8, and Poli Synop. Roman, however, denies the existence of the word in Hebrew, and doubts the derivation of the word from the Arabic. St. Paul, p. 15.

[43] ἀνδρὶ συνετῷ. Acts xiii. 7.

[44] Plin. Nat. Hist. lib. i.; elenchos of lib. ii. and of lib. xviii.

[45] τοῦδε τοῦ νῦν ἐπάρχου τῆς Ῥωμαίων πόλεως, ἀνδρὸς τὰ πάντα πρωτεύοντος ἔργοις τε καὶ λόγοις τοῖς ἐν φιλοσοφίᾳ, Σεργίου Παύλου ὑπάτου. Galen, Anat. 1. Σεργιός τε, ὁ καὶ Παῦλος, ὃς οὐ μετὰ πολὺν χρόνον ἔπαρχος ἦν τῆς πόλεως καὶ Φλάβιος ... ἐσπευκὼς δὲ περὶ τὴν Ἀριστοτέλους φιλοσοφίαν ὥσπερ καὶ ὁ Παῦλος. Galen de Praenot. cited by Wetstein on Acts xiii. 7.

[46] Wordsworth observes that Paul and Barnabas always made the first offer of salvation to the Jews, and then to the Gentiles. They therefore did not *go* to Sergius Paulus, but he *sent for them*.

it was said, was to fulfil and then supersede the dispensation of Moses! There can be no fellowship between light and darkness, and it was evident, that if Sergius Paulus became a Christian, the power of Elymas was at an end. We read therefore without surprise that Elymas "withstood them, seeking to turn away the Proconsul from the faith."[47]

It would seem that as Saul, with his usual eloquence, was urging the great truths of the Gospel upon the Proconsul's attention, the sorcerer answered him with blasphemous mockery, and had recourse to such base artifices as could emanate only from the Father of Lies. What followed shall be related in the words of Luke: "Then Saul (who also is called *Paul*), filled with the Holy Ghost, set his eyes on him, and said, 'O full of all subtilty and all mischief, thou child of the devil, thou enemy of all righteousness, wilt thou not cease to pervert the right ways of the Lord? And now, behold, the hand of the Lord is upon thee, and thou shalt be blind, not seeing the sun for a season.' And immediately there fell on him a mist and a darkness; and he went about seeking some to lead him by the hand. Then the Deputy, when he saw what was done, believed, being astonished at the doctrine of the Lord."[48]

The above passage introduces, for the first time, the familiar name of Paul. Great ingenuity has been exercised, *when* and *wherefore* the Apostle assumed the name, and *why* the historian, having, without exception, spoken of him before as Saul, from this time forward employs exclusively the name of Paul. A not uncommon idea is, that he took the name of Paul out of compliment to Sergius Paulus, whom he converted—just as Josephus took the name of Flavius in honour of his patron, Flavius Vespasianus; and that this is the reason why Luke substitutes, for the first time, Paul for Saul, in narrating the occurrences at Paphos. But it will be observed, that Saul is called *Paul* before the actual conversion of the Proconsul; and it is a very unlikely circumstance, in itself, that Saul should have adopted a new name out of mere compliment to any Gentile. The more natural explanation appears to be, that the Jews of that day—in some cases for more convenient communication with the Gentiles around them, in others from the force of fashion — were in the habit of bearing two names. The second was sometimes a mere translation of the first, and sometimes the only resemblance was in sound, and occasionally the two names were wholly independent. Thomas, we read, was also Didymus, the former being the Hebrew, and the latter the Greek, for 'a twin.' Cephas had also the name of Peter, the former being the Hebrew, and the latter the Greek, for 'a stone.' John bore also the Roman name of Mark; Joses was Barnabas;[49] Joseph (or Barsabas) was Justus;[50]

---

[47] Acts xiii. 8.

[48] Acts xiii. 9-12. It has been conjectured that Pliny may allude to this miracle in the concluding words of the following extract: Est et alia factio a Mose et Jamne et Jotape Judæis pendens, sed multis millibus post Zoroastrem. *Tanto recentior est Cypria.* Plin. N. H. xxx. 2. As Sergius Paulus is often quoted as an authority by Pliny (see note [44] ante), it is not impossible that Sergius Paulus himself may have furnished his version of the miracle to Pliny.

[49] Acts iv. 36.

[50] Acts i. 23.

Simeon was Niger;[51] Judas was Barsabas;[52] Jesus was Justus;[53] and so forth.[54] The circumstance that Saul was a Roman citizen, was an especial reason why he should bear a Roman name;[55] and as he was "freeborn," he may have taken the adjunct of Paul from his birth. Why the name of Paul should have been preferred to any other, it is in vain to inquire, but the choice may have arisen from the mere similarity of it to Saul. The reason for the historian's transition from the one name to the other on this particular occasion is more evident. The Apostle is called Saul until his first circuit among the Gentiles. From that time he took the name of Paul, in order that, being a Roman citizen and carrying a Roman name, he might be more acceptable to his heathen audience—more particularly as the name of Saul, however acceptable in Hebrew, carried with it a degrading idea in Greek.[56] The adoption of a Roman name was also in harmony with the great truth he was promulgating—that henceforth the partition between Jew and Gentile was broken down. But why, it will be said, is not the name of Paul introduced when he first left Antioch to commence his travels? The answer is, that no mention is made of him individually until he reaches Paphos: "*They* departed unto Seleucia,"—"*They* sailed to Cyprus," —"When *they* were at Salamis," &c. It must be admitted that Sergius Paulus "called for Barnabas and *Saul*," and the transition might have been then made; but it occurs more naturally immediately afterwards, when Saul stands forth by himself, and becomes the principal actor: "Then Saul, who also is called Paul," &c.

The passage cited from the Acts relative to the conversion of Sergius Paulus demands our special attention from another circumstance. It is the first relation of a miracle wrought by the hands of the Apostle, and we have transcribed the very words of the sacred historian—as here we stand, as it were, upon holy ground, and must take the shoes from off our feet. In the course of our history, we shall have occasion to relate other miracles by the instrumentality of the same Apostle, and we may now, once for all, subjoin a few obvious remarks upon the subject. It must not be supposed that Paul carried about with him a power of working miracles at his option, or whenever he deemed it a suitable opportunity. He was invested with no such prerogative. Providence was making a revelation of the Divine counsels to man, and Paul was one of the means employed for the purpose. To accredit his testimony, it was necessary, from time to time, to establish the authenticity of his heavenly mission by the display of supernatural gifts; but the circumstances under which such a manifestation was to be vouchsafed depended, not on the will of the agent, but of Him who deputed him. Such communications were made to the Apostle as enabled him to execute the mechanical part of the miracle; but otherwise he was a

---

[51] Acts xiii. 1.
[52] Acts xv. 22.
[53] Col. iv. 11.
[54] Names were also abbreviated, as amongst ourselves: thus, Epaphroditus was Epaphras, Sylvanus was Silas, Artemidorus was Artemas, Demetrius was Demas, and Nymphodorus was Nymphas.
[55] See 1 Gresw. Diss. (1st ed.), p. 77.
[56] Σαῦλος, in Greek, is 'conceited,' 'affected.'

man, and had no privileges beyond the ordinary reach of humanity. He could strike Elymas blind, and could restore the Pythoness at Philippi to her right senses, because in each case he was so directed; but he could not cure Trophimus, or Epaphroditus, when they were sick, or rid himself of the thorn in the flesh, though it so sorely distressed him. So Paul had the gift of tongues ("I thank my God, I speak with tongues more than you all "[57])—yet his knowledge in this respect was limited, as we shall see at Lystra, where the Lycaonian dialect was unintelligible to him. So Paul had the spirit of prophecy as to Antichrist,[58] and could foretell to Ananias that he should be smitten by the Sicarii;[59] and when tossed by the storm in Adria, could predict that not a life should be lost, and that they should be cast away on a certain island. But when he parted from the Ephesian elders, on his third circuit, he could not foresee that he should visit them again;[60] and when imprisoned at Rome the first time, he could not tell whether he should be released or suffer execution, but contemplated either alternative as possible;[61] and when a second time a captive, though he felt the strongest conviction that he was to suffer martyrdom immediately, yet he provided for the contingency of his future labours, by bidding Timothy to come to him, and to bring Mark with him, as useful in the ministry.[62] In short, so far as the Dispensation of the Gospel seemed to the Divine wisdom to call for superhuman agency, either by the working of miracles, or the gift of tongues, or the foresight of future events, so far, and so far only, was Paul invested with any extraordinary powers, but in other respects he was our fellow-mortal.

But to resume the thread of our narrative. Paul and Barnabas had so prospered in the island of Cyprus, that they now proposed to enter upon a wider field, and transfer their labours to the opposite continent. Asia Minor at this time presented a very different aspect from the country of Cyprus. The latter was a province, under a single governor, of a uniform and peaceful character, and the same language was spoken throughout the length and breadth of the land. Asia Minor,[63] on the con-

---

[57] 1 Cor. xiv. 18.
[58] 2 Thess. ii. 3, &c.
[59] Acts xxiii. 3.
[60] Acts xx. 25.
[61] Philipp. i. 20, 25; ii. 17.
[62] 2 Tim. iv. 6, 11.
[63] As to the *geography* of Asia Minor, the writers of the New Testament pay no regard to the *political* division of countries, but look simply to the *nationalities*; or the different peoples, as distinguished by their origin or language. They treat the peninsula, therefore, as composed of the following countries: viz. on the seacoast, Cilicia, Pamphylia, Lycia, Caria, Lydia (called by them Asia), Mysia, Troas, Bithynia, Paphlagonia, Pontus; and in the interior, Cappadocia, Pisidia, Phrygia, and Galatia.

Until recently, there was no good map of these parts, but Kiepert has now done much towards supplying the desideratum. It still remains, however, to adapt Kiepert's labours to the Apostolic age; and this the author has endeavoured to do by adjusting the boundaries generally, as they are laid down by Strabo, who was the contemporary of Paul, and a native of Pontus, so that no one could stand higher as an authority. The variations from Strabo, adopted by the author, are slight, and only in those cases where Strabo himself admits that there was great confusion, and that opinions differed. Thus, Strabo would seem to assign Antioch *of* Pisidia, or (as he writes it) Antioch *on* Pisidia—to Phrygia; but Pliny and Ptolemy, and Stephanus Byzantinus, and others, agree with Luke in reckoning

trary, was broken up into numerous communities, varying in manners, language, and religion, and ruled partly by Roman prefects, and partly by petty kings and potentates, the feudataries of Rome. The geographers enumerate more than seventeen nations as occupying the peninsula west of a line running north and south from

it as situate in Pisidia, and the latter view has been preferred. Again, the tract which contained Laodicea, Colossae, and Hierapolis is also attributed by Strabo to Phrygia; but this region is placed by the author in Lydia.

As to the *political* state of the particular countries now about to be traversed by the Apostle, we had better commence with the kingdom of *Amyntas*. In B.C. 39, Mark Antony appointed Amyntas King of Pisidia, the mountain range at the north of Pamphylia (Appian, B. C. v. 75), and reaching up to the Paroreia, or mountain ridge, which ran from east to west, from Tyriaeum to Olmi: τὴν ἀρχὴν τῆς Παρωρείου τοῖς Ὄλμων ... πέρας τῆς Παρωρείου τὰ Τυριαῖον, Strabo, xiv. 3 (p. 212, Tauchnitz); and see xii. 8 (p. 72, Tauchnitz); see Fasti Sacri, p. 55, No. 480. In B.C. 36, Amyntas became King of Galatia and Lycaonia, with parts of Pamphylia: Γαλατίας ... καὶ Λυκαονίας, Παμφυλίας τέ τινα αὐτῷ προσθεὶς, Dion, xlix. 32; and in Lycaonia was included Isauria (of which the capital was Isaura) and Isaurica (of which the capital was Derbe): ἐφ' ἡμῖν δὲ καὶ τὰ Ἴσαυρα καὶ τὴν Δέρβην Ἀμύντας εἶχεν, Strabo, xii. 6 (p. 59, Tauchnitz); see Fasti Sacri, p. 66, No. 551. In B.C. 31 Augustus gave Amyntas Cilicia Aspera also, with the exception of the city of Seleucia: λυσῶν (Archelaus) τὴν Τραχῶτιν Κιλικίαν ὅλην, πλὴν Σελευκείας, καθ' ὃν τρόπον καὶ Ἀμύντας πρότερον, Strabo, xiv. 5 (p. 224, Tauchnitz); see Fasti Sacri, p. 73, No. 618; p. 64, No. 537. Thus the dominions of Amyntas reached on the coast, from the River Lamus, the eastern limit of Cilicia Aspera, to Coracesium, its western limit; and in the interior, from Coropissus, on the borders of Cappadocia, to Olmi, the western terminus of Paroreia, and, more to the south, as far as the city of Apollonias, near Apamea Cibotus, τὴν μὲν Ἀντιόχειαν ἔχων τὴν πρὸς τῇ Πισιδίᾳ μέχρι Ἀπολλωνιάδος τῆς πρὸς τῇ Ἀπαμείᾳ τῇ Κιβωτῷ καὶ τῆς Παρωρείας τινὰ καὶ τὴν Λυκαονίαν. Strabo, xii. 6 (p. 59, Tauchnitz).

On the death of Amyntas, which event occurred B.C. 25 (see Fasti Sacri, p. 82, No. 675), Cilicia Aspera (Seleucia excepted, as before) was bestowed on Archelaus, King of Cappadocia. Strabo, xiv. 5 (p. 224, Tauchnitz). In another place Strabo writes: τῷ δὲ Ἀρχελάῳ καὶ ἡ Τραχεῖα περὶ Ἐλαιοῦσσαν Κιλικία, καὶ πᾶσα ἡ τὰ πειρατήρια συστησαμένη, xii. 1 (p. 4, Tauchnitz); and by the πᾶσα ἡ τὰ πειρατήρια, &c., must be meant the piratical regions of Isaurica and Isauria, which were famous for their piracies, and adjoined the other dominions of Archelaus—viz. Cilicia Aspera on the south and Cappadocia on the east. It was the policy of the Romans to annex such disturbed and restless regions to some petty kingdom. Strabo, xiv. 5 (p. 224, Tauchnitz). In A.D. 17, Archelaus, King of Cappadocia, died, when his kingdom was reduced to a Roman province (see Fasti Sacri, p. 162, No. 1087); and in A.D. 37 Cilicia Aspera was assigned by Caligula to Antiochus, King of Commagene, τὰ παραθαλάσσια τῆς Κιλικίας, Dion, lix. 8; see Fasti Sacri, p. 250, No. 1505; and these παραθαλάσσια τῆς Κιλικίας must be taken in a liberal and extended sense, for it appears from the coins of Antiochus that he was master also of Lycaonia (Λυκαόνων), by which must be understood Isauria and Isaurica, parts of Lycaonia, and including the cities of Lystra and Derbe. Eckhel, iii. 255. (See fig. 78, p. 153.)

Iconium, another fragment of the dominions of Amyntas, was, either on his death, or not long subsequently, constituted into a tetrarchy; at least, Pliny the Elder, who wrote about A.D. 77, thus refers to it: Datur et tetrarchia ex Lycaonia quâ parte Galatiae contermina est, civitatum xiv. urbe celeberrimâ Iconio. Plin. N. H. v. 25.

The small districts held by Amyntas, carved out of Pamphylia, were, on his death, restored to that jurisdiction: τὰ χωρία τὰ ἐκ τῆς Παμφυλίας πρότερον τῷ Ἀμύντᾳ προσνεμηθέντα τῷ ἰδίῳ νομῷ ἀπεδόθη. Dion, liii. 26.

The remaining dominions of Amyntas, comprising Galatia and Pisidia, up to the Paroreia, and the greater part of Lycaonia, became a Roman province, governed by a Propraetor, named by the Emperor. This was clearly so as to Galatia, for Galatia quoque sub hoc (Augusto) provincia facta est (Eutrop. vii. 10); and Pisidia and Lycaonia were under the same Propraetor; for Strabo writes of Sagalassus, a city of Pisidia: ἐστὶν ὑπὸ τῷ αὐτῷ ἡγεμόνι τῶν Ῥωμαίων ἐφ' ᾧ καὶ ἡ Ἀμύντα βασιλεία πᾶσα, xii. 6 (p. 60, Tauchnitz); and again, of the Pisidians generally: νῦν δὲ

Amisus to the Bay of Issus;[61] and many of these nations used different tongues, or at least different dialects. The dominion of Rome over these parts had been established for more than a century, and the political divisions introduced by Rome, which were quite independent of nationalities, had tended strongly to break down the barriers of race, and fuse the heterogeneous materials into one consistent mass. But, though much had been done in this way, the distinctive features of the discordant peoples were still in the main preserved. Pamphylia, which the Apostles first entered, still retained the Pamphylian tongue;[65] and Pisidia[66] and Lycaonia,[67] which they next penetrated in succession, still spoke Pisidian and Lycaonian. Then there were the Solymian,[68] Carian,[69] Phrygian,[70] Pontine,[71] Cappadocian,[72] and other languages. But in Asia proper, or Lydia (of which Ephesus was the capital), Lydian had in general been superseded by Greek,[73] and Mysia and Bithynia preserved but few traces of their original tongues.[74] We may also assume that Greek, though originally peculiar to the Greek settlements on the west—as Ionia, Æolis, and Doris—yet was more or less diffused over the whole peninsula, and was the common medium of communication, as French is now over the whole continent of Europe.

The entire peninsula was given to idolatry, and the several component states varied only in the particular objects of worship. The prevalent religion appears generally to have come from the East; but Grecian and Roman influences, through so many ages, had so modified the primitive systems, that in the first century of the Christian era the idolatry in vogue was scarcely distinguishable from that of

ἐπήκοοι τελέως γεγόνασι, καὶ εἰσιν ἐν τῇ ὑπὸ Ἀμύντα τεταγμένῃ πρότερον, xii. 7 (p. 63, Tauchnitz); and again: ταύτῃ (Galatiam) καὶ τὴν ὑπὸ τῷ Ἀμύντᾳ γενομένην πᾶσαν εἰς μίαν συναγαγόντες ἐπαρχίαν, Strabo, xii. 5 (p. 56, Tauchnitz), and Pliny the Elder extends the province of Galatia on the west to Milyas and Cabalis, and on the south to Oroanda at the southern end of Lake Trogitis, and on the east to the part of Lycaonia called Oligene (lege Oreine). Plin. N. H. v. 25.

Between the ridge of the Paroreia and Galatia lay a tract of country, accounted by Strabo as part of Phrygia, but reckoned by Pliny the Elder as part of Lycaonia, in a large sense. I do not find whether this district did or not form part of Amyntas's dominions; but in the time of Pliny this portion of Lycaonia was turned over to Proconsular Asia, and formed one of its counties. Hos (Pisidas) includit Lycaonia in Asiaticam jurisdictionem versa, cum quā conveniunt Philomelienses, Tymbriani, Leucolithi, Pelteni, Tyrienses. Plin. N. H. v. 25. All these cities, except Pelte, lay on the north of the Paroreia, between it and Galatia, and as to Pelte, the text may be corrupt, for Pelte was far distant on the west,

and is elsewhere reckoned into the conventus of Apamea. Plin. N. H. v. 29.

The result of the foregoing discussion is, that in the time of the Apostle's visit (A.D. 46), Perga, through which they passed, was subject to the Proprætor of Pamphylia; Antioch of Pisidia was under the government of the Proprætor of Galatia; Iconium was held by an independent Tetrarch not named; and Lystra and Derbe were within the jurisdiction of Antiochus, King of Commagene: so that the Apostles, at each remove, transferred themselves into a new jurisdiction, and so beyond the reach of their persecutors.

[64] Strabo, xiv. 5 (p. 235, Tauchnitz).
[65] Acts ii. 10.
[66] Strabo, xiii. 4 (p. 160, Tauchnitz).
[67] Acts xiv. 11.
[68] Strabo, xiii. 11 (p. 160, Tauchnitz).
[69] Strabo, xiv. 2 (p. 211, Tauchnitz).
[70] Acts ii. 10.
[71] Acts ii. 9.
[72] Ibid.
[73] Strabo, xiii. 4 (p. 160, Tauchnitz).
[74] Strabo, xii. 1 (p. 53, Tauchnitz).

Greece and Rome. One of the most popular of the deities was the Moon, either as a female under the name of Diana, as at Ephesus and Perga; or, as a male, under the name of Mên, or Mensis, or Lunus, as at Antioch of Pisidia. Even the Galatians had lost sight of their Gallic Druidism, and were worshippers of Jupiter and Cybele, and other Pagan divinities, into which their own had been gradually metamorphosed. Such was the adulation of the Asiatics, that the successive Cæsars—as Augustus and Nero, even in their lifetime—had temples erected to their honour, with a regular hierarchy of priests attached.

The only rational faith to be found between the Euxine and the Mediterranean was that of the Jews, who—from their mercantile spirit, and the encouragement given to them, first by the successors of Alexander the Great, and then by the Julian family of Rome—were to be found in considerable numbers in all the principal towns. Exempted from serving in the army, and possessed of other important immunities, they were at this period a favoured race, though always unpopular from their exclusive and unsocial habits. The assemblage of Jews in the leading cities was not the least of the inducements which actuated the Apostles to pass over intervening countries, and open their mission in the various capitals.

In some respects Asia Minor was unfavourable to the progress of missionaries. The roads were scarcely passable, and—what was worse—all the south of the peninsula, to which the Apostles were about to address themselves, was overrun with bandits. More than a century before this, the Romans had made a vigorous effort to extirpate these pests of civilized life, and Pompey was decreed a triumph for his successes over them; but the nature of the country offered such facilities to depredation, that the evil could not be entirely extirpated. Frequent in these parts must have been the "perils of robbers," to which Paul and his companions in the course of their journeyings were exposed.

Such, in outline, was the state of Asia Minor when Paul and Barnabas, accompanied by Mark, embarked at the port of Paphos, and sailed for Pamphylia. This was a region occupying about eighty miles of the seaboard, between Lycia to the west, and Cilicia (the native country of Paul) to the east. How far it extended inland toward the north, where it bordered on Pisidia, is not easy to define, but Pamphylia and Pisidia together reached about a hundred miles from the sea. In general features, the face of Pamphylia was not of so rugged and mountainous a character as Pisidia, which was a highly elevated district intersected by the ridges of Mount Taurus.

The name of Pamphylia signifies All-tribe-land, and the inhabitants are said to have been a medley of many races, but principally of Greek extraction. Pamphylia, like the rest of Asia Minor, was under the dominion of Rome, and on the partition of the Empire between Augustus and the Senate, after the battle of Actium, became an Imperial province, and was governed by a Propraetor, nominated by the Emperor.[70]

---

[70] See Dion, liv. 31; Fasti Sacri, p. 103, No. 792.

Pisidia was given by Mark Antony to Amyntas, King of Galatia.[76] (fig. 68); and on the death of Amyntas, in B.C. 25, formed part of the newly-created Province of Galatia, under the care of the Emperor.[77]

Thus at the time of Paul's visit, Pamphylia was under an Imperial Propraetor of its own, and Pisidia was within the Galatian prefecture.

Fig. 68.—*Coin of Amyntas.* From J. Y. *Akerman.*
Obv. Head of Minerva.— Rev. ΒΑΣΙΛΕΩΣ ΑΜΥΝΤΟΥ (of King Amyntas).

One of the principal rivers of Pamphylia was the Cestus, now the Aksoo. Paul and his company entered the Cestus, and sailed up it till they arrived at Perga (fig. 69), the metropolis of Pamphylia,[78] now Eski Kalessi. This was a considerable town,

Fig. 69.—*View of Perga.* From J. *Murray's Illustrated New Testament.*

surrounded by walls, and lay on the left bank as they ascended, about seven miles and a half from the sea. The inhabitants were Greeks, and they had, as usual, their temples, and a theatre, and a stadium. On a high eminence stood conspicuous a far-famed temple of Diana, the great goddess of the place (fig. 70), in whose honour was celebrated a yearly festival.[79] Here the Apostles landed, but apparently they made no stay, and did not formally commence their evangelical labours.

---

[76] Appian, B. C. v. 75; see Fasti Sacri, p. 55. No. 480.

[77] See Fasti Sacri, p. 82, No. 675.

[78] Cic. Verr. 2nd act. i. 20.

[79] εἶθ᾽ ὁ Κέστρος ποταμός, ὃν ἀναπλεύσαντι σταδίους ἑξήκοντα Πέργη πόλις, καὶ πλησίον ἐπὶ μετεώρου τόπου τὸ τῆς Περγαίας Ἀρτέμιδος ἱερὸν ἐν ᾧ πανήγυρις κατ᾽ ἔτος συντελεῖται. Strabo, xiv. 4 (p. 218, Tauchnitz). Perga est oppidum, et Dianae, quam ab oppido Pergaeum vocant, templum. Mela, i. 14. Pergae fanum antiquissimum et sanctissimum Dianae scimus esse. Cic. in Verr. 2nd act. i. 20. The city is now a ruin, and the stadium has been converted into an inclosure for nursing camels. Fellows's Asia Minor and Lycia (1852), p. 143.

The cause of Christianity may have suffered from the waywardness of Mark, their minister, the cousin of Barnabas. He was a young man, and perhaps not prepared to hazard himself upon the troubled ocean on which the Apostles were now embarking. We have seen that his mother Mary was living at Jerusalem, and that he had accompanied Barnabas to Antioch. He had since attended on Paul and Barnabas in their peregrination over Cyprus, the native country of Barnabas, and where therefore Mark, as the cousin of Barnabas, had, we may suppose, many friends and relations. But, now that the Apostles were extending the sphere of their exertions to more distant regions, Mark, who had not contemplated so wide a circuit,

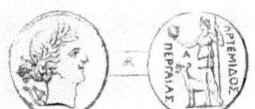

Fig. 70.—*Coin of Perga. From Pellerin.*
(*obv.* Head of Diana.—*rev.* Ἀρτέμιδος Περγαίας (of Diana of Perga).

could not be induced to continue his services, and "went not with them to the *work*."[59] He forsook the Apostles at Perga, and returned to Jerusalem. Charity would lead us to hope that he had private reasons, with which we are not acquainted, but which, if known, might wholly, or in part, be an exculpation. We may conclude that his conduct was not absolutely indefensible, or Barnabas would not afterwards have again made him his fellow-traveller; and we can hardly believe that he was not in some degree blameable, or Paul would not, on his next circuit, have refused to receive him as his companion. Whatever was the offence, it was eventually forgotten, even by Paul himself, for the Apostle, when a prisoner at Rome the first time, was waited upon by Mark; and in writing to the Colossians, the Apostle adds: "Aristarchus my fellow-prisoner saluteth you, and Mark, cousin to Barnabas, (*touching whom ye received commandments: if he come unto you, receive him*;)"[51] and shortly afterwards he observes that Mark had been his "fellow-labourer" and "a comfort" to him.[52] And when Paul was a prisoner at Rome the second time, he writes, in a postscript to his last letter to Timothy: "Take Mark, and bring him with thee, for he is profitable to me for the ministry."[53]

Paul and Barnabas, being thus left to pursue their travels alone,[54] made their way

---

[59] Acts xv. 38. The real work, comparatively, was to begin on the continent, where they had to deal with utter strangers.

[51] Col. iv. 10. Mark, therefore, must have served recently under Paul, or how else could his usefulness have been tested?

[52] Col. iv. 11.

[53] 2 Tim. iv. 11.

[54] As Paul and Barnabas now make their first journey by land in Asia Minor, it may gratify a natural curiosity to say a word about the ancient rate of travelling in this part of the world. Strabo reckons it a six days' journey from Cæsarea Mazaca to the Cilician Gates: ἀφέστηκε δὲ Μάζακα . . . τῶν Κιλικίων Πυλῶν ὁδὸν ἡμερῶν ἕξ, xii. 2 (p. 11, Tauchnitz), and Tyana

across the country to Antioch, the capital of Pisidia,³⁵ but then comprised within the Roman province of Galatia. Of Antioch we have the following description from Strabo: "The Paroreia contains a certain mountainous ridge, and at the foot of it, on each side, extends a great plain, and near the ridge on the north lies the city of Philomelium, and on the other side Antioch, called Antioch on Pisidia—the former standing in the plain, and the latter upon an eminence, having a colony of the Romans; but the Magnetians on the Meander founded it, and the Romans made it a free city, when they gave the rest of Asia to Eumenes; and there was also in it a certain priesthood of Mēn Arcæus (The Moon³⁶), having a multitude of votaries and

---

lay halfway between the two: κατὰ μέσην δὲ τὴν ὁδὸν κεῖται τὰ Τύανα. Ibid. From Cæsarea to Tyana was seventy-three miles (Peutinger Table), and therefore the whole distance was 146 miles, which divided by 6 gives 24⅓ miles per day, or say (in round numbers) twenty-five miles per day.

Greswell, in calculating the rate of travelling generally by the ancients, enumerates the following instances: Procopius, de Rebus Vandal. i. 1, reckons a day's journey at 210 stades, or twenty-six Roman miles; and Livy (xxi. 27) makes twenty-five Roman miles and a day's journey synonymous expressions; and Polybius (iii. 42) designates the day's journey as 200 stades, or twenty-five miles. Horace (Sat. i. v. 506) calls it a day's journey from Aricia to Forum Appii, and the distance by the Antonine Itin. is somewhat more, and by the Jerus. Itin. somewhat less, than twenty-five Roman miles. See Dissert. on the Harmony of the Gospels, vol. iii. p. 316, 1st ed.

From J. B. Lightfoot on the Philippians (p. 37, note) we borrow the following calculations:— From Rome to Brundisium was, according to Strabo (vi. 3, p. 51, Tauchnitz), 360 miles, or, according to the Anton. Itin. 358 miles, and Horace made the journey very leisurely in sixteen days (Horat. Sat. i. 5), which would give somewhat less than twenty-four miles per day. Ovid treats this as an easy ten days' journey (Ovid, Epist. Pont. iv. 5, 8), which would yield thirty-six miles per day. But Horace is speaking of a gentleman travelling leisurely, and Ovid of the post for letters. Again, Cicero, at Dyrrhachium, on the 30th of November, received news from Rome up to the 12th of November (Cic. Ep. Att. iii. 23); and allowing one day for the passage from Brundisium to Dyrrhachium (Ep. Attic. iv. 6) there remain seventeen days for the transit from Rome to Brundisium, a distance of 360 miles, which allows somewhat more than twenty-one miles per day. Again, Cicero left Brundisium on the 30th of April (Ep. Att. iv. 7), and reached Thessalonica on the 23rd of May. The sea-voyage would, as before, be one day, so that the land-journey from Dyrrhachium to Thessalonica, a distance of 270 miles, was accomplished in twenty-two days, and therefore at a rate of little more than twelve miles per day; but apparently Cicero travelled slowly, and made halts upon the road. Again, Cicero, writing from Thessalonica on the 18th of June, mentions that he had received news from Rome up to the 25th of May. If we deduct a day for the sea-passage, we have twenty-five days for the road from Rome to Brundisium, a distance of 360 miles, and from Dyrrhachium to Thessalonica, a distance of 270 miles—making together 630 miles—so that the rate would be about twenty-one miles per day.

Thus, the rate of travelling varied, according to circumstances, from twelve miles to thirty-six miles per day. A person travelling for his amusement would creep along, while the letter-carrier would make all haste. For our present purpose, we may acquiesce in the conclusion drawn from the statement of Strabo, and assume the ordinary rate of travelling in Asia Minor to have been about twenty-five miles per day.

³⁵ Pliny, as Luke, reckons Antioch as in Pisidia: Pisidæ . . . quorum colonia Cæsarea, eadem Antiochia. Plin. N. H. v. 24. And so Ptolemy (v. 5, 4); and Stephanus Byzant., 'Αντιόχεια . . . Πισιδίας. Strabo assigns Antioch to what he calls the Παρώρεια, viz. the ridge running from east to west, from Tyriæum to Olmi, comprised by him in Μεγάλη Φρυγία, Strabo, xii. 8 (p. 72, Tauchnitz); xiv. 2 (p. 212, Tauchnitz), and he does not, as Luke, write 'Αντιόχεια τῆς Πισιδίας, but 'Αντιόχεια ἡ πρὸς τῇ Πισιδίᾳ.

³⁶ The moon, among some nations, was worshipped as a deity of the masculine gender.

[Chap. VIII.] ST. PAUL'S FIRST CIRCUIT. [A.D. 46] 137

sacred grounds, but it was abolished after the death of Amyntas (B.C. 25) by those who were sent into his place."[57] Antioch, as appears from this passage, was originally planted by the Magnetians; but Seleucus, the son of Antiochus, re-settled it, and called it Antioch, after the name of his father. A colony was afterwards planted there by the Romans in the time of Augustus, when it assumed the name of Cæsarea, without, however, losing the name of Antioch, as is mentioned by Pliny."[58] Antioch

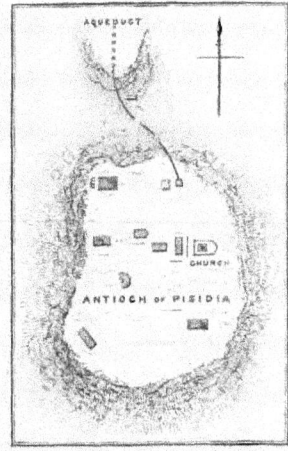

Fig. 73.—*From Arundell's Asia Minor.*

Fig. 72.—*Coin of Antioch of Pisidia. From Cabinet.*

The figure is that of the god Men, Lunus or Mensis, and the crescent of the moon is seen behind his shoulders. It is mentioned by Strabo, xii. 8 (p. 72, Tauchnitz), that this deity was worshipped at Antioch, and that to his temple were attached great multitudes of priests and valuable possessions. The legend on the coin is Mensis Col. Cæs. Antioch. (Mensis of the Colony Cæsarea Antiochia) see Eckhel, vol. iii. p. 19.

had also the Jus Italicum,[59] or immunity from public taxes, with municipal government, and other privileges. The ruins of Antioch are still to be seen, on the eminence or knoll mentioned by Strabo. One of the most striking objects is a very perfect aqueduct of twenty-one arches. Another interesting relic is thus introduced by Arundell:—"A long and immense building, constructed of prodigious stones, and standing east and west, made one entertain a hope that it might be a church—a church of Antioch! It was so, the ground-plan, with the circular end for the bema,

ἔστι δὲ καὶ τοῦτο τῆς Σελήνης τὸ ἱερὸν, καθάπερ τὸ ἐν Ἀλβάνοις, καὶ τὸ ἐν Φρυγίᾳ, τό τε τοῦ Μηνὸς ἐν τῷ ὁμωνύμῳ τόπῳ, καὶ τὸ τοῦ Ἀρκαίου τὸ πρὸς τῇ Ἀντιοχείᾳ τῇ πρὸς Πισιδίᾳ. Strabo, xii. 3 (p. 40, Tauchnitz).

[57] ἡ μὲν οὖν παρώρεια (τῆς Φρυγίας) ὀρεινήν τινα ἔχει ῥάχιν. . . ταύτῃ δ᾽ ἑκατέρωθεν ὑποπέπτωκέ τι πεδίον μέγα, καὶ πόλεις πλησίον αὐτῆς πρὸς ἄρκτον μὲν Φιλομήλιον, ἐκ θατέρου δὲ μέρους Ἀντιόχεια ἡ πρὸς Πισιδίᾳ καλουμένη, ἡ μὲν ἐν πεδίῳ κειμένη, πᾶσα ἡ δ᾽ ἐπὶ λόφου ἔχουσα ἀποικίαν Ῥωμαίων. ταύτην δ᾽ ᾤκισαν Μάγνητες οἱ πρὸς Μαιάνδρῳ. Ῥωμαῖοι δ᾽

ἠλευθέρωσαν τῶν βασιλέων, ἡνίκα τὴν ἄλλην Ἀσίαν Εὐμένει παρέδοσαν· ἦν δὴ ἐν ταύτῃ καὶ ἱερωσύνη τις Μηνὸς Ἀρκαίου, πλῆθος ἔχουσα ἱεροδούλων καὶ χωρίων ἱερῶν, κατελύθη δὲ μετὰ τὴν Ἀμύντου τελευτὴν ὑπὸ τῶν πεμφθέντων ἐπὶ τὴν ἐκείνου κληρονομίαν. Strabo, xii. 8 (p. 72, Tauchnitz).

[58] Insident verticem Pisidæ quondam Solymi appellati, quorum colonia Cæsarea, eadem Antiochia. Pliny, v. 24; and see Eckhel, vol. iii. p. 18.

[59] In Pisidiâ ejusdem (Italici) juris est colonia Antiochiensium. Digest, l. 15, 9.

VOL. I. T

all remaining! Willingly would I have remained hours in the midst of a temple—perhaps one of the very earliest consecrated to the Saviour."[90] The modern town (called Yalabatz) stands at some distance in the valley, between the plateau and the mountains. The inhabitants of Antioch were of a very mixed character. The Roman colonists spoke Latin, and accordingly, many of the inscriptions and coins of the place are in that language;[91] but the Greek settlers ever retained their own tongue, which was intelligible to all; and the lower classes (the native population) still expressed themselves in Pisidian.[92] But besides these nationalities, there was here, as elsewhere, a large admixture of Jews, who were numerous enough to maintain a synagogue. This was probably one reason that drew the Apostles in this direction; for it was principally through the medium of the synagogue that our Saviour himself, and afterwards his Apostles, first promulgated the Christian doctrine.

As we have an account somewhat in detail of Paul's proceedings at Antioch, and they are connected with the synagogue-worship, we shall offer a few explanatory remarks on the constitution and service of the synagogues. The principal officers were the Ἀρχισυνάγωγοι, or Rulers. They in some measure corresponded to the churchwardens of the present day, but had much larger powers. They regulated the sittings; preserved order amongst the people; had authority to inflict scourging for misbehaviour; and gave leave to members of the congregation, or strangers who appeared qualified, to expound the Scriptures, or exhort to good works. The next officer was the Angel, who offered up the prayers of the congregation, which with the Jews, as in our own church, were not spontaneous effusions, but were settled forms. Besides these, there were also the Reader and Interpreter—the former to read the Law and the Prophets in the original Hebrew, and the latter to translate them into the language of the country where the service was performed. In the Law, which was regarded with the greater reverence, one verse only was read at a time, and then translated; but in the Prophets, three verses were read together before any one translated.[93] In Judæa the translation was into the Syro-Chaldaic, the dialect that prevailed after the Babylonish Captivity—a corruption of the old Hebrew, and designated as Hebrew in the New Testament. In the synagogues of the Hellenists, or Jews dispersed beyond Judæa, the Scriptures were generally translated through the medium of the Septuagint, or Alexandrian version.[94] In some synagogues it would appear that no one was permanently appointed Reader, but persons were from time to time selected

---

[90] Arundell's Asia Minor, vol. i. p. 268.
[91] Renan's St. Paul, p. 35.
[92] Strabo, xiii. 4 (p. 160, Tauchnitz).
[93] See Biscoe on the Acts, chap. iv.; and see Kuinoel on Acts ii. 4; Winer, Realwört. 'Synagogen.'
[94] Cæsarea was reckoned into Judæa, and yet was originally a Greek town, and the population was still in great measure Greek. It was therefore fairly a question whether the service should be in Hebrew or in Greek. The latter prevailed, but it shocked Rabbi Levi, as appears from the following: R. Levi Ben Chaiathah adiit Cæsaream atque audiens eos recitantes precationem שְׁמַע (quæ desumpta erat a locis, Deut. vi. 4-9, ix. 13-21; Numb. xv. 37-41) Græcè, voluit eos prohibere. R. Jose id animadvertens iratus dicebat, Qui non potest Hebraicè, num omnino

from the people. Thus, at Nazareth, where Jesus had been brought up, he was called out, as a member of the congregation, to read the Haphtorah, or Lesson for the Day.[95] The lowest officer in rank was the ὑπηρετής, or Clerk, who brought and removed the sacred books—if books they could be called; for they were not composed of separate leaves, but were one continuous piece of vellum, made of a series of skins neatly joined together, written in columns, and wound round two rollers, fastened at the two ends, so that in rolling the book off one roller and on to the other, any part of the Scripture could be readily found.

The first part of the service of the synagogue was the Liturgy, or Prayers, which were offered up by the Angel, and during which the people stood. This was followed by the reading from the Law and the Prophets, which were each divided into fifty-three sections, so that the whole of the Scripture might, by the weekly rota, be recited annually. The third or remaining part of the service was the exposition of Holy Writ, or a sermon by way of exhortation. This duty was committed by the Rulers of the synagogue, as occasion offered, to such as, from sobriety of life and literary attainments, were thought suited to the task.[96] The synagogue was frequented not only by the male sex, who were ranged in seats according to their ages—the elders in the higher, and the younger in the lower[97]—but also by females, but so that the women were seated by themselves apart from the men.[98] The synagogue service was attended not only by Jews, strictly so called, but also by the Proselytes. When a heathen was converted from idolatry, and acknowledged the one true God, if he submitted to circumcision, he became a Jew; but if he declined that rite, he was one of the class called in the New Testament "devout men," "men who feared God," &c., and we shall find the Apostle presently addressing himself to these, as well as to his own countrymen.

---

non recitabit? Imo recitet eâ linguâ quam intelligit et sic officio suo satisfaciat. Hieros. Sota, fol. 21, 2. In Judæa itself, indulgence was shown to the ignorance of the common people. Thus: Sunt qui dicunt precatiunculam istam cujus initium קדש ideo linguâ Arameâ proferri quod sit lingua nobilis et summæ laudis ... In more fuit orationem קדש recitare post concionem; adfuit autem ibi vulgus qui linguam Hebræam non intelligebat; ideo in linguâ Targumisticâ eam instituerunt, ut intelligeretur ab omnibus, nam hæc eorum lingua. Berachoth, fol. 3, 1. See Kuinoel on Acts ii. 4.

[95] Luke iv. 20.

[96] Sometimes the person who read (a priest or elder) was also the person who preached: τῶν ἱερέων δέ τις ὁ παρών, ἢ τῶν γερόντων εἰς, ἀναγινώσκει τοὺς ἱεροὺς νόμους αὐτοῖς, καὶ κατὰ ἕκαστον ἐξηγεῖται μέχρι σχεδὸν δείλης ὀψίας, Philo, Fragm. vol. ii. pp. 630, 631; and sometimes one person read, and another person, who was sufficiently gifted for the purpose, expounded the Scripture to the people, as was the case with Paul at Antioch of Pisidia: εἶθ' ὁ μὲν τοὺς βίβλους ἀναγινώσκει λαβών, ἕτερος δὲ τῶν ἐμπειροτάτων, ὅσα μὴ γνώριμα παρελθὼν ἀναδιδάσκει. Philo, Quod Omn. Prob. c. 12, vol. ii. p. 458. προελθὼν δέ ὁ πρεσβύτατος καὶ τῶν δογμάτων ἐμπειρότατος διαλέγεται. Philo de Vit. Contempl. c. 3, vol. ii. p. 476.

[97] καθ' ἡλικίας ἐν τάξεσιν ὑπὸ πρεσβυτέροις νέοι καθέζονται, Philo, Quod Omn. Prob. vol. ii. p. 458.

[98] καὶ γὰρ καὶ γυναῖκες ἐξ ἔθους συνακροῶνται. Philo de Vit. Contempl. c. 3, vol. ii. p. 476. διπλοῖς ἔστι περίβολος, ὁ μὲν εἰς ἀνδρῶνα, ὁ δὲ εἰς γυναικωνῖτιν ἀποκριθείς, καὶ γὰρ καὶ γυναῖκες ἐξ ἔθους συνακροῶνται, τὸν αὐτὸν ζῆλον καὶ τὴν αὐτὴν προαίρεσιν ἔχουσαι ... ὁ δὲ μεταξὺ τῶν οἰκιῶν τοῖχος, τὸ μὲν ἐξ ἐδάφους ἐπὶ τρεῖς ἢ τέτταρας πηχεῖς εἰς τὸ ἄνω συνῳκοδόμηται, &c. Philo de Vit. Contemp. vol. ii. p. 476.

Paul and Barnabas, having reached Antioch of Pisidia, proceeded to open their mission. On the first Sabbath they attended the synagogue, and took their places, not on the chief seats amongst the Rulers,[99] but on the bench assigned to those who were desirous of addressing the congregation, and thus intimated their wish to deliver a discourse.[100] The service began, as usual, with the Liturgy, and then followed the readings from the Scripture. We are able, curiously enough, to point out, with some degree of probability, what were the Lessons for the day. Thus, in the first chapter of Deuteronomy occurs the passage, " And *in the wilderness* the Lord your God *nursed you in his arms*, as a man nurseth his child, by all the way that ye went until ye came unto this place ;"[101] and in the first chapter of Isaiah we read, "I have nourished and *exalted* children, and they have rebelled against me ;"[102] and the Apostle, in opening his address, and to engage the attention of his audience, refers, as we shall see, to the passages from Scripture which had just been read. Such, at least, is the hypothesis, and it receives some support from the fact, that down to the present day, the first chapter of Deuteronomy and the first chapter of Isaiah are, it is said, the appointed lessons amongst the Jews for the same Sabbath.

At the conclusion of the lessons followed the exhortation, or sermon ; and at this point the Rulers of the synagogue sent a message to the Apostles, "Ye men and brethren, if ye have any word of exhortation for the people, say on."[103] Paul and Barnabas had, perhaps, previously produced testimonials to the Rulers, or had manifested sufficient attainments for the purpose at a personal interview, or probably had attracted the attention of the Rulers by the publication of the new doctrine in the streets of Antioch during the week ; or Paul, who was a member of the Sanhedrim, and Barnabas, who was either a member also, or a person of high rank, may have had, by the Jewish law, a right to preach to the people. At all events, the invitation was given, when Paul stood up and, beckoning with his hand, addressed himself to the Jews and Proselytes in a sermon, the first on record that has been preserved to us, and which we shall give entire, as showing the line of argument adopted by the Apostle in reasoning with the *Jews*. The appeal here is to the Scriptures, and the fulfilment of the prophecies in the person of Jesus. In his discourses to the *Gentiles*, as we shall see at Athens, the topics urged are of a wholly different character. We must not suppose, however, that we have the Apostle's argument at Antioch word for word as it was spoken, for evidently it is a mere summary of the heads, on which the Apostle dilated at far greater length. It may be observed, by the way, that Paul " *stood* up and beckoned with his hand," for such was the custom of the Greeks, who

---

[99] This may be inferred from the expression ἀπέστειλαν οἱ ἀρχισυνάγωγοι, Acts xiii. 15. The Rulers did not give the intimation themselves, but sent a message by the verger to the Apostles.

[100] See Kuinoel, Acts xiii. 15.

[101] In the Septuagint the words are : ἐν τῷ ἐρήμῳ ... ὡς τροφοφορήσει σε Κύριος ὁ θεός σου ὡς εἴ τις τροφοφορήσαι ἄνθρωπος τὸν υἱὸν αὐτοῦ, κατὰ πᾶσαν τὴν ὁδὸν εἰς ἣν ἐπορεύθητε ἕως ἤλθετε εἰς τὸν τόπον τοῦτον. Deut. i. 31.

[102] In the Septuagint, υἱοὺς ἐγέννησα καὶ ὕψωσα, αὐτοὶ δέ με ἠθέτησαν. Isai. i. 2.

[103] Acts xiii. 15.

were the prevailing population of that country; but in Judæa the speaker sat down, as in the case of Jesus at Nazareth: "And he closed the book, and he gave it again to the minister, and *sat down;* and the eyes of all them that were in the synagogue were fastened on him, and he began to say," &c.[104]—and so in numerous other instances. Paul then, having commanded attention by stretching forth his hand, began as follows:[105]—

"Men of Israel, and ye that fear God [viz. Jews and Proselytes], give audience. The God of this people of Israel chose our fathers, and *exalted* the people[106] when they dwelt as strangers in the land of Egypt, and with a high arm brought he them out of it. And about the time of forty years he *nursed them in his arms*[107] in the wilderness. And when he had destroyed seven nations[108] in the land of Chanaan, he divided their land to them by lot. And after that he gave unto them Judges, about the space of four hundred and fifty years,[109] until Samuel the Prophet. And afterward they desired a king; and God gave unto them Saul, the son of Kish, a man of the tribe of Benjamin, by the space of forty years.[110] And when he had removed him, he raised up unto them David to be their king; to whom also he gave testimony, and said, 'I have found David the son of Jesse, a man after mine own heart, who shall fulfil all

---

[104] Luke iv. 20, 21.

[105] The Pisidian tongue is distinguished by Strabo from the Solymian, and Greek, and Lydian: τῇ Πισιδικῇ, τῇ Σολύμων, τῇ Ἑλληνίδι, τῇ Λυδῶν. Strabo, xiii. c. 4 (p. 160, Tauchnitz). Paul therefore, if he spoke Pisidian, must have done so by the gift of tongues which he possessed. 1 Cor. xiv. 18. But it is more likely that in addressing Jews and Proselytes he spoke Greek, which was generally understood in Asia Minor.

[106] τὸν λαὸν ὕψωσεν, in allusion to Isaiah i. 2. υἱοὺς ἐγέννησα καὶ ὕψωσα.

[107] The true reading is no doubt ἐτροφοφόρησεν, in allusion to Deut. i. 31. (See ante, note [101].)

[108] The Hittites, the Girgashites, the Amorites, the Canaanites, the Perizzites, the Hivites, and the Jebusites. Deut. vii. 1; Josh. iii. 10; Nehem. ix. 8.

[109] "Is Saul also amongst the prophets?" and is Paul amongst the chronologists? We have here the statement that the Judges lasted 450 years; but this is contradicted by 1 Kings vi. 1, where the time from the Exodus to the fourth year of King Solomon is reckoned at 480 years; and deducting from this sixty-five years from the Exodus to the Judges, viz. forty years in the wilderness, and twenty-five years under Joshua (Jos. Ant. v. 1, 29), and eighty-four years from the Judges to the fourth year of Solomon—viz. forty years under Saul (Jos. Ant. vi. 14, 9), and forty years under David (1 Kings ii. 11), and four years under Solomon—we have remaining 321 years for the duration of the Judges. The estimate of Paul, however, appears to be the correct one, for on turning to the Book of Judges we find that the periods of the several Judges, when added together, do in fact make 450 years; and this was the chronology adopted in Paul's day by the learned, as is evident from Josephus, who (Ant. viii. 3, 1) computes 592 years from the Exodus to the fourth year of Solomon; and deducting from this sixty-five years from the Exodus to the Judges, and eighty-four years from the Judges to the fourth year of Solomon, we have remaining 443 years, which, in round numbers, may be called 450 years. It will be observed that the expression of Paul is "*about* the space of 450 years." The passage in 1 Kings vi. 1 is therefore corrupt, and that there were different readings in ancient times is attested by the Septuagint, for there instead of 480 years, we read 440 years. See Alford's N. T.; Meyer's Apostg.; Kuinoel.

[110] Here, again, we have Paul employing the chronology received by the learned of his day. The length of the reign of Saul is nowhere stated in the Old Testament, but Josephus, as Paul, assigns to it a duration of forty years. Ant. vi. 14, 9.

my will.'¹¹¹ Of this man's seed hath God, according to his promise, raised unto Israel a Saviour, Jesus: when John had first preached, before his coming, the baptism of repentance to all the people of Israel. And as John fulfilled his course, he said, 'Whom think ye that I am? I am not he. But, behold, there cometh one after me, whose shoes of his feet I am not worthy to loose.'¹¹² Men and brethren, children of the stock of Abraham, and whosoever among you feareth God, to you is the word of this salvation sent. For they that dwell at Jerusalem, and their rulers, because they knew him not, nor yet the voices of the Prophets which are read every Sabbath-day, they have fulfilled them in condemning him; and though they found no cause of death in him, yet desired they Pilate that he should be slain. And when they had fulfilled all that was written of him, they took him down from the tree, and laid him in a sepulchre. But God raised him from the dead; and he was seen many days by them which came up with him from Galilee to Jerusalem, who are his witnesses unto the people. And we declare unto you glad tidings, how that the promise which was made unto the fathers, God hath fulfilled the same unto us their children, in that he hath raised up Jesus again; as it is also written in the second Psalm, 'Thou art my Son; this day have I begotten thee' (Ps. ii. 7).¹¹³ And as concerning that he raised him up from the dead, now no more to return to corruption, he said on this wise, 'I will give you the sure mercies of David' (Isaiah lv. 3).¹¹⁴ Wherefore he saith also in another place, 'Thou shalt not suffer thine Holy One to see corruption' (Ps. xvi. 10).¹¹⁵ For David, after he had served his own generation by the will of God, fell on sleep, and was gathered unto his fathers, and saw corruption; but he, whom God raised again, saw no corruption. Be it known unto you, therefore, men and brethren, that through this man is preached unto you the forgiveness of sins; and by him all that believe are justified from all things, from which ye could not be justified by the Law of Moses. Beware, therefore, lest that come unto you which is spoken of in the Prophets: 'Behold, ye despisers, and wonder, and perish; for I work a work in your days, a work which ye shall in nowise believe, though a man declare it unto you.'"¹¹⁶ (Habak. i. 5.)¹¹⁷

---

¹¹¹ These words are not found verbatim in any part of Scripture; but see 1 Sam. xiii. 14 and Ps. lxxxix. 20.

¹¹² See Matt. iii. 11; Luke iii. 16; Mark i. 7; John i. 26.—But the words of Paul are not identical with those in any of the four Gospels. Was he informed by human testimony, or did he receive the words supernaturally? He tells us himself that he was not taught by man, but received the Gospel by revelation. Galat. i. 12.

¹¹³ Cited verbatim from the Septuagint. Griesbach, Lachmann, Tischendorf, and Alford read πρώτῳ, instead of δευτέρῳ ψαλμῷ. The first and second Psalms were originally one, and πρώτῳ is therefore the true reading; but as, according to the present arrangement, the Psalm has been divided, and the words are found in the second Psalm, the Textus Receptus has substituted δευτέρῳ for πρώτῳ.

¹¹⁴ δώσω ὑμῖν τὰ ὅσια Δαβὶδ τὰ πιστά. Acts xiii. 34. In the Septuagint the words are: διαθήσομαι ὑμῖν διαθήκην αἰώνιον, τὰ ὅσια Δαυὶδ τὰ πιστά.

¹¹⁵ Cited verbatim from the Septuagint.

¹¹⁶ Acts xiii. 16–41.

¹¹⁷ "Ἴδετε, οἱ καταφρονηταί, καὶ θαυμάσατε καὶ ἀφανίσθητε, ὅτι ἔργον ἐγὼ ἐργάζομαι ἐν ταῖς ἡμέραις ὑμῶν, ἔργον ᾧ οὐ μὴ πιστεύσητε ἐάν τις ἐκδιηγῆται ὑμῖν. The Septuagint is: "Ἴδετε, οἱ καταφρονηταί, καὶ ἐπιβλέψατε καὶ θαυμάσατε θαυμάσια καὶ ἀφανίσθητε, διότι ἔργον ἐγὼ ἐργάζομαι ἐν ταῖς ἡμέραις ὑμῶν, ὃ οὐ μὴ πιστεύσητε ἐάν τις ἐκδιηγῆται. Habak. i. 5.

Such was the effect of Paul's impressive address, that as he and Barnabas walked out of the synagogue, the congregation besought them that these words might be preached to them the next Sabbath also;[118] not only so, but many, both of the Jews and Proselytes, followed the Apostles home, to hear further of the new doctrine, and, entering sincerely upon an investigation of the truth, were convinced and became converts. The masterly discourse of the Apostle on the last Sabbath was the theme of conversation in the town of Antioch during the week. The disbelieving Jews were shocked at a doctrine which offered salvation by any other channel than the Law of Moses; and the Proselytes were as loud, on the other hand, in commending to their idolatrous brethren a scheme of religion at once novel and rational, and of universal application. The next Sabbath almost the whole city came together.[119] The multitudes that were assembled attested the popularity of the Christian doctrine among the Gentiles, and the Jews were filled with envy, and became outrageous. Instead of allowing Paul to proceed with his sermon, they ever and anon drowned his voice with contradictions and blasphemous cries. Paul could brook it no longer, and, turning solemnly to the Jews, said: "It was necessary that the Word of God should first have been spoken to you; but seeing ye put it from you, and judge yourselves unworthy of everlasting life, lo, we turn to the Gentiles. For so hath the Lord commanded us, saying, 'I have set thee to be a light of the *Gentiles*, that thou shouldest be for salvation unto the ends of the earth.'"[120]

The Gentiles, on hearing this, rejoiced the more, and "as many as were ordained to eternal life believed,"[121] and the Word of God rapidly spread itself through the whole region.

The Jews, on the other hand, were incensed beyond measure against the Apostles,

---

[118] Griesbach, Scholtz, Lachmann, Tischendorf, and Alford, all agree that the genuine text should run thus: ἐξιόντων δὲ αὐτῶν, παρεκάλουν εἰς τὸ μεταξὺ σάββατον, &c. (Acts xiii. 42), which we should translate—"And as the Apostles went out, the congregation besought them," &c. The Greek is of course very elliptic, and this indistinctness led transcribers to attempt greater clearness by adding τῶν Ἰουδαίων after ἐξιόντων, and τὰ ἔθνη after παρεκάλουν, so that the Textus Receptus now stands—ἐξιόντων δὲ ἐκ τῆς συναγωγῆς τῶν Ἰουδαίων παρεκάλουν τὰ ἔθνη, &c.; and we presume the sense meant to be given to the passage is, that the *Jews*, disgusted with Paul's liberal principles, walked out of the synagogue before the service was ended; while the *Gentiles* were so pleased with the new doctrine, that when the synagogue broke up, they entreated Paul to preach again the next Sabbath. But to this it is objected that *Gentiles*, in the proper sense of the word, would not be found in a Jewish synagogue, and we cannot suppose that Proselytes could be referred to under the term of 'Gentiles.' See, however, Acts xiii. 43.

The words τὰ μεταξὺ σάββατον are rightly translated, 'the next Sabbath.' Thus, τὸν μεταξὺ χρόνον ἐξ οὗ Ῥωμαίοις ἐπετάχθημεν ἐν ἡμέρᾳ τῇ ἡμέραν. Dion. Hal. iii. 23. ἃς εἰς τὸν μεταξὺ χρόνον δυνάμεις οἰόμεθα ἡμῖν ὑπάρχειν. Demos. Phil. i. c. 13. Δαυΐδου τε καὶ Σολομῶντας, ἔτι δὲ τῶν μεταξὺ τούτων βασιλέων. Jos. Bell. v. 4, 2. ταῖς τε μεταξὺ (sequentibus diebus). Ant. xvi, 7, 6. τοῖς μεταξὺ Μακεδονικοῖς βασιλεῦσιν. Plut. Instit. Lacon. ad finem. καὶ μεταξὺ (postea) Παρθυαίοις ἐρεθίζων. Appian, Mithrid. 105, p 263. εἶδε δέ Ἰακὼβ τύπον τῷ πνεύματι τοῦ λαοῦ τοῦ μεταξύ. Epist. Barnab, c. 13. μεταξὺ δὲ τῶν μεσογαίων τινὰς βασιλεύεσθαι παρέδωκε τοῖς ἀπὸ Πυλαιμένους. Strabo, xii. 3 (p. 14, Tauchnitz).

[119] συνήχθη. Acts xiii. 43—viz. in the same synagogue as in the previous Sabbath. See Stier's Reden der Apost. vol. ii. p. 274.

[120] Acts xiii. 46, 47. τέθεικά σε εἰς φῶς ἐθνῶν, &c. In the Septuagint the words are: Ἰδοὺ δέδωκά σε εἰς διαθήκην γένους, εἰς φῶς ἐθνῶν, &c. Isai. xlix. 6.

[121] The word in the original is τεταγμένοι,

and formed a cabal against them. Antioch was a Roman colony, and governed by Roman laws, and blood could not be shed for disputes about creeds; but, though there was no pretext at hand for taking the lives of their victims, the Jews, who had made certain proselytes amongst the wives of the chief men of the city,[122] procured, through their influence, that the Apostles should be driven out of their borders. "The Jews," says Luke, "stirred up the devout and honourable women, and the chief men of the city, and raised persecution against Paul and Barnabas, and expelled them out of their coasts."[123]

The Apostles, being thus ejected from Pisidia, shook off the dust of their feet, as a sign that their enemies, and not themselves, were to blame, and took the road to Iconium. The "shaking off the dust from the feet" was a symbolical act; but as Arundell, who pursued the same track, remarks, it may have been literally true, for no road could be more dusty than that leading from Antioch.[124]

Iconium (fig. 73) has been called the Damascus of Lycaonia. But if so, why does the

Fig. 73.—Coin of Iconium. From Pellerin.

Obs. Head of Nero, with the legend Νερων Καισαρ Σεβαστος (Nero Cæsar Augustus).—Rev. Poppæa seated, with the legend Ποππαια Σεβαστη Κλαυδεικονιεων (of Poppæa Augusta, of the Claud-Iconians). See note 131.

penman of the Acts say, presently, that when they left Iconium, "they fled into Lystra and Derbe, cities of *Lycaonia?*" The passage certainly does not affirm, positively, that Iconium was not also a city of Lycaonia, but the form of the expression rather implies it. Some, indeed (as Xenophon), call Iconium a Phrygian city. Thus, in the Expedition of Cyrus the Younger, we read that he came "to Iconium, *the last city of Phrygia;* thence he pursued his route through *Lycaonia.*"[125] Some (as Ammianus Marcellinus) account it a city of Pisidia.[126] But Cicero,[127] Strabo,[128] and others,[129] ascribe it more

which has been much relied on by many as implying predestination. But non dicuntur nec a Deo præordinati, multo minus immutabiliter præordinati, sed simpliciter tantum ordinati seu τεταγμένοι. Limborch. See the question discussed in Stier's Reden der Apost. vol. ii. p. 276.

[122] ἅπαντες τῆς δεισιδαιμονίας ἀρχηγοὺς οἴονται τὰς γυναῖκας, αὗται δὲ καὶ τοὺς ἄνδρας προκαλοῦνται πρὸς τὰς ἐπὶ πλέον θεραπείας τῶν θεῶν καὶ ἑορτὰς καὶ ποτνιασμούς. Strabo, vii. 3, 4 (p. 75, Tauchnitz).

[123] Acts xiii. 50. Renan writes: "Les deux apôtres en effet furent bannis par arrêté municipal de la ville et du territoire d'Antioche de Pisidie," St. Paul, p. 38; but if a formal decree had been passed, the Apostles could not have returned, as they not long afterwards did; or may we suppose that the edict was only temporary, or that Christianity gained so much ground that the edict was revoked?

[124] Arund. vol. i. p. 319.

[125] ἐς Ἰκόνιον τῆς Φρυγίας πόλιν ἐσχάτην. ἐντεῦθεν διελαύνει διὰ τῆς Λυκαονίας. Anab. i. 2.

[126] Pisidiæ oppidum. Amm. Marcel. xiv. 2, 1.

[127] In Lycaoniâ apud Iconium. Cicero, Epist. ad Divers. xv. 4.

[128] xii. 6 (p. 58, Tauchnitz).

[129] Plin. N. H. v. 25; Stephan. Byzant.

correctly to Lycaonia. Whatever was the origin of Iconium—whether Lycaonian, Phrygian, or Pisidian—it is sufficient to say, in justification of the language of Luke, that Iconium, at the time of the Apostles' visit, formed, with the country about it, a separate and independent principality, governed by a ruler with the title of Tetrarch. In the time of Augustus, Polemo had the tetrarchy,[130] and after him Amyntas, King of Galatia; and in the time of Pliny it was still a distinct tetrarchy, for he observes: "There is also commonly given a tetrarchy carved out of Lycaonia, where it borders on Galatia, composed of fourteen townships, Iconium being the capital."[131] This city lay at the distance of some sixty miles from Antioch of Pisidia, in a south-easterly direction, and on the highroad connecting Ephesus with Antioch of Syria—a well-known track, and traversed by some of the most distinguished characters of antiquity. Iconium still, with a slight variation, bears its ancient name, and is called Cogni. It is pleasantly situate, on the western verge of the largest plain of Asia Minor, and, like Damascus, is an oasis in the desert. The rills that flow from the mountain range on the west of the city irrigate for a little distance the low grounds which stretch away towards the east, and gardens and orchards are seen in luxuriance; but soon the water, the source of vegetation, is exhausted, and from that limit commence the dry, barren, comfortless plains of Lycaonia.[132]

The Apostles, on reaching Iconium, entered, as usual, on the Sabbath-day, into the synagogue of the Jews, who here also, as in other cities of importance, were no inconsiderable part of the population. Such was the force with which the missionaries spake, that a multitude of converts soon came over to the faith, both from Jews and Greeks.[133] It was no time to stand neuter, and the unbelieving Jews exerted all their arts to bring the new doctrine into discredit. The Apostles, however, continued to preach the word at Iconium with great boldness, and miracles were wrought by

---

[130] τοῦτο δ' (Iconium) εἶχε Πολέμων. Strabo, xii. 6 (p. 58, Tauchnitz).

[131] Datur et tetrarchia ex Lycaonia, quâ parte Galatiæ contermina est, civitatum xiv., urbe celeberrima Iconio. Plin. Nat. Hist. v. 25. The tetrarchy was bounded on the north and west sides by the *province* of Galatia. It is also possible that Iconium was at this time an independent municipality as a colony, for it appears, from the coins, that it became a colony by the name of Claudia, and therefore, it is supposed, in the time of Claudius. See Eckhel, vol. iii. p. 33; Renan's St. Paul, p. 39; and coin in preceding page.

[132] "To the east and west the city extends over the plain far beyond the walls, which are about two miles in circumference. To the north is the range of Foudhal Baba (the ancient Lycadnum), of no great elevation; and immediately behind the town to the west, the slopes of the hills are covered with gardens and pleasant meadows. A great portion of the water of a small river, which flows on the north-west side of the town towards the north-east, is absorbed in the irrigation of the gardens and fields; whilst that which remains empties itself into, or rather forms, a small lake or morass. Five or six miles north of the city, mountains, covered with snow, rise on every side, excepting towards the east, where a plain, as flat as the desert of Arabia, extends far beyond the reach of the eye. . . . In the middle of the town is a small eminence, about three-quarters of a mile in circuit, which appears to have been fortified, and where probably the old Castle of Iconium once stood . . . The population is reported to amount to nearly 30,000 souls. . . . Iconium is situate in lat. 37° 51' N." Kinneir's Asia Minor, p. 218, et seq.; and see Leake's Asia Minor, p. 48.

[133] It is at Iconium that the apocryphal Acts of the Apostles place the conversion of Thecla. Acta Pauli et Theclæ, s. 1 (Tischendorf, p. 40).

their hands, by which the truth of the Gospel was confirmed. At length the whole city was divided—some taking part with the Jews, and some with the Apostles. Such a state of things could not last, and violence began. The Jews stirred up the Gentiles, including even the rulers of the city, against the religious innovations, and the Apostles were in danger of being stoned. However, they were apprised of the plot in time, and fled to Lystra, a city of Lycaonia.

This would bring them within a new jurisdiction. The part of Lycaonia here referred to, i.e. the southern portion, comprising Isaurica and the highlands of Isauria, was disconnected both from Pisidia—where the Apostle had first preached, and which belonged to the province of Galatia—and from the separate tetrarchy of Iconium, which they had just left. This southern portion of Lycaonia had been given by

Fig. 74.—*Lycaonian soldier, from the bas-relief of an ancient tomb in Lycaonia.*

At the foot of the bas-relief was an inscription in letters supposed to be Lycaonian, but which C. Texier (from whom the print is taken) was unable, from their height from the ground, to decipher. This is much to be regretted, as a facsimile of the letters might have furnished a clue to the Lycaonian language.

Mark Antony to Amyntas,[134] and was continued to him by Augustus,[135] and on the death of Amyntas (B.C. 25) was assigned to Archelaus, King of Cappadocia, and on his death (A.D. 17) was annexed to the province of Galatia. But in A.D. 37[136] a new

---

[134] Fasti Sacri, p. 65, No. 551.   [135] Fasti Sacri, p. 73, No. 618.
[136] See Fasti Sacri, p. 250, No. 1505.

arrangement was made, and southern Lycaonia was placed under the care of Antiochus IV., King of Commagene,[137] within whose dominions it was comprised at the time of the Apostles' arrival.

Before we proceed to Lystra of Lycaonia, and the better to understand the occurrences there, we must glance at the Grecian fable connected with Lycaonia. The origin of the name Lycaonia is unknown; but as there happened to have been a king of Arcadia called Lycaon, Greek invention soon discovered a connection. It was said that Lycaon had been warned by an oracle to found a city in this part of Asia Minor (why, it does not appear), and that the whole country thence derived its appellation. But, further, Lycus (Λύκος, 'a wolf') was so near in sound to Lycaon, that the resemblance was to be accounted for; and the ready-witted Greeks originated the fable, that when the earth was filled with wickedness, Jupiter (with Mercury) descended from the skies to satisfy himself of the fact; that he visited the house of Lycaon, and that the people around, when the god was recognised, were for paying him adoration; but that Lycaon mocked the servility of his subjects, and questioned the divinity of his inmate, and served up human flesh on the table as a test by which to try the deity's omniscience; that Jupiter was enraged at the attempt, and metamorphosed Lycaon into a wolf. But let Ovid tell the tale. He introduces Jupiter as thus recounting the adventure:—

> "Fame brought the rumour to the courts of heaven
> That rebel man to direst guilt was given:
> I deemed it false, and, gliding from the skies,
> I walked the earth, a god in human guise.
> The scenes I viewed, what need I to rehearse?
> Report was infamy—the truth was worse!
> I passed o'er Mœnala, where beasts of prey,
> That prowl by night, lurk in their dens by day;
> Thence to Cyllene, and Lycæum's shade,
> And Arcady by curst Lycaon swayed.
> Evening had drawn her mantle o'er the earth,
> Ere I approached th' inhospitable hearth.
> Soon as I beckoned that a god was near,
> The people trembled with a holy fear;
> But he (Lycaon) mocked his heavenly guest,
> 'A god!' he cried; 'I will his godship test.
> I know a stratagem shall quickly prove
> An he be mortal or undoubted Jove.'
> It chanced that envoys, on affairs of weight,
> Had just arrived from the Molossian state;
> The blood of one with murderous knife he sheds,
> And of the limbs a loathsome banquet spreads;
> The mangled flesh, part boiled and roasted part,
> Was served upon the board with fiendish art;
> I sickened at the sight, and, stirred with ire,
> My lightnings launched—the palace was on fire!

---

[137] This fact is established upon the evidence of coins. See Eckhel, vol. iii. p. 256; and supra, p. 131, note.

> The caitiff fled, and scoured across the plain,
> The shelter of the distant woods to gain.
> He would have spoke, to speak in vain he tried—
> A savage howl was all the tongue supplied;
> With hungry jaws the gathered foam he churns,
> And on the bleating flock his fury turns.
> His mantle, now his hide, with rugged hairs,
> Cleaves to his back; a famished face he bears;
> His arms descend, his shoulders sink away,
> To multiply his legs for chase of prey.
> He grows a wolf, and in the wolf you scan
> The hoariness and rage that marked the man.
> His eyes still sparkle in a narrower space,
> And still a horrid grin distorts the fiendish face."[138]

Such was the legend attached to Lycaonia, and no doubt believed by many of its rude inhabitants.

Lystra, one of the principal cities, lay about forty miles to the south of Iconium, and was still upon the high road to Syria. It was situate in a hollow, on the north side of a remarkable isolated mountain rising out of the great plain, and now called Kara Dagh, or Black Mountain. Lofty peaks looked down upon the town on all sides, except on the north, where the valley opened into the plain of Iconium. The ruins of Lystra remain, and are called Bin-bir Kilisseh, or "The Thousand-and-one Churches," from the traces still visible of the numerous sacred edifices with which it was once adorned. Its glory has departed, but under the Byzantine emperors it was a place of importance, and an episcopal see.[139]

On arriving at Lystra, the Apostles commenced their labours, as usual, by preaching. Amongst their audience was a man who had been a cripple from his mother's womb. He sat amongst the audience and was listening to the Gospel, when Paul, looking steadfastly at him, and observing the faith depicted on his countenance, said with a loud voice, "Stand upright on thy feet!"[140] and he leaped up and walked. The miracle was wrought in the sight of all the people, and they burst into the exclamation, "The gods are come down to us in the likeness of men!"[141] And they called Barnabas, who was the more commanding figure, Jupiter, and Paul, who was of little stature and the chief speaker, Mercury (fig. 75).

And what did the Apostles? Did they rebuke the blasphemous adulation? Did they suffer the deluded populace to rave in their blindness? The historian adds, that the shout was "in the speech of Lycaonia."[142] The Apostles understood it not. Greek

---

[138] Ovid's Met. lib. i. v. 211. A few lines towards the end are taken from Garth's translation; for the rest the author is responsible.

[139] See Hamilton's Asia Minor, vol. ii. p. 317. We have followed Hamilton. But Kiepert, in his excellent map of Asia Minor, places Lystra on the site of some ruins at the eastern foot of Assar Dagh, on the road from Iconium to Caraman, and halfway between the two. Leake places it at Khatoun Seraï, thirty miles to the south of Iconium. Asia Minor, p. 102.

[140] Acts xiv. 10.
[141] Acts xiv. 11.
[142] Acts xiv. 11.

was the ordinary language among the higher class, and was intelligible to all; but the common folk had a language of their own, and in the astonishment of the moment, their feelings found vent in the tongue familiar from their childhood.[143] Jupiter was the guardian god of their city, and his statue was erected before their gates.[144] They believed that the days of Lycaon had returned, and that Jupiter in person, with Mercury, the constant companion of the god, had again visited the earth.[145]

Fig. 75.—*Representation of Jupiter and Mercury. From an ancient altar. From Millin's Galerie Mythologique.*

Jupiter holds in one hand a sceptre, and in the other a thunderbolt, and the globe or world is beneath him. Mercury holds in one hand the caduceus, and in the other a bag or purse, the emblem of commerce.

The Apostles, unconscious of what was in preparation, retired to their own abode; but soon, the report having spread that Jupiter and Mercury had descended from the skies, the priest of Jupiter, with a crowd at his heels, brought oxen crowned

---

[143] The Lycaonian is supposed by some to have been Cappadocian, by others a bastard Assyrian, by others a corrupt Greek (see Meyer, Apostg. p. 262); but all is conjecture, the only known Lycaonian word being that given by Stephan. Byzantinus: Δέρβη· τινὲς δὲ Δέλβειαν, ὁ ἐπὶ τῇ τῶν Λυκαόνων φωνῇ Ἄρκευθος. Paul tells us, "I speak with tongues *more* than ye all" (1 Cor. xiv. 18), but he did not understand *every* tongue. Some, however, assume that Paul did understand Lycaonian, and that he must have addressed the multitude in Lycaonian, for that they could not have understood any other tongue. But we cannot believe that they did not understand *Greek*, which was the vehicle of communication, both commercially and politically, over the whole of Asia Minor.

[144] τοῦ Διὸς τοῦ ὄντος πρὸ τῆς πόλεως αὐτῶν. Acts xiv. 13. So, Ζεὺς Πρόπυλος τῆς μεγάλης θεᾶς Ἀρτέμιδος πρὸ πόλεως. Boeckh, Corpus Inscrip. Græc. No. 2963 c.

[145] Thus Ovid, F. v. 495:—

Jupiter et Lato qui regnat in æquore frater
Carpebant socias Mercuriusque vias.

So Hyginus, Poet. Astron. 31:—

Cum Jovem et Mercurium hospiter excepisset.

So Euripides, Ion, 4:—

Ἑρμῆς μέγιστος Ζηνὸς, δαιμόνων λάτρις.

And see Wetstein ad loc.

with garlands,[146] as the custom was, before the doors of the house in which Barnabas and Paul were lodged,[147] and was about to offer them sacrifice. Horrorstruck at the

Fig. 76.—*Medal representing the ceremony of a sacrifice. From Pembroke collection.* The legend is Vota soluta pro Salute Populi Romani (vows discharged for the welfare of the Roman people).

profane superstition of the multitude, the Apostles rushed out of the house,[148] rending their clothes, and crying: "Sirs, why do ye these things? We also are men of like passions with you, and preach unto you, that ye should turn from these vanities unto the living God, which made heaven and earth, and the sea, and all things that are therein. Who in times past suffered all nations to walk in their own ways: nevertheless, he left not himself without witness, in that he did good, and gave us rain from heaven, and fruitful seasons, filling our hearts with food and gladness."[149] Thus, and in the like strain, they deprecated the madness of the people, and with difficulty could they restrain them from doing sacrifice to them as gods.

But soon the wind blew from another quarter. The Jews, whom the Apostles had left behind at Antioch of Pisidia and Iconium, had followed hard upon their heels, and now came up with them at Lystra. They denounced Paul and Barnabas as impostors, and so wrought upon the populace, that they, who a moment before could

---

[146] That an ox was the usual sacrifice to Jupiter needs no proof, but that the like victim was slain to Mercury is also evident from the lines of Persius:—

Rem struere exoptas cæsâ bove, Mercuriumque
Arcessis fibrâ.
Pers. Sat. ii. 44.

That the victims were decorated with garlands is evidenced by various passages:—

Tum fera cœruleis intexit cornua sertis.
Stat. Theb. iv. 446.

Huc taurus ingens fronte torvâ et hispidâ,
Sertis revinctus aut per armos floreis,
Aut impeditus cornibus, deducitur.
Prudentius, Peristeph. xiv. 1021.

As to the garlands, we are informed by Tertullian that ipsæ denique fores, et ipsæ hostiæ et aræ, ipsi ministri ac sacerdotes eorum coronantur. Tertull. de Coronâ, c. 10.

[147] ἐπὶ τοὺς πυλῶνας. Acts xiv. 13. πυλῶνες were the outer gates of the *house*. Thus Julius Pollux, in describing the parts of a house, writes: εἰσιόντων δὲ, πρόθυρα, καὶ προπύλαια, καὶ τὸν μὲν πυλῶνα καὶ θυρῶνα καλοῦσι. τὸ δὲ τοῦ πυλωροῦντος οἴκημα, πυλώριον. Julius Pollux, lib. i. c. 8, no. 77. Others, however, think that the gates of the *city* are referred to; and others, again, that the sacrifice was to have been made before the doors of the *temple* of Jupiter.

[148] ἐξεπήδησαν. Acts xiv. 14. In Text. Recept. εἰσεπήδησαν—'they ran in.' But Griesbach, Scholtz, Lachmann, Tischendorf, and Alford, all adopt the reading ἐξεπήδησαν.

[149] Acts xiv. 15-17. Mr. Humphry, in his Commentary on the Acts, hazards the conjecture that the latter part of this passage is a quotation from some lyric poet, and he divides the lines as follows:—

Οὐρανοῦ | θεν ἢ | μὲν ὑ | ετοὺς
διδοὺς καὶ καιροὺς | καρποφόρους,
ἐμπι | πλῶν τρο | φῆς καὶ
εὐφροσύνης | τὰς καρ | δίας

and he calls the first line an iambic, the second a dochmiac and choriambic, the third a trochaic, and the fourth a choriambic and iambic.

scarcely be prevented from worshipping the Apostles as gods, now deemed them unworthy to live as men. This was the character of the Lycaonians, ever a fickle and perfidious race.[150] The Jews, with the connivance of the bystanders, stoned Paul (the retribution for his own stoning of Stephen), and drew him out of the city, and left him for dead. The disciples, however, gathered round their champion, and he revived, and entered into the city, and the next day retired with Barnabas to Derbe.

This was another city of Lycaonia, about twenty miles distant from Lystra, at the south-eastern corner of the great Lycaonian plain, and where commence the highlands which run up to Mount Taurus. Lycaonia, in its largest sense, reached from Galatia on the north, down to the ridges of Taurus on the south; but Lycaonia *proper* did not extend beyond the great plain of Iconium towards the south; and the mountainous country between that and the peaks of Taurus was, towards the east, called Isaurica, and towards the west Isauria, both of them infested with robbers. The capital of Isaurica was Derbe. We gather but few particulars of the place from ancient writers.[151] Strabo tells us that it was on the verge of Isaurica, and knit to

---

[150] ἄπιστοι γὰρ Λυκάονες, ὡς καὶ Ἀριστοτέλης μαρτυρεῖ. Schol. in Iliad δ'. line 88; and see Cic. Ep. Fam. iii. 10.

[151] The exact site of Derbe is still *sub judice*, but the following memoranda will assist in discovering it:—

1. It was in *Isaurica*, which lay between Cilicia Aspera, and Lycaonia. Strabo, xii. 6 (p. 59, Tauchnitz).

2. It was not far from Laranda (now Karaman), for Antipater, issuing from Derbe, took Laranda, and held it with Derbe. Strabo, ibid.

3. It was on the *verge* of Isaurica, Ἰσαυρικῆς ἐν πλεύραις, and clinging to Cappadocia, μάλιστα τῇ Καππαδοκίᾳ ἐπιπεφυκώς. Strabo, ibid.

4. It was on a lake, φρούριον καὶ λίμνη. Stephan. Byzant. (for, unquestionably, λιμὴν is a mistake for λίμνη, as in Isaurica, which was inland, there could be no port).

5. This lake was Ak Ghieul, for the part of Cappadocia touched by Derbe was the county of Castabala and Cybistra: προσεγίνετο δ᾽ ὕστερον παρὰ Ῥωμαίων ἐκ τῆς Κιλικίας ... ἑνδεκάτη στρατηγία, ἡ περὶ Καστάβαλά τε καὶ Κύβιστρα μέχρι τῆς Ἀντιπάτρου τοῦ λῃστοῦ Δέρβης. Strabo, xii. 1 (p. 4, Tauchnitz); and the part of Cappadocia, about Castabala and Cybistra, bordered on Lake Ak Ghieul on the east, as may thus be shown.

In the first place, the Cybistra, here referred to, must not be confounded with that mentioned in the Peutinger Table, and stated to be only nine miles from Caesarea Mazaca. The Cybistra of Strabo was much more to the south, for it was carved out of Cilicia, ἐκ τῆς Κιλικίας (see supra), and therefore adjoined it. And to the same effect is the language of Cicero, who, when Proconsul of Cilicia, marched a little way through the Cilician Gates, with the view of defending Cilicia, and at the same time of taking a view of Cappadocia; and he pitched his camp *in Cappadocia extremâ* non longe a Tauro apud oppidum *Cybistra*. Cic. Ep. Fam. xv. 4, 1.

Again, Castabala and Cybistra were not far from Tyana, but nearer to the Cilician Gates: οὐ πολὺ δ᾽ ἄπωθεν ταύτης (Tyana) ἐστὶ τά τε Καστάβαλα καὶ τὰ Κύβιστρα, ἔτι μᾶλλον τῷ ὄρει πλησιάζοντα πολίσματα. Strabo, xii. 2 (p. 8, Tauchnitz). But further, Strabo, in speaking of the road from Caesarea Mazaca to the Cilician Gates, tells us that Tyana was halfway, κατὰ μέσην δὲ τὴν ὁδὸν κεῖται τὰ Τύανα (Strabo, xii. 2; p. 11, Tauchnitz); and the distance between Caesarea Mazaca and Tyana was, according to the Peutinger Table, seventy-three miles, which was therefore the distance between Tyana and the Cilician Gates. It would not be nearly so much as the crow flies; but the direct line was quite impracticable, from the high mountain range between, and then, as now, the traveller from Tyana had to go round by Eregli to get to the Cilician Gates, and then the distance is seventy-three miles. Strabo, in speaking of this road from Tyana to the Cilician pass, adds, that the distance from Tyana to Cybistra is 300 stades,

Cappadocia.¹⁵² Stephanus Byzantinus calls it a "*stronghold*" of Isauria, with a lake of the same name.¹⁵³ Hamilton, who was pursuing the old route from Tarsus, through the Cilician Gates, by way of Eregli, to the west, informs us that when he started from Eregli, he had the mountains on his left, and Ak Ghieul, or the White Lake, on the right; and that when the snows melted, and the lake rose, the road was impassable. After emerging from this narrow pass, he came to the ruins of an ancient city. The Acropolis stood on an isolated mound, and had been surrounded by a wall and ditch. It was about a quarter of a mile in circumference, and on its summit were foundations of buildings, and fragments of pottery, considerable remains of houses, streets, &c., with fallen columns extending round it in every direction. The Acropolis (which answers to "the stronghold") and the vicinity of the lake (now Ak Ghieul), and other corresponding particulars, seem to identify the spot as the site of Derbe.¹⁵⁴ Strabo (whose geography is very judiciously interspersed with brief historical notices) mentions that Derbe had been the citadel of the famous freebooter Antipater, who, making this his headquarters, scoured the Lycaonian plain and all the adjacent country.¹⁵⁵ Antipater must have been no ordinary person, for, though a robber-chief, he was the friend of Cicero, who for a year was Prætor of Cilicia.¹⁵⁶ Eventually Amyntas, King of Galatia, attacked and slew Antipater, and

or nearly thirty-one miles (Strabo, xii. 2, p. 11, Tauchnitz), and this measurement along the road from Tyana takes us to Eregli, by Lake Ak Ghieul. It is clear, therefore, that Eregli, on Lake Ak Ghieul, or its immediate vicinity, represents the site of the ancient Cybistra, and accordingly, on Kiepert's map, Cybistra is placed there.

6. Derbe, according to the Patriarch Cyril, was two hours from Derbent Bogaz, and nine hours from Iconium. τὸ Μπάμπρα χωρίον πέντε ὥρας ἀφιστάμενον τοῦ Ἰκονίου, δύο ὥρας ἔμπροσθεν ἐστι τὸ ἐρείπιον εἰς τὸ στόμιον τοῦ Δερβέντ Πογαζί, καὶ ἔτι δύο ὥρας τὸ χωρίον Δερβέντι, ἄνω εἰς τὴν ὀφρὺν τοῦ ὄρους εἶναι τὰ ἐρείπια τῆς πάλαι Δέρβης λεγομένης πόλεως. Cyril's Ἀρχισατραπία, cited Arundell's Asia Minor, vol. ii. p. 91.

Upon the whole, we must conclude that Derbe was either upon, or but little removed from, Lake Ak Ghieul, and most probably on the spot above described in the text, where Kiepert also places it.

¹⁵² τῆς Ἰσαυρικῆς ἐστιν ἐν πλευραῖς ἡ Δέρβη, μάλιστα τῇ Καππαδοκίᾳ ἐπιπεφυκὸς τὸ τοῦ Ἀντιπάτρου τυραννεῖον τοῦ Δερβήτου. Strabo, xii. 6 (p. 59, Tauchnitz).

¹⁵³ Δέρβη φρούριον Ἰσαυρίας καὶ λίμνη, Καπίτων δὲ Δέρμην φησί. τινὲς δὲ Δελβείαν, ὅ ἐστι ἐν τῇ τῶν Λυκαόνων φωνῇ Ἄρκευθος, καὶ Ἀρκεύθη ἡ πόλις (Stephanus Byzant.), which shows incidentally that the Lycaonians had a language of their own. For λίμην should be read λίμνη, Derbe being an inland town, and not a port, but in the neighbourhood of an extensive lake—viz. Ak Ghieul. Wetstein adduces an ancient coin with the inscription, Δερβη Κλαυδια Κοινον Λυκαονιας, from which it would appear that the parliament or council of Lycaonia met at Derbe. But Eckhel considers this a mistake, and that the inscription has been miscopied; and it certainly sounds strange that the parliament of Lycaonia should meet at so small a town as Derbe. See Eckhel, vol. iii. p. 32.

¹⁵⁴ Hamilton's Asia Minor, vol. ii. p. 313. Kiepert also, on his map, places it here. Hamilton, however, suggests that Divlé, many miles to the south, may be Derbe which was called Delbia, and of which Divlé may be the corruption; but there does not appear to be any λίμνη (or lake) in that quarter. Colonel Leake thought that Bin-bir Kilisseh (The Thousand-and-one Churches) was Derbe, and that Lystra was at Wiran Khatoun, or Khatoun Ycai, thirty miles to the south of Iconium. Leake's Asia Minor, p. 102; see also Arundell's Asia Minor, vol. ii. p. 91.

¹⁵⁵ See Strabo, xii. 6 (p. 59, Tauchnitz).

¹⁵⁶ Cum Antipatro Derbete mihi non solum hospitium, verum etiam summa familiaritas intercedit. Cic. Ep. Fam. xiii. 73.

then all Isauria and Isaurica, including Derbe, came under the power of Amyntas. On his death, in B.C. 25, the same regions were made over to Archelaus [157] (fig. 77).

Fig. 77.—*Coin of Archelaus, King of Cappadocia. From Pellerin.*
Obv. Head, but no legend. Rev. ΒΑΣΙΛΕΩΣ ΑΡΧΕΛΑΟΥ ΦΙΛΟΠΑΤΡΙΔΟΣ ΤΟΥ ΚΤΙΣΤΟΥ ΤΗΣ ΑΡΧΕΛΑΙΔΟΣ ΣΕΒΑΣΤΗΣ. The Founder, viz. of Eleussa, the island and city of that name, and called, in honour of Augustus, Sebaste).

who died in A.D. 17,[158] when it was annexed to the Roman province of Galatia. But twenty years after, viz. in A.D. 37, the south-eastern part of Lycaonia, which included Derbe, was assigned to Antiochus, King of Commagene,[159] to whom it belonged at the time of Paul's arrival [160] (fig. 78).

Fig. 78.—*Coin of Antiochus IV. of Commagene. From Pellerin.*
Obv. Head, with the legend ΒΑΣΙΛΕΥΣ ΑΝΤΙΟΧΟΣ (King Antiochus).—Rev. A scorpion, with the legend ΛΥΚΑΟΝΩΝ (of the Lycaonians).

Nothing daunted by past persecution, Paul and Barnabas now began their labours at Derbe with fresh zeal. The period of their sojourn there is uncertain, but they made many disciples. This was the utmost limit of their first circuit [A.D. 45–46], but for what reason they here bent their steps back we can only conjecture. Possibly their original intention may have been to proceed along the high road through Eregli, to the Cilician Gates, and so by Tarsus to Antioch, but that the floods were out (which in winter cover all the plain to the north), so that they could not pass round Lake Ak Ghieul. Across the mountains it might not be safe to travel, from the swarms of banditti, nor could they have found the necessary accommodation. It may be in allusion to circumstances connected with this part of his history that Paul afterwards speaks to the Corinthians of his having been "in perils of waters, and in perils of robbers." [161] Besides, Derbe was very near to Cilicia, and the latter province had already been evangelised by Paul from Tarsus, during his residence there some years before. The Apostles may also have been actuated by other prudent considerations, for to render their past labours effective, much still remained to be done. They had been hurried away by persecution, without a moment's notice, from Antioch of

---

[157] See Fasti Sacri, p. 82, No. 675.
[158] See Fasti Sacri, p. 162, No. 1087.
[159] See Fasti Sacri, p. 250, No. 1505.
[160] See ante, p. 131, note.
[161] 2 Cor. xi. 26.

Pisidia to Iconium, from Iconium to Lystra, and from Lystra to Derbe, and they had not had the opportunity of forming their Christian converts into organised societies.

Whatever were their real motives, the Apostles from Derbe retraced their steps successively through Lystra, and Iconium, and Antioch of Pisidia; and as they passed through these cities, composed the minds of the disciples, and strengthened them against the troubles to which they were exposed from their unbelieving townsmen, telling them, with all candour, that the kingdom of heaven was only to be won through much tribulation. In every church also they appointed a day of prayer and fasting, and ordained ministers, or elders, to watch over the flock. Paul and Barnabas had

Fig. 79.—*View of the Port of Attalia, the spectator looking west. From Corne's Syria.*

themselves been ordained Apostles (answering to our bishops) by the church of Antioch, and they now ordained priests to take charge of the churches planted by them.[162] They then committed their converts to the Lord, and crossing Pisidia and Pamphylia, came down to Perga. Here, as they had not proclaimed the Gospel on their arrival from Cyprus, they now made a short pause to preach the Word,[163] which when they had done, they crossed over to Attalia (now Adalia, fig. 79), about sixteen

---

[162] χειροτονήσαντες δὲ αὐτοῖς κατ᾽ ἐκκλησίαν (church by church) πρεσβυτέρους (elders or priests). Acts xiv. 23. This was not the first ordination of priests, but is the first express mention of such ordination.

[163] λαλήσαντες ἐν Πέργῃ τὸν λόγον. Acts xiv. 25. They had, therefore, not preached it there on the occasion of their former visit.

miles to the west of Perga,[164] situate on the north-eastern corner of a fine bay, and possessing a good haven, around which the city arose like a vast amphitheatre (fig. 80). Here they found a ship, in which they embarked, and returned to Antioch in Syria,

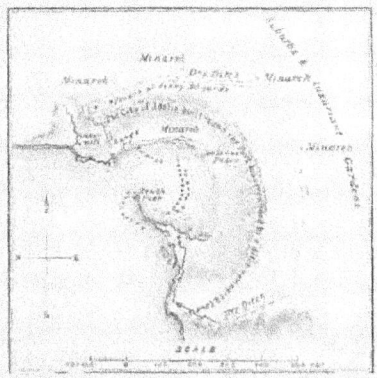

Fig. 80.—*Plan of the port and city of Adalia, the ancient Attalia. From Admiralty Chart.*

Fig. 81.—*Coin of Attalia. From Calmet.*
Obv. Head of Neptune, with trident.—Rev. Figure, with the legend Ἀτταλέων (of the Attalians).

whence they had been commissioned to the work which they had so successfully achieved. On their arrival at Antioch they called together the church, and recounted, to the great joy of the disciples, with what eminent success the door of the Gospel had been thrown open to the Gentiles.[165]

---

[164] The distance is taken from the Handbook for Asia Minor. The ancient Attalia is unquestionably the modern Adalia, a port still much frequented. The exact name has been preserved, and the site agrees. Some, indeed, have doubted the identity from a slight mis-description in Strabo. In tracing the southern coast of Asia Minor from west to east he enumerates the places in the following order: Μετὰ Φασηλίδα δ' ἐστὶν ἡ Ὀλβία, τῆς Παμφυλίας ἀρχή, μέγα ἔρυμα, καὶ μετὰ ταύτην ὁ Καταρράκτης λεγόμενος . . . εἶτα πόλις Ἀττάλεια, xiv. 4 (p. 218, Tauchnitz); so that Attalia would be to the east of the Catarractes, now the Duden Su. But this is a mistake, and corrected by Ptolemy, who gives the coast of Pamphylia thus: Ὀλβία, Ἀττάλεια, Καταρράκτου ποταμοῦ ἐκβολαί, v. 5, 2. So that Attalia was the nearest town to the *west* of the Catarractes, or Duden Su, and the modern Adalia corresponds to this. There can be no doubt that the Catarractes is the Duden Su, for Mela mentions Perga (which was on the right bank of the Cestrus or Ak Su) as between the Cestrus and the Catarractes. "Cestrus et Catarractes . . . Inter eos Perga est oppidum," i. 14; and if so, the Catarractes was the next river on the west to the Cestrus, or Ak Su.

The origin of Attalia was a small settlement called Corycus; but Attalus II. (Philadelphus), King of Pergamus, added a suburb, and inclosed the whole with a wall, and gave it the name of Attalia (fig. 81). Strabo, xiv. 4 (p. 218, Tauchnitz); and see Stephan. Byzant.

[165] Acts xiv. 27. There is nothing to show, as some assume, that Paul and Barnabas kept a written journal of their proceedings, and that they now laid it before the church.

CHAPTER IX.

The Council at Jerusalem on the Question whether the Law of Moses should be observed by the Gentiles.

> The councils called by rulers of the earth
> Are fleeting shadows; for the mightiest state,
> Like to a bubble, has no sooner birth
> Than it is scattered by the blast of fate.
> Not so where saints with holy zeal debate
> Of truths eternal, and the living way
> That leads direct to the celestial gate.
> Their high resolves will be the Christian's stay,
> When time shall be no more, and worlds have rolled away.
>   Anon.

THE duration of this, the first circuit, has not been mentioned, but, considering the countries that were traversed, it may be reckoned at about two years.[1] Their return to Antioch, in Syria, may therefore be placed at the close of A.D. 46.[2]

---

[1] It is difficult to fix the exact commencement or the exact duration of the first circuit. Paul and Barnabas were certainly at Jerusalem at the Passover of A.D. 44, a little before the death of Herod Agrippa I. (see Fasti Sacri, p. 280, No. 1678). The circuit, therefore, was begun some time after this, and as Mark returned with Paul and Barnabas from Jerusalem, and then accompanied them on the circuit, and as Luke records the commencement of the circuit immediately after the return of Paul and Barnabas (Acts xii. 25; xiii. 1), we are led to infer that no long interval elapsed between the two events. We may assume, therefore, that Paul and Barnabas entered upon their first mission in the spring of A.D. 45. The next date of any certainty is the arrival of Paul at Corinth, when he met with Aquila on the expulsion of the Jews from Rome in the first quarter of A.D. 52 (see Fasti Sacri, p. 295, No. 1773); and before reaching Corinth, Paul had spent a long time in Macedonia, long enough to plant permanent churches at Philippi, and Thessalonica, and Berœa, and these labours must have occupied the whole of A.D. 51. Before that, he had evangelised Galatia and Phrygia, and had again revisited the churches of Lystra, and Derbe, Iconium, and Antioch of Pisidia; and the ministry in these countries could scarcely be compressed within one year, and, probably, occupied the consecutive years of A.D. 49 and 50. Before setting out on this, the second circuit, Paul and Barnabas had sojourned a little while in Antioch itself: Παῦλος δὲ καὶ Βαρνάβας διέτριβον ἐν Ἀντιοχείᾳ, ... μετὰ δέ τινας ἡμέρας, &c., Acts xv. 35, 36; and before this, they had gone up to Jerusalem and attended the council there, Acts xv. 1, which event we should assign to the preceding year, A.D. 48; and on their way to the council they spread the news through Phenicia and Samaria, of the great success which had attended their first circuit, xv. 3; from which we may gather that the circuit had closed not very long before. But the council did not follow *immediately* after the close of the circuit, for between the two it is expressly said that they remained

[2] See Fasti Sacri, p. 285, No. 1707.

They continued here "no little time"² (an indefinite expression which may be taken to signify about a year), when a question was agitated at Antioch of the utmost importance to the Gentile converts. The church of Antioch, from its flourishing condition and the great success which had attended the labours of its missionaries, had attracted to it more than ever the attention of the elder sister of Jerusalem. It was while Paul and Barnabas were engaged in their wonted ministry at Antioch that some Jewish converts of the sect of the Pharisees came down from Jerusalem, and, accustomed as they had been in the metropolis of their nation (where the inhabitants were exclusively Jews) to see the strictest observance of the law of Moses, they were shocked to find that at Antioch the barrier between Jew and Gentile had been simply broken down. It was too late for them to contend, since the call of Cornelius [A.D. 40], that the Gentiles were not to be admitted into the Christian pale, but they insisted that the Gospel was never meant to supersede the Law, but to be ingrafted upon it, that baptism, in short, could only be effectual if accompanied with circumcision. Paul and Barnabas resolutely withstood this encroachment, and we wonder only that they should not, by their own authority, have succeeded at once in crushing a doctrine so opposed to the spirit of the new religion. The intruders, however, carried the greater weight, as, having lately arrived from Jerusalem, they claimed to represent the sentiments of a church to whose judgment the infant Christendom must implicitly have deferred.

The dispute at Antioch ran so high that no alternative remained for calming the storm but to send a deputation to Jerusalem, from which the disturbers of the public peace had proceeded, and submit the question for decision at the fountain head. Paul and Barnabas, and some others, were selected for the purpose, and being furnished with the necessary means,⁴ they set forward on their journey by land. Their road, after leaving Syria, lay through Phenicia and Samaria, and as they traversed those countries they published among the brethren the extraordinary progress which the

at Antioch no little time, χρόνον οὐκ ὀλίγον, Acts xiv. 28, which may account for the year A.D. 47. Our conclusion, therefore, upon the whole would be, that the first circuit commenced in the spring of A.D. 45, and ended just before the winter of A.D. 46–47.

The order of events would therefore be as follows:—

A.D. 44. Paul and Barnabas are at Jerusalem at the Passover.
A.D. 45. Paul and Barnabas begin their circuit at Cyprus.
A.D. 46. They continue the circuit in Pisidia and Lycaonia, and return to Antioch.
A.D. 47. They sojourn at Antioch χρόνον οὐκ ὀλίγον, Acts xiv. 28.
A.D. 48. They attend the council at Jerusalem and return to Antioch, where they remain τινὰς ἡμέρας, Acts xv. 36.
A.D. 49. Paul commences his second circuit and revisits the churches of Lycaonia and Pisidia, and evangelises Phrygia.
A.D. 50. He is occupied in Phrygia and Galatia.
A.D. 51. He evangelises Macedonia.
A.D. 52. He meets Aquila and Priscilla at Corinth in the first quarter.

² χρόνον οὐκ ὀλίγον. Acts xiv. 28.
⁴ προπεμφθέντες ὑπὸ τῆς ἐκκλησίας. Acts xv. 3; or, as others understand it, "being escorted by their brethren a part of the way."

Gospel had lately made amongst the Gentiles, and as apparently the successful propagation of Christianity in heathen countries under the auspices of Paul and Barnabas was still new to their ears, no very long interval could have elapsed since the conclusion of their circuit. The mission to Jerusalem may therefore be assigned to A.D. 48.[7]

Paul and Barnabas, on arriving at Jerusalem, were warmly received by the church. They again recounted their labours in the Gentile vineyard, and the astonishing fruits which had been the result. "But," said the deputation, "there rose up certain of the sect of the Pharisees which believed, saying that it was needful to circumcise them, and to command them to keep the law of Moses."[8]

Before proceeding we must advert for a moment to the state of the church at Jerusalem. For some years after the Ascension the Apostles remained in the metropolis to give stability to the newly-formed community, and it is a very ancient tradition that the Apostolic body superintended the formation of the Christian church for a period of twelve years,[7] which would terminate about A.D. 45. Be this as it may, the time would at length arrive when, in obedience to the high behest laid upon them, the Apostles were to disperse themselves into the remotest countries, to carry thither the glad tidings of the Gospel. Some, perhaps, began their commission at an earlier period than others, and some, as Peter and John, might occasionally return, while others might never again revisit their native land. It would seem that from very early times it had been found necessary, from the very nature of things, that some person should be permanently appointed president to maintain order among the members of the church. James the Just, called "the brother of our Lord," the son (and probably the eldest son) of Joseph and Mary,[8] was elected the first bishop. The title of bishop, in the sense now attached to it, had not yet come into use, but that James exercised episcopal functions there can be no reasonable doubt. Thus when Paul returned from Damascus to Jerusalem, in the year A.D. 39,[9] to seek out Peter, "other of the Apostles," he writes, "saw I none, save *James the Lord's brother*;"[10] from

---

[7] See Fasti Sacri, p. 288, No. 1723.
[8] Acts xv. 5.
[7] Euseb. E. H. v. 18; Clem. Alex. Strom. vi. 5, 43.

[8] The genealogy of our Lord's family was this:

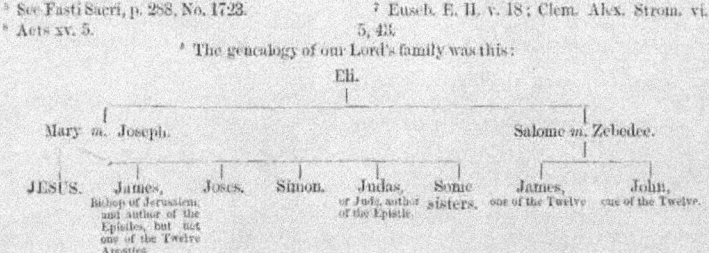

For the proofs of this see Fasti Sacri, p. 181, No. 119.

[9] See Fasti Sacri, p. 264, No. 1551. [10] Gal. i. 19.

which we may infer that James was then constantly resident at the capital in some official capacity. A few years after, when Peter was miraculously released from his incarceration under Agrippa, he said, "Go shew these things unto James, and to the brethren."[11] But why tell it to James unless as representative of the church? Again, in the Galatians, Paul writes, "And when James, Cephas, and John (who seemed to be pillars) perceived the grace that was given unto me," &c.[12] Why should James be now first named, when invariably in the Gospels the precedence is given to Peter? And in the same Epistle, in allusion to a remarkable incident at Antioch, we read, "For before that certain came from James, he (Peter) did eat with the Gentiles."[13] Why is James put forward as head of the church at Jerusalem? So when Paul, at the close of his third circuit, proceeded to Jerusalem to greet the church there, St. Luke adds, "The day following Paul went in with us unto James, and all the elders were present,"[14] which clearly shows that James then held the principal rank. But there cannot be a stronger proof of the supremacy lodged with this Apostle than the authority assigned to him at the great council which led to this discussion, and to which we now return.

We must apprise the reader that the council which was called at Jerusalem was not a general council of different churches by their delegates, but of the Apostles and presbyters and deacons and laity of Jerusalem only, from which church the Pharisaical Christians who maintained the necessity of circumcision had proceeded.

Such of the Apostles as were then found at Jerusalem were no doubt all present, though James and Peter only are expressly named. The presbyters or priests, and deacons, attended generally, and the lay brethren were at least auditors, if they were not invited to take part in the controversy. James, as bishop, took the chair.

The debate appears to have been opened by speakers of inferior note. All eyes, however, were turned towards Peter, who held the keys of the kingdom of heaven, or, in other words, had been the instrument by which the privileges of the Gospel were extended to the Gentiles,[15] and he addressed the venerable conclave as follows:—
"Men and brethren! Ye know how that a good while ago[16] God made choice among us, that the Gentiles by my mouth should hear the word of the Gospel and believe. And God, which knoweth the hearts, bare them witness, giving them the Holy Ghost, even as he did unto us; and put no difference between us and them, purifying their hearts by faith. Now, therefore, why tempt ye God, to put a yoke upon the neck of

---

[11] Acts xii. 17.
[12] Gal. ii. 9.
[13] Gal. ii. 12.
[14] Acts xxi. 18.
[15] Roman Catholics argue that the popes, as successors of St. Peter, are the supreme heads of the church, and infallible. The answer of Protestants is, that Peter himself neither claimed to be supreme nor infallible, for that James the bishop presided at the council and pronounced the decree, and Peter gave his advice only; and that had Peter been pope, the appeal itself would have been to him personally, and he would have issued his bull, whereas the appeal was to the council, and the decree was issued by James.
[16] Viz. eight years before, in A.D. 40. See Fasti Sacri, p. 268, No. 1008.

the disciples, which neither our fathers nor we were able to bear? But we believe that through the *grace* of the Lord Jesus Christ we shall be saved, even as they."

The argument was followed up by Paul and Barnabas, who rehearsed the signs and wonders which God had wrought by their hands among the Gentile nations.

Peter, Paul, and Barnabas, and the other speakers, having concluded, the debate was closed—

When James, who, as bishop, presided, moved that the Gentiles be not bound to observe the law. "Men and brethren," he said, "hearken unto me. Symeon hath declared how God at the first did visit the Gentiles, to take out of them a people for his name; and to this agree the words of the prophets, as it is written, 'After this I will return, and will build again the tabernacle of David, which is fallen down, and I will build again the ruins thereof, and I will set it up; that the residue of men may seek after the Lord, even all the *Gentiles*, who are called after my name, saith the Lord, who doeth all these things.'[17] Known unto God are all his works from the beginning of the world. Wherefore my sentence is, that we trouble not them, which from among the Gentiles are turned to God; but that we write unto them, that they abstain from pollutions of idols, and from fornication, and from things strangled, and from blood; for Moses of old time hath in every city them that preach him, being read in the synagogues every Sabbath day."[18] This resolution, as proposed by James, was acquiesced in and carried without a dissentient voice.[19]

It was a frequent custom in ancient times, when a letter was despatched, to give it in charge to confidential messengers, not only to prevent any suspicion that the document might have been tampered with, but that the sentiments of the writers might be more fully expounded by word of mouth; and on this occasion the church of Jerusalem adopted the precaution of selecting two of the pastors of their flock,

---

[17] In the Septuagint, from which the passage is taken, the words are, 'Ἐν τῇ ἡμέρᾳ ἐκείνῃ ἀναστήσω τὴν σκηνὴν Δαυὶδ τὴν πεπτωκυῖαν, καὶ ἀνοικοδομήσω τὰ πεπτωκότα αὐτῆς, καὶ τὰ κατεσκαμμένα αὐτῆς ἀναστήσω, καὶ ἀνοικοδομήσω αὐτὴν καθὼς αἱ ἡμέραι τοῦ αἰῶνος, ὅπως ἐκζητήσωσιν οἱ κατάλοιποι τῶν ἀνθρώπων, καὶ πάντα τὰ ἔθνη ἐφ' οὓς ἐπικέκληται τὸ ὄνομά μου ἐπ' αὐτῶν, λέγει Κύριος ὁ ποιῶν πάντα ταῦτα. Amos ix. 11, 12. It is evident that the speaker is citing, not from the Hebrew text, which considerably differs, but from the Septuagint version, with just such variations as a person would make who is quoting from memory. Besides, the deputation was from Antioch, a Greek city, and the letter from the church of Jerusalem to the provincials has the Greek salutation and valediction, and Greek was well understood at Jerusalem. Some, however, think that James was speaking in the Aramaic, or Hebrew, the common language at Jerusalem, and that this would account for Peter being referred to by the name of Symeon, the Hebrew form, instead of Simon the Greek form.

[18] The same fact is noticed by Josephus. ἑκάστης ἑβδομάδος τῶν ἄλλων ἔργων ἀφεμένους ἐπὶ τὴν ἀκρόασιν τοῦ νόμου ἐκέλευσεν [Moses] συλλέγεσθαι. Jos. contra Apion. ii. 17. The Law only was originally read, and was divided into sections or parasehioth. But when the reading of the Law was forbidden by Antiochus Epiphanes the Prophets were read and were divided into fifty-four sections, called haphtoroth. When the reading of the Law was again permitted, the Jews, nevertheless, continued also to read the Prophets, so that in the synagogue service, in the time of the Apostles, lessons were read from both the Law and the Prophets. Note by F. M. (F. Martin).

[19] Acts xv. 21.

Judas, surnamed Barsabas, and Silas or Sylvanus, and by their hands a letter was addressed to the Christian communities in Antioch and the adjoining countries. It ran thus:—

"The Apostles, and Elders, and Brethren, unto the brethren which are of the Gentiles in Antioch, and Syria, and Cilicia, greeting.[20]

"Forasmuch as we have heard, that certain which went out from us have troubled you with words subverting your souls, saying ye must be circumcised, and keep the Law, to whom we gave no such commandment, it hath seemed good unto us, being assembled with one accord, to send chosen men unto you, with our beloved Barnabas and Paul, men that have hazarded their lives for the name of our Lord Jesus Christ. We have sent therefore Judas and Silas, who shall also tell you the same things by mouth. For it hath seemed good to the Holy Ghost, and to us, to lay upon you no greater burden than these necessary things—*that ye abstain from meats offered to idols,*[21] *and from blood,*[22] *and from things strangled,*[23] *and from fornication.*[24] From which if ye keep yourselves, ye shall do well. FARE YE WELL."[25]

---

[20] χαίρειν (the Greek salutation in a letter). Acts xv. 23.

[21] When the heathen sacrificed they devoted part (as the entrails) to the gods, and either feasted on the rest in the idol temple, or sent it to the market for sale. A Jew was strictly prohibited from eating it in the idol temple, and also from purchasing it in the market if informed whence it came. But he might buy without asking questions. Thus the Talmud: Si quis omit et nescit ex quâ [tabernâ] emerit, si dubitat, prohibitum ipsi edere. Quod si vero inveniat [in plateâ] ὡς ἐπὶ τὸ πολὺ esse creditur [i.e. licitum]. Ketuvoth, fol. 131, cited Schoettgen's Horæ Hebr. vol. i. p. 465.

[22] To a Jew the blood was the life thereof (Gen. ix. 4) and therefore forbidden, but the Gentile partook of it freely. Thus,

γαστέρες αἵ δ' αἰγῶν εἰσί ἐν πυρί, τὰς δ' ἐνὶ δόρπῳ
κατθέμεθα, κνίσσης τε καὶ αἵματος ἐμπλήσαντες.
Homer, Od. xviii. 44.

And see other passages cited in Schoettgen's Horæ Hebr. vol. i. p. 466.

[23] The heathen had no scruple about eating things strangled; but to the Jews it was forbidden, as they could not eat unless the blood were first poured out. Levit. xvii. 14; De Wette, Apostg. 122. See Athenæus, lib. ix. (p. 316, Tauchnitz); Hesych. sub voce Πνιξαντες; and Horat. Satir. ii. 4, v. 17.

[24] The fact that fornication should be found amongst *ceremonial* matters has occasioned surprise and led to much discussion. Amongst the various explanations are the following:—

1. The simplest, and perhaps the soundest view, is to take the word as signifying fornication in its ordinary acceptation.

2. Others think that idolatry is here meant, which among the Jews was commonly called fornication.

3. Others, that marriage with a heathen is meant, which also by the Jews was classed under the head of fornication.

4. Others, that marriage within the prohibited degrees is referred to under the name of fornication.

5. Others, that the πορνεία θυσία is reprobated, i.e. the practice amongst Gentile courtesans of offering to the gods a portion of the wages of their prostitution.

6. Others, that πορνεία is here derived from πέρνημι, 'to sell,' and that the word means the meats sacrificed to idols and then *sold* in the markets. But see 1 Cor. x. 25, 26.

7. Others, that unnatural crimes are reproved.

8. Others, that the text is corrupt, and that for πορνεία should be read πορκεία or χοιρεία, i.e. swine's flesh. See generally on the subject, Kuinoel and Poli Synopsis ad locum.

[25] Ἔρρωσθε, &c. Acts xv. 29. This was the usual close of a Greek letter, and shows that the epistle, as addressed to churches where Greek was spoken, was written in Greek. Meyer, Apostg. 282. Stier, Reden der Apost. vol. i. p. 48, cites the passage of Artemidorus, Ἴδιον πάσης ἐπιστολῆς τὸ Χαίρειν καὶ Ἔρρωσο λέγειν.

This decree of the Church, as to the *ceremonial* part of it, was founded on the principle that the Law of Moses had been superseded, but that things indifferent in themselves might become sinful, where the use of the liberty would hurt unnecessarily the consciences of weaker brethren. The doctrine is fully set forth in the First Epistle to the Corinthians, and was perhaps enforced by the writer in similar language at the council of Jerusalem. "If meat," he says, "make my brother to offend, I will eat no flesh while the world standeth, lest I make my brother to offend."[26] The intention of the decree of the council was not to impose on Christendom any part of the Mosaic law, but their *recommendation* was, that in order to avoid shocking the consciences of converts, whose prejudices could not be removed in a day, the Gentiles would do well to abstain, where indulgence would by others be accounted criminal.[27]

It will be observed that the missive was directed to the brethren of "Antioch, and Syria, and Cilicia," where the Jews were so numerous that no principal town was without a synagogue, and the ground on which James based the admonition was, that "Moses of old time hath in every city them that preach him, being read in the synagogues every Sabbath day."[28] The *abstinence* from meats and blood and things strangled were not to embrace the whole world, but to be governed by locality and surrounding circumstances; while the general *exemption* of the Gentiles from the observance of the Jewish law was not confined to Antioch, Syria, and Cilicia, but was meant to have a universal application, and James himself afterwards referred to the decree as of this comprehensive character.[29]

It has excited surprise with some, that a caution against fornication, a precept drawn from the code of morality, should have found a place in an enumeration of things in themselves indifferent. At the introduction of Christianity, such was the depravity of mankind, that not only did no opprobrium attach to the vice, but it was often part of the worship of heathens, and entered into their religious rites.[30]

---

[26] 1 Cor. viii. 13.

[27] The ceremonial injunctions as to eating blood, &c., were intended only to be temporary, and were afterwards superseded. See note post to Galat. xi. 1. The Greek church, nevertheless, holds these ordinances to be binding on the consciences of Christians at the present day. See De Wette, Apostg. 123.

[28] Acts xv. 21.

[29] Acts xxi. 25; and so he had stated the question, as a general one, in his address to the council. Acts xv. 19.

[30] The light in which fornication was regarded by the ancients is well expressed by Cicero. Si quis est, qui etiam meretriciis amoribus interdictum juventuti putet, est ille quidem valde severus. Quando enim hoc factum non est? quando reprehensum? quando non permissum? Cic. pro Cælio, c. 20, 48. So in Terence we read,

Non est flagitium, mihi crede, adolescentulum
Scortari.   Adelph. i, 2, 21.

And in Horace,

Quidam notus homo quum exiret fornice, Macte
Virtute esto, inquit sententia dia Catonis.
            Sat. i, 2, 31.

Prostitution was part of the public worship of Venus, and at Corinth her temple, which was one of the attractions of the place, had attached to it more than a thousand courtesans: Τό τε τῆς Ἀφροδίτης ἱερὸν οὕτω πλούσιον ὑπῆρξεν, ὥστε πλείους ἢ χιλίας ἱεροδούλους ἐκέκτητο ἑταίρας, Strabo, viii. 6 (p. 211, Tauchnitz); and the famous Lais was the ruin of hundreds of merchants,

We find it, therefore, in conjunction with "meats offered to idols," for both were, in practice, blended together.

Paul and Barnabas and their company, having concluded their mission, returned to Antioch, taking with them Judas and Silas, the envoys of the church at Jerusalem. On their arrival at Antioch, the letter was publicly read, and the minds of the disciples were at length tranquillised from the storm which had so violently agitated them. Judas and Silas, who were notable speakers,[31] were also instrumental in explaining and enforcing orally the scope of the epistle. When Judas and Silas had executed the high charge committed to them, which must have occupied some time,[32] Judas returned to Jerusalem, while Silas remained at Antioch with Paul and Barnabas.

---

from the high price of her favours. But while no discredit was attached to the use of the courtesan, the profession which she followed was not generally a reputable one, and in the time of Tiberius, A.D. 19, a law was passed that if any daughter, or granddaughter, or widow, of a Roman *knight* became a courtesan it should be a punishable offence. Cautumque, ne quæstum corpore faceret, cui avus, aut pater, aut maritus eques Romanus fuisset. Tac. Ann. ii. 85.

[31] προφῆται ὄντες. Acts xv. 32.
[32] ποιήσαντες χρόνον. Acts xv. 33.

CHAPTER X.

*Paul's Second Circuit—He visits Cilicia, Lycaonia, Pisidia, Phrygia, and Galatia—
Paul's supposed Blindness.*

> Two pilgrims issue forth in poor array—
> No scrip, no purse—with only staff in hand.
> Amongst the heathen folk they wend their way,
> And as they journey on from strand to strand
> Aloud they herald forth their Lord's command :
> " Awake, ye nations ! Lo! the day doth break,
> And dawns the light on your benighted land ;
> Your idols dumb and orgies foul forsake,
> And turn to Israel's God. Ye men of sin, awake!"
>
> Anon.

THE journey to Jerusalem and back, with the proceedings of the council, must have occupied some months, and we may place the return of the Apostles to Antioch, in Syria, at the latter end of A.D. 48.

Having re-united themselves to their own church, they exerted their wonted assiduity in extending and confirming the faith by private instruction and public preaching. After some time,[1] and probably in A.D. 49,[2] Paul became anxious to renew his labours among the Gentiles abroad, and proposed to Barnabas to revisit the churches they had planted, city by city.[3] It was apparently Paul's original intention to retrace their first route through Cyprus, Pamphylia, Pisidia, and Lycaonia; but a sharp contention between Paul and Barnabas led to a separation of the fellow travellers, and this, by dividing their energies, contributed essentially to the more rapid progress of the Gospel. Barnabas was for taking his cousin Mark with them, as before; but Paul could not forget Mark's desertion of them at Perga, and absolutely refused to commit the success of their enterprise to one so infirm of purpose. Barnabas was no less resolute the other way; and eventually the two Apostles agreed to pursue different tracks, each with the companion of his choice. Barnabas chose Mark, and Paul selected Silas, or Sylvanus, whose eminent qualifications as a preacher pointed him out as a suitable instrument. Silas, like Paul, was both a *Jew* and a *Roman*—so at least we should infer from what afterwards occurred at Philippi, where the charge against Paul and Silas before the magistrates

---

[1] μετά τινας ἡμέρας. Acts xv. 36.   [2] See Fasti Sacri, p. 290, No. 1738.
[3] κατὰ πᾶσαν πόλιν. Acts xv. 36.

was, "*These men*, being *Jews*, do exceedingly trouble our city;"[4] and Paul afterwards exclaimed, "They have beaten *us* openly uncondemned, being *Romans*."[5] It would be too much to infer that Paul and Barnabas parted in anger; they differed in opinion as to the means by which the common cause would be most effectually promoted, but there is no trace of any bitterness of spirit. We shall see that at the close of their respective circuits they again, by arrangement, went up to Jerusalem together, and we have already had occasion to remark how Paul repeatedly availed himself in after years of the valuable services of Barnabas's cousin Mark.

As the Apostles had intended to go the round of their first circuit, it was easy to foresee what directions they would respectively take now that they severed. Barnabas, with Mark, proceeded to Cyprus, his native country, where a sufficiently wide field still lay open to his labours; and Paul, with Silas, turned his steps toward the other extreme of their last circuit, namely, Derbe, the road to which was through Cilicia, the native country of Paul. The sacred historian observes of Barnabas merely that he "took Mark and sailed unto Cyprus,"[6] but of Paul, that he "departed, being *recommended by the brethren* unto the grace of God."[7] But we cannot think that any such distinction was intended, as that Barnabas had not the sanction of the brethren, while Paul, as before, was specially commissioned by the Church for the purpose. Probably as the narrative henceforth confines itself to the history of Paul, and dismisses Barnabas, the writer is not so particular as to the mission of the latter, whose progress was not to be traced. In fact, from this period we hear nothing more of Barnabas, except from incidental allusions to him in the Epistles.[8]

Paul and Silas proceeded through Syria and Cilicia, and, no doubt, through Tarsus, the birthplace of Paul, confirming, by the way, the several churches which Paul had planted in those parts some years before, and which, as we have seen, were already so numerous that the council of Jerusalem addressed the decree to them, as well as to the church of Antioch. Between Cilicia and Lycaonia lay the ridge of Mount Taurus, and Paul had to choose what route he would take. The first and most eastern and best known of the passes would conduct him by the ordinary track

---

[4] Acts xvi. 20.
[5] Acts xvi. 37.
[6] Acts xv. 39.
[7] Acts xv. 40.
[8] That Barnabas continued his missionary labours cannot be doubted. At the close of Paul's present (the second) circuit, Barnabas and Paul met again at Jerusalem, when it was agreed between them and the Apostles that Barnabas and Paul should still pursue their ministry among the *Gentiles* (Galat. ii. 9); and accordingly we find Barnabas thus engaged at the date of the First Epistle to the Corinthians, 1 Cor. ix. 6, A.D. 57. As Paul preached only in the western parts of Asia Minor, we should assign, as the scene of the labours of Barnabas and Mark, the eastern portions, viz. Bithynia, Pontus, and Cappadocia. That Mark, the companion of Barnabas, exercised his ministry in parts of Asia Minor, may be inferred from several passages. In the First Epistle of Peter to the converts of Bithynia, Pontus, and Cappadocia, &c. (1 Peter i. 1), the salutation of Mark is sent (1 Peter v. 13), which implies a personal acquaintance; and Paul writes from Rome to the Colossians that they were to receive Mark if he came to them (Colos. iv. 10); and in the very last letter that he penned Paul tells Timothy, who was then in *Asia Minor*, to bring Mark with him. 2 Tim. iv. 11.

from Tarsus through the Cilician Gates to Eregli. Another, the most western, ran from Seleucia on the west of Cilicia, to Laranda; and between these two lay another road still, which, commencing from Soli or Pompeiopolis, pierced the Taurus to the east of Laranda, over against Derbe. As this town was the Apostle's object, it has been suggested that Paul took the route which brought him immediately into that vicinity.[9] This road, however, was the most difficult of the passes, and stretched away for a great distance among the mountains of Isaurica, infested by bandits, while the route by way of the Cilician Gates, after clearing the defile, lay through a comparatively open country, and was much safer, and either ran through Derbe[10] or very near it, and offered far better accommodation upon the road. With all these advantages Paul may have given it the preference. On the Apostle's arrival at Derbe, the terminus of his *first* circuit, the disciples, scarcely yet a compacted body, and pressed perhaps by persecution, would welcome with transport his reappearance from so unexpected a quarter.

The next stage of Paul and Silas was to Lystra, the only other town expressly mentioned by the historian, and noticed only to introduce to the reader one of the most amiable and interesting characters that adorn the Christian scene. We allude to Timothy.

He was at this time a young man, perhaps not five and twenty, and yet Paul, who was nearly twice the age, and possessed transcendent natural powers and great literary accomplishments, and who was entrusted, besides, by his Heavenly Master, with the high commission of carrying the banner of the cross among the Gentiles, could find in Timothy a meet companion; nay, more, the Apostle from this time esteemed him as the most trustworthy of all his coadjutors; frequently joins him with himself in the opening salutations of his Epistles; sends him on the most important and delicate missions to the churches; and, at the close of his career, addresses to him that affectionate letter, the second to Timothy, in which he so touchingly refers to his own exit from a troublesome world, and solemnly implores his favourite disciple not to sink under the persecution that was raging about him, but still to play the good soldier, and be the champion of the church when Paul should be no more. What must have been the self-devotion, the gentle disposition, and ardent attachment of one of whom Paul could write thus: "I have no man like-minded who will unfeignedly care for your state; for all seek their own, not the things which are Jesus Christ's; but ye know the proof of *him*, that, as *a son with the father*, he hath served with me in the Gospel."[11]

Of the lineage of Timothy we know nothing, except that his sire was a Greek[12] and his mother Eunice and grandmother Lois were Jewesses.[13] That the latter two

---

[9] Wieseler's Chronol. Apostol. 24.
[10] Cicero, when in Cilicia, became acquainted with Antipater, the robber-chief, at Derbe, and, as is supposed, from having received attentions from him in passing from Iconium to Cilicia.
[11] Philip. ii. 20—22.
[12] Acts xvi. 1.
[13] 2 Tim. i. 5.

were persons of distinguished piety we may collect from the Apostle's words: "When I call to remembrance the unfeigned faith that is in thee, which dwelt first in thy grandmother Lois and thy mother Eunice,"[14] which we do not understand to imply that Lois and Eunice had been eminent for their Christian virtues after conversion, but had always been of a devotional turn of mind. From the personal acquaintance of Paul, not only with the mother, but also the grandmother, of Timothy, it is likely that an intimacy had subsisted between the two families from the earliest times. We should even surmise that Timothy was in some way connected with the Apostle, either by blood or marriage. The noble character of Timothy was no doubt mainly attributable to the excellent religious education he had received from his mother: "Continue thou," writes the Apostle, "in the things which thou hast learned and hast been assured of, knowing of whom thou hast learned them, and that *from a child* thou hast known the Holy Scriptures."[15] Even the birth-place of Timothy is not expressly mentioned; for though we, for the first time, hear of his name at Lystra during the Apostle's second circuit, he had evidently been a convert at the date of Paul's *first* visit to Antioch in Pisidia, and, in the place of Mark, who had withdrawn his services at Perga, had followed Paul successively to Iconium and Lystra, as we are assured by the Apostle himself. "Thou hast fully known," he says, writing to Timothy, "my doctrine, manner of life, purpose, faith, long-suffering, charity, patience, persecutions, afflictions, which came unto me *at Antioch, at Iconium, at Lystra*—what persecutions I endured; but out of them all the Lord delivered me."[16] It was at Antioch in Pisidia, therefore, that Timothy first met with Paul, but it does not appear that he was a native of that place. Mark had deserted Paul and Barnabas at Perga; and as the Apostles had need of a minister, it is possible that Timothy, at Antioch, the town next visited after Perga, took the place of Mark and attended them throughout the rest of the circuit. The common opinion is, that Timothy was a Lystrian, and such was probably the fact. If his general residence was at Antioch of Pisidia, why should the writer of the Acts, in testifying to his high character, observe, "he was well reported of by the brethren that were" (not at Antioch, but) "at *Lystra and Iconium*."[17] There was no great distance between Lystra and Antioch, and when Paul first visited Antioch, either Timothy was accidentally there, or as the distance between the two places was not great, Timothy, on hearing that a new doctrine was promulgated, might have hastened thither for the express purpose of examining its pretensions. It is clear that Timothy was not of Derbe. The passage in the Acts is: "They came to Derbe and Lystra, and behold, a certain disciple was *there*, named Timothy," and the word "there" refers more naturally to Lystra. Afterwards the historian writes, "and there accompanied him into Asia, Sopater of Berœa, and of the Thessalonians, Aristarchus and Secundus, and Gaius of Derbe, and Timothy."[18] It

[14] 2 Tim. i. 5.
[15] 2 Tim. iii. 14, 15.
[16] 2 Tim. iii. 10, 11.
[17] Acts xvi. 2.
[18] 2 Tim. iii. 11.

follows that Timothy was not of Derbe, or he would have been coupled with Gaius.[19] Besides, had Timothy been of Derbe, the Apostle could hardly have referred so emphatically in his second Epistle to Timothy to his sufferings at Antioch and Iconium and Lystra, and have omitted all allusion to Derbe.

But to proceed, Paul had accepted the companionship of Timothy during the first circuit by way of experiment, to test his resolution under the trials to which a Christian minister was exposed; but Timothy had so approved himself, and his services were so highly appreciated, that Paul now determined to assume him (probably on Timothy's own urgent entreaty) as his coadjutor in the ministry for life. Timothy was peculiarly fitted for this task, as his mother was a Jewess and his father a Greek, and he would thus be acceptable both to Jews and heathen.

The first step taken by the Apostle may appear of questionable propriety, but was in strict accordance with the doctrine which Paul ever preached: he caused Timothy to be circumcised. Christianity, in the hands of the Apostle, was a practical principle; it did not disturb the relations of society, or interfere with any customs that were innocent in themselves. To none was it more distinctly revealed than to Paul that the Mosaic ritual had become a dead letter, yet he saw no harm in complying himself with the Law of Moses, where no Christian duty militated against it. He frequented the synagogues and preached in them; he attended their feasts; he sheared his head at Cenchrea from a vow; he purified himself in the Temple at Jerusalem; he exclaimed in the council, "I am a Pharisee." But when the observance of the Law of Moses was opposed to the Christian scheme, no one more resolute than Paul in maintaining the utter abrogation of Judaism. After the call of Cornelius, a Jew was expressly forbidden to account any Gentile unclean, and accordingly, even in Jerusalem itself, Paul walked about openly with Trophimus the Ephesian;[20] and when Peter, at Antioch, withdrew himself from the Gentiles, out of deference to

---

[19] Some would refer the word Δερβαῖος to Timothy, and argue thus: Aristarchus and Gaius were *Macedonians* (Acts xix. 29), and as Luke here writes Θεσσαλονικέων δέ, Ἀρίσταρχος καὶ Σεκοῦνδος καὶ Γάϊος Δερβαῖος καὶ Τιμόθεος (xx. 4), the Gaius here mentioned, more particularly as he is coupled with Aristarchus, must be the Gaius of Macedonia, and here described as of Thessalonica, which was the capital of Macedonia. Gaius, therefore, they say, was not of Derbe, and the word Δερβαῖος cannot belong to him, but must be carried forward and be attached to Τιμόθεος: "of Derbe also Timothy." Besides, they urge, unless this punctuation be adopted, Timothy's birthplace would be omitted altogether, which is unlikely, as *all* the other names are accompanied with descriptions of their country.

This argument may be ingenious, but cannot prevail. The Greek can only be correctly translated, "of the Thessalonians, Aristarchus and Secundus, and Gaius of Derbe, and Timothy," and this involves no inconsistency or difficulty. The name of Gaius was the commonest of all, as common indeed as that of John amongst ourselves, and it was to distinguish this Gaius from his namesake of Corinth (Rom. xvi. 23) and his namesake of Macedonia (Acts xix. 29), and others, that he is here called "Gaius of Derbe." The name of Timothy naturally follows that of Gaius of Derbe, as Timothy was from the adjoining town of Lystra, and it would have been surplusage and idle repetition to say that Timothy was of Lystra, as Luke had previously (Acts xvi. 1) made especial mention of Timothy as adopted by the Apostle from Lystra.

[20] Acts xxi. 29.

Jewish prejudices, Paul rebuked him publicly.[21] And when Paul was at Jerusalem, accompanied by Titus, who was a Greek, and the Jews strongly insisted that the Gentile convert should be circumcised, the Apostle "gave place by subjection, no, not for an hour,"[22] for in Christ "there was neither Jew nor Greek;" and had Titus, being a Greek, submitted to the initiatory rite of the Mosaic Law, the natural inference would have been that Christianity alone was insufficient. Timothy was a Jew, for the maxim of that day was *partus sequitur ventrem*,[23] and he succeeded to the *status* of his mother, who was a Jewess; he ought therefore by the Law to have been circumcised; but for some reason, perhaps from some objection on the part of his father, who was a Greek, and was entitled to a veto, he had not undergone that ceremony, and the Jews of the neighbourhood were scandalised by the omission. To remove this prejudice, and to enable the disciple to stand before his countrymen without offence, the Apostle caused the rite to be administered. As Timothy was henceforth to accompany the Apostle in his travels it was indispensable that Timothy should be circumcised, for it was the invariable practice of Paul to offer the Gospel first to his own nation, and Timothy, if unclean—that is, uncircumcised—would be of little service to the Apostle, as he could not be allowed to hold any communication with Jews.[24]

To complete Timothy for an Evangelist, it was also necessary that he should be ordained; and as we find several scattered notices in the Epistles relative to this ceremony, we shall collect them together, as it will at least be curious to trace the forms observed in the Apostolic age. They appear in substance to harmonise with our own.

Paul addresses Timothy thus: "Neglect not the gift that is in thee, which was given thee by prophecy (or preaching) with the *laying on of the hands of the presbytery*;"[25] from which we deduce, first, that holy orders were conferred by the assembled clergy. But by whom was the imposition of hands? This we learn from the following text: "Wherefore I put thee in remembrance that thou stir up the gift of God which is in thee, by the putting on of *my* hands."[26] So that Paul, as the bishop then present, and the representative of the church, was the person by whom the orders were conferred. The ceremony was accompanied by solemn charges, called "prophesyings" (or preachings), from the bishop and others of the clergy, as to the serious nature of the office undertaken; and the candidate, on the other hand, made a profession of his faith, and pledged himself to the discharge of the high duties imposed upon him. Paul writes thus to Timothy at Ephesus: "This charge

---

[21] Gal. ii. 14.
[22] Gal. ii. 3.
[23] Ubi sive gentilis, sive servus, concubuerit cum *Israelitide*, proles recta erit. Jebamoth, fol. 45, 2. Filius *Israelitæ* susceptus ex ancillâ aut ex gentili non vocatur filius Israelitæ. Bechorim, i. 4. And so the Civil Law: Ingenui sunt qui ex matre liberà nati sunt, Dig. i. 5, 5. And see the other passages cited in Wetstein. Acts xvi. 3.
[24] 1 Tim. iv. 14.
[25] 2 Tim. i. 6.
[26] 1 Tim. i. 18.

I commit unto thee, son Timothy, according to the *prophesyings pronounced over thee*, that thou *war in them* a good warfare."[28] The Vulgate translation is: "According to the prophecies which went before on thee," but the Apostle rather refers to the charges delivered to him at his ordination.[28] In the following words allusion is also made to Paul's address to him at the same ceremony: "The things that thou *heardest of me before many witnesses*, the same commit thou to faithful men who shall be able to teach others also."[29] But there cannot be a more striking passage on the subject than the solemn exhortation that Timothy while at Ephesus, during the Apostle's absence, should act up to the vows which he had taken upon him at the time of receiving orders. "Fight the good fight of faith, lay hold on eternal life, whereunto thou *wert also called*, and *didst profess* a good profession before many witnesses. I give thee charge in the sight of God, who quickeneth all things, and before Christ Jesus, who before Pontius Pilate witnessed a good confession, that thou keep the *charge* without spot, unrebukable, until the appearing of our Lord Jesus Christ."[30] The ordination of Timothy was at Lystra, and this also leads us to the conclusion that Lystra was his native place, for we can scarcely suppose that Paul would cause him, then a very young man, to be circumcised, and ordain him to the Christian ministry as the Apostle's future companion, unless his family and friends were present to lend their countenance to the proceeding.

We must now [A.D. 49] pursue Paul and Silas, with the addition of Timothy, upon their onward journey. We are not expressly informed what was the next town after Lystra visited by Paul; but as we know what was the primary object of his circuit, namely, to confirm the churches he had planted before, we cannot entertain a doubt but that from Lystra he went to Iconium, and from thence to Antioch of Pisidia. This, we think, sufficiently appears from the sacred narrative itself: " And as they went through *the cities* they delivered them the decrees for to keep that were ordained of the Apostles and Elders which were at Jerusalem; and so were *the churches* established in the faith, and increased in number daily."[31] What *cities*, and what *churches?* The cities he had before traversed, and the churches that Paul had previously planted. We may safely conclude, therefore, that Paul, after leaving Cilicia, pursued the track of his first circuit (but reversing the direction of it), through Derbe, Lystra, Iconium, and Antioch.

Paul, it is said, delivered the decrees of the council of Jerusalem to the churches, and the statement is not without significance. The decrees themselves had been addressed to the disciples of Antioch and Syria and Cilicia,[32] and had been forwarded to them accordingly. But Lycaonia, including Isaurica and Isauria, bordered upon

---

[27] See Biscoe on the Acts, xix.
[28] It may be thought, perhaps, by some, that the Apostle is here only reminding Timothy of the injunctions laid upon him by Paul, when they had parted at Ephesus.
[29] 2 Tim. ii. 2.
[30] 1 Tim. vi. 12-14.
[31] Acts xvi. 4, 5.
[32] Acts xv. 23.

Cilicia, and next to Isaurica and Isauria lay Pisidia, and in all these countries the Jews were nearly as numerous as in Cilicia itself. The same reasons, therefore, that called forth the decrees as regards Cilicia would apply to the regions in immediate proximity, and that there was a close political connection between Cilicia and these western provinces appears from the coins, in which Tarsus is called the metropolis of Lycaonia and Isauria, as well as of Cilicia.[33] The ordinance of the Apostles had been necessitated by the zeal of the Jewish converts for the Law of Moses;[34] and Paul, to accommodate the like prejudices, had caused Timothy to be circumcised, and with the same view he now delivered the decrees.

The immediate object of Paul at starting from Antioch had been to revisit the churches planted during his first circuit.[35] This he had accomplished, but an ardent spirit like his could little brook to rest while aught remained to be done. His watchword was ever "Forwards!"

In quitting Antioch, then, did he continue his progress along the high road toward Ephesus, or did he turn to the right toward Galatia? It is clear that Paul did not reach Ephesus itself, as he visited it for the first time on his way from Corinth in A.D. 53. But Colossæ, Laodicea, and Hierapolis lay on the road from Antioch of Pisidia to Ephesus; and as Paul wrote Epistles to the Colossians and Laodiceans (the latter miscalled the 'Epistle to the Ephesians'), it may be contended that Paul advanced as far as Colossæ, and then turned about towards Galatia. But on opening the Epistles to the Colossians and Laodiceans (or Ephesians), it cannot escape notice that the Apostle is corresponding with strangers, and not with churches with whom he was personally acquainted. Thus, to the Colossians he speaks of "the word of the truth of the Gospel which is come unto you as it is in all the world, and bringeth forth fruit, as it doth also in you since the day ye heard of it, and knew the grace of God in truth, as ye also *learned of Epaphras*, our dear fellow servant, who is for you a faithful minister of Christ, who hath also *declared unto us* your love in the Spirit. For this cause also *since the day we heard of it*," &c.[36] So that the Apostle refers to Epaphras as the harbinger from whom they had received the Gospel, and Paul only expresses the joy which he had experienced on being informed of their conversion. So also to the Laodiceans: "Wherefore I also, after I *heard* of your faith in the Lord Jesus, and love unto all the saints, cease not to give thanks for you, making mention of you in my prayers;"[37] so that he had not witnessed their reception of the Gospel in his own person, but it had been reported to him, and he thanked God for the intelligence. And again: "For this cause I, Paul, the prisoner of Jesus Christ for you Gentiles, *if at least* (εἴγε) *ye have heard* of

---

[33] Acts xv. 21.
[34] Some have Ταρσου Μητρ. των Κιλικων, Ισαυρια, Καρια, Λυκαονια. Others have Κοινος των τριων επαρχιων, viz. Isauria, Lycaonia, and Caria. Eckhel, vol. iii. pp. 74, 75. And see Wieseler Chron. Apostol. 27.
[35] Acts xv. 36.
[36] Coloss. i. 5–9.
[37] Ephes. i. 15, 16.

the dispensation of the grace of God which is given me to you-ward,"[38] &c. But how could they by any possibility have been ignorant of Paul's apostleship, if he had ever himself laboured amongst them in that very character? However, the decisive argument lies in another text addressed to the Colossians. "I would," he says, "that ye knew what great conflict I have for you, and for them at Laodicea, and for *as many as have not seen my face in the flesh.*"[39] Is it not here distinctly stated that the Colossians and Laodiceans had never been favoured with the presence of the Apostle? The same was, no doubt, the case with the Hierapolitans, for evidently all the three cities owed their enlightenment to the same missionary, Epaphras, of whom Paul writes to the Colossians, " Epaphras, who is one of you" (the Colossians), "a servant of Christ, saluteth you, always labouring fervently for you in prayers, that ye may stand perfect and complete in all the will of God. For I bear him record that he *hath a great zeal* for *you* and them that are at *Laodicea*, and them in *Hierapolis.*"[40]

The brief summary of Luke is, that they "passed through *Phrygia* and the region of *Galatia*, but were forbidden of the Holy Ghost to preach the word in Asia."[41] Paul then was making for Galatia, which lay to the north of Antioch in Pisidia; and if so, it is very unlikely that he should have journeyed about one hundred and fifteen miles from Antioch of Pisidia, to Colossæ, Hierapolis, and Laodicea, in a south-western direction, and so away from Galatia for which he was bound, and on the road to Ephesus, which he had certainly no intention of now visiting. Besides, we shall see presently, that Colossæ, Laodicea, and Hierapolis were all probably in the Asia of the New Testament, i.e. in Lydian Asia, and if so, as Paul at this time was forbidden to preach the Word in Asia, he could not have visited those cities.

We must conclude, then, that Paul, after revisiting the churches planted by him on his first circuit in Lycaonia and Pisidia, decided, after arriving at Antioch of Pisidia, not to proceed farther westward on the road to Ephesus, but to bend his steps northward.[42]

---

[38] Ephes. iii. 1.
[39] Coloss. ii. 1.
[40] Coloss. iv. 12, 13.
[41] Acts xvi. 6.

[42] In the former edition the author advocated the view that Paul visited Colossæ, but not Laodicea or Hierapolis. He has since doubted the correctness of this assumption, and inclines to the opinion that Paul did not visit any of these cities. However, the arguments pro and con. are so nearly balanced that, to enable the reader to exercise his own judgment, the following advocacy of the hypothesis that Paul reached *Colossæ* but did not penetrate to *Laodicea* or *Hierapolis*, which appeared in the former edition, is now subjoined as a note:—

"If we regard the Epistles to the Ephesians, to the Colossians, and to Philemon, the hypothesis that Paul visited Colossæ, but not Laodicea or Hierapolis, is the only solution of many passages otherwise inexplicable. The reader, in examining these Epistles, will carry in his mind two things: first, that what is called the Epistle to the Ephesians, is in fact the Epistle to the Laodiceans, referred to in the following passage to the Colossians: 'When this Epistle is read among you, cause that it be read also in the church of the Laodiceans, and that ye likewise read *the Epistle from Laodicea*;[1] and, secondly, that the Epistles to the Ephesians, or

[1] Col. iv. 16.

Round about Antioch of Pisidia, to the north, east, and west, lay Phrygia. This name originally comprised a great square block of country in the heart of Asia Minor, but in after ages its dimensions were greatly curtailed. The north-eastern portion, about a quarter of Phrygia, had long since been detached from Phrygia and made

Laodiceans, and to the Colossians and to Philemon, were all written at one and the same time.[1]

"We open first the Epistle to the *Laodiceans*, and the whole tissue of it shows that Paul had *never visited Laodicea*. From beginning to end the Epistle is entirely destitute of any personal allusion, but contains, first, a general exposition of the Christian doctrine, and then a compendium of Christian duty. In short, the letter is evidently one addressed to strangers in the flesh though brethren in Christ, and is a summary of the Gospel scheme which Paul had never been present to deliver orally.

"If we examine the contents in detail, we find at every step something inconsistent with the notion that Paul had been amongst them. The Epistle begins thus: 'Paul, an Apostle of Jesus Christ, by the will of God, to the saints,' &c.; but in the Colossians it is 'Paul, an Apostle of Jesus Christ, by the will of God, and *Timothy our brother*, to the saints,' &c.; and in Philemon, 'Paul, a prisoner of Jesus Christ, *and Timothy our brother*, unto Philemon,' &c. As Timothy was with Paul when all three Epistles were written, why is he joined with him in the Epistles to the Colossians and Philemon, and not in that to the Laodiceans? The only satisfactory explanation is, that Paul and Timothy had been at Colossæ, and were known to them and to Philemon, but that they had not visited Laodicea, and therefore Paul wrote only in his character of Apostle of the Gentiles, and, if we may so express it, in a formal and distant manner. Paul, at the date of the Epistle to the Romans, had never seen *them*, and though Timothy was with him at that time, the opening address of the Epistle is, in like manner, from Paul only.

"We may point out another remarkable contrast, of a similar nature, between the Epistle to the Laodiceans, whom Paul had not seen, and the Epistles to the Colossians and Philemon, with whom Paul was familiar. In the Epistle to the Laodiceans there are no salutations at the close, but in the Epistles to the Colossians and Philemon there are several, as from Mark, Aristarchus, Demas, and Luke. The absence or presence of these greetings would be of no weight taken by itself, but when three letters are written at the same time, and a marked distinction is observable, we have to account for the difference. The solution is, that the letter to the Laodiceans was an explanation of the Christian scheme to strangers, while the letters to the Colossians and Philemon were a correspondence between persons mutually acquainted.

"There are two passages in the Epistle to the Laodiceans which alone almost carry conviction that the Apostle had never instructed them himself. In c. iii. v. I, he writes thus: 'For this cause, I, Paul, the prisoner of Jesus Christ, *if at least* (εἴγε) ye have *heard* of the dispensation of the grace of God, which hath been given me to you-ward, how that by revelation he made known unto me the mystery, as I have *written above* in few words, whereby ye may understand by *reading* my knowledge in the mystery of Christ,' &c. Thus the writer supposes that they *might not be aware* of his Apostleship by express revelation, and appeals in support of his claims to that character, not to what they had seen of him, or received from his lips, but to what they would read in his letter. In the corresponding text in the Colossians there is no such hesitation, but his apostleship is assumed as a known fact, 'according to the dispensation of God which hath been given me for you.' Col. i. 25. The other passage referred to is the following: 'But ye have not so learned Christ, *if at least* (εἴγε) ye have heard him, and have been taught by him, *as the truth is in Jesus*.' Ephes. iv. 20. Had Paul himself been their spiritual teacher, how could he doubt whether they had been rightly instructed or not? How differently does he address the Colossians, to whom he had himself preached, 'We give thanks to God and the Father of our Lord Jesus Christ, praying always for you, having heard[a] of your faith in Christ Jesus, and of the love which ye have to all the saints, for the hope which is laid up for you in heaven, whereof

over to the Galatians, and was now called Galatia. The three other quarters of Phrygia, viz. the south-eastern quarter and the two western quarters, still retained the ancient name, but were much mutilated and confused. The tract that lay between Antioch of Pisidia and Galatia contained a mongrel population of Phrygians,

ye *heard long since in the word of the truth of the Gospel*,' Col. i. 3; and again, 'as ye have therefore received Christ Jesus the Lord, so walk ye in him, rooted and built up in him, and stablished in the faith, *as ye have been taught*.'[1]

"At the close of the Epistle to the Laodiceans there is a single word, καί, 'also,' which, however apparently insignificant, may be construed to have a peculiar force. It is thus introduced: 'But that ye *also* may know my affairs, and how I do, Tychicus our beloved brother and faithful minister in the Lord shall make known to you all things.'[2] The meaning of the word 'also,' we take to be this: 'I have had occasion to write to the church I planted at Colossæ, and send it by Tychicus, and as he will pass through Laodicea on his way, I charge him with a letter to yourselves *also*, and have instructed him to acquaint you *also* with the state of affairs at Rome.'

"Turn we now to the Epistle to the *Colossians*, the perusal of which will convince the reader that Paul *had been personally present at Colossæ*. We have already anticipated some remarks upon this Epistle, but a few more remain.

"After telling them of their reconciliation to God by Christ, he adds, ' *if at least* (εἴγε) ye *continue* in the faith grounded and rooted, and be not moved away from the hope of the Gospel which ye have heard,' &c. Col. i. 23. With the Laodiceans it is, ' *If at least* ye have *heard* of the dispensation,' and ' *if at least* ye have been *taught as the truth is in Jesus*;' but here he assumes that the Colossians had been instructed in the truth, and exhorts them only to abide in it and hold it fast.

"The text we cite next has greatly perplexed commentators, and has been employed as an argument in aid of very opposite opinions. It runs thus: 'For I would that ye (Colossians) knew what great conflict I have for you and for them at Laodicea and for *as many as have not seen my face in the flesh* that their hearts might be comforted,' &c. Col. ii. 1. Some contend that the Colossians and Laodiceans, and those who had not seen the Apostle, are all coupled together, and that consequently Paul had never been either at Colossæ or Laodicea. Others, as Lardner, insist that the Apostle is discriminating between the Colossians and Laodiceans whom he had seen, and the brethren whom he had not seen, and they rely on the change from the second person, 'what great conflict I have for *you*,' to the third person, 'that *their* hearts might be comforted.' The passage, as we read it, supports neither hypothesis, but fortifies the position we have advanced, that Paul had been at Colossæ and not at Laodicea. The authorised translation, subject to a slight correction, may be admitted, but the punctuation has been misplaced, and sufficient regard has not been paid to the style of the Apostle in interposing parentheses. The occasion of writing the Epistle to the Colossians was to warn them against the Gnostic doctrines which had invaded the church; and accordingly in the second chapter the Apostle opens the subject by expressing his solicitude on account of the Colossians; but, before he proceeds, he guards himself against being supposed to be indifferent to the interests of the neighbouring churches by the parenthetical remark, that not for the Colossians only was he anxious, but also for the Laodiceans, and all others (viz. in those parts) who had not seen him; and then returns to the matter in hand. The text should run thus: 'For I would that ye knew what great conflict I have for *you* (and for them at Laodicea and for as many as have not seen my face in the flesh, that *their* hearts may be comforted, being knit together in love, and unto all riches of the full assurance of understanding to the knowledge of the mystery of God, and of the Father, and of Christ, in whom are hid all the treasures of wisdom and knowledge), but this I mean, lest any man should beguile *you* with enticing words, for, though I be absent in the flesh, yet am I with you in the spirit, joying and beholding your order and the steadfastness of your faith in Christ,' &c. The passage, read in this manner, gives a force to every

---

[1] "Col. ii. 6, 7. In order to avoid the effect of the word εἴγε, 'at least,' in the two texts above commented upon, some, as Lardner, have translated it 'since.' But is there any passage in which it can fairly bear such an interpretation? It never signifies the affirmative certain, but always implies a possible negative.

[2] "Eph. vi. 21, 22. However, it may mean only, 'As I, Paul, have heard of your welfare by Epaphras, I send Tychicus, that you *also* may hear of my welfare.'

Lydians, Carians, and Mysians,[43] and was bounded on the east by Lycaonia (Tyriæum being the last city of Phrygia in that direction), and was at this time part of the province of Galatia. The two western quarters of Phrygia which bordered on Galatia contained some very considerable cities, such as Synnada, Docymeum, and Dorileum,

word without any repugnance or inconsistency. The tenor of the latter part furnishes an additional argument that Paul had visited Colossæ, for the allusion to his absence strongly implies that he had once been present. He employs a similar expression to the Philippians, with whom he was familiar: 'Only let your conversation be as it becometh the gospel of Christ, that whether I come and see you, or else be absent, I may hear of your affairs,' &c. Philip. i. 27.

"Again, amongst the salutations at the end of the Epistle to the Colossians, we read thus: 'Aristarchus, my fellow soldier, saluteth you, and Mark, cousin to Barnabas, touching whom ye received commandments, if he come unto you, receive him.' Col. iv. 10. Does not this show that there was occasional communication between Paul and the Colossian church, and if so, how can we account for it, but because Paul had planted it? We are reminded of a similar charge to the Corinthian church: 'If Timothy come, see that he be with you without fear, for he worketh the work of the Lord, as I also do. Let no man, therefore, despise him; but conduct him forth in peace, that he may come unto me.' 1 Cor. xvi. 10, 11.

"The last text we shall cite from the Epistle to the Colossians is one on which Lardner has greatly relied, as proving that Paul had been at Laodicea. It is this: 'Salute the brethren which are in Laodicea, and Nymphas, and the church which is in his house.' Col. iv. 15. The Apostle, therefore, it is argued, was personally acquainted with some of the Laodiceans, and how did he become so, but by visiting the city? But, surely, there is a satisfactory explanation. Paul charges the Colossian church to transmit a copy of their epistle to Laodicea, and to procure from the Laodiceans a copy of the epistle written to them, but as the Laodicean church, and Nymphas, their bishop, were personally strangers to the Apostle, he, with a feeling of delicacy, accompanies the request to them with the ordinary complimentary language. The whole passage runs thus: 'Salute the brethren which are in Laodicea and Nymphas and the church which is in his house, and when this epistle is read among you, cause that it be read also in the church of the Laodiceans, and that ye likewise read the epistle from Laodicea.' The paraphrase of the learned Wetstein is, 'Salute the Laodiceans in my name, and request in my name that they will communicate to you the letter I have written to them.' By the church in the house of Nymphas is not meant his family, but the congregation of Laodicea, who were wont to assemble there for public worship, it being the custom of the early Christians, before they had the means of erecting suitable edifices, to meet together in some private dwelling; and what place so proper for the purpose as the house of their bishop?

"It remains only that we offer a very few remarks on the Epistle to *Philemon*, as supporting the hypothesis that Paul had visited Colossæ. It begins thus: 'Paul a prisoner of Jesus Christ, and Timothy our brother, unto Philemon our dearly beloved, and fellow-labourer, and to our beloved Apphia, and Archippus, our fellow-soldier, and to the church in thy house.' Philemon was undoubtedly a Colossian, and we have no reason to suppose that he had ever travelled from his native place; yet we here find the Apostle on terms of intimacy with him, as we may collect from the epithet 'dearly beloved,' and not only so, but acquainted also with Apphia and Archippus, thought to be the wife and son of Philemon. A subsequent expression leads us to infer that Paul had first converted Philemon, 'Albeit, I do not say unto thee how thou *owest unto me even thine own self* besides.' Philem. 19. Onesimus, a Colossian ('who is one of you'[a]), and the slave of Philemon, had been converted by Paul at Rome, but he had probably introduced himself to Paul from having seen him before at the house of his master Philemon at Colossæ. Epaphras, a fellow-labourer of the Apostle, and who sends his salutation in the

[a] Col. iv. 9.

---

[43] Strabo, xiii. 4 (p. 156, Tauchnitz).

and were comprised in the province of Proconsular Asia. But Phrygia generally, though subject to the Roman rule, was allowed to live under its own peculiar laws.

We have now to determine, on the best grounds we can, whether Paul crossed direct from Antioch of Pisidia to Galatia, or evangelised the main portion of Phrygia to the west of Galatia.

Much to our regret this portion of the circuit is passed over by Luke in comparative silence. He had given us details of the commencement of the circuit as at Lystra, and he again particularises the Apostle's movements after the time of which we are now speaking, when Paul went down to Troas. But between these two extremes is unhappily a wide hiatus. The explanation may be, that Luke had started with Paul from Antioch of Syria, and accompanied him as far as to Antioch of Pisidia, but there parted from him, and remained behind to take care of the churches just visited. Whatever may be the reason, Luke remarks only that they "went through *Phrygia and the region of Galatia*,"[44] from which, however, we should infer, as indeed was necessary from the relative positions of the two countries, that they evangelised Phrygia before entering Galatia.

In the almost equally brief account of Paul's third circuit the order in which these two countries are referred to is reversed, for it is said on the latter occasion that Paul went over all the country of *Galatia and Phrygia* in order.[45] On the *third* circuit, therefore, Paul entered Galatia first, and thence passed into Phrygia; but what we have here to notice is, that he did this "*in order*" (καθεξῆς). Now Luke is so accurate in all his minutest details, that every word deserves attention, and when therefore it is said that Paul visited these churches "*in order*" we cannot doubt that he kept in his former track, but moved in an opposite direction; and as Paul, on his third circuit, started from Antioch of Syria and traversed Galatia and Phrygia,

---

Epistle to the Colossians and to Philemon. Col. iv. 12; Philem. 23, was also a Colossian, as we learn from the description, 'who is one of you,' Col. iv. 12. Thus we have Philemon, Apphia, Archippus, Onesimus, Epaphras, five Colossians, all acquainted with the Apostle; and the almost necessary conclusion is, that this was not the result of mere accident but that Paul had actually visited Colosse.

"The only other extract we shall make from the letter to Philemon (for brevity has compelled us to omit many remarks on all three Epistles) is the following: 'But, withal, prepare me a lodging, for I trust that through your prayers I shall be given unto you.' v. 22. Had Paul never been at Colosse, the injunction to prepare a lodging would be extremely vague; but if the Apostle had stayed there before, and had then occupied a lodging, as was his custom, Philemon, recollecting what the Apostle had required on the former occasion, would be able to make suitable provision. The words 'That through your prayers I shall be given unto you' (v. 22) also seem to imply that the Apostle had once identified himself with them by personal presence. It is very like the language to the Hebrews, 'Pray for us; but I beseech you the rather to do this, that I may be *restored to you* the sooner.'"[1]

[44] διελθόντες δὲ τὴν Φρυγίαν καὶ τὴν Γαλατικὴν χώραν. Acts xvi. 6.

[45] διερχόμενος καθεξῆς τὴν Γαλατικὴν χώραν καὶ Φρυγίαν. Acts xviii. 23.

---

[1] "Heb. xiii. 18, 19. Should the reader not adopt the position that Paul visited Colosse, and not Laodicea, there remain the two alternatives: first, that Paul visited both places; and, secondly, that he visited neither. Of these two, the latter appears to the author the more probable, and has been adopted in the text."

and finally arrived at Ephesus, we must conclude that Paul, on his *second* circuit, advanced from west to east. From the light, therefore, thus gathered from the third circuit, we should say that Paul, in the course of his second circuit, after quitting Antioch of Pisidia, did not evangelise generally the south-eastern part of Phrygia, between Antioch of Pisidia and Galatia, but journeyed to that part of Phrygia which lay to the west of Galatia, the far more important tract as regards extent, and studded with the chief cities. Just north of Antioch of Pisidia ran a mountain ridge called Paroreia, from west to east, Antioch lying in the valley to the south, and Philomelium in the valley to the north. From Philomelium, a main road, according to the Peutinger Table, communicated with Synnada, the assize town of the vicinity.[16] We should surmise, therefore, that Paul, starting from Antioch of Pisidia, crossed the mountain range to Philomelium, and exercised his ministry there, and then travelled by the high road to Synnada, a distance of sixty-three miles. From Synnada, according to the same Table, the high road led to Docymeum, a distance of thirty-two miles, and thence to Doryleum, at a further distance of thirty-two miles. Paul would naturally visit these towns, and from Doryleum would perhaps turn eastward and pass along the high road to Midaeium, a distance of twenty-eight miles, and thence to Tricomia (the last town of Phrygia), a further distance of twenty-eight miles along the same road.

The Phrygian soil, however, appears, religiously, not to have been very productive. That Paul made some converts in Phrygia is evident, for on the next circuit he went through Phrygia "strengthening all the disciples."[17] But on the other hand, they were perhaps few in number and widely scattered, for we have no mention of any Phrygian churches in particular, nor did the Apostle ever write any letter to them. There is also this further remarkable circumstance, that Paul, before commencing the next, his third circuit, promised the apostles at Jerusalem that he would make a collection for the poor Hebrews amongst the Gentile churches planted by him; and we read that a collection was made accordingly in Galatia, and again in Macedonia, and again in Achaia, but not a word is said about any collection in Phrygia. It would seem, therefore, that either no churches of importance existed in Phrygia, or that they were too poor to be called upon for an eleemosynary contribution. It is possible, however, that a collection may have been made there also, but that, as it was quite distinct from the others in its time and circumstances, it did not call for any especial reference to it in the Epistles.

The Apostles having concluded their ministry in Phrygia, now transferred their labours to Galatia; but before we enter its confines we must give some account of this singular people. They were not aborigines of the country, but had migrated from Gaul. In the most ancient times the Gauls, or Galatians, or Celts (for it is the same word under different forms) occupied all the west of Europe. They were a powerful

---

[16] Plin. N. H. v. 29.   [17] Acts xviii. 23.

and prolific race, and for many centuries poured out their swarms to foreign climes.⁴⁷ Shortly after the death of Alexander the Great, when the Gauls were still in their zenith, a horde of some three hundred thousand warriors issued forth under Brennus,⁴⁸ to seek their fortune in other climes. They advanced along the banks of the Danube till they reached the confluence of the Save. Here they divided themselves into three bodies, under different leaders, one halting in Pannonia, another crossing into Illyricum and Macedonia, and a third pushing on to Thrace. Of the last band, one part, under Leonorius, passed the Hellespont, and another, under Lutatius, the Bosporus, and the two then again united their forces in Asia Minor. Nicomedes, King of Bithynia, was at that time at war with his brother Zipetes, and as the Gauls were hardy soldiers, Nicomedes hired their assistance against the enemy. But called in as allies, they soon domineered as masters, and all Asia Minor became subject to their predatory incursions. At length, in B.C. 230, they were utterly defeated by Attalus, King of Pergamus, and thenceforth were confined within moderate limits, viz. the north-eastern part of Phrygia, thenceforth called Galatia, or Gallo-Græcia. It was bounded by Cappadocia and Pontus on the east, by Phrygia on the west, by Phrygia and Lycaonia on the south, and by Bithynia and Paphlagonia on the north. In a general way their country may be taken to have been between the Halys in the east and the Sangarius on the west. The Gauls for many centuries continued a distinct people, neither changing their language nor their manners. Even in the time of Jerome, more than six hundred years after their severance from their native country, it is said that he could detect traces of the tongue which he had heard spoken at Treves, part of ancient Gaul.⁴⁹ It would seem, however, from the inscriptions found in

---

⁴⁷ By these repeated efforts they seem to have exhausted the strength of the original stock, for, by degrees, invaders pressed upon them at home, and so straitened them that they could only maintain themselves in fastnesses, or in some corner where the impossibility of escape gave them the courage of despair. In France, for instance, they were forced into Brittany; in England they retired before the Saxons into Cornwall (or Corner-Wales) and into Wales (called from them Wallia or Gallia, the *w* and *g* being interchangeable letters, as in *guerre*, war, *gardien*, warden, &c.) and indeed the principality of Wales is to this day called by the French, Pays de Galles. In Scotland the Celts (or Gauls, or Gaels) sought for shelter in the Highlands and abandoned the Lowlands to their invaders. In Ireland the Celts were more fortunate, and retained the greater part of the island, losing only the north-eastern portion. It is almost unnecessary to remark, that the language of Brittany, the Cornish (now extinct), the Welsh, the Gaelic, and the Erse, are all substantially the same; and indeed the Irish and the Highlanders can at the present day, it is said, speak intelligibly to each other, and there is an almost equal similarity between the Welsh and Cornish and the Breton. But between the Erse and Gaelic, on the one hand, and the Welsh and Cornish and Breton on the other, there is considerable diversity, as may be seen on comparing the Lord's Prayer, for instance, in those languages.

⁴⁸ This was also the name of the leader who sacked Rome. But in fact, Brennus, though passing for a proper name amongst the Greeks and Romans, is in Celtic a generic term, signifying a prince or chieftain, and is not the name of an individual. The Welsh for 'a king' at the present day is *brain*.

⁴⁹ Galatas, excepto sermone Græco, quo omnis oriens loquitur, propriam linguam eandem pene habere quam Treveros, nec referre si aliqua inde corruperint, quum et Afri Phœnicum linguam nonnulla ex parte mutaverint, et ipsa Latinitas et regionibus quotidie mutetur et tempore. Hieron. in Epist. Galat. lib. ii. præf.

Galatia, that Greek was the language, at least of the educated classes, in the time of the Apostle. Amongst the common people the Celtic, though greatly corrupted, may still have been spoken; but no Celtic inscriptions have been discovered.

The Galatians consisted of three tribes, the Tolistobogii, the Troemi, and the Tectosages. The two first, according to Strabo, were so called after the names of their leaders,[51] while the Tectosages were a swarm from the hive of the Tectosages in Aquitain, well known in the time of Strabo. Each tribe was divided into four tetrarchies, having each of them distinct civil and military rulers. Originally the affairs of the nation were regulated by a parliament,[52] composed of representatives from the different tetrarchies, but by degrees the constitution underwent great alterations. The twelve Tetrarchs became reduced to three and then to two, and eventually the supreme power over the whole people was acquired [B.C. 65], in the time of Pompey, by Dejotarus, the Tetrarch of the Tolistobogii.[53] When the East became subject to Mark Antony, Amyntas, who had been originally employed in the capacity of secretary to Dejotarus,[54] was [B.C. 36][55] raised to the sovereignty of Galatia.[56] In the war between Augustus and Antony, Amyntas went over to Augustus, and after the battle of Actium was confirmed in his kingdom.[57] Amyntas was slain in an ambush in B.C. 25, and on his death Galatia, with Lycaonia, became a Roman province, under a Proprætor named by the Emperor.[58] Thus at the time when Paul visited Galatia it was under the jurisdiction of an Imperial Proprætor. The principal towns (in all of which there is little doubt that the Apostle preached) were Ancyra (now Angora), Pessinus, and Tavium. The Galatians, like their neighbours, were idolaters. They had brought the Druidical system and their own peculiar deities from Gaul, but ancient writers have not distinguished the Galatian superstition from that of the Greeks and Romans. Jupiter was worshipped at Tavium and Ancyra, and both Jupiter and Cybele at Pessinus.[59]

It is a great disappointment that neither in the Acts nor even in the Epistles can we trace any details of Paul's ministry in Galatia,[60] and we must therefore content ourselves with reasonable probabilities.

---

[51] δύο μὲν τῶν ἡγεμόνων ἐπώνυμοι Τρόκμοι καὶ Τολιστοβόγιοι. Strabo, xii. 5 (p. 55, Tauchnitz); and see iv. 2 (p. 305, Tauchnitz). However, it is more probable that the Tolistobogii or Tolosatobogii (which appears to be the best of several readings) were the people of Tolosa, referred to by Mela as Tolosa Tectosagum. Mela, ii. 5, and see Plin. iii. 5. Thus some of the Gauls are said to have returned "to their ancient country Tolosa" (in antiquam patriam Tolosam, Justin. xxxii. 3), and a similar name is found in Galatia itself, viz. Tolosocorium, Peuting. Tab., and Τολαστάχωρα (Τολασταχώριον) in Ptolemy, v. 4. See J. B. Lightfoot on Galatians, p. 213.

[52] Called Δρυνέμετον. Strabo, xii. 5. The meaning of this word is clear, viz. the Grove-Temple, from the Celtic derw, 'an oak,' and nemed, 'a temple.' See J. B. Lightfoot, Galatians, p. 212.

[53] Strabo, xii. 3, 5 (p. 56, Tauchnitz); Appian, B. C. ii. 71; Flor. iv. 2, 5.

[54] Dion, xlix. 32.

[55] See Fasti Sacri, p. 65, No. 551.

[56] Dion, xlix. 32.

[57] Dion, l. 13; b. 2, 7.

[58] Fasti Sacri, p. 83, No. 676.

[59] Strabo, xii. 5.

[60] I have assumed above that the Galatians were Celts, but it has been disputed (for what has not been disputed?) whether they were Celts

The first town that Paul would approach from Phrygia[51] would be Pessinus, the capital of the Tolistobogii, seated on the southern slope of Mount Dindymus. The great idol of the city was Agdistis, or, in the language of the Greeks and Romans,

or Teutons. The arguments mainly urged for the latter view is the fact mentioned by Jerome, that he traced the identity of the Galatian language with that spoken at Treves, for the Treveri or people of Treves (they say) were not Gauls but Germans. This however seems to be a mistake. The Treveri bordered upon the Germans, and, from the versatility of the Gallic mind, adopted many features of their character. Treveros, quorum civitas propter Germaniæ vicinitatem . . . non multum a Germanis differebat. Cæs. B. G. viii. 25. And as the Germans stood higher in repute than the Celts, were desirous of passing themselves off as of German origin. Treveri et Nervii circa affectationem Germaniæ originis ultro ambitiosi sunt, tanquam per hanc gloriam sanguinis, a similitudine et inertia Gallorum separentur. Ipsam Rheni ripam haud dubie Germanorum populi colunt, Vangiones, Triboci, Nemetes. Tac. Germ. 28. But while the Treveri themselves claimed to be of German lineage, the world at large, judging from their language, manners, and features, set them down as Gauls, or at least as Belgæ, an impure branch of the Gauls. See Tac. Ann. i. 43, 44; iii. 44; Hist. iv, 71, 73; Cæs. B. 9, ii. 4, 24; v. 3, 45; vi. 2, 7, 8; vii. 63. Mela, iii. 2. It has been further insisted that the names of the leaders of the Galatian immigrants, Lutatius and Leonorius, are rather German than Celtic, but apparently these names have in them quite as much of the Celtic as the German element.

On the other hand, the arguments in favour of the *Celtic* origin of the Galatians are overwhelming. Thus:—

1. The very fact that they have been called Galatians attests the general agreement of mankind that they came from Gaul—i.e. were Galli, as opposed to the Germani.

2. One of the Galatian tribes was called Tectosages, and we find this tribe in the west of Gaul, in Aquitain, and it is all but certain that the Tolistobogii also were the people of Tolosa, now Toulouse, in the immediate neighbourhood of the Tectosages. It seems that *part* only of the Tectosages, but the *whole* of the tribes of Troemi and Tolistobogii, migrated; for in the time of Strabo no tribes of the name of Troemi or Tolistobogii were known in any part of Gaul. Strabo, iv, 1 (p. 302, Tauchnitz).

3. The names of places in Galatia have in their terminations a clear affinity to the names of places in Gaul. Thus we have in Galatia—

The termination '-briga,' as in Eccobriga, Peut. Tab., Anton. Itin.; and in Ipetobrogen, Itin. Hieros.

The termination '-iacum,' as in Rosologiacum, Anton. Itin.; Acitorihiacum, Peut. Tab.

So the terminations of names of persons in Galatia are the same as in Gaul. Thus we have the termination '-gnatus,' as in Eposognatus, Livy, xxxviii. 18; '-marus' in Combolomarus, Livy, xxxviii. 19; '-orius,' as in Aeichorius, Paus. x. 19; Orestorius, Paus. x. 22, 2; Comontorius, Polyb. iv. 46, 3; Leonorius, Strabo, xii. (p. 565, Tauchnitz); '-rix,' as in Adiatorix, Cic. Fam. ii. 12; Strabo, xii. 3 (p. 17, Tauchnitz), Albiorix, Ateporix, Boeckh, Insc. No. 4039; '-tarus,' as in Dejotarus, Cic. pro Rege Dejotaro; Brogitarus, Cic. Harusp. Resp. 28, 59.

4. The language generally of the Galatians was that of Gaul. Thus the place where the Galatian parliament met was Δρυναίμετον (Strabo, xii. 5, p. 56, Tauchnitz), which unquestionably is the "grove temple" (as we should expect in a nation amongst whom the Druidical system prevailed), *drw* in Celtic being 'an oak,' from which the Druids are so called, and νεμετον, or nemetum, being the Celtic *named*, 'a temple.' At Clermont, in Auvergne, was the temple of Augustus, called in the vernacular tongue Augustonemetum. So Vernemetum, at Bordeaux, was "the great temple," whence the lines—

Nomine Vernemetis voluit vocitare vetustas,
Quod quasi *Fanum ingens* Gallica lingua refert.
Venant. Fortun. Poematum lib. i. No 9, l. 9.

And another Vernemetum, and for the same reason, was in Britain. Anton. Itin. The identity

---

[a] Renan adopts the strange notion that Paul never visited Galatia at all, and that the Epistle to the Galatians was addressed to the churches planted in his first circuit at Antioch, Iconium, Lystra, and Derbe; all which as he supposes were comprised in the Roman province of Galatia. Renan's St. Paul, p. 51.

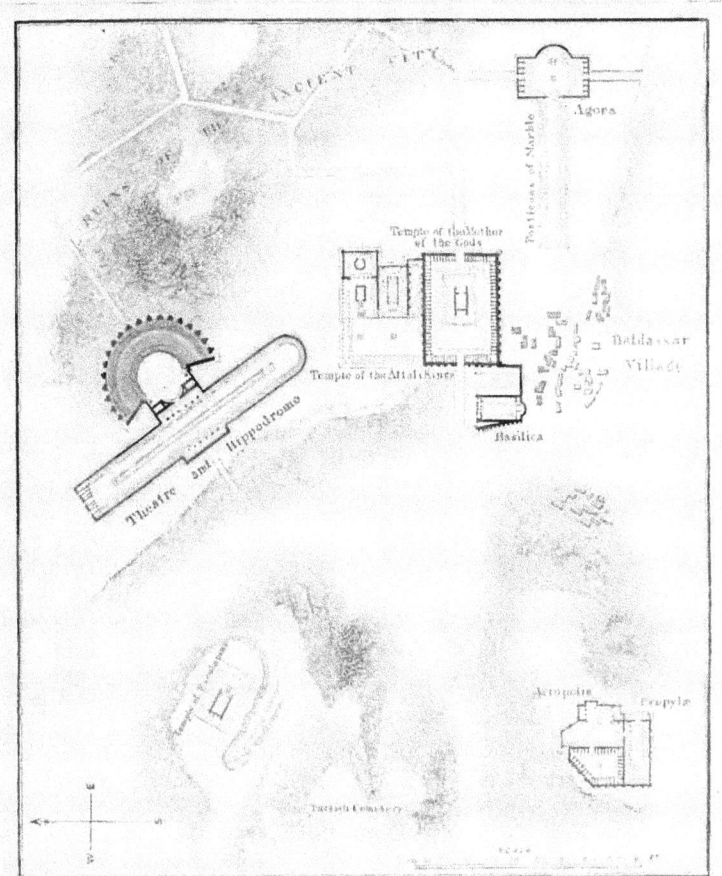

Fig. 82.—Plan of the ruins of Pessinus. From C. Texier.

Fig. 83.—Coin of Pessinus, capital of Tolistobogii. From Pellerin.
Obv. Head of emperor Aurelius.—Rev. Tek. Tower. Hermogenes (or the Pessinuntians of the Tolistobogii of Galatia).

Cybele Dindymene. Indeed, the city itself is said to have derived the name of Pessinus, or Fallingdon, from the legend that the statue of the goddess had here fallen from the skies. Such was the celebrity of this idol over the whole world that in B.C. 204 the Romans, in obedience to a Sibylline oracle, carried it away from Pessinus, and planted it in Rome as the only palladium of their safety. The loss of the image, however, did not impair the veneration for the goddess at Pessinus, but rather increased her fame, and the kings of Pergamus erected a magnificent temple, with porticoes of white marble, in her honour, and surrounded it with a spacious grove. Pessinus, like the rest of Galatia, must have contained a Jewish element, though not perhaps to any great extent. It is remarkable, however, that, as recorded by Pausanias, the inhabitants religiously abstained from swine's flesh,[42] and thence the opinion of some that the population generally was descended from Abraham. But the abhorrence of swine's flesh was not peculiar to the Jews, but common to many other people, and therefore no argument can be built upon it. As Paul addresses his Epistle to the *Churches* of Galatia,[43] and Pessinus was one of the capitals, we must conclude that the Apostle not only preached, but established an organised community there. Pessinus has long since been obliterated from the map of Asia; indeed, we never hear of it after the sixth century, and now the ruins only are traceable (fig. 82). They are to be found about three hours or nine miles to the south of Sèvri Hissar, and extend over three hills, which are covered with blocks of marble, shafts of columns, and other fragments. The principal object is a well-preserved theatre, the marble seats of which are nearly entire.[44]

From Pessinus the Apostle could scarcely fail to follow the direct road laid down on the Antonine Itinerary to Ancyra (fig. 84), a distance of ninety-nine miles. Ancyra was the central point of Galatia, and the capital, not only of the Tectosages (fig. 85), but of the whole country. It existed long before the inroad of the Gauls, and is said to have derived its name "Άγκυρα from the circumstance of Midas, who founded the town, having dug up an anchor in excavating the foundations. Such are the natural advantages of its position that it retains much of its ancient importance, and has undergone but little change even in its name, being still called Angora. The beautiful silken hair of the Angora goat has contributed not a little to this continued prosperity.

---

of the two languages appears also in many other words. Thus Brennus, the leader of the Galatians, signifies 'a prince.' Prasus, another name for the same (Strabo, iv. 4, p. 302, Tauchnitz), 'Terrible.' Cerethrius, the name of another of their leaders (Paus. x. 19, 4), means 'Glorious,' &c. The same phenomenon appears also in many parts of words found in composition. Thus the termination '-briga,' as in Eccobriga, signifies a hill. The termination '-rix,' a king. In the termination '-marus,' 'mar' is 'great.' In the termination '-gnatus' 'gnath' is 'accustomed.'

The substance of the above note is taken from J. B. Lightfoot on the Galatians, where the reader who desires to pursue the subject, will find it most learnedly discussed.

[42] Paus. Achaic. vii. 17, 5.
[43] Galat. i. 2; 1 Cor. xvi. 1.
[44] Smith's Geograph. Dict. Exploration Archéologique de la Galatie, &c., p. 297. See the plan, planche iv., referred to and explained at p. 213 of the latter work.

At Ancyra were the usual idol temples, the tutelary god of the place being Jupiter, in whose shrine, down to the time of Pausanias, the anchor turned up by Midas was still preserved. But amongst the sacred edifices one in particular deserves our notice, viz. the gorgeous temple of white marble erected at the expense of all Asia in the lifetime of the Emperor Augustus, in honour of the Emperor himself as a divi-

Fig. 84.—View of Ancyra, now Angora. From Tournefort.

Fig. 85.—Coin of Sebaste at Ancyra, capital of the Tectosages. From D'Anville.
Obv. Head of emperor.—Rev. Σεβαστηνων Τεκτοσαγων (of the Augustan Tectosages).

nity, and of the goddess Roma (fig. 86). There was the usual staff of priests attached to the temple, and incense and sacrifices were constantly offered up upon the altar. Parts of the fabric still remain, and in a literary point of view are of inestimable value. It is well known that Augustus composed with his own hand a statement of the most glorious transactions of his reign, and directed by his will that it should be engraved on bronze tablets in front of his mausoleum by way of epitaph. A transcript of this valuable record in the original Latin was cut on the walls of the temple at Ancyra in the interior, and a Greek translation was added on the exterior. Great part of the Latin copy, with some portion of the Greek, is legible at the present day, and is commonly known as the Monumentum Ancyranum. The temple not only set forth the achievements of Augustus himself, but there were also inscribed the Imperial decrees affecting the interests of the Asiatic provinces, and amongst them on a pillar of the temple was one issued by Augustus in favour of Paul's own countrymen the Jews, by virtue of which Paul was enjoying much of his present liberty

Fig. 34. Front of the Temple of Rome and Augustus at Ancyra. From C. Texier.

in preaching the Gospel. The decree which Paul may have read *in situ* was as follows: "The proclamation of Cæsar Augustus, Pontifex Maximus," (which fixes the date between the 6th of March, B.C. 12, and 19th of Aug. A.D. 14,[65]) "Tribune of the people. Since the nation of the Jews has been found grateful, not only in the time present, but also in time past, and more especially in the time of my father Cæsar, the Emperor . . . it is decreed by me and my council, with the sentence and oath of the people of Rome, that the Jews be at liberty to use their own customs according

---

[65] See Fasti Sacri, p. 99, No. 775.

to the law of their forefathers," &c., "and this decree I order to be posted up in that most famous place which hath been dedicated to me by the community of Asia at Ancyra."[68]

Fig. 87.—*Specimen of the Inscription in the Temple of Augustus at Ancyra. From the French vol. Exploration Archéologique de Galatie.*

The lacuna is most unfortunate, as mention is made of the "Britanni" and "Dumnobellaunus" their king, and if the passage were entire it would have supplied a missing link in the ancient history of Britain.

Paul's invariable habit was to publish the Gospel in great capitals (as at Damascus, Jerusalem, Antioch, Ephesus, Thessalonica, Corinth, and Rome), and he could not have missed the opportunity of publishing the Gospel at Ancyra, the capital of Galatia, and here therefore was unquestionably another of "the churches of Galatia" to whom Paul afterwards addressed his Epistle.

From Ancyra the high road, according to the Antonine Itinerary, was continued eastward to Tavium, or, as sometimes written, Tavia, the capital of the Trocmi (fig. 88), a distance of 116 miles. Tavium was near the right bank of the river Halys, and was then a place of great commercial consequence. Besides the road which led to it from Ancyra, four other great routes branched out from it on the east into Pontus

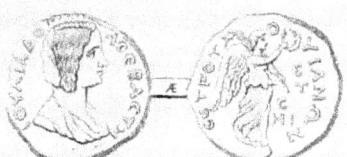

Fig. 88.—*Coin of Tavium, capital of the Trocmi. From Sestini.*
Obv. ΙΟΥΛΙΑ ΣΕΒΑΣΤΗ (Julia Augusta).—Rev. ΣΕ. ΤΡΟ. ΤΡΟΚΜΩΝ (of the Augustan Trocmi of Tavium)

and Cappadocia, a sure sign of the immense traffic that was constantly streaming through its gates. It was also famous for a colossal bronze statue of Jupiter, the deity worshipped in common by all the tribes of the Galatians. The splendour of Tavium has disappeared, and the very site of it has been questioned in modern times.

[68] Jos. Ant. xvi. 6. 2.

Some, as D'Anville, would place it at Tchorum; but this is highly improbable, from the distances given in the Itineraries, and modern geographers with much more probability refer it to Boghaz Kieui, six leagues to the north-west of Jazgat or Juzghat, where are found abundant sculptures in relief, with the wreck of an immense building supposed to be the famous temple of Jupiter.[67] Tavium must have been another of the Galatian "churches" selected by the Apostle,[68] and in after times it was the seat of an episcopal see.[69]

The general result of the Apostle's campaign amongst the Galatians must have been eminently successful. They seem to have embraced Christianity with singular readiness, and quite to have loved the Apostle, the harbinger of such good tidings. There is a most remarkable passage to this effect in the Epistle to the Galatians, upon which we cannot forbear pausing to offer a few comments, as it communicates to us, not indistinctly, something of the Apostle's personal appearance at this his first visit to Galatia.

The Epistle was written after his *second* visit, and the words are as follows: "Ye know how in infirmity of the flesh I preached the Gospel unto you *the former time*,[70] and my temptation which was in my flesh ye despised not, nor *spit me out*,[71] but received me as an angel of God, even as Jesus Christ. What then *was your blessing of me*?[72] For I bear you record, that, if it had been possible, *ye would have plucked out your own eyes and have given them to me*."[73] Here the Apostle alludes to the *thorn in the flesh*,[74] upon which so many different opinions have been entertained, but of which the above words convey the evident explanation. His eyes were so affected by ophthalmia, a state of constant inflammation, as not only to injure the vision, but also to render him a distressing object to every beholder. The Galatians were so enraptured with their spiritual deliverer on this his first visit, that could they, by so doing, have removed so sad an infliction, they would have plucked out their own eyes and have given them to him. Unless we suppose that the Apostle was nearly blind, there is no force in the words, "if it had been possible," for it was quite possible for them to pluck out their own eyes, but the impossibility was to give them to him and so restore *his* vision. The Apostle at his conversion had been subjected to the blaze of the heavenly light, and his eyes may ever afterwards have been more or less affected. For a time he was perfectly blind; the scales then fell from his eyes by the touch of Ananias, but a memento of his sinful career still remained. The climate of Damascus is peculiarly injurious to the sight, and almost all the inhabitants suffer more or less from ophthalmia; and as Paul resided there for nearly

---

[67] Smith's Geograph. Dict.
[68] Galat. i. 2; 1 Cor. xvi. 1.
[69] Cramer's Asia Minor, vol. ii. p. 98.
[70] τὸ πρότερον. Gal. iv. 13.
[71] ἐξεπτύσατε. Galat. iv. 14.
[72] ὁ μακαρισμὸς ὑμῶν. Gal. iv. 15.
[73] Gal. iv. 13–15.
[74] σκόλοψ τῇ σαρκί, 2 Cor. xii. 7; ἀσθένειαν τῆς σαρκός, Gal. iv. 13; πειρασμὸν τὸν ἐν τῇ σαρκί, ib. 14. It is evident from this expression, that whatever the disorder was, it was of the *body* and not of the *mind*.

three years after his conversion, a permanent affection of the vision may have been contracted.

Many texts may be cited, which convey an intimation more or less distinct of the nature of the malady by which Paul was oppressed. Thus in the same Epistle to the Galatians we meet with two other allusions. The Galatians had questioned whether his Apostleship were direct from Christ. He appeals to his miraculous conversion as the ground of his Apostleship, and at the close of the Epistle cuts the matter short by saying, "From henceforth let no man trouble me, for I bear in my body the *brands*[75] of the Lord Jesus."[76] In other words: "If any man doubt my Apostleship, let him but look at me, and he will see the marks which the Lord Jesus imprinted on me as his servant at my conversion." The Greek word refers to the well-known practice amongst the ancients of impressing marks on the forehead with a hot iron. The stamp was sometimes a word, sometimes a letter, sometimes a device, as a horse or a fox.[77] One case in which the custom prevailed, was, where a person was devoted to the service of some god, when the name of the god was burnt upon the forehead. Another was, where a runaway slave was caught and punished, when he was branded with his master's symbol, that on again deserting his master he might not escape detection.[78] In either of these senses, the words of the Apostle are full of meaning; for Paul became at his conversion the servant of the Lord Jesus for life, and the loss of sight was the symbol of his servitude. Or he might look on himself as the fugitive slave who had run from Christ, and was in the midst of his mad career when he was overtaken by him; and in allusion to this he afterwards speaks of himself as *arrested* by Christ: "Not as though I had already attained, either were already perfect; but I follow after, if that I may apprehend that for which also I *was apprehended* of Christ Jesus."[79]

The other passage in the Galatians, referring to the Apostle's infirmity, is the following: "Ye see how large a letter I have written unto you with mine own hand."[80] From the weakness of sight under which he laboured, the operation of writing was always an effort; and his general habit was to employ an amanuensis for the body of the epistle, and to authenticate the letter by inditing with his own hand the closing benediction, "The grace of our Lord Jesus Christ be with you all." Of this he informs us himself in the Epistle to the Thessalonians: "The salutation" or benediction "of Paul with mine own hand, which is the token in every epistle: so I write. The

---

[75] στίγματα. Gal. vi. 17.

[76] Gal. vi. 17.

[77] τούτους ὡς οἰκέτας ἐπώλουν, στίζοντες ἵππον εἰς τὸ μέτωπον, Plut. Nicias, c. 29. ἐπὶ τοῦ μετώπου στίγματα ἐπιβαλλέτω, ἢ ἐγκαυσάτω, κατὰ τὸ μεσόφρυον. ὁ δὲ τύπος τοῦ καυτῆρος ἔστω ἀλώπηξ, ἢ πίθηκος. Lucianus Revivisc. c. 46. And see numerous other passages cited by Wetstein, Gal. vi. 17.

[78] Implevit Eumolpus frontes utriusque ingentibus literis et notum *fugitivorum* epigramma per totam faciem liberali manu ducit. Petronius, 105. Ilerisa deletura diu fronti data signa fugarum. Columel. Hort. 125; and see Wetstein, Gal. vi. 17.

[79] Phil. iii. 12.

[80] Gal. vi. 11.

GRACE OF OUR LORD JESUS CHRIST BE WITH YOU ALL. AMEN."[1] At the time of writing the Epistle to the Galatians he was so deeply concerned for their welfare that, to make the greater impression upon them, he enforced the doctrines he was expounding by penning them (suffering though he was from ophthalmia) with his own hand. At the same time he apologizes to them for the large size and inelegance and almost illegibility of his handwriting. "See," he says, "in what large characters"[2] (not how large a letter, for it was comparatively a short one,) "I have written unto you with mine own hand." They knew his infirmity, and they would attribute the indifferent penmanship to the right cause, and would thence appreciate the zeal that prompted him when their everlasting interests were at stake to struggle against such natural difficulties.

In another epistle (the second to the Corinthians), the Apostle again refers to his besetting infirmity: "Lest I should be exalted above measure through the abundance of the revelations, there was given to me *a thorn in the flesh*, the messenger of Satan, to buffet me, lest I should be exalted above measure. For this thing, I besought the Lord thrice, that it might depart from me. And he said unto me, My grace is sufficient for thee, for my strength is made perfect in weakness. Most gladly, therefore, will I rather glory in my infirmities, that the power of Christ may rest upon me. Therefore, I take pleasure in infirmities, in reproaches, in persecutions, in distresses, for Christ's sake: for when I am weak, then am I strong."[3] The word "thorn" may be derived from two Greek words, signifying "to wither the sight."[4] The term "thorn" is peculiarly applicable to ophthalmia. A writer upon the subject of the Apostle's *thorn* in the flesh, expresses himself thus: "The pain of ophthalmia, when severe, exactly resembles that of a thorn or pin. I once had it very severely indeed in the West Indies. It made me blind, in a manner, for about three weeks; and during that time, if a ray of light by any means broke into my darkened chamber it was like a thorn or pin run into my eye, and so I often described it. I felt, also, the subsequent effect for years (which I suppose to have been experienced by St. Paul), a predisposition to inflammation in the eyes, which extreme care and timely applications prevented from recurring."[5] We have instances in Scripture itself of the application of the word "thorn" to the eye. Thus, in Numb. xxxiii. 55, we read, "If ye will not drive out the inhabitants of the land from before you, then it shall come to pass that those which ye let remain of them shall be pricks" (or thorns) "in your eyes." And again, in Josh. xxiii. 13: "They shall be snares and traps unto you, and scourges in your sides, and *thorns* in your eyes." We can readily imagine how painful

---

[1] 2 Thess. iii. 17, 18. All the fourteen Epistles of Paul (including the Hebrews) are thus authenticated, as will be seen by reference to the closing verses of the several Epistles.

[2] πηλίκοις γράμμασιν. Gal. vi. 11. Had a letter been referred to, the accusative case would have been used, viz. πηλίκα γράμματα.

[3] 2 Cor. xii. 7-10.

[4] σκόλοψ, from σκέλλω and ὄψ.

[5] See Life and Corr. of Hannah More, by Roberts, vol. iii.

such a disorder must have been to one whose life was a constant journey through the open air. How it must have exposed him to insult and ridicule in the presence of unbelieving brethren! In what straits and difficulties he must have been occasionally placed from personal helplessness! It is to these, perhaps, he alludes in the words "Therefore I take pleasure in infirmities, in reproaches, in necessities, in persecutions, in distresses, for Christ's sake; for when I am weak, then am I strong."[76]

Another confirmation of the affection of the Apostle's eyes may be deduced from his conduct before Ananias. When the bystanders said, "Revilest thou God's High Priest?" Paul answered, "I wist not, brethren, that he was the High Priest."[87] The explanation is, that his imperfect sight had not enabled him to distinguish who it was that spoke, and when informed that he had insulted the High Priest he immediately made an apology and pleaded his ignorance of the personage whom he had addressed.

We shall only refer to one other circumstance as connected with the Apostle's infirmity, and it is this, when a tumult arose at Beroea, the disciples "sent away" Paul, and "they that *conducted* him brought him to Athens;"[88] and in writing to the Thessalonians he mentions it as a proof of his regard for them, that when Timothy had come up with him at Athens, he had sent him to Thessalonica, so that he was *left alone*.[89] Is it not reasonable to suppose, that, as the Apostle was more especially suffering during this circuit from an impaired eyesight, he could neither travel by himself without danger, nor could he be left alone in a strange place without great personal inconvenience?

Paul had now preached successively in the three capitals, Pessinus, Ancyra, and Tavium, and had thus evangelised the whole region of Galatia. But whither next was he to bend his steps? Was he to push forward into Cappadocia or Pontus on the east, or was he to turn his face again to the west?

On his first circuit, after evangelising successively Antioch of Pisidia, Iconium, Lystra, and Derbe, he retraced his steps through Derbe, Lystra, Iconium, and Antioch, for the purpose of confirming the new disciples; and we may suppose that on the present occasion, on this his second circuit, Paul adopted a similar policy, and followed back his own footsteps in a reverse order from Tavium, through Ancyra and Pessinus, until he re-entered Phrygia. There is also this further parallelism between the first and second circuit: not only did Paul, on his first circuit, *plant and revisit* the churches of Antioch in Pisidia, Iconium, Lystra, and Derbe, but he *again revisited* them at the commencement of his second circuit; and so in Galatia, not only did he plant and probably revisit the churches during his second circuit, but he again returned to them at the commencement of the next, his third, circuit.[90]

The concise account by Luke of this part of the second circuit is pregnant with

---

[86] 2 Cor. xii. 10. [87] Acts xxiii. 5. [88] Acts xvii. 15.
[89] 1 Thess. iii. 1. [90] Acts xviii. 23.

meaning, and we give it entire: "Now when they had gone throughout Phrygia and the region of Galatia, and were forbidden of the Holy Ghost to preach the Word in Asia, after they were come to Mysia, they essayed to go into Bithynia, but the Spirit suffered them not; and they, passing by Mysia, came down to Troas."[91] As the Apostles were advancing from Galatia westward there lay round about them, in a semicircle, three contiguous countries, viz. Asia, or Lydia, on their left hand to the south;[92]

---

[91] Διελθόντες δὲ τὴν Φρυγίαν καὶ τὴν Γαλατικὴν χώραν, κωλυθέντες ὑπὸ τοῦ Ἁγίου Πνεύματος λαλῆσαι τὸν λόγον ἐν τῇ Ἀσίᾳ, ἐλθόντες κατὰ τὴν Μυσίαν, ἐπείραζον κατὰ τὴν Βιθυνίαν πορεύεσθαι, καὶ οὐκ εἴασεν αὐτοὺς τὸ πνεῦμα· παρελθόντες δὲ τὴν Μυσίαν, κατέβησαν εἰς Τρωάδα. Acts xvi. 6–8.

[92] The word 'Asia' has been used from time to time in various senses.

1. The name seems to have originated from the plain of the Cayster, on which Ephesus was situate, and which is called by Homer "the Asian meadow":—

Ἀσίῳ ἐν λειμῶνι, Καϋστρίου ἀμφὶ ῥέεθρα.
Iliad, ii. 461.

and so Virgil, his imitator:—

Asia . . . prata Caystri.
Georg. i. 383.

2. From the banks of the Cayster the name communicated itself to the whole of Lydia, the country occupied by the people through whose domain the Cayster flowed. The Lydi or Mæones, for they were the same people, were called Ἠϊονεῖς, the Ionic for Ἀσιονεῖς, and hence all Lydia or Mæonia came to be known as Asia. Strabo, xiii. 1 (p. 151, Tauchnitz).

3. When Crœsus, King of Lydia, extended his conquests over all the tract west of the Halys and north of the Taurus, the whole of his dominions, extensive as they were, passed by the name of Asia.

4. Subsequently, the name propagated itself over the entire continent now called Asia, and this enlarged application of the term was in common use as early as the time of Herodotus.

5. In after times the Kings of Pergamus established a kingdom bounded by the Halys on the east and the Mæander on the south, and called themselves Kings of Asia; and when Attalus III. (B.C. 133) bequeathed his dominions to the Romans, the new acquisition was known as Asia. οἱ δ' [Romans] ἐπαρχίαν ἀπέδειξαν τὴν χώραν, Ἀσίαν προσαγορεύσαντες ὁμώνυμον τῇ Ἠπείρῳ, Strabo, xiii. 14 (p. 149, Tauchnitz).

6. In the time of the Apostles, Asia was generally understood amongst the Greeks and Romans to mean the proconsular province of that name, which consisted principally of the kingdom of Pergamus, which had been left by Attalus III. to the Romans, but with various additions from the surrounding countries, as by the incorporation of Caria. See Wieseler, Apostg. 32.

7. When Agrippa, in the time of Augustus, had the government of the East (B.C. 23), he divided the peninsula into two parts by drawing a line of demarcation from north to south, across the middle of it, Plin. N. H. v. 28; but this distribution is passed over in silence by other historians, and never came into vogue.

8. The name of Asia Minor, or Anatolia, by which we now distinguish the peninsula, was not known to the ancients; but it was a natural division, and Strabo is very particular in describing it under the name of the "Chersonese" or "Peninsula," and makes the eastern boundary run from the Bay of Issus on the south to Amisus on the Euxine on the north. The name of Asia Minor, in opposition to Asia Major, did not obtain currency until the 4th century of our era, and is first mentioned by Orosius. Asia regio, vel (ut proprie dicam) Asia Minor. Or. lib. i. c. 2.

We are here more particularly concerned with the Asia of the New Testament, and this we take to be identical with Lydia. The limits of Lydia were these: on the north it was bounded by the Caicus, which separated it from Mysia. No doubt it was the opinion of some that Mysia extended as far south as Thyatira; ἣν [Thyatira] Μυσῶν ἐσχάτην τινές φασιν, Strabo, xiii. 1 (p. 151, Tauchnitz); but Strabo himself did not agree to this, for he places Mysia to the north of Pergamus, which was on the Caicus: τὰ δὲ προσάρκτια τῷ Περγάμῳ τὰ πλεῖστα ὑπὸ Μυσῶν ἔχεται. Ib. From the Caicus, Lydia extended along the coast, southward as far as the Mæander, which divided it from Caria: τὰ δὲ πέραν ἤδη τοῦ Μαιάνδρου . . . πάντα ἐστὶ Καρικά, οὐκέτι τοῖς Λυδοῖς ἐπιμεμιγμένων τῶν Καρῶν. Strabo, xiv. 2 (p. 191, Tauchnitz). There was, however, to the north

Bithynia on their right hand to the north; and between the two, and in front of them on the west, was Mysia. Their first impulse upon quitting Phrygia was to make for Asia, but "they were forbidden of the Holy Ghost to preach the Word in Asia;" then they turned their eyes towards Bithynia, but "the Spirit suffered them not;"[93]

of the Mæander an admixture of the Carian blood. Thus, says Strabo, on the road from Ephesus towards the east, through Tralles, you have ἐν δεξιᾷ τὸ Μαιάνδρου πεδίον, Λυδῶν ἅμα καὶ Καρῶν νεμομένων, Strabo, xiv. 1, 42 (p. 188, Tauchnitz). But the Carian element to the north of the Mæander was never recognised nationally.

Thus much for the boundaries of Lydia on the north and west and south; but towards the east there is more difficulty. To begin from the north and descend southward, there lay to the east, at some distance from the sea border, the Mæonians, with Thyatira for their capital, whom some distinguished from the Lydians, but in Strabo's opinion they were the same people under another name, and Mæonia, therefore, was part of Lydia: οἱ μὲν τοὺς αὐτοὺς τοῖς Λυδοῖς, οἱ δ' ἑτέρους ἀποφαίνοντες· τοὺς δ' αὐτοὺς ἀμεινόν ἐστι λέγειν, xiii. 4 (p. 151, Tauchnitz); and so Ptolemy, Λυδίας δὲ τῆς καὶ Μῃονίας, v. 2, 16. To the south of Mæonia was the region called Κατακεκαυμένη, the Burnt country, from the subterranean fires and constant earthquakes, and Strabo gives the dimensions of it as sixty-two and a half miles in length, by fifty in breadth. As it commenced to the south of Philadelphia (Strabo, xii. 8, p. 76, Tauchnitz), it would apparently comprise Laodicea, Colossæ, and Hierapolis, which were notoriously subject to these convulsions of nature; and if so, these cities would be Lydian, for Katakekaumene was certainly either Mæonian or Mysian, and Mysia did not in the Apostle's time extend so far south. Μετὰ δὲ ταῦτ' [the Mæonians] ἔστιν ἡ Κατακεκαυμένη λεγομένη χώρα, μῆκος μὲν καὶ πεντακοσίων σταδίων, πλάτος δὲ τετρακοσίων, εἴτε Μυσῶν χρὴ καλεῖν εἴτε Μῃονίαν, λέγεται γὰρ ἀμφοτέρως. Strabo, xiii. 4, 11 (p. 155, Tauchnitz). Katakekaumene, however, may not have been intended by Strabo to include Laodicea, Colossæ, and Hierapolis, and if not, these cities would be comprised in the region next described by him as lying between Katakekaumene and Cibyra, which was at the northern part of the Lycian Taurus. As to this territory geographers were entirely at fault, from the mixture of races. It was occupied confusedly by Lydians, Phrygians, and Carians, with a sprinkling of Mysians, so that no one could separate them: ὥστε καὶ τὰ Φρύγια καὶ τὰ Λύδια καὶ τὰ Καρικὰ καὶ ὅτι τὰ τῶν Μυσῶν δυσδιάκριτα εἶναι. Strabo, xiii. 1, 12 (p. 156, Tauchnitz). Strabo, after throwing out these doubts about the nationalities, treats these parts as Phrygian, xiv. 2 (p. 212, Tauchnitz); xii. 8 (p. 72, Tauchnitz). It is remarkable, however, that while he locates Laodicea and Colossæ in Phrygia (Strabo, xii. 8, p. 72, Tauchnitz) he comprises Hierapolis, which was close to Laodicea, and visible from it, under Lydia: Strabo, xiii. 4 (p. 157, Tauchnitz); and see Cramer's Asia Minor, vol. ii. p. 36.

It is difficult also to reconcile Strabo's assumption that Laodicea was Phrygian with his other statements, for in tracing the course of the Cayster upward to its source, he makes Phrygia commence as far eastward as Peltæ: τὸ Πελτηνὸν πεδίον ἤδη Φρύγιον, xiii. 4 (p. 157, Tauchnitz); and again, in describing the range of Messogis as running from Celænæ on the east to Mycale on the west, he speaks of the Phrygians as occupying that part of it only which lay about Celænæ and Apamea Cibotus. τὰ μὲν αὐτοῦ Φρύγες κατέχουσι, τὰ πρὸς Κελαιναῖς καὶ τῇ Ἀπαμείᾳ· τὰ δὲ Μυσοὶ καὶ Λυδοί· τὰ δὲ Κᾶρες καὶ Ἴωνες. xiii. 4 (p. 156, Tauchnitz).

Ptolemy assigns Laodicea to Caria, v. 2, 18. But Stephanus Byzant. more correctly to Lydia: ἔστι δὲ καὶ ἑτέρα (Λαοδίκεια) Λυδίας, Ἀντιόχου κτίσμα τοῦ παιδὸς τῆς Στρατονίκης, τῇ γὰρ γυναικὶ αὐτοῦ ὄνομα Λαοδίκῃ, Steph. Byz. Λαοδίκεια; and so also does St. John in the Apocalypse, for he includes Laodicea amongst the seven churches of Asia, Rev. i. 4; iii. 14. This view harmonises best with surrounding geography, for the Laodicean district is close upon Lydia, and if the debatable territory were divided between the competing countries of Lydia, Phrygia, and Caria, would naturally fall to the share of Lydia. We have also the authority of Renan for saying that the people of these parts were not of the Greek, but, as is evidenced by the names of the mountains and rivers and towns, and other peculiarities, of the

---

[93] Acts xvii. 7.

and thus the will of man was foiled a second time. The world was to be Christianised by a few fishermen from Galilee and a tentmaker from Tarsus, and it was necessary that their labours should be so husbanded that the Christian ministry might be the most effective. For this purpose the Apostles were not at liberty to preach as their own inclination or judgment dictated; but their course was prompted by a higher power. Paul and Silas being thus precluded from pursuing their journey either to the left towards Asia or to the right towards Bithynia, they "passed by"[34] Mysia; that is, they did not stop to preach the Word in it (for it was of a mountainous character and thinly peopled), and came down to Troas—the port for embarkation for any country to which the Holy Spirit might send them.

---

emitic stock, and he considers the district as properly belonging to Lydia: "une annexe de la Lydie." Renan's St. Paul, p. 359.

The Asia of the New Testament, then, is not Proconsular Asia, or any political division, but a country distinguished from others by its nationality and language. Thus, at the gift of tongues on the day of Pentecost, "the dwellers in *Asia*" heard the Apostles speak "in their own language," Acts ii. 9. In short, the Asia of the New Testament is neither more nor less than the Lydian Asia.

This is further confirmed by the fact that all the seven churches of Asia addressed in the Apocalypse are found in Lydia, and fill up its whole space without exceeding the limits. Thus, Pergamus is on the left bank of the Caïcus, at the northern extremity of Lydia; Smyrna and Ephesus are on the western coast; Laodicea is at the southern end; while Sardes, Thyatira, and Philadelphia are spread over the central and eastern parts. If Asia be Lydia, we see also why, in the New Testament, it is distinguished from Mysia, Troas, Bithynia, Phrygia, &c., which has often occasioned embarrassment.

[34] The Greek word is παρελθόντες (Acts xvi. 8), which has been variously interpreted. According to some, it means simply 'passing *through*.' According to others, 'passing *by*,' in the sense of passing alongside of it. And according to others, and with more reason, 'passing *by*,' in the sense of neglecting it, and omitting to preach in it—the view adopted in the text.

1. Those who advocate the first opinion, say that Mysia lay between Galatia and Troas, and that in passing from one to the other it was impossible to avoid Mysia, and that παρελθόντες therefore can only be taken to mean 'passing *through*.' This translation, however, does violence to the Greek word, which will not properly bear such an interpretation.

2. Those who advance the second opinion, suggest that there were two Mysias, the Greater and the Less—that the Greater was to the south of Troas and to the west of Galatia; and that the Less lay between Bithynia and the mouth of the Æsepus, along the sea coast, and reached back to Olympus. ὅμως δ᾽ ἐφ᾽ ὅσον εἰσιέζειν οἰόν τε, τῆς μὲν Βιθυνίας μέσην ἄν τις θείη καὶ τῆς ἐκβολῆς τοῦ Αἰσήπου τὴν Μυσίαν, ἀποτομένην τῆς θαλάσσης καὶ διήκουσαν μέχρι τοῦ Ὀλύμπου σχεδὸν δὲ παντός. Strabo, xii. 4, 4 (p. 52, Tauchnitz), and that the Troad extended from the Æsepus, which disembogued a little to the west of Cyzicum, to the Promontory of Lectum, a few miles to the south of Alexandria Troas, and lay between the two Mysias (see Strabo, xiii. 1 (p. 88, Tauchnitz); Plin. N. H. v. 32, 10); so that the Apostles might thus have passed from Galatia to the Troad, between the two Mysias, without entering either. There is a want of proof, however, that any interval between the two Mysias existed, and it would rather seem, as we should expect, that they bordered upon each other.

3. The third opinion is thought to be the more correct one. On the right lay Bithynia, which the Apostles could not enter, and on the left was Asia, from which they were also debarred. Between the two lay Mysia, divided into the Greater and the Less. Paul and Silas would, therefore, necessarily have to cross Mysia, and as παρελθόντες can only signify 'passing *by*' and not '*through*,' it is better to interpret it as 'passing by,' not in a geographical, but in a metaphorical sense; that is, they omitted to preach the Word in Mysia, and hastened down to Troas. The reason of the omission may have been the paucity of inhabitants in the mountainous region at the back of the Troad.

The town of Troas was on the sea-coast, about four miles from ancient Troy and six miles south of the entrance to the Hellespont, and was properly called Alexandria Troas (fig. 89). It was founded by Antigonus, one of the successors of Alexander the Great, and called by him Antigonia Troas, but finished by Lysimachus, another of Alexander's generals, and by him called Alexandria Troas.[35] It afterwards received the honour of being a Roman colony,[36] with the Italicum jus,[37] or immunity from direct taxes, as the land tax and poll tax,[38] with municipal government; and this honour was acquired

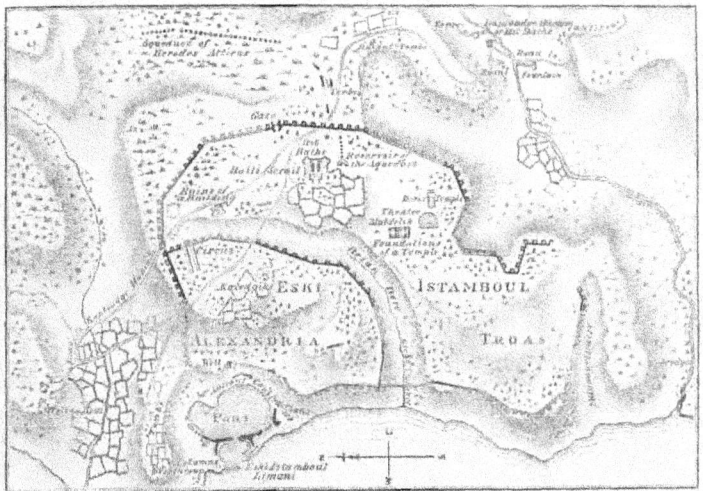

Fig. 89.—Plan of the remains of Alexandria Troas. From Choiseul Gouffier.

as early as in the time of Augustus, for we read on coins " Col. Aug. Troas "[39] (fig. 90). It stood on a gentle eminence sloping down to the sea, flanked on each side by an extensive plain, and divided from Mount Ida at the back or east by a deep ravine. It owed its importance to an artificial port, consisting of an inner and outer basin, and for many centuries it was the key of the traffic between Europe and Asia. Some idea may be formed of its ancient greatness from the fact, that the walls which can still be traced enclose a circuit of several miles. It is now an utter ruin. There are the few remains

---

[35] Winer's Realw. 'Troas.'

[36] νῦν δὲ καὶ Ῥωμαίων ἀποικίαν δέδεκται καὶ ἔστι τῶν ἐλλογίμων πόλεων. Strabo, xiii. (p. 100, Tauchnitz). Ipsaque Troas Antigonia dicta, nunc Alexandria, colonia Romana. Plin. N. H. v. 33.

[37] Juris Italici sunt Τρωάς, Βήρυτος, Δυρράχιον. Id est Troas, Berytus, Dyrrachium. Digest, l. 15, 7. In provincia ' Asia' duæ sunt juris Italici, Troas et Parium. Digest, l. 15, 8, 9.

[38] Winer's Realw. 'Colonie.'

[39] Eckhel, vol. ii. p. 481.

of a theatre and odeum and a stadium and gymnasium, and on the ground that environs the port are still to be seen the low granite pillars to which the cables of the vessels in which Paul sailed were fastened; but a sand-bank has blocked up the mouth of the port and no ship can enter (fig. 91). When Chandler was there it was a perfect desolation. "A solemn silence," he says, "prevailed, and we saw nothing alive but a

Fig. 90.—*Coin of Troas. From the British Museum.*
Obv. Col. Troa. (colony of Troas).—Rev. Col. Aug. Tro. (colony of Augusta Troas).

fox and some partridges."[100] It is now called Eski Stamboul, or Old Constantinople. The most imposing of all the relics which time has left is the gymnasium, which crowns the hill and stands a conspicuous object to the passing mariner. The building fronted towards the west, and was 413 feet from north to south, and 224 feet from

Fig. 91.—*View of Port of Troas. The spectator is standing at the extreme end of the port, and is looking westward, that is, to the mouth of the port and toward the sea. From J. Murray's Illustrated New Testament.*

east to west. The portico was beautified with sculptures of the finest marble in the Corinthian style.

The Apostles, it is said, "*came down*" to Troas, and the expression shows that they descended from the highlands of Mount Ida, and must have approached the very site of Troy. Bent as he was upon his high calling, Paul, a classical scholar,

---

[100] Chandler's Travels in Greece and Asia Minor, vol. i. p. 28.

and so imbued with Grecian literature that he could familiarly cite Aratus and Epimenides and Menander, could scarcely have passed unmoved over the scene of the immortal Iliad. The towers of Troy above, and the Simois and Scamander below, and the plumes of the panoplied heroes and the harnessed steeds, must have been present to the mind's eye. But twelve hundred years had intervened, and nothing remained but the mountain and plain—of Troy itself not a vestige! And who would recognise, in those shallow reedy streams, the Simois and Scamander of the poet's fancy? The storm of war had swept over the spot, and now it was the path of the messengers of peace. Europe had poured forth her thousands to desolate and destroy; and Asia, in return, sent her three way-worn pilgrims—Paul, Silas, and Timothy—to proclaim to Europe the healing truths of the Gospel. They passed on and entered Alexandria Troas.

It was during this circuit, and while Paul and Silas were bringing Galatia and Phrygia into subjection to the Gospel, that the Romans, after a struggle of many years, succeeded at length in establishing their power in Britain by the capture of the famous chieftain Caradoc, better known by his Latinised name of Caractacus. For nine years (that is, from the first invasion by Aulus Plautius in A.D. 42 to A.D. 50) had the hero Caractacus, with the stubborn courage of a true Briton, maintained himself with honour against the Imperial armies. But his allies, one after another, had been destroyed or succumbed, and Ostorius, the Proprætor, now pressed upon him with overwhelming force. Caractacus had retreated to the fastnesses of Wales, and, taking up a strong position in the north, awaited the attack of the enemy. The Britons, without helm or corslet, and unskilled in military tactics, could ill stand against the charge of the disciplined veterans of Rome. Caractacus was defeated, and his wife, daughter, and brothers were all made captives. He himself escaped to Cartismandua, the Queen of the Brigantes, (will Yorkshiremen acknowledge their ancestors?) when the British hero was treacherously put in chains and delivered up to the victors. The fame of Caractacus had been noised throughout Italy, and, when the captive was brought to Rome, curiosity was on the stretch to see the man who had so long defied the armies of the Empire. Not Perseus, the last King of Macedonia and the successor of Alexander the Great, had excited by his presence a more lively interest. The Prætorian bands (the household troops) stood under arms in the open area before the camp, and the Emperor Claudius ascended the tribunal or throne erected for the purpose on a raised stage, and the people of Rome hemmed in the pageant with a dense living mass. First were paraded the trophies taken in war; then followed the wife and daughter and brothers of Caractacus; last of all came the hero himself—

Pride in his port, defiance in his eye.

"Had my moderation," he said, addressing the Emperor, "been equal to my success, I had appeared here as a friend, not as a captive—the Emperor of Rome would not have spurned the alliance of one nobly descended, and the chieftain of many states. My present lot redounds indeed as much to your glory as to my ignominy. I once had horses, men, arms, treasures. What wonder if I resolved to keep them? If you would lord it over all, it follows not that all would be lorded over by you. Had I yielded without a blow, neither had I won a name nor you your laurels. Wreak your vengeance on me, and the deed will soon pass into oblivion; preserve my life and the memorial of your clemency will endure for ever." Claudius on this, as on other occasions, was actuated by generous sentiments, and pardoned Caractacus, and gave him back his family.[161] Caractacus had been a prisoner in the Prætorium, and though now his life was spared he probably remained at Rome under some surveillance. Some years after Paul also arrived at the Prætorium, and was two years prisoner at Rome, in the neighbourhood of the Prætorium. Is it not possible that Paul and Caractacus, men who had both perilled their lives in a great cause, may have met at Rome, and even that the ex-king of Britain may have become a Christian?

[161] Tac. Ann. xii 37.

CHAPTER XI.

Paul carries the Gospel into Europe—He preaches at Philippi, Thessalonica, and Berœa.

> No more shalt thou, by oracling abuse
> The Gentiles; henceforth oracles are ceased,
> And thou no more with pomp and sacrifice
> Shall be inquired at Delphos or elsewhere;
> At least, in vain, for they shall find thee mute.
> God hath now sent his living oracle
> Into the world to teach his final will,
> And sends his Spirit of Truth, henceforth to dwell
> In pious hearts; an inward oracle
> To all truth requisite for man to know.
>
> Paradise Reg. b. i.

It was not improbably the anxious wish of Paul at this time, A.D. 51, to transfer his labours to Rome. The Apostle of the Gentiles would naturally desire to visit the metropolis of the Gentile world and about six years after this he wrote to the Romans, "Oftentimes I purposed to come unto you, but was let hitherto."[1] And again, "I have had a great desire *these many years* to come unto you."[2] But "Man proposes and God disposes." A voyage to Rome at this time would have been of little avail, for an edict was shortly afterwards issued by the Emperor Claudius that all Jews should depart from the Imperial city, and Paul, as a Jew, would have been within the terms of the proclamation.

The Apostle was a humble instrument in the hands of his Maker for the accomplishment of a great purpose; and while he was ruminating whither to direct his steps, a divine interposition resolved the doubt, and pointed to Macedonia. "A vision appeared to Paul in the night. There stood a man of Macedonia, and prayed him, saying, 'Come over into Macedonia, and help us.'"[3] The sacred narrative proceeds, "And after he had seen the vision, immediately we endeavoured to go into Macedonia, assuredly gathering that the Lord had called *us* to preach the Gospel unto them."[4]

This remarkable passage ushers for the first time upon the stage, and only thus incidentally, the affectionate companion of Paul, the zealous minister of the Gospel, and the accomplished writer, Luke, the author of the Gospel, and of the Acts of the Apostles. From the words "assuredly gathering that the Lord had called *us* to preach the Gospel unto them," it is evident that Luke was not now a convert for the first time, but that he had long been associated with Paul in the Christian cause.

---

[1] Rom. i. 13.   [2] Rom. xv. 23.   [3] Acts xvi. 9.   [4] Acts xvi. 10.

Had there been no previous acquaintance between them, it is not conceivable that Luke should have spoken of himself and Paul as then jointly commissioned to preach, or that he would have said afterwards, "*We sat down (at Philippi), and spake unto the women.*"[5] There can be little doubt that Luke and Paul had been previously labouring together in the same vineyard at Antioch, the chief seat of the Gentile church.

That Luke was a native of Antioch[6] is a tradition handed down by Eusebius[7] and Jerome;[8] but perhaps the fact was an inference drawn by themselves from the circumstance of Luke's constant abode there. The Cambridge manuscript has a reading of Acts xi. 28,[9] "And *when we were gathered together*,[10] there stood up one of them, named Agabus," &c., from which it would appear that Luke was at that time (A.D. 43) a member of the church at Antioch; but the words in italics have been rejected by all the best critics, and cannot be relied on. Whether they be genuine or not, they at least show a very ancient opinion in favour of a circumstance highly probable in itself.

What was Luke's worldly occupation we learn from the Epistle to the Colossians, "Luke, the beloved *physician*, and Demas, greet you;"[11] and perhaps, though it is mere conjecture, his professional skill may have been the cause of his presence at Troas. We know from the Apostle's own statement, that in the circuit which he had just concluded through Galatia, he had been labouring under great infirmity, and a message may have been transmitted to the "beloved physician" to join him at that seaport, the common resting-place of all voyagers between Asia and Europe. That they crossed each other's path accidentally, we cannot believe.

So little is known of the private history of Luke, that it has been much disputed whether he was a Jew or a Gentile; but we concur with Grotius (though in opposition to the learned Lardner), that the following passage from the Colossians evinces conclusively that Luke was a Gentile: "Aristarchus, my fellow-prisoner, saluteth you; and Mark, cousin to Barnabas (touching whom ye received commandments, if he come unto you, receive him), and Jesus, which is called Justus, *who are of the circumcision.* These only are my workfellows unto the kingdom of God, which have been a comfort unto me. Epaphras, who is one of you, saluteth you, always labouring fervently for you in prayers, that ye may stand perfect and complete in all the will of God; for I bear him record that he hath a great zeal for you, and them that are in Laodicea and them in Hierapolis. *Luke, the beloved physician, and Demas, greet you.*"[12] Luke was a fellow-labourer, and was so regarded by the Apostle,[13] and

---

[5] Acts xvi. 13.
[6] But if Luke be identical with Lucius, he was of Cyrene, see ante, p. 113, note [4]. Renan makes Luke a native and proselyte of Philippi; but his reasons are not convincing.
[7] Λουκᾶς δὲ, τὸ μὲν γένος ὢν τῶν ἀπ' Ἀντιοχείας. Euseb. iii. 4.
[8] Λουκᾶς ἰατρὸς Ἀντιοχεύς. Hieronymus de Illustribus Viris.
[9] See Wetstein and Alford ad loc.
[10] συνεστραμμένων δὲ ἡμῶν. Acts xi. 28.
[11] Col. iv. 14.
[12] Col. iv. 10–14.
[13] Philem. 24.

had he been a Jew, it is impossible that Paul should have said of Aristarchus, Mark and Justus, "who are of the circumcision, *these only* are my workfellows." There is an evident contrast between the circumcision and the uncircumcision, and amongst the latter Luke is classed. The name of Luke, whether an abbreviation of Lucanus, Lucius, or Lucilius, is heathen; and it is nowhere suggested that he had any Jewish name. It has also been remarked that while Paul, as a Jew, uses the expression "by night and day," Luke reverses it and writes as would a Greek, "by day and night."[14] There is also a passage in the Acts which would lead to the same inference: "Now this man [Judas] purchased a field with the reward of iniquity; and falling headlong, he burst asunder in the midst, and all his bowels gushed out; insomuch as that field

Fig. 92.— *View of Alexandria Troas. From a sketch by the author in passing.*

is called *in their proper tongue*,[15] Aceldama, that is to say, the field of blood."[16] This has been thought by some to be part of the speech of Peter, and that "in *their* proper tongue" means, in the *dialect* of Judea, as opposed to that of Galilee. But Peter would scarcely so address his own countrymen at Jerusalem, and the same phrase is used presently in the sense of a distinct language: "We hear every man *in our own tongue*,[17] wherein we were born, Parthians and Medes," &c.[18] It is probable, therefore, that the citation is the passing remark of Luke the historian, and if so, it would furnish an argument that the writer was of a different nation from those who spoke Hebrew.

Paul and Sylvanus, and Timothy, with the addition of Luke, set sail from Troas, and pursued the usual track towards Macedonia (fig. 92). As they had a fair wind,

[14] See note of Wordsworth on 1 Thess. ii. 9.
[15] τῇ ἰδίᾳ διαλέκτῳ αὐτῶν. Acts i. 19.
[16] Acts i. 18, 19.
[17] τῇ διαλέκτῳ ἡμῶν. Acts ii. 8.
[18] Acts ii. 8.

they voyaged the same day as far as Samothrace (still called Samothraki), lying about halfway between Troas and the Macedonian port (fig. 93). Samothrace was an island

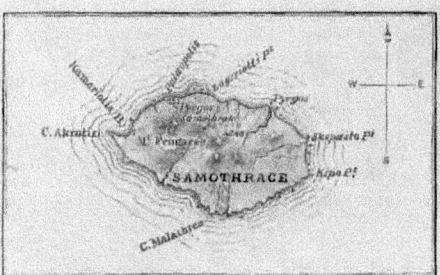

Fig. 93.—Island of Samothrace. From Admiralty Chart.

Fig. 94.—Coin of Samothrace. From the British Museum.

Obv. Head of Pallas.—Rev. Σαμο (Samothrace) Μητρωνα.

Fig. 95.—The view eastward from the foreshore of the Troad. From a sketch by the author in passing.

Showing the truthfulness of Homer's description that the mountains of Samothrace, which are 5248 feet high, commanded a view of the plains of Troy. The island immediately in front is Imbros, and the mountain beyond in the centre of the picture is Samothrace.

some eight miles long and six miles broad, and from its lofty ridges might be seen the battle-field of Troy:—

> ὑψοῦ ἐπ' ἀκροτάτης κορυφῆς Σάμου ὑληέσσης
> Θρηϊκίης, ἔνθεν γὰρ ἐφαίνετο πᾶσα μὲν Ἴδη,
> φαίνετο δὲ Πριάμοιο πόλις. Homer, Il. v. 12.

> The lofty peaks of woody Samothrace,
> The eye can thence in shadowy distance trace,
> The plain where Simois and Scamander flow,
> And Priam's town and Ida's beetling brow.[20]

[20] This passage is a remarkable instance of the geographical accuracy of Homer. Looking at the charts, one would think it impossible that the plains of Troy should be seen from Samothrace, as Imbros and the Rabbit Islands lie between; but, in fact, in sailing by Troy, you see the explanation (as Eöthen first pointed out), viz. the Rabbit Islands are insignificant and low, and though Imbros is of great extent, and the country mountainous, yet the peaks of Samothrace are far higher, and easily overlook it (see fig. 95).

The next day they sailed to Neapolis,[20] or New Town, now Cavallo, and thus for the first time carried the Gospel from Asia into Europe. Neapolis was no inconsiderable town, lying just opposite Thasos, at the northern end of the Thasian Bay. It was seated on a rocky peninsula, running out as an advanced sentinel from Mount Pangæus, which here lined the coast from west to east. The principal object, as one approached by sea, was the Parthenon, or Temple of Diana, which crowned the highest point of the saddleback which supported the city. This temple so closely resembled the Parthenon of Athens, that an opinion (not improbable on other grounds) has been hazarded that Neapolis was an Athenian colony. It had not, properly speaking, a port, but there was a roadstead on the east side of the peninsula,[21] where was found good holding ground for anchorage and protection on three sides from the violence of the elements; but the vessels suffered when it blew from the south-west, and in that case they were obliged to take shelter under the neighbouring island of Thasos.[22]

---

[20] Acts xvi. 11. At a subsequent time, Paul and Luke reversed the voyage, and sailed from Neapolis to Troas in *five* days. Acts xx. 6. The wind, therefore, must have been against them on the latter occasion.

[21] The writer of the article 'Neapolis' in Smith's Dict. of the Bible, places a harbour on the west side also of the peninsula.

[22] Mission Archéologique de Macédoine, par ordre de Napoléon III. p. 11 et seq. (1864). Cousinery places Neapolis, the port of Philippi, not at Cavallo, but at Eski Cavallo, about fifteen miles to the south-west of Cavallo. This port, called Lentere Liman, is described as follows: "L'entrée de ce port est au nord-est. Nous y pénétrâmes par la seule bouche qu'il présente aux navigateurs qui souvent y cherchent un abri contre les vents du sud et du sud-ouest. Ce passage a une largeur suffisante pour que deux bâtiments de guerre y entrent en même temps. . . Ce port est très-vaste; c'est un grand ovale d'un bon quart de lieue de profondeur." Cousinery, vol. ii. p. 116. But Eski Cavallo cannot be Neapolis, for the following reasons.

1. When Brutus and Cassius, advancing from the east, pitched their camp a little to the west of Philippi, on the River Gangites, now the Bournabaschi, it is expressly said that the port from which they drew their supplies at Neapolis was *behind* them, ἣν δὲ . . . θάλασσα ὄπισθεν, ἐν ᾗ καὶ τὰ ταμιεῖα καὶ ἐνορμίσματα ἔμελλον ἕξειν. Appian, B. C. iv. 106. Now, Cavallo answers this requisite exactly, but Eski Cavallo would not be *behind* them, but rather in *front* of them, so that their supplies might be cut off by the enemy. How, then, could Eski Cavallo have been fixed upon as the base of their operations?

2. The Via Egnatia, or great road across Macedonia and Thracia, from west to east, passed successively, according to all the Itineraries (Anton., Hieros., and Peut. Tab.) through Amphipolis, Philippi, Neapolis, and Acontisma. But how is it conceivable that the road, after passing by Eski Cavallo, on the way from Amphipolis to Philippi, should turn twenty miles back again to Eski Cavallo, and then again resume an eastern direction? On leaving Philippi, the road must necessarily have gone to Cavallo direct, and not to Eski Cavallo; for to the east of Philippi the mountains bar further progress, but on the south-east, and just at the back of Cavallo, is a gap in Mount Pangæus, as if for the very purpose of giving access to the sea, and through this opening is still the Turkish high road from Philippi to the sea. As the Via Egnatia was running eastward, it would naturally take advantage of the first practicable passage in that direction.

3. The distances given by the Itineraries and the historians agree with Cavallo, but not with Eski Cavallo. Thus, Neapolis, according to the Jerus. Itinerary, was ten miles, and according to the Antonine Itinerary, was twelve miles from Philippi. The exact distance is thirteen kilomètres, or a little more than eight miles English, and about nine miles Roman, which agrees well enough with the Itineraries; but Eski Cavallo is about twenty miles from Philippi, and therefore could not be Neapolis. Again, Appian describes the camp of Brutus and Cassius, or rather perhaps Philippi itself, as seventy stades, or about nine miles, from Neapolis (App. B. C.

Neapolis, notwithstanding these drawbacks, was the invariable landing-place for travellers who were bound for the great military road through Macedonia, called the Via Egnatia, which here had its commencement, and led through Philippi,[23] across Macedonia to Epidamnus and Apollonia.

We must here, on entering Macedonia, introduce a hasty sketch of the country as it presented itself to the Christian missionaries.

The successors of Alexander the Great upon the throne of Macedon maintained the independence of the kingdom until the year B.C. 167, when Perseus, the last of the line, was utterly defeated at Pydna by Paulus Æmilius, and Macedonia became a Roman province. The conquerors, for the better prevention of a general rebellion, divided Macedonia into four districts, called respectively Macedonia the First, Second, Third, and Fourth. The first division extended from the River Nestus, the

Fig. 96.—Coin of Macedonia Prima. From the British Museum.
Obv. Head of Diana.—Rev. Μακεδονων Πρωτης (of the Macedonians, First division).

eastern boundary of Macedonia, to the River Strymon on the west, and the capital was at first Amphipolis, but afterwards, and at the time of which we are speaking, Philippi (fig. 96). The second region lay between the Strymon to the east and the River

---

iv. 106), which again approximates to the actual distance from Cavallo; but is wholly at variance with the distance from Eski Cavallo.

4. The next station to Neapolis, eastward, on the Via Egnatia, was Acontisma, which according both to the Antonine and Jerusalem Itinerary, was at the distance of nine miles. The theory of those, who advocate Eski Cavallo as Neapolis, places Acontisma at Cavallo; but the distance between these two is not nine miles but fifteen miles; and, again, Acontisma must have been much more eastward than Cavallo, for it was beyond the limits of Macedonia, and lay in Thrace. Ex angulo tamen orientali [Thraciæ] Macedonicis jungitur [Thracia] collimitiis per arctas præcipitesque vias, quæ cognominantur Acontisma. Ammian Marcell. xxvii. 4, 8.

5. As Neapolis was the port of Philippi, which was the capital of that part of Macedonia, it must have been a Roman station of some consequence, and accordingly we find there numerous and important Roman remains, as "a massive aqueduct, which brings water into the town from a distance of ten or twelve miles . . . built on two tiers of arches a hundred feet long, and eighty feet high . . . marble sarcophagi, with Latin inscriptions of the age of the Emperor Claudius; columns with chaplets of elegant Ionic workmanship, blocks of marble, fragments of hewn stone," &c. Smith's Dict. of Bible. But at Eski Cavallo it does not appear that there are any remains which can be carried back beyond the middle ages.

6. It has been objected to Cavallo that in fact it is not a port at all. But is not this an argument in its favour? For nowhere is it said that

---

[23] ἐνόρμιτρα ταῖς τριήρεσι Νέαν πόλιν. Appian, B. C. iv. 106.

Axius to the west, with the capital Thessalonica (fig. 97). The third was bounded by the Axius on the east, and the Peneus on the west, with the capital Pella, the birthplace of Alexander the Great. The fourth portion of the kingdom was at the rear on the west

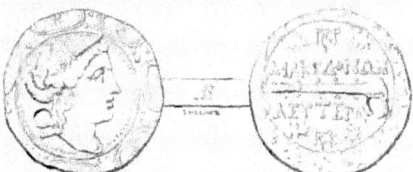

Fig. 97.—*Coin of Macedonia Secunda. From the British Museum.*
Obv. Head of Diana.—Rev. Μακεδονων Δευτερας (of the Macedonians, Second division).

of the second and third divisions, along the confines of Illyria, with the capital Pelagonia or Heraclea (fig. 98).[24] These different districts were kept wholly distinct, and the

Fig. 98.—*Coin of Macedonia Quarta. From the British Museum.*
Obv. Head much defaced. Rev. Μακεδονων Τεταρτης (of the Macedonians, Fourth division).
N.B.—There is no coin extant of the Third division.

inhabitants of one were not allowed to intermarry with those of another, or to have any dealings with them in respect of lands or houses.[25] Subject, however, to arbitrary decrees, emanating from time to time from the Roman Senate, the Macedonians were permitted to live under their ancient laws. The cities had their own magistrates, and the general affairs of each division were settled by a council summoned to the capital of the district, and consisting of delegates sent from the principal cities.[26] The supreme power over the whole province was vested in the Proconsul, who fixed his residence at Thessalonica, as the capital of the entire country.

No part of the Roman policy was more useful to mankind than their solicitude, for state reasons, to facilitate intercourse between Rome and her dominions by the construction of military roads. Thus, the approaches to Macedonia from Italy were by

---

Neapolis was a *port*, but only that it was ἐπίνειον (App. B. C. iv. 106), i.e. a roadstead or good anchoring ground; and that is remarkably the character of Cavallo, for while there is no close port, there is a roadstead on the east side of the little peninsula on which Cavallo stands (Mission Archéol. de Macédoine, iii. 11); and also, it seems, on the west side. Smith's Dict. of Bible.

[24] Livy, xlv. 29.

[25] Neque connubium neque commercium agrorum aedificiorumque inter se placere cuiquam extra fines regionis suae esse. Livy, xlv. 29.

[26] In quatuor regiones describi Macedoniam, ut suum quaeque concilium haberet, placuit. Livy, xlv. 18.

the two ports of Apollonia, and Dyrrhachium or Epidamnus, the Calais and Boulogne of Macedonia. From these points two converging roads were carried up the country and met at Claudiana, whence the great highway called the Via Egnatia traversed Macedonia from west to east, and passing through Heraclea, Pella, Thessalonica, Amphipolis, and Philippi, united the capital cities by a ready communication. From Philippi the road was continued to the seaport of Neapolis, whence the traveller might take ship and pursue his route by sea.

It was probably the design of Paul to effect the conversion of Macedonia by visiting successively the capitals of the four districts, viz. Philippi, Thessalonica, Pella, and Heraclea. This intention was carried out in the present circuit as regards the *three first divisions*, but we shall see that the storm of persecution which burst out at Thessalonica, and followed him to Berœa, obliged him to abandon a portion of his original plan, and that he had no opportunity of visiting the *fourth division* to the west of Macedonia until about six years after, viz. in A.D. 57.

Paul and his fellow-travellers, having landed at Neapolis, took the road to Philippi.

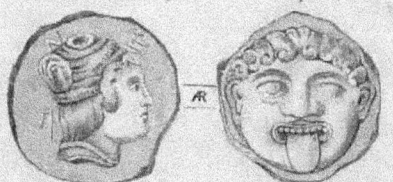

Fig. 90.—*Coin of Neapolis. From Clarke's Travels.*
Obv. Head of Diana with the legend NEAΠ (Neapolis).—Rev. Head of a monster.

Thanks to his Imperial Majesty Napoleon III. we have now a perfect knowledge of this part of the country, from the archæological survey lately made under his auspices by Messrs. Henzy and Daumet, who have executed their task with great ability. Quitting Neapolis by its western gate, Paul and his companions ascended the hollow way which led in a north-westerly direction to the pass (a miniature Thermopylæ) over Mount Pangæus (fig. 100).[27] This range, which separates the valley of Drama from the sea, here makes a dip, and from the facility of the ascent the Via Egnatia naturally took this direction. Upon gaining the summit of the pass our travellers had before them a magnificent view. On the northern side of the valley to their left was seen Philippi, with its walls and towers crowning a spur of the mountain that bounded the valley on the north. Just below them was a little fertile plain, the apex or commencement of the valley of Drama, shut in by mountains on the north, south, and east, and watered by the stream of the Zygactes, now the Zygosto,[28] which, flowing from the north-east to the south-west of the valley, pours itself into the vast marsh, bristling with gigantic reeds, between Pangæus on the south and the suburbs of Philippi on the north. Zygactes, in Greek, has the meaning of 'pole-break,' and

[27] Mission Archéol. de Macédoine, p. 12 (1864). [28] Mission Archéol. &c. p. 34 (1864).

hence the fanciful Greeks invented a legend to account for the name. The young lass Proserpine, they said, was gathering flowers in the luxuriant meadows on the banks of the rivulet, when Pluto fell in love with her and carried her off in his chariot, but as he drove across the bed of the stream he broke the pole of the car, and thence the name of Zygactes, or Pole-break. To the west of this little plain the marshes between Philippi and Pangæus stretch away for several miles, and are then succeeded by the rich pastures and ploughed lands of the valley of Drama, as far as the Strymon.

Fig. 199.—View of the road by which Paul started from Neapolis over Mount Pangæus for Philippi. From Mrs. Walker's Albania.

Paul could scarcely have failed to pause for a moment on the heights of Pangæus to sweep with his eye the beautiful and interesting prospect before him, and he must at the same time have breathed a prayer for the success of his mission in so glorious a vineyard. The travellers now descended into the little plain watered by the Zygactes, and then, skirting the marsh on their left, pursued the road in a northerly direction, and next turning westward along the foot of the northern mountain range, traversed the beaten road, still lined on either side by tombs, until they reached Philippi. The distance from Neapolis to Philippi was, according to Appian, about nine miles,[20] and according to the Jerusalem Itinerary ten miles, and according to the Antonine

[20] ἐνώρμισμε δὲ ταῖς τριήρεσι Νέαν πόλιν, ἀπὸ ἑβδομήκοντα σταδίων. App. B. C. iv. 106.

Itinerary twelve miles, and according to Galen even fifteen miles;[30] but recent admeasurement has ascertained the exact distance to be from twelve to thirteen kilometres, or about eight miles.[31]

Luke describes Philippi as " the chief city of that part" (or division) " of Macedonia, and a colony,"[32] and the accuracy of the sacred penman is remarkable ; but to appreciate it we must trace for a moment the history of Philippi. The place was at first

Fig. 101.—*The Tomb of Vibius on the road to Philippi. From Mission Archéologique de Macédoine.*

Fig. 102.—*Coin of Philippi. From the British Museum.*
Obv. Head of Augustus, with the legend Cæsar Aug. P. M. Tr. P. Imp. (Cæsar Augustus Pontifex Maximus, with the Tribunitian Power, Imperator).—Rev. Figures of Julius Cæsar and Augustus, and the legend Col. Aug. Jul. Philip.

called Crenides, or Fountains, from its numerous springs, which, rising in the mountains on the north, ran down into the marsh to the south of Philippi. It also at one time bore the name of Datum. Crenides, or Datum, was originally in Thrace, for Macedonia was anciently bounded on the east by the Strymon ; but Philip of Macedon, the father of Alexander the Great, having triumphed over the Thracians, extended the limits of Macedonia to the river Nestus, now the Kara Su. As the Thracians were a warlike and restless people, it was necessary to establish a garrison on the frontier to repress their incursions ; and Philip fixed on Crenides as the most suitable spot,

[30] ἐν Φιλίπποις ἐγενόμην, ἥπερ ἐστὶ ὅμορος τῇ Θρᾴκῃ πόλις. ἐντεῦθεν ἐπὶ τὴν πλησίον θάλασσαν κ ἐπὶ τοῖς ρ΄ ἀπέχουσαν στάδια κατελθών, ἔπλευσα πρότερον μὲν εἰς Θάσον ἐγγὺς τοῦ α΄ σταδίους, ἐκεῖθεν δὲ εἰς Λῆμνον ψ΄, εἶτ' αὖθις ἀπὸ Λῆμνου τοὺς ἴσους ψ΄ εἰς Ἀλεξάνδρειαν Τρωάδα. Galen de Facult. Medic. [31] Mission Archéol. p. 19. [32] Acts xvi. 12,

and erected a fortress on the crown of the hill, on the southern slope of which Crenides stood, and called the name of the place after himself, Philippi.[23] He at the same time worked the mines in the neighbouring mount, called Bacchus's Mount, now Raktcha, about a mile to the north of Philippi,[24] and made them yield the enormous sum of one

Fig. 103.—Coin of Octavius and Antony and Lepidus (the Triumvirate). From C. W. King's *Antique Gems*. Octavius (the most to the left) and Antony are placed side by side, and Lepidus by himself, facing them.

thousand talents per annum. Indeed he is said to have attained his supremacy over the rest of Greece by means of the ample treasures which were thus poured into his coffers.[25] What gave Philippi its greatest celebrity was the famous battle of Philippi (A.D. 42) between Octavius and Antony on the one side and Brutus and Cassius on the other. About two kilometres, or ten furlongs, to the west of Philippi, a small river, called the

[23] The name of Philippi was long preserved in the village of Filibedjik, but has now disappeared. Renan's St. Paul, p. 140.

[24] See Mission Archéol. &c. p. 58.

[25] The identity of Philippi with Crenides and Datum has been assumed in the text, and is the result of the following authorities:—Δάτος· Μετωνομάσθη μέντοι ἡ πόλις τῶν Δατηνῶν, Φιλίππου τοῦ Μακεδόνων βασιλέως κρατήσαντος αὐτῆς. Harpocration. πλεῖστα μέταλλα ἐστὶ χρυσοῦ ἐν ταῖς Κρηνίσιν ὅπου νῦν οἱ Φίλιπποι πόλις ἵδρυται, πλησίον τοῦ Παγγαίου ὄρους. . . . ἡ νῦν Φίλιπποι πόλις Κρηνίδες ἐκαλοῦντο τὸ παλαιόν. Strabo, Excerpt. ex lib. vii. 17 and 20 (p. 133, Tauchnitz); and see Diod. xvi. 8. οἱ δὲ Φίλιπποι πόλις ἐστὶν ἡ Δάτος ὠνομάζετο πάλαι, καὶ Κρηνίδες ἔτι πρὸ Δάτου, κρῆναι γὰρ εἰσὶ περὶ τῷ λόφῳ ναμάτων πολλαί. Φίλιππος δ' ὡς εὐφυὲς ἐπὶ Θρᾴκης χωρίον ὠχύρωσέ τε, καὶ ἀφ' ἑαυτοῦ Φιλίππους προσεῖπεν . . . Φιλίππων μὲν οὖν ἕτερος λόφος οὐ μακρὰν, ὃν Διονύσου λέγουσιν, ἐν ᾧ καὶ τὰ χρυσεῖά ἐστι, τὰ Ἄσυλα καλούμενα. Appian, B. C. iv. 105, 106. And in the following fragments from Strabo, it is evident from the description that by Datum is meant Philippi: εἰσὶ δὲ περὶ τὸν Στρυμονικὸν κόλπον πόλεις καὶ ἕτεραι, οἷον Μύρκινος, Ἄργιλος, Δραβῆσκος Δάτον, ὅπερ καὶ ἀρίστην ἔχει χώραν καὶ εὔκαρπον καὶ ναυπήγιον καὶ χρυσοῦ μέταλλα, ἀφ' οὗ καὶ παροιμία Δάτον ἀγαθῶν, ὡς καὶ Ἀγαθῶν ἀγαθίδες. Strabo, excerpt. ex lib. vii. 16 (p. 133, Tauchnitz). It will be observed here, that Amphipolis is not mentioned at all, while Philippi or Datum is put prominently forward as commanding great resources by land, and enjoying commercial prosperity. This countenances what is otherwise probable, that Amphipolis had at that time been superseded by Philippi as the capital of Macedonia Prima. The ναυπήγια, or docks, were probably at Neapolis, now Cavallo. This would appear from Appian, iv. 108, who observes that Brutus and Cassius had this advantage over Augustus and Antony, that while the latter were distressed for provisions, the former, being in possession of Philippi, could procure unlimited supplies from Neapolis. When Appian states that Brutus's army advanced to Philippi, ἔνθα αὐτοῖς καὶ ὁ Τύλλιος ἐπικατήχθη (iv. 105), it is not meant, as Biscoe understands it, that Tullius sailed up to Philippi, which was impossible, but only that he landed his troops at the port of Philippi. Pliny distinguishes Datum from Philippi, and places it on the coast to the east of Neapolis. Plin. N. H. iv. 18. The identity of Datum with Philippi has been doubted by J. B. Lightfoot, on Philipp. p. 46, but recent explorations assume Philippi to occupy the very site of Datum. See Mission Archéol. &c. p. 62.

Gangas or Gangites, now the Bournabachi, flowed from the mountain on the north across the valley of Drama, into the western end of the great marsh to the south of Philippi. The armies of Brutus and Cassius lay behind, i.e. on the eastern bank of

Fig. 104.—*Coin of Brutus. From the British Museum.*
Obv. Head of Brutus with the legend Brutus Imp.—*Rev.* Trophy with the legend Casca. Longus. The features of Brutus as represented on this and other coins are extremely mean, and not at all corresponding to one's preconceived idea of Brutus the patriot.

Fig. 105.—*Coin of Cassius. From Pembroke collection.*
Obv. Head of liberty with the legend C. Cassius Imperator Leibertas.—*Rev.* The pontifical emblems, with the legend Lentulus Spinther.

this stream, Brutus fixing his headquarters on the natural platform or terrace on the slope of the northern mount, and Cassius on an eminence, a spur of Pangæus, at the south of the plain on the borders of the marsh. Between the two camps, and connecting them together, was thrown up an earthwork, consisting of a fosse and vallum

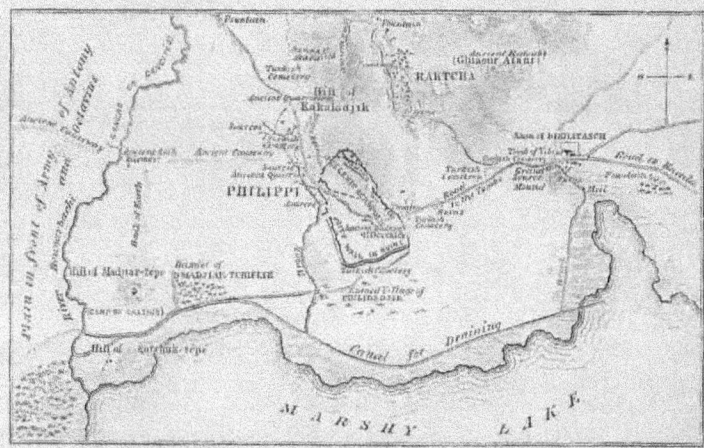

Fig. 106.—*Plan of Philippi. From the French Mission Archéologique de Macédoine.*

for barring the passage to the armies of Octavius and Antony encamped on the plain of Drama, to the west of the River Gangas (fig. 106). The remains of this earthwork can be traced to a considerable distance, even at the present day.[26] The advance of Octavius and Antony from Amphipolis was thus checked, while, at the same time,

[26] Mission Archéol. p. 103.

delay would be fatal to them from the want of supplies. Antony, however, by an unexpected attack at mid-day, gained possession of the mount occupied by Cassius and plundered his camp. Brutus, on the other wing, was victorious against Octavius, though, on the defeat of his colleague, he could not push his success. Cassius fled back to Philippi, and looking from the summit of the hill saw the enemy ransacking his camp. The sight overwhelmed him, and, in the agony of the moment, he commanded Pindarus, his armour-bearer, to despatch him with the sword. Two days after, Brutus, from the imprudence of his officers and the pusillanimity of his troops, was utterly routed, when he escaped to the mountainous region northward, in the vain hope of again rallying his forces. But deserted by all, and choosing to die by the hand of a friend rather than a foe, he implored his comrade Strato to take his life, a behest which was obeyed.[37]

In honour of so signal a victory, Philippi was patronised by Augustus, and a colony of Romans was settled there,[38] with the Italicum Jus, which carried with it immunity from taxes and other privileges,[39] so that Latin was the language of the colonists, while Greek was spoken by the native population. As Amphipolis, the former capital, had fallen into decay, Philippi, now a flourishing city and a Roman colony, with Neapolis for a seaport, was adopted as the metropolis of Macedonia Prima, and made the seat of government. In the Peutinger Table, accordingly, Philippi is represented as a city of consequence, for houses are drawn on the site, but Amphipolis is merely mentioned and no houses are annexed. Thus it was rightly designated by Luke as at that time the "first city of that division of Macedonia, and a colony."[40]

Philippi itself was situate on the rounded termination of a hill or mount, which stood out into the plain from the north. Its walls inclosed all the southern slope of the hill from the castle on the summit, and stretched a considerable distance into the plain below, though not quite so far as the marsh.[41] The circuit of the walls as now traced

---

[37] Appian, B. C. iv. 109, et seq.

[38] τοὺς γὰρ δήμους τοὺς ἐν τῇ Ἰταλίᾳ τοὺς τὰ τοῦ Ἀντωνίου φρονήσαντας ἐξοικίσας, τοῖς μὲν στρατιώταις τάς τε πόλεις, καὶ τὰ χωρία αὐτῶν, ἐχαρίσατο· ἐκείνων δὲ δὴ τοῖς μὲν πλείοσι τό τε Δυρράχιον καὶ τοὺς Φιλίππους ἄλλα τε ἐποικεῖν ἀντέδωκε. Dion Cass. li. 4. Intus Philippi colonia, Plin. N. H. iv. 18. Wetstein (Ep. to Philip. sub initio) also mentions an ancient stone with the inscription "Col. Jul. Philippensis;" and Eckhel, vol. ii. p. 76, describes coins of Philippi with the inscription on the obverse "Col. Aug. Jul. Phil. Juss. Aug." and on the reverse, two figures, one of Augustus and the other of Julius Cæsar, and elicits from them that a colony was planted at Philippi by Augustus. The full title would appear from inscriptions to be, "Colonia Augusta Julia Victrix Philippensium." See Mission Archéol. p. 18.

[39] Colonia Philippensis juris Italici est. Digest, l. xv. 6. In provinciâ Macedoniâ, Dyrrhachieni, Cassadrenses, Philippenses, Dienses, Stovenses juris Italici sunt. Digest, l. xv. 8, 9.

[40] Others, however, think that Amphipolis retained its rank, and have recourse to other interpretations of the passage in Luke. Thus, according to some, πρώτη πόλις means only a principal city and not the principal city of this division. According to others it means the primæ coloniæ city of the division. According to others it was the first city in point of locality to a person approaching it from the east, Neapolis being, as they say, either a marine suburb or port of Philippi, or beyond the limits of Macedonia, and deemed part of Thrace. Meyer, Apostg. 292.

[41] ἔστι δὲ ἡ πόλις ἐπὶ λόφου περιερῥωγυῖαν, τοσαύτη τὸ μέγεθος ὅσον ἐστὶ τοῦ λόφου τὸ εὖρος. ἔχει

incloses a space only of twelve hundred metres from north to south, and eight hundred metres from east to west.[42] But the city must anciently have extended far beyond these narrow limits.

The town comprised within it two distinct quarters, divided by the Via Egnatia, viz. the High Town to the north and the Low Town to the south. The former, the original Greek city, had once been surrounded by an Hellenic wall, and portions of it may still be distinguished. The Low Town was a subsequent accretion, as the place rose into importance. The High Town contained the citadel, or fortress, at the summit, and a theatre for scenic representations at the south-east corner. The northern part, the High Town, was so interrupted by projecting rocks as to be unfit in places for human habitation; and here and there the rock has been scarped, and figures of the popular deities have been carved upon it. Amongst other divinities are found Bacchus, the tutelary god of the whole district; Minerva, Diana, Mercury, Hercules, and Mēn, or Lunus, i.e. the Moon, as a god, and not as a goddess.[43] Next to the theatre, on the west, was a temple to Sylvanus, which opens a curious chapter of heathen mythology. Sylvanus was what may be called a vulgar god, not one of the fashionable deities, like Apollo or Diana. Sylvanus had been mightily honoured by Rome in its rudest state, but as civilisation increased the rustic gods gave way to the patrons of refined life. When Philippi became a colony, the Romans who settled there were the rough soldiers who had stood on the side of Antony and Octavius on the field of battle,[44] and these hardy veterans, as drawn from the lower ranks of life, brought with them a deep veneration for the primitive but neglected deity, Sylvanus. A temple was erected to him at Philippi, and some inscriptions found upon the spot contain interesting particulars about the construction and fitting up of the edifice.[45] One tablet furnishes a list of benefactions. The first name is that of Publius Hostilius Philadelphus, the ædile or chief of the collegiate body incorporated for the worship of the god. Another subscriber is the donor of a bronze statue of the deity, with a shrine to contain it; another helps to roof the building, another advances a

δὲ πρὸς μὲν ἄρκτῳ δρυμούς, ... πρὸς δὲ τῇ μεσημβρίᾳ ἕλος ἔστι καὶ θάλασσα μετ' αὐτό, κατὰ δὲ τὴν ἕω τὰ στενὰ τὰ Σαπαίων τε καὶ Κορπίλων· ἐκ δὲ τῆς δύσεως πεδίον μέχρι Μυρκίνου τε καὶ Ἀμφίπολου καὶ ποταμοῦ Στρυμόνος, τριακοσίων που καὶ πεντήκοντα σταδίων, εὔφορον πᾶν καὶ καλόν (now the valley of Drama). Appian, iv. 105. The old traveller Belon thus describes it: "Philippi maintenant n'est qu'un village, ou il n'y a que cinque ou six maisons basties, hors le circuit des murailles près de l'eau. Philippi enceinet et contient une grande plaine et une partie de la prochaine montaigne, jusqu'à la sommité où la muraille comprend un chateau bien faite qui est dessus la montaigne et a des cisternes qui sont encore entières. Les murailles de Philippi sont quasi totallement ruinées, faites de brique et cément, et en quelques endroits de pierre de taille mais sans aucunes fossez ne douves. Philippi est située en plain du coté de levant, ayant la montaigne du coté de l'occident qui lui sert de forteresse. La plaine est si humide qu'elle semble estre quasi un marez." Belon, c. 56, p. 57. And see the Missionary Herald, vol. xxxii. No. 9; and more recently still the Mission Archéologique de Macédoine.

[42] Mission Archéol. p. 67.

[43] So in German, der (not die) Mond. See the figures of the gods of Philippi in Mission Archéol.

[44] See Mission Archéol. p. 119.

[45] See Mission Archéol. p. 71.

sum of money, &c. A second tablet sets forth the sodales, or members of the sacred college, and many of the names are already familiar to us from the Acts of the Apostles and the letters of St. Paul, such as Crescens, Secundus, Trophimus, Aristobulus, Pudens, Urbanus, and Clemens.[46] The social positions also of the persons inscribed convey to us a distinct idea of the motley crowd amongst whom Paul sought for converts; some are freemen and some are slaves (either the public slaves of the colony or of individuals), some (and these constitute a large class) had been slaves, but became freedmen.[47] In short, the inscriptions show how truly the features of the period are reflected on the pages of the writers of the New Testament.

The Lower Town, on the south of the Via Egnatia, presents but one relic of antiquity, which however is of paramount interest, viz. the forum where Paul and Silas were publicly scourged. Just within the eastern gate, and on the south side, are four massive pillars, which are so conspicuous an object as to have given to the spot the name of Derekler, or the Columns. They were supposed by Belon to have belonged to a temple of Claudius, but this has been disproved;[48] and recent explorations lead to the inference that here was the forum or market-place of Philippi. A minute examination of the ruins by a competent judge has elicited the general outline of the original plan. The four imposing columns already referred to stood at the four corners of an open court, which was surrounded by the courts of justice and other public buildings.[49] This was properly the forum, answering to the Forum Romanum of the mother city, of which Philippi, as a Roman colony, was the miniature. This first and more ornamented court led to another and larger quadrangular area, which served as the market-place for the sale of commodities.[50] The forum and the market-place, though often confounded, were quite distinct. The first, being the exchange or bourse, employed for public meetings and the administration of justice, and the latter (the market-place) being used for the sale of commodities.

To return to the Apostles. Paul and Silas and their company entered Philippi by the eastern gate, and following the broad street that continued the Via Egnatia, had on their right hand the theatre and then the temple of Sylvanus, and on their left the forum, soon to become the scene of an unjustifiable outrage against themselves.

There were no doubt many public hostelries in the town, but it was Paul's custom to seek the calm and retirement of a private lodging. Having secured the necessary accommodation, he lost no time in addressing himself to the duties of his ministry.

It would seem that there was not a synagogue at Philippi, but that in lieu of it there was a proseucha, an oratory or place of prayer.[51] The Jews did not form any

---

[46] See Mission Archéol. p. 72.
[47] See Mission Archéol. p. 75.
[48] See Mission Archéol. p. 87.
[49] See Mission Archéol. p. 89.
[50] See Mission Archéol. p. 90.
[51] That 'proseucha' was the common term for a Jewish meeting-house may be collected from the words of the poet:

Ede ubi consistas, in quâ te quæro proseuchâ?
Juv. Sat. i. 3. 296.

See Philo, Leg. ad Caium, c. 23; and Renan's St. Paul, p. 146.

considerable part of the population, as may be inferred from the fact that the persecution which followed arose, not as usual from the Jews, but from the Gentiles. This paucity of the Jews may be readily accounted for, as Philippi was a military garrison, a colony of soldiers, and as almost all Jews out of Judea were engaged in trade, and on account of their religious peculiarities were exempt from serving in the Roman armies, the atmosphere of Philippi would be little adapted to commerce. Not only was there no synagogue at Philippi, but even the proseucha or oratory was without the walls, as if the strict laws of an unenlightened and intolerant soldiery had not permitted a despised and hated race to erect a place of worship so at variance with idolatry in close proximity to the temples of their own deities. These proseuchæ were commonly in the open air and uncovered, being spacious areas, like *fora* or market-places.[52] The Jewish ceremonial law was accompanied with frequent ablutions; and the public worship was generally conducted for convenience in the immediate vicinity of water;[53] and Luke places the oratory in question without the city, by the side of a river,[54] and as the Pythoness met them on the way and followed after them,[55] it would seem that this river was not immediately under the walls of the city, but at some little distance. Now Philippi is surrounded by numerous little springs, whence its old name of Κρηνῖδες; but there is only one river (ποταμός) in the vicinity, viz. the stream (which is also designated by Appian as a river or ποταμός), which was called the Gangas or Gangites, and is now known as the Bournabachi.[56] It takes its rise from the mountain range at the north of the valley of Drama, a little to the west of Philippi, and runs across the plain in a southward direction, until it falls into the great marsh at the northern foot of Pangæus. The Via Egnatia, after leaving Philippi on the west, cuts the river at right angles at the distance of about two kilometres, or a little more than a mile, from the town. On the road from Philippi, along the Via Egnatia westward, and just before reaching the river, you come to a triumphal arch (of which there are still some remains) at the point where the entrenchments of Brutus and Cassius were carried across the plain to connect their two camps. This arch, erected to commemorate the victory of Philippi, was perhaps the commencement of the suburbs of Philippi; at least, up to this point the sides are lined with the remains of tombs.[57] The oratory of the Jews may have been just beyond the arch, and on the banks of the Bournabachi.

---

[52] ἔξω τῆς πόλεως ἐν τῇ πεδιάδι ὡς ἀπὸ σημείων δύο θεατροειδῆς, οὕτως ἐν ἀέρι καὶ αἰθρίῳ τόπῳ. Epiphan. Hæres. lxxx. 1. lib. iii. tom. 2, p. 1068.

[53] Thus there is a decree of Halicarnassus, permitting the Jews to build oratories by the seaside. δέδοκται ἡμῖν Ἰουδαίων τοὺς βουλομένους, ἄνδρας τε καὶ γυναῖκας, τά τε σάββατα ἄγειν, καὶ τὰ ἱερὰ συντελεῖν κατὰ τοὺς Ἰουδαϊκοὺς νόμους, καὶ τὰς προσευχὰς ποιεῖσθαι πρὸς τῇ θαλάσσῃ κατὰ τὸ πάτριον ἔθος, κ.τ.λ. Jos. Ant. xiv. 10, 23. And see Lardner, vol. i. p. 115, ed. 1838. And when the προσευχαί at Alexandria were destroyed, the Jews ἐπὶ τοὺς πλησίον αἰγιαλοὺς ἀφικνοῦνται, τὰς γὰρ προσευχὰς ἀφῄρηντο, καὶ ἐν τῷ καθαρωτάτῳ στάντες ἀνεβόησαν. Phil. in Flac. 14.

[54] ἔξω τῆς πόλεως παρὰ ποταμόν. Acts xvi. 13.

[55] Acts xvi. 16, 17.

[56] App. B. C. iv. 106.

[57] Mission Archéol. 118.

As Paul's invariable practice was to make the first appeal to his own countrymen, the missionaries on the Sabbath day attended divine service at the oratory for the purpose of preaching the new doctrine. "And on the Sabbath," says Luke, "we went out of the city by a river side, where prayer was wont to be made, and we sat down and spake unto the women which resorted thither."[58] Why the congregation should have consisted of women has not been satisfactorily explained; but as in the synagogue the women sat separately from the men, and were generally screened by a lattice-work, it has been conjectured, and it is very possible, that from straitness of room the service may have been performed at one time of the day to one sex and at another time to the other. The address of the Apostle was not without fruit; for at least one of his audience, Lydia by name, a seller of purple, from the city of Thyatira (fig. 107), a proselyte or worshipper of the true God, was deeply impressed

Fig. 107.—*Thyatira. From a photograph by A. svoboda.*

with the great truths advocated by the preacher, and became a convert, and herself and "her whole house" were baptized. Lydia only is mentioned by name, and it has been surmised that she was a widow, and that her "whole house" consisted of her children and domestics.[59] A woman thus became the first convert by the preaching

---

[58] Acts xvi. 13.
[59] See Stier, Reden der Apost. 54. It has been pointed out by J. B. Lightfoot (Philippians, p. 55) that the female sex of Philippia, and of all Macedonia, was evidently on a much higher relative position than in other countries. Lineage

of Paul in Europe; and it is probable that Euodia and Syntyche, who figure in the Epistle to the Philippians, and had some disagreement which called for the Apostle's animadversion, were also converted by the Apostle at or about the same time.

Fig. 108.—Coin of Thyatira, the birthplace of Lydia. From the British Museum.
Obv. Ιερα Συγκλητος (Sacred Senate).—Rev. Θυατειρηνων (of the Thyatirans).

Thyatira was a city of Lydia, and the Lydian women had, from the time of Homer downwards, been famous for their purple dyes:

> Ὡς δ' ὅτε τίς τ' ἐλέφαντα γυνὴ φοίνικι μιήνῃ
> Μῃονὶς ἠὲ Κάειρα.   Iliad. iv. 141.
>
> And as by Lydian or by Carian maid
> The purple dye is on the ivory laid.

And Claudian (thought by some to have been a Christian poet) thus describes the blushes of Proserpine:

> Niveos infecit purpura vultus,
> Per liquidas succensa genas, castæque pudoris
> Illuxere faces; non sic decus ardet eburnum
> Lydia Sidonio quod fœmina tinxerit ostro.
>   Claud. Rapt. Proserp. i. 270.
>
> Blushes o'erspread the features of the maid,
> And modesty was in the downcast eye;
> Her purpling cheek was ivory overlaid
> By Lydian damsel with Sidonian dye.

And Sir G. Wheler found, amongst the ruins of Thyatira, an inscription, Οἱ Βαφεῖς, 'The Dyers.'[60] Lydia had probably in her own country borne another name; but when she removed to Philippi, for the sale of the dye, she was called, as a stranger, Lydia, or the Lydian. As purple in ancient times was of a very costly description, and the manufacture of it would require considerable capital, Lydia must have been a lady of

---

here was traced by matronymics as well as by patronymies, i.e. from the mother as well as the father; as in the following inscriptions: Σωσιπάτρου τοῦ Κλεοπάτρας. Boeckh, No. 1967. Ταύρου τοῦ Ἀμμίας, ib. Ἀλέξανδρος καὶ Εὐβούλιος οἱ Μαρίας, ib. 1997, c. (add.). Ἕσπερος Σεμέλης, ib. Εἰούλιος Καλλίστης, ib. &c. Women again were allowed to have property, for they are found contributing from the common earnings of themselves and their husbands. ἐκ τῶν κοινῶν καμάτων, Boeckh, No. 1958; ἐκ τῶν κοινῶν κόπων,

ib. No. 1977. In short, they were treated conventionally as the mistresses of the house. Εὐτύχης Στρατονίκῃ τῇ συμβίῳ καὶ κυρίᾳ μνείας χάριν, Boeckh, No. 1965; and occasionally public monuments were erected in their honour. τὸ κοινὸν τῶν Μακεδόνων Μανλίαν Ποντείαν Λουκούλλαν Ἆθλον Ποντίου Βήρου τοῦ λαμπροτάτου ἀνθυπάτου γυναῖκα ἀρετῆς ἕνεκεν. Boeckh, No. 1999, b. (add.), &c.

[60] Spon's Misc. iii. 93.

some wealth and influence; and certainly, as will be seen, she had the means of exercising a noble hospitality.[61]

It had been the practice of Paul and his followers not to become the inmates of any convert, lest the cause of Christianity might suffer from the imputation of interested motives; but such was the importunity of Lydia that Paul deemed it best to waive his ordinary usage, and he and his company became her guests. "'If,' said she, 'ye have judged me to be faithful to the Lord, come into my house, and abide there.' And she constrained us." The liberality of the whole Philippian church was indeed very remarkable throughout the Apostle's life. From them only, and from them no less than four times, did Paul receive a contribution to his necessities.

The next event that occurred led, in its consequences, to the Apostle's bidding farewell (but not for ever) to the thriving church of Philippi. There was a damsel in the place who was subject to ravings, and at the present day would simply be committed to the charge of a keeper; but at that time the aberrations of mind arising from epileptic attacks were attributed to the presence of some good or evil spirit. Amongst the Jews it would have been said she had a devil, but amongst the Greeks and Romans (and they comprised chiefly the population of Philippi) the common notion was that she was possessed by Apollo, and was in fact a Pythoness,[62] or had a spirit of divination. She had fallen into the hands, and was, perhaps, the *slave* of crafty men, who, disseminating the notion that she had the gift of soothsaying, and that in her wild moments she uttered oracles, had made by her means considerable gains. It is well observed by Mr. Biscoe, that "the ancient Greeks and Romans sometimes happened to have slaves that were astrologers, or magicians, or diviners. Ἐγγαστρίμυθοι,[63] or those who had the spirit of Python, were doubtless very rare, and the purchase of one must have been exceedingly high. The maid servant (at Philippi) is represented as having more than one owner. Her price, it is likely, was too great to be advanced by a single person—at least no one in prudence cared to risk so large a sum upon the uncertainty of a life; for though she brought much gain, how soon might it be cut off by her decease."[64] We may conjecture, from her being constantly on the road to the oratory, that she was in some way connected with the house of Israel, and had, perhaps, some indistinct notions of the long-expected Messiah, and the tidings of the Gospel now proclaimed by Paul had a powerful effect on her disordered mind. Whenever the Apostle and his company proceeded to the oratory she followed them, crying, "These men are the servants of the Most High God, which show unto us the way of salvation."[65] The vociferations of the damsel were at first

---

[61] That large fortunes were often made by dyeing, we learn from the old epigram.

Βάπτων πάντα, Βαφεῦ, καὶ χρωματίοις μεταβάλλων,
καὶ πενιχρὸς βαφεὺς πλούσιος ἐξεβάφης.
Greek Anth. xi. 423.

Our dyer was poor, but by dint of his art
He has dipped all his rags, and has dyed himself smart.

[62] From Python, a name given to Apollo as the destroyer of the great serpent, called Python.

[63] Literally ventriloquists. Ἐγγαστρίμυθοι· οἱ κεκλεισμένον τοῦ στόματος φθεγγόμενοι, διὰ τὸ δοκεῖν ἐκ τῆς γαστρὸς φθέγγεσθαι. Galen. Gloss. Hippocrat., cited by Kuinoel on Acts xvi. 16.

[64] Biscoe on the Acts, c. 8, note.

[65] Acts xvi. 17.

but little heeded, but day after day the same cry was heard, till the orderly ministry of the Apostle suffered no little interruption. Paul therefore, on the Divine impulse, was enabled to work the cure of the poor demoniac, and said to the spirit (for so a Jew would express himself), "I command thee in the name of Jesus Christ to come out of her." The damsel recovered her sober senses, and the inspired Pythoness was metamorphosed into a sane woman. The dealers in soothsaying had lost their stock-in-trade, purchased perhaps at an extraordinary price, and their rage was unbounded against Paul and Silas, who were regarded as the ringleaders, and were the more obnoxious as being Jews, the objects of general detestation. They resolved on wreaking vengeance on the two mischief-making meddlers, and they might well reckon on the co-operation of the ignorant multitude, who would lament the loss of their favourite oracle. The outbreak that followed is remarkable as the *first instance of Gentile persecution*. Hitherto Jews only had been the active adversaries, but now at Philippi, as afterwards under Demetrius the silversmith at Ephesus, the Pagans were the aggressors. But at Philippi, as at Ephesus, the outbreak was not on religious grounds, but from the prejudicial effect of Christianity upon private pecuniary interests.

Philippi, we must remember, as a colony of Romans sent thither from the parent state, was governed by Roman laws. While, on the one hand, the Romans permitted every nation to practise freely its own religion, they prohibited by penal enactments the unauthorized introduction among themselves of any new object of worship.[66] However, the aid of the magistrate (unless there were a violation of the peace) was seldom invoked to protect the gods of their fathers from the encroachments of foreign superstitions. The fraternity of soothsayers at Philippi, not being able to impeach the moral conduct of the Apostles, laid hold of the doctrines preached by them as contrary to the established usages and tenets of a Roman community.

Philippi, a Rome in miniature, had a senate, or curia, answering to the senate of Rome, in whose hands was the municipal legislation; and justice was administered by two annual officers called duumviri, corresponding to the two consuls of the parent city,[67]

---

[66] Qui novas et usu vel ratione incognitas religiones inducunt, ex quibus animi hominum moveantur, honestiores deportantur, humiliores capite puniuntur. Jul. Paulus, Sentent. v. 21. Cautum fuerat et apud Athenienses et apud Romanos, ne quis novas introduceret religiones, unde et Socrates damnatus est, et Chaldæi et Judæi urbe depulsi. Servius ad Virgil. Æn. viii. 187. τὸ μὲν θεῖον πάντῃ πάντως αὐτός τε σέβου κατὰ τὰ πάτρια, καὶ τοὺς ἄλλους τιμᾶν ἀνάγκαζε, τοὺς δὲ ξενίζοντάς τι περὶ αὐτὸ καὶ μίσει καὶ κόλαζε. Dion, vii. 36; and see Euseb. H. 2; and numerous other passages cited by Wetstein on Acts xvi. 2, and Matt. xxiii. 15, and by Kuinoel on Acts xvi. 21.

[67] J. B. Lightfoot (Philippians, p. 50) cites two inscriptions in which the duumviri of Philippi are mentioned. Thus, *Q. Vibius C. F. Vol. Florus Bos. ii vir et munerarius Philippis Fil. Car. C.*, Orell. No. 3746; and *Decurionatus et ii viralicis Pontifer Flamen Divi Claudi Philippis*, Mission Archéologique, p. 15. The latter duumvir was contemporary with Paul, and may have been one of those who insulted him by a public scourging in the market-place.

Philippi had also its censor, as appears from the inscription at Philippi, "*Mag. Quinquenn.*" The censor was called Quinquennalis from the censorship recurring only every fifth year. The censor, when in office, took precedence in rank and in like manner attended by lictors (fig. 109).[58] The term 'duumviri' was rendered in Greek by the word στρατηγοί, or prætors; and accordingly we find Luke referring to them under this designation.[69] Originally in colonies the chief magistrates were called duumviri, and prætors were known only at Rome; but so early as the time of Cicero certain towns had begun to arrogate the title used at Rome, for he mentions

Fig. 109.—Coin of Brutus. From Pembroke collection.
Obv. Head of Liberty.—Rev. Brutus attended by Lictors.

the vanity of Capua in parading its *prætors* with lictors marching before them with the fasces;[70] and by degrees the example spread until 'prætors' became the common appellation of the chief magistrates in the various colonies.[71] Wetstein remarks that down to the present day the inhabitants of Messina call the prefect of their city 'stradigo,' the corruption of the Greek word στρατηγός.[72]

Paul and Silas were tumultuously arrested and dragged into the forum (fig. 110), and the leaders of the infuriated mob were open-mouthed with the accusation, "These men, being Jews, do exceedingly trouble our city, and teach customs which are not lawful for us to receive, neither to observe, being Romans." Paul, and Silas too, were Romans, and as such entitled to an impartial hearing, and one of them at least had the ability to defend himself. But before their voices could be heard to claim the privilege of Romans the mob set upon them, and the dastardly prætors, instead of checking the lawless violence, lent their magisterial power to the gratification of the popular passions. The prætors themselves, the representatives of justice, before the cause was heard, before any evidence was adduced, indulging only the madness of the crowd and despising the mean appearance of the prisoners, ordered the lictors to

even of the duumviri.

Philippi had also its ædiles. Thus we meet with the inscription "P. Hostilius Philadelphus ob honorem ædilitatis," &c., Mission Archéol. p. 71.

[58] Called by Luke ῥαβδούχους. Acts xvi. 35.
[69] οἱ στρατηγοί. Acts xvi. 22.
[70] Cum cæteris in coloniis duumviri appellentur, hi se prætores appellari volebant. Quibus primus annus hanc cupiditatem attulisset, nonne arbitramini paucis annis fuisse consulum nomen appetituros? Deinde anteibant lictores non cum bacillis, sed, ut hic prætoribus antevunt,

cum fascibus duobus. Cic. de Leg. Agrar. 34, in speaking of Capua.

[71] This, observes Biscoe, is very evident from the book of Modestinus, the Roman lawyer, D. Excusationibus, which he wrote in the Greek language, wherein, speaking of the magistrates of colonies, he calls them στρατηγοί. And Theophilus, a Greek interpreter of the laws, does the same. If the Roman lawyers gave them that name, we may be sure it was only because it had been the prevailing practice. Biscoe on the Acts, c. 9, s. 3.

[72] Wetstein, Acts xvi. 20.

strip the culprits and lay on the rods. Paul and Silas had their clothes rent from their backs down to the waist, and thus were scourged before the public eye amidst the scoffs and jeers of the assembled crowd.[73] Paul and Silas may each have exclaimed, in the famous words ascribed by Cicero to the Roman beaten by Verres publicly in the forum of Messina, "*Civis Romanus sum!*"[74] But their voices, if raised, were drowned in the general din and the fast-falling blows of the rods; or possibly they expressed themselves in Greek, which the Roman prætors, who spoke only Latin, did not sufficiently understand. This unjust and ignominious treatment was keenly felt by one of Paul's natural spirit and nice sense of propriety, and we find him afterwards pointedly alluding to it in writing to the Thessalonians: "Yourselves, brethren, know our entrance in unto you, that it was not in vain; but even after we had suffered before, and were *shamefully entreated*, as you know, at Philippi, we were bold in our God to speak unto you the Gospel of God with much contention."[75]

But the prætors had not yet sufficiently humoured the blind fury of the populace.

[73] As this infliction of punishment was in a Roman colony, we may assume that it was after the Roman fashion. That is, the culprit was stripped either entirely or to the waist, and lashed to a post erected for the purpose in the market-place. The relation of such a scene is thus given by C. Gracchus: Palus destitutus est in foro: vestimenta detracta sunt; virgis cæsus est. Aulus Gell. x. 3. In forum venit [the prætor] . . . hominem proripi atque foro medio nudari ac deligari et virgas expediri jubet. Ib. So, Stabant deligati ad palum nobilissimi juvenes . . missique lictores ad sumendum supplicium nudatos virgis cædunt. Liv. ii. 5. So M. Cato speaks feelingly, as did Paul, of the insult and ignominy of such a public exhibition. Jussit vestimenta detrahi atque flagro cædi. Videre multi mortales! quis hanc contumeliam, quis hoc imperium, quis hanc servitutem ferre potest? . . . Insignitas injurias, plagas, verbera, vibices, eos dolores atque carnificinas, per dedecus atque maximam contumeliam, inspectantibus popularibus suis atque multis mortalibus, te facere ausum esse? Aul. Gell. x. 3.

Another form of scourging was to strip the culprit and tie the hands behind the back: οἱ δὲ [ὑπηρέται], εὐθὺς συλλαβόντες τοὺς νεανίσκους, περιέρρηγνυον τὰ ἱμάτια, τὰς χεῖρας ἀπῆγον ὀπίσω, ῥάβδοις ἔξαινον τὰ σώματα. Plut. Poplic. c. 6. προσέταξε τοῖς ὑπηρέταις τοῦ μὲν ἀνθρώπου καταρρηγνύναι τὰ ἱμάτια, καὶ τὰς χεῖρας ὀπίσω περιάγειν, τοῖς δὲ παισὶ διδόναι ῥάβδους καὶ μάστιγα. Plut. Camill. 10.

That the Roman scourging was upon the naked body, is attested by numerous other passages. Lacerantibus vestem lictoribus. Liv. viii. 32. Nudatum virgis lacerari in conspectu populi Romani. Ib. viii. 133. O spectaculum admirabile! magister equitum scissâ veste, spoliatoque corpore, lictorum verberibus lacerandus! Valer. Max. ii. 7, 8. τοῖς ῥαβδούχοις ἐκέλευσαν τὴν ἐσθῆτά τε περικαταρρῆξαι καὶ τὰς ῥάβδοις τὸ σῶμα ξαίνειν. Dionys. Halicarn. ix. 39. τὰ χιτώνιον περιρρήξας ἡμιστέγιον γυμνήν. Plut. de Virtut. p. 251 B. οἱ δὲ τὰς ἐσθῆτας περιρρηγνύντες. Diod. Sic. xvii. 35. παραγαγὼν εἰς μέσον καὶ περιρρήξας τὴν ἐσθῆτα, ἐπέδειξε τὰ στέρνα τῆς γυναικός. Plut. V. Orat. p. 849. παραγαγὼν αὐτὴν εἰς τοὐμφανὲς καὶ περιρρήξας τοὺς χιτωνίσκους γυμνά τε τὰ στέρνα ποιήσας. Athen. xiii. 59 (p. 590. Tauchnitz).

[74] Cædebatur virgis in medio foro Messanæ civis Romanus, judices. Cum interea nullus gemitus, nulla vox alia istius miseri inter dolorem crepitumque plagarum audiebatur nisi hæc, "Civis Romanus sum." Hâc se commemoratione civitatis omnia verbera depulsurum cruciatumque a corpore dejecturum arbitrabatur. Cic. in Verr. actio ii. lib. v. sect. 62.

[75] 1 Thess. ii. 1, 2. Philo the Jew in like manner refers to the disgrace of a public scourging in similar terms. προστάττει [Flaccus] πάντας περιδυθέντας αἰκισθῆναι μάστιξιν αἷς ἔθος τοῖς κακούργων πονηροτάτους προπηλακίζεσθαι. Philo in Flac. 10.

Not content with having beaten two innocent men, they treated them as already convicted of a heinous crime, and cast them into prison with an innuendo to the gaoler to keep them "safely." The gaoler knew well enough what his masters meant by "safe" custody, and he executed his orders by thrusting Paul and Silas into the inner prison, and making their feet fast in the stocks.[26] What occurred during the night is graphically described by Luke, who was with Paul at Philippi at the time. "And at midnight Paul and Silas were praying and singing praises unto God; and the prisoners were listening to them. And suddenly there was a great earthquake, so that the foundations of the prison were shaken; and immediately all the doors were opened

Fig. 116.—Ruins in the market-place of Philippi, where Paul was scourged. From Missionary Herald.

and every one's bands were loosed. And the keeper of the prison awaking out of his sleep, and seeing the prison doors open, he drew out his sword, and would have killed himself, supposing that the prisoners had been fled. But Paul cried with a loud voice, 'Do thyself no harm, for we are all here.' Then he called for lights,[27] and sprang in, and came trembling, and fell down before Paul and Silas, and brought them out, and said, 'Sirs, what must I do to be saved?'[28] And they said, 'Believe on the Lord Jesus

---

[26] εἰς τὸ ξύλον, Acts xvi. 24. The ξύλον or "nervus" resembled our stocks, and was a wooden frame in which the feet, and sometimes the head and hands also, were held fast in narrow holes, from which they could not be drawn out by any struggles of the culprit. See Kuinoel, Acts xvi. 24.

[27] φῶτα, Acts xvi. 29, not a light, as in the English translation.

[28] How, it has been asked, could a heathen know anything about salvation? The answer is twofold. First, the gaoler does not necessarily refer to salvation at all, though Paul, in order to

Christ, and thou shalt be saved, and thy house.' And they spake unto him the word of the Lord, and to all that were in his house. And he took them the same hour of the night, and washed their stripes, and was baptized, he and all his, straightway. And when he had brought them into his house he set meat before them, and rejoiced, believing in God with all his house."[79]

The prætors meanwhile had, during the night, reflected upon their scandalous conduct, not that they had any conscientious scruples, but it was evident that they had grossly violated their magisterial duties, and were liable to impeachment, and should the facts be correctly represented to the proconsul of Macedonia might themselves at any moment be arrested and sent to Rome, to answer for it before the Emperor. In short, they had committed themselves, and they very properly deemed it the wisest course to hush up the matter, and to release the prisoners with as little stir as possible. In the morning, accordingly, they dispatched their lictors with a message to the gaoler, "Let those men go." The keeper of the prison, rejoicing at the liberation of those whom he, as a convert, now so much venerated, hurried with the glad tidings to Paul and Silas. "The magistrates have sent to let you go; now, therefore, depart and go in peace." But what answered Paul? Had he and his fellow-prisoner simply quitted their dungeon the report would have been spread that they had made their escape. Paul well understood the motives by which the prætors were actuated, and, a scribe and lawyer himself, he knew the danger they had incurred by beating and imprisoning Roman citizens without even the form of a trial, and, standing up for the honour in the eyes of the Philippians of the holy cause he was advocating, demanded that the prætors should make some apology for the insult. Paul's reply to the lictors was, "They have beaten us openly" (publicly), "*uncondemned*, being *Romans*,[80] and have *cast us into prison*, and now do they thrust

---

have an opportunity of discoursing upon the subject of salvation, gives it that sense. All that the gaoler meant was, what must I do to save myself from the immediate danger? Secondly, the gaoler may well have heard of salvation in its proper sense, for the Pythoness had made the city ring with her exclamations, "Those men are the servants of the most high God, and show unto us the way of *salvation*." Acts xvi. 17. See Stier's Reden der Apost. vol. i. p. 61.

[79] Acts xvi. 25-34. The "whole house" of the gaoler, as before the "whole house" of Lydia, are baptized, and it is scarcely credible that there were none but adults in the two households, and hence an argument in favour of infant baptism.

[80] Causâ cognitâ, multi possunt absolvi: incognitâ quidem condemnari nemo potest. Cic. in Verrem, actio ii. lib. i. sect. 9. ἀκρίτως ἐφθάρη. Dion, lviii. 1. μηδενὸς ἀκρίτου προκαταγινώσκειν ἀξιοῦντες. Philo in Flaccum, s. 12, &c.

Proh Deum atque hominum fidem,
Hoc pacto indemnatum atque intestatum me abripi?
Plaut. Curcul. v. 2, 16.

Great stress is to be laid on the fact that Paul and Silas had been scourged when *uncondemned*, for after conviction scourging was a legitimate form of punishment of *Romans* as well as of others; and the Roman franchise did not protect Paul, who also was a *Jew*, from being whipped after conviction by the law of the *Jews*. Paul was thrice beaten with rods at the hands of the *Romans*, and was five times whipped at the hands of the *Jews*. 2 Cor. xi. 24, 25. And we may be sure that Paul would not have submitted to these indignities had they not been legal.

us out privily? Nay, verily, but let them come themselves and fetch us out."[31] These words were reported to the prætors, and if they were uneasy before, what was their alarm when informed that the prisoners whom they had so illegally chastised and had incarcerated, were not the mere friendless strangers they had supposed, but Roman citizens, entitled to especial protection, and the more so in a Roman colony, and quite conscious of their Roman privileges. The prætors felt themselves at the mercy of their former victims. They were liable to an action for damages, or might be criminally indicted, and if convicted would become infamous and incapable of again serving in the magistracy. As abject in submission as they had been tyrannical in oppression, they went in person to the prison, and making apologies to Paul and Silas, led them forth and besought them, as a matter of favour, to calm the minds of the people by quitting the city.

Paul and Silas were now at liberty, and returning to the house of Lydia, comforted the disciples, and as, from the popular excitement, it was not likely that they could for the present preach the Gospel there with effect, it was arranged that Luke, against whom, as not being a Jew, the rage of the multitude had not been directed, should remain at Philippi to establish order in the church there, and sustain the disciples against the persecution which had been commenced, but that Paul and Silas should proceed upon their circuit. We are not informed what was the length of the Apostle's stay at Philippi, but it must have been several weeks, and though Lydia and the gaoler and their households are the only converts expressly named, it is evident that the Gospel had been attended there with remarkable success, and that the strong foundations were firmly laid of a flourishing church.

Luke, in relating the voyage from Troas to Neapolis and the proceedings at Philippi, uses the first person plural, so that he was certainly the companion of Paul during this part of the circuit, but at the close of the proceedings at Philippi this phraseology ceases, and Luke again recurs to the use of the third person plural: "*they went out*,"[32] &c.; so that he must have remained behind at Philippi. The next time we hear of Luke is on Paul's arrival in Macedonia, in the course of his next circuit, A.D. 57, and the natural inference is that during the interval Luke had continued at his post at Philippi. It was probably during this period that Luke composed his Gospel for the Greeks, as Matthew had done before for the Hebrews, and as Mark did afterwards for the Latins. When Paul returned to Philippi, in A.D. 57, and wrote the Second Epistle to the Corinthians, the Gospel of Luke had been recently published, for Paul speaks of him as "the brother whose praise is in the Gospel."[33]

Paul and Silas, parting from Luke at Philippi, and accompanied by Timothy,[34] bent their steps towards Thessalonica, the capital of Macedonia Secunda. The

---

[31] Acts xvi. 37.
[32] ἐξῆλθον. Acts xvi. 40.
[33] 2 Cor. viii. 18.
[34] Timothy was certainly with Paul at Berœa, for "Timotheus abode there still." Acts xvii. 14.

route lay along the Via Egnatia,[55] the great military road, and the distance was, according to the Antonine Itinerary, one hundred miles; (viz. Philippi to Amphipolis[56] thirty-three miles, thence to Apollonia thirty miles, thence to Thessalonica thirty-seven miles;) but according to the Peutinger Table, one hundred and six

[55] As the Via Egnatia was the great highway through Macedonia, and was more than once traversed by Paul, we shall here give some particulars of it. The two ports on the Adriatic were Dyrrhachium (or Epidamnus) and Apollonia, and the two roads from them met at Clodiana, and ran thence in a pretty direct line to Philippi. We have accounts of the Via Egnatia in the Antonine Itinerary, the Peutinger Table, and the Jerusalem Itinerary, and the following summary is taken chiefly from Cramer's Greece. The reader will bear in mind that the names of places are generally in the ablative case.

FROM APOLLONIA TO CLODIANA.

ANCIENT NAME.	MODERN NAME.	ANTON. ITIN.	JERUS. ITIN.
Apollonia	Pollina		
Stephanaphora			xviii.
Ad Novas		xxiv.	
Apons Fluv.	Ergent River		xii.
Marusio			xiv.
Clodianis		xxv.	xiii.
		xlix.	lvii.

FROM DYRRHACHIUM THROUGH ILLYRIA TO HERACLEA.

ANCIENT NAME.	MODERN NAME.	ANTON. ITIN.	JERUS. ITIN.	PEUT. TABLE.
Dyrrhachio	Durazzo			
Clodiana		xliii.		xxvi.
Ad Quintum			xv.	
Scampis	El Bassan	xxii. alias xxiii.	xi.	xx.
Ad Gemisium or Trajectus	Scumbi River		ix.	viii.
Ad Dianam				vii.
In Candavia			ix.	viii.
Pons Servilii	Over the Drina			viii.
Tres Tabernas		xxx. alias xxviii.	ix.	
Claudanon			ix.	
Patras			iv.	
Lychnido		xxvii.	xii.	xxviii.
Brucida			xiii.	
Nicia	Presba Nikia?	xxxiv.		
Parembole or (Latine) Castra			xix.	
Heraclea or Pelagonia	Erekli	xi.	xii.	xi. from Nikia.
		clxiii.	ccvii. from Clodiana, or clx. from Dyrrhachium.	

FROM HERACLEA THROUGH MACEDONIA TO PHILIPPI.

ANCIENT NAME.	MODERN NAME.	ANTONIN. ITIN.	JERUS. ITIN.	PEUT. TABLE.
Heraclea or Pelagonia	Erakleh			
Melitonus			xiii.	
Grande			xiv.	
Cellis	Kezl Derbend	xxxiv.	xiv.	xxxiv.
Ad duodecimum			xvi.	
Edessa	Vodina	xxviii.	xii.	xiv.
Scurio			xx.	
Pella	Palatica	xxviii.	xv.	xiv.
Gephyra			x.	
Ad decimum				
Thessalonica	Saloniki	xxvii.	x.	xxvii.
Duceira			xiii.	
Melisurgin		xx.		xx.
Herachostibus			xiv.	
Apollonia	Polina	xvii.	xi.	xviii.
Euripus (Furnius)				
Peraana			xi.	
Amphipoli	Jenikeuy	xxx.	x.	xxx.
Domeros			xiii.	
Ad duodecimum			vii.	
Philippis	Felibah	xxxiii.	xii.	xxxiii.
		ccxvii. making cclxxx. from Dyrrhachium.	ccxxx. making cccxc. from Dyrrhachium.	

[56] Amphipolis lay on the Strymon, about three miles from the mouth, and westward Lake Cercinitis (now Lake Takenos) stretched away for about twenty miles with overhanging mountains on the north. The consequence was that the only practicable passage from north to south or from south to north was at the eastern end of the lake at Amphipolis. Hence all the roads on both banks of the Strymon converged to this point, and the most ancient and original name of the town was Ἐννέα ὁδοὶ, or Nine-Ways. One of these roads was the Via Egnatia, described in the foregoing note, which traversed Macedonia from east to west. A little to the east of Amphipolis there still remains a fragment (perhaps the only genuine one) of the old Roman causeway. Cousinery, p. 122.

The situation of Amphipolis was also eligible on strategic grounds, for it was built on a tongue of land formed by the bend of the River Strymon, which flowed round it on the west and south and east, so that artificial protection was needed only on the north, where a wall was carried

Fig. 111.—*Coin of Amphipolis. From Anachassis.*
Obv. A laureated head.—Rev. A torch burning, with the legend Αμφιπολιτων (of the Amphipolitans).

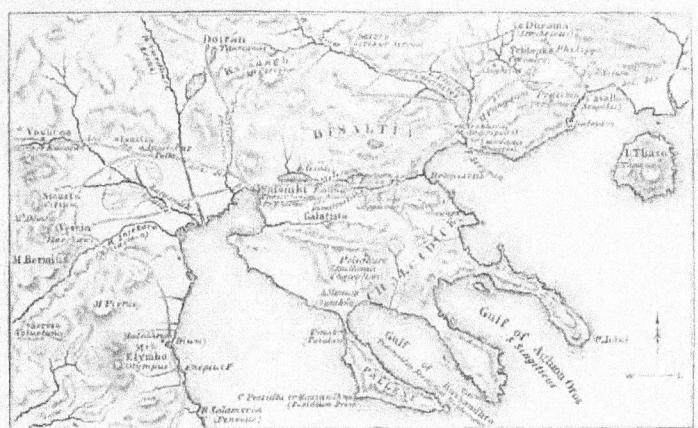

Fig. 112.—*Map of part of Macedonia. Grounded on Leake's Northern Greece.*
N.B.—'Ant.' indicates the route as given by the Antonine Itinerary, and 'Jer.' by the Jerusalem Itinerary.

Fig. 113.—*Coin of Thessalonica. From the British Museum.*
Obv. Head of Caius with the legend Γαιος Σεβαστου υιος (Caius son of Augustus). We have here the portrait of the young Caius, the adopted son of Augustus, and who was one of the assessors when Archelaus and Herod Antipas and Philip were heard before Augustus on the death of Herod the Great. Jos. Ant. xvii. 9, 5. The features of Caius are strikingly like those of Augustus.
Rev. Head of Augustus and the legend Θεσσαλονικεων (of the Thessalonians).

miles (viz. Philippi to Amphipolis, thirty-four miles, thence to Apollonia thirty miles, then to Thessalonica thirty-eight miles). Paul and Silas made no pause at either Amphipolis or Apollonia,*¹ apparently as the Jews were not in sufficient numbers at

across the isthmus. τείχει μακρῷ ὑπολαβὼν ἐκ ποταμοῦ εἰς ποταμόν. Thucyd. iv. 102.

A position presenting such natural advantages was from the first an object of contention amongst the leading states of Greece. The Athenians, at the height of their prosperity, twice made an attempt to seize it, but were defeated and driven off. Nothing daunted, however, they made a third descent in B.C. 437 under Agnon, the son of Nicias, and succeeded in establishing a colony there, and changed the name to Amphipolis or Round-about Town, as being girt in on three sides by the river. Ἀμφίπολις Ἄγνων ὠνόμασεν, ὅτι ἐπ' ἀμφότερα περιρρέοντος τοῦ Στρυμόνος, κ.τ.λ. Thucyd. iv. 102. The Athenians did not long retain their conquest, for eight years after, in B.C. 429, the Spartan general Brasidas, in the course of the Peloponnesian war, carried it by surprise. Thucydides, the celebrated historian, who commanded the Athenian fleet at Thasos, arrived too late to save the city: a most fortunate circumstance for mankind, as he was banished in consequence, and hence the production of a work (the History of the Peloponnesian War) allowed universally to be the masterpiece of its kind. The Athenians sent a strong force under the demagogue Cleon to retrieve their loss, but without success, and in the battle which was fought under the walls of Amphipolis both Brasidas and Cleon fell, and Brasidas was buried with great pomp within the city. There is still a tumulus among the ruins which Cousinery supposes to mark the spot where the Spartan hero was interred. Cousinery, vol. i. p. 126.

Amphipolis was never recovered by the Athenians, and subsequently submitted to the yoke of the Macedonian kings. In the time of Philip, the father of Alexander the Great, Stratocles and another were sent by a party in Amphipolis to Athens, with the view of negotiating a return to the Athenian sway, but Philip discovered the intrigue, and Amphipolis was held in check. Curiously enough, an inscription has been recently found at Amphipolis confirming a decree of banishment against one Stratocles, and Cousinery infers, with some probability, that the Stratocles of the monument is the Stratocles who went to Athens, and who on his return was visited with vengeance by the Macedonian faction. Cousinery, vol. i. p. 128.

On the subjugation of Macedonia by the Romans, Amphipolis with the rest of the country fell under the domination of Rome, and on the partition of Macedonia into four provinces, Amphipolis was declared the metropolis of Macedonia Prima; but subsequently was fought the great battle of Philippi, when the city from which the battle took its name was highly favoured by the victors, and became a Roman colony, and thenceforth Amphipolis began to lose its pre-eminence, and in the time of the Apostle Philippi was regarded as the capital of that division of Macedonia.

Amphipolis is now a mere village, called by the Greeks, Neochorion, and by the Turks, Jeni Kene, i.e. New Town.

*¹ Cousinery and Leake (Northern Greece) are probably correct in placing Apollonia at Polina, for not only the name but the distances agree. Apollonia, according to the Itineraries, was thirty miles from Amphipolis and thirty-seven miles from Thessalonica, and such, or nearly so, is the position of Polina.

T. L. F. Tafel (de Viâ Egnatiâ) would place Apollonia at Clisali, at the north-western end of Lake Bolbe, but this cannot be, for Clisali is twenty-one miles only from Thessalonica, and therefore much nearer to Thessalonica than to Amphipolis, whereas Apollonia, according to the Itineraries, was much nearer to Amphipolis than to Thessalonica, viz. thirty miles from Amphipolis and thirty-seven from Thessalonica.

Little light is to be gained from ancient authors. Apollonia, according to Livy, was a day's journey to the west of Amphipolis. Id dici iter est. Liv. xlv. 28, which agrees with Polina.

Scylax after following the coast line northward from the River Peneus, where Macedonia began on the south, concludes his description of the coast line which ended for Macedonia at the mouth of the Strymon thus, Ἀρεθοῦσα Ἑλληνίς. Βολβὴ Λίμνη· Ἀπολλωνία Ἑλληνίς· εἰσὶ δὲ καὶ ἄλλαι Μακεδονίας ἐν μεσογείᾳ πολλαί, and all that we can collect from this is, that Apollonia was an inland city not far from Lake Bolbe, which again answers to Polina.

ST. PAUL IN MACEDONIA. [A.D. 51]

either Amphipolis or Apollonia to maintain a synagogue—so at least we should infer from the expression applied to Thessalonica, "where was *the* synagogue" (and not, as translated, "*a* synagogue") "of the Jews."

Thessalonica is situate on a declivity at the north-eastern corner of the Bay of Thermæ. It was originally an inconsiderable town, and known successively as Emathia, and Halia, and Thermæ from the hot salt springs in the neighbourhood; but Cassander, one of Alexander's generals, was pleased with the spot, and having, according to the usage of the age, depopulated some of the neighbouring villages, transferred the inhabitants to Thermæ, which he thenceforth called Thessalonica, in honour of his wife, the daughter of Philip.* The main street runs from east to west, and near the western end are the remains of a triumphal arch erected in honour of

---

So Pliny describes Apollonia as an inland city in the region "under (that is to the south of) Mygdonia," and therefore to the south of Lake Bolbe. Regio Mygdoniae subjacens, in quâ recedentes a mari Apollonia, Arethusa. Plin. N. H. iv. 17. Apollonia is placed before Arethusa, and therefore, as Pliny is advancing from west to east, Apollonia was to the west of Arethusa.

Athenæus, viii. p. 334 (vol. ii. p. 206, Tauchnitz), speaks of two rivers, the Ammites and Olynthiæus, as flowing past Apollonia into Lake Bolbe (Βολβὴν λίμνην), and this passage has led some to place Apollonia on Lake Bolbe. But the writer is evidently referring to the other Apollonia, viz. that near Olynthus, and for Βολβὴν λίμνην should be read Βολυκὴν λίμνην, the lake close to Olynthus. This notice, therefore, throws no light on the Apollonia, the town on the Via Egnatia.

The Itineraries run thus,—

ANTONINE ITIN.	PEUTINGER TAB.	ITIN. HIEROSOL.
Amphipolis to Apollonia . xxx.	Amphipolis to Apollonia xxx.	Amphipolis to Pennana x.
Melissureis . xvii.	Melissurgis xviii.	Mutatio Peripidis x.
Thessalonica . xx.	Thessalonica xx.	Mansio Apollonia xi.
(But in another p. are xxi.)		Mutatio Heracleustibus . xi.
lxvii.	lxviii.	Mutatio Duodea . xiv.
(or lxviii.)		(hoc ad duodecimum)
		Thessalonica xiii.
		lxix.

Melissurgis, in the Antonine and Peutinger Itineraries, lies to the south of the stream connecting the two lakes Prasias and Bolbe, and is still called Melissurgis, and is inhabited by honey-workers, as the name implies. Leake's Northern Greece, iii. 461.

In the Jerusalem Itinerary, Mutatio Peripidis is a corruption of Mutatio Euripidis, viz. at the tomb of Euripides, which was at the Anion or Bromiscus, and near Arethusa, where Lake Bolbe discharges itself into the sea. Thucyd. iv. 103.

Heracleustibus is a corruption of Ἡρακλέους στίβος, and indicates that the road there ascended some steep.

At present there are two ordinary roads from Amphipolis to Thessalonica, viz. one along the northern brink of Lake Bechik, the ancient Bolbe, and then along the northern foot of Mount Cortiach or Disoron; and the other along the southern bank of the lake, and then as before along the northern foot of Mount Cortiach or Disoron. But Apollonia, now Polina, does not lie exactly on either of these roads, but on the rising ground a little to the south of the most southern of these two tracks. Cousinéry remarks that the two routes along the banks of the lake are liable to be flooded, and this may be the reason why the Via Egnatia on which Apollonia lay was not carried along the low grounds, but over the adjoining hills. As Paul passed through Apollonia, Cousinéry infers that he could not have followed either of the present roads to Thessalonica, but on leaving Apollonia must have passed along the south of Mount Cortiach or Disoron to Thessalonica.

* μετὰ τὸν Ἀξιὸν ποταμὸν ἡ Θεσσαλονίκη ἐστὶν πόλις, ἡ πρότερον Θέρμη ἐκαλεῖτο. κτίσμα δ᾽ ἐστὶ Κασσάνδρου, ὃς ἐπὶ τῷ ὀνόματι τῆς ἑαυτοῦ γυναικὸς, παιδὸς δὲ Φιλίππου τοῦ Ἀμύντου, ὠνόμασεν, κατασκάψας δὲ τὰ περὶξ πολίχνια εἰς αὐτήν, οἷον Χαλάστραν, Αἴνειαν, Κισσὸν, καί τινα καὶ ἄλλα. Strabo, excerpt. ex lib. vii. s. 10 (p. 131, Tauchnitz). But there are other accounts of the origin of the name. See Smith's Geograph. Dict.

the victory of Octavius and Antony over Brutus and Cassius at Philippi (fig. 114). At the time that Paul was there it was a free city,[89] the most populous of all the towns of Macedonia, and the capital of the whole province.[90] The Roman proconsul, attended by his six lictors with their fasces,[91] there held his court, assisted by his privy council, or board of advice, composed of select illustrious Romans, with whom he conferred on all matters of state. Thessalonica had also considerable mercantile importance, and to its trade and constant communication with all parts of the globe

Fig. 114. Triumphal arch across the main street at Thessalonica, erected in honour of the victory of Octavius and Antony over Brutus and Cassius at Philippi. From Cousinery.

we must ascribe the rapidity with which the intelligence of the success of the Gospel there was disseminated. Only a short time after Paul had left it he writes from Corinth to his new converts, "From you hath sounded out[92] the word of the Lord, not only in Macedonia and Achaia, but also *in every place* your faith to Godward is spread abroad, so that we need not to speak anything."[93] Thessalonica, now by a slight change Salonica, still carries on an extensive trade and is a place of consequence (fig. 115). The walls are five miles round, and, as you sail up the Bay of Thermae, have a very striking appearance, being whitewashed and painted, and rising up the hill in a theatrical form (fig. 116). Thessalonica, from its commercial character, had

---

[89] Thessalonica liberae conditionis. Plin. N. H. iv. 17.

[90] ἣ νῦν μάλιστα τῶν ἄλλων εὐανδρεῖ. Strabo, lib. vii. c. 7.

[91] τί δέ, αἱ πεντακόσιαι τῆς Ἀσίας πόλεις; οὐχὶ δίχα φρουρᾶς ἕνα προσκυνοῦσιν ἡγεμόνα καί τὰς ὑπατικὰς ῥάβδους; Jos. Bell. ii. 16, 4; and see Fasti Sacri, p. 89, No. 666.

[92] ἐξήχηται. 1 Thess. i. 8.

[93] 1 Thess. i. 8.

always a large proportion of Jews, and what is remarkable is, that one-half of the population is said at the present day to be of the Israelitish race.

Paul, Silas, and Timothy having arrived at Thessalonica, provided themselves with a lodging at the house of a Jew, one Jesus,[34] who had taken the Gentile name

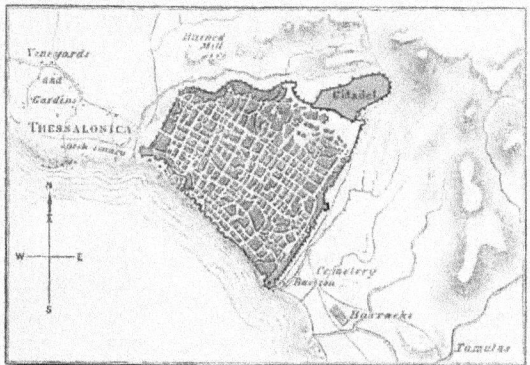

Fig. 115.—*Plan of Thessalonica. From Admiralty Chart.*

of Jason,[35] to whom, perhaps, they had brought letters of introduction from the disciples at Philippi. Paul's next step was to obtain employment for himself as a tentmaker, and for this purpose he might either hire himself to some artisan in that

Fig. 116.—*View of Thessalonica. From J. Barcenty's Illustrated New Testament.*

calling, or work at home and carry his manufacture to some vendor of the article. These preliminaries settled, he addressed himself to the great object of his mission.

His first appeal was as usual to his own countrymen, and on the Sabbath day he attended their synagogue, and reasoned with them out of the Scriptures.[36] The Jews,

---

[34] Rom. xvi. 21.   [35] See a similar instance in Jos. Antiq. xii. 5, 1.

as is well known, expected the Messiah to be a temporal king, and had so interpreted the prophecies. Under David and Solomon they had been a powerful people, and their hope was that the mighty Deliverer who was promised would restore the sceptre to Israel. This was the great stumbling-block and stone of offence, and of this deeply-rooted error the Apostle on this occasion endeavoured, but in vain, to disabuse their minds. He taught, writes the historian, that Christ (or the Messiah) "must needs have suffered, and risen from the dead, and that this Jesus, whom I preach unto you, is Christ" (or the Messiah).[97] You seek, he argued, in the Messiah a king, and Jesus is a king; but the kingdom of which he is sovereign is a spiritual and not a temporal one. For three consecutive Sabbaths Paul urged the Gospel upon the benighted Jews, but with little effect. A few only of them believed; but of the devout Greeks or proselytes (including some of the chief women of the city) a considerable number.

At the end of three weeks all further efforts for the conversion of the Jews being hopeless, Paul devoted himself more particularly to the idolatrous population, and here his success was as remarkable as the want of it had been amongst the Jews. That the church which he founded at Thessalonica consisted chiefly of Pagans we learn from his boast in the Epistle: "They themselves" (the world at large) "shew of us what manner of entering in we had unto you, and how ye *turned to God from idols to serve the living and true God;*"[98] language which would not apply to either Jews or proselytes, who both acknowledged one God and did not participate in the heathen abominations. The nature of his address to the idolaters the historian has not declared; but as no arguments could be drawn from the Scriptures, as not yet admitted,[99] the Apostle must have contrasted the grossness and impiety of their own superstition with the purity and beauty of the Christian scheme. The great engine that the Apostle wielded was the gift conferred upon him of displaying miracles. "Our Gospel," he says, "came not unto you in word only, but also in *power*, and in the Holy Ghost,"[100] where the word 'power' has evidently the sense, attached to it in other similar passages, of supernatural agency. One thing is clear, that Paul made no use of any such carnal weapons as the employment of artifice, by humouring their passions, for plainness of speech on this, as on every occasion, was his leading characteristic. "Our exhortation," he writes to them, "was not of *deceit*, nor of *uncleanness*, nor in *guile*; but as we were allowed of God to be put in trust with the Gospel, even so we speak, *not as pleasing men*, but God, which trieth our hearts."[101] Nay, he went so far as to declare to his hearers, while he was endeavouring to win them over to Christ, that he

---

[96] διελέγετο αὐτοῖς. Acts xvii. 2. Discussion in the way of dialogue was allowed in the synagogues of the Jews, as appears from John vi. 25, 59. Matt. xii. 9. Luke iv. 16. See Meyer, Apostg. 307.

[97] Acts xvii. 3.

[98] 1 Thess. i. 9.

[99] Accordingly in the two Epistles to the Thessalonians we find no quotation of the Old Testament, except perhaps in one solitary instance, viz. I Thess. iv. 9.

[100] 1 Thess. i. 5.

[101] 2 Thess. ii. 3, 4.

invited them, not to a life of pleasure and enjoyment, but of trial and persecution. When he afterwards alludes to their afflictions, he says, "Yourselves know that we are appointed thereunto; for verily, when we were with you, *we told you before that we should suffer tribulation*, even as it came to pass, and ye know."[102]

A strong persuasive to all about him must have been the eminent personal example set by the Apostle himself. Though still smarting under the stripes he had received at Philippi, he preached with unabated boldness at Thessalonica—and why? For the sake of gain? He would accept nothing at their hands. For the sake of honour? He humbled himself among them, and would not avail himself of the ordinary privileges of an Apostle. "Neither at any time used we flattering words, as ye know; nor a cloak of *covetousness* (God is witness); nor of men sought we *glory*, neither of you, nor yet of others, when we might have been burdensome as the Apostles of Christ."[103] As ordained to the ministry, Paul was entitled to support from his followers, for "the labourer is worthy of his reward;"[104] but this right the Apostle waived, that no man might charge him with interested motives. It was also necessary to set an example, more particularly at Thessalonica, where the prevailing fault was, that the converts, charmed with the new religion, were disposed to abandon their ordinary business and make no provision for this life. In his First Epistle to the Thessalonians the Apostle exhorts, "That ye study to be quiet, and to do your own business, and to *work with your own hands*, as we commanded you."[105] And again, Paul charges the church to "warn them *that are unruly;*"[106] and in the Second Epistle he speaks still more plainly: "Now we command you, brethren, in the name of our Lord Jesus Christ, that ye withdraw yourselves from every brother that walketh disorderly, and not after the tradition which he received of us. For yourselves know how ye ought to follow us; for we behaved not ourselves disorderly among you, neither did we eat any man's bread for nought, but *wrought with labour and travail night and day*, that we might not be chargeable to any of you; not because we have not power, but to make ourselves an ensample unto you to follow us. For even when we were with you this we commanded you, that *if any would not work neither should he eat;* for we hear that there are some among you which walk disorderly, working not at all, but are *busybodies*. Now them that are such we command and exhort by our Lord Jesus Christ, that with quietness they work, and eat their own bread."[107]

The Apostle, indeed, while at Thessalonica was at one and the same time the Christian advocate and the industrious artisan. He had no private fortune. He had either already expended it upon the Gospel, or perhaps it had been confiscated by the Jews. "I have suffered the loss of all things,"[108] where the Greek word would rather signify, 'I have been fined (or mulcted) of all.' It mattered little to one who looked to an everlasting crown whether he was or not surrounded by the comforts of life, for "I

---

[102] 1 Thess. iii. 4.
[103] 1 Thess. ii. 5, 6.
[104] Luke x. 7.
[105] 1 Thess. iv. 11.
[106] 1 Thess. v. 14.
[107] 2 Thess. iii. 6–12.
[108] ἐζημιώθην. Philipp. iii. 8.

have learned," he says, "in whatsoever state I am, therewith to be content. I know both how to be abased and how to abound; everywhere and in all things I am instructed both to be full and to be hungry, both to abound and to suffer need."[109]

But it is likely that, notwithstanding his toil night and day, the Apostle at this time underwent very unusual privations. There had been recently throughout Greece so severe a famine, that a modius or peck of wheat was sold for six drachmæ, or nearly five shillings, being six times the usual price.[110] It is also probable that the Apostle still continued to labour under no little bodily infirmity from his besetting disorder, ophthalmia; so that he was less able to earn the wonted wages by personal exertion in the art of tentmaking.

Fortunately, under such a concurrence of difficulties, assistance was rendered to him from an unexpected quarter. The cruel usage he had experienced at Philippi seems to have kindled amongst the Philippians a strong feeling towards him, and perhaps Luke, who was still there, may have given a proper direction to their liberality. Certain it is, that while Paul was at Thessalonica he twice received relief from the Philippians, and eleven years after, when a prisoner at Rome, he gratefully recalls the circumstance to their recollection. "Ye Philippians, know that in *Thessalonica also* ye sent once and again unto my necessities."[111]

Paul had now been some months at Thessalonica, and a church had been planted which was destined to be one of the brightest ornaments of early Christendom. Amongst the converts were several who became afterwards the constant companions and fellow-labourers of the Apostle, as Caius, Aristarchus, and Secundus, and perhaps Jason his host.[112] As the numbers increased he appointed ministers;[113] and though Paul himself would not receive any stipend as an Apostle, we may assume from the necessity of the case that those who were constituted the regular pastors of the church were supported by it. The instrument by which order was preserved in the Christian community was, excommunication. If any one submitted not to the commands of the Apostle or the ordinances of the church, he was, after sufficient warning, expelled from the society. "If any man," writes the Apostle to the Thessalonians, "obey not our word by this epistle, note that man, and have no company with him, that he may be ashamed; yet count him not as an enemy, but admonish him as a brother."[114]

The question may perhaps suggest itself to the reader how, when the Apostle should take leave of the Thessalonians, were they to regulate their faith? While he was with them, he would unfold the Christian scheme by word of mouth; but to

---

[109] Philipp. iv. 11, 12.
[110] Fasti Sacri, p. 200, No. 1735.
[111] Philipp. iv. 15, 16. The fact that relief was twice sent to him from Philippi shows that the sojourn of Paul at Thessalonica was of long continuance.
[112] Acts xix. 29; xx. 4.
[113] προϊστάμενοι. 1 Thess. v. 12.
[114] 2 Thess. iii. 14, 15.

whom were they to refer in his absence? I think the answer is, that Paul, upon their conversion, placed in their hands the Old Testament, as the groundwork of the new covenant, and containing the prophecies relating to it, and that he also delivered to them the Gospel of St. Matthew,[115] the only one of the four which had then been published. The Second Epistle to the Thessalonians appears to refer plainly to St. Matthew, and assumes that the Gospel was in their hands. In speaking of the last day, he says, "But of the times and the seasons, brethren, *ye have no need that I write unto you*, for yourselves *know perfectly* that the day of the Lord *so cometh as a thief in the night.*"[116] The allusion evidently is to the following passage in St.

Fig. 117.—The church in which according to tradition Paul preached at Thessalonica. From Cousinery.

Matthew: "But of that day and hour knoweth no man, no, not the angels of heaven, but my Father only. Watch, therefore, for ye know not what hour your Lord doth come; but *know this*, that if the good man of the house had known in *what watch the thief would come*, he would have watched, and would not have suffered his house to be broken up."[117]

The labours of Paul at Thessalonica were soon to be brought to a close. The Jews had rejected the Gospel themselves, but they were not the less jealous of its reception by the Gentiles. Their indignation against Paul and Silas was such, that apparently they meditated their destruction by lawless violence. They instigated the lowest vagabonds of the place to break out into a riot, and the whole town was

[115] See note on 1 Thess. v. 2. [116] 1 Thess. v. 1, 2. [117] Matt. xxiv. 36, 42, 43.

soon thrown into confusion. The mob made an attack upon the house of Jason, where Paul and Silas lodged, with a view of dragging them forth, when they would easily fall victims to the fury of the people. An intimation, however, of their intention was secretly conveyed to the Apostles, and they were not to be found. The rabble then laid hold of Jason himself with some of the brethren, who chanced to be there, and carried them before the civic authorities, called the politarchs.[118]

We are now involved in legal proceedings, and must premise a few words upon the administration of justice in a Greek city enjoying its freedom, like Thessalonica. In general, the accuser served a summons upon the delinquent to attend at a certain time before the magistrate; but in criminal matters, where from the nature of the crime or other circumstances an escape was to be apprehended, the informer was permitted to arrest the person of the accused, and drag him before the tribunal. When the parties met before the judge the plaintiff preferred his indictment, and if on the assumption of the facts alleged the charge was sustainable, the magistrates received it; and thereupon the accusation was copied upon a tablet and posted in court, and a day was named for the trial. The prisoner, at the discretion of the judge, was either placed in confinement, or was allowed to be at large on giving satisfactory bail. When the matter came on to be heard the plaintiff pledged his oath to the truth of the charge, and then opened his case, and substantiated it in the usual manner by oral testimony or documentary evidence. The accused was then sworn to his defence, and proceeded to answer the several counts, and offered his proofs. Both plaintiff and defendant were allowed only a limited time for their address, and the duration was measured by a clepsydra or water-clock (fig. 118). The judges were a certain number of jurors, selected by lot from those liable to serve. When both sides had concluded, the jurors voted by ballot, and the opinion of the majority determined the result.[119]

What was the crime of which Jason and his associates were now accused? It was treason! The law of the Twelve Tables (the Magna Charta of Rome) had simply

---

[118] ἐπὶ τοὺς πολιτάρχας. Acts xvii. 8. We have here again an instance of the extreme accuracy of Luke in describing the magistrates of Thessalonica by a title not given to them in books, from which an impostor might have gathered the fact, but found only in ancient monuments accidentally brought to light in comparatively modern times.

It appears from an inscription (Boeckh, 1967; and Cousinéry, p. 27) that there were seven politarchs. Πολειταρχούντων Σωσιπάτρου τοῦ Κλεοπάτρας, καὶ Λουκίου Ποντίου Σεκούνδου, Πουβλίου Φλαυίου Σαβείνου, Δημητρίου τοῦ Φαύρου, Δημητρίου τοῦ Νικοπόλεως, Ζωίλου τοῦ Παρμενίωνος, τοῦ καὶ Μενίσκου, Γαίου Ἀγιλληοῦ Ποτείτου Ταμίου τῆς πόλεως Ταύρου τοῦ Ἀμμίας τοῦ καὶ Ῥήγλου, Γυμνασιαρχοῦντος Ταύρου τοῦ Ἀμμίας τοῦ καὶ Ῥήγλου. It is also remarkable that in this short inscription we have no less than six names that are mentioned in the New Testament, viz. Sosipater, Lucius, Pontius, Secundus, Publius, Demetrius, and Gaius, some of whom were the companions of Paul. Secundus was, as we learn from the Acts, a Thessalonian, and Sosipater was of a neighbouring city, viz., Beroea. Acts xx. 4. Further, we find two of those mentioned in the inscription, called each by two names, as Ζώϊλος ὁ καὶ Μενίσκος and Ταῦρος ὁ καὶ Ῥῆγλος, corresponding to the expression in Luke, Σαῦλος ὁ καὶ Παῦλος. Acts xiii. 9.

[119] See Smith's Greek and Rom. Antiquities, art. Δίκη.

enacted, that "whoever excited an enemy against the state, or betrayed a citizen to an enemy, was to be punished with death."[120] But under the Emperors (Julius Cæsar, Augustus, and Tiberius) the provisions of the Twelve Tables had been extended by what were called the Julian Laws, and by them treason was made to comprise various offences. "Whoever violated the majesty of the state" (qui majestatem publicam læserit)[121] was declared a traitor; and upon the construction of this general and vague clause it was impossible to say within what bounds the Imperial jealousy was to be confined. If a person sold a statue of the Emperor,[122] or if he insulted the Cæsar by casting at it a stone, it was treason.[123] Indeed eventually, if one desired to overwhelm an enemy, and could find no plausible pretence for a prosecution, it was a common resource to call in aid the law of treason.[124] It was on a groundless charge of this kind that the Jews succeeded in wresting from Pilate the condemnation of our Saviour, for as he had declared himself to be a king, the decrees of the Cæsars, or the Julian

Fig. 118.—*A clepsydra or water-clock. From C. W. King's Antique Gems.*
The water is held in an egg-shaped vessel, and escapes through a small orifice at the pointed end, and measures a space of twenty minutes. The vessel is supported by a pair of Cupids.

Laws, were said to have been violated by such an assumption of royalty. The punishment probably varied according to the heinousness of the offence. In some cases, the penalty was death; in others, "interdiction from fire and water," which was equivalent to outlawry, and drove the traitor into exile.[125] The mildest sentence was confiscation of property.

It was to the Julian Laws that the mob of Thessalonica now had recourse against Jason and his companions. They dragged them before the politarchs, saying, "These that have turned the world upside down are come hither also, whom Jason hath received; and these all do contrary to the decrees of Cæsar" (the Julian Laws), "saying, that 'There is another king, one Jesus.'" The Roman Proconsul was resident at Thessalonica, and the authorities would be alarmed at the idea of being thought disloyal. True it was that the kingdom of which Paul had spoken was a spiritual, and not a temporal one, but might not the Cæsar, the arbitrary disposer of

[120] Dig. xlviii. 4, 3. [127] Tac. Ann. i. 73. nium accusationum complementum erat. Tac.
[121] Dig. xlviii. 4, 3. [122] Dig. xlviii. 4, 5. Ann. iii. 38.
[123] Addito majestatis crimine, quod tum om- [124] Tac. Ann. iii. 38.

life and death, consider even such a doctrine treasonable? The indictment carried a difficulty with it, and is said to have "troubled the people and the rulers of the city." The politarchs dared not dismiss the complaint; they contented themselves with taking bail[126] from Jason and the rest, to appear upon the day named for their trial, and then set them at liberty. When night came, the disciples, fearful of the result, sent away Paul and Silas to Berœa.

How long Paul remained at Thessalonica is not said, but he preached in the synagogue for three Sabbath days,[127] which would give three weeks; and besides this, he appeals, in the Epistles to the Thessalonians, to their knowledge of his way of life,[128] as if he had lived amongst them for some considerable period; and further, he mentions in the Epistle to the Philippians (who were one hundred miles distant from Thessalonica) that they had twice sent relief to his necessities while he was at Thessalonica,[129] and we must therefore conclude that his stay there extended to several months.

Timothy, on Paul's departure, remained behind at Thessalonica. The popular fury had been directed against Paul and Silas as the principal offenders, but the youthful Timothy was not an object of their indignation. He therefore sojourned a little longer in the incipient church,[130] but was directed to follow the Apostles soon after, which he did, and rejoined them at Berœa.[131]

Before we dismiss Thessalonica, we may add that Jason and the rest were probably afterwards put upon their trial, and their property either wholly or partially confiscated. We may also conjecture that the persecution thus begun against the Christians of Thessalonica was of some continuance, for allusion is made to it in both the Epistles which Paul afterwards wrote to them. "Ye, brethren, became followers of the churches of God which in Judea are in Christ Jesus; for ye also have *suffered like things* of your own countrymen, even as they have of the Jews; who both killed the Lord Jesus, and their own prophets, and have persecuted us; and they please not God, and are contrary to all men; forbidding us to speak to the Gentiles that they might be saved."[132] One of the inflictions on the Christians of Judea had been the spoiling of their goods,[133] and as the Thessalonians were suffering like things, we may infer that they had at least been subjected to heavy fines. In the Second

---

[126] λαβόντες τὸ ἱκανόν. Acts xvii. 9. See LXX. Levit. xxv. 26. But others, as Meyer (Apostg. 300) consider that the matter was now finally disposed of, and that the expression of Luke means that Jason and the rest were bound over to good behaviour and to keep the peace.

[127] Acts xvii. 2.

[128] 1 Thess. ii. 9; 2 Thess. iii. 7.

[129] Philipp. iv. 16.

[130] ἐξέπεμψαν τόν τε Παῦλον καὶ τὸν Σίλαν εἰς Βέροιαν. Acts xvii. 10. The name of Timothy is no doubt purposely omitted by so accurate a writer as Luke.

[131] That Timothy rejoined Paul at Berœa appears from the words, ὑπέμεινον δὲ ὅ τε Σίλας καὶ ὁ Τιμόθεος ἐκεῖ. Acts xvii. 14. It is well observed by Wordsworth, on 1 Thess. iii. 6, that Paul confided each of his three Macedonian churches to a beloved follower, viz. Philippi to Luke, Thessalonica to Timothy, and Berœa to Silas.

[132] 1 Thess. ii. 14—16.

[133] Heb. x. 34.

Epistle, Paul again adverts to their sufferings thus: "We ourselves glory in you in the churches of God for your patience and faith in *all your persecutions and tribulations* that ye endure."[134]

We now proceed with Paul and Silas to Berœa. This was a walled town, and was included in Macedonia Tertia.[135] As you approach it from Pella, an open plain stretches away on the left down to the seaside, and on the right tower the heights of Mount Bermius, part of the Olympic range. The city itself (for it still exists) is situate on the eastern slope of the mount,[136] and just before entering it from Pella flows a rivulet from which numerous rills are diverted into the city. Partly from these artificial ducts, and partly from natural springs, there is scarcely a street that

Fig. 110.—*Coin of Berœa. From Pellerin.*

Obv. Ἀλέξανδρος (Alexander).—Rev. A man sacrificing at an altar, and before him a table with two urns, and beyond it a caduceus. The legend is Κοιν. Μακε. Β. Νεω. Βεροιαω, (community of the Macedonians. Of the Beroeans twice Neocori). It is observable that the name is spelt Βεροια, not Βερροια as in Acts xvii. 10. Some by mistake have connected the B, not with νεωκορος, but with Μακεδονων, as if Berœa were in Macedonia Secunda, whereas it was in Macedonia Tertia.

is not enlivened by a running rivulet; all these waters when collected join the River Haliacmon. Berœa was founded by one Pheres, and was called after him Pherœa, but the Macedonians, from a peculiar lisp, changed Φ into B, and Pherœa in their mouths became Berœa.[137] At the present day the original pronunciation has been resumed, and the name is still Pheria, or more commonly Kara-Pheria. Its ancient importance has disappeared, and the principal occupation of the inhabitants is hewing red marble from the quarries of the adjoining mountain.[138]

The reasons why the Apostle was conducted to Berœa can only be conjectured, but we may arrive at some probability. In the first place it was in the course of his progress through Macedonia, and as Berœa was a town beyond the limits of Macedonia Secunda, the jurisdiction of the magistrates of Thessalonica would not extend to it. But the principal inducement was, perhaps, the comparative seclusion of Berœa. Had Paul proceeded along the Via Egnatia to Pella, the *capital* of

---

[134] 2 Thess. i. 4.

[135] Edessa quoque et Berœa eodem [to Macedonia Tertia] concesserunt. Livy, xlv. 29.

[136] ἡ Βέροια πόλις ἐν ταῖς ὑπωρείαις κεῖται τοῦ Βερμίου ὄρους. Strabo, excerpt. ex lib. vii. (p. 131, Tauchnitz).

[137] Βέροια πόλις Μακεδόνων, ἥν φασιν ὑπὸ Φέρητός τινος κτισθεῖσαν, Φέροια καὶ κατὰ Μακεδόνων βέρροια τραπῆ τοῦ Φ εἰς Β. Etymol. Βέροια πόλις Μακεδονίας, ἥν Φέρωνα κτίσαι φασίν, αὐτοὺς δὲ τὸ Φ εἰς Β μετατονεῖν, ὡς Βαλοκρὸν, Βιλιππον, Βεδαλινος. Stephanus Byz. See Wetstein, Acts xvii. 10.

[138] See Malte-Brun; Leake's Travels in Northern Greece, &c.

Macedonia Tertia, and there remained, his enemies at Thessalonica would immediately have discovered his retreat, and have followed up their designs against his life. In order to baffle his pursuers, the Apostle seems, in parting from Thessalonica, to have struck off into a byroad. The great highway, the famous Via Egnatia, ran from Thessalonica to Pella, a distance, according both to the Antonine Itinerary and the Peutinger Table, of twenty-seven miles, and from Pella a branch road ran to Beroea, which, according to the Peutinger Table, was a distance of thirty miles, making in the whole, from Thessalonica to Beroea by way of Pella, fifty-seven miles. But the Antonine Itinerary gives another and apparently a direct road from Thessalonica to Beroea, and makes the distance fifty-one miles only; and as we hear nothing in the Acts of Paul passing through Pella, he probably took the less frequented route referred to in the Antonine Itinerary. There is a passage in Cicero which furnishes a remarkable illustration of this part of the Apostle's circuit. In his bitter invective against Piso, who had been prefect of Macedonia, and whose base practices had so exasperated the province against him that he was fain to avoid any appearance in public, he thus addresses him: "You came to *Thessalonica* without the knowledge of any, and by night; and when you could not endure the laments of the mourners and the storm of complaints, you stole away to the *secluded town of Beroea*."[139]

Considering the hostility that Paul had just encountered from the Jews of Thessalonica, it could scarcely be matter of surprise if on reaching Beroea he should pass by the children of Abraham and appeal at once to the Gentiles. Paul, however, acted only on the purest motives, and his affection to his own countrymen was far too deep-rooted to be shaken by a systematic persecution from them. He now, as heretofore, attended the synagogue at Beroea, and argued with the Jews, as before at Thessalonica, on the nature of the Messiah's kingdom. To the credit of the Beroeans be it spoken, that they were more noble than those of Thessalonica, and applied themselves daily to the study of the law and the prophets, to ascertain whether the doctrines promulgated by Paul were well founded. Many of them were convinced, and professed themselves Christians, and their example was followed by a considerable number of the Gentiles, both men and women; and amongst the latter sex were some of the highest rank. Things had never gone on so prosperously, when all at once the clouds gathered and a storm broke over his head, and the Apostle was obliged to fly for his life.

Intelligence had reached the Jews of Thessalonica that Paul was preaching with his wonted success at Beroea. They were furious, and made all haste to come up with him, and overwhelm the apostate from the Law of Moses. Presently all Beroea was in commotion, and an assault was meditated. The danger was imminent; and as

---

[139] Thessalonicam omnibus inscientibus noctuque venisti, qui cum concentum plorantium et tempestatem querelarum ferre non posses, in oppidum devium Beroeam profugisti. Cic. in Pis. 36.

the Jews were plainly with venomous malice pursuing the Apostle from place to place, so that no more good could be effected in that quarter without exposing a valuable life to almost certain destruction, it was resolved that Paul should quit Macedonia altogether for the present, and, as the safest route, should cross the country to the nearest seaport, and embark on board the first vessel he could find. Silas, and Timothy who had since come from Thessalonica to Beroea, had not been marked out as the objects of vengeance, and they were to remain at Beroea[140] until they heard of the Apostle's arrival at some place of safety. The presence of Silas and Timothy at Beroea would strengthen the faith of the new converts, and when the tumult had subsided they might carry the last tidings with them to Paul. But how was the Apostle to pursue his journey? Afflicted with weakness of sight, amounting almost to blindness, was he to travel alone, and that by night, through a strange country? The affectionate brethren of Beroea furnished him with trusty guides, who were not to part from him until he was beyond the reach of danger. Paul and his attendants left their enemies behind them, and found their way down to the seaside[141] at Dium, to which there was a direct road from Beroea. The distance of Dium from Beroea, according to the Antonine Itinerary, was seventeen miles. There can be no doubt that Paul and his guides followed the beaten track as far as Dium, but it has been much disputed whether from this point they passed to Athens by land or sea. In favour of the first hypothesis are the expressions οἱ καθιστῶντες and ἤγαγον,[142] which are more applicable to a land journey than to a voyage. On the other hand, the statement that the disciples "sent him forth to *go down to the sea*"[143] seems almost decisive that at Dium they took ship. Again, in tracing Paul's journey from Philippi to Thessalonica, Luke notices that they passed through Amphipolis and Apollonia, though they did not stop at either place. How then is it conceivable that if Paul went by land from Beroea to Athens, Luke should not have adverted to the important cities that Paul must have visited by the way. Besides, had Paul travelled by land he would more naturally have gone direct to Corinth, and then (if at all) to Athens, and not have deviated from his route to visit Athens first. The sea route is also confirmed by the fact that Paul read at Athens the inscription on the altar to the unknown gods, for this altar lay on the road from Port Phalerens to Athens.[144]

The duration of Paul's ministry at Beroea is not stated, but it was probably some weeks, for many converts were made;[145] and intelligence of this success had reached

Thessalonica, which was more than fifty miles distant,[146] and the Thessalonian Jews had taken counsel and sent their emissaries to Berœa, who created the disturbance which obliged Paul eventually to take his departure. It is also probable that one at least of the "two hindrances,"[147] whatever they were, which prevented his return to Thessalonica, occurred while he was at Berœa, which again would argue some interval.

The time consumed on the way from Berœa to Athens would depend on the route taken. The road by *land* was, according to the Antonine Itinerary, two hundred and fifty-one miles, which might be accomplished in about ten days. But assuming that Paul took ship, and that the distance by sea was much the same as that by land, the *voyage*, if they sailed in the daytime only, would occupy about six days, and if they sailed by night also about three days.[148]

Fig. 120.—View of Athens from the entrance to Port Piræus. From a sketch by W. Simpson.

The time of Paul's arrival at Athens is, to a great extent, matter of conjecture. If Paul proceeded to Athens by land he might have made the journey either in winter or summer, for the roads were always open; but if, as we think most likely, he sailed thither, then as the navigation of the ancients was considered to be closed about 11th November,[149] though subject to exceptions, particularly in the coasting trade,[150] the voyage must be placed at some time previously to 11th November. We shall see hereafter that when Paul quitted Athens he went to Corinth, and had been there a year and six months when Gallio arrived, about 4th June, A.D. 53. Paul had quitted

[146] Acts xvii. 13.
[147] 1 Thess. ii. 18.
[148] Wieseler's Chronol. Apost. 43.
[149] See Roman Cal.
[150] Plin. N. H. ii. 47.

Athens therefore about 4th December, A.D. 51, and as his sojourn at Athens must have been several weeks (say a month), we should place his arrival there about the beginning of November, A.D. 51.

So soon as Paul's companions had conducted him to Athens, and seen him safely lodged there, they returned to Beroea charged with a message from him to Silas and Timothy, to rejoin the Apostle in Greece with all convenient expedition.

CHAPTER XII.

Paul at Athens—Corinth—Ephesus—Jerusalem.

> Athens, the eye of Greece! Mother of arts
> And eloquence! Native to famous wits!
> See there, the olive groves of Academe,
> Plato's retirement, where the Attic bird
> Trills her thick-warbled notes the summer long;
> There—flowery hill—Hymettus, with the sound
> Of bees' industrious murmur, oft invites
> To studious musing; there Ilissus rolls
> His whispering stream. Within the walls then view
> The schools of ancient sages—his who bred
> Great Alexander to subdue the world,
> Lyceum then, and painted Stoa next.
>   Milton.

PAUL at Athens! Once the bigoted Jew, now the champion of Christianity, amongst the vaunted sages and philosophers of the great metropolis of letters! How curiosity is on the stretch to know his reception! They who were stirred by the trumpet-blast of Demosthenes, will they listen to one no less eloquent, and of deeper feeling, and advocating a cause of far higher and of everlasting import? They who followed with delight the speculative flights of Plato in his vain searchings after truth, can they fail to be ravished by the full light poured upon their darkened vision by direct revelation from the Deity? Oh! that Paul could have met Socrates in the market-place, and that Plato had written the dialogue! But Socrates and Plato had long since passed away. Socrates had fallen the victim of an age of which he was far in advance; and how was Paul, a preacher of sublimer doctrines in more degenerate days, to escape a similar fate?

Athens at this time was no longer, what she had been under the rule of Pericles, the centre and focus of a little empire. Sparta and the Allies had humbled her by the Peloponnesian war, and after many vicissitudes she fell, with the rest of Greece, under the dominion of the Macedonians and finally of Rome. The part taken by her in the political struggles for power was invariably unfortunate. In the war between Pompey and Cæsar, Athens, under the influence of noble motives, attached herself to Pompey, and it was only the generosity of the victor that spared the living for the sake of the dead. Again, when Brutus and Cassius strove to maintain the liberties of their country against the usurpations of Octavius and Antony, Athens, which ever adopted the liberal cause, ranged herself under the banners of the two last of the Romans. Brutus indeed spent his last winter before the battle of Philippi in the pursuit of philosophy at Athens, under Cratippus and Theomnestus.[1] Again, when the dissensions between Octavius and Antony broke out into open hostilities, Athens once more unluckily (but perhaps unavoidably) took the part of Antony, and after the battle of Actium lay at the feet of the young autocrat. Octavius was, happily, of a merciful and forgiving temper, and Athens was once more spared. It was not to be expected that the Julian family should regard the city with any degree of favour, and until the close of the twelve Cæsars Athens was discountenanced, and pined under the cold shade of Imperial displeasure.

Extraordinary as it may appear, yet such was the prestige of Athens, from the fame of her ancestry, that notwithstanding these repeated offences the most unrelenting victor never went to the extreme of depriving her of liberty. Even under the twelve Cæsars Athens was still a *free* city[2]—free in a Roman sense; that is, when the interests of Rome did not interfere she had the privilege of living under her own customs and making laws for her own citizens. The constitution at this time, as appears from inscriptions, consisted of the three estates: the Areopagus, the Council of Six Hundred, and the People.[3] The Areopagus took precedence in rank, and not improbably also in power.

The city was wholly divested of political consequence, but in the world of letters it still maintained a conspicuous place. It was no longer the fountain of light, the only source from which flowed all the streams of philosophy and rhetoric among surrounding nations; but it still shone as a university for education, on a par with Alexandria and Tarsus. It so happened, however, that Athens was not now prolific of talent. The preceding age had furnished many illustrious names, and the succeeding one, in the time of Adrian, was also not wanting in luminaries; but the golden age of the past had expired, and the silver age of the future had not yet commenced. Philosophers and rhetoricians there were in abundance, for learning was the staple in which Athens traded, but none of them rose to any world-wide celebrity.

There was the same fall in respect of the fine arts. The types of excellence in architecture, statuary, and painting, met the observer at every turn; but there were no living artists who could rival the immortal works of their fathers. It is likely that when any transcendent merit rose to the surface, it was drafted off to Rome to gratify the vanity of the Emperor.

Let us now take a survey of the outward aspect presented to the eye of a stranger as he perambulated the city.

---

[1] Plutarch, Brutus, 24.
[2] ἡ βουλὴ ἡ ἐξ Ἀρείου πάγου, ἡ βουλὴ τῶν ἑξακοσίων, ὁ δῆμος. See Renan's St. Paul, p. 193, note.
[3] For the details of Athenian history, see p. 260, note.

Let us first follow the footsteps of the Apostle, from Phalerus[4] to Athens. As he steps on shore at the port, he sees before him the splendid temple of Ceres, another of Minerva, and another of Jupiter. A little farther on are some altars, and pausing

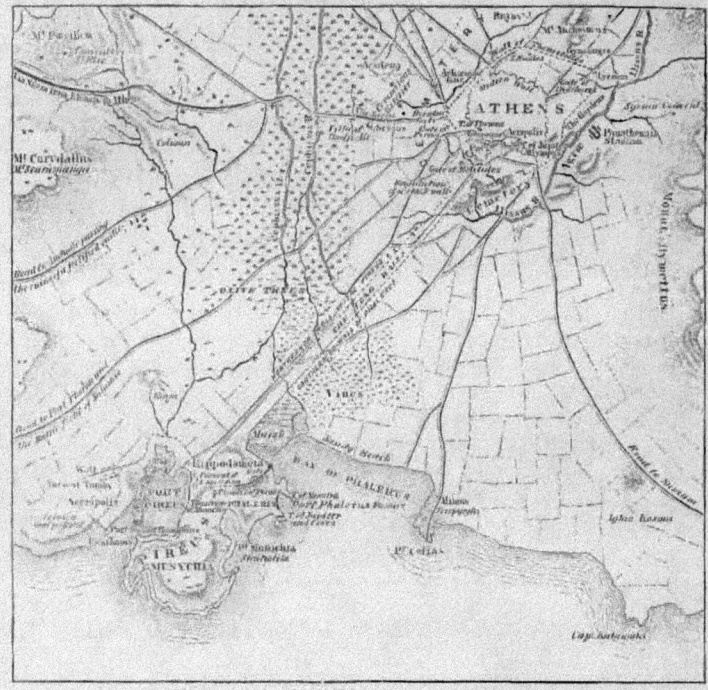

Fig. 121.—*Plan of Ports and Long Walls of Athens. From Anacharsis.*

to read the inscription, he finds on one of them the dedication, "To the unknown God;"[5] perhaps Jehovah, the great God of the Jews, or rather of all peoples and of

---

[4] Phalerus was the nearest Athenian port to one coming from Macedonia; and the altars of the unknown gods were on the road from it to the city. Pausan. Attic. i. 1, 4. Piræus, however, was no doubt at this time the more usual port. See Philost. Vit. Apoll. iv. 17; Tac. Ann. v. 10; Lucian, Navig. v. 20. And Paul *may* have landed there.

[5] Frequent reference is made to these unknown gods. Thus, βωμοὶ δὲ θεῶν τε ὀνομαζομένων Ἀγνώστων. Pausan. Attic. i. 1, 4. οἳ καὶ Ἀγνώστων δαιμόνων βωμοὶ ἵδρυνται. Philost. Vit. Apoll. vi. 3. ἡμεῖς δὲ τὸν ἐν Ἀθήναις Ἄγνωστον ἐφευρόντες καὶ προσκυνήσαντες, &c. Lucian, Philoptaris, 29; and see Hesych. Ἀγνῶτες θεοί: Pausan. Eliac. v. 14, 6. It is said that in the time of a plague, and it being uncertain what god was offended, a number of sheep, some white and some black,

the universe. What is yonder temple, with neither doors nor roof? It is Juno's, burnt by Mardonius at the time of the Persian invasion.

Let us now approach Athens itself, following Pausanias as our guide. Ascending from the Piræus, we pass between the ruins of the two Long Walls, and along the great carriage road[6] to the Piraic gate,[7] which opens upon a street running, between the Pnyx on the left and Museum Hill on the right, to the Agora, the forum or market-place. On passing the gate we observe on either side a splendid colonnade, under the porticoes of which are ranges of shops, furnished with all the costly and attractive wares of the age, while in front of the shops are seen rows of statues in bronze of the most celebrated heroes and heroines of antiquity.[8]

As we advance we pass the house of Polytion, where Alcibiades and his dissolute companions evoked the wrath of their fellow citizens by their mockery of the Eleusinian Mysteries.[9] We now stand at the end of the street, in the very heart of the Agora, the forum or market-place, where several roads meet. The original city was built for security on the Acropolis, and the country people used to

---

were, by the advice of Epimenides (the Cretan who is quoted by St. Paul), let loose on the Areopagus, and wherever any one lay down an altar was erected τῷ προσήκοντι θεῷ, Diog. Laërt. Epimenides, lib. i. c. 10, s. 3; and it is easy to conceive that on one of these altars was the inscription Ἀγνώστῳ θεῷ.

It is a common error to assume that the altars referred to in the citations were respectively inscribed to the unknown gods in the plural. The correct meaning unquestionably is, that each altar was dedicated "to the unknown god," in the singular. See Meyer, Apostg. 315; Olshausen, Apostg. by Ebrard, 238. And the Philopatris of Lucian speaks of the Ἀγνώστων θεόν in the singular number. Philop. 29. However, no such inscription has been found. See Renan's St. Paul, p. 174, note.

Others suggest that the altar may have been dedicated to some idol, but that in the course of time, by some mishap, the name of the idol had been lost, and that to secure its sanctity it was inscribed with the words, "To the god whose name is now unknown."

According to others, the altar was really dedicated to the true God, that of the Jews, whom the Athenians would fain conciliate. There can be no doubt that from the time of Alexander the Great, there had been constant intercourse between the Jews and the Greeks, and leagues of friendship were entered into between them (Jos. Ant. xii. 4, 10), and the Athenians had even erected a statue at Athens in honour of Hyrcanus, the high priest of the true God. Jos. Ant. xiv. 8, 5; see Biscoe, c. 8, p. 212.

[6] ἁμαξιτός. Xen. Hellen. ii. 4, 10. Leake places this highway *outside* the Long Walls and on the north side of them. Topog. of Athens, 92. But in this he has not been followed by later writers. See Smith's Geogr. Dict. vol. i. p. 260.

[7] Many think that Pausanias entered by the Dipylum gate, which was outside the Long Walls and more to the west. But this cannot be, for the Dipylum gate divided the outer Ceramicus from the inner Ceramicus, and Pausanias did not reach the Ceramicus until he came to the end of the street by which he had entered; στοαὶ δέ εἰσιν ἀπὸ τῶν πυλῶν ἐς τὸν Κεραμεικόν. Pausan. i. 2, 4. The reason why some fix on the Dipylum gate is, that they suppose it to be the general thoroughfare from the Piræus (Leake, 91); but this has been shown to be erroneous. Forchhammer, p. 236, cited Smith's Dict. vol. i. p. 263. Dipylum, otherwise the Ceramic or Thriasian gate, was the most frequented of all the gates, but the neighbourhood about it was of a low description, and it was called the Prostitutes' gate (Δημώδεις πύλαι) from its being the haunt of all the courtesans of the city. See Leake, pp. 75 and 80.

[8] στοαὶ δὲ εἰσιν ἀπὸ τῶν πυλῶν ἐς τὸν Κεραμεικὸν, καὶ εἰκόνες πρὸ αὐτῶν χαλκαῖ, καὶ γυναικῶν καὶ ἀνδρῶν, ὅσοις τι ὑπῆρχε καὶ ὧν τις λόγος ἐς δόξαν. Pausan. Attic. i. 2, 4.

[9] Pausan Attic. i. 2, 4.

bring their products for sale to the foot of the rock on the western side, where was the ascent. This undercliff accordingly became the market.[10] But in course of time, as the city grew, the population flowed over from the heights into the plain below and streets began to be formed there. The part first occupied was that about the market, and hence the new town was itself called the Agora, or Market. Eventually the whole hollow between the Acropolis and the Areopagus on the north, the Pnyx on the west, and the Museum Hill on the south, became populous, and was all known by the name of the Agora.[11]

Taking our stand then at the end of the street which descends from the Piraic gate, we find ourselves in the heart of the city where the principal ways meet. Behind us is the street of the Piraic gate, by which we entered. On the right runs off the Royal Portico,[12] and in front of us is a triumphal gateway, opening upon the road which passes in front of the Painted Portico, or Porch of the Stoics.[13] This gateway is one of the best known objects in Athens, and is celebrated for the sculpture upon it, which represents the victory of the Athenians over the cavalry and mercenaries of Cassander.[14] Here also is the statue of Hermes Agoraeus, or

---

[10] Thucyd. ii. 15.

[11] It reached northward to the foot of the Acropolis, for the statues of Harmodius and Aristogeiton were in the Agora (Arist. Rhet. i. 9; Lucian, Parasit. 48; Aristoph. Lysist. 633), and yet were at the commencement of the ascent to the Acropolis. ἡ ἄνωμεν ἐς πόλιν, Arrian Anab. iii. 16; πέτραν παρ' αὐτὴν Παλλάδος, Eurip. Hippol. 30 (see Smith's Geogr. Dict. vol. i. p. 297). On the west the Agora reached to the Pnyx, which was said to be in it. ἐν ἀγορᾷ πρὸς τῷ λίθῳ, Plutarch, Solon, 25. On the south it neared Colonus, a knoll connected with the Museum, παρὰ τῷ Κολωνῷ εἰσέρχεσαν οὗ ἐστι πλησίον τῆς ἀγορᾶς. Harpocrat. Κολωνίτας. The Ceramicus, also, seems to be used as almost an equivalent expression to the Agora; but there was this distinction, that the Ceramicus reached up to the gate Dipylum, whereas the Agora did not extend beyond the place called the Mercuries by the side of the Gymnasium of Ptolemy, which was halfway between the Porch and the gate Dipylum, for Xenophon recommends that the horsemen before joining a procession should, to show their respect for all the gods, begin by riding round the Agora, and he starts them from the Mercuries. εἰ ὅσων (θεῶν) ἱερὰ καὶ ἀγάλματα ἐν τῇ ἀγορᾷ ἐστι, ταῦτα ἀρξάμενοι ἀπὸ τῶν Ἑρμῶν κύκλῳ περὶ τὴν ἀγορὰν καὶ τὰ ἱερὰ ἀγυικλαύνοιεν, Xenoph. Hipparch. iii. 1. Again, the Gymnasium of Ptolemy is said by Pausanias to be not in, but "not far from the Agora," ἐν δὲ τῷ γυμνασίῳ τῆς ἀγορᾶς ἀπέχοντι οὐ πολὺ. Pausan. i. 17, 2.

[12] πρώτη δέ ἐστιν ἐν δεξιᾷ καλουμένη στοὰ βασίλειος. Pausan. i. 3.

[13] This follows from the three routes taken by Pausanias after arriving at the end of the Piraic Street. The first route turns to the right, ἐν δεξιᾷ, to the στοὰ βασίλειος. He then returns to the same spot and goes forward to the Painted Porch. ἰοῦσι δὲ πρὸς τὴν στοὰν, ἣν Ποικίλην ὀνομάζουσιν ἀπὸ τῶν γραφῶν, ἔστιν Ἑρμῆς χαλκοῦς καλούμενος Ἀγοραῖος καὶ Πύλη πλησίον, Pausan. i. 15, 1; and then after apparently passing the Painted Porch he turns to the left, going up the Ceramicus till he comes to the Mercuries and the Gymnasium of Ptolemy. ἐν δὲ τῷ γυμνασίῳ τῆς ἀγορᾶς ἀπέχοντι οὐ πολὺ, Πτολεμαίου ἀπὸ τοῦ κατασκευασαμένου καλουμένῳ, λίθοι τέ εἰσιν Ἑρμαῖ, &c. Pausan. i. 17, 2. The στοὰ βασίλειος and the στοὰ Ποικίλη were apparently contiguous, for the Mercuries began from both Porches, ἀπὸ γὰρ τῆς Ποικίλης καὶ τῆς τοῦ βασιλείου στοᾶς εἰσιν οἱ Ἑρμαῖ. Harpocrat. and Phot. Ἑρμαῖ. The explanation perhaps is, that the Mercuries commenced from Ἑρμῆς Ἀγοραῖος, the Mercury of the market, which stood at the western end of the Royal Porch, and were thence continued in front of the Painted Porch and up the street leading to the Dipylum Gate. They might thus be said to run from the two porches, viz. first from the Royal Porch northward, and thence from the Painted Porch westward.

[14] Pausan. i. 15, 1.

Mercury of the Market, and this is regarded as the very centre of the Agora.[15] It was erected by the nine archons, and is one of the most admired pieces of casting in bronze in all the city.[16] It is sometimes also referred to as the Mercury of the Gate,[17] or the Mercury of the Porch.[18]

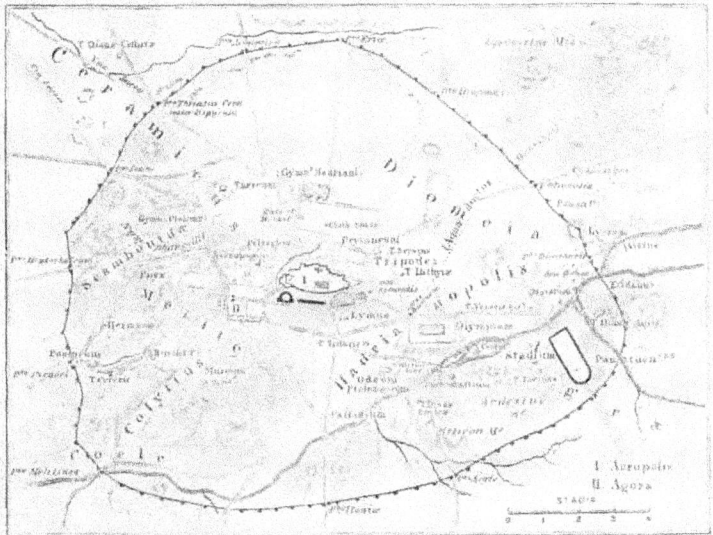

Fig. 122.—*Plan of Athens. From Spruner's Atlas.*

The Royal Porch (Στοὰ Βασίλειος), the colonnade on our right, as we stand at the end of the Piraic Street, is so called because here the king archon sits for the trial of causes,[19] and upon the summit are mounted the statues of Theseus throwing Sciron into the sea and of Aurora carrying away Cephalus,[20] and before the cloister stand the statues of Conon and of his little less celebrated son Timotheus.[21] The colonnade in front of us as we stand at the end of the Piraic Street, the colonnade which lines the west side of the street which continues the Piraic Street, is the celebrated Painted Porch, so called from the numerous paintings with which it is

---

[15] ἐν μέσῃ ἀγορᾷ ἵδρυται Ἑρμοῦ Ἀγοραίου ἄγαλμα. Scholiast ad Aristoph. Equit. 297.

[16] αἱ ἐννέα ἄρχοντες ταῖς φυλαῖς ἀνέθεσαν Ἑρμῆν παρὰ τὸν πυλῶνα τὸν Ἀττικόν (lege Ἀγοραῖον). Harpocrat. and Photius.

[17] περὶ τὸν Ἑρμῆν τὸν πρὸς τῇ πυλίδι. Demosth. c. Energ. et Mnesib. p. 146.

[18] ὁ Ἀγοραῖος ὁ παρὰ τὴν Ποικίλην. Lucian.

Jupit. Trag. 33.

[19] τὸ δὲ χωρίον, ὁ Κεραμεικός . . . πρώτη δέ ἐστιν ἐν δεξιᾷ καλουμένη στοὰ βασίλειος, ἔνθα καθίζει βασιλεὺς ἐνιαυσίαν ἄρχων ἀρχὴν καλουμένην βασιλείαν. Pausan. Attic. i. 3. 1.

[20] Pausan. Attic. i. 3. 1.

[21] Pausan. Attic. i. 13. 1.

decorated.[22] Here Zeno, the Stoic, founded his school of philosophy, and here his followers, the philosophers of the Porch, may still be seen in their loose-flowing gowns, with venerable beards and pale faces and thoughtful brows, either seated in deep study and pondering over some abstruse problem, or perambulating up and down discussing the subtlest questions of morals and metaphysics.[23] The paint-

Fig. 135.—*A Philosopher studying a roll of papyrus before a gnomon, or sun-dial. From C. W. King's Antique Gems.*

ing on one of the side walls of the porch represents the battle between the Athenians and the Lacedemonians at Œnoe, while in one compartment of the central wall are the Athenians under Theseus fighting with the Amazons; and in another compartment Troy is taken, and the assembled chieftains are debating the outrage of Ajax upon Cassandra, the prophetic daughter of Priam. The other side wall, at the farther end, displays a painting of stirring interest, the battle of Marathon. Miltiades and Callimachus, the polemarchs, are seen cheering on the little patriot band, and the turbaned host of Datis and Artaphernes are flying in disorder to their ships. The gallant Cynegirus, to prevent their escape, has seized a boat first with one hand and then with the other, and both have been severed by the Persian scimitars, and lie bleeding on the ground, and he now gripes the boat with his teeth. There in the thickest of the mêlée is the poet-warrior Æschylus, and there is the faithful dog of an Athenian, who, while his master is engaged in combat, has fastened on the heels of his adversary.[24] In front of the porch are erected the bronze statues of the great men, and amongst the most honoured is that of the immortal Solon, the founder of the Athenian constitution.[25]

Passing the Painted Porch, we now turn to the left and walk up the Ceramicus, the street leading to the Dipylum Gate, which opens upon the Sacred Way, the road to Eleusis. This street is remarkable for the stone pillars called the "Mercuries," square blocks of about a man's height, and surmounted with the head of Mercury.[26]

---

[22] Pausan. Attic. i. 3, 1.

[23] ὠχρὸς περιπατῶν, φιλοσόφων τὸ χρῶμ' ἔχων. Lucian, Jupiter Trag. 1. Καὶ ἔτυχον γὰρ νεφέλην τῶν παχειῶν περιβεβλημένος (Jupiter), σχηματίσας ἐμαυτὸν εἰς τὸν ἐκείνων τρόπον, καὶ τὸν πώγωνα ἐπισπασάμενος εὖ μάλα ἐῴκειν φιλοσόφῳ. Lucian, Jupiter Trag. 16. The scene is laid in the Στοᾷ Ποικίλῃ of the Agora.

[24] Pausan. Attic. i. 15, 2, et seq.

[25] Pausan. i. 16, 1. And see Demosth. in Aristog. 27, p. 807; Ælian, Var. Hist. viii. 16.

[26] ἀπὸ γὰρ τῆς Ποικίλης, καὶ τῆς τοῦ βασιλέως στοᾶς εἰσὶν αἱ Ἑρμαῖ καλούμενοι· διὰ γὰρ τὸ πολλοῖς κεῖσθαι καὶ ὑπὸ ἰδιωτῶν καὶ ἀρχόντων ταύτην εἰληφέναι τὴν προσηγορίαν συμβέβηκεν. Harpocrat. and Phot. Ἑρμαῖ.

They are inscribed with moral sentences for the edification of the wayfarer, and some are as old as Hipparchus, the brother of Hippias the tyrant, for on one of them we read, "The gift of Hipparchus: Go and think no ill;" and on another, "The gift of Hipparchus: Never betray thy friend."[27] The Mercuries serve also as direction posts; for when a single road, as Vesta Street, branches off from the Ceramicus, there stands at the corner a three-faced Janus, with the three routes underwritten;[28] and where a street crosses so that four ways meet, we find a four-faced Mercury as a guide to the embarrassed traveller.[29] About halfway up the street is an open space, called specially "the Mercuries," from the number of Mercuries here congregated to indicate the various routes.[30] A little to the right is one of the

Fig. 124.—Temple of Theseus. From T. H. Dyer's Athens.

oldest and at the same time one of the grandest works in all Athens, viz., the Theseum, or Temple of Theseus, erected in the fifth century before the Christian era, and still standing (fig. 124). The temples and statues and public buildings that are crowded into the area of the Agora between the Areopagus and Acropolis on the north, the Pnyx on the west, and the Museum on the south, are countless.[31] There is the Temple of Apollo, called the Patroum, and the Temple of the Mother of the Gods, or the Metroum, and the circular Tholus, where the prytanes take their meals and offer their sacrifices, the council house, where the six hundred meet, the famous altar of the Twelve Gods, the statues of the heroes from whom the wards or quarters of Athens take their names, called the Eponymi, the statues of Eirene, Amphiaraus, Lycurgus, Demosthenes, Harmodius and Aristogeiton, Hercules, Apollo, and Pindar, the Temple of Ares, or Mars, at the foot of the Areopagus, the Temples of Aphrodite, Pandemus, and Vulcan, the Odeum, the Eurysaceum, &c.,[32] and near the western limit of the Agora is the statue of the Cretan poet Epimenides,[33]

Fig. 122.—*View of Athens from the south, from a point near the Monument of Philopappus.*

In the centre is the Acropolis. Below, on the extreme left, is the hill of Areopagus. The open space to the south of the Areopagus, and of the Acropolis, is the site of the ancient Agora, or Market, or Forum, now uninhabited.

whose testimony to the lying rascality of his countrymen is cited by St. Paul in the Epistle to Titus;[34] and in another part may be seen the statue of a Jew in pontifical robes, the High Priest Hyrcanus, whose friendship for the Athenians had called forth this testimony of their regard.[35] The traveller may gaze also on the statue of a Jewish Princess, viz. the beautiful Berenice, the sister of Agrippa II., that

[31] προσέλθετε οὖν τῇ διανοίᾳ καὶ εἰς τὴν Στοὰν τὴν Ποικίλην, ἁπάντων γὰρ ὑμῖν τῶν καλῶν ἔργων τὰ ὑπομνήματα ἐν τῇ Ἀγορᾷ ἀνάκειται. Æschin. in Ctesiphon. c. 62, p. 437 (the Porch, therefore, was in the Agora, and must have formed the western side of it); and see the passage cited from Xenophon, ante, p. 244, note [1].

[32] See Smith's Geogr. Dict. vol. i. p. 296.
[33] Pausan. i. 14, 3.
[34] Tit. i. 12.
[35] Jos. Ant. xiv. 8, 5.

very Berenice before whom Paul was some years after this to plead the cause of Christianity.[36]

The Agora of Athens, in its widest sense, was not what according to modern conception is meant by a market, but was an extensive quarter of the city. It is probable, however, that an open area at the foot of the Acropolis was still exclusively occupied as a market, and that it reached thence to the Royal Cloister on the south

Fig. 120.—Gate of the Agora, or market on the north of the Acropolis.   From Fisher's Belgium, &c.

and the Painted Porch on the west, and this we may almost infer from the fact that the Mercury which stood at the junction of these two porticoes or colonnades was called distinctively the Mercury of the Market. In one sense, indeed, the whole quarter known as the Agora was a market, for at the same time that it contained all the finest temples and statues and public edifices of Athens, it was one great bazaar of an irregular form, but everywhere presenting the busy scene of commercial life. Here was the flower piazza, there the fish-stalls, here the mart for men's clothing, there for women's clothing, here a stand for slaves, there a bookstall, not to mention

---

[36] The inscription of the statue was as follows: Ιουλιαν Βερενικην βασιλισσαν Ιουλιου Αγριππα βασιλεως θυγατερα και μεγαλων βασιλεων ευεργετων της πολεως εκγονον. Acad. Inscript. vol. xxvi. p. 451, citing Spon, Misc. p. 319.

the stores of pottery, perfumes, garlic, onions, walnuts, apples, and vegetables and fruits of every description.[37]

Such was the Agora at the south of the Acropolis, but at the north of the Acropolis was also a market in the strictest sense of the word, that is, there was an open space, isolated from the rest of the city, and devoted exclusively to the sale of commodities. The site of this market (which, as more useful than ornamental, is scarcely mentioned in ancient writers[38]) has been ascertained by the testimony of monuments and inscriptions which still exist.[39] On the north side of the Acropolis, and fronting westwards, is a Doric portico of four columns (fig. 126), and on the acroterium, or summit of the pediment, was, but no longer is, an equestrian statue.[40] On the entablature is an inscription to the effect that the portico was erected from donations presented by Julius Cæsar and Augustus, and was dedicated to Minerva Archegetis in the prætorship of Eucles of Marathon (who had succeeded in the care of the work to his father Herodes), and in the archonship of Nicias the son of Serapion.[41] The date of the erection, from the mention of Eucles as archon, is supposed by Boeckh to be somewhere between B.C. 12 and A.D. 1. The inscription at the foot of the statue which stood on the acroterium proves the person thus honoured to have been Lucius, the grandson and adopted son of Augustus.[42] The portico had a peculiar configuration, just such as we should expect for the vestibule of a market,[43] and at the entrance of the portal was found the base of a statue erected in honour of Julia, the mother of Tiberius, and the inscription upon it shows that the expense of the monument was defrayed by Dionysius when he and Quintus Nævius Rufus were clerks of the market.[44] It is justly remarked by Boeckh, that the clerkship of the market is

---

[37] Leake's Athens, p. 380.

[38] The existence of a second market is evidenced by the fact that the market at the south of the Acropolis is distinguished as the *old* market. Ἀπολλόδωρος ἐν τῷ περὶ θεῶν Πανδημόν (Ἀφροδίτην) φησὶν Ἀθήνησιν ἀφιδρυθεῖσαν περὶ τὴν Ἀρχαίαν ἀγοράν, διὰ τὸ ἐνταῦθα πάντα τὸν δῆμον συνάγεσθαι τὸ παλαιὸν ἐν ταῖς ἐκκλησίαις ἃς ἐκάλουν ἀγοράς. Harpocrat. and Phot. Πανδημὸς Ἀφροδίτη. The quarter where the new market lay was called Eretria. Ἐρέτριαν δ' οἱ μὲν ἀπὸ Μακίστου τῆς Τριφυλίας ἀποικισθῆναί φασιν ὑπ' Ἐρετριέως· οἱ δ' ἀπὸ τῆς Ἀθήνῃσιν Ἐρετρίας, ἣ νῦν ἐστιν ἀγορά. Strabo x. 1 (p. 324, Tauchnitz).

[39] Some, however, still dispute (but, as appears, on insufficient grounds,) the existence of a second market. See Smith's Geogr. Dict. vol. i. p. 291.

[40] That the statue was equestrian appears from the measurements of the acroterium. See Stuart.

[41] ὁ δῆμος ἀπὸ τῶν δωρεῶν ὑπὸ Γαΐου Ἰουλίου Καίσαρος θεοῦ καὶ Αὐτοκράτορος Καίσαρος, θεοῦ υἱοῦ σεβαστοῦ, Ἀθηρᾷ Ἀρχηγέτιδι, στρατηγοῦντος ἐπὶ τοῖς ὁπλίτας Εὐκλέους Μαραθωνίου, τοῦ καὶ διαδεξαμένου τὴν ἐπιμέλειαν τοῦ πατρὸς Ἡρώδου, τοῦ καὶ πρεσβεύσαντος. ἐπὶ ἄρχοντος Νικίου τοῦ Σεραπίωνος Ἀθμονέως. Boeckh, No. 477. Boeckh suggests that this Herodes was of the family of Herodes Atticus, and gives the following pedigree:

Herodes
|
Eucles
|
Hipparchus
|
Atticus
|
Herodes Atticus.

[42] ὁ δῆμος Λούκιον Καίσαρα Αὐτοκράτορος, θεοῦ υἱοῦ, Σεβαστοῦ Καίσαρος υἱόν. Boeckh, No. 312.

[43] See Stuart's Antiq. of Athens, vol. i. p. 1.

[44] Ἰουλίαν θεὰν Σεβαστὴν Πρόνοιαν ἡ Βουλὴ ἡ ἐξ Ἀρήου πάγου καὶ ἡ βουλὴ τῶν ἑξακοσίων καὶ ὁ δῆμος, ἀνεθέντος ἐκ τῶν ἰδίων Διονυσίου τοῦ Ἄθλου Μαραθωνίου, Ἀγορανομούντων αὐτοῦ τε Διονυσίου Μαραθωνίου καὶ Κοΐντου Ναυΐου Ῥούφου Μελιτέως. Boeckh, No. 313. From Julia being described as θεά, Boeckh supposes the date to be some time under the Emperor Claudius. See a facsimile of the inscription in Stuart and Revett.

here mentioned because the statue was erected within the limits of the market, and it is difficult, if not impossible, to give any other explanation. There is yet another inscription confirmatory of the same view, for close to the portal was found a stone upon which was engraved a decree of the Emperor Adrian, which declares the amount of dues to the state in respect of oils, and subjects the sale of this product to various stringent restrictions.[15] It is also worthy of note, that at a little distance to the east of the portal, and where we should suppose would be the other extremity of the market, we find the famous Temple of the Winds, erected by Andronicus

FIG. 127.—Temple of the Winds, or Clock Tower. From T. H. Dyer's Athens.

Cyrrhestes, and very appropriate to the site of a market. It is an octagon, with the eight winds, into which the Athenian compass was divided, represented by appropriate figures and costumes on the eight sides, and on the summit was a Triton turning on a spindle and holding in his hand a switch, pointing from time to time to the quarter of the wind; and on the exterior was a sun-dial with lines cut in the stone (which are still traceable) to indicate the hour while the sun was shining,[16] and within was a clepsydra,

[15] The inscription is too long to be copied, but will be found in Boeckh, No. 355.
[16] See Leake's Athens, 64.

or water clock, to tell the hour when the weather was cloudy. The tradition is, that Socrates used to take his stand at the foot of this clock tower and there instruct the rising youth of Athens.[47] Considering the extent of ancient Athens, there must have been a market, either concentrated or dispersed, for the north as well as for the south of the Acropolis, and we cannot well avoid the conclusion that here, between the Doric portico on the west and the clock tower on the east, was an open space, answering strictly to the modern idea of a market. We have dwelt thus long upon the Agora at the south and the market at the north as possessing an unusual interest from the fact that the Apostle Paul discoursed for weeks with all comers in one or other of these areas.

Another site that also claims our attention is the Areopagus, or Mars Hill. This was a rocky elevation on the west of the Acropolis, and divided from it by a narrow valley. It sloped gently toward the west, and the line of it formed the northern limit of the old Agora, of which so much has been said. At the eastern and highest end was the place of meeting of the celebrated court of Areopagus, otherwise called the Upper Court, as opposed to the Council of Six Hundred, which sat in the Agora below. It was the most august of all the courts, and it was at this bar that Socrates was arraigned and condemned on the ground of innovating upon the state religion. The name of Mars Hill is traced to the fable that here Mars was tried before the assembled gods for the murder of a son of Neptune.[48]

---

[47] ἑστία δὲ τῆς πόλεως ἐστι τὸ διδασκαλεῖον τοῦ Σωκράτους, ἐν ᾧ ἐστι κύκλῳ οἱ ἄνδρες καὶ οἱ ἄνεμοι ἱστοριαμένοι. From a MS. of the 15th century.

[48] When at Athens, in 1851, I examined the Areopagus with some minuteness. The hill is a bare and rugged rock, lying east and west, abrupt on the east, north, and south, but toward the west descending by a gradual slope. The length of the platform at the top, from the eastward extremity to the commencement of the slope on the west, is about sixty paces, and the width at the eastern end from north to south is about twenty-four paces, but increasing toward the west. The stairs are at the south-eastern corner. Sixteen steps still remain, and four others can be traced. After ascending a little more than half-way, an opening, formerly used as a passage, leads up on the left to an open area on the summit, covering about sixteen paces N. to S. and ten paces E. to W., which perhaps anciently served as an apartment for the suitors and officials, until their presence was required in court. Near the top of the stairs are two steps to the right, by which probably the Areopagites mounted to their seats. At the top of the stairs is the court of Areopagus itself. There is first a quadrangular excavation, seven paces from right to left and three paces across, divided into two equal compartments; that to the left is hollowed about two feet deep in the middle, so as to leave solid benches round the sides, apparently for seats. The right compartment has no corresponding excavation. I observed that the cutting forming the eastern side has been streaked, so as to imitate large square stones, from which I conclude that the face of the rock remains much as it ever was. At the southern corner of the left compartment is a rude stone, levelled at the top, which may be that mentioned by Pausanias as the Stone of Insolence, on which the accuser stood, and to the south of the right compartment is a smoothed stone, of a corresponding level, and ascended by a step from the head of the stairs, which may be the stone called by Pausanias the Stone of Impudence, on which the prisoner was placed. τοὺς δὲ ἀργοὺς λίθους ἐφ᾽ ὧν ἑστᾶσιν ὅσοι δίκας ὑπέχουσι, καὶ οἱ διώκοντες, τὸν μὲν Ὕβρεως, τὸν δὲ Ἀναιδείας αὐτοὶ ὀνομάζουσι. Pausan. i. 28, 5. From the side of each of these two stones rises a higher stone, of an irregular and massive form, upon which the accuser or the accused might lean at his convenience. These are, perhaps, the βάθρα

CHAP. XII.] ST. PAUL AT ATHENS. [A.D. 51] 253

We now mount the Acropolis, an isolated rock rising majestically from the heart of the city. We ascend successive flights of steps, and at last reach the Propylæa or vestibule, leading by five marble portals to the elevated platform above. On our left, as we go up, is the gallery of paintings, and on our right is the Temple of Victory.

Fig. 120.—Site of the court of Areopagus. From a model made by the author from personal examination and measurement in 1851. Paul must have ascended the Areopagus from the Agora by these steps, and have stood in the hollow excavated at the top, and must have addressed the Areopagites ranged in tiers on the benches of the surrounding court.

We pass the gorgeous gateway and stand before the gigantic bronze statue of Minerva Promachus, with helmed head and spear in hand, the presiding goddess of the city, a well-known landmark for miles and miles to the mariner at sea and the pilgrim on

referred to by Euripides:

ἐν δὲ νῷ λαμπραὶ μὲν ἧλιου βολαί,
ὄντες, ἕνα καὶ Ποσειδῶν λαθρίαν θάσσων,
τὸ δ' ἄλλο προσβλέπει πέτρᾳ ἐν Ἄρειον·
                    Iphig. Taur. 961.

The quadrangular excavation of which I have spoken may have answered to what in an English court is called the well, viz. the hollow space immediately under the judges, de-shore; on our left is the Erechtheum, or temple of Minerva Polias, and on our right the Parthenon itself, unrivalled for its marble columns, and sculptured frieze the work of Phidias[49] (fig. 131).

To describe all the temples and statues in Athens would be an endless task. There was every conceivable variety of structure and sculpture. Temples of marble, temples of stone, temples quadrangular, temples round; statues colossal, statues full size, and statues diminutive; some in bronze, some in marble, some in stone, some in wood, some in pottery, some plain, some painted, some overlaid with ivory, or gold, or silver, some isolated, some projecting in relief from the wall. Well might the sacred historian add that Paul's spirit was stirred within him as he scanned a city so crowded with idols.[50] It was a common saying about Athens that it was easier to find there a *god* than a *man*. The sight, too, must have been the more striking to one who had passed his early life at Jerusalem, within whose circuit not an image was to be seen.[51]

Athens, however, after all, was a strange compound of grandeur and meanness. Nothing could exceed the magnificence of the Acropolis itself and of the city below. The Ceramicus, from the Dipylum gate down to the Agora or Market, was broad and imposing,[52] and the street from the Piraic gate to the Ceramicus was lined on each side, as we have seen, with handsome porticoes; but, in general, where the public monuments did not preoccupy the ground, the streets were narrow and crooked, and there were the usual little alleys and passages of a crowded Eastern

---

voted to the officials interested in the pleadings. The surface of the rock round the quadrangle chamber rises toward the north, and upon this upper platform were probably ranged the judges. There is room for benches on the east, and west, and north, and also on the south on each side of the stairs. On the north may have been two or three rows of benches, one above another, and one of them can still be traced by a cutting. The whole space occupied by the court was probably a square of sixteen paces each way. Near the north-eastern corner the rock has been cut into the shape and size of an altar, and possibly this may be the altar of Minerva Martia, dedicated by Orestes. καὶ βωμός ἐστιν Ἀθηνᾶς Ἀρείας, ὃν ἀνέθηκεν [Orestes] ἀποφυγὼν τὴν δίκην. Pausan. i. 28, 5. At the north-western corner of the court the rock has been levelled for two or three yards, as for a passage, and at the end are two steps leading to the west. Beyond the court, on the north-west, but still on the summit, is another open area, where some public building may have stood, but I did not distinguish any remains. On the slope to the west were several excavations for buildings and some dry walls. At the foot of the hill, on the north, the ruins of the church of Dionysius the Areopagite may be seen toward the east, the building apparently having been erected on the nearest site to the court of Areopagus above. The form of it was a rectangle, with an apsis at the eastern end. Under the hill, a little more to the west, the rock has been excavated, so as to form two sides of another edifice, probably a church, and there are steps up the rock, but I could not trace them to the summit, and it seemed to me doubtful whether they had formed a staircase to the top of the Areopagus, or only to a gallery of the church. Under the rock, still farther to the west, I observed a cross cut in the rock, and my guide informed me that it was from the height above that St. Paul, according to tradition, preached to the people below.

[49] The greater part of the frieze is in the British Museum.

[50] κατείδωλον. Acts xvii. 16. See Wetstein ad loc.

[51] Nulla simulacra urbibus suis, nedum templis sinunt. Tac. Hist. v. 5. οὐ δ' ἄγαλμα οὐδὲν ἐν αὐτοῖς ποτέ τοῖς Ἱεροσολύμοις ἔσχον. Dion. xxxvii. 17.

[52] ἄρχεται μὲν εὐθὺς ἐκ πυλῶν (Κεραμεικῶν).

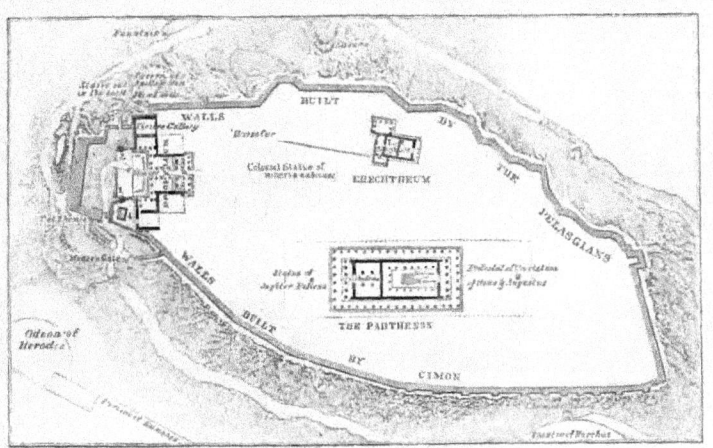

Fig. 129.—*Plan of the Acropolis. From Anacharsis.*

Fig. 130.—*Coin of Athens. From Pellerin.*

On the right is the ascent by stairs to the Acropolis, and on the top are first the Propylæa to the right, then the statue of Minerva in the centre, and then on the left the Parthenon. At the foot of the rock is the cave of Pan.

Fig. 131.—*The Parthenon, or Temple of Minerva. From T. H. Dyer's Athens.*

city. The Agora may perhaps not be improperly compared to the City of London as it was in the days of Queen Elizabeth, or still more appropriately to the great bazaar of some Eastern capital, as that of Constantinople.

Paul had come to Athens as a temporary refuge. His intention previously had been to evangelise Macedonia, but at Beroea his progress had been broken off, and that so suddenly that no other plan of operations had yet been substituted. He was now waiting at Athens for the arrival of Silas and Timothy from Beroea, that he might concert with them the course of future operations. He was alone, and among strangers, and, bowed by infirmity, he had not proposed to unfold the banner of the Gospel where the prospect was so inauspicious. But one of Paul's earnest and ardent temperament could ill brook to remain long an idle spectator while the grossest superstition was staring him in the face. "His heart was hot within him, and while he was musing the fire kindled, and at the last he spake with his tongue."[53] But not even then did he neglect the preference he invariably showed to his own countrymen. On each Sabbath day he entered into the synagogue (for there was one at Athens as elsewhere) and preached to the Jews and proselytes,[54] but during the week he daily frequented the Agora, and opened the truths of religion to the casual passers by.[55]

The word "Agora" at Athens might, as we have seen,[56] be understood in three senses: 1st, as the quarter of the city so called, lying between the Acropolis, the Areopagus, the Pnyx, and the Museum hill; 2nd, as the market or forum at the south of the Acropolis; and, 3rd, as the market for commodities at the north of the Acropolis. In the first place, we cannot think that Luke, by "the market," meant any particular quarter of the city, as such. An Athenian might by "the market" well intend a portion of the city commonly known by that name; but Luke, a native of Antioch, and writing for the general reader, could scarcely have so expressed himself. Besides, the object of the Apostle evidently was to take up a post where he could command the largest audience. The market which Luke had in view was a market proper, and might be either that on the south or that to the north of the Acropolis. We lean to the hypothesis that it was the one to the south, for the following reasons: 1. In the time of the Apostle, when the market simply was spoken of, as here by Luke, the old market to the south of the Acropolis was invariably and without exception the one referred to. 2. Paul, in his discourse, was encountered by the Stoics, which, if we look to the relative positions of the market and the Porch,

κινηθεῖσα δὲ ἐκεῖθεν διὰ μέσου τοῦ δρόμου κομίζεται, ὃς εὐθύνης τε καὶ λείος καταβαίνων ἄνωθεν σχίζει τὰς ἑκατέρωθεν αὐτῷ παρατεταμένας στοάς, ἐφ᾽ ὧν ἀγοράζουσιν Ἀθηναῖοί τε καὶ οἱ λοιποί. Himerius Sophist. Orat. 3, p. 146. Ab Dipylo accessit Porta ea, velut in ore urbis posita, major aliquanto potentiorque quam cæteræ est, et intra eam extraque latæ sunt viæ, ut et oppidani dirigere aciem a foro ad portam possint. Liv. xxxi. 24.

[53] Psalm xxxix. 3.

[54] ἐν τῇ συναγωγῇ τοῖς Ἰουδαίοις καὶ τοῖς σεβομένοις. Acts xvii. 17.

[55] ἐν τῇ ἀγορᾷ πρὸς τοὺς παρατυγχάνοντας. Acts xvii. 17.

[56] See p. 244.

was the most natural thing in the world, for the Porch of the Stoics formed the western side of the southern market. 3. When the philosophers laid hands on Paul they took him up to Mars Hill, and this also is strictly in keeping with the view that Paul was preaching in the old market, for the stairs leading up to the Areopagus started from the north side of the old or southern market.

Fancy portrays to the mind's eye the Apostle in humble garb encircled in the southern market by dealers and chapmen, busybodies and idlers, listening with curiosity to strange doctrines flowing from a tongue, eloquent indeed, but betraying a foreign accent. The orator whom accident had thrown upon their shores was apparently highly gifted by nature, for he could return a ready answer to the caviller, and had even some store of learning, for he could quote their best writers with fluency. A passion for novelty was the prominent feature of the Athenian character. Students were there assembled from all quarters of the globe to cultivate letters, to imbibe knowledge, and carry home with them the very newest fashion of philosophy. "All the Athenians and strangers which were there," says Luke (and the observation is fully confirmed from other sources),[57] "spent their time in nothing else but either to tell or to hear some new thing."[58] Amid such a population the daily harangues of Paul could not fail to create an intensity of interest. It was evident that sooner or later the zeal of the Apostle would bring him into collision with the Athenian system of idolatry. But before we narrate the circumstances which led to this catastrophe, let us advert for a moment to an intervening incident.

After Paul had been a short time at Athens Timothy arrived from Beroea, but alone. Such was the critical situation of the rising church at Beroea, that Silas, the colleague of Paul, and himself an Apostle, and to whose care the Beroean church had been more particularly confided, had not deemed it advisable to take his departure. The youthful and active Timothy, whose authority was less weighty amongst the Beroean converts, had started by himself to join the Apostle. He brought with him no consolatory news from Macedonia, more particularly as regards Thessalonica. When Paul had quitted Thessalonica in such haste he had anticipated a very brief absence —"for an hour's time,"[59]— he had expected that the storm would soon blow over, and that after preaching awhile at Beroea he might again return. On the contrary, new troubles had overtaken him at Beroea, and he had fled for his life to a distant city. At Athens he still cherished the idea that as soon as Silas and Timothy joined him

---

[57] ἡμεῖς δὲ ... οὐδὲν ποιοῦντες ἐνθάδε καθήμεθα ... πυνθανόμενοι κατὰ τὴν ἀγορὰν εἴ τι λέγεται νεώτερον. Demosth. Philippic. Epist. 5. ἢ βούλεσθε, εἰπέ μοι, περιιόντες αὑτῶν πυνθάνεσθαι κατὰ τὴν ἀγοράν, λέγεταί τι καινόν, Philipp. i ; 5; and there are other passages to the like effect, as μετὰ καινότητος μὲν λόγου ἀπατᾶσθαι ἄριστοι (Thucyd. iii. 38), upon which the scholiast remarks, ταῦτα πρὸς τοὺς Ἀθηναίους αἰνίττεται, οὐδὲν τι μελετῶντας, πλὴν λέγειν τι καὶ ἀκούειν καινόν. So the scholiast on Arist. Eq. 975. δεῖγμα τόπος ἐστὶν ἐν Πειραιεῖ, ἔνθα πολλοὶ συνήγοντο ξένοι καὶ πολῖται καὶ ἐπωπτείσαν, cited with other passages by Kuinoel on Acts xvii. 21. It is said that in Athens were 360 λέσχαι, or resorts for gossip. Ibid.

[58] Acts xvii. 21.

[59] πρὸς καιρὸν ὥρας. 1 Thess. ii. 17.

circumstances might have so changed for the better that they all might revisit Thessalonica. But now when Timothy arrived and brought the intelligence that the Jews of Thessalonica were still mad against the Apostle, and had banded themselves together to pursue him from place to place, the delusive hopes in which he had indulged all vanished, and it was evident that a return to Thessalonica was for the present impracticable.

But what anxiety of mind did Paul now suffer for the fate of the Thessalonians! The Jews of that city were the acknowledged and bitter enemies of the Gospel, and yet the Thessalonian church had been left to itself. Luke had remained at Philippi — Silas was still at Beroea — but at Thessalonica there was no Apostle to pilot the vessel, though the tempest there still raged with the utmost violence. Paul had not even any intelligence of their present state. He determined therefore to remain at Athens alone, and to send Timothy to Thessalonica, the church more particularly confided to his care, to comfort them in their affliction, to strengthen their faith, and to bring him news of their welfare. In the following passage from the First Epistle to the Thessalonians the Apostle has beautifully expressed his earnest longing to revisit that church, and his trouble of mind lest they should have fallen away from the faith: "But we, brethren, being bereaved of you for a short time in presence, not in heart, endeavoured the more abundantly to see your face with great desire. Wherefore we would have come unto you, even I Paul, *once and again*, but Satan hindered us. For what is our hope, or joy, or crown of rejoicing? Are not even ye in the presence of our Lord Jesus Christ at his coming? For ye are our glory and joy. Wherefore *when we could no longer forbear*, we thought it good to be left at Athens alone;[60] and sent Timothy, our brother, and minister of God, and our fellow-labourer in the Gospel of Christ, to establish you, and to comfort you concerning your faith: that no man should be moved by these afflictions, for yourselves know that we are appointed thereunto. For verily, when we were with you, we told you before that we should suffer tribulation; even as it came to pass, and ye know. For this cause, when I could no longer forbear, I sent to know your faith, lest by some means the tempter have tempted you, and our labour be in vain."[61]

Timothy now set out from Athens for Thessalonica, and the Apostle was again

---

[60] Wieseler suggests that Timothy never arrived at Athens, but that Paul, after having desired Silas and Timothy to come to him ὡς τάχιστα, Acts xvii. 15, countermanded the injunction, and directed Timothy to proceed to Thessalonica, and that Paul, by saying that he was left at Athens alone, means only that he waived the order that Silas and Timothy should join him there. Wieseler, Chronol. Apost. 248. But as those who conducted Paul to Athens carried the message back to Silas and Timothy to come ὡς τάχιστα, "with all haste," the countermand, to be effectual, must have been sent off immediately after the departure of Paul's guides; and if so, how could the events at Athens be said to have occurred as he was waiting for their arrival (Acts xvii. 16)? more particularly as his encounter with the Epicureans and Stoics was while he was so waiting, and this encounter was toward the close of his sojourn, for he left Athens in consequence of it.

[61] 1 Thess. ii. 17 to 20; and 1 Thess. iii. 1 to 5.

left alone to declaim against Pagan idolatries. His ability and learning had by this time attracted public observation, and even the Epicureans and the philosophers who paced the Painted Porch adjoining the market did not deem it beneath their dignity to enter the lists against so formidable an antagonist.

Fig. 122.—*Portrait of Epicurus, Founder of the Sect of Epicureans. From C. W. King's Antique Gems.*

The Epicureans, so called from their founder Epicurus, an Athenian, supposed the world to have been formed by a fortuitous concourse of atoms, and that the Deity was a purely contemplative being, insensible to pain or pleasure, and taking no interest in the affairs of mankind[62] that the soul was material and had no consciousness after death, but was dispersed into its primitive elements. Their axiom was,

Fig. 123.—*Portrait of Zeno, Founder of the Sect of the Stoics. From Fulvius.*

"Death is nothing to us; for what is dissolved is insensible, and what is insensible is nothing to us."[63]

The Stoics, founded by Zeno, a native of Cyprus, but who taught at Athens, were of a different and somewhat more rational school. They believed in one God, the

[62] Diog. Laërt. x. 1, 31.   [63] Diog. Laërt. x. 1, 31.

Alpha and Omega, the beginning and the end; that by him the world had been created and was sustained;[64] that under him were divine beings, called Demons, who sympathised with mankind and superintended all their actions;[65] that the souls of the good were exalted after death to superior intelligences called Heroes;[66] but that the souls of others on their separation from the body became amalgamated with the general mass of animated matter, and ceased to have any distinct or personal consciousness.[67]

Such were the Epicureans and Stoics (the Sadducees and Pharisees of the Greeks), who, loitering about Athens in learned leisure, now proffered battle to the Apostle. Paul was little disposed to indulge their passion for literary trifling, or to involve himself in the subtleties with which human reason had entangled itself. He disclaimed all the weapons of sophistry, and preached matters of fact plain and simple in themselves, however repugnant to the preconceived notions of philosophy, viz., that Jesus of Nazareth had come into the world to save sinners, and had risen from the dead, the first-fruits of them that sleep. The Epicureans turned contemptuously to the bystanders and said, "What can this babbler mean?" while the Stoics assumed a more serious air, and charged him with an innovation on the state religion. He had preached unto them Jesus and the Resurrection, and as there were altars at Athens to Modesty, Fame, Impetuosity, Persuasion, Pity, Health, Peace, Democracy, and such like,[68] the foolish philosophers of the Porch conceived Jesus and Resurrection to be a god and goddess, and exclaimed, "He seemeth to be a setter forth of strange gods!" No people ever showed more courtesy to the forms of worship practised by other nations than the Athenians. They were even solicitous to enrol as their own every god that was adored on the face of the earth,[69] but at the same time it was death for any private person to disturb the religion of the State by the introduction of any foreign god that had not been publicly recognised.[70] Such had been the law in the time of Socrates, and such it was still; for the Romans, when they became masters of the city, allowed the descendants of so illustrious an ancestry to retain their laws and continue their courts of judicature.[71]

---

[64] Diog. Laërt. vii. 1, 70 and 72.
[65] Diog. Laërt. vii. 1. 79.
[66] Diog. Laërt. vii. 79.
[67] Diog. Laërt. vii. 84.
[68] See Pausan. Attic.
[69] Jerome mentions that there was an altar at Athens to the gods of Asia, and Europe, and Africa—to the unknown and foreign gods. Com. ad Tit. i 12.
[70] νόμῳ δ' ἦν τοῦτο παρ' αὐτοῖς (Atheniensibus) κεκωλυμένον, καὶ τιμωρία κατὰ τῶν ξένον εἰσαγόντων θεῶν ὥρατο θάνατος. Jos. contra Ap. ii. 37.
[71] When Macedonia was reduced to a Roman province, Athens, with the rest of Greece, became nominally free. Afterwards, Archelaus, an officer of Mithridates, occupied Athens; but Sylla, B.C. 86 (Fasti Hellen.), took it by storm from Aristion, the tyrant who held it for Mithridates, and again gave the Athenians their liberty. L. Sulla Athenas, quas Archelaus Præfectus Mithridatis occuparat, circumsedit, et cum maximo labore expugnavit. Urbi libertatem et civibus quæ habuerant reddidit. Liv. lxxxi.; Appian, Mithrid. 38.

In B.C. 48, the general of Cæsar took Athens, but the conqueror spared it. Dion xlii. 14; Fasti Sacri, p. 33, No. 282.

After the battle of Philippi, Mark Antony, B.C. 42 (Fasti Sacri, p. 48, No. 422), rewarded the servilities of the Athenians by giving them Ægina,

[Chap. XII.]   ST. PAUL AT ATHENS.   [A.D. 54]   261

The Areopagus, which still retained its ancient authority, or had even extended it,[12] had exclusive jurisdiction of determining what objects of worship should be admitted, and of inflicting punishment when persons made any wanton inroad upon the national creed.[13] Paul, therefore, by propagating the doctrines of one God, and a resurrection from the dead, and that Jesus would be the Judge of all men, had furnished a handle to the disputants, whom he had offended, to bring his life into jeopardy. They might urge with great plausibility that if the gods whom Paul preached were really such, they ought to be recognised by the State; but if they were no gods, the impostor who was obtruding them as such should be punished, and in either case the matter ought to be brought before the Areopagus.

The court sat originally for three consecutive days in every month,[14] but afterwards oftener, as occasion required, on the crown of the Hill of Areopagus, at the eastern end, and were ranged in concentric circles, one above another, while, in case of a trial, the cave or hollow in the middle was occupied by the accuser and the accused and their legal advisers, the accuser standing on an elevated stone on the one side and the accused on an elevated stone on the other.[15] Paul was now laid hold of.[16]

Iccs, Cos, Sciathus, and Peparethos. Appian, B. C. v. 7.

In the war that followed between Augustus and Antony, Athens favoured Antony, for which Augustus, B.C. 21 (Fasti Sacri, p. 89, No. 720), deprived them of Ægina and Eretria, but left them their liberty. Dion, liv. 7. And Strabo tells us that Athens remained free until his day, A.D. 20; μέχρι νῦν ἐν ἐλευθερίᾳ τέ ἐστι καὶ τιμῇ παρὰ τοῖς Ῥωμαίοις. Strabo, ix. (p. 214, Tauchnitz). And Germanicus, in the reign of Tiberius, recognised their nominal freedom; for, in Athens, he was preceded by one lictor only. Foederi sociae et vetustae urbis datum, ut uno lictore uteretur. Tac. Ann. ii. 53. It was still free in the time of Pliny the elder (Libera hæc civitas, Plin. N. H. iv. 11); and so it continued till long after the Apostolic age; see Plin. Epist. viii. 24. But Athens, though municipally free, was obliged to submit to the Imperial edicts, whence Josephus introduces Agrippa as saying: Ἀθηναῖοι . . . νῦν δουλεύουσι Ῥωμαίοις, καὶ τὴν ἡγεμονίδα τῆς Ἑλλάδος πόλιν δοκεῖ τὰ ἀπὸ τῆς Ἰταλίας προστάγματα. Jos. Bell. B. ii. 4.

[12] Val. Max. ii. 6, 4; Tacit. Ann. ii. 55; Aul. Gell. xii. 7; Amm. Marcell. xxix. 2, 19.

[13] Renan's St. Paul, p. 194, citing Lysias Areopagit.; Demosth. cont. Neær. s. 80 et seq.; Æschin. cont. Timarch. 81 et seq.; Diog. Laert. ii. 8, 15, and ii. 5, and vii. 5, 2; Xenoph. Mem. iii. 5, 20; Cic. Ep. Fam. xiii. 1; Attic. v. 11; De Divin. i. 25; Athen. iv. 64, 65; vi. 46; xiii. 21; Plut. de Plac. Philos. i. 7, 2; Corp. Inscrip. Græc. 123; Ross, Demen von Attica, Inscr. Gr. No. 163. A good dissertation on the court of Areopagus will be found in the 7th volume, p. 174, of Académie des Inscriptions.

[14] The constitution of the Areopagus is thus explained by Julius Pollux: ἐδίκαζε δὲ φόνου καὶ τραύματος ἐκ προνοίας, καὶ πυρκαϊᾶς καὶ φαρμάκων ἐάν τις ἀποκτείνῃ δούς. ἐγίγνετο δὲ διωμοσία, καὶ μετὰ αὐτὴν κρίσις. προωμνύζεσθαι δὲ οὐκ ἐξῆν, οὐδὲ ἀκτείρεσθαι. μετὰ δὲ τὸν πρότερον λόγον ἐξῆν φεύγειν, εἴ τις γονέας ἢ ἀπέκτονας. καθέκαστον δὲ μῆνα, τριῶν ἡμερῶν ἐδίκαζον ἐφεξῆς, τετάρτου φθίνοντος, τρίτου, δευτέρου. οἱ δὲ ἐννέα ἄρχοντες, οἱ καθ' ἕκαστον ἐνιαυτὸν, μετὰ τὸ δοῦναι τὰς εὐθύνας, ἀεὶ τοῖς Ἀρεοπαγίταις προσετίθεντο. ἐπαίθριοι δὲ ἐδικάζοντο, φόνου δὲ ἐξῆν ἐπεξιέναι μέχρις ἀνεψιῶν, καὶ ἐν τῷ ὅρκῳ προσεπειρωτᾶν, τίς προσήκων ἐστὶ τῷ τεθνεῶτι, κἂν οἰκέτης ᾖ, ἐπισκήπτειν συγκεχώρηται. Jul. Poll. lib. viii. c. 10: Περὶ τῶν ἐν Ἀθήνῃσι δικαστηρίων.

[15] Eurip. Iphig. Taur. 961. See the passage cited ante, p. 253.

Pausanias calls these stones Insolence and Impudence: τοῖς δὲ ἀργοῖς λίθοις ἐφ' ὧν ἑστᾶσιν ὅσοι δίκας ὑπέχουσι, τὸν μὲν Ὕβρεως τὸν δὲ Ἀναιδείας αὐτοῖς ὀνομάζουσι. Pausan. Attic. i. 28, 5. But, according to others, Insolence and Impu-

[16] Ἐπιλαβόμενοι, Acts xvii. 19. And see xviii. 17.

and was carried up the steps—the very steps which still remain—to the platform on the Areopagus, where the court was assembled, and placed in the dock. Paul was alone, and one of a nation that was despised and hated. The Areopagites were the noblest blood of Athens, the first politicians, the first orators, the first philosophers; a court the most august, not only of Athens, but of Greece, and indeed of the whole world. The charge against the Apostle was expressed with Athenian politeness. "May we know what this new doctrine whereof thou speakest is? for thou bringest certain strange things to our ears. We would know, therefore, what these things mean?" Paul then, standing in the midst of Areopagus,[74] addressed his audience as follows:

"Ye men of Athens, I perceive that in all things ye are devout to excess.[75] For

---

dence were the names of two altars: ὥσπερ ἡμέλει καὶ Ἐπιμενίδης ὁ παλαιός, Ὕβρεως καὶ Ἀναιδείας Ἀθήνησιν ἀνέστησεν βωμούς. Clem. in Protrep. c. 2, s. 26. Illud vitiosum, quod Cylonio scelere expiato, Epimenide Crete suadente, fecerunt Contumeliæ fanum et Impudentiæ. Virtutes enim, non vitia consecrare decet. Cicero de Leg. c. 11. The court is also said to have sat in the open air, but, according to Vitruvius, there was a roof though of a very rude description. Athenis Areopagi antiquitatis exemplar ad hoc tempus luto tectum. Vitruv. ii 1, 5.

[74] ἐν μέσῳ τοῦ Ἀρείου πάγου. These words are applicable to the Areopagus as a court of justice. But if the hill generally, and not the court, be meant, how could Paul be better heard by standing in the middle of the hill than in the plain below? The question then is, whether the proceeding was, 1st, a solemn indictment of Paul for an infraction of the state religion; or, 2nd, an inquisition by the state whether Jesus and Resurrection were to be admitted amongst the recognised divinities; or 3rd, a formal development by Paul of the theory of Jesus and the Resurrection for the fuller information of the Epicureans and Stoics. The text, which adopts the first view, has not been disturbed, but the balance of evidence appears to be in favour of the last view. Luke, after stating that they took Paul up to the Areopagus, adds immediately, by way of explanation, that the Athenians busied themselves about nothing but to hear some new thing, and when Paul stood in the midst of them the question put to him, "May we know what this new doctrine is?" was couched in the form of any legal process but of a friendly invitation to enunciate his doctrine; and at the close of his address there was no verdict of condemnation or acquittal, or report, but, as individuals, some mocked, and some doubted, and some believed. Had Paul been put upon his trial he would not have been still left at liberty, which he evidently was, for ἐξῆλθεν ἐκ μέσου αὐτῶν (Acts xvii. 33) "he went away from amongst them," and shortly afterwards departed for Corinth.

The argument in favour of a judicial proceeding is the expression, ἐπιλαβόμενοί τε αὐτοῦ ἐπὶ τὸν Ἄρειον πάγον ἤγαγον, v. 19, as if a legal arrest were intended. But the persons who thus took him were not the officers of the court, but the Epicureans and Stoics; nor does the word ἐπιλαβόμενοι imply a forcible apprehension, or anything more than a friendly guidance of him to a more convenient place of discussion. We cannot do better than make Luke his own interpreter. When Paul came from Damascus to Jerusalem and was disavowed by the disciples, it is said that Βαρνάβας δὲ ἐπιλαβόμενος αὐτὸν ἤγαγε πρὸς τοὺς ἀποστόλους (Acts ix. 27), "Barnabas took him by the hand and introduced him to the Apostles;" and so here the words ἐπιλαβόμενοί τε αὐτοῦ ἐπὶ τὸν Ἄρειον πάγον ἤγαγον may very well mean, they took him by the hand courteously and led him up to the Areopagus. Paul had been declaiming in the market-place at the foot of the Areopagus, amongst the vagabonds who frequented it, and had casually attracted the attention of the Epicureans and Stoics. These philosophers thought him worthy of notice, and condescended to dispute with him; but the busy and stirring scene of the market was not the proper arena for sober discussion, and, for the convenience of both parties, and in order to give him a fair hearing for the exposition of his views, they withdrew him from the crowd of buyers and sellers, and allowed him the privilege of addressing them from the tribune of a regular court, where both speaker and audience would be free from disturbance.

[75] δεισιδαιμονεστέρους, Acts xvii. 22; used in

as I passed by, and beheld your objects of worship, I found an altar with this inscription, 'To the *Unknown God*.'[80] Whom therefore ye ignorantly worship, him I declare unto you. God, that made the world and all things therein, seeing that he is Lord of heaven and earth, dwelleth not in temples made with hands; neither is served by men's hands, as though he needed any thing, seeing he giveth to all life, and breath, and all things; and hath made of one blood all nations of men for to dwell on all the face of the earth, and hath determined the times before appointed, and the bounds of their habitation; that they should seek the Lord, if haply they might feel after him, and find him, though he be not far from every one of us: for in him we live, and move, and have our being; as certain also of your own poets have said, 'For we are also his offspring.'[81] Forasmuch, then, as we are the offspring of God, we ought not to think that the Godhead is like unto gold, or silver, or stone, graven by art and man's device. And the times of this ignorance God winked at; but now commandeth all men everywhere to repent, because he hath appointed a day in the which he will judge the world in righteousness by that man[82] whom he hath ordained; whereof he hath given assurance unto all men, in that he hath raised him from the dead."[83]

The address as recorded by the historian contains the summary only of the Apostle's argument; but even in this compendium we cannot but admire the singular adroitness with which Paul adapted to his purpose existing circumstances, and the still more extraordinary boldness with which he enunciated his doctrines. He had been charged with introducing new divinities, and true, he had inculcated the one Supreme Being; but how admirably does he avail himself of the inscription on the altar! Who could accuse him of innovation when he only expounded to the Athenians the attributes of the God whom they had ignorantly worshipped? Even if by the Unknown God were meant some Deity with whose nature they were unacquainted, he was justified in making such an appeal; but there is a reasonable probability that by " the Unknown God" was actually meant Jehovah. Since the conquest of Alexander the Great an intimacy had subsisted between the Jews and the Greeks, and in particular, the Athenians had entered into a treaty with that singular people, and had greatly honoured Hyrcanus the High Priest; and it is scarcely credible that

---

the same sense, Acts xxv. 19. The Athenians prided themselves on their excessive devotion, and ancient writers make repeated allusions to it. τούτοις καθίστηκεν ἐν θεοὺς εὐσεβεῖν ἄλλων πλέον. Pausan. i. 17, 1. 'Αθηναίους περισσότερόν τι ἢ τοῖς ἄλλοις ἐς τὰ θεῖά ἐστι σπουδῆς. Pausan. i. 24, 3, &c.; and see Renan's St. Paul, p. 173.

[79] σεβάσματα, Acts xvii. 23.

[80] See ante, p. 242.

[81] Τοῦ γὰρ καὶ γένος ἐσμέν. Acts xvii. 28. The same sentiment is found in the Latin as well as in the Greek poets. Thus Lucretius,

Isonique exitiali sanres omnes semine oriundi;
Omnibus ille idem pater est.
Lucret. ii. 992

[82] Had Christ been a mere man, he would not have been thus designated, for Paul and Peter are not called men, as their humanity was self-evident; but as Christ was also God, reference is here made to His human nature, as that which fitted Him to be our judge, and also to be the mediator, for " there is one God and one mediator between God and man, *the man* Christ Jesus," 1 Tim. ii. 5. [83] Acts xvii. 23 to 31.

the Athenians, who adopted the gods of all foreigners, should have excluded Jehovah, whose mighty acts could not but be familiar to the neighbouring nations. Had Jehovah, like the false Gods, been worshipped as an idol, the Athenians would have erected to him a statue and a temple; but the Jews religiously abstained from uttering any name, and adored him only as a Spiritual Being. Dion Cassius speaks of the God of the Jews as ἄῤῥητον, "not to be expressed;"[54] and the Emperor Caligula, in his answer to the Jews, calls him τὸν ἀκατονόμαστον ὑμῖν, "him that may not be named by you;"[55] and Lucan[56] and Trebellius Pollio[57] call him "incertus Deus;" and Justin Martyr relates, that among the heathen the God of the Jews was commonly called Πάγκρυφος, or All-hidden.[58] No wonder, then, that the Athenians should inscribe an altar to him as "The Unknown God."

Again, what felicity, and at the same time what moral courage, is there in the reference of the Apostle to the scene by which he was surrounded! Above him was only the canopy of Heaven; around him was plain and mountain; and in the distance was the expanse of ocean. Immediately before him was the Acropolis, with the glorious Parthenon,[59] and the colossal statue of Minerva, and a thousand other images, many of them glittering with gold and silver. How impressively, but with what peril, must he have uttered the words, "God that made the world, and all things therein, seeing that he is Lord of Heaven and Earth, dwelleth not in *temples made with hands!* Forasmuch as we are the offspring of God, we ought not to think that the Godhead is *like unto gold or silver, or stone, graven by art and man's device.*"

How happy, too, amongst a literary people, was Paul's citation of the poets; not, it will be observed, of a poet, but of poets, for both Aratus and Cleanthes had expressed the same sentiment. The reader may be curious to see the originals, for passages that made an impression on the mind of an Apostle can be of no ordinary character. Aratus, a Cilician (fig. 134), and therefore a fellow-countryman of the Apostle, opens his poem thus:

> Ἐκ Διὸς ἀρχώμεσθα, τὸν οὐδέποτ' ἄνδρες ἐῶμεν
> Ἄῤῥητον, μεσταὶ δὲ Διὸς πᾶσαι μὲν ἀγυιαὶ
> Πᾶσαι δ' ἀνθρώπων ἀγοραί· μεστὴ δὲ θάλασσα,
> Καὶ λιμένες· πάντη δὲ Διὸς κεχρήμεθα πάντες,
> Τοῦ γὰρ καὶ γένος ἐσμέν, &c.
>
> Aratus, Phænom.

> From Jove begin we—who can touch the string
> And not harp praise to Heaven's eternal King?
> He animates the mart and crowded way,

---

[54] Dion Cass. xxxvii. 17.
[55] Philo, Leg. ad Caium, s. 44.
[56] Pharsalia, ii. 592:
    Et dubitat sacris
    Incerti Judæa Dei.
[57] Claud. p. 351, cited by Biscoe on Acts, c. 8.
[58] Param. ad Græc. s. 38.
[59] The Parthenon, however, was not actually visible. When standing at the eastern end of the Areopagus, I observed, not without some surprise, that the Parthenon was obscured by the intervening buildings.

The restless ocean, and the sheltered bay.
Doth care perplex? Is lowering danger nigh?
We are his offspring, and to Jove we fly.

And Cleanthes begins his sublime hymn to Jupiter, thus:

Κύδιστ' Ἀθανάτων, πολυώνυμε, παγκρατὲς αἰεί,
Ζεῦ, φύσεως ἀρχηγέ, νόμου μετὰ πάντα κυβερνῶν,
Χαῖρε. Σὲ γὰρ πάντεσσι θέμις θνητοῖσι προσαυδᾶν.
Ἐκ σοῦ γὰρ γένος ἐσμὲν, ἴης μίμημα λαχόντες
Μοῦνοι, ὅσα φύει τε καὶ ἕρπει θνητ' ἐπὶ γαίαν.
   Hymn of Cleanthes.

Most glorious of the gods, immortal Jove!
Supreme on earth beneath, in heaven above!
Thou great first cause, whose word is Nature's law.
Before thy throne we mortals bend with awe;
For we thine offspring are. To man is given—
To man alone—to lift a voice to heaven.

The words also,

———For in him we live
And move and have our being,

have been traced by some to an old iambic—

Ζῶμεν δ' ἐν αὐτῷ θνητὰ, καὶ κινούμεθα,
Καί ἐσμεν.

But probably the order of things has been reversed, and the iambic ought rather to be traced to the beautiful sentiment that easily assumed a poetical garb.

The closing part of the Apostle's discourse was directed against the mistaken notions of the Athenians as to Jesus and the Resurrection. The latter was no goddess,

---

As the Hymn of Cleanthes is not found in the ordinary anthologies, we subjoin the original:

[Greek text of the hymn]

But thus the words are changed from those used by Paul, and the quotation from a poet which immediately follows, shows that what preceded was the Apostle's own language.

as they supposed; but the Apostle meant to teach that *all* should rise at the last day, and should be judged by that man whom God had appointed.

Simple throughout as is the language of the preacher, yet observe how, in the compass of a few words, he tells them the noblest truths: that there was one God; that he dwelt not in temples; that the world was not only made, but sustained, by him; that all mankind were of one blood; that they had fallen away from righteousness; that God had sent his son Jesus to redeem them; that he had raised him from the dead, as an earnest of future life; that all men must be judged at the last day.

The address was not without some fruit. Had any one, acquainted with the Athenian character, heard the sentiments so boldly expressed by Paul, he would have trembled for the speaker's life. But no such result followed. Some, indeed, as the Epicureans, when they heard of the resurrection of the dead laughed aloud, for even Orpheus, who could draw after him the brute beasts and the very woods in which

Fig. 134.—*Portrait of Aratus the Cilician Poet, Author of the Phænomena, quoted by St. Paul. From Bellorius.*

they made their lair, could not recover his lost Eurydice. But others, as the Stoics, were of a more thoughtful turn, and said they would think about it. "We will hear thee again of this matter." And so the court adjourned.

Paul had probably gained many wellwishers amongst his audience (for they were the most enlightened men of Athens), and they may have given him the friendly hint that although he had then escaped, yet Athens was no place for the propagation of a creed which aimed at the overthrow of idolatry; for the interested votaries of the numerous temples would soon be active to inflict the heaviest penalties of the law. Paul, with a sigh for the foolishness of human wisdom, retired from amongst them and set out for Corinth. The converts at Athens are summed up by the historian in these few words: "Dionysius, the Areopagite, and a woman named Damaris, and others, with them."[92] These may have been the germ of the church which eventually

---

[92] Acts xvii. 34. The name Damaris is not found elsewhere, and hence the conjecture that the true name was Δάμαλις, a heifer, and that Δάμαρις is the mistake of the transcriber. Kuinoel.

was undoubtedly established there, and of which Dionysius is said to have been ordained the first bishop.

Before we quit so interesting a theme, we cannot help adverting very briefly to the analogous case of Socrates. He too had frequented the market-place, instilling into the Athenian youth juster notions of religion. He too was arraigned before the Areopagus on the charge of introducing strange gods, and had pleaded his own cause. It cannot be expected that one who felt his way through the surrounding darkness by the dim light of nature should give utterance to as sublime sentiments as were declared by the Apostle; but a few extracts from his celebrated Apology, as recorded by his pupil Plato, will show how superior he rose to the age that condemned him. He addressed his judges by the same title as did the Apostle, "Ye men of Athens," though but for this instance such a form might have appeared inappropriate to the court of Areopagus. "Ye men of Athens!" he said, "I know not how yourselves have been affected by my accusers; but I have well-nigh forgotten myself, so persuasively have they spoken."

Fig. 135. *Portraits of Socrates and Plato, Socrates on the left and Plato on the right. From C. W. King's Antique Gems.*

"If you hear me defending myself in the same language that I am wont to use in the market-place, where and elsewhere most of you have heard me, let me entreat you not to be surprised, or take it in ill part, for thus it is: now for the first time, at the age of more than seventy years, I appear at the bar of the court." "Let us take the accusation. It runs to this effect: 'Socrates hath violated the laws by corrupting the youth, and by acknowledging, not the gods whom the city acknowledges, but other strange deities.'" Socrates then expatiates on the principles in which he had trained their youth, and proceeds thus: "But some one may say, 'Do you not repent, Socrates, at having followed a course that now endangers your life?' I would return him this just answer: 'You are wrong, my friend, if you think that man should have respect to life and death alone; for his single thought in every action should be, whether what he is about to do is just or unjust, whether it is the work of a good or a wicked man.' If you were to say to me, 'Socrates, we acquit you, but on this condition only, that you abandon your former courses; but if you are again detected in them you die.' Ye men of Athens! I am obliged to you, and thank you; but I must obey God rather than you."⁵³ "This which hath befallen me will, I doubt not, turn out a blessing, and it cannot be that their opinion is right who esteem death to be an evil." "The dead are more happy than the living, both in other respects, and thenceforth they die no more for ever, if at least we may believe what is said of them." And, in conclusion, after imploring the Athenians to corrupt his own sons as he had corrupted their youth, viz. by instilling into them the principles of virtue, he adds, "And now the hour is come for us to depart; I go to death, and you to life, but which of the twain is the better choice is known only to God." The venerable sage was condemned by a large majority, and the cup of hemlock was placed in his hands. He drank it with an equanimity worthy of the noblest heathen that the world had produced.

How long Paul remained at Athens can only be collected by inference. The companions who conducted him thither from Berœa returned to Macedonia with orders that Silas and Timothy should join him with all speed.⁵⁴ Paul on reaching Athens had proposed to wait until the arrival of Silas and Timothy;⁵⁵ and he did wait until the arrival of Timothy.⁵⁶ And as the return of Paul's conductors to Berœa (a distance of two hundred and fifty-one miles), and the passage of Timothy from Berœa to Athens would necessarily occupy a considerable interval, we cannot allow less than a month at least for Paul's sojourn. His stay there was certainly some weeks, for he was wont to preach to the Jews in the synagogue every Sabbath-day.⁵⁷ He had reached Athens the beginning of November, A.D. 51, and his departure, therefore, may be placed (to name a day) about 4th December, A.D. 51. This date would tally with the fact that Paul, on leaving Athens, retired to Corinth, and had been there a year and six months when Gallio arrived in the province about 4th June, A.D. 53.⁵⁸

Did Paul pass from Athens to Corinth by land or sea? If by land he would pass through Eleusis, famous for its sacred Mysteries; so sacred indeed, that even the hardened Nero durst not defile them by his presence. From Eleusis the route would lie through ancient Megara, and so onward to Port Schœnus (now Kalamaki), at the narrow neck of the isthmus (three miles and a half in breadth), over which the vessels were wont to be dragged formerly, as they still are, from one gulf to the other, to avoid the dangerous circumnavigation of the Morea.⁵⁹ Paul would also traverse the spacious arena of the great national festival, the Isthmia, and would regard with wonder the stadium for the chariot races, the theatre, the temples, and especially that of Neptune, the tutelary god, with its long avenue in front, and lined on each side with the statues of the Isthmian victors, and shaded by overhanging pines. The

---

⁵³ How forcibly the last sentiment reminds us of the words of St. Peter on a similar occasion! "Whether it be right in the sight of God, to hearken unto you, more than unto God, judge yo." Acts iv. 19.

⁵⁴ Acts xvii. 15.   ⁵⁵ Acts xvii. 16.

⁵⁶ 1 Thess. iii. 6.
⁵⁷ Acts xvii. 17.
⁵⁸ Acts xviii. 11. For the date of Gallio's arrival, see post.
⁵⁹ ὁ Σχοινοῦς καθ' ὃν τὸ στένον τοῦ διόλκου. Strabo, viii. 6 (p. 214, Tauchnitz).

remains of the Isthmia have scarcely received the attention they deserve. Nothing, even in Athens, conveyed to myself so forcible an impression of the greatness of ancient Greece as the vast and extensive ruins scattered over the site of the Isthmia.

However, the most expeditious and least expensive transit from Athens to Corinth was by sea. It was a day's sail;[100] and Paul, as a native of Tarsus, a commercial city with a port nigh at hand, must have been familiar with the seas from childhood; and that he was not deterred from taking ship by the uncertainty of the season we may infer from the fact, that before the date of the second Epistle to the Corinthians he had suffered shipwreck thrice.[101] It is also noticeable that Luke states merely that " Paul departed from Athens and *came to Corinth*;"[102] for when Paul journeyed by *land* from Philippi to Thessalonica, Luke mentions that " they passed through Amphipolis and Apollonia."[103] Had Paul, therefore, on his way to Corinth, passed through cities of such celebrity as Eleusis and Megara, we should expect to find it so recorded. There can be no certainty upon a subject where the materials for judging are so scanty; but it is likely that Paul resolved on a voyage to Corinth in preference to a slower journey by land; nay, we may even conjecture, from the inclemency of the season, that he was overtaken on the way by one of those squalls to which the narrow channels of that part are subject, and that he suffered on this occasion one of those shipwrecks to which he alludes in his letter to the Corinthians.

If Paul accomplished the voyage without mishap, he would arrive at Cenchrea, the eastern port of Corinth, at the south-western corner of the Saronic gulf, and would thence proceed to Corinth by land.

We are now about to shift the scene to Corinth, the capital of Achaia, the name by which all Greece, as distinct from Macedonia, was then known. Corinth was the seat of government, and lay at a distance of forty miles from Athens, and was situate at the south-western extremity of the isthmus, on an elevated table land at the foot of Acrocorinthus, a mountain which towered to the skies on the south, and overlooked the city spread along its northern base. Corinth was five miles round, and where not sufficiently defended by nature was fortified by a wall. Acrocorinthus was not quite half a mile in perpendicular height, and was approached by an ascent of nearly four miles. The crest of it was a fortress surrounded by a wall.[104] Corinth had always possessed great importance, not only as a military position, as holding the keys of the Peloponnesus, but also from the extensive trade that flowed thither both by land and sea. All the land traffic between Peloponnesus and northern Greece necessarily passed

---

[100] In 1851 I sailed myself in one day from Athens to Cenchrea in an open boat.
[101] 2 Cor. xi. 25.
[102] Acts xviii. 1.
[103] Acts xvii. 1.
[104] When I was there in 1851 the area within the wall was a picture of utter desolation. In the war between the Greeks and Turks the place had been burnt, and the blackened, roofless, and tenantless walls proclaimed aloud what must have been the amount of human suffering before Greece recovered her independence.

along the neck of the isthmus, and was made subject to a toll; and from the dangerous navigation round the Peninsula the commerce by sea was carried on principally across the Isthmus, and for this purpose Corinth had two ports, Lechæum in the Corinthian bay, and Cenchrea in the Saronic bay. Lechæum was only a mile and a half from

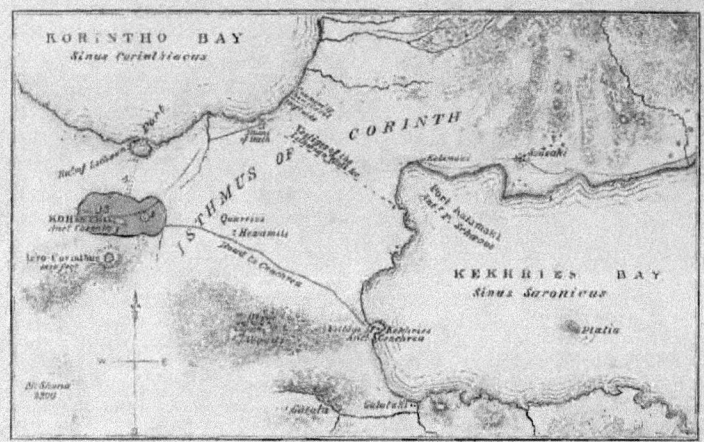

Fig. 138.—*Plan of the Isthmus. Grounded on Admiralty Chart.*
1. The Forum or market; 2. The Theatre; 3. Temple of Apollo; 4. Long walls connecting Corinth with Port Lechæum.

Corinth, and was connected with it by long walls, as the Piræus was with Athens; Cenchrea, on the eastern shore, lay at a distance of eight miles and three-quarters from Corinth.[105]

In the time of Alexander the Great, Corinth, like the rest of Greece, had been under the Macedonian sway; but on the conquest of Macedonia by the Romans (finally achieved at the battle of Pydna, B.C. 168), the Greeks were declared a free people. The Achæans, occupying the north of Peloponnesus to the west of Sicyon, now formed a league, and were joined by Corinth and other neighbouring states, and the influence thus gained having excited the jealousy of the Romans, Greece was to be brought under subjection. The ground for hostilities was, that the Corinthians had insulted some Roman legates. The Achæans constituted Critolaus their general, who, with his allies, the Bœotians and Chalcidians, was defeated by Metellus at Thermopylæ, and then put an end to his life by poison. Diæus was elected in his stead, who, the following year (B.C. 146), was defeated by Mummius at the Isthmus, when Corinth was taken and utterly destroyed,[106] and Achaia became a Roman province.[107] Corinth

[105] Strabo, viii. 6 (p. 213, Tauchnitz); and see Plin. N. H. iv. 5.
[106] See Livy, lii. 52.
[107] As to the political state of Achaia from this time, see Pausan. Achaic. vii. 16, 6.

lay in ruins for a century, and then Julius Cæsar founded it anew, and sent thither a Roman colony, consisting principally of freedmen,[108] among whom were great numbers of the Jewish race.[109] The city, when Paul arrived, was still governed as a Roman colony, as appears from its coins, for they are stamped with the names of its duum-

Fig. 137.—*Coin of Corinth. From Morell.*

Obv. Head of Claudius with the legend, Claud. Cæsar Aug. P.P.—Rev. The Acrocorinthus with the Temple of Venus on the summit, and the legend, Luscino Octavio iter. iivir. Cor. (Luscinus and Octavius, Duumvirs for the second time, Corinth).

viri, the peculiar designation of the two chief magistrates in the colonies, and corresponding to the two consuls at Rome. This constitution continued during the successive reigns of Augustus, Tiberius, Caligula, Claudius, and Nero.[110] Corinth, from its extraordinary natural advantages, very soon recovered itself after its colonisation and rose to a wonderful prosperity.

In the time of Augustus, Achaia (that is, Greece, as opposed to Macedonia,) was allotted to the Senate and ruled by proconsuls;[111] but under Tiberius it was transferred to the Emperor, and subject to proprætors.[112] In the fourth year of Claudius (A.D. 44)[113] it was restored to the Senate, and became proconsular.[114] Under Nero, who succeeded him, Achaia was once more taken from the people, and declared free;[115] and in the reign of Vespasian it became a province again.[116] When Paul started from Athens to Corinth, in the time of Claudius, Achaia was under the government of proconsuls, and considering what singular vicissitudes the province experienced, it is remarkable that Gallio, of whom we shall speak presently, is accurately described by Luke as proconsul, such being the force of the word in Greek, though in the received translation it has been rendered "deputy."[117]

As Paul advanced to the capital of Achaia, his eye would trace under the walls the

---

[108] Strabo, viii. 6 (p. 216, Tauchnitz); Pausan. ii. 1; Plin. N. H. iv. 5.

[109] Philo, Leg. ad Caium, s. 36.

[110] Pellerin, Mélanges, vol. i. See the coins of Corinth in p. 251, et seq.

[111] Fasti Sacri, p. 79, No. 666.

[112] Achaiam ac Macedoniam, onera deprecantes, levari in præsens proconsulari imperio tradique Cæsari placuit. Tac. Ann. i. 76.

[113] Fasti Sacri, p. 281, No. 1682.

[114] Provincias Achaiam ac Macedoniam, quas Tiberius ad curam suam transtulerat, senatui reddidit. Suet. Claud. xxv. τήν τε Ἀχαΐαν καὶ τὴν Μακεδονίαν αἱρετοῖς ἄρχουσιν, ἐξ οὗπέρ ὁ Τιβέριος ἧρξεν, διδομένας, ἀπέδωκεν ὁ Κλαύδιος τότε τῷ κλήρῳ. Dion. lx. 24.

[115] Decedens deinde provinciam universam libertate donavit. Suet. Ner. 24. Ἐλεύθερον Νέρων ἀφίησιν ἁπάντων. Pausan. vii. 17, 2.

[116] Achaiam . . . libertate adempta . . . in provinciæ formam redegit. Suet. Vesp. viii.; Pausan. Achaic. vii. 17, 2.

[117] ἀνθυπατεύοντος. Acts xviii. 12.

grove of cypress, the burial ground of Corinth; and among the tombs was that of Lais, the famous courtesan, surmounted with the emblem of a lioness with her fore paws upon a ram. Close to the gate was a monument to the memory of Diogenes, the cynic. The traveller entered the city, and the market-place opened to his view. In the centre was a bronze Minerva, and around were temples and statues and a fountain gushing from the mouth of a dolphin, supporting the figure of Neptune. At

Fig. 138.—*Portrait of Lais. From Anacharsis.*

Fig. 139.—The Tomb of Lais was, according to Pausanias, surmounted by a sphinx with her forepaws upon a ram. The design became common, and this engraving is taken from a sepulchral monument dug up in the Roman cemetery at Colchester; and preserved in the Museum there.

a little distance to the south rose majestically the Acrocorinthus, and on the summit of it stood the temple of Venus.[118] By what a scene of iniquity was the Apostle surrounded! He who had mortified the flesh, and had even refrained from marriage, that he might be the unencumbered soldier of his Divine Master, was now within a city where lasciviousness held her obscenest revels. Suffice it to say, that to the temple of Venus were attached more than a thousand courtesans, who, under the cover of religious rites, pandered to the passions of citizens and foreigners.[119] Such was the Augean stable which the Christian Hercules now addressed himself to purify.

Paul arrived at Corinth early in December, A.D. 51,[120] and it would seem that he was still a sufferer from his besetting disorder, "the thorn in the flesh," for he afterwards reminds the Corinthians, "And I was with you in *weakness*" (or *sickness*), " and in fear, and in much trembling."[121]

Paul had been not long at Corinth when he met with Aquila, a Jew, a native of

---

[118] Pausan. ii. 4, 7. Corinth is now so absolute a desolation, that even the sites of the ancient buildings cannot be traced. The well-known Doric columns are the only architectural remains of the Apostolic age which have survived. In 1851 I counted forty or fifty wretched houses which then constituted the modern village, and in the midst of them was an open area which might pass for a market-place; but very different from that in which Gallio took his seat.

[119] Strabo, viii. 6, and see xii. 3.

[120] See Fasti Sacri, p. 297, No. 1778; and see the discussion of the time, c. viii. p. 72 of the same work.

[121] 1 Cor. ii. 3.

Pontus,[122] and a tentmaker like Paul himself. Aquila, with his wife Priscilla,[123] had been previously settled at Rome, but circumstances, which we shall now refer to very briefly, had obliged him and his countrymen to remove from the great capital.

Fig. 140. *Doric Temple at Corinth. From Stuart and Revett's Athens.*

Since this view was taken many of the columns have fallen. This temple is the only monument of the former magnificence of Corinth. It is singular that the Corinthian order of architecture takes its name from Corinth, and yet no specimen of the style is to be found there.

The wealth and importance of Rome attracted to it a vast multitude of Jews, who lived chiefly in the quarter of the city called Trans-Tiberim, or Over-Tiber, where they had their proseuchæ, or oratories,[124] in which they held their solemn assemblies on the Sabbaths and other festivals. They were also to be found dispersedly in other quarters, as in the Campus Martius, the Insula Tiberis, the Suburra, and without the

---

[122] Ποντικὸν τῷ γένει. Acts xviii. 2. As there was a Pontius Aquila in the time of Cicero (Epist. Fam. x. 33, Suet. Cæs. 78), it has been conjectured by some that Aquila may have been a freedman, named after this Pontius Aquila, and that Luke was thus led into the mistake of supposing that Aquila was a *native of Pontus*. See Meyer, Apostg. 326. This, however, is mere conjecture, and not to be reconciled with the known accuracy of Luke. Aquila was a Jew, and is another instance of a Jew bearing a Roman name.

[123] Priscilla is the diminutive of Prisca, as Terentilla, Quintilla, Prisilla, Claudilla, Marulius, Catullus, are diminutives of Terentia, Quinta, Prima, Claudia, Marius, Catius, &c. Kuinoel. It does not follow, however, that Priscilla was a Roman, as Jewesses as well as Jews according to the fashion of the day, often bore Roman names.

[124] προσευχὰς ἔχουσαι, καὶ συνιοῦσαι εἰς αὐτάς, καὶ μάλιστα ταῖς ἱεραῖς ἑβδόμαις ὅτε δημοσίᾳ τὴν πάτριον παιδεύονται φιλοσοφίαν. Philo, Leg. ad Caium, 24; and see Martial, i. 42. They had also at one time at least four synagogues. Renan's St. Paul, p. 103, note.

Porta Capena.[125] The germ of this Jewish colony had been the captives from Judea whom Pompey brought with him on his return from the East, and who from time to time were manumitted by their masters.[126] The exact number of Jews at Rome in the first century after Christ has not been stated, but eight thousand of them concurred at one time in the petition against Archelaus,[127] and the whole Jewish population must therefore have been immense.

Christianity had found its way amongst them at a very early period, and it was probably first carried thither by some of the converts made by St. Peter on the day of Pentecost next after the Ascension, for amongst his hearers are expressly mentioned "Strangers from Rome, both Jews and proselytes."[128] Two Jews, named respectively Andronicus and Junias, may have been the first preachers of the Gospel at Rome, for they were certainly Apostles, and had been converted to Christianity before Paul, and their ordinary residence was apparently at Rome. Thus much we may collect from the Epistle to that church. "Salute Andronicus and Junias, my kinsmen, and my fellow prisoners, who are *of note among the Apostles, who also were in Christ before me.*"[129] The very fact that the most important of all Paul's Epistles was a few years after addressed to the Romans, proves how extensively Christianity had been propagated in that quarter. It was not without a struggle that the new religion obtained a footing in the imperial city; on the one side was the force of truth, on the other deep-rooted prejudice. The unbelieving Jews would naturally persecute the new sect, and the tumults that were excited by the Jews of Antioch, Iconium, and Lystra, of Thessalonica and Berœa, were probably enacted with no less violence in the capital of the ancient world.

At the very commencement of A.D. 52[130] Claudius issued an edict or proclamation that all Jews should depart from Rome; and Suetonius, in his brief summary of the occurrences of the time thus states the fact, and assigns the reason: *Judæos, impulsore Chresto, assidue tumultuantes Româ expulit.*[131] "The Jews, who were constantly making disturbances, Chrestus being the mover, he banished from Rome." Here by Chrestus is plainly intended Christus: a grammatical error not at that day uncommon, the word Chrestus, or Good, being familiar enough,[132] but the term Christus, or Anointed, however intelligible to a Jew, not conveying any definite notion to one who had never heard of the Messiah.[133] The mistake, however, is the more remarkable, as Suetonius

---

[125] See Renan's St. Paul, p. 101. And two Jewish cemeteries near to each other have been found on the Via Appia. Ib. p. 102, note.

[126] αἰχμάλωτοι γὰρ ἀχθέντες εἰς Ἰταλίαν, ὑπὸ τῶν κτησαμένων ἠλευθερώθησαν, οὐδὲν τῶν πατρίων παραχαράξαι διασθέντες. Philo, Leg. ad Caium, c. 23.

[127] Jos. Ant. xvii. 11, 1.

[128] Acts ii. 10.

[129] Rom. xvi. 7.

[130] See Fasti Sacri, p. 295, No. 1773.

[131] Suet. Claud. xxv.

[132] Appian, Mithrid. 10; Cic. Epist. Fam. ii. 8; Gruter, Inscript. 331, 2; 339, 5; and see Renan's St. Paul, p. 99.

[133] We have adopted Kuinoel's view, that by Chrestus was meant Christus, and the following pregnant passages may be cited in support of it: Cum perperam Chrestianus pronuntiatur a vobis (nam nec nominis est certa notitia penes

himself afterwards calls the sect Christiani.[134] Under the term Jews were often included Christians; and by the commotions existing among the Jews at the instance of Chrestus we must understand the hostilities of the Jews (properly such) against the rising Church of Christ, which in their eyes would be a heresy.[135]

The religious dissensions among the Jews are assigned by Suetonius as the occasion of the edict of expulsion, but the real cause was a political one, arising out of the state of Judea, which just at this time[136] was all but in open rebellion;[137] indeed the Roman legions and tumultuary bands of Jews and Galileans had, toward the close of the preceding year, already come into collision, and the Romans, having gained the day, had inflicted on many capital punishment.[138] At such a juncture it was not thought safe to harbour so many thousands of a hostile people within the precincts of Rome itself, and the edict for their expulsion followed.[139] Dion Cassius (but who lived at a much later period, and might not be well informed), tells us that the Emperor was afraid to eject so vast a multitude, and forbade only their assembling together.[140] The fact, however, of the actual banishment, attested by St. Luke, and supported by the authority of Suetonius, cannot be questioned.

Aquila, as a Jew, was obliged, amongst the rest, to take his departure from Rome, and, till the storm passed over, sought an asylum at Corinth. Or perhaps, being a native of Pontus, he was pursuing his route homeward by the ordinary maritime track in the winter, across the Isthmus of Corinth, when, finding at Corinth an opening for his trade, he took a house and workshop there, and commenced his occupation of tentmaking. The opulence of the place would of itself furnish a reasonable prospect of carrying on a lucrative business.[141] Here he shortly afterwards met with Paul. Aquila, it is likely, was already a convert,[142] and if so, the Apostle was fortunate in falling in with one who, like himself, was at the same time a Jew, a tentmaker, and a Christian.

vos) de suavitate vel benignitate compositum est [for χρηστός is suavis or benignus]. Tertull. Apol. c. 3. Sed exponenda hujus nominis ratio est propter ignorantiam eorum, qui cum immutatâ literâ Chrestum solent dicere. Lactant. Instit. iv. 7.

Others, however, are of opinion that Suetonius has made no mistake, but that Chrestus was the name of the ringleader at Rome who had been busy in exciting insurrection. See Meyer, Apostg. 327.

[134] Suet. Nero, xvi.
[135] See Renan's St. Paul, p. 99.
[136] Fasti Sacri, p. 293, No. 1759.
[137] Arsissetque bello provincia, ni Quadratus Syriæ rector subvenisset. Tac. Ann. xii. 54.
[138] Jos. xx. 6, 1; Bell. ii. 12, 3–5.
[139] It was the common practice, when a people was in rebellion, to expel all of that nation from the city. This was done by Augustus, who banished the Gauls, when Varus lost his legions in Gaul. Dion, lvi. 23.

[140] Dion, lx. 6.
[141] It has been questioned whether Aquila's domicile was at Rome, or whether he carried on business at other capitals also, as at Corinth and Ephesus, at both of which places we find him occasionally residing, and in which cities the disciples were in the habit of assembling for worship at his house. Rom. xvi. 5; 1 Cor. xvi. 19. It is not improbable that his principal place of business was at Rome, but that he had branch establishments at Corinth and Ephesus.
[142] This is the more probable supposition, as nothing is said as to the conversion of Aquila and Priscilla by Paul, but it is merely said that he (Paul) joined himself to them, προσῆλθεν αὐτοῖς. Acts xviii. 2. See Kuinoel ad locum. This, however, is disputed by others. See Meyer, Apostg. 326.

Paul took up his abode with him, and wrought with him;[143] and not only continued an inmate in his house while he remained at Corinth (a space of a year and a half and upwards), but an intimacy now commenced which terminated only with the Apostle's life, and in the course of it Aquila rendered to him the most important services, particularly in the tumult at Ephesus, as we shall see hereafter.

Paul, in exercising his ministry at Corinth, adhered to his usual practice in making the first appeal to the Jews, by preaching every Sabbath day in their synagogue; but he no doubt at the same time availed himself of every opportunity of publishing the Gospel amongst the Gentiles also. He converted many, both of Jews and Greeks. The first whom he won over was Stephanas with his family, as he tells us in his Epistle to the Corinthians: "Ye know the house of Stephanas, that it is *the first-fruits of Achaia*, and that they have addicted themselves to the ministry of the saints."[144] Epænetus is also called in another place the first-fruits of Achaia,[145] but a different reading, and the correct one, substitutes Asia for Achaia. Another convert, and a man of note, was Crispus, a ruler of the synagogue.[146] There were usually two or more rulers of the synagogue,[147] and here Crispus and Sosthenes were the two rulers; and Crispus, one of them, became a convert, while Sosthenes, the other, remained for the present a Jew, but eventually became a Christian also. Another believer was Gaius, or Caius, with whom Paul, on a subsequent occasion, lodged.[148] Paul, we must remember, was now at Corinth *alone*, and it is a remarkable circumstance that these three converts, Stephanas, Crispus, and Gaius, were *baptized by Paul personally*. It was not his usage to administer this rite, lest his enemies might make a handle of it, and accuse him of enlisting Paulites, and not Christians—a precaution of which the history of the Corinthian church soon proved the necessity, for only a few years after such parties actually arose. "I thank God," writes the Apostle to the Corinthians on a subsequent occasion, "that I baptized none of you but *Crispus* and *Gaius*, *lest any man should say that I had baptized in mine own name*. And I baptized also the household of *Stephanas*; besides, I know not whether I baptized any other. For Christ sent me not to baptize, but to preach the Gospel; not with wisdom of words, lest the cross of Christ should be made of none effect."[149]

Paul had been labouring at Corinth some two or three months, when Silas and Timothy arrived together from Macedonia. Timothy had been despatched by Paul

---

[143] A passage of Chrysostom on this subject is very striking: "St. Paul, after working miracles, stood in his workshop at Corinth, and stitched hides of leather together with his hands, and the angels regarded him with love, and the devils with fear." Chrysostom, cited by Wordsworth, on Acts xviii. 3.

[144] 1 Cor. xvi. 15.

[145] Rom. xvi. 5.

[146] Acts xviii. 8.

[147] Thus the ἀρχισυνάγωγοι of the synagogue of Antioch in Pisidia are spoken of, Acts xiii. 15; and Jairus of Capernaum is described as *one* of the rulers of the synagogue, εἶς τῶν ἀρχισυναγώγων. Mark v. 22. Corinth was so populous a city, and so abounded with Jews, that there may have been several synagogues, and possibly Crispus may have been the ruler of one, and Sosthenes of another.

[148] Rom. xvi. 23.

[149] 1 Cor. i. 14, 16.

from Athens by sea to Thessalonica, a church which was under the particular charge of Timothy; and, having executed his mission, he had passed by land from Thessalonica to Berœa,[150] and there rejoined Silas, who had been left in care of that church. Luke meanwhile was superintending the church of the Philippians, who now, under his auspices, forwarded by Silas and Timothy a contribution for the relief of the Apostle's necessities at Corinth.[151] The arrival of Silas and Timothy was in every way calculated to give him comfort. In the first place, Paul had been enduring great privations from the famine which had of late prevailed throughout Greece. To the day of his death, he would receive no support from the Corinthian church,[152] that his enemies (and he had many there) might not misconstrue it. He wrought night and day, with his own hands, at his craft of tentmaking;[153] yet, from the severity of the times, he could not earn the necessaries of life in sufficient abundance. It was while he was in this strait that Silas and Timothy brought him relief from Macedonia. The Apostle afterwards, in writing to the Corinthians, alludes to this seasonable supply, and anxiously justifies his conduct in refusing aid from the Corinthians themselves. "Have I committed an offence," he says, "in abasing myself that ye might be exalted, because I have preached to you the Gospel of God gratuitously? I robbed other churches, taking wages of them to do you service. And *when I was present with you, and wanted*, I was chargeable to no man, for that which was lacking to me *the brethren which came from Macedonia* (Silas and Timothy) *supplied*: and in all things I have kept myself from being burdensome unto you, and so will I keep myself. As the truth of Christ is in me, no man shall stop me of this boasting in the regions of Achaia. Wherefore? Because I love you not? God knoweth. But what I do, that I will do, that I may cut off occasion from them which desire occasion; that wherein they glory, they may be found even as we."[154] This passage does not tell us from what church in particular the liberality proceeded, but in another Epistle, written eleven years after, the Apostle still gratefully remembers the kindness, and tells us that he was indebted for it to the amiable Philippians. "Now ye Philippians, know also, that in the beginning of the Gospel, *when I departed from Macedonia*, no church communicated with me as concerning giving and receiving, but ye only."[155]

The report of Timothy from Thessalonica was in the main highly satisfactory. The converts had maintained their faith against the persecution of their enemies, and, retaining their devotion to the Apostle, had been as anxious for his safety as he had been for theirs, and longed to see him again. On the other hand, Timothy had found some disorders in the church that required correction. They had not yet

---

[150] That Timothy was not accompanied by Silas when he quitted Thessalonica, is evident from the passage—ἄρτι δὲ ἐλθόντος Τιμοθέου πρὸς ἡμᾶς ἀφ' ὑμῶν, κ.τ.λ., 1 Thess. iii. 6; and that he rejoined Silas before passing on to Corinth appears from the passage in Acts xviii. 5—ὡς δὲ κατῆλθον ἀπὸ Μακεδονίας ὅ τε Σίλας καὶ ὁ Τιμόθεος.

[151] Philipp. iv. 15; 2 Cor. xi. 9.

[152] 2 Cor. xi. 8; xii. 13, et seq. 1 Cor. ix. 12 et seq.

[153] 1 Cor. iv. 12; ix. 6.

[154] 2 Cor. xi. 7 to 12. [155] Philipp. iv. 15.

learnt to subdue their carnal appetites; there were still busybodies within the Christian pale, who, pretending to devote themselves to religion, had abandoned their lawful callings and luxuriated in idleness; some of the brethren also, since the Apostle's departure, had paid the debt of nature, and the Thessalonians, under the misconception that Christ's second appearance was immediately at hand, imagined that those already dead would lose some benefit of his coming; the internal economy of the church also was imperfect, and there had been symptoms of insubordination to their spiritual pastors.

Upon this information Paul, though he had full occupation for his thoughts at Corinth, where his enemies occasioned him much tribulation and distress,[156] found time to write them a letter, for the purpose of further strengthening their faith, and admonishing them as to their faults.[157] To give the letter greater authority, he joined with himself the names of Silas and Timothy, who had both been his coadjutors in their conversion.

The Epistle consists of three parts.

In the first (i. 2), the Apostle recurs to his recent presence amongst them, how he had on his side preached the Gospel at Thessalonica with boldness, not for honour or lucre, but as the servant of God, and had sacrificed his own ease for their sakes, as a nurse for her children, and that the Thessalonians for their part had received the Gospel worthily as a revelation from God, and had since, like the churches in Judea, continued steadfast in the faith, notwithstanding the incessant persecutions carried on against them by their fellow-citizens.

In the second part (ii. 17) the Apostle dwells on the anxiety of mind which he had suffered on their account since his flight from Thessalonica; that twice he had made an attempt to see them, but had been foiled, and that, unable to bear such suspense any longer, he had endured to be left alone in a strange city, and had sent Timothy from Athens to inquire into their state, and that Timothy having now returned with such gratifying tidings of their welfare, he had more joy and thankfulness than he could express.

In the third part (iv. 1) he introduces such exhortations as appeared most appropriate, as that they should avoid the lust and concupiscence with which the heathens so defiled themselves; that they should abound more and more in brotherly love, a virtue so necessary in a time of persecution; that they should not sorrow for those who had died in the Lord, for all would rise together at the general resurrection; and that inasmuch as the last day would come as a thief in the night, as declared in the Gospel of Matthew which was in their hands, they ought to be watchful, always standing armed with the breast-plate of Faith and the helmet of Hope; that they

---

[156] 1 Thess. iii. 7.

[157] Hitherto Paul had written no letters, for the limits of his labours had been circumscribed, and he could regulate the churches by his personal presence or by his missionaries, but now that he had extended Christendom beyond the limits of Asia into Europe, it became absolutely necessary to resort to occasional correspondence.

should submit themselves to the pastors who had been newly appointed over them, and should cultivate various other Christian graces which the Apostle recommends.[158] The Epistle ran thus:—

[*The italics indicate the variations from the Authorized Version; and the words in brackets, thus [ ], are not expressed, but only implied, in the Greek.*]

Ch. I "PAUL,[159] AND SILVANUS, AND TIMOTHY, UNTO THE CHURCH OF THE THESSALONIANS WHICH IS IN GOD THE FATHER AND IN THE LORD JESUS CHRIST: GRACE BE UNTO YOU, AND PEACE,[160] FROM GOD OUR FATHER, AND THE LORD JESUS CHRIST.

2 "We give thanks to God always for you all, making mention of you in our
3 prayers without ceasing, remembering your work of faith, and labour of love, and patience of hope of our Lord Jesus Christ, in the sight of God and our
4, 5 Father; knowing, brethren *beloved of God*,[161] your election. For our Gospel came not to you in word only, but also in power,[162] and in the Holy Ghost, and in much *fruitfulness*;[163] as ye know what manner of men we were among you
6 for your sake. And ye became *imitators* of us, and of the Lord, having
7 received the word in much affliction,[164] with joy of the Holy Ghost; so that ye

---

[158] The date of the Epistle may be collected as follows:—It was written not long after the time when Paul had been insulted (viz. by public scourging) at *Philippi*. προπαθόντες καὶ ὑβρισθέντες, καθὼς οἴδατε, ἐν Φιλίπποις, ἐπαρρησιασάμεθα ἐν τῷ Θεῷ ἡμῶν λαλῆσαι πρὸς ὑμᾶς τὸ εὐαγγέλιον τοῦ Θεοῦ ἐν πολλῷ ἀγῶνι, 1 Thess. ii. 2; and his success at *Thessalonica* was still a common topic of conversation: αὐτοὶ γὰρ περὶ ἡμῶν ἀπαγγέλλουσιν, ὁποίαν εἴσοδον ἔχομεν πρὸς ὑμᾶς, 1 Thess. i. 9; and Paul had since been in *Athens*. εὐδοκήσαμεν καταλειφθῆναι ἐν Ἀθήναις μόνοι. 1 Thess. iii. 1. And Timothy and Silas had recently returned to Paul from Thessalonica. ἄρτι δὲ ἐλθόντος Τιμοθέου πρὸς ἡμᾶς ἀφ' ὑμῶν. 1 Thess. iii. 6. Παῦλος καὶ Σιλουανὸς καὶ Τιμόθεος τῇ ἐκκλησίᾳ Θεσσαλονικέων, κ.τ.λ. 1 Thess. i. 1. And that this arrival of Timothy and Silas was when Paul was at Corinth, appears from the Acts. χωρισθεὶς ὁ Παῦλος ἐκ τῶν Ἀθηνῶν ἦλθεν εἰς Κόρινθον . . . ὡς δὲ κατῆλθον ἀπὸ τῆς Μακεδονίας ὅ τε Σίλας καὶ ὁ Τιμόθεος. Acts xviii. 1, 5.

[159] It is observable, that in this his first Epistle, and in the second Epistle to the Thessalonians, written not long after, Paul does not style himself an *Apostle*, though his Apostleship is asserted and assumed in ii. 6 of the present Epistle. At the close of this circuit, Paul and Barnabas went up together to Jerusalem, when the Apostles, who were there, viz. James, Peter, and John, made a compact with Paul and Barnabas, that the latter should be regarded as the Apostles of the Gentiles, as James and Peter and John were of the Jews. Galat. ii. 9. The other Epistles of Paul were all written subsequently to this compact, and in all (except the Hebrews, which was not addressed to a *Gentile* church) Paul styles himself an Apostle.

[160] The words of the Author. Vers., "from God our father, and the Lord Jesus Christ," are omitted by Griesbach, Lachmann, Tischendorf, and Alford, and are thought to have found their way into the text from 2 Thess. i. 2; Rom. i. 7; 1 Cor. i. 3; 2 Cor. i. 2; Philipp. i. 2; Ephes. i. 2; Coloss. i. 2; Galat. i. 3; 1 Tim. i. 2; 2 Tim. i. 2; Tit. i. 4; Philem. 3. The universality of this form, however, in St Paul's other Epistles, furnishes a strong argument in favour of the MSS which insert the words.

[161] ἀδελφοὶ ἠγαπημένοι ὑπὸ Θεοῦ, "*Beloved* of God" not "Your *election* of God." So in 2 Thess. ii. 13: ἀδελφοὶ ἠγαπημένοι ὑπὸ Κυρίου.

[162] ἐν δυνάμει, in the working of miracles, as in Acts x. 38; Matt. vii. 22; Rom. xv. 19; 2 Cor. xii. 9.

[163] πληροφορίᾳ.

[164] Therefore, not only Paul was persecuted in Thessalonica, but the church also planted there suffered persecution.

8 were ensamples to all that believe in Macedonia and Achaia ;[165] for from you *hath* sounded out the word of the Lord, not only in Macedonia and Achaia, but in every place your faith to God-ward is spread abroad; so that we need
9 not to speak anything. For they themselves shew of us what manner of entering in we had unto you, and how ye turned to God from idols to serve the living
10 and true God,[166] and to wait for his Son from the heavens, whom he raised from the dead, even Jesus, which delivereth us from the wrath to come.

Ch. II. "For yourselves, brethren, know our entrance in unto you, that it was not in
2 vain: but even after that we had suffered before, and were shamefully entreated, as ye know, at Philippi,[167] we were bold in our God to speak unto you the Gospel
3 of God in much *conflict*.[168] For our exhortation [was] not of deceit, nor of
4 uncleanness, nor in guile: but as we were *approved* of God to be put in trust with the Gospel, even so we speak; not as pleasing men, but God, *who proveth*
5 our hearts. For neither at any time *were we in the word of flattery* (as ye
6 know), nor *under the* cloke of covetousness (God is witness); nor of men sought we glory, neither of you, nor of others, when we might have been burdensome,
7 as Apostles of Christ;[169] but we were gentle among you, as a nurse *would*
8 cherish her *own* children. So being affectionately desirous of you, we are willing to impart unto you, not the Gospel of God only, but also our own
9 souls, because ye were dear unto us. For ye remember, brethren, our labour and travail: [for] working night and day,[170] because we would not be chargeable
10 unto any of you, we preached unto you the Gospel of God. Ye are witnesses, and God also, how holily, and justly, and unblameably we behaved ourselves
11 among you that believe, as ye know, exhorting and comforting and charging
12 every one of you, as a father doth his children, that ye would walk worthy of
13 God, who calleth you unto his kingdom and glory. For this cause also thank

---

[165] The Romans, under Paulus Æmilius, conquered Perseus, the last King of *Macedonia*, and reduced the countries formerly possessed by the Macedonian monarchs into a Roman province, which was governed by a Prætor or Proconsul sent from Rome, whose usual residence was in Thessalonica. Some time after, when Mummius defeated the *Achean* league and destroyed Corinth, Mummius with the commissioners sent from Rome to regulate the affairs of Greece, abolished the assemblies held by the Acheans, Bœotians, Phocians, and the rest, and reduced the states composing the Achean league, that is, all to the south of Macedonia and Illyricum, into a Roman province, which was called *Achaia*, because, at the taking of Corinth, the Acheans were the leading people. καλοῦσι δέ, οὐχ Ἑλλάδος, ἀλλ' Ἀχαίας ἡγεμόνι οἱ Ῥωμαῖοι, διότι ἐχειρώσαντο Ἕλληνας δι' Ἀχαιῶν τότε τοῦ Ἑλληνικοῦ προεστη- κότων. Pausan. vii. 16, 7. Thus the whole of the countries in Europe occupied by the Greeks were distributed by the Romans into two great divisions, one called Macedonia, with Thessalonica for its capital, and the other Achaia, with Corinth for its capital.

[166] The living and true God is opposed to the lifeless and false idols. The members of the Thessalonian church, therefore, did not consist mainly of Jews, but of heathen.

[167] Viz. by the public scourging there. See Acts xvi. 19, and ante, p. 279.

[168] ἐν πολλῷ ἀγῶνι. In the English version, "with much contention."

[169] The Apostles, therefore, looked to their flock for their support.

[170] Paul as a Jew places the night before the day, the twenty-four hours being with them a νυχθήμερον, or 'night-day,' commencing at sunset.

we God without ceasing, because, when ye received the word of God which ye heard of us,[171] ye received it not as the word of men, but as it is in truth,
14 the word of God, which effectually worketh[172] also in you that believe; for ye, brethren, became *imitators* of the churches of God, which are in Judea, in Christ Jesus, for ye also suffered like things of your own countrymen,[173] even
15 as they of the Jews, who both killed the Lord Jesus and their own prophets, and have *driven us out*;[174] and please not God, and are contrary to all men;[175]
16 forbidding us to speak to the Gentiles that they might be saved; that they
17 might fill up their sins alway. But wrath *overtaketh them at the last*.[176] But we, brethren, being *bereaved of*[177] you for *an hour's time* in presence, not in heart, *were anxious*[178] the more abundantly to see your face with great desire.
18 Wherefore we would *fain* have come unto you, yea, I Paul, *both* once and again;
19 but Satan hindered us.[179] For what is our hope, or joy, or crown of *boasting*?
20 Are not even ye in the presence of our Lord Jesus Christ at his coming? For ye are our glory and joy.

Ch. III. "Wherefore, when we could no longer forbear, we thought it good to
2 be left at Athens alone; and sent Timothy,[180] our brother, and minister of God, and our fellow-labourer in the Gospel of Christ, to establish you,
3 and to comfort[181] you concerning your faith: that no man *cring*[182] in

---

[171] λόγον ἀκοῆς παρ' ἡμῶν, literally "the word of hearing from us."

[172] "Effectually worketh" is expressed in the Greek by one word, ἐνεργεῖται.

[173] συμφυλετῶν. The *Gentiles* therefore were persecutors.

[174] ἐκδιωξάντων. In Eng. ver. "have persecuted." Paul had been driven by the Jews out of Damascus, and then, after a sojourn of fifteen days, out of Jerusalem, Acts ix. 23, 29; Gal. i. 18. Since that time he had been driven by the Jews out of Antioch of Pisidia and Iconium and Lystra, and recently again out of Thessalonica and Berœa.

[175] This was the character of the Jews generally: Adversus omnes alios hostile odium. Tac. Hist. v. 5.

[176] ἔφθασε δὲ ἐπ' αὐτοὺς ἡ ὀργὴ εἰς τέλος. For the use of εἰς τέλος in the sense of 'at the last,' see Sophocles, Philoctetes, 409:

ἀφ' ἧς
μηδὲ λιμνὴν τι τέλος φτάνει ποτίν.

In Eng. ver. "for the wrath is come upon them to the uttermost," which meaning is also allowable. The foreboding of the Apostle was accomplished eighteen years after this by the utter destruction of Jerusalem and the dispersion of the nation.

[177] ἀπορφανισθέντες ἀφ' ὑμῶν πρὸς καιρὸν ὥρας. In Eng. ver. "being taken from you for a short time." The Greek word ἀπορφανισθέντες literally carries with it the sense of orphanage.

[178] ἐσπουδάσαμεν. In Eng. ver. "endeavoured."

[179] He had wished to return to the Thessalonians from Berœa, but had been obliged to fly to Athens. He would have come to them from Athens, but again was prevented by untoward circumstances (perhaps by an attack of ophthalmia, the thorn in the flesh, which he calls a messenger of Satan, 2 Cor. xii. 7; or by his encounter with the Stoics and Epicureans, and consequent hearing before the Areopagus; or by some plot against him not recorded); and therefore, as the Apostle could not return himself from Athens, he sent Timothy.

[180] Timothy had been left at Berœa when Paul was obliged to fly from it, Acts xvii. 14; but Paul on arriving at Athens sent a message to Silas and Timothy to come to him with all speed, Acts xvii. 15, which Timothy appears to have done.

[181] Or, 'to exhort,' παρακαλέσαι.

[182] σαίνεσθαι.

[183] The persecution that followed at Thessalonica upon the arrest of Jason and his associates, Acts xvii. 5.

these afflictions:[183] for yourselves know that we are appointed thereunto;
4 for verily, when we were with you, we told you before that we should suffer
5 tribulations; as *also* it came to pass, and ye know. For this cause *I also*, when
I could no longer forbear, sent to know your faith, lest *haply* the tempter
6 *had* tempted you, and our labour be in vain.[184] But now when Timothy
came from you unto us, and brought us good tidings of your faith and *love*,
and that ye have good remembrance of us always, desiring greatly to see us,
7 as we also to see you, therefore, brethren, we were comforted over you in all
8 our affliction and distress by your faith: for now we live, if ye stand fast in
9 the Lord. For what thanks*giving* can we render to God again for you, for all
10 the joy wherewith we *rejoice* for your sakes before our God; night and day
praying exceedingly that we *may* see your face, and perfect that which is
11 lacking in your faith? Now God himself, even our Father, and our Lord
12 Jesus Christ,[185] direct our way unto you: and the Lord make you to increase
and abound in love one toward another, and toward all [men], even as we do
13 toward you: to the end *that* he may stablish your hearts unblameable in
holiness before God, even our Father, at the coming of our Lord Jesus Christ
with all his saints.

Ch. IV. "Furthermore, then, we beseech you, brethren, and exhort you *in* the Lord
Jesus, that, as ye have received of us how ye ought to walk and to please God,[186]
2 so ye would abound more and more. For ye know what commandments we
3 gave you by the Lord Jesus—for this is the will of God, your sanctification,—
4 that ye should abstain from fornication—that every one of you should know
5 how to possess his *own* vessel in sanctification and honour—not in the lust of
6 concupiscence, even as the Gentiles which know not God—that no man *transgress*, and *covet his brother* in *the* matter;[187] because that the Lord is the avenger
7 of all such, as we also forewarned you and testified. For God hath not called
8 us unto uncleanness, but unto holiness. He, therefore, that *dishonoureth*,
dishonoureth,[188] not man, but God, who hath also given unto us his Holy Spirit.
9 "But, as touching brotherly love, ye need not that I write unto you, for ye
10 yourselves are taught of God to love one another (*Lev*. xix. 18); and indeed
ye do it toward all the brethren which are in all[189] Macedonia. But we beseech
11 you, brethren, that ye *abound* more and more; and that ye study to be quiet,

---

[184] I.e. lest the Thessalonians had relapsed into idolatry.

[185] Lachmann, Tischendorf, and Alford, reject the word Χριστός.

[186] Lachmann and Alford add the words καθὼς καὶ περιπατεῖτε, "as also ye are walking."

[187] τὸ μὴ ὑπερβαίνειν καὶ πλεονεκτεῖν ἐν τῷ πράγματι τὸν ἀδελφὸν αὐτοῦ. The Apostle alludes to a crime which the delicacy of his mind forbids him to refer to in plainer language. The heathen not only "coveted their neighbour's wives" but one another. In Eng. ver. "that no man go beyond and defraud his brother." There is a similar use of the expression ἐν τῷ πράγματι in 2 Cor. vii. 11; and see Wetstein, 1 Thess. iv. 6.

[188] ἀθετεῖ. In Eng. ver. "despiseth."

[189] ἐν ὅλῃ τῇ Μακεδονίᾳ. Literally, "in whole Macedonia."

and to do your own business, and to work with your own hands, as we com-
12 manded you; that ye may walk *decorously* toward them that are without, and
that ye may have lack of nothing.

13 "But I would not have you to be ignorant, brethren, concerning them which
14 are asleep, that ye sorrow not, even as others which have no hope. For if we
believe that Jesus died and rose again, even so them also which sleep in Jesus
15 will God bring with him. For this we say unto you *in* the word of the Lord,[120]
that we which are alive and remain unto the coming of the Lord shall not
16 *have the start of*[121] them which are asleep; for the Lord himself shall descend
from Heaven with a shout, with the voice of an archangel, and with the trump
17 of God; and the dead in Christ shall rise first; then we[122] which are alive and
remain shall be caught up together with them in the clouds, to meet the Lord
18 in the air, and so shall we ever be with the Lord. Wherefore comfort one
another with these words.

Ch. V. "But of the times and the seasons, brethren, ye have no need that I write
2 unto you; for yourselves know perfectly that the day of the Lord so cometh
3 as 'a thief in the night.'[123] (*Matt.* xxiv. 43.) For when they shall say 'Peace
and Safety,' then sudden destruction cometh upon them, as travail upon a
4 woman with child; and they shall not escape. But ye, brethren, are not in
5 darkness, that that day should overtake you as a thief. Ye are all *sons* of
light, and *sons* of the day; we are not of the night, nor of darkness: there-
6, 7 fore, let us not sleep, as do *the rest*, but let us watch and be sober; for they
that sleep sleep in the night, and they that be drunken are drunken in the
8 night. But let us, who are of the day, be sober, having put on the breastplate
9 of faith and love, and for a helmet the hope of salvation. For God hath not
10 appointed us to wrath, but to obtain salvation by our Lord Jesus Christ, who
died for us, that, whether we wake or sleep, we should live together with him.
11 Wherefore comfort *one another*, and edify one another even as also ye do,

---

[120] By express revelation. Paul therefore claimed to be inspired.

[121] φθάσωμεν. In Eng. ver. "shall not prevent," in the sense, now disused, of *anticipating*, from the Latin prævenio.

[122] In 2 Cor. iv. 14, we read ἡμᾶς διὰ Ἰησοῦ ἐγερεῖ, which shows that St. Paul did not by 'we' and 'us' refer to himself personally, for if amongst the living in the text above, "we which are alive," he could not be amongst the dead whom Christ should "raise," in the Epistle to the Corinthians. But the Thessalonians seem not to have understood this, and imagined the Day of Judgment to be at hand in Paul's time, a delusion which called forth the second Epistle to them.

[123] The Apostle says—"yourselves know," for he had placed in their hands the Gospel of St. Matthew, in which the warning was contained. The first eleven verses of this fifth chapter suppose the reader to have before him the twenty-fourth chapter of St. Matthew, from the thirty-sixth verse to the end. There are other references to St. Matthew's Gospel in 1 Cor. vi. 3; vii. 10; xiii. 2; Heb. xi. 4. It is satisfactory to find that wherever Paul planted a church, whether at Thessalonica, or at Corinth, or elsewhere, he delivered into the hands of the converts the Gospel of St. Matthew as an authentic record of our Lord's ministry. From the frequent citation by Paul of this Gospel as an infallible guide, it is evident that in the earliest as in the

12 "And we beseech you, brethren,[194] to know them which labour among you,
13 and are over you in the Lord, and admonish you, and to esteem them very
14 highly in love for their work's sake. Be at peace among yourselves. *And* we
exhort you, brethren,[195] warn them that are *disorderly*, comfort the feeble-
15 minded, support the weak, be *longsuffering* toward all men. See that none
render evil for evil unto any *one*, but ever follow that which is good, both *to*
16, 17 *one another*, and to all men. Rejoice evermore.[196] Pray without ceasing. In
18 every thing give thanks: for this is the will of God in Christ Jesus concerning
19, 20 you. Quench not the Spirit.[197] Despise not prophesyings.[198] Prove all things.
21, 22 Hold fast that which is good.[199] Abstain from all appearance of evil. And
23 the[200] very God of peace sanctify you wholly; and *may* your whole spirit
and soul and body be preserved blameless *in* the coming of our Lord Jesus
24, 25 Christ. Faithful is he that calleth you, who also will do it. Brethren, pray
26 for us.[201] Greet all the brethren with a holy kiss.[202] I *adjure* you by the Lord
27 that this Epistle be read unto all the holy brethren.[203]
28 "THE GRACE OF OUR LORD JESUS CHRIST BE WITH YOU."[204]

This Epistle was not penned by Paul himself, but was dictated to an amanuensis. It was authenticated, however, by Paul's salutation or benediction with his own hand at the end, "The grace of our Lord Jesus Christ be with you." Constantly suffering, as he was, from a feeble vision, he could not write without pain. He therefore adopted the practice of employing a scribe, as he tells us himself in his second Epistle to the Thessalonians. "The salutation of Paul with mine own hand, which is the token in every Epistle: so I write. THE GRACE OF OUR LORD JESUS CHRIST BE WITH YOU."[205] It will be found, on referring to them, that *all the fourteen Epistles (including*

---

latest ages, the Gospel of St. Matthew was regarded as inspired scripture. We shall see that at a later period when Luke's Gospel was written Paul refers to that also.

[194] Addressed to the laity, who are exhorted to submit themselves to their pastors.

[195] Addressed to the ministers of the gospel, who are reminded of their duties to their flock.

[196] Though the persecution of you continue, heed it not, but rejoice that ye are counted worthy to suffer for Christ's sake.

[197] The Spirit of God is supporting you in your trials. Quench it not by backsliding.

[198] προφητείας or preachings, in which sense the word is commonly used in the New Testament.

[199] Listen to those who prophesy or preach, but prove what they say, and adopt the good.

[200] The Eng. ver. inserts the words "I pray God," which are not in the original.

[201] Paul is the only writer of the New Testament who asks for the prayers of his correspondents, and this is an argument, and a weighty one, that he was the author of the Epistle to the Hebrews, as the writer of it asks for their prayers on his behalf. Heb. xiii. 18.

[202] According to the practice of the ancient Christians, and in order to guard against impropriety, the males saluted the males only, and the females the females. Bingham's Antiq. xv. 3. 3, where the authorities for this practice are stated at large. This custom, so general in the earliest ages of the church, fell afterwards into desuetude.

[203] It was not a private epistle, but written for the church generally, and to be read as Scripture.

[204] Griesbach, Scholtz, Lachmann, Tischendorf, and Alford, all omit the Amen which is in the Authorized Version.

[205] 2 Thess. iii. 17, 18.

that to the Hebrews) conclude with this benediction, and have all, therefore, the stamp of authenticity.[206]

Paul, Silas, and Timothy were now joint labourers at Corinth, and united their efforts to convince the Jews that Jesus was the Messiah,[207] and to convert the Gentiles.

Fig. 141. *Representation of a tragic poet dictating to an amanuensis. From Zinc and Barré's Herculanum and Pompeii.*

Their appeal to the Jews was all in vain. The more earnest they were, the more violent was the opposition. It at last came to this; that whenever Paul began to preach in the synagogue, the Jews interrupted him by horrid blasphemies against the name of Jesus. Paul was ready to break his heart at such a result;[208] but to persevere was useless, and shaking his raiment, he bade them solemnly farewell, exclaiming as

---

[206] Such authentication was not an uncommon practice amongst the ancients. Thus Cicero writes to Atticus, "in eâ Pompeii epistolâ erat in extremo in ipsius manu, Tn, censeo," &c. See Renan's St. Paul, p. 233, note (1).

[207] "Preached among you by us, even by me and Sylvanus and Timotheus." 2 Cor. i. 19.

[208] συνείχετο τῷ πνεύματι. Acts xviii. 5. In 2 Cor. ii. 4, is a similar expression: ἐκ γὰρ πολλῆς θλίψεως καὶ συνοχῆς καρδίας ἔγραψα ὑμῖν διὰ πολλῶν δακρύων.

he walked out of the synagogue, in the words of the prophet Ezekiel, "Your blood be upon your own heads;[209] I am clean. From henceforth I will go unto the Gentiles."

The next step was to provide a lecture-room, in which the Apostle might impart instruction to the Gentiles, though not to the exclusion of any Jews that would attend; and for this purpose he hired an apartment from one Justus, a proselyte, whose house was next door to the synagogue. The Jews were nettled at a Christian meeting-house being opened in such immediate contiguity, and the more so as Paul began to preach there with extraordinary success; but they could find no handle against him, and sulkily abided their time. The Apostle, indeed, was divinely protected—"The Lord spake to Paul in the night by a vision, 'Be not afraid, but speak, and hold not thy peace; for I am with thee, and no man shall set on thee to hurt thee, for I have much people in this city.'"[210]

About this time the messenger whom Paul had despatched with his letter to Thessalonica returned, and brought with him news of a somewhat singular character, viz. that he left the church in a panic from the expectation that the world was coming to an end. Some deceivers had spread the notion, and alleged inspiration for it. Nay, they had quoted a passage from the letter of the Apostle himself: "For this we say unto you by the word of the Lord, that *we* which are alive and remain unto the coming of the Lord, shall not have the start of them which are asleep."[211] Here, said they, the Apostle himself plainly indicates that the advent of Christ is to take place in his own time. It must be obvious to any one acquainted with the style of Paul, that by "we" he designated all Christians, and was not referring to himself and his correspondents individually.[212] The ignorant part of the Thessalonian church may, however, be well pardoned for this mistake, when the same text has been seriously urged in our own time as an argument that Paul himself entertained this belief.[213] Another communication from Thessalonica was, that, notwithstanding the admonitions contained in the Apostle's letter, there were still busybodies in the church who were leading a life of idleness under the cloak of religion.

Paul, under these circumstances, addressed a second letter to the Thessalonians. He begins with the usual salutation, and then (i. 3) commending their continued steadfastness in the faith, notwithstanding the troubles which had beset them, he proceeds (ii.) to allay their fears by removing the cause. He reminds them that when present with them he had explained how the second advent of Christ was to be preceded by an apostasy, which would not happen until the obstacle to which he had then referred, and which still operated, was removed. "Now we beseech you, brethren, as concerning the coming of our Lord Jesus Christ, and our gathering together unto him, that ye be not soon shaken in mind, or be troubled, neither by spirit, nor by word, nor by letter as from us, as that the day of Christ is at hand. Let no man

---

[209] Ezekiel xxxiii. 4. [210] Acts xviii. 9, 10. [211] 1 Thess. iv. 15.
[212] See note ante, p. 278. [213] By Jeremy Bentham.

[CHAP. XII.]   SECOND EPISTLE TO THESSALONIANS.   [A.D. 52]

deceive you by any means, for that day shall not come, except there come a falling away first, and that man of sin be revealed, the son of perdition. Remember ye not, that, when I was yet with you, I told you these things? And now ye know what withholdeth that he might be revealed in his time."[214]

In the latter part of the Epistle (iii. 1) the Apostle asks their prayers, that, for the Gospel's sake, he may be delivered from the ungodly men that were persecuting him at Corinth; and he then (iii. 6) sharply rebukes the drones of the church of Thessalonica, who were living upon other men's labours, and reminds them of the precept which they had received from him, that if a man would not work, neither should he eat, and if any were refractory, the church should excommunicate him. "If any man obey not our word by this Epistle, note that man, and have no company with him, that he may be ashamed." As wicked men had been imposing on the credulity of the Thessalonians, he tells them, in conclusion, how to test the genuineness of his Epistles, namely, that the Benediction at the close was always in his own handwriting. The letter was as follows:—

[The *italics* indicate the variations from the Authorized Version; and the words in brackets thus [ ] are not *expressed*, but only *implied*, in the Greek.]

CH. 1. "PAUL, AND SILVANUS, AND TIMOTHY, UNTO THE CHURCH OF THE THESSALONIANS
2 IN GOD OUR FATHER AND THE LORD JESUS CHRIST, GRACE UNTO YOU, AND PEACE FROM GOD OUR FATHER AND LORD JESUS CHRIST.

3 "We are bound to thank God always for you, brethren, as it is meet, because that your faith groweth exceedingly, and the *love* of every one of you all
4 toward each other *overfloweth*;[215] so that we ourselves glory in you in the churches of God, for your patience and faith in all your persecutions and
5 *afflictions* that ye endure: [which is] a token of the righteous judgment of God, that ye may be counted worthy of the kingdom of God, for which ye also
6 suffer: seeing it is a righteous thing with God to recompense *affliction* to them
7 that *afflict* you, and to you who are *afflicted* rest with us, *in the revelation of*
8 the Lord Jesus from heaven with the angels *of his might*, in flaming fire, *administering* vengeance to them that know not God, and that obey not the
9 Gospel of our Lord Jesus Christ, who shall be punished with everlasting destruction from the presence of the Lord, and from the glory of his power,
10 when he shall come to be glorified in his saints, and to be admired in all them that believe (because our testimony among you *hath been* believed) in That
11 day.[216] *To which end* also we pray always for you, that our God would count

---

[214] 2 Thess. ii. 1 to 6.
[215] πλεονάζει. In the Eng. ver. "aboundeth."
[216] By "that day" is meant the Day of Judgment. So in 1 Cor. iii. 13, and 2 Tim. i. 18, iv. 8. So when our Lord was asked by the disciples *when* the Temple should be destroyed, and *when* should be the end of the world, he said, in answer to the first question, that all should be fulfilled before that generation had passed away. "But," he continued, "of *That day and hour* knoweth no man." Matt. xxiv. 36; Mark xiii. 32.

you worthy of this calling, and fulfil all the good pleasure of his goodness, and
12 the work of faith with power, that the name of our Lord Jesus Christ may be glorified in you, and ye in him, according to the grace of our God and the Lord Jesus Christ.

Ch. II. "Now *as concerning* the coming of our Lord Jesus Christ, and our gathering
2 together unto him,[217] we beseech you, brethren, that ye be not *lightly*[218] shaken in mind, or be troubled, neither by spirit, nor by word, nor by letter as from
3 us,[219] as that the day of Christ is at hand. Let no man deceive you *in any manner:* for [that day shall not come] except there come *the* falling away
4 first, and that man of sin be revealed, the son of perdition, who opposeth and exalteth himself above all that is called God, or that is worshipped, so that he as God sitteth in the temple of God, showing himself that he is God.[220]

---

[217] In the Eng. ver., "Now we beseech you, brethren, *by* the coming of our Lord Jesus Christ, and *by* our gathering together unto him," &c. But the Apostle is evidently referring to the main subject of his letter, viz. the panic in the Thessalonian church from the erroneous notion that the Day of Judgment was at hand—a panic which had arisen in part from a misconstruction of the Apostle's first Epistle (see ante, p. 278), and which he now sought to allay. The preposition ὑπέρ is here to be taken in the sense given by the lexicons as equivalent to περί, viz. 'of' or 'concerning.'

[218] ταχέως. In Eng. ver. "soon."

[219] 'Let nothing which I may have *said* when I was present, or have *written* since, be misinterpreted to have this meaning.'

[220] The interpretations of this mysterious passage have been almost numberless. It will be sufficient to select a few.

1. According to some the apostasy referred to was the Gnostic heresy, and the Man of sin, or Antichrist, was Simon Magus, and he who "withholdeth," or checked the development of the iniquity, was Paul himself; and in support of this view it is argued that the apostasy meant must have been a practical question of the Apostle's own time, as he had by word of mouth cautioned the Thessalonians against the Man of sin, and it is certain that Gnosticism struck root in the Apostle's day, and is frequently adverted to in his letters, though the Apostle's personal influence in the church would naturally "withhold" the canker from spreading.

2. According to others, the apostasy was the relapse from Christianity to Paganism in the time of the Neronian persecution, A.D. 64-66, and the Man of Sin was Nero, and he who withheld or prevented for a time the outbreak of heathen violence against the true faith was Claudius, the predecessor of Nero, and whose principles of universal toleration gave free play to the growth of Christianity. The name of Claudius (= 'qui claudit') has been ingeniously suggested as the translation of ὁ κατέχων applied in 2 Thess. ii. 7, to the person who warded off the Antichrist.

3. Others insist that Mahomedanism (which was an offshoot from Christianity) was the apostasy, and that Mahomet was the Man of sin.

4. Others say that the apostasy was the falling away of the church from the purity of the early believers to the idolatries of the Romish community; that the Man of sin is the Pope, and that he who withholds, ὁ κατέχων (2 Thess. ii. 7), or rather that which withholds, τὸ κατέχον (2 Thess. ii. 16), is the temporal power of Rome, for so long as Paganism subsisted, a strong line of demarcation was drawn between it and Christianity, but when the empire itself became Christian, it introduced into the church the worship of the Virgin and of the Saints, idolatries substituted for those which had been practised by the heathen. (See the argument of Wordsworth in support of this view.)

5. The writers of the Romish church, in retaliation, insist that the apostasy was the Reformation, and that Martin Luther was the Man of sin.

6. Others, until the theory was falsified by the event, maintained the hypothesis that the atheism of the French Revolution was the apostasy, and that Napoleon I. was the Man of sin.

7. Others again urge, with much plausibility, that the prophecy yet remains to be fulfilled, and

[Chap. XII.] SECOND EPISTLE TO THESSALONIANS. [a.d. 52]

5 Remember ye not, that, when I was yet with you, I told you these things?
6 And now ye know what withholdeth that he might be revealed in his time.
7 For the mystery of iniquity doth already work: only [there is] who with-
8 holdeth,[221] until he be taken out of the way. And then shall that *lawless one* be revealed, whom the Lord shall consume with the *breath* of his mouth, and
9 shall destroy with the brightness of his coming—even him, whose coming is after the working of Satan with all power and signs and lying wonders,
10 and with all deceivableness of unrighteousness in them that perish; because
11 they received not the love of the truth, that they might be saved. And for this cause God *sendeth*[222] them strong delusion, that they should believe *the*
12 lie,[223] that all *may* be *judged* who believed not the truth, but had pleasure in
13 unrighteousness. But we *ought* to give thanks alway to God for you, brethren beloved of the Lord, because God hath from the beginning chosen you to
14 salvation through sanctification of the spirit and belief of the truth: whereunto he called you by our Gospel, to the obtaining of the glory of our
15 Lord Jesus Christ. Therefore, brethren, stand fast, and hold the traditions which ye have been taught, whether by *our* word, or our epistle.[224]
16 Now our Lord Jesus Christ himself, and God, even our Father, which hath loved us, and hath given us everlasting consolation and good hope
17 through grace, comfort your hearts, and stablish you in every good word and work.

Ch. III. "Finally, brethren, pray for us,[225] that the word of the Lord may have free
2 course, and be glorified, even as it is with you, and that we may be delivered
3 from unreasonable and wicked men:[226] for all men have not faith: but the
4 Lord is faithful, who shall stablish you, and keep you from evil. And we have confidence in the Lord touching you, that ye both do and will do the things
5 which we command you. And the Lord direct your hearts into the love of God, and into *endurance* for Christ.
6 "Now we command you, brethren, in the name of our Lord Jesus Christ,

---

that as the apostasy is immediately to precede the second and triumphant advent of Christ, the Man of sin will not be revealed until the approach of the end of all things.

We have by no means exhausted the various hypotheses which have been broached, but to pursue them further would tend rather to confuse than edify. The reader is referred upon this subject to Alford's Introduction to the 2nd Epistle to the Thessalonians, and to the works there quoted.

[221] ὁ κατέχων, the same word as that translated before in Eng. ver., "what *withholdeth*." The Eng. ver., therefore, unnecessarily translates it here, "he who letteth," instead of "he who withholdeth."

[222] Lachmann, Tischendorf, and Alford read πέμπει instead of πέμψει.

[223] τῷ ψεύδει—*the* lie, not *a* lie.

[224] I.e. 'The doctrines which ye learned of me orally when I was present, and now, when I am absent, learn of me by letter.' The word παράδοσις here corresponds to the word παρέδωκα, 1 Cor. xv. 3; and see post, iii. 7.

[225] See note ante, 1 Thess. v. 25.

[226] From whose opposition and persecution Paul was suffering at Corinth at the date of the Epistle.

that ye withdraw yourselves from every brother that walketh disorderly, and
7 not after the tradition which he received of us; for yourselves know how ye
ought to *imitate* us; for we behaved ourselves not disorderly among you,
8 neither did we eat any man's bread for nought, but wrought with labour and
travail night and day,[227] that we might not be chargeable to any of you;
9 not because we have not power,[228] but to make ourselves an ensample unto you
10 to *imitate* us. For even when we were with you, this we commanded you, that
11 if any would not work, neither should he eat; for we hear that there are some
among you which walk disorderly, *having no business*,[229] but *being* busy-
12 bodies. Now them that are such we command and exhort by our Lord
Jesus Christ, that with quietness they work, and eat their own bread.
13, 14 But ye, brethren, be not weary in well-doing; *but* if any man obey not our
word by this Epistle, note that man, and have no company with him, that he
15 may be ashamed; yet count him not as an enemy, but admonish him as a
16 brother. *And* the Lord of peace himself give you peace always by all means.
17 The Lord be with you all. The salutation of *me* Paul with mine own hand,
18 which is the token in every Epistle: so I write.[230] THE GRACE OF OUR LORD
JESUS CHRIST BE WITH YOU ALL."[231]

The state of things at *Corinth* when the Epistle was written may be collected from the following passage in it: "Finally, brethren, pray for us, that the word of the Lord may have free course, and be glorified, even as it is with you: and *that we may be delivered from unreasonable and wicked men; for all men have not faith*."[232] The unbelieving Jews were constantly on the watch to take his life. But, notwithstanding their opposition, the word *had* its free course, and the Apostle *was* delivered; for during the first year and six months that he continued at Corinth his career was undisturbed and the disciples multiplied daily. Nowhere did Paul make more converts than at Corinth. Besides Justus[233] and Crispus,[234] we read of Stephanas, Fortunatus, and Achaicus,[235] Erastus,[236] Caius,[237] and Chloe,[238] to whom we may perhaps add Quartus[239] and Tertius.[240]

The eminent success of the Gospel at Corinth must, of course, be ascribed, not exclusively to the *preaching* of Paul and his companions, but to the display of the supernatural powers with which Paul was endowed. The sacred penman has not

---

[227] Observe the Jewish education of Paul in making the night precede the day, whereas others would have said 'day and night.'

[228] For the Apostles generally looked to their flocks for their support.

[229] μηδὲν ἐργαζομένους. In Eng. ver. "working not at all." One object of the altered translation is to preserve in English the play in Greek between ἐργαζομένους and περιεργαζομένους—between 'the busy' and 'the busybodies.'

[230] By the salutation or greeting is of course meant, not the greeting at the opening of the Epistle, but the parting benediction at the close. This has been already explained.

[231] Griesbach, Tischendorf, and Alford omit the "Amen" which is in the Authorized translation.

[232] 2 Thess. iii. 1, 2.
[233] Acts xviii. 7.
[234] Acts xviii. 8.
[235] 1 Cor. xvi. 17.
[236] Rom. xvi. 23.
[237] Rom. xvi. 23.
[238] 1 Cor. i. 11.
[239] Rom. xvi. 23.
[240] Rom. xvi. 22.

particularised instances, as the narration of all that occurred was not within the compass of his design; but that Paul was enabled to work many miracles amongst them appears incidentally from his Second Epistle to that community, in which he appeals to miracles in proof of his Apostleship. "Truly," he says, "the signs of an Apostle were wrought among you in all patience, in *signs, and wonders, and mighty deeds*."[241]

At the expiration of a year and six months, and about the beginning of June, A.D. 53,[242] Gallio arrived at Corinth to assume the government of Achaia.[243] At the period of which we are speaking the prefects of provinces were bound by an edict of the Emperor to quit Rome before the middle of April.[244] Gallio, therefore, would start from Rome about the 15th of April, A.D. 53. The time occupied in passing from Rome to Corinth we may best collect from the analogous case of Cicero, who set out from Tarentum to take possession of his province of Cilicia on the 18th of May, B.C. 51 (Ep. Attic. v. 6), and arrived at *Athens* on the 25th of June (Ep. Attic. v. 10),[245] and was thus about forty days on the road, without including the journey from Rome to Tarentum, for which we must allow ten days more,[246] making in all fifty days. Gallio, at this rate, would reach his province about the 4th of June, A.D. 53. Who had been proconsul before Gallio is uncertain, but whoever he was, he must have entertained a very favourable view of Christianity, or Paul could scarcely have been allowed for so long a space to pursue his ministry without interruption. Gallio (whom Seneca calls "my Lord Gallio," from his having attained the honour of the prætorship), was one of a distinguished family. Marcus Annæus Seneca, the famous rhetorician, had three sons, Marcus Annæus Novatus (afterwards called Junius Annæus Gallio, from the adoption of him by Lucius Junius Gallio, the rhetorician), and Lucius Annæus Seneca, the philosopher, and M. Annæus Mela. L. A. Seneca, the philosopher, had not long before been appointed by Claudius private tutor to the young Nero.[247] Mela was best known as the father of Lucan the poet, the author of the Pharsalia. The love of letters was but ill requited at Rome; for a few years after, both Seneca and his nephew Lucan were put to death at the same time by Nero, on the charge (a groundless one, at least as regards Seneca,) of their having concurred in Piso's conspiracy against the life of the Emperor; and Gallio and Mela eventually shared the same fate. Gallio was possessed of ability and accomplishments, and wrote a book on natural questions;[248] but more than that,

---

[241] 2 Cor. xii. 12.

[242] See Fasti Sacri, p. 300, No. 1793.

[243] That is, of Greece, called by the Romans Achaia, as distinguished from the provinces of Macedonia and Illyria, which bounded it on the north. καλοῦσι δὲ οὐχ Ἑλλάδος, ἀλλ' Ἀχαΐας ἡγεμόνα οἱ Ῥωμαῖοι, διότι ἐχειρώσαντο Ἕλληνας δι' Ἀχαιῶν τότε τοῦ Ἑλληνικοῦ προεστηκότων. Pausan. vii. 16, 7.

[244] Dion. lx. 17. See Fasti Sacri, p. 276, No. 1655.

[245] See Fasti Sacri, p. 24, Nos. 192-194.

[246] Horace, in his journey from thence to Brundisium, spent ten or eleven days upon the road. Hor. Sat. i. 5.

[247] Tac. Ann. xii. 8.

[248] Senec. Nat. Quæst. v. 11.

he was a man of the most imperturbable good humour, and of such gentleness of manner as to ingratiate himself with all that approached him. Statius refers to him as the sweet Gallio.[249] Seneca speaks of his brother as without a fault, " whom every one loved too little, even he who loved him to the utmost;"[250] and again, " Gallio is more delightful to *all*, than any other to *one*."[251] This amiable temper was the more praiseworthy, as he was a person of delicate health from a consumptive tendency, and shortly after his proconsulship was obliged on that account to make a voyage to Egypt.[252] One of his *bons-mots*, recorded by Seneca, is this. The Etesians went by the name of the 'Sleepers,' and when Gallio was asked why, he said, " Because they don't get up till morning;" for it was commonly observed that the Etesiæ began to blow at sunrise.[253] We have, unfortunately, no account of Gallio's administration of Achaia, the only anecdote recorded of him there being a remark of his incidentally mentioned in Seneca's letters, and which, perhaps, was remembered, not so much from its piquancy as because it fell from " my Lord Gallio." " The saying of my Lord Gallio recurred to me, who, when he was taken ill of a fever in Achaia, immediately stepped on board a ship, saying, the disorder was not of the man but of the place."[254]

Gallio had no sooner arrived in his province than the Jews, who had quailed before the austerity of his predecessor, thought they might presume with impunity upon the easy temper of the new proconsul. They also argued, perhaps, that Gallio, as unaccustomed to office, might be so little acquainted with the exact duties of it that they could extort the infliction of a punishment by clamour, which could not be obtained by legitimate means. Some time would be required for the forms of legal procedure, but we may suppose that about the 14th of June, A.D. 53, i.e. about ten days after Gallio's arrival, the Jews, with Sosthenes, a chief ruler of the synagogue, at their head, indicted Paul, and brought him before the judgment-seat on the charge —" This fellow persuadeth men to worship God contrary to the law"—in other words, that Paul, a Jew, was preaching a doctrine subversive of the Jewish polity, and was maintaining, contrary to all reason, that Jesus was the Messiah. Gallio, however, knew well enough that the governor of a province was not called upon to interfere in the religious differences of his subjects, where no civil offence was involved, and he was perhaps equally well aware of the malice by which the Jews were actuated, and of the innocence of the Christian doctrine. He therefore heard the Jews patiently to an end, and then, without even waiting for the defence (for Paul was

---

[249] Hoc plus quam Senecam dedisse mundo
Aut dulcem generasse Gallionem.
Stat. Sylv. ii. 7, 31.

[250] Solebam tibi dicere Gallionem fratrem meum (quem nemo non parum amat, etiam qui amare plus non potest) alia vitia non nôsse, hoc etiam odisse. Nat. Quæst. iv. Præf.

[251] Nemo enim mortalium uni tam dulcis est, quam hic omnibus. Nat. Quæst. iv. Præf.

[252] Plin. N. H. xxxi. 33.

[253] Seneca, Quæst. Nat. v. 11.

[254] Illud mihi in ore erat domini mei Gallionis, qui cum in Achaia febrem habere cœpisset, protinus navem ascendit clamitans, non corporis esse, sed loci morbum. Sen. Epist. 104.

ready to reply), he dismissed the complaint very summarily for want of jurisdiction. "If," said he, "it were a matter of wrong or wicked lewdness, O ye Jews, reason would that I should bear with you; but if it be a question of words and names (as whether Jesus be the Christ or Messiah), and of your Law, look ye to it, for I will be no judge of such matters."[255] The sentence of the judge was pronounced, but the Jews could not take an answer. They persisted in the charge till they were forcibly removed from the court—Gallio "drave them from the judgment-seat"—nay, the Greeks, who detested the Jews, and looked with complacency on the Christian scheme as propounded by Paul, laid hold of Sosthenes, the ruler of the synagogue,[256] the mouthpiece of the Jews, and, from indignation at the indictment, beat him in the presence of the judge. The Jews were open-mouthed, that this was an insult to the court; but Gallio (not sorry, perhaps, to see the persecutor caught in his own snare) refused to interpose. "Gallio cared for none of those things." Sosthenes shortly afterwards, though we know not under what circumstances, himself became a convert, and is joined with Paul in the opening salutation of the First Epistle to the Corinthians."[257]

---

[255] Acts xviii. 14, 15.

[256] τὸν ἀρχισυνάγωγον. Acts xviii. 17. Sosthenes may have been the ruler of one synagogue, while Crispus, who was invested with the same office (Acts xviii. 8), may have been ruler of another synagogue; for Corinth must have supported more synagogues than one. But there were often, if not generally, two or more rulers of the same synagogue, so that Sosthenes and Crispus may both have belonged to the same synagogue. Sosthenes may be here spoken of as "*the* ruler," Crispus, his only colleague, having lost the office by becoming a convert; or Sosthenes may have been designated as "the ruler of the synagogue" to distinguish him from others of the name of Sosthenes who were not rulers.

[257] The view advanced in the text is that the assailants were *Greeks*, and that Sosthenes was a *Jew*; but another opinion is that the assailants were *Jews*, and that Sosthenes was a *convert* to Christianity.

The Greek text is not decisive either way, for Lachmann, Griesbach, Tischendorf, and Alford all agree that the passage should stand ἐπιλαβόμενοι δὲ πάντες Σωσθένην (omitting οἱ Ἕλληνες, which is found in the Textus Receptus, and omitting οἱ Ἰουδαῖοι, which appears in various MSS.). The word Ἕλληνες, or Ἰουδαῖοι, has crept into the text from the marginal glosses for the purpose of clearing away an ambiguity.

1. The hypothesis adopted—viz. that the assailants were Greeks, and that Sosthenes was a Jew—rests mainly on the following argument. Luke had stated a little before, as the result of Paul's labours at Corinth, that "*Crispus*, the *chief ruler of the synagogue*, believed on the Lord with all his house; and many of the Corinthians hearing, believed and were baptized." Acts xviii. 8. If Sosthenes, "chief ruler of the synagogue" (τὸν ἀρχισυνάγωγον, v. 17), was also a Christian, it is incredible that Sosthenes should not have been mentioned as such as well as Crispus. They were both rulers of the synagogue, and if both believed, Luke could scarcely have singled out Crispus and passed over Sosthenes. Besides, when it is said that they beat "Sosthenes, the chief ruler of the synagogue," the emphasis is evidently to be laid on his being such ruler—i.e. he was beaten, not because he was a Christian, but as the representative of the Jewish party, who were the prosecutors. Had Sosthenes been a Christian he could not have been a ruler of the synagogue at all, but would necessarily, on adopting the new faith, have been ejected from the office.

The obvious inconsistency that would result from the supposition that Crispus and Sosthenes were both of them converts is attempted to be met by the assertion that they were one and the same person—that Crispus was the Roman name, and that Sosthenes was the Hebrew name, derived from the root שוש, which is found in the Hebrew "Susanna." But who can believe that

Though Paul thus escaped through the liberality of the Roman Proconsul, yet the danger had been imminent. Thankful for so great a deliverance, the Apostle, in accordance with the common practice of the Jews of that period, took upon himself the vow of the Nazarite."[258] What this was is explained to us in few words by Josephus. "It is customary," he says, "for those who have been afflicted with any distemper, or have laboured under any other difficulties, to make a vow, that for thirty days before they offer sacrifices, they will abstain from wine, and will at the expiration shave the head."[259] In the Book of Numbers we have the following particulars: "He (the Nazarite) shall separate himself from wine and strong drink, and shall drink no vinegar of wine, or vinegar of strong drink, neither shall he drink any liquor of grapes, nor eat moist grapes, or dried. All the days of the vow of his separation there shall no razor come upon his head; until the days be fulfilled, during which he separateth himself unto the Lord, he shall be holy, and shall let the locks of his head grow; all the days that he separateth himself unto the Lord, he shall come at no dead body. And this is the law of the Nazarite—when the days of his

---

Luke, in the same chapter, could speak of a person as Crispus, and then, without notice of the change, speak of him as Sosthenes? not to mention that Crispus is also called the ruler of the synagogue; and if he were identical with Sosthenes, it would be an idle repetition to describe Sosthenes as such. Besides, not only Luke, but Paul also makes mention of Sosthenes (1 Cor. i. 1), and then of Crispus (1 Cor.), without the least indication of their identity.

2. We must now advert to the opposite view—viz., that the assailants were Jews and Sosthenes a Christian, which is advocated in the manner following: first, it is urged that a Corinthian of distinction by the name of Sosthenes was some years afterwards a Christian (Σωσθένης ὁ ἀδελφὸς, 1 Cor. i. 1), and well known to the church at Corinth. He is therefore presumptively the Sosthenes that was beaten as a Christian before the tribunal. To this it is answered that, even admitting the Sosthenes of the Acts and the Sosthenes of the Epistle to be the same person, it does not follow that Sosthenes was a Christian at the time of the assault upon the Apostle at Corinth, for Sosthenes may very well have become a convert subsequently. Besides, Sosthenes was a common Greek name (see Achill. Tat. v.), and there may have been two of the name of Sosthenes at Corinth, and perhaps on this very account the Sosthenes in question is purposely distinguished as Sosthenes ὁ ἀρχισυνάγωγος.

It is next urged that the assumption that Sosthenes was a convert chimes in with the rest of the narrative, for the Jews, it is said, had come to accuse Paul, and failed; and it is natural that when they were denied justice by the Court they should take the law into their own hands, and beat the principal convert. But to this it may be replied that the beating of Sosthenes, if a Jew, by the Greeks, harmonizes equally with the context. For the Jews were hated by the Greeks; and when Gallio forcibly removed the Jews from the court, the Greeks (including, perhaps, many Christian converts whose zeal could not be checked), taking their cue from the the judge, would gladly follow it up by the chastisement of Sosthenes, the prime mover of the illegal attempt upon Paul. Besides, if the Jews beat any one, why not Paul, the great offender, and not Sosthenes, a simple convert?

There are, no doubt, difficulties on both sides, and we leave the decision to the reader's judgment.

[258] Others think that the vow was undertaken to obtain a prosperous voyage to Jerusalem. See Meyer, Apostg. 331. Others, that as Paul was intending a voyage to Jerusalem, and had it in view to soften the prejudices of the Jews there by performing the sacrifices of the Nazarite, he now laid the foundation for it by taking the vow of the Nazarite, not under the pressure of any actual danger, but from motives of policy. See Schrader, ii. 270. But this hypothesis must be rejected as unworthy of the Apostle.

[259] τοὺς γὰρ ἢ νόσῳ καταπονουμένους, ἢ τισιν ἄλλαις ἀνάγκαις, ἔθος εὔχεσθαι πρὸ τριάκοντα ἡμερῶν, ἧς ἀποδώσειν μέλλοιεν θυσίας, οἴνου τε ἀφέξεσθαι καὶ ξυρήσασθαι τὰς κόμας. Jos. Bell. ii. 15, 1.

separation are fulfilled, he shall be brought unto the door of the tabernacle of the congregation, and he shall offer his offering unto the Lord, one he lamb of the first year without blemish for a burnt offering, and one ewe lamb of the first year without blemish for a sin offering, and one ram without blemish for peace offerings; and the Nazarite shall shave the head of his separation at the door of the tabernacle of the congregation, and shall take the hair of the head of his separation, and put it in the fire which is under the sacrifice of the peace offerings."[260]

Such were the ceremonies where the vow was concluded within reach of the Temple. But frequently, as in the case of Berenice, the sister of the younger Agrippa,[261] the vow was taken in a foreign land, and then, during the continuance of the vow, which was usually a month,[262] the hair was allowed to grow, and at the expiration of the month, the head was not (as commonly supposed) *shaven*, which could only be done at Jerusalem after a purification of seven days, and after performance of the requisite sacrifices. But as the vow was at an end, as regarded the growth of the hair, the shears or scissors (not the razor) were applied, and the hair was sheared or polled, and thenceforth the hair was cut from time to time, in the ordinary course, until the Nazarite had an opportunity of going up to Jerusalem.[263] He then purified himself seven days in the Temple, and offered the accustomed sacrifices during that period,[264] and then finally shaved his head, and having burnt the hair (with what had been sheared at the termination of the thirty days) thus completed the vow. "If he polled his head in the country," says Lightfoot, "as Paul did at Cenchrea, he was to bring his hair and burn it under the cauldron where his peace-offering was boiling, which was in this place of the Temple that we are speaking of," (i.e., at the south-east angle of the court of the women in the Temple).[265] The shearing or cutting of the hair at the

---

[260] Numb. vi. 3, 5, 6, 13, 14, 18.

[261] She is described by Josephus as having come to Jerusalem to complete the vow taken in a foreign land: ἐπεδήμει δὲ ἐν Ἱεροσολύμοις εὐχὴν ἐπιτελοῦσα τῷ θεῷ. Bell. ii. 15, 1.

[262] Absolute si quis voverit Nazireatum, est xxx. dierum. Mischna de Nazir. iii. 148. Nazireatus absolute votus est xxx. dierum. Ib. 164.

[263] Nazireus nequit commorari extra terram Israelis propter immunditiem. R. Mosche. fil. Maimon. Mischna de Naziræis, vol. iii. p. 156.

[264] ἔθος δὲ ἦν τοὺς ἔχοντας εὐχὴν κείρεσθαι τὴν κεφαλὴν μετὰ τὸ ἁγνισθῆναι, καὶ οὕτως ἐπὶ ἑπτὰ ἡμέρας ποιεῖν προσφορὰν ὑπὲρ ἑαυτῶν. Theophylact. p. 157. Aspergit se aquâ tertiâ et septimâ die, tondeturque eâdem septimâ. Mischna de Nazir. vol. iii. p. 166. Where the vow had been made abroad, it was disputed amongst the learned Rabbis what should be the period of purification in Judea, before completing the vow by shaving the head. The school of Hillel said that the purification must be of the same length as the vow, and they cited the instance of Helen, Queen of Adiabene, who made a vow of seven years in her own country, and then on coming to Jerusalem purified herself for seven years, but just at the close became defiled, and so had to repeat the purification over again, making in all a period of twenty-one years. The school of Schammai, on the contrary, laid down that a purification of thirty days was sufficient, whatever the length of the vow. Mischna de Nazir. iii. 156. There was thus no rule universally acknowledged, and in the time of Paul a much shorter period seems to have been permitted, viz. seven days; for Paul on his return from the next circuit proceeded with four other Nazarites to complete the vow, and it is said, ὡς δὲ ἤμελλον αἱ ἑπτὰ ἡμέραι συντελεῖσθαι. Acts xxi. 27.

[265] Lightfoot, vol. i. p. 1092.

expiration of the vow in a foreign land (κειράμενος, Acts xviii. 18), and the *shaving* of the head on completion of the vow in the Temple at Jerusalem (ἵνα ξυρήσωνται, Acts xxi. 24), were two different things, though often confounded. The distinction between the words κειράμενος and ξυρησάμενος is borne out by the language of Paul himself, where he writes, "It is a shame for a woman to be *shorn* (κείρασθαι) or *shaven* (ξυρᾶσθαι)."[266]

It is surely unnecessary to say anything in defence of Paul's undertaking a vow, as there would be no unlawfulness in a Christian now subjecting himself to the same obligation; and it was then the received custom of the Jews, and Paul was an observer of the law of Moses, though he denied its efficacy in respect of salvation. Let it always be remembered that Paul, though a Christian, remained a Jew.[267]

---

[266] 1 Cor. xi. 6. So in Dion Cassius we read that when the Prefect of Egypt to curry favour sent to the Emperor Tiberius an unusually large amount of tribute procured by extortionate imposts, the Emperor returned the cutting rebuke, that he wished his sheep to be *shorn* (κείρεσθαι), and not to be *shaved* (ἀποξύρεσθαι). Dion, lvii. 11.

[267] Luke, just before narrating the indictment of Paul by the Jews before Gallio, mentions that Paul was settled at Corinth for "a year and six months." ἐκάθισέ τε ἐνιαυτὸν καὶ μῆνας ἓξ, διδάσκων ἐν αὐτοῖς τὸν λόγον τοῦ Θεοῦ. Γαλλίωνος δὲ ἀνθυπατεύοντος τῆς Ἀχαίας, κ.τ.λ. Acts xviii. 11. While all or most agree that the interval thus particularly mentioned by Luke commences from the *arrival* of Paul at Corinth, it is much disputed at what period it should terminate, viz. whether with the trial of Paul before Gallio, or with his final departure from Corinth. The difference is not great, as Paul remained only a month, or a little more, after the trial, and yet the question is not unimportant. Assuming, for instance, that the year and six months represent the whole sojourn of Paul at Corinth, the consequences are these: the arrival of Gallio must be placed about the 4th of June, A.D. 53, and if so the impeachment of Paul before Gallio would follow soon after, say within ten days, or about the 14th of June, A.D. 53, and the departure of Paul at the expiration of his vow (usually undertaken for a month) would be thirty days later, i.e. about the 14th of July, A.D. 53, and if we measure back a year and six months from this period, it will take us to the 14th of January, A.D. 52, as the time of Paul's departure from Athens, and arrival at Corinth. But as he sojourned about a month at Athens, his arrival there must then be placed about the middle of December, A.D. 51. But Paul appears to have come to Athens by ship, and if so we must assume that he sailed in December, when the seas were closed for general navigation.

It is much more probable, therefore, that the year and six months are meant by Luke to mark the duration of Paul's undisturbed ministry up to the arrival of Gallio, which immediately follows the mention of the year and six months, and that Luke, after relating the scene before Gallio, intends a further period, when he writes that Paul tarried (or more literally 'stayed-on,' προσμείνας, Acts xviii. 18, as in Josephus, Vit. 12, 44, '49, 58) a good many days. Indeed, the word 'stayed-on' imports an addition to the interval of a year and six months previously mentioned.

Luke in a similar manner marks the time of Paul's three-years sojourn at Ephesus by successive periods of three months, and then two years, and then another interval: ἐπὶ μῆνας τρεῖς (Acts xix. 8), ἐπὶ ἔτη δύο (ib. 10), and then ἐπέσχε χρόνον (ib. 22); and in the case of Ephesus (as of Corinth) does not in his own narrative mention the length of the whole sojourn which, as is gathered from the address of Paul to the Ephesian elders, was for three years. Acts xx. 31.

So again at Troas the words διετρίψαμεν ἡμέρας ἑπτά, ἐν δὲ τῇ μιᾷ τῶν σαββάτων (Acts xx. 6) probably mark not one period of seven days, but seven days and one day more, making together eight days. See p. 297.

As it is of great importance to the chronology of the New Testament that we should interpret rightly the notes of time employed by Luke, we shall present in a tabular form the three instances above referred to.

The Apostle tarried but little longer at Corinth, not that he fled before his enemies, but the church was now firmly established, and the presence of Paul could be dispensed with. The expression of Luke is that Paul tarried there yet "a good many days,"[268] which may mean one or two months,[269] and as we have placed the impeachment before Gallio soon after the 4th of June, A.D. 53, we should date St. Paul's final departure from the city about the middle of July, A.D. 53. The Feast of Tabernacles[270] of the Jews was approaching, and Paul was expressly commanded by revelation to keep the festival at Jerusalem.[271] Had he been free to choose his own course, he would probably have returned to Thessalonica. He had twice made the attempt, and had twice been hindered by Satan.[272] Even when he wrote the first Epistle to the Thessalonians, he still entertained a hope of revisiting them. "God Himself, even our Father, and our Lord Jesus Christ, *direct our way* unto you."[273] However, the counsels of Heaven were otherwise, and he was not to see their face until after an interval of several years.[274]

That the number of Corinthian converts was very considerable, we may collect from the Epistle to the Romans, in which, writing from Corinth, he says, "The *churches* of Christ salute you"[275]—a greeting, not from individuals, but from whole congregations! The light of the Gospel had also penetrated into the neighbouring

At Ephesus.			At Corinth.			At Troas.	
	Years.	Months.		Year.	Months.		Days.
1. ἐπὶ μῆνας τρεῖς . . Acts xix. 8.	0	3	1. ἐνιαυτὸν καὶ μῆνας τρεῖς . . . . . Acts xviii. 11.	1	6	1. ἡμέρας ἑπτὰ . . . . 2. ἐν τῇ μιᾷ τῶν σαββάτων Acts xx. 7.	7 1
2. ἐπὶ ἔτη δύο . . . Acts xix. 10.	2	0	2. ἡμέρας ἱκανὰς (say).	0	1	Whole sojourn . . .	8
3. ἐπέσχε χρόνον—further sojourn for an indefinite time . Acts xix. 22.	0	9	Whole sojourn .	1	7		
Whole sojourn was τριετίαν . . . . Acts xx. 31.	3	0					

[268] ἡμέρας ἱκανάς. Acts xviii. 18.

[269] Wieseler reckons this at one or two months. Chronol. Apost. p. 46.

[270] The feast which Paul attended could not, at all events, have been the Passover (which this year was the 22nd of March), for in that case, as the voyage from Corinth must have occupied about seven weeks, he must have started before the seas were open for navigation.

[271] Gal. ii. 2.

[272] 1 Thess. ii. 18. See ante, p. 281, note 179.

[273] 1 Thess. iii. 11.

[274] It may seem strange that Paul should start so early as about the middle of July to keep a feast at Jerusalem on the 16th of September. But judging of this voyage from Corinth by the next in A.D. 58, we shall not find the time excessive. In A.D. 58, just as he was about to sail (μέλλοντι ἀνάγεσθαι, Acts xx. 3) a plot against his life was discovered, and he was obliged to go round overland by Macedonia, reaching Philippi at the Feast of the Passover. Acts xx. 6. Philippi

[275] Rom. xvi. 16.

cities, as may be inferred from the salutations in the Epistles to the Corinthians, the First of which is addressed to their church, " with all that *in every place* call upon the name of Jesus Christ;" and the Second is addressed to the Corinthians, " with all the saints which are in *all Achaia.*" There certainly was a church at Cenchrea, as Phebe is called a deaconess of it.[276]

It may be remarked, for the information of the curious, that at Corinth we find the first mention of a church or public edifice for the celebration of divine worship. " Now in this that I declare unto you," he afterwards writes to them, " I praise you not,—that ye come together, not for the better, but for the worse. For, first of all, when ye come together *in the church*,[277] I hear that there be divisions among you, and I partly believe it. What, have ye not *houses* to eat and to drink in? or despise ye the *church of God*, and shame them that have not? What shall I say to you? shall I praise you in this? I praise you not."[278] " Let your women keep silence in the *churches*, for it is not permitted unto them to speak; but they are commanded to be under obedience, as also saith the law. And if they would learn anything, let them ask their husbands *at home*: for it is a shame for women to speak in the *church*."[279]

---

according to the Antonine Itinerary, was about four hundred and sixty-two miles from Corinth:

	Millia passuum
PHILIPPI to Amphipolis	xxxiii
Apollonia	xxx
Mellissurgis	xvii
Thessalonica	xx
Berœa	li
Dium	xvii
Larissa	xxiiii
Demetrias	xliiii
Opus	xiii
Chalcis	xlviii
Thebæ	xxiiii
Oropos	xxxvi
Athens	xliiii
CORINTH (not in Itin.)	lx
	ccclxii

As the ordinary rate of travelling was twenty-five miles a day (see ante, p. 135), Paul would thus consume about eighteen days from Corinth to Philippi. We must then add the three days of the Passover, up to and inclusive of the Sheaf-offering, from which the fifty days to Pentecost were counted, and these, added to the eighteen days, make twenty-one days. Then come the fifty days from the Sheaf-offering to the Feast of Pentecost, by which time he proposed to reach Jerusalem, making in all seventy days. Paul, therefore, had intended, with the view of keeping the Pentecost at Jerusalem in A.D. 58, to quit Corinth seventy days before the Feast. If we apply the same rule to the Feast of Tabernacles, which fell on the 16th of September, A.D. 53, Paul would set out upon his voyage from Corinth seventy days before that date, i.e., about the 8th of July.

[276] Rom. xvi. 1.

[277] ἐν τῇ ἐκκλησίᾳ. But Griesbach, Scholtz, Lachmann, Tischendorf, and Alford all read ἐν ἐκκλησίᾳ, and it is said there is no instance of ἐκκλησία being used in a local sense for a building. Alford therefore would translate it " in assembly," and so equivalent to the Apostle's expression, "when ye come together " ἐπὶ τὸ αὐτὸ, in 1 Cor. xi. 20. If no building be referred to, it might be rendered very literally " *at* church." But with all deference, we have an instance of the use of the word ἐκκλησία in the sense of a building in Eusebius, thus: ἔνθα τῶν ἐκκλησιῶν αἱ μὲν ἐξ ὕψους εἰς ἔδαφος τοῦτο τὸ δεύτερον μετὰ τὰς πρώτας καθῃροῦντο πολιορκίας, τὰς δ᾽ ἀπείκλειον οἱ κατὰ τόπους ἡγεμόνες. Vita Const. ii. 2. Liddell and Scott give ἐκκλησία as meaning in ecclesiastical writers *the church*: 1. The body; 2. The place (whence Fr. *église*). And the word '*église*' shows conclusively that ἐκκλησία must in early times have been used in the sense of an edifice.

[278] 1 Cor. xi. 17, 18, 22.

[279] 1 Cor. xiv. 34, 35.

[Chap. XII.] ST. PAUL AT CORINTH. [A.D. 53]

Paul now passed from Corinth to Cenchrea, the eastern port of Corinth, to embark for Syria, and as the month of his vow expired while he was at Cenchrea, he there

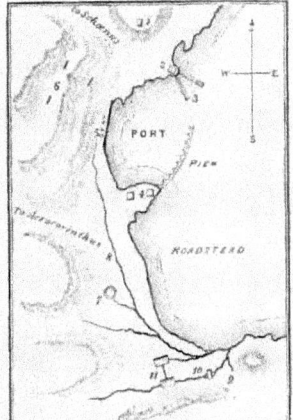

1. Temple of Diana which lay on the road from the Isthmus to Cenchrea, but the exact site is uncertain.
2. Site of the Temple of Venus at the northern end of the port.
3. Probable site of the bronze statue of Neptune holding a trident in one hand and a dolphin in the other.
4. Site of the Temples of Æsculapius and Isis at the southern extremity of the port.
5. Blocks of granite traceable for a length of one hundred paces, and forming anciently the quay of the port for the embarkation and debarkation of goods and passengers. Here Paul must have stepped on board for Ephesus.
6. Site of the city of Cenchrea, which spread itself from the port up the rising ground on the west. The foundations are still traceable over an extensive tract. The name of Cenchrea appears to be derived from the κέγχρος or millet, then as now grown in the vicinity. So Schœnus the next port was so called from its σχοῖνοι or rushes, and Cromnyon, near it, from the κρόμμυα or onions which abounded there.
7. A circular pool, and assuming this form from one of the numerous springs with which this low ground abounds.
8. A clear running stream flowing from north to south parallel to the sea, and discharging itself at the southern end of the bay.
9. A natural salt-water spring which issues from the rock several feet from the ground. This is the Bath of Helen described by Pausanias, i. 19.
10. A mill.
11. Reservoirs for feeding the mill.

Fig. 142.—*The port of Cenchrea. From E. Curtius.*

sheared his head.[250] The accompanying sacrifices prescribed to the Nazarite, as Paul was in a foreign country, were necessarily to be deferred until he reached Jerusalem.[251] At Cenchrea[252] he took ship for the East, and Sylvanus and Timothy, who had gone the

---

[250] Acts xviii. 18.

[251] ἐξέπλει εἰς τὴν Συρίαν, καὶ σὺν αὐτῷ Πρίσκιλλα καὶ Ἀκύλας, κειράμενος (not ξυρησάμενος), κ.τ.λ. Acts xviii. 18 (see ante, p. 296). It has been much disputed, and always will be, whether the word κειράμενος refers to Paul or Aquila. See Kuinoel, Acts xviii. 18. I have adopted the view that Paul is referred to, for he is the principal personage, and the vow itself was a natural consequence of the danger he had experienced from the attack of the Jews before Gallio. Besides, if Aquila took the vow, why did he not go up to Jerusalem to complete it, instead of stopping short at Ephesus? Indeed it does not appear that Aquila ever went to Jerusalem at all. Those who adopt the hypothesis that Aquila is meant, rely on the circumstance that Priscilla is placed before her husband Aquila, which they argue could only have been for the purpose of connecting Ἀκύλας with the word κειράμενος. But no reliance can be placed upon this, as Priscilla elsewhere (e.g. Rom. xvi. 3, and 2 Tim. iv. 19) is placed before Aquila. And the reason of this precedence may be, that Priscilla was the most active in the Christian cause, Aquila being constantly engaged in his trade. The only reason for Luke's mentioning Priscilla and Aquila at all, is the part they took in the further instruction of Apollos at Ephesus, where Paul left them (Acts xviii. 19, 26), and any notice of a vow taken by Aquila would be foreign to the subject and have no meaning. See contra, Wieseler, Chronol. Apost. 400, note.

[252] Cenchrea at this time was a thriving town situate at the south-western corner of the Saronic bay, in a little cove which formed the harbour. Here, as at Corinth, Venus was the presiding deity, and her temple was a conspicuous object to the mariner on the north of the port; and at the southern end of it were the temples of Æsculapius and Isis; and by the side of the stream which ran (and still runs) along the

round with the Apostle, the one from Antioch and the other from Lystra, were also in his company when he set sail. Aquila and Priscilla, who had joined themselves to the Apostle at Corinth, and were now his faithful coadjutors in the Gospel, were also

border of the sea from north to south before discharging its waters, was, according to Pausanias, a bronze statue of Neptune. Pausanias, Corinth. ii. 2.

A coin of Corinth represents on the obverse the head of Anton. Pius, and on the reverse the haven of Cenchrea as lying between two temples with the statue of Neptune above referred to between them, with the letters C. L. I. COR., i.e. "Colonia Laus Iulia Corinthus." The 'Iulia' refers, of course, to Caius Julius Cæsar, by whom the colony was planted.

Fig. 143.—*Coin of Corinth. From Killinger.*
Obv. Head of Antoninus with the legend Antoninus Aug. Pius. Rev. Port of Cenchrea with a temple at each end, and a statue of Neptune with a trident in the centre. Below are ships, and above are the letters C. L. I. COR., i.e. "Colonia Laus Iulia Corinthus."

In this coin the statue of Neptune is placed in the sea itself at the entrance of the port, and hence Leake (Morea, iii. 235) suggests that in Pausanias's description of the statue as standing ἐπὶ τῷ ῥεύματι τῷ διὰ τῆς θαλάσσης we should read ἐπὶ τῷ ἕρματι, 'upon the rock,' and others propose that the words should be ἐπὶ τῷ χώματι, 'upon the jetty.' But neither emendation is quite satisfactory, for Pausanias does not speak of the statue as standing ἐπὶ ἕρματι or ἐπὶ χώματι but ἐπὶ τῷ ῥεύματι τῷ διὰ τῆς θαλάσσης (not on a rock or a jetty, but upon the ῥεῦμα, whatever it was, which was διὰ τῆς θαλάσσης), i.e. on something altogether distinct from the statue itself. I would suggest another reading still, which involves no change, but only a transposition of letters, viz. ἐρύματι for ῥεύματι, and then the statue would be represented as standing 'upon the breakwater which runs out into the sea.' The remains show that the port had a breakwater both on the north and also on the south, and conjecturally the statue was at the end of the northern pier, for the order in which Pausa-

nias describes the objects (which he visited personally) is this: first, on the road from the Isthmus to Cenchrea, a temple of Diana, and then on reaching Cenchrea, a temple of Venus, which by implication was at the northern end of the port, and after that (μετὰ αὐτό) the statue, and then at the other or southern end of the port (κατὰ τὸ ἕτερον πέρας τοῦ λιμένος) were the temples of Æsculapius and Isis. Thus the statue is placed between the two extremes of the port as portrayed on the coin, and from the order observed by Pausanias, the probability is that it occupied the southern extremity of the northern pier. It forms no objection to this view that on the coin the statue is seen rising out of the sea itself, for the breakwaters which only rose a few feet above the sea-level are altogether omitted on the coin. This is evident from the fact that all round the port are depicted warehouses, and these would not be found on the breakwaters, but only on the mainland.

In 1851, when I was at Kalamaki, the northwestern corner of the Saronic bay, I inquired of the natives if they knew Cenchrea. After some confusion arising from the pronunciation of the word, they recognised the name, and described it as a creek, where there was a corn-mill and a stream of water flowing from the rock. I crossed in an open boat and as I approached the spot, the bay appeared to lie between two mountains confronting each other in the dusk like crouching lions. The elevation on the left was precipitous, and standing forward into the sea served as a barrier against the waves from the east. That on the right was approached from the sea by a gentle slope. The pine and olive grew luxuriantly in this direction, the brilliant green of the pine, and the grey foliage of the olive, showing a most striking contrast. The boat was run ashore (for the water was deep to the edge), and we landed on a beach of fine pebbles. Beyond the beach was a row of shrubs covered with red berries, and resembling the arbutus. Having passed this, we found ourselves in a triangular plot of ground shut in by the mountains, the sea forming the base of the triangle, and its apex ending in a valley which swept away to the left. A clear and swift stream flowed from north to south, parallel to the sea, as mentioned by

his companions for a part of the voyage. Titus not only started with Paul, but also went up with him to Jerusalem itself, as we learn from the Epistle to the Galatians, "and took Titus with me also."[243]

But who was Titus, now for the first time introduced upon the stage? It is difficult to give a satisfactory answer. That he was converted by Paul himself, we may infer from the Apostle's calling him "his own son after the common faith,"[244] and that, like Timothy, he was a young man, we may reasonably conjecture from several passages in the Epistle to Titus.[245] That he was a Greek is expressly stated.[246] He was certainly with Paul on his present voyage from Corinth to Jerusalem, and it seems that he was also a fellow-labourer with Paul during this the Apostle's first visit to Corinth, for in the Second Epistle to the Corinthians, and written before Paul returned to them again, we read, "Whether any do inquire of Titus, he is my partner and *fellow-helper concerning you*; or our brethren (Luke and Trophimus) be inquired of, they are the messengers of the churches, and the glory of Christ."[247] Observe, also, that while Paul here sets forth the claims of Titus on account of his ministry amongst the Corinthians, he recommends Luke and Trophimus (who clearly were not Corinthians) as the Apostles of other churches. There is a various reading in Acts xviii. 7, which is as ancient as Chrysostom, and, if genuine,[248] would show that Titus was a Corinthian, for instead of Paul's transferring himself to the house of one "named Justus," as in the received text, some copies have it the house of "Titus."

Pausanias (Corinth. ii. 2, 3): ἐπὶ τῷ ῥεύματι τῷ διὰ τῆς θαλάσσης—"on the stream alongside of the sea." Having crossed it we found about the middle of the area a circular pool resembling a bath, for the purposes of which it was admirably adapted by its size, and the depth and clearness of its waters. A stream was running rapidly from it, betokening the power of the spring by which it was fed. Beyond was another rivulet running towards the sea; and thinking it must come down the valley, I traced it for a little distance, but all the water was from the springs in the fairy ground we stood upon, and the channel was dry long before we reached the valley. We then turned to the left, and traversed the southern side, and here were two small millponds, or reservoirs, enclosed in stone walls, and connected together with springs in them, so abundant that while a stream flowed from them at one end to supply the mill below, the water poured from the other end into the rivulet which was finding its way to the sea by the side of the mill. At the south-eastern corner of the triangular plot, and near the sea, a stream leapt out of the rock at the height of several feet from the ground. The pool formed by this spring is Pausanias's "Bath of Helen" (Corinth. ii. 2, 3): Κεγχρεῶν δὲ ἀπαντικρὺ τὸ Ἑλένης ἐστὶ λουτρόν· ὕδωρ ἐς θάλασσαν ἐκ πέτρας ῥεῖ πολὺ καὶ ἁλμυρόν, ὕδατι ὅμοιον ἀρχομένῳ θερμαίνεσθαι. It had excavated a channel for itself, and ran into the millstream below the mill. All the waters discharged themselves into the sea at the north-eastern corner of the bay, and all were salt as the sea itself. There was no building in sight but the mill, and a small storehouse near it. I had not time to examine the ground to the north, where was the site of the ancient city of Cenchrea. The cove which I had examined was that of Galataki, which was the open port or roadstead of Cenchrea, as opposed to the close or proper port of Cenchrea which adjoined on the north.

[243] Gal. ii. 1.
[244] Tit. i. 4.
[245] Titus ii. 6, 7, 15. Compare 1 Tim. iv. 12.
[246] Gal. ii. 3.
[247] κοινωνὸς ἐμὸς καὶ ἐν ὑμᾶς συνεργός. 2 Cor. viii. 23.
[248] But the reading ὀνόματι Τίτου Ἰούστου is supposed to have arisen from a confusion of the words ονοματιωνιουστου in a MS. not pointed, and is rejected by the best critics. See Alford.

Whatever be the true reading, we are led to conclude that Titus was a Corinthian; and this is the reason why, a few years after, he was selected by the Apostle to manage the collection of the alms at Corinth. But to proceed.

Paul and his company on their voyage from Cenchrea touched at Ephesus. The ship, perhaps, was bound for that port, and there unloaded. While Paul waited for another vessel to take him on to Cæsarea, he availed himself of the interval to preach in the synagogue of the Jews. How different was their reception of him at this time to their rough usage of him at his next visit! They now requested him to prolong his stay. This the Apostle could not do, as a divine revelation had expressly summoned him to Jerusalem; but he made them a promise (which he shortly afterwards redeemed) of coming to them again. "He bade them farewell, saying, 'I *must* by all means keep *this* feast that cometh [the Tabernacles] in Jerusalem;[289] but I will return unto you again, if God will.'"[289] The fact that he "must" keep this feast at Jerusalem is explained to us by the notice of this journey in the Epistle to the Galatians, where the Apostle tells us that he went up by revelation;[291] and from the context it seems that the object of the divine communication was that, as Paul had now spread the Gospel over such an extended area, not only in Asia, but also in Europe, he should explain to the Hebrew church what was the Gospel which he preached amongst the Gentiles, in order that there might be no schism in the Church, and Titus went up with Paul, as representing the Gentile church.

Paul, Silas, Timothy, and Titus made the whole voyage from Ephesus to Judea; but Aquila and Priscilla, having no call to Jerusalem, remained at Ephesus, and continued there until the Apostle joined them again. Paul landed at Cæsarea, and thence (accompanied also by Barnabas, from whom he had separated at the commencement of the circuit,) went up to Jerusalem. Paul and Barnabas met each other by arrangement, but whether their rendezvous was at Cæsarea, or whether Paul took up Barnabas by the way at Cyprus, the native country of Barnabas, and where Barnabas had been making a circuit, it is in vain to conjecture. We know only what the Apostle himself tells us, "Then fourteen years after I went up again to Jerusalem, with Barnabas, and took Titus with me also."[292] It is even possible that Barnabas may have visited Corinth itself, before Paul's departure, and laboured there, and then made the whole voyage

---

[289] These words, "I must by all means keep this feast," &c., are omitted in some MSS., but the genuineness of the passage is defended on good grounds by Wieseler, Chron. Apost. 47. The subsequent words, ἀναβὰς καὶ ἀσπασάμενος τὴν ἐκκλησίαν, Acts xviii. 22, have evidently a reference to and therefore authenticate, the passage in dispute, since, but for the previous notice of the Apostle's object to keep the feast at Jerusalem, Luke would have said, ἀναβὰς εἰς Ἱεροσόλυμα, and not ἀναβὰς simply. It is impossible that ἀναβὰς, as some contend, can refer to the church at Cæsarea, for Paul is said to have gone *down* and not *up* to Cæsarea (κατελθὼν εἰς Καισάρειαν, Acts xviii. 22); and if Paul went up to Cæsarea, he could not be said (as he is said) to have gone *down* from Cæsarea to Antioch (κατέβη εἰς Ἀντιόχειαν, ib.), as Cæsarea was on the coast, and Antioch at a distance from the coast and higher up.

[290] Acts xviii. 21.

[291] Gal. ii. 2. See Fasti Sacri, p. 30, Nos. 1794–1796.

[292] Gal. ii. 1.

with Paul; for it is observable that the Apostle, in writing to the Corinthians before he visited them again, speaks of Barnabas as familiarly known to them, "or I only and Barnabas, have not we power to forbear working?"[293]

The presence of Paul and Barnabas at Jerusalem was connected with matters of high import. Previously to the call of Cornelius, the Gospel had been preached exclusively to the Jews. When upon that event the doors of the Christian Temple were thrown open to the world at large, the Apostles of Jerusalem were not withdrawn from their proper province of publishing the Gospel to the *Jews*, but other instruments were by divine appointment selected for the conversion of the *Gentiles*, and Paul and Barnabas, as we have seen, were specially ordained for that great work. Not that the Twelve at Jerusalem were forbidden to preach to the heathen, or that Paul and Barnabas were prohibited from addressing the Jews, but the Twelve made it their primary office to evangelize their own countrymen, and Paul and Barnabas the Gentiles. Paul and Barnabas had since pursued their career with eminent success, and numerous churches had been established in Asia, Macedonia, and Achaia. During the interval they had held but little communication with Jerusalem. They had never visited it in their Apostolic character, and only twice as Ambassadors of the church of Antioch. On the first occasion they had carried up alms to the Hebrew church; on the second they were joined with others to take the opinion of the Apostles on the circumcision of the Gentiles. The latter occasion was immediately after the conclusion of the first circuit, and before the results of their labours had become publicly known, and accordingly the letter of the Hebrew church was directed to the brethren of *Antioch, Syria, and Cilicia* only. Since that time, however, Paul and Barnabas had traversed a much wider field, and the important results of their labours were in every one's mouth, and were the fruitful subject of discussion amongst the Hebrews of Jerusalem. The Gospel which they taught, and which Paul calls distinctively "my Gospel," was this—that the cross of Christ was the only means of salvation; that the ceremonial dispensation of Moses had been the schoolmaster for a time, but the end having been answered, it had become a matter indifferent; that *Jews* might lawfully conform to it, except in the article that the Gentiles were unclean, which had been abrogated; but that the *Gentiles* ought not to comply with it, as then the inference would be drawn, that the Law was essential to salvation. The doctrines, however, of Paul and Barnabas had been misrepresented, and the rumour was rife at Jerusalem that they had simply taught the Jews of the dispersion to abandon the law of Moses. Another position taken up by Paul's adversaries was plausible in appearance, though unfounded in substance. The council of Jerusalem had decreed an abstinence from things offered to idols, and from blood, and from things strangled.[294] But Paul, in the churches planted by him in Galatia and Macedonia and Achaia, had dispensed with these ordinances, except under special circumstances, and hence the

---

[293] 1 Cor. ix. 6.   [294] Acts xv. 29.

malicious rumour that Paul was at variance with the Apostles of Jerusalem, and that while Paul preached the total abolition of the ceremonial law, the Apostles maintained, at least partially, its continued obligation. The truth of the matter appears to have been this. The decree of the council at Jerusalem had manifestly been of a temporary and local character—in short, a rule of convenience. It had not been addressed to all Christians, but to those of Antioch and Syria and Cilicia;[295] and the reason assigned was a local one—because the law of Moses was read in their synagogues every Sabbath-day;[296] or, in other words, because the mass of the converts in those parts consisted of Jews, whose consciences would be shocked by the open breach of these ceremonials. Paul himself had approved of this policy, and therefore, where the same principle applied, as in the churches immediately adjoining to Cilicia, and where the Jews were equally numerous, he had himself delivered to them the decrees of the council for their observance.[297] But as the ambit of the Christian pale enlarged itself, and churches were planted in Galatia and Macedonia and Achaia, where the Jews were few, and the Christian community was chiefly Gentile, Paul boldly declared that the decrees of the council were not binding on the converts *foro conscientiæ suæ*, but only *foro conscientiæ alienæ*, or, as he afterwards explained himself to the Corinthians respecting things offered to idols,[298] that there was no harm, *per se*, in eating any meat, whether coming from the sacrifice offered to idols or not; but that, if the act offended the conscience of any weak brother, then it was uncharitable and wrong to eat. Paul's conduct was perfectly justifiable, and in accordance with the spirit of the new religion, but it furnished a specious handle to the Apostle's enemies, who gave out that Paul's doctrine was not that of Peter, and that the Gospel preached by Paul was spurious and contrary to that sanctioned by the holy synod of Jerusalem. Barnabas, the colleague of Paul in the Apostleship of the Gentiles, had, we may be sure, concurred in the views of Paul; and it was under these circumstances that, in order to maintain the unity of the church, and insure the cordial co-operation of all the Apostles, Paul and Barnabas were sent by revelation to Jerusalem, that they might come to an understanding with the Hierarchy there as to the true faith. But Paul is careful to tell us that in seeking this interview he was not deferring to any authority of the Hebrew church over the Gentile churches, but that he went up to Jerusalem, as no doubt was Barnabas also, by express revelation.

Perfect harmony between Paul and Barnabas as the Apostles of the Gentiles, and James, the bishop or head of the Jerusalem church, and the leading Apostles, was the more called for at this particular juncture, inasmuch as now that so many Gentile churches had been planted, a design was entertained by certain Judaizers of Jerusalem to make the Gentile converts their own proselytes, and bring them into captivity to the law of Moses. The Twelve Apostles themselves, who were divinely illuminated, must

---

[295] Acts xv. 23.
[296] Acts xv. 21.
[297] Acts xvi. 4.
[298] 1 Cor. viii. 1, &c.

have known well enough that the Law had been superseded, but not so the disciples at Jerusalem in general. "Thou seest, brother," said James to Paul, a few years after, "how many thousands of Jews there are which believe, and they are *all zealous of the Law*."[299] They would not even eat with a Gentile, notwithstanding the injunction, "What God hath cleansed that call not thou common."[300] And a sect had risen up in the bosom of the Hebrew church who, notwithstanding the decrees of Jerusalem, still inculcated the doctrine that the Gentile converts must be circumcised. We shall see that not long after this they sent emissaries abroad to propagate the same principle, and it required the united vigilance of all the Apostles, whether Apostles of the Jews or Gentiles, to prevent the error from spreading.

We must now advert to what passed at Jerusalem between Paul and the Hebrew church at the Feast of Tabernacles (the 16th of September, A.D. 53), and fortunately the Apostle himself has left us a brief account of the matter. "I went up," he says, "by revelation, and communicated unto them that Gospel which I preach among the Gentiles, but privately to them of reputation, lest by any means I should run, or had run, in vain."[301] The mass of the Hebrew Christians, blinded by Jewish prejudices, could not yet bear the full light of the Gospel. When Paul afterwards wrote to them, he tells them, "For when for the time ye ought to be teachers, ye have need that one teach you again which be the first principles of the oracles of God, and are become such as have need of milk, and not of strong meat."[302] But the Apostles themselves, to whom alone Paul explained his Gospel, at once acknowledged that Paul was but preaching the truth; and particularly James the bishop, and Peter and John, the Apostles of the greatest weight, when they had heard Paul, and were informed of the wonderful works which he and Barnabas had been enabled to perform, gave them the right hand of fellowship, and it was agreed, that, as had been done before, Paul and Barnabas should prosecute their ministry amongst the Gentiles, and the other Apostles amongst the Jews. "But of those," says Paul, "who seemed to be somewhat,[303] whatsoever they were, it maketh no matter to me; God accepteth no man's person; for they who seemed to be somewhat conferred nothing on me, but contrariwise, when they saw that the Gospel of the uncircumcision was committed unto me, as the Gospel of the circumcision was unto Peter (for he that wrought effectually in Peter to the Apostleship of the circumcision, the same was mighty in me toward the Gentiles): when, I say, James, Cephas, and John, who seemed to be pillars, perceived the grace that was given unto me, they gave to me and Barnabas the right hands of fellowship, that we should go unto the heathen, and they unto the circumcision."[304] To this compact one additional article was proposed by the Apostles, which was at once acceded to by Paul and Barnabas, viz. that as the Jews of the

---

[299] Acts xxi. 20.
[300] Acts x. 15; xi. 9.
[301] Gal. ii. 2.
[302] Heb. v. 12.
[303] James, as bishop of Jerusalem, had precedence of all, but Peter and John were the two leading characters of the twelve Apostles. James the brother of John had been previously put to death. Acts xii. 2.
[304] Gal. ii. 6–9.

dispersion had been wont to send alms to Jerusalem for the relief of the poor, and as the disciples of Christ had been excommunicated, and were therefore excluded from further participation in these remittances, Paul and Barnabas should, in their next circuit among the Gentiles, make a collection for the Hebrew church and forward it to Jerusalem: "Only they would" (writes Paul to the Galatians) "that we should remember the poor, the same which I also have been forward to do."[305] Indeed, Paul's affections ever yearned towards his own countrymen, and he joyfully undertook so pleasing a task. A charitable act of this kind might also have the effect of somewhat mitigating the prejudices which the Hebrews entertained against him, from the rumour, grossly exaggerated, that he was poisoning the minds of the Jews of the dispersion against the observance of the law of Moses; and the Apostles, who were ever anxious for the safety of Paul, as the great pillar of the Gentile church, may, in suggesting the contribution, have had this object also in view, as well as the alleviation of Hebrew distress.

Such was the harmony amongst the Apostles. What was the conduct of the Judaizing party to whom we have alluded? No sooner was it known that Paul and Barnabas were at Jerusalem with Titus, a Gentile, than they insisted that Paul, in conformity with their erroneous views, should cause Titus to be circumcised. They might as well have attempted to shake the rock on which Jerusalem was built. No one more deferential than Paul to the prejudices of others in matters purely indifferent; no one more resolute in maintaining his principles in points material. "But neither Titus," writes the Apostle, "who was with me, being a Greek, was compelled to be circumcised; (and that because of false brethren unawares brought in, who came in privily to spy out our liberty which we have in Christ Jesus, that they might bring us into bondage;) to whom we gave place by subjection, no, *not for an hour*, that the truth of the Gospel might continue with you."[306] Timothy had some years before been circumcised by the direction of Paul himself, but Timothy was by birth *a Jew*, and it was by accident only that the rite had been previously omitted. Titus was *a Greek*, and circumcision in this case would have negatived the sufficiency of the Gospel, without the Law, for salvation. The attempt of the Judaizers was frustrated and the Gentiles were exempted from the yoke, which the Jews, neither of that nor of any preceding age, had been able to bear.

When the Feast of Tabernacles was over, and the week required for performing the sacrifices of the Nazarite had expired, and the other purposes for which Paul and Barnabas had been summoned to Jerusalem, were accomplished, they went down to Antioch.

It would seem, however, that Sylvanus, Paul's companion throughout the circuit, did not, when the meeting at Jerusalem broke up, accompany Paul to Antioch, but transferred his services thenceforth to Peter. The Apostle of the Gentiles was, by

---

[305] Gal. ii. 10.   [306] Gal. ii. 3–5.

the compact, to go westward, even, if possible, to Spain, the very extremity of Europe; and Peter eastward, to the headquarters of the Jews in Babylonia, and we find Sylvanus in the company of Peter, some time after this, in Babylon.[207] The inference is, that Sylvanus, as the more fitting instrument for the conversion of Jews than of Gentiles, now quitted Paul and attached himself to Peter.

---

[207] 1 Peter v. 12, 13.

CHAPTER XIII.

Paul rebukes Peter at Antioch—He commences his Third Circuit, and visits Galatia, Phrygia, and Ephesus—Writes the Epistle to the Galatians, and the First Epistle to the Corinthians—The Riot of Demetrius.

> How fallen is Antioch! Once the Eastern queen,
> Whose sceptre reached beyond Euphrates' flood,
> The Rome of Asia! Drear is now the scene
> On which her palaces and temples stood.
> Where too the champions of the holy rood
> The saints and martyrs, who the church upreared,
> Where Jew and Gentile met in brotherhood?
> Strange that where Paul and Peter preached the word
> No font should now be found, no Sabbath bell be heard!
>
> *Anon.*

PAUL had not been long at Antioch when a very painful circumstance occurred. Peter, the great Apostle of the circumcision, had shortly after the conclave held at Jerusalem, commenced another circuit for the confirmation of the churches already planted by him, and the conversion of such of his countrymen as were still without the pale. The Jews considered all Syria to the east of Mount Amanus as part of the Holy Land, and peculiarly appropriated to God's chosen people.[1] The church of Antioch had thus naturally sent relief during the famine to their Christian brethren at Jerusalem, and again had despatched their deputies to Jerusalem upon the subject of the mooted question of circumcision. Antioch, therefore, though the metropolis of the Gentile church, was, at the same time, not beyond the limits of the Jewish church. The Jewish converts of Antioch differed, at least in one respect, from their brethren of Jerusalem, viz. that the Antiochians, while they observed the law of Moses in general, yet, in obedience to the heavenly mandate, "not to call the Gentiles unclean," lived on terms of familiarity with them as members of the same church. There could be no disagreement between Paul and Peter upon this point, for to Peter himself the injunction not to call a Gentile unclean, had been given; and accordingly Peter, without scruple, conformed to the practice of the Antiochian

---

[1] Renan's St. Paul, p. 4, citing Mischna Schebiit vi. 1; Challah iv. 8; Tosiphta Challah, ch. 2; Talm. de Jer. Schebiit vi. 2; Talm. de Bab. Gittin 8 a; Targum de Jerus. Numbers xxxiv. 8. Jerome, Epist. ad Dardanum (Martianay, ii. 609). Cf. Neubauer, la Géographie du Talmud, p. 5 et seq.

Jews, and fraternised with the Gentiles. In a little time, however, there came down certain Jewish converts of the church of Jerusalem, where the Law was strictly observed, and then the unfortunate weakness that caused Peter thrice to deny his master, again betrayed itself. He was alarmed at the idea of being seen by Hebrews to eat with the Gentiles, and he withdrew himself from their company; and such was the force of example, that the Antiochian Jews dissembled likewise, and at last even Barnabas concurred in the hypocrisy. Now shone forth the strength of Paul's character. He stood alone, but his courage did not forsake him. As the Apostle of the Gentiles, and the champion of their religious liberty, he foresaw the consequences, and he grappled with the danger at once. He openly, in the face of the congregation, called the Apostle of the circumcision to account. "If thou," said he, "being a *Jew*, livest after the manner of the *Gentiles*, and not as do the *Jews*, why compellest thou the *Gentiles* to live as do the *Jews*?"[2] To understand the force of these words, it must be remembered that a Judaizing sect had lately, as we have seen, sprung up at Jerusalem, and the Christians of that party had even endeavoured to procure the circumcision of Titus, but had been foiled in the attempt, and the Hebrew Jews who now visited Antioch brought the same bigoted opinions along with them. Previously to their arrival, Peter, though a *Jew* himself, had conversed freely with the *Gentiles*; but his countrymen from Jerusalem now so wrought upon him by their representations, that he separated himself from the Gentiles, and the Judaizers, pushing their advantage, sought (notwithstanding the decree of Jerusalem many years before) to bring over the Gentiles to the observance of the Jewish law. Paul, therefore, at this critical moment, boldly came forward with the cutting rebuke to Peter, "If thou, who art a *Jew*, didst before, as it were, go over to the *Gentiles* by living with them, why now dost thou countenance the doctrine of the Judaizers, that the *Gentiles* should come over to the *Jews*?"

This reproof of Peter, in the face of the Antiochian church, is one of the most remarkable incidents in the New Testament. Both Paul and Peter were inspired, and yet one of them was in error. But the question at issue, it will be observed, was one, not of *doctrine*, but of *conduct*. Both were agreed as to the article of faith, viz. that henceforth the Jew was not bound by the Law of Moses; but what called the vehement spirit of Paul into action was the duplicity of Peter, in at one time associating with the Gentiles, and at another avoiding the contamination of their company. Inspiration (if the author's view be correct) did not paralyse a person's free agency, or exempt him from a mistake of judgment; otherwise, either Peter or Paul was not inspired; for if Peter's demeanour towards the Gentiles was right, Paul was in fault in passing censure upon it. No doubt Peter was the one to be blamed; and we may infer from the narrative that he at once confessed his indiscretion, and corrected it. We may also add that the harmony between the two Apostles was not

[2] Gal. ii. 14.

long—if at all—disturbed, for Peter afterwards took occasion to call his fellow Apostle "*our beloved brother Paul.*"[3]

While Paul was thus actively engaged at Antioch, he did not forget his promise of preaching the Gospel at Ephesus. At the beginning of A.D. 54[4] (the Church of Antioch being in a highly flourishing state, and not requiring his personal superintendence), he commenced his third circuit, with the intention of reaching Ephesus, the capital of Asia, by way of Galatia and Phrygia.[5] He took Titus with him, but by whom else he was accompanied we have no data upon which even to form a conjecture, unless we may infer that Gaius and Aristarchus were with him, from their being called three years after at Ephesus his fellow-travellers.[6]

Paul and Titus proceeded from Antioch, through Cilicia direct to Galatia. This is implied by the language of Luke. In his *second* circuit Paul, it is said, passed from Pisidia "through *Phrygia* and the region of *Galatia;*"[7] but now, in the *third* circuit, Luke varies the expression, and writes that Paul "went over the country of *Galatia* and *Phrygia,* strengthening all the disciples,"[8] that is, he traversed Galatia before he entered Phrygia. Paul did not at this time visit the churches of Lystra, Derbe, Iconium, and Antioch of Pisidia, as they had already thrice enjoyed the personal presence of the Apostle on previous occasions, and he was now pressed for time, and anxious to make his way expeditiously to Ephesus. He therefore (we may suppose) took the direct route from Antioch of Syria to Tarsus, a distance of 141

---

[3] 2 Pet. ii. 15.
[4] See Fasti Sacri, p. 263, No. 1815.
[5] The direct route from Antioch to Ephesus would occupy, it is estimated, about thirty days. Wiesel, Chron. Apost. 51. But as Paul by the way strengthened the disciples in Galatia and Phrygia, we must allow about three months. He left Ephesus at the end of May, A.D. 57 (1 Cor. xvi. 8), after a sojourn of three years (Acts xx. 31), so that he arrived at the end of May, A.D. 54, and must have started from Antioch about three months before, or at the end of February. Now his stay at Antioch is described by Luke as some time: ποιήσας χρόνον τινά. Acts xviii. 23. What is the force of this expression? The Feast of Tabernacles, which Paul had attended at Jerusalem in A.D. 53, began on the 16th of September, and ended 23rd September. The journey from Jerusalem to Antioch would commonly occupy about a fortnight (Anger, p. 20) but as Paul would probably pass some days with the several churches on the road, we should assign about a month for his passage from Jerusalem to Antioch, which would bring us to the latter part of October. From this time to the close of February would be four months, which, if we are right, must be the period indicated by Luke's expression of χρόνον τινά. This, in fact, is just about the interval which, as appears from other texts, is commonly meant by χρόνον τινά. Thus, in the first Epistle to the Corinthians, Paul holds out the expectation that he would "*pass the winter*" with them (1 Cor. xvi. 6), and then adds, "I will not now see you by the way, but I trust to tarry a while (χρόνον τινά) with you. Ib. v. 7. Again, Paul, some time before the Passover, A.D. 57, sent Timothy and Erastus to Macedonia (compare Acts xix. 22, 1 Cor. xvi. 10, v. 7), and remained at Ephesus himself until Pentecost, or seven weeks after the Passover, and if Timothy and Erastus set out five weeks before the Passover, the interval from their departure to that of Paul would be about three months, which is described by Luke under the terms αὐτὸς ἐπέσχε χρόνον. Acts xix. 22. See Anger, p. 60. Thus the expression, χρόνον τινά implies generally some three or four months, and Paul therefore sojourned at Antioch, the capital of Syria, during the winter A.D. 53–54.
[6] συνεκδήμους. Acts xix. 29. See note [15], p. 312.
[7] Acts xvi. 6.
[8] Acts xviii. 23.

miles,[a] and thence through the celebrated Cilician Gates (fig. 144) by way of Mazaca, or Cæsarea of Cappadocia, to *Tavium*, the nearest capital of Galatia, and which according to the Peutinger Table, lay at a distance of 271 miles from Tarsus, viz. first, 191 miles to Cæsarea, and then 80 miles from Cæsarea to Tavium. A journey of this length, at the rate of twenty-five miles a day,[10] would occupy about eleven days, without allowing any rest for the sabbath, or thirteen days if we allow two days rest for the sabbaths. From Tavium Paul would revisit, in succession, the churches before planted by him at Ancyra and Pessinus. By his converts in Galatia the Apostle was

Fig. 144.—*The Cilician Gates, the pass over Mount Taurus from Cilicia into Cappadocia.* From Carne's *Syria*.

somewhat less rapturously received than on his former visit. Then the faith of the Gentiles, being for the first time planted, was pure and unadulterated. But during his lengthened absence, the Jews interspersed amongst the Galatian converts had, as in other places, sown the seeds of discord on the subject of the Jewish law. Paul was now called upon to check the spreading leaven, and he rebuked them sharply. In the letter which he afterwards wrote to them, he recalls to their recollection his plainness of speech, while he was yet amongst them; for alluding to the hatred, variance, emulations, wrath, strife, seditions, and heresies which were again rife in Galatia, he adds, " Of the which I tell you before, as *I also told you in time past*, that they which do such things shall not inherit the Kingdom of God."[11] The Apostle's labours on this

---

[a] Itin. Hieros.
[10] See note ante, p. 135.

[11] Gal. v. 21. Paul by this reprimand on his second visit lost ground in their affections, and

his second visit, were attended with success, and before he left Galatia, the church was again at unity with itself—an orthodox member of the Christian community; so at least we should infer, from the language which he afterwards addressed to them, " It is good to be zealously affected *always* in a good thing, and not only *when I am present with you;*"[12] and, again, " Ye *were running well*; who hath hindered you that you should not obey the truth."[13] The Judaizing missionaries from Jerusalem, who propagated so much mischief in Christendom, had not at the time of Paul's arrival in Galatia yet made their appearance in that province; but the disorders which the Apostle corrected were those only which the Jews of Galatia itself had mischievously started.

When Paul last parted from the Apostles at Jerusalem, he had undertaken, as we have seen, to raise a contribution among the Gentile churches for the poor brethren of Judea, and he now redeemed his pledge in Galatia. Luke has not expressly mentioned the fact, but it appears incidentally from the Epistles. We may gather from a passage in the first Epistle to the Corinthians, that Paul, before setting out from Antioch, had despatched a messenger to Galatia to announce his intention, and bid them make preparation. " Now concerning the collection for the saints," he writes to the Corinthians, " *as I gave order to the churches of Galatia*, even so do ye. Upon the first day of the week let every one of you lay by him in store, as God hath prospered him, that there be *no gatherings when I come;* and when I come, whomsoever ye shall accredit by your letters, them will I send to carry your liberality unto Jerusalem; and if it be meet that I go also, they shall go with me.'[14] The alternative, however, offered to the Corinthians either of despatching the bounty by the hands of trusty messengers, or of the Apostle taking it himself, could not apply to the Galatians, as Paul was under a promise to proceed to Ephesus. It is likely, therefore, that the contribution from Galatia was carried to Jerusalem by some special envoys.[15] It seems not to have been mixed up with the collection afterwards made in Macedonia and Achaia, for in writing to the Galatians he speaks of their alms as complete, " Only they would that we should remember the poor, the same which I also *have been forward to do,*"[16] whereas, at the date of the first Epistle to the Corinthians, the contribution in Macedonia and Achaia was only in progress. Had the Galatian liberality been simultaneous with that of the Macedonian and Achaian churches, the Apostle could scarcely have omitted to refer to it in the following passage of the Epistle

---

he afterwards alludes to it in the passage— " Am I therefore become your enemy because I tell you the truth?" Gal. iv. 16.

[12] Gal. iv. 18.
[13] Gal. v. 7.
[14] 1 Cor. xvi. 1-4.
[15] It is singular that Luke, who was chosen by the Macedonian churches *to carry their collection to Jerusalem*, should be designated by Paul as his συνέκδημος (2 Cor. viii. 19), and that Gaius and Aristarchus are called by Luke, in the riot of Demetrius, the συνέκδημοι of Paul, Acts xix. 29. It is not improbable that Gaius and Aristarchus may have been the persons chosen by the Galatian churches to carry their contribution to Jerusalem.
[16] Gal. ii. 10.

to the Romans: "But now I go unto Jerusalem to minister unto the saints; for it hath pleased them of *Macedonia and Achaia* to make a certain contribution for the poor saints which are at Jerusalem."[17] Not a word here of Galatia!

Paul having "strengthened all the disciples"[18] in Galatia, advanced into Phrygia, and here, too (though we have no information), a similar collection for the poor may have been made, and forwarded to Jerusalem. St. Luke mentions that Paul went through Galatia and Phrygia "in order,"[19] from which we may infer that Paul visited successively the churches he had planted in those countries about three years before. Luke adds, that Paul, before arriving at Ephesus, passed through the *upper coasts*.[20] As Paul was making all haste to Ephesus in fulfilment of his promise, it cannot be supposed that he would break new ground. All that he did on this circuit was to confirm the disciples already made in Galatia and Phrygia, and then in fulfilment of the pledge he had given the year before, he made his way to Ephesus. He therefore passed with all the haste he could through the churches planted by him on his former circuit in Galatia and Phrygia, and then took the direct route to the capital of Proconsular Asia.

We shall here give some account of this province. It extended along the coast from Telmessus, the most northerly town of Lycia, to the River Rhyndacus, which separated it from Bithynia,[21] and included the Greek settlements of Doris, Æolis, and Ionia, and also Caria, Lydia, Phrygia, Mysia, and Troas; but not Lycia, Pamphylia, Lycaonia, Galatia, or Bithynia. The province was governed by a Roman Proconsul, chosen by lot from men of consular dignity, namely, those who had passed the chair of the consulship. In the distribution of the provinces made by Augustus between himself and the people, B.C. 27,[22] as there were two Consuls and ten Prætors, the Emperor allotted to the people two Consular provinces and ten Prætorian provinces. Asia and Libya were the two consular provinces, and the Prefects appointed to these were always selected from men of consular dignity, and were attended, like consuls, by *twelve* lictors, with the fasces. The Prefects of the ten Prætorian provinces might either be of consular or only prætorian rank; and if the former, they too had twelve lictors, but if the latter, they had only *six* lictors. The other provinces of the empire were retained by Augustus himself, and he appointed to them Prefects, called Proprætors, who

---

[17] Rom. xv. 25, 26.
[18] Acts xviii. 23.
[19] καθεξῆς, Acts xviii. 23.
[20] τὰ ἀνωτερικὰ μέρη, Acts xix. 1. The sea being necessarily at a lower level than the land, the Greeks considered any advance from the shore into the interior as an ascent. Thus the expedition of Cyrus into Persia is called by Xenophon the 'Ανάβασις. So Severus, the provincial governor of Asia, is described by Aristides, as Paul is by Luke, as coming from the *upper parts* to Ephesus: Σεβῆρος μὲν ἐκ τῶν ἄνωθεν χωρίων εἰς τὴν Ἔφεσον κατῄει. Arist. Ἱερῶν λόγος α΄, p. 339, ed. Jebb. Luke therefore means by ἀνωτερικὰ μέρη the upland or back country, i.e. Phrygia and Galatia, which Paul, according to the narrative, had just traversed.

[21] A Telmesso Asiaticum mare et quæ proprie vocatur Asia. Plin. N. H. v. 28. Rhyndacus, ante Lycus vocatus. . . . Asiam Bithyniamque disterminans. Plin. N. H. v. 40.

[22] See Fasti Sacri, p. 79, No. 666.

might be of any rank, and were invariably preceded by six lictors.[23] Thus, the Proconsul of Asia was one who had been Consul at Rome, and still displayed all the ensigns of the office, being arrayed in purple, and attended by twelve lictors, with the *fasces*.[24] During the year (for the appointment was usually, though not invariably, annual) the Proconsul of Asia exercised supreme power in all matters, whether military, civil, or religious, over the provincials; but the jealousy of the Emperor did not permit one who was the delegate of the senate to take the life of a Roman soldier, and therefore, he was regarded as a civil magistrate, and did not wear a military uniform, or carry a sword. The officers under him were a Quæstor (ταμίας or ταμιεύων), and three Assessors (πάρεδροι) or Legates (πρεσβευταί); and the Emperor, besides, appointed his own Procurator (ἐπίτροπος). The Quæstor collected the *public* revenue as opposed to the *imperial* revenue (though, in fact, both the Ærarium and the Fiscus were at the disposal of the Emperor), and assisted the Proconsul in his judicial functions. The three Legates had the command of the military, and were nominated from men of consular dignity with the sanction of the Emperor.[25] The Procurator collected the *imperial* revenue and regulated the financial affairs of the whole province.[26] The Procurator had originally no civil or military jurisdiction.[27] But recently, in A.D. 53,[28] the powers of the Procurator had been enlarged, and he now exercised supreme judicial authority, and could issue edicts that were binding as law.[29]

Subject to this despotic dominion of the Proconsul, qualified by the power of the Procurator, the province governed itself. Matters of general interest were debated in Congress (συνέδριον), a council composed of representatives from the different states of which Asia consisted. Subordinate to this collective legislature, were the separate governments of the cities which returned members to Congress. Each town of importance was a kind of municipal corporation. There was a council

of influential citizens (βουλή) and an assembly of the people (ἐκκλησία).[30] In Ephesus, the council, though latterly called βουλή, had been anciently known as the γερουσία, or court of aldermen, and is said to have been first instituted by Lysimachus, the general of Alexander.[31] The lower house or assembly usually met in the theatre,[32] and probably three times every month upon stated days.[33] This ἐκκλησία is alluded to by the recorder or town-clerk of Ephesus in the following passage:—
"If ye enquire any thing concerning other matters, it shall be determined in the assembly legally convoked."[34]

The Recorder was so called from his having the custody of the public records. He was, in fact, during the year he was in office, the representative of the civil power, and was the President or Speaker both of the senate and the assembly.[35] This will account for the tone of authority which was assumed by him on the

---

[30] That the cities in Asia thus governed themselves, see the several decrees, Jos. Ant. xiv. 10. Cicero thus traduces the character of the popular assemblies of Asia: Quum in theatro imperiti homines rerum omnium rudes ignarique consederant, tum bella inutilia suscipiebant, tum optime meritos cives e civitate ejiciebant. Quod si haec Athenis tum, quum illae, non solum in Graeciâ, sed prope cunctis gentibus enitebant, accidere sunt solita, quam moderationem putatis in Phrygiâ, in Mysiâ concionum fuisse.... Mementote igitur quum audietis psephismata, non audire vos testimonia—audire temeritatem vulgi, audire vocem levissimi cujusque, audire strepitum imperitorum, audire concionem concitatam levissimae nationis. Cic. pro Flac. vii. and viii. The βουλή and δῆμος of Ephesus, in particular, are mentioned in their decree, Jos. Ant. xiv. 10, 25; and in the edicts addressed to them, Jos. Ant. xvi. 6, 4, and 7; xiv. 10, 12. Philostratus thus speaks of the Senate: Σεγκλήτου γὰρ βουλῆς ἀξιοῦνται πάντες ἐπ' εὐδοξίᾳ θαυμαζόμενοι καὶ ἐπεμψίᾳ χρημάτων. Phil. Vit. Sophist. ii. 23. The Assembly of the people at Ephesus is thus alluded to by Appian: καὶ συνελθεῖν οἱ τοὺς Ἐφεσίους ἐς ἐκκλησίαν ἐκήρυττεν. Appian, Mithrid. xlviii. Augustus, on defeating Antony, deprived many cities of their popular assembly: τὰς μὲν πόλεις χρημάτων τε ἐσήμιξε καὶ τῆς λοιπῆς ἐς τοὺς πολίτας σφῶν ἐν ταῖς ἐκκλησίαις ἐξουσίας παραιρέσει μετῆλθε, Dion Cass. li. 2; but this was not the case with Ephesus, which was highly favoured by him. Dion Cass. li. 20. There is also an ancient inscription which illustrates the constitution of Ephesus in a most remarkable manner. It has been edited by various persons, but the most correct copy is that perhaps which is given by Boeckh, Corpus Inscrip. No. 2966, and is as follows: Σωθεῖσαν Σεβαστὴν γυναῖκα Αὐτοκράτορος Καίσαρος θεοῦ Τραϊανοῦ Παρθικοῦ υἱοῦ θεοῦ Νέρωνος υἱοῦ Τραϊανοῦ Ἁδριανοῦ Σεβαστοῦ ἡ φιλοσέβαστος Ἐφεσίων Βουλή, καὶ ὁ νεωκόρος Δῆμος καθιέρωσαν, ἐπὶ Ἀνθυπάτου Πεδουκαίου Πρεισκείνου, ψηφισαμένου Τιβ. Κλ. Ἰταλικοῦ τοῦ Γραμματέως τοῦ Δήμου, ἐργεπιστατήσαντος Τιβ. Κλ. Πεισωνείνου. Here we have mention made of the Senate and the People, and the people's Recorder, and all subject to the Proconsul, who is again subject to the Emperor.

[31] ἦν δὲ γερουσία καταγραφομένη. τούτοις δὲ συνῄεσαν οἱ ἐπίκλητοι καλούμενοι, καὶ διῷκουν πάντα. Strabo, xiv. 1 (p. 174, Tauchnitz).

[32] At least the ἐκκλησία at Antioch met in the theatre. τοῦ δήμου τῶν Ἀντιοχέων ἐκκλησιάζοντος εἰς θέατρον παρελθών. Jos. Bell. vii. 3, 3. Antiochiensium theatrum ingressus, ubi illis consultare mos est. Tac. Hist. ii. 80. And so, very frequently, at Athens. Veniebat autem in theatrum, quum ibi concilium populi haberetur. Corn. Nep. Timol. iv. 2. And see the passage from Cicero, cited above, note [30]; and Appian, Mithrid. xlvii.; Plut. Demetr. 34.

[33] It was so at Athens, and, Ephesus being a colony from that city, the Athenian constitution appears in a great measure to have been adopted. Thus we have the βουλή, and ἐκκλησία, and γραμματεὺς and πρύτανις. An Ephesian decree, recorded by Josephus, runs in this form: Ψήφισμα Ἐφεσίων. Ἐπὶ πρυτανέως Μηνοφίλου, μηνὸς Ἀρτεμισίου τῇ προτέρᾳ ἔδοξε τῷ δήμῳ... Ἐπεὶ, &c. δέδοκται τῇ βουλῇ καὶ τῷ δήμῳ, &c. Jos. Ant. xix. 10, 25.

[34] ἐν τῇ ἐννόμῳ ἐκκλησίᾳ. Acts xix. 39.

[35] See the description of the γραμματεὺς in Julius Pollux, lib. viii.

riot of Demetrius. The recorder had the honour of being the Ἐπώνυμος, that is, the year at Ephesus was distinguished by his name, as it was at Rome by that of the consuls. Thus we have coins of Ephesus with such inscriptions as the following:— ΕΠΙ ΠΑΙΤΟΥ ΓΡΑΜΜΑΤΕΩΣ ΑΡΤΕΜΙΣ ΕΦΕΣΙΩΝ. "Under Pætus, Recorder. Diana of the Ephesians." ΕΦΕΣΙΩΝ ΑΡΧΙΕΡΕΥΣ ΓΡΑΜΜΑΤΕΥΣ ΓΛΑΥΚΩΝ ΕΥΘΥΚΡΑΤΟΥΣ. "Glaucon, the son of Euthycrates, High Priest and Recorder of the Ephesians," &c.[36]

Justice was administered in Asia in a manner so similar to our own, that, after all the boasted enlightenment of modern times, one is ready to exclaim, "There is nothing new under the sun." The province was divided into shires,[37] and in each shire was an assize town, at which the assizes were annually held, and thither, during the session, the inhabitants of the county went up for the adjudication of their

Fig. 145.—*Coin of Ephesus. From the British Museum.*
Obv. Heads of Augustus and Livia.—Rev. A stag, the emblem of Ephesus, with the legend Γραμματευς Αριστιων Μηνοφαντος. Εφε. (Aristion Menophantus, Recorder of the Ephesians).

various pleas. The proconsul every year made a circuit to each assize town in succession, and when he opened the court he was said ἀγοραίους ἡμέρας ἄγειν, or *forum agere*, or *conventum agere*. He either sat in person, with the assistance of a jury, or nominated judges to act as his deputies. Ephesus was of course a principal assize town, and not only the immediate neighbourhood, but also remote districts were under the necessity of travelling up to the capital for the trial of their causes.[38] The recorder of Ephesus makes the following allusion to these assizes held at stated periods:—"If Demetrius, and the craftsmen which are with him, have a matter against any man, the law is open, and there are deputies;" but which should be more literally translated, "assizes are held, and there are proconsuls."[39]

The constitution of the Pagan *Hierarchy* in the Province of Asia, bore not a little resemblance to the Levitical Priesthood. Thus, in each metropolitan city were the priests of the different gods and goddesses, and over them a college of chief priests, in whom was vested the general superintendence of the religious worship, and from

---

[36] And so Εφεσος Κυζικος επι Παιτου Γραμματεως ὁμονοια. Van Dale, Dissert. v. p. 425; and see Eckhel, vol. ii. pp. 514, 519.

[37] Διοικήσεις. Strabo, xiii. 4 (p. 156, Tauchnitz).

[38] Ephesum vero, alterum lumen Asiæ, remotiores conveniunt Cæsarienses, Metropolitæ, Cibiani inferiores et superiores, Mysomacedones, Mastaurenses, Briulitæ, Hypæpeni, Dioshieritæ.

Plin. N. H. v. 31.

[39] Ἀγοραῖοι ἄγονται, καὶ ἀνθύπατοί εἰσιν. Acts xix. 38. So in Strabo, τὰς ἀγοραίους (omitting ἡμέρας) ποιοῦνται (the Romans) καὶ τὰς δικαιοδοσίας. Strabo, xiii. 4 (p. 156, Tauchnitz). Why Proconsuls in the plural should be spoken of, will be explained presently.

the college of chief priests, and occasionally from the priests, was annually elected the High Priest (ὁ ἀρχιερεύς), or, to adopt the corresponding title amongst the Romans, the Pontifex Maximus—a dignity not disdained by the Emperors themselves. The High Priest, as well as the Recorder, was sometimes an ἐπώνυμος, that is, the year was distinguished by his name. Thus we read on Ephesian coins, ΑΡΧΙΕΡΕΥΣ ΑΣΚΛΗΠΙΟΣ ΤΡΥΦΩΝ ΕΦΕ., "Asclepius Tryphon, High Priest of the Ephesians;" and, ΑΡΧ. ΚΟΤΣΙΝΙΟΣ Τ. Δ. ΕΦ., "Cusinius, for the fourth time High Priest of the Ephesians;"[40] and in the martyrdom of Polycarp, at Smyrna, the narrative closes with the remarkable notice that the event occurred "in the *High Priesthood* of Philip of Tralles, and the proconsulship of Stratius Quadratus, and in the reign of Jesus Christ for ever, to whom be glory, honour, might, and everlasting dominion from generation to generation. Amen."[41] We may

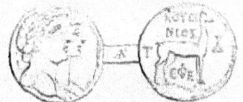

Fig. 116.—*Coin of Ephesus. From J. Y. Akerman.*

Obv. Heads of Perseus and Andrada.—Rev. A stag with the legend Κουσινιος τ. δ. Εφε. (Cusinius, for the fourth time of the Ephesians). Cusinius was both High Priest for the fourth time and Recorder for the fourth time. See Eckhel, ii. 51.

remark, by the way, that amongst the Greeks and Romans, the civil magistracies and the priesthood were often united in the same person. Thus, on the coin before referred to, we read that Glaucon was Recorder as well as High Priest, and at Rome the consul was often Pontifex Maximus.

There was in the Province of Asia another board of Hierarchs, quite distinct from and independent of the ordinary Priesthood, viz. the *Asiarchs*,[42] or, as the word is translated in the authorized version, "The Chief of Asia." The office arose thus: the festivals of the heathen gods were accompanied with games, which every year increased in splendour, and were at last, and particularly after the introduction of beast fights by the Romans, of a very costly description. The public funds provided for the purpose, partly from the temple lands, and partly, perhaps, from a kind of rate levied on the inhabitants, were wholly insufficient, and to meet the expense, distinguished honours were conferred on those who would undertake to exhibit them. The Asiarchs then were like the ædiles at Rome, the benefactors who, either wholly or principally, defrayed the charges of the public amusements. They were the presidents of the games, and as the pastime was part of the idol worship, they were invested, at least for the year, with the character of priests. From the nature of the

---

[40] See Van Dale, Dissert. iii. p. 233.

[41] ἐπὶ ἀρχιερέως Φιλίππου Τραλλιανοῦ, Ἀνθυπατεύοντος Στρατίου Κοδράτου, Βασιλεύοντος δὲ εἰς τοὺς αἰῶνας Ἰησοῦ Χριστοῦ, ᾧ ἡ δόξα, τιμή, μεγαλοσύνη, θρόνος αἰώνιος, ἀπὸ γενεᾶς εἰς γενεάν. Ἀμήν.

[42] On the subject of the Asiarchs, see particularly Kuinoel, Acts xix. 31.

office they were taken from the wealthiest men of Asia. Strabo mentions as a proof of the opulence of Tralles, that some of the Asiarchs were always selected from that city;[43] and such was the outlay involved in the appointment, that if a person had five children he might claim exemption, and no one was compelled to discharge the office twice.[44] In return for these onerous duties they had a patent of precedence, and were styled the Primates of the Province.[45] The Asiarchs were annually elected,[46] and they are said to have been ten in number,[47] and to these, allusion is perhaps made on the coins of Asia, under the description of ΟΙ ΔΕΚΑ ΠΡΩΤΕΤΟΝΤΕΣ, the ten primates.[48] As to the manner in which they were appointed, there is a difference of opinion. We know, however, what was the proceeding in the case of the Lyciarch (for not only were there Asiarchs in Asia, but there were corresponding officers in the other provinces, as Lyciarchs, Syriarchs, Bithyniarchs, Cappadociarchs, Ciliciarchs, Cypriarchs, Phœniciarchs, Helladarchs, &c.).[49] In Lycia then, which,

Fig. 147.—*Coin of Laodicea. From the British Museum.*
Inscribed Επι Αιλ. Πιγρητος Ασιαρ. Λαοδικεων Νεωκορων (under Ælius Pigres Asiarch of the Laodiceans Neocori). As the Laodiceans are here described as Neocori, the medal was struck in honour of some games at which Pigres was Asiarch.

Fig. 148.—*Coin of Hypæpa. From J. Y. Akerman.*
Inscribed Επι Μενανδρου Β. Ασιαρ. Στρ. Υπαιπηνων (under Menander twice Asiarch, Prætor. Of the Hypepians).

until A.D. 43,[50] was allowed by the Romans to govern itself, and was a free country, the course was this. Twenty-three cities who composed the union returned members to Congress, viz., the capital cities three, the next in importance two, and the rest one. As soon as the representatives met, they elected the Lyciarch, in the first

---

[43] συνοικεῖται καλῶς, εἴ τις ἄλλη τῶν κατὰ τὴν Ἀσίαν, ὑπὸ εὐπόρων ἀνθρώπων, καὶ ἀεί τινες ἐξ αὐτῶν εἰσιν οἱ πρωτεύοντες κατὰ τὴν ἐπαρχίαν, οὓς Ἀσιάρχας καλοῦσιν. Strabo, xiv. 1 (p. 188, Tauchnitz).

[44] Sponte sacerdotium provinciæ iterare nemo prohibetur, Dig. l. 4, 17. In Asiâ sacerdotium provinciæ suscipere non coguntur numero liberorum v submixi, Dig. l. 5, 8. See Wetstein on Acts xix. 31.

[45] Οἱ πρωτεύοντες κατὰ τὴν ἐπαρχίαν. Strabo, xiv. 1 (p. 188, Tauchnitz).

[46] Potestas erat annua in Asia Minori, ut præsiderent in ludis et sumptus in eos facerent. Wetstein ubi supra.

[47] In F. M. (Fred. Martin's) notes they are stated to have been thirteen.

[48] Μάρκον Νώνιον, εὐτύχητον, ἀξιολογώτατον, Γραμματέα Βουλῆς Δήμου, Σειτωνησαντα, Εἰρηναρχήσαντα, Στρατηγήσαντα, Δεκαπρωτεύσαντα, &c. Inscription from Leake's Asia Minor, p. 340.

[49] Wetstein on Acts xix. 31.

[50] See Fasti Sacri, p. 277, No. 1656.

DESCRIPTION OF EPHESUS. [A.D. 54]

place, as the highest dignity of the state, and then the inferior officers in succession.[51] It is probable from an ancient author, that the Asiarchs were appointed in a somewhat similar manner, viz. each city that returned members to the congress of Asia, sent annually by its representatives the name of some person who had been selected for the purpose in their own assembly, as a candidate for the Asiarchate, and from all the candidates thus proposed, the Congress chose ten, who then became Asiarchs.[52] It is possible, however, that as the office was an influential one, the election by the Congress may not have been final without some ratification by the Proconsul.[53]

We must now say something more particularly of Ephesus itself. It was not only the capital of the province, and as such the residence of the Proconsul, but was the city of the greatest importance in all Asia Minor, and the principal emporium of trade in the East. It was called one of the eyes of Asia,[54] Smyrna being the other. Indeed, Ephesus and Smyrna, both of them on the sea coast, and both great commercial marts, at the distance of about forty miles from each other, looked forth like eyes from the projecting forehead of the Peninsula. The inhabitants of Ephesus were of course Greeks, and the principal colony had been led thither by Androclus, the son of Cadmus, King of Athens; and they seemed to have carried with them the natural genius and fine taste of the Attic stock, for Ephesus held no contemptible position in letters, and in sculpture it rivalled, and in painting excelled, the parent city. Apelles and Parrhasius, the two matchless masters of the pencil, were both of them natives of Ephesus.[55]

The topography of the place is very simple.[56] The city stood on the south of a plain about five miles long, from east to west, and three miles broad, the northern boundary being Mount Gallesius, the eastern Mount Pactyas, the southern Mount Prion,

---

[51] ἐν δὲ τῷ συνεδρίῳ πρῶτον μὲν Λυκιάρχης αἱρεῖται, εἶτ' ἄλλαι ἀρχαὶ τοῦ συστήματος. Strabo, xiv. 3 (p. 214, Tauchnitz).

[52] συμβαίνει μετὰ ταῦτα συνέδρους μὲν ἐξιέναι Σμυρναίων εἰς Φρυγίαν ἄνω, καὶ μέλλειν φέρειν τοὐμὸν ὄνομα ἐν τῷ συνεδρίῳ τῷ κοινῷ, προαισθέσθαι δέ με καὶ πέμψαι τὸν τροφέα τὸν Ζώσιμον, καὶ γέγραμμαι τρίτος ἢ τέταρτος τῇ χειροτονίᾳ. Aristides, S. S. iv. ad finem. The Asiarchs were not confined to the Lydian Asia, for we read of Asiarchs at Cyzicus. ΣΤΡ. Λ. ΑΥΡΗΛΙΟΥ ΑΣΙΑΡΧΟΥ ΚΥΖΙΚΗΝΩΝ. Van Dale, Dissert. iii. In Fellows's Asia Minor, p. 49, an inscription from Assus is given thus: Ὁ ἱερεὺς τοῦ Σεβαστοῦ Θεοῦ Καίσαρος, ὁ δὲ αὐ νασίαρχος ὁ Καιντος Λοος καὶ πατριος βασιλευς. But there is some error or hiatus, and the word may have been Γυμνασιαρχος.

[53] Van Dale, who has examined into these matters with great research, thinks that the Asiarchs were appointed in the same manner as the Irenarchs (Εἰρηναρχοί) or High Constables, and which resembled the pricking of sheriffs among ourselves; that is, each city returned every year to the proconsul ten names of the most influential inhabitants and the one that appeared the most eligible, and it is likely, in the absence of any violent objection, the first on the list, was the one fixed upon. ἐπέμπετο ταῖς ἡγεμόσι κατ' ἐκείνους τοὺς χρόνους ἀφ' ἑκάστης πόλεως, ἑκάστου ἔτους, ὀνόματα δέκα ἀνδρῶν τῶν πρώτων. ταῦτα ἔδει σκεψάμενον τὸν ἡγεμόνα, ἕνα, ὃν προκρίνειεν ἐξ ἁπάντων, καθιστάναι φύλακα τῆς εἰρήνης. . . . ὁ δὲ . . . προέκρινεν ἄρχειν ἐρί. Aristides, Ἱερῶν λόγος δ', p. 338, ed. Jebb. See Van Dale, Dissert. iii. c. 3.

[54] Alterum lumen Asiæ. Plin. N H. v. 31

[55] Strabo, xiv. 1 (p. 177, Tauchnitz).

[56] For the natural features of the plain in which it stood, and the line of coast, see the Admiralty chart.

or Pion, and on the west it was washed by the sea. The sides of the mountains were precipitous, and shut up the plain like a *stadium*, or racecourse. About half-way along the southern side of the plain stood a little forward the circular hill of Coressus, famous for its quarries of beautiful marble, the source of the surrounding magnificence. To the north-east of Coressus rose out of the middle of the plain a little mount, the seat of the modern village of Ayasaluch, or the Holy Divine (Ἅγιος Θεόλογος), as St. John was called, who passed his latter days at Ephesus. The Cayster entered the plain at the north-east corner, and flowed diagonally across it (but with many meanders) to the south-western side, where it discharged itself into the sea. As one entered the broad mouth of the river, and after ascending a little distance, but before reaching the city, one came to an opening on the right-hand, leading in a south-eastern direction to what had originally been an extensive lake,

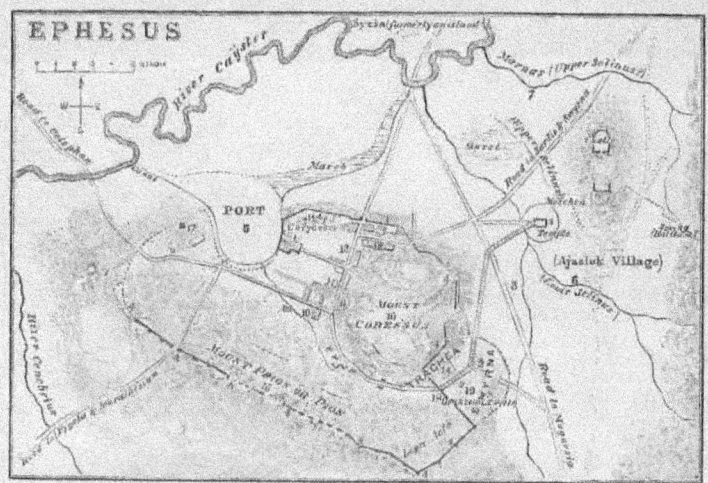

Fig. 149.—*Plan of Ephesus. Grounded on that of Guhl.*

1. Site of the Temple of Diana, lately discovered by J. T. Wood. It is singular that the true site, now ascertained by actual exploration, should have been hit upon long before by Guhl on historical grounds only. At p. 178 of his Ephesiaca he places it near the marsh (E. f. on his map), and at pp. 12 and 13 he assumes it to lie between the two streams marked Selinus and Marnas on his map—an exact position. Kiepert, however, who prepared the map, places the site of the temple erroneously on the spot indicated by the letter d, which is much too far to the northwest, and at variance with the text of Guhl. These remarks must not be taken to detract in any way from the merit of J. T. Wood, who, proceeding upon quite independent grounds, made the discovery of the temple itself.

The temple was situate at the village of Pokia (τόκια, "the site"). Ἐν δὲ καὶ Ἀρτεμίδος ἱερόν ἐστι.—Stephan. Byz. Ephesus. And an ancient coin of Ephesus (fig. 151) represents the temple with a tree at the side of it. It is remarkable that olive-trees flourish there at the present day (Guhl. p. 8). For a description of the temple, see Plin. N. H. xxxvi. 21. It stood on a platform ascended by ten steps. τοιοῦτον εἶν ἐξαιθοῦν ἐβαλλετο κρηπῖδα δεκαβάθμου διεγύρωσε πρὸς βάσιν μετατροφίσιν. Philo Byzant. de Sept.

Orbis Spectaculis, Gronov. Thesaur. viii. 2682. This number of the steps has been found to be correct.

2. The old town called Smyrna, situate at the mouth of the Hypelaeum, the valley between Coressus on the north, and Prion, or Pion, on the south, and spread itself eastward round the Gymnasium and the Athenaeum or Temple of Minerva. It occupied on the north the part called Trachea ("The Rough"), at the eastern end of Coressus, and on the south Lepre Acte ("Scrubbyside"), the bluff eastern end of Prion, or Pion. ἡ δὲ πόλις (Ephesus) ἦν τὸ παλαιὸν παρὰ τὸ Ἀθήναιον, τὸ νῦν ἔξω τῆς πόλεως, ὃ κατὰ τὴν καλουμένην Ὑπέλαιον· ὥστε ἡ Σμύρνα ἦν κατὰ τὸ νῦν Γυμνάσιον, ὀπίσθεν μὲν τῆς νῦν πόλεως, μεταξὺ δὲ Τρηχείης τε καὶ Λέπρης Ἀκτῆς. Strabo, xiv. 1. φησιον (Androclus) . . . . . περὶ τὸ Ἀθήναιον καὶ τὴν Ὑπέλαιον προσπεριλαβεῖν καὶ τῆς περὶ τὸν Κορησσὸν παρωρείας. Strabo, xiv. 1 (p. 174, Tauchnitz). Τρηχείαν καὶ τὰ περὶ Κορησσὸν. Athen. viii. 62 (p. 234, Tauchnitz).

Trachea was the eastern end of Coressus. Τρηχείη δ᾽ ἐκαλεῖτο ἡ ὑπὲρ ("beyond") as from the sea) τοῦ Κορησσοῦ παρώρεια. Strabo, xiv. 1 (p. 164, Tauchnitz). And Lepre Acte was the precipitous eastern end of Prion, or Pion, where commenced the wall

DESCRIPTION OF EPHESUS. [A.D. 54]

once famous for its fish, but was now a broad basin artificially embanked, and filled with shipping. This was the celebrated port, the busy scene of the commerce of all nations. Ephesus itself covered Mount Coressus, and part of the plain of Lysimachus, which ran westward and overlooked the city. ἐκαλεῖτο γὰρ Λεπρὴ μὲν Ἀκτὴ ἡ Πρίων ὁ ὑπερκείμενος τῆς νῦν πόλεως ἔχων μέρος τοῦ τείχους αὐτῆς· τὰ γοῦν ὄπισθεν τοῦ Πρίωνος ἀκμαῖον ἔτι νῦν λέγεται ἐν τῇ Ὀπισθολεπρίᾳ. Strabo, ib.

The old town of Smyrna was seven stadia or furlongs from the Temple of Diana. ἔστι δὲ μεταξὺ τῆς τε παλαιᾶς πόλεως ἣ τοὺς ἑπτακοσίους καὶ τοῦ ναοῦ ἑπτὰ στάδιοι. Herod. i. 26. And as the temple is now a fixed point, the boundary of the old city on the north can be approximately determined.

Such was the city down to the time of Croesus. Strabo, xiv. 1 (p. 174, Tauchnitz); but in after-times it descended northwards into the plain in the direction of the temple. ἀπὸ τῆς παρεμβολὰς κατάβασις περὶ τὸ ἱερὸν ἔχοντας μέχρι Ἀλεξάνδρου. Strabo, ib.; Stephan. Byzant. Ἔφεσος; and Pococke found traces of it in that quarter. Pococke, vol. ii. part 2, p. 47.

But this part of the city was on low ground, and suffered from inundations; and Lysimachus, the successor of Alexander, transplanted the population from the plain on the east of Coressus to the plain on the west of Coressus, between Coressus and the port (Strabo, xiv. 1, p. 174, Tauchnitz; Stephan. Byzant. Ἔφεσος), which from this time became the heart of the city, and comprised all the principal buildings. The plain, however, on the east of Coressus in the direction of the temple, was still partially inhabited down to the time of Augustus; for when Mark Antony extended the asylum of the temple to two stadia, it comprised part of the city itself; and this leading to inconvenience, Augustus reduced the limits of the asylum to one stadium. Strabo, xiv. 1 (p. 178, Tauchnitz).

2. The colonnade from the Magnesian Gate to the temple. For the length of a stadium it was all of stone; the character of the remainder is not given. As the asylum of the temple was exactly a stadium the more magnificent stone-work not improbably commenced at the boundary of the asylum, and was thence continued to the temple itself. στοιχηδὸν δὲ (Damianus) καὶ τὸ ἱερὸν τῆς Ἐφεσίας κατασκευασθέντες αὐτῷ τῆν διὰ τῶν Μαγνητικῶν καθόδων. ἔστι δὲ αὕτη στοὰ ἐπὶ στάδιον λίθου πᾶσα. Philost. Soph. ii. 23, 2.

On the road from the Magnesian Gate to the temple was the tomb of Androclus, the founder of Ephesus as a Greek city. δείκνυται δὲ καὶ ἐς ἐμὲ τὸ μνῆμα (of Androclus) κατὰ τὴν ὁδὸν τὴν ἐκ τοῦ ἱεροῦ παρὰ τὸ Ὀλυμπιεῖον καὶ ἐπὶ πύλας τὰς Μαγνητικάς. Pausan. vii. 2, 6. Recent explorations identify the tomb of Androclus at a little distance without the Magnesian Gate, on the right-hand of the road leading down to the Temple of Diana.

4. The line of the walls of the city in the time of the Apostle. According to Pococke, the circuit was about four miles. Pococke, vol. ii. part 2, p. 4.

5. The inner or city port. The entrance to it was originally of great breadth, and the sea washed into it: αἱ παραυγάδες καὶ ἡ καθήκουσα τοῦ πελάγους ῥόμβη τῆς γοῦν καὶ ἄνωθεν πρὸς τὸ εἴσω. Strabo, xiv. 1 (p. 177, Tauchnitz), and at the eastern end was probably still more communication with the Cayster, which gradually silted up the port. διὰ τὸ ἐκ τοῦ Καΰστρου χωσις. Strabo, 26. Guhl, on his map, represents this to have been the case, and Falkener, in confirmation, draws the line of the marsh from the port to the Cayster in the same direction. However, it is possible that the slit of the Cayster may have found its way into the port through the broad mouth of it on the west. The open western channel was narrowed by Attalus Philadelphus, with the idea of checking the silting by increasing the current; but just the opposite result followed, and the port was ruined. Strabo, ib.

This inner port appears to have been called the Sacred Port, from the Temple of Apollo which overlooked it. ὁ ἱερὸς λιμήν, Athenaeus, viii 62 (p. 254, Tauchnitz); unless the marsh close to the great Temple of Diana was then a port, and called the Sacred from the temple of Diana.)

The outer port called Panormus was the channel of the river with the bay into which it discharged itself. Quod in Ephesiis medium longum et angustum et vadosum ostium portus sit. Liv. XXXVII. 14. εἶτα λιμὴν Πάνορμος καλούμενος ἔχων ἱερὸν τῆς Ἐφεσίας Ἀρτέμιδος. Strabo, xiv. 1 (p. 173, Tauchnitz). In the most ancient times the sea had flowed up the valley as far as the great Temple of Diana. Ephesi, ubi quondam telum Dianæ (mare) alluebat. Plin. N. H. ii. 87; Herod. ii. 10. The temple at Panormus was a temple, but not the great temple of Diana.

6. The lower selinus. This stream is traced on Guhl's map and the Admiralty chart, and forms a marsh before it joins the Cayster. It passed very close to the Temple of Diana. See next note.

7. The upper selinus. This on Guhl's map is marked Marnas, and according to him was the Upper Selinus. The two Selinuntes shut in the Temple of Diana, one on the west, and the other on the east, as described by Pliny. Templum Dianæ complexi e diverso regionibus duo Selinuntes. Plin. N. H. v. 31.

Neither of the two Selinuntes must be confounded with the river Cayster, for Xenophon, who was familiar with the Cayster, speaks of the river Selinus as distinct: Ἐκεῖσε δὲ ῥεῖ μὲν ὁ τῆς Ἐφεσίας Ἀρτέμιδος ἱερὸς Σέλινους ποταμὸς παραρρέων. Xenoph. Cyr. Exped. v. 3. And so Pliny, who notices the two Selinuntes, speaks in the same breath of the Cayster as flowing by Ephesus. Alluitur (Ephesos) Cayster. Plin. N. H. v. 31. And the two streams called Selinus are not to be confounded with the lake of that name referred to by Strabo, xiv. 1 (p. 177, Tauchnitz).

8. The Temple of Apollo, at the head of the port. Ἀπόλλωνος τε τοῦ Πυθίου καὶ τοῦ Ἀπόλλωνος. Athen. viii. 62 (p. 254, Tauchnitz).

9. The Agora or Forum opposite the great Theatre. Another temple of Diana was in the vicinity of the Agora. Ἱερὸν Ἀρτέμιδος ἐπὶ τῇ ἀγορᾷ. Athen. viii 12 (p. 234, Tauchnitz). And this, perhaps, is the temple referred to in the coin which represents a temple of Diana Ephesia with four columns in front, where on the

Fig. 150.—Coin of Ephesus. From Pembroke collection.

Great Temple of Diana has eight columns in front. It tends to confirm this view that the inscription on the four-columned coin is in Latin 'Diana Ephesia,' and the headquarters of the Romans were about the Forum.

10. A hollow square which Pococke took to be the site of a naumachium. There is sloping ground all round with the appearance of seats, and to the west may be traced a depression like the bed of a canal to the port. Here perhaps were the scopæ, or docks, referred to by Strabo, xiv. 1 (p. 176, Tauchnitz).

11. The Great Theatre in which occurred the riot of Demetrius the silversmith. The chord or base of the theatre where was the proscenium, according to Pococke, about 458 feet long, and the diameter from the chord to the arc of the semicircle is about 300 feet. Pococke, vol. ii. pt. 2, pp. 50 and 52. But according to Cockerell, the diameter is 660 feet, and if so, it was the largest theatre known, and capable of holding 56,700 spectators. Falkener's Ephesus, p. 102.

12. The stadium. For a description of which see Pococke, vol. ii. pt. 2, p. 51.

13. The principal street of Ephesus running from the theatre to the stadium.

14. The gymnasium, which was within the old city, but was without the city as it stood in the time of Paul. ἐν τῷ γυμνασίῳ ὁπόθεν μὲν τῆς νῦν πόλεως. Strabo, xiv. 1 (p. 184, Tauchnitz).

15. Mount Prion or Pion, called by most travellers Coressus. Coressus is stated as the name of Prion, on the authority of Strabo and Pliny, but Pausanias calls it Pion, and this, according to the coins, is the more correct appellation.

Fig. 151.—Coin of Ephesus. From Calmet.

The legend of the coin is Ἡ διὸς Ἐφεσίων (Pion of the Ephesians). It exhibits the leading features of Ephesus, viz. the river Cayster, Mount Pion, and the Temple. At the foot is seen Mount Pion...

to the north of it, and extended on the west to the port, and on the south along the valley between Mount Coressus and Prion or Pion, and covered part of Prion, or Pion, itself. No city ever changed its name or its site so frequently as Ephesus. In the time of the Trojan war it was called Alopes, then Ortygia, then Morges, then Smyrna Trachea, then Samornion, then Ptelea, and lastly Ephesus.[37] The city stood originally

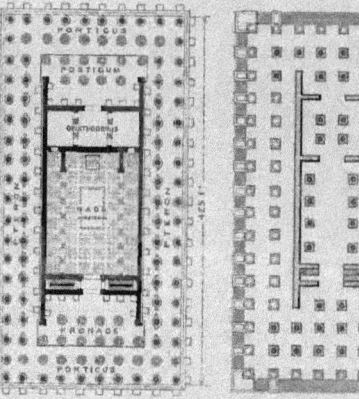
Fig. 152.—*Plan according to Falkener.*

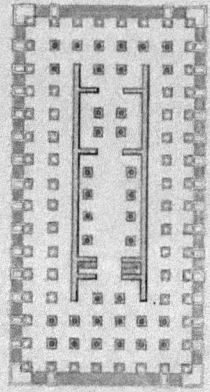
Fig. 153.—*Plan according to J. Fergusson.*
This is the nearest approach to the actual plan so far as the same has been at present ascertained by exploration on the spot.

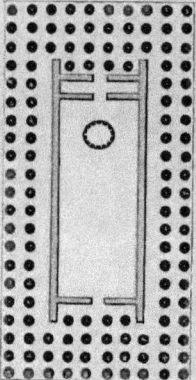
Fig. 154.—*Plan according to Leake.*

to the east of Mount Coressus, but this part, in the days of the Apostle, had been abandoned in favour of Mount Coressus and the parts adjoining it on the west.[38]

It would require a volume to describe the city at length; but three objects of

---

the source of the Cayster; and the recumbent figure is the Cayster personified, pointing in the direction of the stream. On the left bank of the river is a building which may either represent the city itself or the temple. In favour of the former, it is observable that the building has windows, which is less appropriate in a temple than to a house. The received opinion, however, is that a temple is intended, and this is confirmed by the tree standing by it. The temple was erected at Ortygia, or 'The Elm,' and that kind of tree still flourishes there. In the centre of the coin is Mount Pion, the predominant mountain, supporting Jupiter, who scatters plenty from a cornucopia with one hand, and holds thunderbolts, the emblem of power, in the other. The coin agrees with the textual features, for on the right, or east, is the river, and then the temple, and then, more to the left, or west, is Pion, commonly called Prion.

16. Mount Coressus, commonly but erroneously called Prion, or Pion. In reading the books of travels, it must be carefully borne in mind that, when they speak of Prion, or Pion, they mean what has now been ascertained to be Coressus; and that, when they speak of Coressus, they mean what is now known as Prion, or Pion.

17. The tower called the Prison of St. Paul. There is no certain account of his imprisonment at Ephesus, but he was finally arrested in Asia, and seems to have been incarcerated at Ephesus, and sent thence to Rome, where he suffered martyrdom.

18. The Magnesian Gate, from which the road out of the city after running a little distance branched off into two roads, the one on the right leading to Magnesia, and the one on the left leading to the temple and called from its sloping down to the temple, ἡ διὰ τῶν Μαγνησιακῶν καθοδος. Philost. Soph. ii. 23, 2.

19. The Athenæum, or Temple of Minerva, which was within the old city of Smyrna, but was just outside the city of Lysimachus. Strabo, xiv. 1 (p. 184, Tauchnitz).

20. The watercourse from the spring in the Hypelæan Valley, called ἡ κρήνη ὑπέλαιος καλουμένη καὶ ὁ τόπος Ἀρηρ. Athen. viii. 62 (p. 254, Tauchnitz). The stream is marked on the Admiralty chart as flowing between Prion or Pion and Coressus into the port. Both Guhl and Falkener place a fountain also on the south of the port at the foot of the mount on which stands the Prison of St. Paul.

Falkener in his sketch plan notices another fountain on Coressus (called by him Prion), and Tournefort another to the north of the port, and Guhl another still at the foot of Mount Pactyas near the aqueduct.

---

[37] In orâ autem Manteium, Ephesus Amazonum opus, multis ante expetita nominibus—Alopes cum pugnatum apud Trojam est—mox Ortygia, et Morges vocata est, et Smyrna cognomine Trachea, et Samornion, et Ptelea. Plin. N. H. v. 31.

[38] Strabo, xiv. 1 (p. 174, Tauchnitz).

interest, as connected with our subject, cannot be passed over in silence—viz, the Temple of Diana, the Theatre, which was the scene of the riot of Demetrius, and the Stadium, or Circus, the arena of the beast-fights.

The temple, one of the wonders of the world, and which was 220 years in building, and erected at the joint cost of all Asia,[59] stood without the walls, at some little distance to the north-east, and being constructed of the purest marble, is said to have gleamed like a meteor to the gaze of the approaching mariner.[60] It was built upon marshy ground, and the foundations were laid at a vast expense. The first superstructure, or basement, was ascended by a grand flight of ten steps, and upon

Fig. 155.—*Coin of Ephesus representing the Temple with eight columns in front. From Pembroke collection.*

this platform was erected the temple, facing the east, 425 feet long, and 220 broad, and supported by columns of Parian marble, sixty feet high, of which thirty-six were beautifully carved, and one by the hand of the famous Scopas.[61] The building was of the Ionic order, and an octastyle dipteros—that is, the portico in front *in pronao*, and at the back *in postico*, consisted each of thirty-two columns, eight abreast, and four deep, and round the sides were two rows of columns.[62]

It was the custom with the ancients to place at the entrance of the temples a

---

[59] Liv. i. 45; Plin. N. H. xvi. 79; xxxvi. 21.

[60] μετεωροφανές. Philo Byzantius de Septem Orbis Spectaculis.

[61] Magnificentiæ vera admiratio exstat templum Ephesiæ Dianæ, ducentis viginti annis factum a totâ Asiâ. In solo id palustri fecere, ne terræ motus sentiret aut hiatus timeret. Rursus ne in lubrico atque instabili fundamenta tantæ molis locarentur, calcatis ea substravere carbonibus, dein velleribus lanæ. Universo templo longitudo est cccccxxv. pedum, latitudo duccentorum viginti, columnæ centum viginti septem a singulis regibus factæ. lx. pedum altitudine: ex iis xxxvi. cælatæ, una a Scopâ. Plin. N. H. xxxvi. 21, and see xxxvi. 58.

This passage as to the number of columns may be pointed in three several ways: as,

(1) Columnæ centum, viginti septem a singulis regibus factæ;

so that the columns were 100, and 27 by as many kings.

(2) Columnæ centum viginti, septem a singulis regibus factæ;

so that the columns were 120, and 7 by as many kings. And

(3) Columnæ cxxvii. [lege cxxviii.] a singulis regibus factæ;

so that the columns were 127, by as many kings.

Fergusson adopts the first punctuation; Falkener is in favour of the second; and Leake supports the third. The restorations of the temple as given by each of them are annexed. All are agreed that the columns could not be the uneven number 127.

[62] Dipteros autem octastylos et pronao et postico, sed circa ædem duplices habet ordines columnarum, sicut est ædes Quirini Dorica, et

περιρραντήριον, or lavatory, that the worshippers might first purify themselves, and such a lavatory appears to have stood in front of the Temple of Diana.[63]

Let us now survey the interior of the temple. We mount the outer steps, and, standing under the portico, look on the massive doors framed of carved cypress.[65] On each side are the jambs of marble, and at the top is the enormous transom, a single block of such vast dimensions that the beholder marvels at the mechanical skill that could have raised it. The legend runs that the architect despaired of the undertaking, but that while he slept the goddess herself came to the rescue, and in the morning the ponderous stone was found adjusted to its place.[66] We pass the doorway, and find ourselves in a court or hall, in which are the most famous pieces of sculpture from the hands of Praxiteles and Scopas, and the most eminent artists. There stands, radiant with gold, the figure of Artemidorus, who was thus highly honoured for having successfully advocated the cause of the temple at Rome against the Imperial revenue officers, who had sacrilegiously appropriated to the Exchequer the fisheries of the Selinusian Lakes, which formed part of the sacred possessions.[67] There is a group of Amazons, one by Polycletus, another by Phidias, another by Ctesilaus, another by Cydon, and another by Phradmon; but the work of Polycletus is the finest, excelling even that by Phidias.[68]

Here, also, is the gallery of paintings,[69] and nobler specimens of the art are not to be found in the world. There hangs the masterpiece of Calliphon, the Samian—Patroclus preparing for battle, with attendant damsels buckling on him the armour of Achilles.[70] There may be seen the *chef-d'œuvre* of Apelles, the prince of painters—Alexander the Great grasping a thunderbolt. This grand work cost the temple twenty talents of gold, or £7000,[71] estimated by Chandler to be equivalent to £38,650 at the present day.[72]

Ephesiæ Dianæ Ionica, a Chersiphrone constituta. Vitruv. iii. 2, 7. Leake and Falkener translate this, "The Dipteros style must have had eight columns (at least) both in front and at the back," &c., as any less number would be out of proportion with the double row at the sides, but any greater number than eight might be introduced. This interpretation is admissible as a general principle, but as Vitruvius gives the Temple of Diana as an *instance* of the octastylus, the natural inference is, that the temple had eight columns abreast in front, and not more; and this agrees with the coins, which represent the temple as having eight columns only in front.

[64] Λυκίου τοῦ Μύρωνος χαλκοῦν παῖδα, ὃς τὸ περιρραντήριον ἔχει. Pausan. Attic. i. 23, 8. Τὰ πρὸ τῶν ἱερῶν περιρραντήρια. Julius Pollux i. 8, 32; and again, Εἴη δ' ἂν ὁ μὲν εἴσω τῶν περιρραντηρίων τόπος ἔνθεος, ἱερός, &c. Ib. i. 1, 6.

Μὴ γὰρ ἔνδον τοῦτο ποιήσαιμι ἐγώ, μὴ καὶ τὸ ἱερὸν ὕδωρ τῷ τῆς ὕβρεως αἵματι μιανθῇ. Achilles Tatius, lib. viii.

[65] Τούτων δὲ χρονιώτατα δοκεῖ τὰ κυπαρίττινα εἶναι, τὰ γοῦν ἐν Ἐφέσῳ ἐξ ὧν αἱ θύραι τοῦ νεὼ τεθησαυρισμέναι τέτταρας ἐκεῖντο γενεάς. Theophrast. Hist. Plant. v. 5. Valvas esse e cupresso, et jam quadringentis prope annis durare materiem omnem novæ similem. Plin. N. H. xvi. 79.

[66] Plin. N. H. xxxvi. 21.

[67] Strabo, xiv. 1 (p. 177, Tauchnitz).

[68] Plin. N. H. xxxiv. 19.

[69] Ἐν δὲ Ἀρτέμιδος τῆς Ἐφεσίας πρὸς τὸ οἴκημα ἐρχομένῳ τὸ ἔχον τὰς γραφάς. Pausan. Phocic. x. 38, 3.

[70] Καὶ ἐν Ἀρτέμιδος τῆς Ἐφεσίας Καλλιφῶν ὁ Σάμιος Πατρόκλῳ τοῦ θώρακος τὰ γυαλὰ ἁρμοζούσας ἔγραψε γυναῖκας. Pausan. Phocic. x. 26, 2.

[71] Plin. N. H. xxxv. 36, 15.

[72] Asia Minor, p. 159.

In the centre of the court or hall is the *naòs*, or shrine, containing the image of the goddess. We enter, and the roof, which is of cedar,[72] is supported by a row, on each side of four columns, of green jasper.[74] Against the walls hang the votive offerings of the worshippers of the goddess: some the gorgeous presents of kings and princes, and one the humble psaltery of Alexander the musician of Cythera.[75] In front of us is the altar, rich with the carvings of Praxiteles,[76] and beyond it hangs from the ceiling the purple embroidered veil screening the image that all the world worshippeth.[77] The veil is raised, and we look on the goddess herself. Can this be Diana, the great goddess of the Ephesians?—a wooden image so time-worn that whether the material be vine,[78] or cedar,[79] or ebony,[80] the nearest examination cannot discover. In either hand is a staff or trident (see fig. 156, and the coins ante, pp. 321, 323, and post, p. 326), and the body is covered with paps, the emblem of prolificness. Mutianus was profane enough to say that the image was

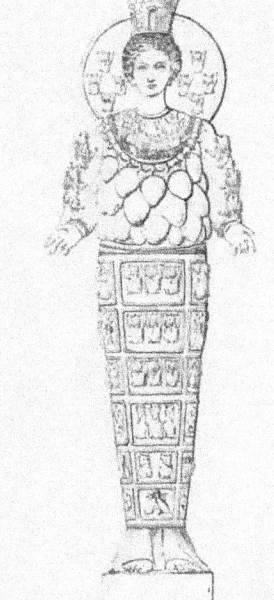

Fig. 156.—From an alabaster image of Diana of Ephesus in the museum of Naples.
The figure, however, is in great measure ideal, and a much more faithful representation of the goddess will be found in the coin that follows.

[72] Conveuit tectum ejus esse cedrinis trabibus. Plin. N. H. xvi. 79. Ephesi in æde simulacrum Dianæ, etiam lacunaria ex eâ [cedro] et ibi et in cæteris nobilibus fanis propter æternitatem sunt facta. Vitruv. ii. 9, 13.

[73] These eight columns were afterwards transported to Constantinople, and may now be seen in the mosque of St. Sophia. Τοὺς δὲ ὀκτὼ πραςίνους, κίονας τοῖς ἀξιοθαυμάστοις ἐκόμισε Κωνσταντῖνος στρατηγὸς ἀπὸ Ἐφεσίων λελατομημένους. Bauduini Imperium Orientale, tom. i. lib. iv. p. 66, n. 186. The shafts only are of green jasper. The capitals are of white marble with tracery upon them, somewhat resembling leaves. The bases are also of white marble.

[75] Τόδε ψαλτήριον Ἀλέξανδρος Κιθήρως συνετελήρωσε χρυσαῖς, καὶ ἐγγηράσας τῇ Ἐφεσίων πόλει, ὡς σοφώτατος τῆς ἑαυτοῦ τέχνης, τουτὶ τὸ εὕρημα ἀνέθηκεν ἐν Ἀρτέμιδος. Athenæus, iv. 81. (183.)

[76] Τοῦ δὲ δὴ δωμοῦ εἶναι τῶν Πραξιτέλους ἔργων ἅπαντα σχεδόν τι πλήρη. Strabo, xiv. 1 (p. 176, Tauchnitz). Τέτηπται παρ' αὐτῷ τῷ βωμῷ, βλεπούσης, οἶμαι, τῆς θεοῦ. Achilles Tat. viii. sub initio.

[77] Ἐν δὲ Ὀλυμπίῳ παραπέτασμα ἐρεοῦν κεκοσμημένον ὑφάσμασιν Ἀσσυρίοις καὶ βαφῇ πορφύρας τῆς Φοινίκων ἀνέθηκεν Ἀντίοχος. . . . Τοῦτο οὐκ ἐς τὸ ἄνω τὸ παραπέτασμα πρὸς τὸν ὄροφον, ὥσπερ γε ἐν Ἀρτέμιδος τῆς Ἐφεσίας, ἀνέλκουσι, καλῳδίοις δὲ ἐπιχαλῶντες καθιᾶσιν ἐς τὸ ἔδαφος. Pausan. Eliac. v. 12, 2.

[78] Mutianus, ter consul, ex his qui proxime vivo eo, scripsere, vitigineum [tradit], et nunquam mutatum, septies restituto templo. Plin. N. H. xvi. 79.

[79] Vitruv. ii. 9, 13.

[80] De ipso simulacro Deæ ambigitur. Cæteri ex ebeno esse tradunt. Mutianus, &c., ut supra Plin. N. H. xvi. 79.

the work of Pandemion,[51] but the air of antiquity about it carries us back to a period long anterior to the records of written history. Whence it came or by whom it was shaped is a mystery, but the common belief is that it fell from heaven.[52]

Fig. 157.—*Coin of Claudius. From Akerman.*

Obv. Portraits of Claudius and Agrippina, and therefore struck some time between A.D. 49 and A.D. 54. The legend is Tiberius Claudius Cæsar Augustus, Agrippina Augusta. The coin may have been struck and was certainly current when Paul was at Ephesus.—*Rev.* The image of Diana, with the legend Diana Ephesia (Diana of the Ephesians).

At the back of the ναός is an apartment which we may not enter; it is the repository where nations and potentates have stored their most valuable treasures, for such is the sanctity of the temple that no safer bank can be found in Asia, or even in the world.

Let us next ascend to the roof of the temple.[53] The staircase is said to have been constructed from the wood of a single vine from Cyprus.[54] A gigantic tree to have yielded all this material! We arrive at the top, and look down upon the scene below. Immediately beneath us, before the portico of the temple, our attention is drawn to a crowd of people listening, with gaping mouths, to an orator who is holding forth from the edge of the platform.[55] The speaker is Apollonius of Tyana, a sophist or philosopher, who travels from country to country, and from his knowledge of sorcery imposes himself on the vulgar as a kind of oracle. If any one has lost an article of value, Apollonius is the cunning man to say where it will be found. If a famine or pestilence visits the city, Apollonius is the magician who can provide a charm against it. Here, at the corner of the roof, stood Mithridates when he shot the arrow to mark the boundary of the sanctuary or asylum of the temple, and the shaft flew to the length of more than a furlong.[56] On the east are gardens, and orchards, and luxuriant fields,[57] till the view is interrupted by the towering ridges of Mount Paetyas. On the south we look down on the broad thoroughfare, with a portico on

---

[51] Plin. N. H. xvi. 79.

[52] Acts xix. 35.

[53] That the temple was roofed is evident from Strabo: Μετὰ δὲ τὴν ἔμπρησιν τῆς ὀροφῆς ἠφανισμένης, ἐν ὑπαίθρῳ τῷ σηκῷ τίνα ἂν ἐθελήσαι παρακαταθήκην κειμένην ἔχειν; Strabo, xiv. 22 (p. 175, Tauchnitz). And apparently the roof was tiled. Μιθριδάτου δὲ τόξευμα ἀφεῖτος ἀπὸ τῆς γωνίας τοῦ κεράμου. Id. xiv. 23. See Pliny, N. H. xiv. 2; Vitruv. ii. 9, 13, and see next note.

[54] Etiam nunc scalis tectum Ephesiæ Dianæ scanditur, unâ e vite Cypriâ, ut ferunt, quoniam ibi ad præcipuam amplitudinem exeunt. Plin. N. H. xiv. 2.

[55] Τὴν μὲν δὴ διάλεξιν τὴν πρώτην ἀπὸ τῆς κρηπῖδος τοῦ νεὼ πρὸς τοὺς Ἐφεσίους διελέχθη. Philost. Vict. Apoll. iv. 2.

[56] Strabo, xiv. 1 (p. 176, Tauchnitz).

[57] See Achill. Tat. lib. v.

each side, running from the temple to the Magnesian Gate between Prion or Pion and Coressus. We turn our eyes westward, and gaze upon Ephesus, and beyond it the harbour bristling with innumerable masts, and still further westward the blue waters of the Ægean. To the north we see the Cayster winding its sluggish way along the plain, and beyond it are the rugged heights of Gallesius.

Quitting the Temple of Diana, we walk along the broad road to the Magnesian Gates, and then pass down the valley which lies between Mount Prion or Pion and Coressus, and come to the theatre, excavated from the sloping side of Coressus, looking to the west, and faced with a portico. It is the largest structure of the kind ever erected by the Greeks, and is capable of containing some 50,000 spectators. Like all other theatres, it has no roof, but the spectators protect themselves from the sun either by head-gear adapted for a screen, or by holding a parasol in the hand, and occasionally a light tarpauling is drawn across part of the theatre itself. Here are exhibited the scenic representations, and here, at stated intervals, are held the assemblies of the people (see fig. 158 and 159).

After passing the theatre, another broad paved street leads off to the north along the foot of Mount Coressus; and at the end of this street, and on the right, is the stadium or circus, lying east and west, 685 feet long, and 200 wide. The rows of seats on the south are excavated from the hill, and those on the north towards the plain are supported on arches. The eastern end of the stadium is of a circular form, like a theatre; the other extremity is fenced in by a straight wall drawn across it, with open spaces left on the north and south for the two entrances into the stadium. This is the arena in which the Ephesian population witnesses the foot-races, and wrestling, and pugilistic combats,[88] and here, more particularly, are enacted the θηριομάχιαι, or beast-fights, the wild beasts being kept in the vaults beneath the northern limb of the building. The bestiarii or combatants are mostly condemned malefactors, and are sent naked into the arena to be torn to pieces. To these (called the ἔσχατοι ἐπιθανάτιοι, "the last victims," as usually exposed at the close of the games), Paul, writing in the neighbourhood of the scene, compares himself and the other champions of the Gospel: "I think that God hath set forth us, the Apostles, last, as men doomed to death; for we have been made a *spectacle* unto the world, and to angels, and to men."[89] It has been thought by some that the words also of the Apostle, "I have fought with beasts at Ephesus,"[90] are to be taken literally, and that he had survived one of these terrible conflicts; but unquestionably the expression is metaphorical, or, as he qualifies it himself, κατὰ ἄνθρωπον, "figurative," and nothing but a love of the marvellous could ever attach to it any other signification. The words, however, have annexed an interest to the circus or stadium which it would not otherwise have possessed (see fig. 160 and 161).

Such was Ephesus at the time of the Apostle's visit, and now it is an utter desola-

---

[88] 1 Cor. ix. 24, 25.   [89] 1 Cor. iv. 9.   [90] 1 Cor. xv. 32.

Fig. 154.—View of the theatre at Ephesus in its present state. From a photograph by A. Svoboda.

The circular rows of the benches are seen in the centre of the plate, with the main passage to them running up the middle. The masses of masonry below, on the right and left, are the lateral ends of the semicircular theatre, and are the remains of the proscenium. The hill at the back is part of Mount Coressus, the theatre itself occupying the south-western foot of the hill.

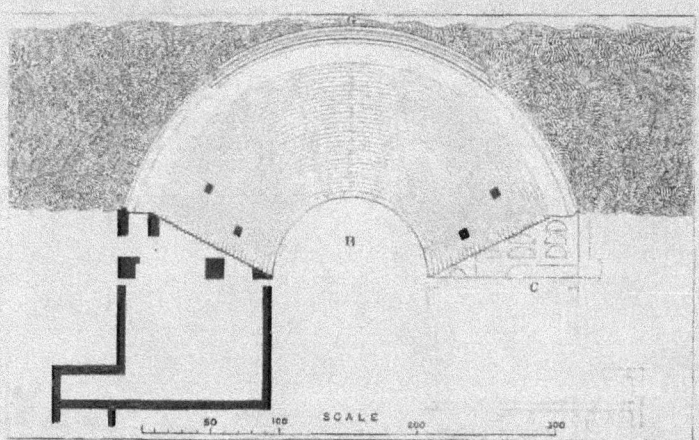

Fig. 155.—Ground plan of the great theatre at Ephesus. From Pococke.

B. The area. C. Section showing the arches by which the circular seats were supported. G. Rows of seats at the top of the theatre, and separated by a corridor from the seats below.

tion. So completely has "the candlestick been removed out of its place," that not a living soul resides within the walls. The beasts of the field and the birds of the air

Fig. 160.—View of the remains of the stadium at Ephesus. From Mayer and Ainslie.

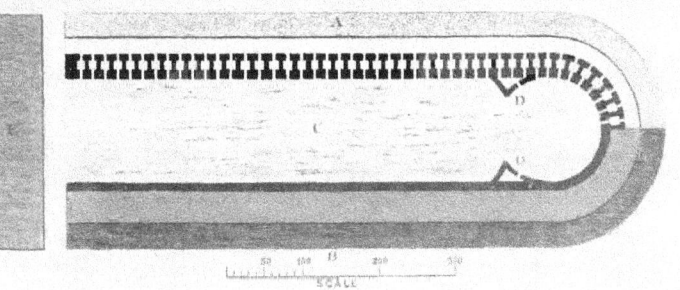

Fig. 161.—General plan of the stadium at Ephesus. From Pratt.

A. The northern limb, built upon arches. B. The southern limb, resting against the side of Mount Coressus. C. The area where the sports were carried on. D. Two projections of a semicircular shape, and apparently intended to form an amphitheatre. E. Additional seats for spectators, commanding a view of the whole stadium.

haunt the spot where living myriads rent the skies with their acclamations, "Great is Diana of the Ephesians!" It was the port that advanced the city to her greatness, and the loss of it laid her in the dust. In the course of ages the soil that was washed into the port filled up the basin. In the time of Attalus Philadelphus, King or Regent of Pergamus, B.C. 150, the vessels had already some difficulty in entering, and in a fatal moment the counsellors of Attalus suggested that, if the outlet of the port, where it joined the Cayster, were narrowed and embanked, the increased rapidity of the current would carry away the accumulation of soil. The work was executed,

Fig. 162.—*Coin representing a beast fight. From St. Non.*

and the remains of it may still be seen, but the result was exactly the reverse of their fond expectation.[91] The mud of the stagnant waters increased in a still more rapid ratio, and when the Apostle was there, the celebrated haven could with difficulty be entered. In A.D. 65[92] Barea Soranus, the Proconsul of Asia, bestowed great pains on scouring the port,[93] but eventually the force of nature prevailed against the efforts of man, and gradually Ephesus disappeared from the face of the earth.[94]

Paul arrived at Ephesus in the second quarter of A.D. 54.[95] The preceding year he had touched there on his way to Jerusalem, and we must recur for a moment to what had passed at Ephesus during the interval. Aquila and Priscilla had been left by the Apostle in the capital of Asia, while he himself proceeded on his route. Ephesus was celebrated for its manufacture of tents, so much so that the luxurious Alcibiades thought his furniture not complete unless he had a tent from Ephesus.[96] Here, then, Aquila hired a factory to carry on his trade of tent-making. It is nowhere stated that he personally stood forth as a preacher of the Gospel; all that we find is that the disciples met for divine service at his house,[97] and that Paul, in writing to the Romans a few years after, calls Priscilla and Aquila his "fellow-helpers in Christ Jesus."[98]

Ephesus, as a mercantile city, was replete with Jews who had acquired important privileges, and, though living amongst Gentiles, formed a separate and distinct community.[99] Aquila, as a Jew, was, of course, an attendant at the synagogue.

---

[91] Strabo, xiv. 1 (p. 176, Tauchnitz).

[92] See Fasti Sacri, p. 336, No. 1977.

[93] Portui Ephesiorum aperiendo curam (Barea Soranus) insumpserat. Tac. Ann. xvi. 23.

[94] I was there in A.D. 1862. I could not even discover a hut on the site of the capital of Asia.

[95] See Fasti Sacri, p. 303, No. 1816. The circuit he made from Antioch round about to Ephesus, would occupy several months. See Wieseler, Chron. Apost. 51, and ante, Chap. XII. note [?].

[96] Plut. Alcib. 12; Athenæus, xii. 47 (534).

[97] 1 Cor. xvi. 19.

[98] τοὺς συνεργούς μου ἐν Χριστῷ Ἰησοῦ. Rom. xvi. 3.

[99] See Jos. Ant. xiv. 10, 11, et seq.; xvi. 6, et seq.; Philo, Leg. ad Caium, 40.

It happened that one Sabbath, when the lessons from the Law and the Prophets had been read, a stranger rose to address the congregation. His manner was bold; his language eloquent; his knowledge of the Scriptures profound; and his argument, to prove Jesus the Messiah, unanswerable. At the same time, though he reasoned closely, he betrayed upon some vital points an ignorance of the Christian scheme—an ignorance the more remarkable from the great compass of his learning in other respects. This was Apollonius, or Apollos, a Jew of Alexandria, a man possessing an extraordinary insight into the mysteries of Holy Writ, and singularly gifted with the power of exposition.[160] He had imbibed from various sources, as chance threw them in his way, the general outline of the Christian doctrine, and these limited means had been improved by natural talents and scriptural attainments. Still his instruction had been so defective, that he had not even been made acquainted with the rite of Christian baptism as instituted by Jesus and imparting the gift of the *Holy Spirit*, but only that of John, the baptism of *Repentance*. He had lately landed at Ephesus, and being of a fervent temperament, had, by zealous declamation, both in public and private, argued from Holy Writ that Jesus was the Christ. He had at last ventured on preaching in the synagogue when Aquila and Priscilla happened to be his hearers. They were so charmed with the earnest but somewhat rude appeal which had been addressed to the congregation, that when the service was concluded, they introduced themselves to Apollos, and invited him to their house, and communicated to him the full light of the Gospel, as themselves had received it from Paul. Apollos did not stay long at Ephesus, but having occasion to pass over to Corinth, Aquila and Priscilla, and the other brethren who were then at Ephesus, gave him letters of recommendation to the Corinthian church.[161] During his short sojourn at Corinth (for he not long after returned to Ephesus), he rendered important services to the Christian community, for the Jews there were quite unable to resist the torrent of eloquence and argument by which he evinced that Jesus was the Christ.

It was while Apollos was at Corinth that Paul entered the gates of Ephesus. His first step was to seek out Aquila and Priscilla. At Corinth he had lived in their house, and found employment in Aquila's tent-manufactory; and it is not unlikely that Paul lodged with them again at Ephesus, and again provided for his own support by working under Aquila, or in partnership with him. We are assured by himself that, during his whole abode at Ephesus, he gained his own livelihood by manual labour;

---

[160] He is described as λόγιος, that is, either a *learned* man or an *eloquent* man, and the word probably here reflects both meanings. See Philo. Vit. Mos. i. 5; Jos. Bell. vi. 5, 3; id. xvii. 6, 2; and Kuinoel, Acts xviii. 24.

[161] Paul had been at Ephesus just before the Feast of Tabernacles, which was on the 16th of September, A.D. 53, and returned to Ephesus about Pentecost, 31st of May, A.D. 54, and during the interval Apollos had come to Ephesus, and had then sailed to Corinth before Paul's arrival. This he might well do, as the seas were open about the 8th of February, and Paul did not arrive at Ephesus until at least after the vernal equinox.

for, writing from Ephesus to Corinth, he says: "Even *unto this present hour* we both hunger and thirst, and are naked, and are buffeted, and have no certain dwelling-place; and *labour, working with our own hands.*"[102] And he some time afterwards reminded the Ephesians: "Yea, ye yourselves know that *these hands* have ministered unto my necessities, and to them that were with me."[103] From these passages we collect that, not only at Thessalonica, Corinth, and Ephesus, but indeed in all other places, he pursued the same course of industry, and that, from the returns of his labour, he sustained not himself only, but also some of his followers. We must conclude that Paul possessed remarkable skill in his craft, and that the wants of himself and his companions were but few.

The first occurrence at Ephesus related by the historian is this: Paul, soon after his arrival, fell in with some twelve men, professing to be members of the Church,[104] and the Apostle, as they were strangers to him, proceeded to interrogate them. He asked them, amongst other things, "Have ye received the Holy Ghost since ye believed?" and they said, "We have not so much as heard whether there be any Holy Ghost"—an answer that surprised Paul,[105] who perhaps had not heard of Apollos. Until Paul had touched at Ephesus, the year before, on his voyage to Jerusalem, the name of Jesus had not been preached there. Apollos, during Paul's absence, had promulgated the Christian scheme, but until he met with Aquila and Priscilla, he had known only the baptism of John, and had not heard of the miraculous powers conferred by the rite of baptism at the hands of Christ's ministers. The Baptist had forewarned his disciples that himself baptized with *water*, but that Christ, who should follow him, would baptize with the *Holy Ghost*. (Luke iii. 16.) But it had not yet reached the ears of Apollos that the Holy Ghost had been actually given. These men were apparently converts of Apollos, while in his state of ignorance, and before he had been instructed in the baptism of Jesus. Paul said, "Unto what, then, were ye baptized?" for had baptism been in the name of the Father, and of the Son, and *of the Holy Ghost*, they could not fail to have heard of the Holy Ghost. They said, "Unto John's baptism;" the only one with which Apollos had been acquainted. Then said Paul, "'John verily baptized with the baptism of *repentance*, saying unto the people, that they should *believe on him which should come after him*, that is, on *Christ Jesus*, who was to baptize with the *Holy Ghost and with fire.*"[106] When they heard this, they were baptized in the name of the Lord Jesus; and when Paul had laid his hands upon them, the Holy Ghost came on them, and they spake with tongues, and prophesied."[107] This communication of the Holy Ghost

---

[102] 1 Cor. iv. 11, 12.
[103] Acts xx. 34.
[104] Luke calls them μαθηταs. Acts xix. 1.
[105] It is well observed by Schrader that baptism in those days must have been followed, as matter of course, by spiritual gifts, as speaking with tongues, &c., or else why should Paul have been surprised? Schrader, Ap. P. vol. ii. p. 274.
[106] In allusion to the tongues of fire on the day of Pentecost. Acts ii. 3.
[107] Acts xix. 4, 5, 6.

by the imposition of the Apostle's hands, and the miraculous effects that followed, furnish a clue to the full meaning of the few words that Paul shortly afterwards addresses to the Galatians, for referring to himself, though using the third person, he writes: "He that *ministereth to you the Spirit and worketh miracles among you*, doeth he it by the works of the law, or by the hearing of faith?"[108] The scene particularly described at Ephesus had, no doubt, occurred again and again in Galatia.

Paul now, according to his practice, proceeded to unfold the Gospel scheme to his own countrymen, the *Jews*, who had invited him the year before to come amongst them. He entered into the synagogue, and for three months argued with them, and pressed the kingdom of God upon their acceptance. It cannot but be interesting to know who was his first convert. It was Epenetus, for in the best MSS. he is called the first-fruits, not of Achaia, but of Asia.[109] At the expiration of three months (which would be in the autumn of A.D. 54) the greater part of the Jews assumed a tone of decided opposition. Some of them became so hardened in unbelief, that they openly blasphemed the name of Christ in the face of the congregation. To persevere would lead to the disturbance of the public peace, and Paul bade adieu to the synagogue, taking with him all those (and they were not a few) whose minds had been open to conviction. He now hired the school or lecture-room of one Tyrannus,[110] and here for two years he opened the mystery of the Gospel to all who would attend, both Jews and Greeks. In so populous a city, the eloquence and argumentative powers of the Apostle soon drew about him a crowded audience.

At the same time that Paul was thus declaiming publicly, he exerted himself no less in private, by going from house to house, wherever he had access, and inculcating amongst individuals the doctrines of the Gospel.[111] The seed thus industriously sown soon sprang up, and ripened into an abundant harvest. The disciples became so numerous, that presbyters, or bishops, as they were then called, were ordained by Paul,[112] and churches were regularly established, not only in Ephesus, but throughout Asia.[113] In vain did the Jews try to thwart his success by secret machinations against his life. The vigilance and adroitness of the Apostle eluded them all. Luke, indeed, does not expressly say that, when Paul quitted the synagogue, the Jews continued their persecution, but we know, from their acrimonious spirit, that such must have been the case, and we learn it as a fact from Paul's touching address to the Ephesians on a

---

[108] Gal. iii. 5.

[109] Rom. xvi. 5. This is the reading adopted by Griesbach, Lachmann, Tischendorf, Scholtz, and Alford.

[110] This was possibly Tyrannus the Sophist mentioned by Suidas: Τύραννος σοφιστής, περὶ στάσεως καὶ διαιρέσεως λόγου βιβλία δέκα. Some, however, have objected that this could scarcely be, as the Tyrannus of Suidas was a heathen, and the Tyrannus of Saul must have been a Jew or Christian. But the argument appears destitute of weight, as Tyrannus, the owner of the lecture-room, would be willing enough to let the use of it for hire to anyone that required it, without reference to the doctrines to be promulgated in it. See Meyer, Apostg. 317. Some critics, as Lachmann and Tischendorf, reject the word τινος after Τυράννου, and then the expression ἐν τῇ Σχολῇ Τυράννου would simply designate a lecture room called the 'School of Tyrannus.'

[111] Acts xx. 20.

[112] Acts xx. 17, 28.

[113] 1 Cor. xvi. 19.

subsequent occasion: "And when they were come to him, he said unto them, ye know from the first day that I came into Asia, after what manner I have been with you at all seasons, serving the Lord with all humility of mind, and *with many tears and temptations which befell me by the lying in wait of the Jews.*"[114] Indeed, the life of Paul at Ephesus must have been one continued escape from the most imminent perils. How else could he have drawn such a picture of himself as the following, in the first Epistle to the Corinthians, written during his sojourn at Ephesus: "I protest by your rejoicing which I have in Christ Jesus our Lord, *I die daily*. If, after the manner of men, *I have fought with beasts* at Ephesus, what advantageth it me, if the dead rise not? let us eat and drink, for to-morrow we die."[115] Not that Paul fought with beasts literally, but only, as already explained, "after the manner, or in the language, of man"—that is, in a metaphorical sense. But the strength of the metaphor shows what fearful struggles he must here have encountered.

The most effective instrument wielded by Paul at Ephesus for the establishment of the Gospel was the open display by him of supernatural powers. It seems that at Ephesus more particularly Paul was accredited by this divine testimony. "And God," says Luke, "wrought special miracles by the hands of Paul; so that from his body were brought unto the sick handkerchiefs[116] or aprons,[117] and the diseases departed from them, and the evil spirits went out of them."[118] But if such wonders were enacted, how, it will be said, was not all Ephesus a convert to Christianity? Who could resist such ocular demonstration of the Divine Power? But the heart of man is slow to believe, and there was a peculiar cause at Ephesus why such miracles should lose half their effect. The prevailing ignorance ascribed them to magic. In no city upon the face of the globe at that day was sorcery so much practised as at Ephesus. The incantations used there had acquired a high degree of celebrity, and were known by the name of Ephesian charms. The most famous of their charms was not unlike the gibberish of modern conjurors, "Aski Cataski Lix Tetrax Damnameneus Aision."[119] The black art was there exercised, not merely by the strolling

---

[114] Acts xx. 18, 19.
[115] 1 Cor. xv. 31, 32.
[116] σουδάρια, the Latin *sudaria*—handkerchiefs for wiping off perspiration, &c.
[117] σιμικίνθια, another Latin word—*semicinctia*. It is uncertain what the exact nature of them was. Some think they were half-girdles, i.e. narrow girdles, of only half the usual width. Suidas renders the word by φακιώλιον ἢ σουδάριον, and he defines φάκελλος as τὸ τῆς κεφαλῆς φόρημα ὃ καὶ φακιώλιον λέγεται, and φακιόλιον as παρὰ Κυπρίοις τὸ τῆς κεφαλῆς περικάλυμμα, so that in his opinion the *semicinctium* was a kind of turban. Hesychius adds other explanations: Σιμικίνθια φακιόλια [fasciolæ], ζωνάρια, ὡράρια [horaria] τῶν ἱερέων. The English translation "aprons" may be taken as the most correct. They were the aprons worn by persons who lived by manual labour, and we know that Paul by his own account supported himself during his three years' residence at Ephesus by the labour of his own hands as a tent-maker. *Why* aprons were called *semicinctia*, or *half-cinctures*, may perhaps be explained by the fact that they did not, like the ordinary garments, reach *all round* the body, but only *halfway round*. These aprons, like the handkerchiefs, would be generally of linen, and so would require constant change; and this, the text implies, was the case with the *semicinctia*.

[118] Acts xix. 11, 12.
[119] Ἐφέσια γράμματα ἦν μὲν πάλαι ς′, ὕστερον

vagabond for extracting a few pence from the credulity of silly women and illiterate artisans, but, like astrology in more recent times, was in the hands of the polite, and was studied as a science by philosophers and men of letters. Volumes and volumes had been written by professors, setting forth the various incantations proper to be used for the desired end. Many of these books, where the proficiency of the writer was acknowledged, and the secret recipes contained in them had not been disclosed to the public, were sold at enormous prices.

To magic were equally addicted both Greeks and Jews, but amongst the latter there was one form of it which was peculiar, namely, exorcism. The Jews ascribed the disorders of the mind to the possession of devils; and they had various adjurations by which the evil spirits were to be cast out. Josephus tells us that Solomon had, in his manifold wisdom, composed incantations, by which evil spirits might be so effectually ejected as not to return any more, and " this method of cure," he adds, " has been continued in use amongst us down to our own time." Nay, he informs us that he himself had witnessed an instance, " having beheld one Eleazar, a Jew, in the presence of Vespasian, his sons, and the great officers of the army, curing demoniacs by holding a ring to their nose, under whose seal was hid the root of a certain plant prescribed by Solomon, at the scent whereof the demon presently took leave and was gone, the patient falling to the ground, while the exorcist, by naming Solomon and reciting some charms made by him, stood over him, and charged the evil spirit never to return. And to let them see that he was really gone, he commanded the demon as he went out to overturn a cup full of water, which he had caused to be set in the room before them."[120]

We can now readily conceive that when Paul displayed those miraculous gifts, he only gained credit with the multitude for having acquired (they knew not how) a superior system of magic not yet publicly known. However, a judgment that overtook some exorcists tended much to open the eyes of the Ephesians, and to prove that the hand of God was indeed amongst them. Some itinerant exorcists, conceiving the name of Jesus to be used as a spell, would fain try their skill, and attempted to cast out evil spirits, saying, " We adjure you by Jesus whom Paul preacheth." " And there were," writes St. Luke, " seven sons of one Sceva, a Jew,[121] and chief of the priests, which did so. And the evil spirit answered, and said, ' Jesus I know, and Paul I know ; but who are ye?' And the man in whom the evil spirit was leaped on them, and overcame them, and prevailed against them, so that they fled out of that house naked and wounded."[122] The fame of this soon spread through Ephesus, and

---

δὲ προσέθεσάν τινες ἀπατεῶνες καὶ ἄλλα. Φασὶ δὲ τῶν πρώτων τὰ ὀνόματα τάδε—Ἀσκι, Κατάσκι, Λίξ, Τέτραξ, Δαμναμενεύς, Αἴσιον—Δηλοῖ δὲ τὸ μὲν Ἀσκι σκότος, τὰ δὲ Κατάσκι φῶς, τὰ δὲ Λίξ γῆ, [Τέτραξ δὲ ἐνιαυτὸς.] Δαμναμενεύς δὲ ἥλιος, Αἴσιον δὲ ἀληθές. Ταῦτα οὖν ἱερά ἐστι καὶ ἅγια. Hesych. sub Ἐφέσια γράμματα. See the authorities upon this subject collected by Renan, St. Paul, p. 344.

[120] Jos. Ant. viii. 2, 5.

[121] The name of Sceva, however, is Roman, and is another instance of the fashion of the day for a Jew to bear a Roman name, and most likely together with some Jewish name. Sceva occurs in Horat. Epist. i. 17, 1. See Kuinoel, Acts xix. 14.

[122] Acts xix. 14-16.

fear overtook both Jews and Greeks, and sorcery vanished before the withering influence of the name of Jesus. Such, indeed, was the sensation produced, that divers of the believers, who had, notwithstanding, continued their evil practices in secret, now came and confessed their deeds. "Many of them, also, which used curious arts brought their books together, and burned them before all men; and they counted the price of them, and found it fifty thousand pieces of silver. So mightily grew the word of God and prevailed."[123] These pieces of silver were either Attic drachmæ of 9¾d. each, or (which is more probable) Roman denarii of 8½d. each. If the former, the amount would be £2031; and if the latter, £1770;[124]—in either case,

---

[123] Acts xix. 19, 20.

[124] These were, we may assume, the Roman denarii, which at this time had superseded the Attic drachmæ, and were the common currency over the whole Roman empire. The tribute money shown to our Lord was a denarius, for the image and superscription were Cæsar's.

The coinage current in the first century was either gold or silver or brass, as in the charge of our Lord to his disciples: "Provide neither *gold* nor *silver* nor *brass* in your purses," Matt. x. 9; where, however, in the original the word is 'girdles,' and not 'purses;' for anciently the girdle had pockets attached to it for carrying articles of frequent use, as money, handkerchiefs, &c.

The common *gold* coin was the Roman aureus, or χρυσοῦς (fig. 163), of the weight of 120 grains, and of the value of 25 denarii = 17s. 8½d. (fig. 164).

Fig. 163.—*Aureus of Augustus. From the British Museum.*
Obv. Head of Augustus with legend, Cæsar Augustus Divi F. Pater Patriæ.—Rev. C. L. Cæsares Augusti F. Cos. Desig. Princ. Juvent.

These aurei, or χρυσοῖ, are frequently mentioned by Josephus (Vit. 26, 57) and other writers. There were also, but not so much in use, smaller pieces of the same metal containing fractional parts of the aureus, as the half and quarter aureus.

The common *silver* coin was the Roman denarius, the Greek δραχμή (fig. 164). Originally the denarius and drachma were of different values, the former being 8½d. and the latter 9¾d.; but in the time of the Apostle the drachma was coined of precisely the same weight as the denarius, viz. 56 grains; and the words 'denarii' and 'drachmæ' were used indifferently. Thus, Dion calls the Roman denarii 'drachmæ.' Dion, lv. 23, lvi. 32, lix. 2. When drachmas, therefore, are

Fig. 164.—*Denarius of Tiberius. From the British Museum.*
Obv. Head of Tiberius with the legend, Ti Cæsar Divi Aug. F. Augustus.

spoken of by Josephus (Vit. 13) or the writers of the N. T. (Luke xv. 8), denarii must be understood. Besides the denarius, or drachm, which was the common circulating medium, there were also the tetradrachm and didrachm. The tetradrachm (or stater, or shekel, for they were the same) (fig. 15) was the highest silver coin minted, and, as the name imports, was equal to four drachms = 2s. 10d. The didrachm, or half-shekel (fig. 16) was equal to two drachms = 1s. 5d., and was the Temple tax paid by every Jew; and therefore it was that our Lord said of the tetradrachm, or stater (the double didrachm), taken from the fish's mouth, "that take and give unto them *for thee and me*." Matt. xvii. 27.

The ordinary *copper* coinage was the Roman as, or Greek ἀσσάριον (answering to our penny);

Fig. 165.—*As of Antioch. From the British Museum.*
Obv. Head of Tiberius with the legend, Ti. Cæsar Aug. Tr. Pot xxxiii, and therefore struck A.D. 31, in the third year of our Lord's ministry.—Rev. S. C. (By decree of the Senate).

the quadrans, or χαλκοῦς (answering to our farthing), and the λεπτόν (answering to our mite).

more particularly if we take into account the value of bullion at that period, an enormous sum to be sacrificed by Christian converts, not perhaps the most wealthy part of the Ephesian community.[125]

It was during Paul's sojourn at Ephesus, viz. on 13th October, A.D. 54,[126] that the Emperor Claudius died. This event was a heavy blow to Christendom. Claudius may have been the butt of the court, and even have been kicked and cuffed by the madman Caligula,[127] but with all his faults, he had many noble qualities. He had been schooled in adversity, and could feel compassion for others. He was no bigot, and would never lend his sanction to religious persecution. Universal toleration was with him a sacred principle,[128] and Gallio but represented the feelings of his master when he drave the Jews from the judgment-seat. It was during his reign that Christianity extended itself with such rapidity throughout the provinces of the Roman empire. The loss of Claudius was felt the more severely from the succession of that execrable monster, the Emperor Nero.

At the very commencement of the new reign a bloody tragedy was enacted at Ephesus. Junius Silanus, at the arrival of Paul at Ephesus, and also at the death of Claudius, was Proconsul of Asia, and Celer and Ælius were the Procurators of the Emperor, or the collectors of the Imperial revenue. Silanus was of the lineage of Augustus himself, and a person of inoffensive and even lethargic habits—insomuch so, that he went by the sobriquet of the "golden sheep."[129] But the fact that he was descended from Augustus, and might therefore draw aside the eyes of the public from the young Nero to himself, was the sealing of his death-warrant. Agrippina, the mother of Nero, and now in full power at the court of Rome, had some time before procured the murder of Lucius Silanus, the brother of the Proconsul; and now, from a fear of some movement in favour of Junius Silanus, and being also in constant

---

The as, or ἀσσάριον (see fig. 165) was the twelfth part of the denarius or drachm, and therefore in strictness of the value of ½d. The quadrans, or χαλκοῦς (see fig. 166) was the fourth part of

Fig. 167.—1 χαλκοῦς. Entry the Jewish Hammer obv. An anchor, a common emblem on Jewish coins, with the date RK or 26.—Rev. The Legend χαλκοῦς.

the as, and therefore somewhat less than the farthing; and the λεπτὸν was half the quadrans (Mark xii. 42), and therefore somewhat less than the mite. See the coins of Chios, p st.

It was the advice of Mæcenas to Augustus that subject provinces should be compelled to use Roman coins and weights and measures (Dion, lii. 331), and this policy seems in the main to have been adopted. Thus the provinces, and even the feudatory kings, while they were allowed to mint copper, were prohibited from coining gold, and only some highly-favoured municipalities had the liberty of coining silver. Even Herod, with all his Court influence, was not privileged to coin gold or silver—at least, only copper coins of his reign have been discovered; and we may be sure that, with his magnificent ideas, he would have coined gold and silver, had it not been treasonable to Rome.

[125] Others think that Jewish sicli, or shekels, and others that Attic minae are referred to, but neither supposition is probable. See Kuinoel, Acts xix. 19.

[126] See Fasti Sacri, p. 302, No. 1892.

[127] Seneca ἀπόκολ. ad finem.

[128] See the rescript of Claudius, Jos. Ant. xix. 6, 3; Dion, lx. 5.

[129] Tac. Ann. xiii. 1.

apprehension, from a guilty conscience, that Junius would avenge his brother's death, she sent private instructions to Celer and Ælius to remove Junius out of the way, and he was shortly afterwards poisoned at a banquet. By a decree of Claudius, passed shortly before his death, the Emperor's procurators had been invested with irresponsible power in their respective provinces, and were to be regarded in the Emperor's absence as his vicars;[130] and Celer and Ælius, the Procurators, now assumed jointly the proconsular authority in Asia until the appointment of another proconsul. This circumstance may assign a meaning to that remarkable expression in the speech of the town clerk to the Ephesians—"Wherefore if Demetrius, and the craftsmen which are with him, have a matter against any man, the law is open, and there are *Deputies* (or Proconsuls); let them implead one another."[131] There had never previously been more than one Proconsul of Asia, but at the particular juncture when the riot occurred, Celer and Ælius may still have been acting jointly in the execution of the office. It may be mentioned, by the way, that Celer was afterwards tried at Rome for maladministration, but was screened by the court.[132]

Paul had been at Ephesus little more than a year,[133] when he received the heart-breaking intelligence of the partial defection of the Galatian church. They had a few years before thrown themselves into the arms of the Apostle, and had almost worshipped the man who was the herald of such glad tidings. But Gallic fickleness was proverbial, and they had recently given their allegiance to some artful emissaries, who had come amongst them to corrupt their faith. We have already had occasion to trace the movement of the Judaizing party—how they had assailed the Apostle of the Gentiles at Jerusalem, and had followed him down to Antioch. They had now tracked his footsteps onward, and had succeeded in undermining the foolish Galatians. There were several false teachers who had thus busily disseminated their dangerous doctrines in Galatia. "There be *some*," writes the Apostle, "that trouble you, and would pervert the Gospel of Christ;"[134] but it would seem that one in particular led the van: "*He* that troubleth you shall bear the blame, whosoever he be."[135] Such weakness in the Galatian converts, so contrary to the firm and uncompromising character of the Apostle himself, filled him with indignation. He would gladly, on the instant, have hurried thither to rescue them from their Jewish thraldom, but other duties required his presence at Ephesus at that time; and the only corrective he could apply was to dispatch one of his trusty followers to them with an expostulatory letter. This he did; and the Epistle bears strong marks of the circumstances under which it was written. It is penned in haste—it expresses by turns astonishment at their tergiversation—pity for their weakness—anger against the mischief-making firebrands—ardent love towards the misguided. The Apostle now plies them with irony—now

---

[130] Tac. Ann. xii. 60. See Fasti Sacri, p. 299, No. 1787.
[131] Acts xix. 38.
[132] Tac. Ann. xiii. 33.
[133] See Fasti Sacri, p. 305, No. 1825.
[134] Gal. i. 7.
[135] Gal. v. 10.

with argument—at one time pronounces authoritatively, and at another makes a touching appeal to their affection.

After saluting the church, he at once gives expression to his wonder at the readiness with which, since he had parted from them little more than a year before, they had abandoned their first faith. "I marvel," he says, "that ye are so soon removed from him that called you in the grace of Christ unto another gospel,"[136] viz. that of bondage to the Law; and then, with a solemnity almost dreadful, he recalls them to the truth in these impressive words: "Though we, or an angel from heaven, preach any other gospel unto you than that which we have preached unto you, LET HIM BE ACCURSED; as we said before, so say I now again—If any man preach any other gospel unto you than that ye have received, LET HIM BE ACCURSED."[137]

He next (i. 11) meets the charge which had been brought against him personally. The Judaizers in Galatia had propagated the calumny that Paul was not an Apostle at all, as he was not one of the Twelve;—that he had received his gospel at second-hand, not the pure Gospel, but in a corrupt form;—that the Apostles and the church at Jerusalem observed the Law, and disclaimed Paul's doctrine that the dispensation of Christ had superseded that of Moses. The Apostle answers, that the Gospel which he preached had been revealed to him directly from God;—that so far from having derived it at second-hand from other Apostles, he had been three years in the ministry before he saw an Apostle;—that (with the exception of having twice gone to Jerusalem as the messenger of others) he had never visited Jerusalem but on two occasions—on the first he had voluntarily sought a private interview with Peter, and had remained only fifteen days with him, and on the other he had been called thither by revelation; and so far from the Apostles having discountenanced the gospel which he preached, he had fully explained it to Peter, James, and John, who were accounted the chiefs of the Apostles, and they had given him and Barnabas the right hand of fellowship, and had fully recognized them as the Apostles of the Uncircumcision in the same sense as Peter was of the Circumcision;—that the false brethren had made the same stir at Jerusalem then, as now in Galatia, and insisted that Titus, who travelled with Paul and was a Greek, should be circumcised, but that they had not prevailed for a moment— nay, more, that when the Judaizers shortly afterwards came down to Antioch, and had some countenance from the inconsistent conduct of Peter, he, Paul, had openly rebuked even the great Apostle of the Circumcision; and he then (ii. 15) adds the corollary, that if *Jews* by birth had been obliged to have recourse to Christ as a means of salvation, *a fortiori* the *Gentiles* could not be justified by the Law.

The Apostle next (iii. 1) addresses himself to the main point, and proves by a variety of arguments, that justification could be only by faith in Christ—that the promise had been made to Abraham four hundred years before the Law, "In thy seed (that is, in Christ) shall all the nations of the earth be blessed;" and then he explains

---

[136] Gal. i. 6. [137] Gal. i. 8, 9.

the use of the Law by this striking illustration—that for a length of time after the promise was given, the Jewish family, as the offspring of Abraham, was in its infancy; that as the child grew up it was requisite that a schoolmaster should discipline and form the mind, and the Mosaic dispensation had been instituted for that purpose; but the heir had now attained to manhood; the schoolmaster was dismissed; and the promise having been fulfilled by the coming of Christ, the Jews who believed in him had become the sons of God, and were put in possession of their inheritance.

The Apostle then (iv. 12) endeavours to touch the chord of their affections, and reminds them of the tender feelings they had entertained towards him when he first preached amongst them in a state of almost total blindness; that such were their transports of joy and gratitude, that if they could have served him, they would have plucked out their own eyes and given them to him. "Am I, therefore," he continues, "become your enemy because I tell you the truth?"[138] "But," he continues, "it is good to be zealously affected in a good thing *always*, and not only when I am *present with you*, my little children, of whom I travail in birth again until Christ be formed in you."[139]

Here (iv. 21) a new argument suddenly crosses his path, and he pursues it on the instant. "Tell me, ye that desire to be under the Law, do ye not hear the Law?"[140] and then he traces out the allegory that Abraham had two sons, one of the bondwoman, which was Ishmael, or the Jewish Church, and one of Sarah, the freewoman, which was Isaac, or the Christian Church; that Agar, the mother of Ishmael, was Mount Sinai, from which the Law was delivered that held Agar and her children in bondage; that the freewoman was the heavenly Jerusalem, the mother of all Christians, and who were under no thraldom; that as the freewoman had cast out the bondwoman and her child, so must the Church of Christ put away the Jewish dispensation, which was now abrogated.

The Apostle then (v. 1) tries the influence of his personal authority, for he might well suppose that, degenerate as they were, they had not yet lost all respect for the name of Paul. "Behold, *I, Paul*, say unto you, that if ye be circumcised, Christ shall profit you nothing; but I testify again to every man that is circumcised, that he is a debtor to do the *whole* Law."[141]

The Apostle now (v. 13), as usual with him at the close of an Epistle, addresses to them some admonitory precepts arising out of the previous matter, and exhorts them not to make "their freedom in Christ a cloak for maliciousness," but that they should walk after the Spirit, and not after the flesh, &c.

Here the Apostle might have concluded his letter; but, no! he is so anxious for their welfare, that he must again recur to the mischievous doctrines of the Judaizers. Hitherto he had dictated to an amanuensis, but he cannot be easy in his conscience while any means remain of adding force to his appeal. He therefore takes the pen

[138] Gal. iv. 16.
[139] Gal. iv. 18, 19.
[140] Gal. iv. 16.
[141] Gal. v. 2, 3.

himself, and half blind as he is, and scarcely capable of forming the letters, he sits down to impress upon his converts with his own autograph the great truths he had been advocating. "See," he says, "in what large characters I have written unto you with mine own hand!"[142] and then, pointing out the insidious designs of the Judaizing party, he recapitulates the great doctrine by which they should be guided: "*In Christ Jesus neither circumcision availeth anything, nor uncircumcision, but a new creature; and as many as walk according to this rule, peace be on them, and mercy, and upon the Israel of God.*"[143]

He now appends the benediction, but as the contents of the letter might have created something of an irritated feeling, it will be observed what inexpressible tenderness is conveyed by the closing words: "The grace of our Lord Jesus Christ be with your spirit, *my brethren*. Amen." The Epistle ran as follows:[144]—

[The *italics* indicate the variations from the Authorized Version, and the words in brackets, thus [ ], are not *expressed*, but only *implied*, in the Greek.]

CH. I. "PAUL, AN APOSTLE (NOT *from* MEN, NEITHER BY MAN, BUT BY JESUS CHRIST, 2 AND GOD THE FATHER, WHO RAISED HIM FROM THE DEAD), AND ALL THE 3 BRETHREN WHICH ARE WITH ME,[145] UNTO THE CHURCHES[146] OF GALATIA; GRACE

---

[142] Gal. vi. 11.
[143] Gal. vi. 15, 16.
[144] The date is thus ascertained:—

1. The Epistle was written after a collection amongst the Gentiles for the poor Hebrews, for in writing to the Galatians the Apostle thus alludes to it: "Only they" (the Apostles of Jerusalem) "would that we should remember the poor, the same which also I have been forward (ἐσπούδασα) to do." Gal. ii. 9. Now, in the preceding year (A.D. 54) Paul had passed through Galatia, and had made a collection there, as appears from the first Epistle to the Corinthians: "Concerning the collection for the saints, as I have given order to the churches of *Galatia*, even so do ye." 1 Cor. xvi. 1.

2. The Epistle to the Galatians was subsequent to the Apostle's *second* visit to Galatia, for he thus alludes to the former of his two visits: "Ye know how, under infirmity of the flesh, I preached the Gospel unto you *the former time* (τὸ πρότερον)." Gal. iv. 13. And again, he contrasts the welcome they gave him at his first visit with the coldness of their treatment of him at his second visit, in consequence of the rebukes administered by him Gal. iv. 16. The first visit was in A.D. 50 and the second in A.D. 54, and therefore the Epistle must have been written either in or subsequently to the year A.D. 54.

3. The Epistle was written *not long after* the second visit, for the Apostle frequently alludes to his *recent* presence amongst them: "I marvel that ye are *so soon* removed from him that called you." Gal. i. 6. "It is a good thing to be zealously affected *always* in what is good, and not only *when I am present with you*." Gal. iv. 18. "Ye *were running well*; who hath tripped you up that you should not obey the truth?" Gal. v. 7. Indeed the whole Epistle breathes the spirit of one who had, not long before, been personally amongst them.

4. The very year of the Epistle is indicated in the following passage: "Ye are observing days and months and times and *years*." Gal. iv. 10. The Galatians are here represented as in the actual observance of days and months and *years*; and by the latter can only be meant sabbatic years. The date of the Epistle, then, was at a time when Paul, having recently left the Galatians, heard that they were observing the sabbatic year. But the first sabbatic year after his *second* visit to Galatia was from 1 Nisan A.D. 55 to 1 Nisan A.D. 56, and during that interval, therefore, the letter was written, and probably in the latter half of A.D. 55.

[145] Viz. Titus, Gaius, Aristarchus, &c., who had been with Paul in Galatia.

[146] This is the only epistle in which Paul addresses the churches as such. The expression implies that the Epistle was meant to be publicly read in the churches.

[A.D. 55]   EPISTLE TO THE GALATIANS.   [CHAP. XIII.

UNTO YOU AND PEACE FROM GOD THE FATHER, AND FROM OUR LORD JESUS
4 CHRIST, WHO GAVE HIMSELF FOR OUR SINS, THAT HE MIGHT DELIVER US FROM
THIS PRESENT EVIL WORLD, ACCORDING TO THE WILL OF OUR GOD AND FATHER,
5 TO WHOM BE GLORY FOR EVER AND EVER. AMEN.

6   "I marvel[147] that ye are so soon removed[148] from him that called you *in* the
7 grace of Christ,[149] unto a *different* gospel, which is not another;[150] but there be
8 some that trouble you, and would pervert the Gospel of Christ. But though
even we, or an angel from heaven, preach any other Gospel unto you, than
9 that[151] which we have preached unto you, let him be accursed. As we said
before, so say I now again, if any *one* preach any other Gospel unto you than
10 that ye have received, let him be accursed.[152] For do I now *urge* men or
God?[153] or do I seek to please men? for if I yet pleased men, I should not be
the servant of Christ.

11   "But I certify you, brethren, that the Gospel which was preached of me is
12 not after man; for I neither received it *from* man, neither was I taught it, but
13 by the revelation of Jesus Christ. For ye have heard of my conversation
in time past in the Jews' religion, that beyond measure I persecuted the church
14 of God, and *destroyed* it; and *advanced* in the Jews' religion above many my
equals *in age* in mine own nation, being more exceedingly zealous of the tra-
15 ditions of my fathers. But when God, who separated me from my mother's

---

[147] J. B. Lightfoot (ad locum) has well observed that here "an indignant expression of surprise takes the place of the usual thanksgiving for the faith of his converts. This is the sole instance in which St. Paul omits to express his thankfulness in addressing any church."

[148] It was somewhat more than a year since the Apostle had quitted Galatia, and considering the total change wrought in that church, and allowing some time for the transmission of the intelligence, the interval was a short one, and the Apostle might well express surprise—"I marvel that ye are so *soon* removed!" Others think, however, that the word ταχέως does not refer to the short period which had elapsed since the Apostle's presence among the Galatians, but may denote the celerity with which, when the leaven began to work, the whole community had been corrupted. If, for instance, the Apostle had heard six months before that the Galatian church was in a healthy state, and was now all at once informed of their total alienation from him, he might express his astonishment at the lubricity of the Gallic character—"I marvel that ye so quickly (or readily) fall away!" The word ταχέως is used in this sense in 2 Thess. ii. 2, where the Apostle exhorts them εἰς τὸ μὴ ταχέως σαλευθῆναι ἀπὸ τοῦ νοός, 'not lightly to be shaken from their sobriety.'

[149] ἐν χάριτι Χριστοῦ. There is great force in these words, and they are in fact the keynote of the whole epistle. The Apostle throughout dwells on the *grace* or *free gift* of Christ, in opposition to those who held out salvation by the *works* of the Law.

[150] εἰς ἕτερον εὐαγγέλιον, ὃ οὐκ ἔστιν ἄλλο, κ.τ.λ. ἕτερον denotes a difference in *kind*, ἄλλο in number. Wordsworth.

[151] παρ᾽ ὅ. "On the interpretation of these words," says J. B. Lightfoot, "a controversy on tradition has been made to hinge, Protestant writers advocating the sense of 'besides' for παρά, and Roman Catholics that of 'contrary to.'"

[152] Let him be excommunicated, i.e. regarded by you as an outcast and alien. The Greek word is ἀνάθεμα, 'what is devoted to Satan,' and not ἀνάθημα, 'what is devoted to God.'

[153] πείθω. In Eng. ver. "persuade." 'In urging the pure Gospel upon you, am I the advocate of what is human or divine? not of what is human, for I did not "receive it of man;" but of what is divine, for it was revealed to me by God.' Or πείθω may mean 'conciliate,' i.e. 'do I seek to conciliate man or God?'

16 womb, and called me by his grace, *was pleased* (A.D. 37) to reveal his Son in
me, that I might preach him among the heathen, immediately I *applied* not
17 *myself to* [154] flesh and blood, neither went I up to Jerusalem to them which were
Apostles before me, but I went *away* into Arabia, and returned again unto
18 Damascus. Then *the third year* after [155] (A.D. 39) I went up to Jerusalem to
19 *seek out* [156] Peter, and abode with him fifteen days; [157] but other of the Apostles
20 saw I none, save James the Lord's brother. [158] (Now the things which I write
21 unto you, behold, before God, I lie not.) *Then* I came into the regions of Syria
22 and Cilicia; [159] and was unknown by face unto the churches of Judea which
23 were in Christ, but they heard only, that he which *once* persecuted us now
24 preacheth the faith which once he destroyed; and they glorified God in me.

Ch. II. "Then, fourteen years after (A.D. 53), [160] I went up again to Jerusalem with
2 Barnabas, *taking* Titus with me also. And I went up by revelation, [161] and

[154] προσανεθέμην. In Eng. ver. "conferred not with."

[155] μετὰ τρία ἔτη, i.e. in the third year *current* from his conversion, which was in the spring of A.D. 37. His visit to Jerusalem was towards the close of A.D. 39. That μετὰ τρία ἔτη means the third year current is beyond question. See Fasti Sacri, p. 264, No. 1581.

[156] ἱστορῆσαι. In Eng. ver. "to see."

[157] We have here an undesigned coincidence strongly confirmatory of Luke's accuracy. A sojourn of fifteen days was a very short one, and while Luke does not in express terms say whether the visit of Paul on this occasion was long or short, he assumes that it was very brief; for Paul is warned in a vision to make haste out of Jerusalem: σπεῦσον καὶ ἔξελθε ἐν τάχει. Acts xxii. 18.

[158] Whom Paul would see of course, for James, the half-brother of our Lord, was bishop of the church at Jerusalem, and permanently resident there. See Fasti Sacri, p. 181, No. 1198.

[159] Paul therefore passed through Syria on his way to Cilicia.

[160] Viz. fourteen years from his last visit in A.D. 39, that is, at the Feast of Tabernacles of A.D. 53. The word διὰ implies 'after the expiration of fourteen years complete,' as in ἡ δι' ἐξ ἡμερῶν ἱερὰ ἑβδόμη. Philo de Septen. s. 6. See Fasti Sacri, p. 300, No. 1795.

[161] It has been much disputed what was the particular journey here referred to. We find recorded in the Acts five occasions on which the Apostle went up to Jerusalem—1. In A.D. 39, in the third year current after his conversion (see Fasti Sacri, p. 264, No. 1581). 2. In A.D. 44, when Barnabas and Paul (observe the order of the names) carried up the bounty of the Antiochian church at the great famine (see Fasti Sacri, p. 279, No. 1669). 3. In A.D. 48, when Paul and Barnabas (observe the order of names reversed) were envoys from the church of Antioch to take the opinion of the council at Jerusalem on the subject of the Jewish law. 4. In A.D. 53, when Paul sailed from Corinth, after the indictment of him before Gallio, and attended the Feast of Tabernacles at Jerusalem (see Fasti Sacri, p. 300, No. 1794). 5. In A.D. 58, when Paul again started from Corinth, and was present at the Pentecost at Jerusalem (see Fasti Sacri, p. 313, No. 1857).

Of these five journeys the first and last may be dismissed at once. The *first* is distinctly mentioned in the Galatians as having occurred in the third year current from the conversion, and then follows the journey in question, which is placed after an interval of fourteen years. The two, therefore, could not be identical. The *fifth* of the five journeys is also easily disposed of, as this occurred in A.D. 58, and as the Epistle to the Galatians was written in A.D. 55 (see Fasti Sacri, p. 305, No. 1825), the journey in question, which is referred to in the Epistle, must have been of a previous date, that is, it could not have been the one in A.D. 58. The only journeys therefore that admit of discussion are the second, third, and fourth.

A. It could not have been the second journey in A.D. 44, when Barnabas and Paul took up the Antiochian bounty, for

1. Barnabas and Paul went up at the desire of the Antiochian church on a mission of charity,

communicated unto them that Gospel which I preach among the Gentiles, but privately to them which were of reputation, lest by any means I should run, 3 or had run, in vain. But neither Titus, who was with me, being a Greek, was

not on their own account, but as the agents or instruments of others. But the journey in the Galatians was "by revelation," and with a view to the adjustment of religious differences. Galat. ii. 2.

2. When Barnabas and Paul arrived at Jerusalem they found the church in great tribulation, from Agrippa having just before put to death James, the brother of John; and as this pleased the Jews, he laid hold of Peter also and put him in prison with the intention of bringing him also to the block, when the Passover was concluded (Acts xii. 1); but Peter was miraculously delivered, and departed "to another place" (εἰς ἕτερον τόπον, Acts xii. 17), until the death of Agrippa. Now, in the Galatians Saul is represented as holding a peaceful discussion with James the Bishop, and Peter, and John. Galat. ii. 9. How, then, could this have happened at the time of a persecution against the church? It is no doubt conceivable that Paul arrived before the imprisonment of Peter, and notwithstanding the general consternation from the death of James, Paul may have debated the scheme of Christianity with James the Bishop, and Peter, and John, but this is highly improbable, and not to be admitted if there be any other alternative.

3. Paul in the Galatians speaks of himself individually as the Apostle of the Uncircumcision, or Gentiles, as Peter was of the Circumcision, or Jews. Galat. ii. 7. But at the date of the mission of Barnabas and Paul in A.D. 48 (Acts xi. 30) these Apostles had not yet made their first circuit amongst the Gentiles. Acts xiii. 1. Besides, the envoys from Antioch were Barnabas and Saul, i.e. Barnabas had as yet the precedence and Saul had not yet taken the name of Paul. But the Epistle to the Galatians is from *Paul* the Apostle, and manifestly assumes the pre-eminence of himself as an Apostle over Barnabas, Galat. ii. 7; and so, "I went up with Barnabas," &c., ibid. ii. 1.

4. Again, in the Galatian visit, Paul took Titus with him. But how could Titus have been his companion when Barnabas and Saul took up the Antiochian alms? Titus is expressly said to have been a *Greek* (Galat. ii. 3), and from his missionary labours amongst the Corinthians, it is generally believed that he was a Corinthian (see post), and he was certainly converted by Paul himself. Tit. i. 4. Who, then, can doubt that Titus was brought over to the faith by Paul in the course of his ministry at Corinth in A.D. 53? and if so, Titus could not have gone up with Barnabas and Saul from Antioch in A.D. 44.

5. The Galatian visit was fourteen years after the preceding visit in A.D. 39, ἔπειτα διὰ δεκατεσσάρων ἐτῶν, κ.τ.λ. (Galat. ii. 1), or as some think, fourteen years from the conversion, but the mission of Barnabas and Saul by the Antiochian church in A.D. 44 was not fourteen years from either the one period or the other, and this objection alone would be fatal to the hypothesis.

B. We have next to consider whether the Galatian visit can be identified with the mission of Paul and Barnabas to Jerusalem in A.D. 48, when the Council was convoked. If we look only to the surface there are accidental coincidences which primâ facie might lead one to infer the identity. Thus, on both occasions Paul had Barnabas for his companion (Galat. ii. 1; Acts xv. 2); on both, Paul takes precedence of Barnabas (Acts xv. 2); on both, Peter is at Jerusalem (Galat. ii. 9; Acts xv. 7); on both, the question was how far the law of Moses was binding on the Gentile converts. These circumstances induced Wieseler at first to adopt this theory, but the more he considered it the less confidence he felt in it and eventually was obliged to abandon it. Indeed, the arguments against it are overwhelming and unanswerable.

1. The Galatian visit was "by revelation," but on the mission to the Council Paul and Barnabas went up from no Divine communication to themselves, but were sent by the church of Antioch. Acts xv. 2, 3.

2. At the Galatian visit Paul had an interview with James, and Cephas, and John, and all three evidently took part in the deliberations, but at the Council James and Peter only are mentioned, and either John was absent or took no part in the debate.

3. In the Galatians it is expressly stated that Paul conferred with the Apostles only, and did not communicate his views publicly. κατ' ἰδίαν τοῖς δοκοῦσι. Galat. ii. 2. But the Council was a

4 compelled to be circumcised;[104] (and that[105] because of *the* false brethren
unawares brought in, who came in privily to spy out our liberty which we
5 have in Christ Jesus, that they might bring us into bondage; to whom we

public one, and attended by the Apostles and elders (Acts xv. 6), and even the laity (see Acts xv. 22, 23).

4. If the Galatian visit was the journey of Paul and Barnabas to the Council of Jerusalem, how could Paul have avoided referring to the decree of the Council in the Epistle itself? Instead of that, he makes not the most distant allusion to it, or rather negatives its existence by appealing to the private communications between himself and the leading Apostles. This omission of all notice of the decree of the Council is very remarkable, and we shall see presently that at the date of the Epistle it had merged in a still greater freedom from the ceremonial law, and had, in fact, become a dead letter.

5. At the time of the visit recorded in the Galatians, not only had the Gospel been extensively propagated amongst the heathen, but what is particularly to be noted is, that Paul speaks of his own labours as distinct from those of Barnabas: "When they saw that the Gospel of the Uncircumcision was committed unto *me*, as the Gospel of the Circumcision was unto Peter, for he that wrought effectually in Peter to the Apostleship of the Uncircumcision the same was mighty in *me* towards the Gentiles," &c. Galat. ii. 7. Now, Paul made his *first* circuit in company with Barnabas, and had Paul in the Galatians referred to his journey up to Jerusalem with Barnabas at the close of this circuit he could scarcely have put himself forward as the only missionary whose labours had been crowned with such signal success; he could not have said: "When they (the Apostles of Jerusalem) saw that *I* was entrusted with the Gospel of the Uncircumcision as Peter was with the Gospel of the Circumcision." Galat. ii. 7. But on the *second* circuit Paul parted from Barnabas and took Silas with him, and then carried forward the banner of the Gospel in the most triumphant manner through Phrygia and Galatia, and then into Europe through Macedonia and Greece. It was, no doubt, this marvellous progress that called forth the admiration of the Apostles at Jerusalem; and, if so, the meeting at Jerusalem was after the close of the second circuit; that is, it could not have been at the meeting of the Council which was after the first but before the second circuit.

6. If any further argument were required, it would be furnished by chronology, for the Council was held in A.D. 48, and this would not be fourteen years either from the conversion in A.D. 37, or from the Apostle's first visit to Jerusalem after the conversion in A.D. 39.

C. We come lastly to the journey when Paul (A.D. 58) sailed from Cenchrea, having shorn his head for a vow, and passed by way of Ephesus to Cæsarea, and thence went up to Jerusalem, and this visit is unquestionably the one to which the Apostle refers, as is evidenced by various circumstances peculiar to this visit, and not common to any other.

1. The Galatian visit was "by revelation," which agrees with what we know of the fourth journey. Thus, the Apostle at Ephesus was requested to make some sojourn there, but "he *must* keep the coming *feast* at Jerusalem": δεῖ με πάντως τὴν ἑορτὴν τὴν ἐρχομένην ποιῆσαι εἰς Ἱεροσόλυμα. Acts xviii. 21. As he did not keep other feasts, why was he obliged to keep this, except that he had received a divine command to that effect, and had arranged in consequence to meet Barnabas there? But why was he to be present at Jerusalem, at a *feast* in particular? Because then James, and Peter, and John and the other heads of the church would be assembled, and the Apostles would be able to confer with Paul and Barnabas on the question under discussion. Luke certainly makes only a passing allusion to this visit, viz. that he "went up and saluted the church" (Acts xviii. 22), but this does not negative the importance of the matters transacted. Though Luke tells us only that Paul "saluted the church," he had before intimated that Paul was going up, not only to salute the church, but to keep a feast under some circumstances that obliged him to do it. Why Luke does not

---

[104] Renan assumes that Titus was allowed to be circumcised, but that it was done from policy and not from compulsion. But how can this be reconciled with the Apostle's statement that he did not give way for a moment?

[105] The Apostle means that he opposed the circumcision of Titus because of the false brethren, that their doctrines might not spread.

gave place by subjection, no, not for an hour; that the truth of the Gospel
6 might continue with you); but of those who seemed to be somewhat—whatsoever they were, it maketh no matter to me: God accepteth no man's person;

give any particulars of Paul's interview with James and Peter and John is easily enough accounted for by the fact that as Paul informs us he communicated his Gospel not to the public, but exclusively to the heads of the church, and that privately. Galat. ii. 2.

2. As this journey was at the close of the second circuit which was made by Paul without Barnabas, and had been attended with most wonderful results both in Asia and in Europe, we can now understand why Paul should have spoken of the Gospel of the Uncircumcision as specially committed to himself, and not to himself and Barnabas jointly.

3. It is now also intelligible how Titus came to be in Paul's company, viz. he was a native of Corinth, where the Apostle had resided for more than a year and a half, and Titus now accompanied the Apostle from Corinth to Jerusalem.

4. When James and Cephas and John gave the right hand of fellowship to Paul and Barnabas, it is added, "only they would that we should remember the poor (Hebrews); the same also which I have been forward to do." Galat. ii. 10. We should expect, therefore, from this injunction that Paul in his next circuit would make a collection for the Hebrews, and if we find any circuit on which this was done we may be sure it was the circuit which immediately followed the interview with the Apostles at Jerusalem. But we know that Paul in his *third* circuit did make a collection in the churches of Galatia, and Macedonia, and Achaia, and the inference, therefore, is, that the visit to Jerusalem recorded in the Galatians, immediately preceded the third circuit, and if so, it was the journey up to Jerusalem when Paul sailed from Cenchrea at the close of the second circuit.

5. Paul tells us that in the third year after his conversion, and therefore in A.D. 39 he went up to Jerusalem for the first time, and that fourteen years after that, and therefore in A.D. 53 he went up again upon the occasion of the visit in question. How then can this visit have been any other than that when the Apostle sailed from Corinth at the close of the second circuit, for this actually fell in A.D. 53?

It has been made an objection by some, but without the least reason, that in the Galatian visit Paul went up *with Barnabas* (Galat. ii. 1), but that Luke in the journal of Paul's voyage from Corinth to Jerusalem at the close of the second circuit does not mention Barnabas. But if, as is most probable, Barnabas had during the second circuit been employed in Cyprus, his native country, and merely joined the Apostle at Cyprus or Cæsarea, what occasion had Luke to mention Barnabas? The interview at Jerusalem between Paul and Barnabas on the one hand and the Apostles on the other was a private one, and as Luke passes over this interview in silence, he would naturally omit any reference to Barnabas, who was present only to assist at the conference.

The companionship of Barnabas on this visit may be almost assumed as a necessity. From their earliest years they had been intimately acquainted. Natives the one of Cyprus and the other of the neighbouring province of Cilicia, they had both probably been trained together in the Tarsian school, and both, according to tradition, had been fellow-disciples at Jerusalem at the feet of Gamaliel, and on the conversion of Saul Barnabas had introduced him to the Apostles at Jerusalem, and when Saul retired to Tarsus Barnabas fetched him thence to assist him in the ministry at Antioch. They were then deputed together by the Antiochian church to go up to Jerusalem in charge of the collection, for the relief of the poor Hebrews, and were afterwards solemnly ordained together by the church at Antioch to go forth as the Apostles specially designated for the conversion of the Gentiles. On their return, when the question arose whether Gentile converts were to be bound by the law of Moses, they were together sent up to consult the Apostles at Jerusalem. Being thus continually associated together, they would naturally be found again united at Jerusalem upon the discussion of any important question affecting the Gentiles, to whose conversion their joint labours were devoted.

The occasion that required their presence at Jerusalem at this juncture may be thus explained. Paul and Barnabas had made their first circuit together and at the close of it had arisen the question whether the Gentiles were to observe the law of Moses. The result of the Council upon this subject was a letter addressed to the Christians of Syria and Cilicia (amongst

7 for they who seemed to be somewhat added nothing to me; but contrariwise
when they saw that *I was entrusted with*[164] the Gospel of the uncircumcision,
8 as *Peter was with* the Gospel of the circumcision; (for he that wrought in
Peter to the Apostleship of the circumcision, the same *wrought* in me toward
9 the Gentiles)—when, *I say*,[165] James,[166] *and* Cephas, and John, who seemed to
be pillars, perceived the grace that was given unto me, they gave to me and
Barnabas the right hands of fellowship; that we should go unto the *Gentiles*,
10 and they unto the circumcision; only that we should remember the poor; the
11 same which I also *have been* forward to do.[167] But when *Cephas*[168] was come

whom the dispute had arisen) to the effect that the Gentiles of those countries should abstain only "from things offered to idols, and from blood, and from things strangled, and from fornication." On setting out on a second circuit, Paul and Barnabas, for the first time, severed, and while Barnabas with his cousin Mark proceeded to Cyprus, Paul and Silas took the direction of Cilicia. Paul then passed successively through Derbe and Lystra and Iconium, and as the Jews were numerous in these cities also, Paul delivered to them the decree of the Council of Jerusalem. Acts xvi. 4. But after this we hear no more of the decree, and in evangelizing Phrygia, Galatia, Macedonia, and Achaia Paul preached the unqualified and absolute abolition of the ceremonial law, which he calls emphatically in the Epistles "my Gospel." This entire freedom of the Gentiles from the Mosaic dispensation was continually calling forth the hostility of the Jewish element in the Church; and the malicious report was widely circulated that the Gospel of Paul was not the Gospel of the Apostles. It was to counteract this prejudice, and to cement the harmony between the Hebrew and Gentile branches of the Church that Paul was now commanded by revelation to go up to Jerusalem, and seek an explanation with the Apostles. As the views of Barnabas were identical with those of Paul on this subject (see Acts xv. 2) we must suppose that Barnabas also, either by revelation, or on the dictates of human policy, met Paul at Cyprus or Cæsarea, and accompanied him to Jerusalem on this important question. The conference at Jerusalem had the desired effect, and the Apostles there fully approved of the Gospel as preached by Paul and Barnabas, and gave to them the right hand of fellowship, i.e. they admitted that the whole ceremonial law had been abolished, and that the former decree of the Council, though enjoined to the churches of Syria and Cilicia, on the ground of expediency on account of the numerous Jews in those parts, who were zealous for the Law, was not binding on Gentile converts generally. Accordingly, the Apostle in his Epistle to the Corinthians, instead of requiring them to refrain from things offered to idols, allows them to buy whatever was sold in the shambles asking no questions for conscience sake. 1 Cor. x. 25; and see viii 1.

On the subject of this note see particularly Wieseler, Chronol. Apostg. p. 176, and Schott, Erörterung einiger wichtigen chronol. Punkten in der Lebensgeschichte des Apostel Paulus, p. 13, ed. 1832.

[164] πεπίστευμαι τὸ εὐαγγέλιον. In Eng. ver. "the Gospel was committed unto me."

[165] This seems to be the force of the word καί; but the whole sentence, or rather, string of sentences, is such a tangled web of involved construction, that, though the meaning is sufficiently clear, it is difficult to reduce the language to grammatical propriety.

[166] The James here referred to is James the half-brother of our Lord and Bishop of Jerusalem, and therefore the same person as "James, the brother of the Lord," mentioned before, Gal. i. 19. The reason why James was before distinguished as the "brother of the Lord," and is now named simply, is that at the former date James the brother of John was still living, so that it was necessary to mark which James was meant, but at the date of the present Epistle James the brother of John was dead. Acts xii. 2.

[167] ὃ καὶ ἐσπούδασα αὐτὸ τοῦτο ποιῆσαι. In Eng. ver. "*was* forward to do;" but the original expresses something of recent occurrence, and the Apostle had a little time before the date of the Epistle completed the collection amongst the Galatians to whom he was writing, and was about to commence a collection in Macedonia and Achaia.

[168] In Eng. ver. Peter, but according to the

12 to Antioch, I withstood him to the face, because he was *self-convicted*.[169] For
before that certain came from James, he did eat with the Gentiles; but when
they were come, he withdrew and separated himself, fearing them which were
13 of the circumcision;[170] and the *rest of the* Jews dissembled likewise with him,
14 insomuch that Barnabas also was carried away with their dissimulation. But
when I saw that they walked not uprightly according to the truth of the
Gospel, I said unto Cephas[171] before them all, 'If thou, being a Jew, livest *as
do the* Gentiles, and not as do the Jews, why compellest thou the Gentiles to
15 *Judaize?*' We who are Jews by nature, and not sinners of the Gentiles,
16 knowing that a man is not justified by the works of the Law, but only by the
faith of Jesus Christ, even we have believed in Jesus Christ, that we might be
justified by the Faith of Christ, and not by the works of the Law; for 'By
17 the works of the Law shall no flesh be justified' (Ps. cxliii. 2).[172] But if, *in
seeking* to be justified *in* Christ, we ourselves[173] also *have been* found sinners, is
18 therefore Christ the minister of sin? *Far be it!*[174] For if I build again the
19 things which I destroyed, I make myself a transgressor; for I through the
20 Law *was* dead to the Law, that I might live unto God; I *have been* crucified
with Christ; nevertheless I live; yet not I, but Christ liveth in me; and the
life which I now live in the flesh I live by the Faith of the Son of God, who
21 loved me, and gave himself for me; I do not frustrate the grace of God; for
if *justification* be by the Law, then Christ is dead in vain.

Ch. III. "O foolish Galatians! who hath bewitched you,[175] before whose eyes Jesus
2 Christ crucified *was portrayed*[176] among you? This only would I learn of you
—received ye the Spirit by the works of the Law, or by the hearing of Faith?
3 Are ye so foolish? Having begun in the Spirit, *do* ye now *end in* the flesh?
4, 5 Have ye suffered so many things in vain? if it be yet in vain. He therefore
that ministereth to you the Spirit, and worketh miracles among you, doeth he
6 it by the works of the Law, or by the hearing of Faith?[177] Even as 'Abraham

---

best MSS. the word is Cephas, which has been adopted by Scholtz, Lachmann, Tischendorf, and Alford. The mention of Cephas in ver. 9 as a pillar of the church in connection with James and John shows that Peter had no supremacy over the other Apostles.

[169] κατεγνωσμένος. In Eng. version " to be blamed."

[170] The Jewish converts.

[171] The note [169] above, applies equally here.

[172] Οὐ δικαιωθήσεται ἐξ ἔργων νόμου πᾶσα σάρξ. In the LXX. the words are, Οὐ δικαιωθήσεται ἐνώπιόν σου πᾶς ζῶν. The same text is quoted in Rom. iii. 20, and in the same words, but not in the same order as in this Epistle.

[173] I.e. "We who are Jews by nature." See ante, ver. 15.

[174] Μὴ γένοιτο. In Eng. ver. the words are rendered "God forbid," which appears to the author objectionable, as it might be thought that Paul was taking the name of God in vain. The German version renders it more correctly. "Das sey fern!"

[175] The words τῇ ἀληθείᾳ μὴ πείθεσθαι—"that ye should not obey the truth"—though adopted in the Authorized Version, are not found in the best MSS., and are rejected by Griesbach, Scholtz, Lachmann, Tischendorf, and Alford.

[176] προεγράφη. In Eng. ver. "hath been evidently set forth."

[177] The Apostle alludes to the spiritual gifts communicated by *himself* to the Galatians. This

CHAP. XIII.]   EPISTLE TO THE GALATIANS.   [A.D. 55]   349

believed God, and it was *reckoned* to him for righteousness' (*Gen.* xv. 6).[137]
7 Know ye, therefore, that they which are of Faith, *these* are the sons of Abra-
8 ham. And the Scripture, foreseeing that God would justify the *Gentiles* through
  Faith, preached before the Gospel unto Abraham, saying, 'In thee shall all
9 nations be blessed' (*Gen.* xviii. 18); so then they which be of Faith are
10 blessed with faithful Abraham. For as many as are of the works of the Law
  are under *a* curse: for it is written, 'Cursed is every one that continueth not
  in all things which are written in the book of the Law to do them'
11 (*Deut.* xxvii. 26);[138] but that no man is justified by the Law in the sight of God
12 is evident: for 'The just shall live by Faith' (*Hab.* ii. 4). And the Law is
  not of faith; but, 'The man that *hath done* them shall live in them.'
13 (*Lev.* xviii. 5.) Christ hath redeemed us from the curse of the Law, being
  made a curse for us: for it is written, 'Cursed is every one that hangeth on a
14 tree' (*Deut.* xxi. 23);[139] that the blessing of Abraham might come on the
  Gentiles through Jesus Christ; that we might receive the promise of the
15 Spirit through Faith. Brethren, I speak after the manner of men—though
  it be but a man's *disposition*, if it be confirmed,[140] no man annulleth, or
16 addeth thereto. Now to Abraham 'and his seed' (*Gen.* xxii. 18)[141] were the
  promises *spoken*.[142] He saith not, 'and to seeds,' as of many; but as of one
17 'and to thy seed,' which is Christ. And this I say, that the *disposition*, that
  was confirmed before of God in Christ, the Law, which was four hundred and
  thirty years after (*Exod.* xiii. 40),[143] *doth not* annul, that it should make the

passage is illustrated by Acts xix. 6, where Paul laid his hands on the disciples, and they straightway received the Holy Spirit, and spake with tongues, and prophesied.

[137] Ἀβραὰμ ἐπίστευσεν, κ.τ.λ. In the LXX. καὶ ἐπίστευσεν Ἀβραάμ, κ.τ.λ. The faith of Abraham, so much relied upon here and in the Epistle to the Romans, was a common topic with the learned Jews. Thus Philo observes of Abraham, Διὸ καὶ πιστεῦσαι λέγεται τῷ Θεῷ πρῶτος. Philo de Mundo, s. 1.

[138] Ἐπικατάρατος πᾶς ὃς οὐκ ἐμμένει ἐν πᾶσι τοῖς γεγραμμένοις ἐν τῷ βιβλίῳ τοῦ νόμου τοῦ ποιῆσαι αὐτά. In the LXX. the passage is—'Ἐπικατάρατος πᾶς ἄνθρωπος ὃς οὐκ ἐμμένει ἐν πᾶσι τοῖς λόγοις τοῦ νόμου τούτου ποιῆσαι αὐτούς.

[139] The Apostle, in the citation, substitutes ἐπικατάρατος for κεκατηραμένος ὑπὸ θεοῦ, in the LXX.

[140] That is, to clothe the idea in English dress, 'When a man's testamentary disposition or will has been proved, it is implicitly carried out. The probate is conclusive. So the disposition or dispensation given by God to Abraham can-

not be set aside by the interposition of the Law of Moses.'

[141] And see Gen. xii. 7; xv. 5; xvii. 7.

[142] ἐῤῥέθησαν. In Eng. ver. "made."

[143] The Hebrew text gives 430 years for the sojourning in *Egypt*; and if so, the period from the promise to Abraham to the delivery of the Law at the Exodus would be 430 years + 215 years = 645 years. That the interval from the Promise to the going down to Egypt was 215 years may be thus shown: Abraham had been 25 years in *Canaan* (i.e. it was 25 years after the date of the Promise) when Isaac was born (compare Gen. xii. 4 with xii. 5), and Isaac was 60 years old when Jacob was born (Gen. xxv. 26), and Jacob was 130 years old when he went down to Egypt. Gen. xlvii. 9. Thus 25 + 60 + 130 = 215. But the Hebrew text of Exodus xii. 40, which gives 430 years for the sojourning in Egypt, is no doubt corrupt, and the LXX. version of it is correct, which gives 430 years for the sojourning of the children of Israel, not exclusively in Egypt, but in Canaan and in Egypt together, so that as the sojourning

18 promise of none effect. For if the inheritance be of the Law, it is no more of
19 promise: but God gave it to Abraham by promise. Wherefore then the Law?
   It was added because of transgressions, till the seed should come to whom *it*
20 *was promised*; ordained by angels[183] in the hand of a mediator. Now a medi-
21 ator is not of one, but God is one.[184] Is the Law, then, against the promises
   of God? *Far be it!*[185] for if there had been a law given which could have
22 made alive, verily *justification would* have been by the Law. But the Scripture
   hath *shut up* all under sin, that the promise by Faith of Jesus Christ might
23 be given to them that believe. But before Faith came we were kept under the
24 Law, shut up unto the Faith which should afterwards be revealed. *So that*
   the Law was our schoolmaster[186] to bring us unto Christ, that we might be
25 justified by Faith; but Faith *being* come, we are no longer under a school-
26, 27 master; for ye are all sons of God by Faith in Christ Jesus; for as many of you
28 as have been baptized into Christ have put on Christ. There is neither Jew
   nor Greek, there is neither bond nor free, there is neither male nor female,
29 for ye are all one in Christ Jesus; and if ye be Christ's, then are ye Abraham's
   seed, and heirs according to promise.

in Canaan was 215 years, the sojourning in Egypt would be also 215 years. This interval for the sojourning in Egypt is confirmed by collateral writers, for which the reader is referred to Alford upon Galat. iii. 17. It follows that Paul's chronology harmonizes with the LXX. version and with the facts, and must therefore prevail against the erroneous Hebrew text.

[183] That is, ordained by God by the intervention of angels, for all the works of God were ascribed by the Jews to the ministration of angels. Thus in Exod. iii. 2, "the *angel* of the Lord appeared unto him," and directly afterwards, at v. 4, "when the *Lord* saw;" so that "the angel of the Lord," and "the Lord" are equivalent expressions. So in the Hebrews, the Law is spoken of as ὁ δι' ἀγγέλων λαληθεὶς λόγος, Heb. ii. 2; and the same phraseology occurs elsewhere in the Scriptures, as in Acts vii. 30 (compare Ex. iii. 2, 4); Acts vii. 53; 1 Cor. xi. 10, &c. So in Josephus: ἡμῶν τὰ κάλλιστα τῶν δογμάτων, καὶ ὁσιώτατα τῶν ἐν τοῖς νόμοις, δι' ἀγγέλων παρὰ τοῦ θεοῦ μαθόντων. Ant. xv. 5, 3. See further, Schoettgen's Horæ Heb. i. 738.

[184] The train of thought in the Apostle's mind may be this: You that Judaize say that the promise was fulfilled in Moses, and that justification is by the law of Moses. But how can this be? for you admit that Moses was a mediator, and a mediator is not a principal at all, but an agent or medium between two others. God who gave the promise is one of the principals, and if Moses is the mediator or agent between God and some other principal in whom the promise is fulfilled, how can Moses himself be that other principal? Or the explanation may be this: The promise was made by God to Abraham, and the promise was to be fulfilled in the person of Christ. But between the promise and Christ came the Law; and Moses is therefore called the mediator as intervening between the promise and Christ. For a mediator, continues the Apostle, is a person who comes between two others; and as God, who gave the promise, is one only, the word mediator implies some other than God, which is Christ, in whom the promise is fulfilled. In the Rabbinical writers, Moses is commonly called the μεσίτης or mediator. See Wetstein, and Heb. viii. 6. For numerous other meanings given to this difficult passage, see Alford.

[185] See note [87] ante.

[186] παιδαγωγός, more properly, one who is not himself the schoolmaster, but conducts the child to the schoolmaster, as in the passage cited by J. B. Lightfoot from Plato: Ἀλλ' ἄρχει τίς σου; Ὁ δὲ, παιδαγωγός, ἔφη. Μῶν δοῦλος ὤν; Ἀλλὰ τί μήν; ἡμέτερός γε, ἔφη. Ἡ δεινόν, ἦν δ' ἐγώ, ἐλεύθερον ὄντα ὑπὸ δούλου ἄρχεσθαι. τί δὲ ποιῶν αὖ οὗτος ὁ παιδαγωγός σου ἄρχει; Ἄγων δήπου, ἔφη, εἰς διδασκάλου. Μῶν μὴ καὶ αὐτοί σου ἄρχουσιν, οἱ διδάσκαλοι; Πάντως δήπου. Plato, Lysis. s. 12.

Ch. IV. "Now I say, that the heir, as long as he is a child, differeth nothing from a
2 servant, though he be lord of all; but is under *guardians* and *stewards*[189]
3 until the time appointed of the father. Even so we, when we were children,
4 were in *servitude* under the elements of the world: but when the fulness of
    the time was come, God sent forth his Son, made of a woman, made under
5 the Law, to redeem them that were under the Law, that we might receive the
6 adoption of sons. And because ye are sons, God hath sent forth the Spirit of
7 his Son into your hearts, crying, 'Abba, Father;'[190] *so that* thou art no more
    a servant, but a son; and if a son, an heir *also* of God through Christ.[191] *But*
8 then, when ye knew not God, ye did service unto them which by nature are no
9 gods; but now, after that ye have known God (but are more known of God),
    how turn ye again to the weak and beggarly elements, whereunto ye desire again
10 to be in bondage? Ye observe days, and months, and *seasons*, and years.[192] I
11 am afraid of you, lest *haply* I have bestowed upon you labour in vain.
12 "Brethren, I beseech you, be as I am, for I am as ye are;[193] ye have not
13 injured me at all; *nay*, ye know how through infirmity of the flesh I preached
14 the gospel unto you the *former time*,[194] and my temptation which was in
    my flesh ye despised not, nor rejected, but received me as an angel of God,
15 even as Christ Jesus. *What then was your blessing [of me]?*[195] for I bear you

---

[189] ἐπιτρόπους καὶ οἰκονόμους—the former to take care of the person, the latter, of the property.

[190] The Apostle seems here to allude to the opening words of the Lord's Prayer, in which we call God our Father.

[191] For the various readings of this passage, see Alford.

[192] The "days" are the sabbaths, the "months" are the new moons, the "seasons" are the yearly festivals, and the "years" are the sabbatic years. We find in Josephus much the same classification: Ταῖς δ' ἑβδομάσι, καὶ νουμηνίαις, καὶ εἴ τις ἑορτὴ πάτριος, ἡ πανήγυρις πάνδημος ἀγομένη δι' ἔτους. Jos. Bell. v. 5, 7. And so Philo: κατὰ πάντας χρόνους ἡμερῶν καὶ μηνῶν καὶ ἐνιαυτῶν, de Septen. s. 10; ἔν τε ἡμέραις καὶ μησὶ καὶ ἐνιαυτοῖς, de Festo Cophin. s. 4. When the Apostle reproves them for observing the Sabbath, it must be borne in mind that the Galatians were *Gentiles*. The Apostle never objected to the Jews keeping the Law; and, indeed, to avoid offence, he kept it himself. From the Apostle's rebuke, that they were observing "years," it may be inferred that the Epistle was written in the course of a Sabbatic year, and, as will appear presently, after the Apostle's second visit to Galatia. The recurrence of the sabbatic years has been ascertained with certainty; and the first that fell after the Apostle's second visit to Galatia was in A.D. 55, in which year, accordingly, we must place the Epistle. That A.D. 55 was a sabbatic year may be shown without long discussion by the simple testimony of Josephus. According to Josephus, Herod and Sosius took Jerusalem in the consulship of M. Agrippa and Caninius Gallus, i.e. B.C. 37, on the day of the νηστεία, or atonement, which fell on the 5th of October (Ant. xiv. 16, 4), and the siege had lasted for five or six months (Bell. i. 18, 2, id. v. 9, 4), or at least for three months (Ant. xiv. 16, 4), and during that period the city had been straitened for want of provisions, because the sabbatic year was then current (Ant. xiv. 16, 2), and when the siege was over the land could not be sown for the same reason, Ant. xv. 1, 2. But if B.C. 37 was a sabbatic year, we have only to reckon forward every seventh year, and we shall find that A.D. 55 was a sabbatic year likewise. See further on this subject Fasti Sacri, p. 60, No. 525.

[193] 'Be one with me as I am one with you—let us be united together.'

[194] τὸ πρότερον. It appears from this expression that the Epistle was written after the Apostle's *second visit* to Galatia. This is the natural sense, though the phrase may not be conclusive. See John ix.

[195] Τίς οὖν ἦν ὁ μακαρισμὸς ὑμῶν; 'When I first brought you the tidings of the Gospel, you

witness, that, if it had been possible, ye would have plucked out your own eyes,
16 and have given them to me.[196] Have I therefore become your enemy *by telling*
17 *you the truth?*[197] They *are* zealous *of* you, but not well; yea, they would
18 exclude you,[198] that ye *may be zealous of* them. But it is good to be zealous in
19 a good thing *always*, and not only when I am present with you,[199] my little
20 children, of whom I travail in birth again until Christ be formed in you; *and
   I would that I were* present with you now, and *might* change my *tone*, for I
   stand in doubt of you.

21 "Tell me, ye that desire to be under the Law, do ye not hear the Law?
22 For it is written, that Abraham had two sons, the one by a bondmaid
23 (*Gen.* xvi. 15), the other by a freewoman (*Gen.* xxi. 2); but he who was of the
   bondwoman was born after the flesh, but he of the freewoman was by promise.
24 Which things are an allegory: for these are the two *dispensations*—the one
25 from the mount Sinai, which gendereth to bondage, which is Agar; for this
   Agar is mount Sinai in Arabia,[200] and answereth to Jerusalem which now is,
26 and is in bondage with her children. But Jerusalem which is above is free,
27 which is the mother of us all; for it is written, 'Rejoice, thou barren that
   bearest not; break forth and *shout*, thou that travailest not: for the desolate
   woman hath many more children than she which hath an husband' (*Is.* liv. 1).[201]
28, 29 Now we, brethren, *like* Isaac, are the children of promise. But as then he that
   was born after the flesh persecuted him [that was born] after the Spirit, even
30 so is it now. *But* what saith the Scripture? 'Cast out the bondwoman and
   her son: for the son of the bondwoman shall not be heir with the son of the
31 freewoman' (*Gen.* xxi. 10).[202] So then, brethren, we are not children of the
   bondwoman, but of the free *woman*.

---

looked upon me as a blessed one, and now you regard me as your enemy."

[196] The Apostle here refers to his partial blindness. See ante, p. 186.

[197] When did the Apostle thus tell them the truth? Some have thought that the Apostle alludes only to the wholesome but not very pleasing truths contained in the former part of the Epistle. But the objection to this is that the Galatians had not yet read the letter. The Apostle more probably refers to the severe rebuke which he had administered on his second visit, with a view to correct the abuses in the Galatian church, and more particularly to counteract the Jewish propensities which were even then beginning to show themselves.

[198] They would separate you from the true faith to be sectarians following them.

[199] The Apostle then at his last visit had succeeded in bringing the church into a satisfactory state.

[200] Sinai is said to be called "Hagar." This was first suggested by Chrysostom, who, in commenting on this Epistle, speaks of the mountain Sinai as called by the same name with Abraham's handmaid: τῷ ὄρει ὁμωνύμῳ τῇ δούλῃ (Hagar). Comment. on c. iv. 4; and again: τὸ δὲ Σινᾶ ὄρος οὕτω μεθερμηνεύεται τῇ ἐπιχωρίῳ αὐτῶν γλώσσῃ, s. 3; and Chrysostom has been followed by Theophylact and others. Of modern travellers, Havant writes: "The Arabian and Mauritanian heathen call Mount Sinai Agar, or Tur." Der Christliche Ulysses. Nürnb. 1678. But the fact is not referred to in other travels. Hagar, or, as more properly written, Chagar or Chajar, signifies in Arabic a rock or stone generally. See on the subject of Hagar, J. B. Lightfoot ad loc.

[201] The citation is word for word from the LXX. version.

[202] The citation is word for word from the LXX., except that for υἱοῦ τῆς ἐλευθέρας the LXX. has υἱοῦ μου Ἰσαάκ.

Ch. V. "Stand fast, therefore, in the liberty wherewith Christ has made us free, and be not entangled again with the yoke of bondage. Behold, I Paul say unto you, that if ye be circumcised, Christ shall profit you nothing;[202] for I testify again[203] to every man that is circumcised, that he is a debtor to do the whole Law. *Ye have no effect from* Christ,[204] whosoever *justify yourselves* by the Law; ye are fallen *away* from Grace; for, we through the Spirit, wait for the hope of *justification* by Faith; for in Jesus Christ neither circumcision availeth anything, nor uncircumcision, but Faith, which worketh by love. Ye *were running* well; who *hath tripped you up*[205] that ye should not obey the truth? This persuasion cometh not of him that calleth you.[206] 'A little leaven leaveneth the whole lump.'[207] I have confidence in you *in* the Lord, that ye will be none otherwise minded;[208] but he that troubleth you shall bear *the guilt*,[209]* whosoever he be. And I, brethren, if I yet preach circumcision, why *am* I yet *persecuted*? then *hath* the offence of the cross *been done away*. I would they would even CUT THEMSELVES OFF[210] which trouble you.

"For, brethren, ye have been called unto liberty; only [use] not liberty for an occasion to the flesh, but by love serve one another; for all the law is fulfilled in one word, even in this: 'Thou shalt love thy neighbour as thyself.' (*Lev.* xix. 18).[211] But if ye bite and devour one another, take heed that ye be not consumed one of another. *But* I say, Walk in the Spirit, and ye shall not fulfil the lust of the flesh; for the flesh lusteth against the Spirit, and the Spirit against the flesh, and these are contrary the one to the other, so that ye cannot do the things that ye would; but if ye be led of the Spirit, ye are not under the Law. Now the works of the flesh are manifest, which are these:[212] Fornication, uncleanness, lasciviousness, idolatry, witchcraft, hatreds, *strifes*, emulations, wrath, *contentions, divisions*,[213] heresies, envyings, murders, drunkenness, revellings, and such like; of the which I *forewarn* you, as also *I* told you *before*[214] that they which do such things shall not inherit the kingdom

---

[202] That is, if ye look to circumcision as the means of salvation.

[203] He had said the same thing before, iii. 12.

[204] κατηργήθητε ἀπὸ Χριστοῦ. In Eng. ver. "Christ is become of no effect unto you."

[205] ἀνέκοψε. In Eng. ver. "hindered you."

[206] 'This new doctrine is not of God.' See the same expression 1 Thess. v. 24.

[207] This was a proverb, and is found also at 1 Cor. v. 6.

[208] 'I trust that ye will not fall away from the purity of the Gospel as it was preached by me.'

[209]* τὸ κρίμα—the sentence passed on the guilty.

[210] ἀποκόψονται. An allusion to the doctrine of the circumcision, περιτομή, preached by the Judaizers. 'I would they were *excised* as well as *circumcised*.'

[211] Cited from the LXX., except that the Apostle substitutes ἑαυτὸν for σεαυτόν.

[212] μοιχεία, 'adultery,' which appears in the Eng. version, is omitted by all the best critics, as Griesbach, Scholtz, Lachmann, Tischendorf, and Alford.

[213] διχοστασίαι. In Eng. ver. "emulations."

[214] προεῖπον. In Eng. ver. "I told you in time past." The Apostle apparently alludes to his second visit; for it is unlikely that, on his first visit, when they received him so rapturously, and before the Judaizers had arisen, he should have dwelt on the subject of " hatred, variance, emulations, wrath, strife, *divisions, heresies.*" At the time of his second visit, his mind was full of

22 of God. But the fruit of the Spirit is love, joy, peace, long-suffering, gentle-
23 ness, goodness, faith, meekness, temperance; against such there is no law.
24 And they that are Christ's have crucified the flesh with the *passions* and lusts.
25, 26 If we live in the Spirit, let us also walk in the Spirit; let us not be *vain-glorious*,[215] provoking one another, envying one another.

CH. VI. "Brethren, if a man be overtaken in a *transgression*, ye which are spiritual restore such a one in the spirit of meekness; considering thyself, lest thou also
2 be tempted. Bear ye one another's burdens, and so fulfil the law of Christ;
3 for if a man think himself to be something, when he is nothing, he deceiveth
4 himself. But let *each one* prove his own work, and then shall he have *boast*[216]
5 of himself alone, and not *over* another; for *each* shall bear his own burden.
6 And let him that is taught the word communicate unto him, that teacheth, all
7 good things.[217] Be not deceived: God is not mocked; for whatsoever a man
8 soweth, that shall he also reap; for he that soweth to his flesh shall of the flesh reap corruption, but he that soweth to the Spirit shall of the Spirit reap
9 life everlasting. And let us not be weary in well doing; for in due season we
10 shall reap, if we faint not. As we have therefore opportunity, let us do good unto all men, especially unto them who are of the household of faith.

11 "SEE *in what large characters*[218] I HAVE WRITTEN UNTO YOU WITH MINE OWN
12 HAND!"[219] AS MANY AS DESIRE TO MAKE A FAIR SHEW IN THE FLESH, THEY CONSTRAIN YOU TO BE CIRCUMCISED, ONLY LEST THEY SHOULD SUFFER PERSECUTION FOR THE
13 CROSS OF CHRIST; FOR NEITHER THEY THEMSELVES WHO ARE CIRCUMCISED KEEP THE LAW, BUT DESIRE TO HAVE YOU CIRCUMCISED, THAT THEY MAY GLORY IN YOUR FLESH.
14 BUT *far be it from me to* GLORY,[220] SAVE IN THE CROSS OF OUR LORD JESUS CHRIST,
15 BY WHOM THE WORLD IS CRUCIFIED UNTO ME, AND I UNTO THE WORLD; FOR IN CHRIST JESUS NEITHER CIRCUMCISION AVAILETH ANY THING, NOR UNCIRCUMCISION,
16 BUT A NEW CREATURE; AND AS MANY AS WALK ACCORDING TO THIS RULE, PEACE BE
17 ON THEM, AND MERCY, AND UPON THE ISRAEL OF GOD. FROM HENCEFORTH LET NO MAN TROUBLE ME; FOR I BEAR IN MY BODY THE *brands* OF THE LORD JESUS."[221]

---

the mischiefs created by the Judaizers, which he had so lately witnessed, first at Jerusalem, where they had endeavoured to procure the circumcision of Titus, and afterwards at Antioch, where Paul had rebuked Peter himself; and as they had followed him into Galatia, or rather had preceded him, he may well have warned the converts on his second visit against their machinations.

[215] κενοδόξοι. In Eng. ver. "desirous of vainglory."

[216] καύχημα. In Eng. ver. "rejoicing."

[217] In other words, "The labourer is worthy of his hire;" and the Apostle enjoins the flock to support their own pastor by sharing with him their temporal good things.

[218] Not πηλίκην ἐπιστολήν, 'how large a letter,' but πηλίκοις γράμμασιν, 'in what large characters.' In Eng. ver. "how large a letter;" but 'how large a letter' would be πήλικα γράμματα ἔγραψα, not πηλίκοις γράμμασιν ἔγραψα.

[219] This verse and the remainder of the Epistle the Apostle writes with his own hand. See ante, p. 187.

[220] ἐμοὶ δὲ μὴ γένοιτο καυχᾶσθαι. In Eng. ver. "God forbid that I should glory," which is objectionable. See ante, p. 348, note [17].

[221] The Apostle here refers to the custom among the ancients of branding their slaves. Paul, at his conversion, had been afflicted with blindness, and though he recovered his sight, the permanent

18 "THE GRACE OF OUR LORD JESUS CHRIST BE WITH YOUR SPIRIT, [MY] BRETHREN, AMEN."

This Epistle was dispatched by the hands of some faithful follower, and as we find the Apostle afterwards holding communication with the Galatian church,[222] it cannot be doubted that so salutary an appeal was attended with the desired success.

Paul himself, it appears, never quitted Ephesus until his final departure; "Ye know," he says to the Presbyters of Ephesus, "from *the first day* that I came into Asia after what manner I was with *you the whole time*."[223] But we should do little justice to the labours of Paul and his comrades, if we supposed the results confined within the walls of the city. Paul's long sojourn there was owing to the "great door" that was opened to him for spreading the Gospel throughout the whole proconsulate. The provincials of Asia, some on business at the assizes, and some for pleasure at the festivals, flocked from all quarters to Ephesus, the capital, and when there, could not fail to hear of the new religion recommended by the faultless life and powerful argumentation of the Apostle, and forced upon their attention by the miraculous gifts by which it was authenticated. Many were thus converted, and on returning home carried the seeds of the Gospel with them, and not unfrequently planted them with success in their native towns. Thus Ephesus was the centre from which the truth radiated to all the surrounding districts; and Demetrius, the silversmith, was not far wrong when he exclaimed, "Ye see and hear, that not alone at Ephesus, but almost throughout all Asia, this Paul hath persuaded and turned away much people, saying, that they be no gods which are made with hands."[224]

The writer of the Acts has not indulged our curiosity by stating into what cities of Asia Christianity was thus introduced by the influence of Paul, but without his personal presence. From the Epistles, however, we learn that, amongst others, Colossæ, Laodicea, and Hierapolis, were evangelised, and all these were comprised within the proconsulate of Asia. The province was divided into circuits for holding assizes, and Laodicea and Hierapolis, and probably Colossæ also, were included in the circuit of Cibyra,[225] one of the most important and influential of them all.[226]

The position of Colossæ, Laodicea, and Hierapolis, was this. The traveller who landed at Milétus, and pursued his course up the country along the banks of the Meander, would, after a journey of something more than 100 miles, come to the mouth

---

ophthalmia which settled in his eyes probably produced a disfigurement. He had also been stoned, and had received various scourgings (as in the market-place of Philippi, the traces of which may have been still visible. See ante, p. 187.

[222] 2 Tim. iv. 10.
[223] τὸν πάντα χρόνον. Acts xx. 18.
[224] Acts xix. 26.
[225] Una (jurisdictio) appellatur Cibyratica.

Ipsum oppidum Phrygiæ est. Conveniunt eo xxxv. civitates, celeberrima urbe *Laodicea*. Imposita est Lyco flumini, latera alluentibus Asopo et Capro, appellata primo Diospolis, dein Rhoas. Reliqui in eo conveniunt, quos nominare non pigeat, Hydrelitæ, Themisones, *Hierapolitæ*. Plin. N. H. v. 29.

[226] οὐδὲν δ' ἧττον ἐν ταῖς μεγίσταις ἐξετάζεται διοικήσεσι τῆς Ἀσίας ἡ Κιβυρατική. Strabo, xiii. 4 (p. 170, Tauchnitz).

of the River Lycus, on the right, falling into the Meander. If he then traced the valley of the Lycus for about sixteen miles, he would have in sight two considerable and very conspicuous cities, on opposite sides of the Lycus, and facing each other, and

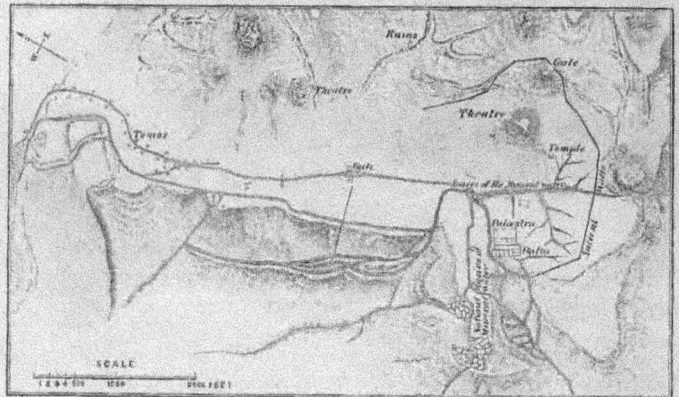

Fig. 167.—Plan of Hierapolis. From Laborde's Syria.

some five miles apart. The one on the left, Hierapolis, was the less important, but in the more commanding situation (fig. 167); it stood on the summit of a cliff, but with a

Fig. 168.—Coin of Hierapolis. From the British Museum.
Obv. A laureated female head with the legend Βουλη (senate). Rev. Equestrian figure with the legend Ἱεραπολειτων (of the Hierapolitans).

still higher mountain towering behind, and the slope before it down to the plain had a white dazzling appearance like a glacier. This phenomenon arose from the springs that issued above, and which, being strongly impregnated with a cretaceous substance, covered the rocks, over which they trickled, with an incrustation of brittle stone. Under a brow of the overhanging mountain was the famous Plutonium, or Temple of Pluto, the mouth of a subterraneous cavern, from which arose a caliginous noxious vapour, most destructive to life. About half an acre of ground around the orifice was fenced in, and any animal that was driven within the paling immediately expired, while the priests of Pluto could venture in with impunity.[227] The solution of the

---

[227] Strabo, xiii. 4 (p. 157, Tauchnitz).

mystery was, that the exhalation from the cavern being carbonic acid gas, was heavier than the external air, and being confined within the fence settled upon the ground, so that cattle carrying their heads low, and inhaling the poison, died from the effects; but the priests, who stood erect, and breathed above the height of the enclosure, were out of reach of the danger. This was foisted upon the vulgar as a miracle. The city at that day was a flourishing one, with an amphitheatre and a stadium, and a multitude of gorgeous buildings, but is now a ruin. It was called Hierapolis, or the Holy City,

Fig. 108.—Remains of the Plutonium at Hierapolis. From a photograph by Robedo.

from the extraordinary nature of the waters, and the wonder of the Plutonium. The name at the present day amongst the Turks is Tambouk,[22] or Cotton, from the fleecy appearance of the cliff on which it stands.

The town on the traveller's right, as he passed up the Lycus and situate about half a mile from the river, was Laodicea. It was built upon three or four sand hills at the foot of Mount Cadmus, and two small streams, the Asopus on the west, and the Cadmus on the east, ran on either side of the city into the Lycus.[23] The ruins at the present day are of vast extent, and indicate the ancient importance of Laodicea. Amongst the most curious of these remains are stone pipes, for conveying water from a neigh-

---

[22] The commonly received name of Pambouk or Pambook is said by Renan to be a mistake for Tambouk. St. Paul, p. 357, note.
[23] Strabo, xii. 8 (p. 75, Tauchnitz).

bouring eminence into the valley, and then up to the town, which proves (what had been denied before) that the ancients understood the great hydraulic principle, that water when confined can be made to flow down a descent, and up again to the height of the original level.[230] In A.D. 60 it was overwhelmed by an earthquake,[231] but from the

Fig. 170.—*Coin of Laodicea. From the British Museum.*
Obv. Head with legend Ιερὰ Σύγκλητος (Sacred Senate).—Rev. Figure seated, with legend Λαοδικέων...(of the Laodiceans...).

wealth of its inhabitants it soon recovered itself to be again overthrown. Its utter destruction by violence from the struggles of nature has been referred to as a striking illustration of the warning uttered in the Apocalypse, "Because thou art lukewarm, and neither cold nor hot, I will *spue thee out of my mouth.* Behold, I *stand at the door and knock.*"[232]

If the traveller, after leaving Laodicea and Hierapolis, continued his route up the valley of the Lycus for twelve miles farther, he came to Colossæ, a city on his right hand—i.e. on the south bank of the river—standing on a plain about one league wide from north to south, and four long from east to west.[233] The ruins, consisting of a

Fig. 171.—*Coins of Colossæ. From Pellerin.*
These three coins are given to show how, even in the most ancient times, the name of this city was differently spelt. In the first coin we have Κολοσσηνῶν, in the second Κολοσσηνῶν, and in the third Κολοσηνῶν. But they all confirm the reading of Colossæ instead of Colossæ.

theatre and other public buildings, with broken columns strewn over a considerable space, still mark the spot. On the left, or northern, bank was the Necropolis, and

---

[230] Hamilton's Asia Minor, i. 515. The fact of their knowledge of this principle is also confirmed by Pliny, who observes: Aquam surgere in sublime opus fuerit e plumbo veniat. Subit altitudinem exortus sui. N. H. xxxi 31.
[231] See Fasti Sacri, p. 319, No. 1889.
[232] Rev. iii. 16, 20.

[233] For an account of Colossæ see Hamilton's Asia Minor, and Arundell's Asia Minor. The name is sometimes written Colossæ and sometimes Colassæ, but according to the general usage of the coins, though they vary, Colossæ is the true spelling. See Mionnet, iv. p. 267–268; vii. p. 540, 541; Waddington, Voy. Num. p. 29.

the tombs are still to be seen. There is now not a single inhabitant of Colossæ; they all rest in their last homes. There can be no doubt that this is the site of the town, but the wonder spoken of by Herodotus is still a problem. He speaks of Colossæ thus: "Colossæ is a great city of Phrygia, at which the Lycus entering into a chasm in the ground disappears, then after little more than half a mile rises again and discharges itself into the Meander."[234] The Lycus has been traced all the way from the Meander to its source, and no such marvel appears. Hamilton has suggested the following solution:[235] He says that a little below Colossæ the Lycus enters a narrow gorge, with steep banks on each side, which have been gradually raised by the extraordinary nature of the streams which there run into it from the north and south. The waters of these rills, he says, are so impregnated with calcareous matter, that they incrust everything they touch; insomuch that they are continually filling up old channels and forming others, and the high banks through which the Lycus here flows have, in the course of centuries, been raised by successive layers from these deposits. He supposes that anciently the river was actually overarched in this way, but that by some violence of nature the superstructure has been broken down. That this gorge is the chasm alluded to by Herodotus he thinks probable, from the statement of the Byzantine historian, Curopalates, who speaks of it as being at the confluence of certain rivulets,[236] and it is the fact that several tributary streams which run past Colossæ all unite with the Lycus at this narrow channel. One of them is the Ak Soo, or White River, which has the same peculiar property of incasing any substance cast into it with a thick incrustation. This explains the remarkable observation of Pliny, that there is a river at Colossæ which will convert brick into stone.[237] Indeed, such is the petrifying power even of the main stream of the Lycus, from the influx of these waters, that the mills erected upon it, unless they are frequently scoured, would soon become choked up by the accumulation of the calcareous silt. Xenophon describes Colossæ in his time as a great city, populous and flourishing;[238] and Pliny classes it amongst the *oppida celeberrima* of Phrygia;[239] and so it continued for some centuries after the Christian era, but gradually it decayed, and Chonas, three miles to the south, at the foot of the mountain, grew up in its place. By many Chonas has been identified with Colossæ.[240]

[234] Κολοσσὰς, πόλιν μεγάλην Φρυγίης, ἐν τῇ Λύκος ποταμὸς ἐς χάσμα γῆς ἐσβάλλων ἀφανίζεται, ἔπειτα διὰ σταδίων ὡς μάλιστά κῃ πέντε ἀναφαινόμενος ἐκδιδοῖ καὶ οὗτος ἐς τὸν Μαίανδρον, Herod. vii. 30; and so Pliny: Subeunt terras, rursusque redduntur Lycus in Asia, Erasinus in Argolica, Tigris in Mesopotamia. N. H. ii. 106; and see Strabo, xii. 8 (p. 75, Tauch.).

[235] Vol. i. p. 511.

[236] Μηδὲ τὰς τοῦ χάσματος σήραγγας ἐν ᾧπερ οἱ παρῤῥέοντες ποταμοὶ ἐκεῖσε χωνευόμενοι διὰ τῆς τοῦ ἀρχιστρατήγου παλαιᾶς ἐπιδημίας καὶ θεοσημείας.

Curopalat. Hist. p. 652, cited 2 Arundell, 178.

[237] In Colossis flumen est quo lateres conjecti lapides extrahuntur. Hist. Nat. xxxi. 20.

[238] Κῦρος δὲ ὡρμᾶτο ἀπὸ Σαρδέων καὶ ἐξελαύνει διὰ τῆς Λυδίας σταθμοὺς γ' παρασάγγας κϛ' ἐπὶ τὸν Μαίανδρον ποταμόν· τοῦτον διαβὰς, ἐξελαύνει διὰ Φρυγίας σταθμὸν ἕνα παρασάγγας η' εἰς Κολοσσάς, πόλιν οἰκουμένην εὐδαίμονα καὶ μεγάλην. Xenoph. Anab. ii. 2.

[239] Plin. N. H. v. 41.

[240] As Leake, Asia Minor, p. 254, and Arundell, Asia Minor, p. 161. Arundell is thought to be in

Who was the energetic preacher that first converted the Colossians, Laodiceans, and Hierapolitans, is not recorded expressly; but that it was one of Paul's followers, we may conclude from the fact of Paul having addressed letters to them. A passage in the Colossians leads us to surmise that this envoy was Epaphroditus, or Epaphras.

Fig. 172.— View of Chonas. From Arundell, who thinks that Chonas represents the ancient Colossae.

Born at Colossae,[241] he had heard the word at Ephesus, and became a disciple and attached follower of Paul. We shall find him hereafter, sometimes in Asia, sometimes in Macedonia, and sometimes even at Rome, in the service of the Apostle.

error in placing Colossae at Chonas (fig. 172), but he furnishes some curious details which illustrate the temporary submergence of the Lycus, and its reappearance. In journeying to Chonas from Denizli (which lay on the south-west), he had for some time a rivulet on his left-hand, but imperceptibly he lost it, and on advancing further he again discovered it issuing from the limestone rock, and making its way northward into the plain. This stream (called the Kionk Bonar) he imagined to be the Cadmus, which is described by Strabo, xii. 8 (p. 75, Tauch.), as earthing itself as well as the Lycus. He made some attempt to ascertain the spot where the rivulet had buried itself, but the want of time prevented his finding it. He arrived at Chonas itself fifty minutes afterwards. The city was situate at the northern foot of mount Cadmus, and at the back, or south, was a deep ravine, from which a stream issued, and he was informed that on reaching the town the stream sank underground, and rose again a little below. He was also told that the river Ak-khan, which struck the road two hours from Denizli, and two and a half from Chonas, secreted itself in a chasm at three hours higher up, and re-emerged at an interval of 800 fathoms.

[241] Coloss. iv. 12.

A man of this active and enterprising character would naturally, when the light dawned upon himself, be anxious to impart it to his fellow-countrymen. With a commission from Paul, he set about the work of planting a church at Colossæ, and with the assistance of Philemon, a wealthy Colossian who had also been converted by Paul,[242] his efforts were crowned with success. "The Gospel," writes Paul to the Colossians, "is come unto you as it is in all the world, and bringeth forth fruit as it doth also in you, *since the day ye heard of it, and know the grace of God in truth, as ye also learnt it of Epaphras, our dear fellow-servant, who is for you a faithful minister of Christ.*"[243] Epaphras, when he quitted Colossæ on his return to Paul, appears to have constituted Archippus the bishop or presbyter of the city, under whose auspices the rising church flourished and increased. But there was as yet no public building for divine worship, and they met in the private house of the wealthy Philemon. Almost the last words in the Epistle to the Colossians are, "Say to Archippus, Take heed to the ministry which thou hast received in the Lord, that thou fulfil it;"[244] and again, Paul, in writing to Philemon, sends his benediction to "*Archippus, our fellow-soldier, and to the church in thy* (Philemon's) *house.*"[245]

We have still fewer particulars respecting the conversion of Laodicea and Hierapolis; but as these cities were not far distant from Colossæ, and were all included in one and the same circuit of Asia (the Cibyratic), and must have had frequent communication with each other, we can readily suppose that the light of the Gospel would soon shine upon them also. Epaphras, again, was either the original founder of these churches, or, at least, was an earnest promoter of the cause, or Paul in his Epistle to the Colossians, would not have used such language as this: "I bear him (Epaphras) record that he hath a great zeal for you, and for *them at Laodicea and them in Hierapolis.*"[246] The church at Laodicea seems to have been placed under the care of Nymphas, in whose house they met for public worship; for Paul writes, "Salute the brethren which are in Laodicea, and Nymphas and the church which is in his house."[247]

Paul had been now (October, A.D. 56) between two and three years at Ephesus, and as he "had no certain dwelling-place," it was time to struggle on towards the prize of his high calling, through other scenes. He was particularly anxious to visit Rome, the more so as Paul at Corinth had become acquainted with so many Romans, who, like Aquila and Priscilla, had retired to the capital of Achaia for refuge. But even Rome was to be only a temporary resting-place, for the ulterior object was Spain, a country in which Christianity had never been planted, and therefore a field of labour ardently coveted by an Apostle who was ever reluctant to reap where he had not sown. Paul, however, had much on his hands before he could gratify the secret yearning of his heart. He had but recently laid the foundations of the

---

[242] Philem. 19.
[243] Coloss. i. 6.
[244] Coloss. iv. 17.
[245] Philem. 2.
[246] Coloss. iv. 13.
[247] Coloss. iv. 15.

churches in Macedonia and Achaia, and it was necessary to examine into their state, to supply defects in the fabrics hastily erected, and to counteract the inroads of invading disorders. He had also undertaken to make a collection amongst them for the poor saints of Jerusalem. Of all the churches which he planted, none, perhaps, had a stronger hold on his affections than Corinth—in none was there so much evil mixed up with so much good—and the training of so wayward a child required the utmost care of the watchful parent. Paul also had made a longer stay with them than at any other place, except Ephesus, and a degree of intimacy had sprung up which bound the Apostle to them by the most tender ties. The plan therefore he now proposed to himself was, after remaining some months longer at Ephesus, to sail direct for Corinth, and proceed thence to Macedonia, then to return again to Corinth on his route to Jerusalem, and finally to pass through Rome into Spain. Paul, referring to this period, writes thus to the Corinthians: "I was minded to come unto you before, that ye might have a second benefit; and to pass by you into Macedonia, and to come again out of Macedonia unto you, and of you to be brought on my way toward Judea."[248]

Having resolved upon this plan, he conveyed an intimation of it to the Corinthian church, and at the same time announced his purpose of setting on foot a collection amongst the Corinthians for the poor Hebrews. The Corinthians in reply expressed great pleasure at the prospect of the Apostle's return, and they seem also to have cheerfully, and even joyfully, accepted the invitation to open a subscription for the church of Jerusalem; for the Apostle writes to them the year following: "As touching the ministering to the saints, it is superfluous for me to write to you; for I know the forwardness of your mind, for which I boast of you to them of Macedonia, that Achaia was *ready a year ago*, and your zeal hath provoked very many."[249]

It was at the beginning of A.D. 57, and when the Apostle was thinking of commencing his journey, that he received from Corinth, through the household of Chloe, intelligence of a distressing character, and which totally deranged his preconceived intentions. The information thus communicated was—*First*, that serious divisions had sprung up in the Corinthian church. After the Apostle had left them his steps had been followed by Apollos, who, as we have seen, had originally possessed a very imperfect knowledge of the Christian scheme, and had since been better instructed by Aquila and Priscilla, but he had still carried with him to Corinth some peculiar views. He was a powerful preacher, and had become very popular there, and his congregation, standing aloof from the rest of the community, had formed itself into a separate sect. Some indiscreet Christians of Jerusalem, where the law of Moses was still rigidly observed even by the church, had also found their way to Corinth, and by magnifying the dignity of Peter as the chief of the twelve, and insisting on obedience to the Mosaic ritual, had given rise at Corinth to a Judaizing

---

[248] 2 Cor. i. 15, 16.   [249] 2 Cor. ix. 1, 2; and see viii. 10.

party, entertaining opinions not in conformity with the Pauline creed. Certain it is that at Corinth the robe of Christ, which should be without seam, was rent by schism. "It hath been declared unto me of you, my brethren," writes the Apostle, "by them which are of the house of Chloe, that there are contentions among you. Now, this I say, that every one of you saith I am of Paul, and I of Apollos, and I of Cephas, and I of Christ."[250]

A *second* charge laid at the door of the Corinthian church was that of gross immorality. Corinth had ever been the seat of the lustful passions, and some of the brethren had not yet learnt to wear the white garment of Christian purity. The Apostle received private information that one of the converts was living in fornication with his father's wife, his own stepmother! This was an enormity which, even among the heathen, who indulged otherwise the carnal appetites with little scruple, was deemed an offence of unpardonable wickedness, and in some places was even punishable with death.[251] "It is reported commonly that there is fornication among you, and such fornication as is not so much as named among the Gentiles, that one should have his father's wife."[252]

A *third* scandal in the Corinthian church was of a less aggravated character, but bringing great discredit on the Christian community, viz. a revengeful prosecution of wrongdoers before the heathen tribunals. Even in the instance of fornication before referred to, it is not unlikely that the father, who had been robbed of his wife by his own son, had commenced an action for damages in some court of law. Certainly the church had suffered by a spirit of resentment in some of its members, who had taken legal proceedings for the redress of either real or supposed injuries. Such a course was as unnecessary as it was contrary to the Christian spirit. Private arbitration was then the common mode of settling differences, and the award could be enforced by law; not only so, but the Jews were forbidden by the Rabbinical traditions to go before a Gentile judge,[253] and were permitted by the Romans throughout the empire to have a special judicature of their own; and the early Christians, who, from worshipping one God and rejecting polytheism, were accounted Jews, were not improbably allowed the same privilege.[254] "Dare any of you," writes the Apostle, "having a matter against another, go to law before the unjust and not before the saints? Do ye not know that the saints shall judge the world? and if the world shall be judged by you, are ye unworthy to judge the smallest matters? Know ye

---

[250] 1 Cor. i. 11.

[251] Nubit genero socrus nullis auspicibus, nullis auctoribus, funestis ominibus omnium omnibus. O mulieris scelus incredibile et præter hanc unam in omni vitâ inauditum! O libidinem effrenatam et indomitam! O audaciam singularem! Cic. pro Cluentio, v. 14. And see Suet. Tib. 35, and numerous passages cited by Wetstein, 1 Cor. v. 1, from writers sacred and profane.

[252] 1 Cor. v. 1.

[253] Statutum est, ad quod omnes Israelitæ obligantur, cum qui litem cum alio habet, non debere eam tractare coram Gentilibus. Tanchuma, f. 92, 2, cited by Wetstein, whom see on 1 Cor. vi. 1.

[254] Thus the Essenes determined their own controversies. Jos. Bell. ii. 8, 9.

not that we shall judge angels? how much more things that pertain to this life? If then ye have judgments of things pertaining to this life, set them to judge who are little esteemed in the church. I speak to your shame. Is it so, that there is not a wise man among you? no, not one that shall be able to judge between his brethren? But brother goeth to law with brother, and that before the unbelievers."[255]

A *fourth* ground of complaint, and almost incredible at the present day, was connected with the celebration of the Eucharist. This sacrament, in the Apostolic age, was either itself a feast or was accompanied with one, and the Corinthian congregations had outraged all Christian decency, not only by an exclusive spirit in forming themselves into parties at the Lord's table, but by eating and drinking as if they were partaking of an ordinary banquet. The rich brought their luxuries, and the poor had not enough to eat. "Ye come together," says the Apostle, "not for the better, but for the worse. For first of all, when ye come together in the church, I hear that there be divisions among you, and I partly believe it; for there must be also heresies among you, that they which are approved may be made manifest among you. When ye come together therefore into one place, this is not to eat the Lord's supper; for in eating every one taketh before other his own supper, and one is hungry and another is drunken. What! have ye not houses to eat and drink in? or despise ye the church of God, and shame them that have not? What shall I say to you? shall I praise you in this? I praise you not."[256]

These painful tidings, indirectly conveyed to the Apostle, caused him infinite anxiety. What course was he to adopt under circumstances so embarrassing? If he persevered in the intention of an immediate visit to Corinth, it was impossible for him not to inflict exemplary punishment on the offenders; yet how repugnant was this to the feelings of warm affection which he entertained towards them! His more than parental love dictated a total alteration of his plans. Instead of crossing direct to Corinth, as he had before intended, and passing thence to Macedonia, he now resolved on *first* visiting Macedonia (which would give the Corinthians an opportunity of repentance), and *then* proceeding to Corinth and spending the winter there. He also proposed to dispatch two of his most trustworthy followers to Corinth to rectify, if possible, the prevailing abuses, that when the Apostle himself arrived he might come in peace, and not with the rod. It is to this project of passing through Macedonia *first*, contrary to his former purpose, that the Apostle alludes in the following passage of his letter to the Corinthians, and which, without a knowledge of the above circumstances, would not be fully understood. "Now I will come unto you, when I shall pass through Macedonia; for *I do pass through Macedonia*;"[257] or, as it might be paraphrased, "I say, when I shall pass through Macedonia, for I have changed the route before laid down, and intend now, instead of sailing from Ephesus to Corinth direct, to visit Macedonia in the first instance."

---

[255] 1 Cor. vi. 1–6. [256] 1 Cor. xi. 17–22. [257] 1 Cor. xvi. 5.

The disciples whom the Apostle selected to send to Corinth were Timothy and Erastus. The former had now served an apprenticeship of several years in the Christian ministry, and his ardent zeal, and amiable manners, and unaffected piety, rendered him the fittest instrument to be employed on so delicate a mission. "For this cause have I sent unto you Timotheus, who is my beloved son, and faithful in the Lord, who shall bring you into remembrance of my ways which be in Christ, as I teach every where in every church."[258] Erastus was a Corinthian, and a man of authority amongst them, and the following year was chamberlain of the city.[259] It might well be hoped, therefore, that their united labours would produce the happiest results. Having thus settled his plans anew, the Apostle conveyed an intimation to Corinth of what was proposed.

Timothy and Erastus proceeded on their journey by way of Macedonia. This would interpose a little delay; but as Paul was now about to visit Macedonia first, and intended to start at an early day, it was necessary to put the Macedonians on their guard, that they might prepare for his reception, particularly with reference to the collection for the poor saints at Jerusalem. Timothy was charged on reaching Corinth to await the Apostle's arrival there, and Erastus would naturally remain at Corinth as his native place. It is to the particular juncture of the foregoing circumstances that the writer of the Acts refers in the following passage: "After these things were ended, Paul purposed in the spirit, when he had passed through Macedonia and Achaia to go to Jerusalem, saying, after I have been there I must also see Rome. So he sent into Macedonia two of them that ministered unto him, Timotheus and Erastus, but he himself stayed in Asia for a season."[260]

Timothy and Erastus probably took their departure from Ephesus about February, A.D. 57. While they were on their passage, the announcement that the Apostle had delayed his visit to Corinth reached that city by a more direct route, and excited a variety of feelings, and was made the subject of much strange comment. Some affected to say that he was trifling with them, and though he had promised to return, he never meant to return at all; others may have conjectured the true cause, but at present it was only conjecture, for it was not until the sincere contrition of the Corinthian church that the Apostle opened his heart to them in these solemn words, "I call God for a record upon my soul, that *to spare you* I came not as yet unto Corinth."[261]

The end of the matter at Corinth was, that as various questions were then agitating the Corinthian church, and the Apostle was not to be expected for some time, they should address a letter to him upon the subject of their doubts. An epistle from the Corinthians was drawn up accordingly, and was forwarded to Paul at Ephesus. It does not appear who was the bearer of it, but Stephanas, the first convert at Corinth, and Fortunatus and Achaicus (who were perhaps his sons), either

---

[258] 1 Cor. iv. 17. [259] Rom. xvi. 23. [260] Acts xix. 21, 22. [261] 2 Cor. i. 23.

carried it themselves, or accompanied those who did.[262] The letter, so far as the contents can be collected, was something to the following effect:—

"THE ELDERS AND BRETHREN OF THE CHURCH OF CORINTH, TO PAUL, AN APOSTLE OF JESUS CHRIST,—GREETING.

"We give thanks unto God, that the church planted by you at Corinth increases more and more. The disciples multiply daily, both at Corinth and in the parts adjacent. We trust also that the lives of the saints are an example to unbelievers, and many have been converted to Christ from seeing, we think, the fruits of faith in the conduct of the brethren.[263]

"We certify you, that we have been longing for your coming as promised, and that when lately your message reached us that your journey to us was deferred for the present, we had great sorrow, and many amongst us fear lest we should be again disappointed.[264]

"Seeing that the time of your return to us is uncertain, we have deemed it meet to write unto you touching various questions which have arisen amongst us, and which (to put an end to disputes amongst ourselves) we would fain refer to your determination.

"Upon the subject of marriage there are such doubts as these: some think that the purity of the Gospel requires that man and wife should no longer live as they have been wont, but that they should lead a life of total abstinence.[265]

"Again, it is the opinion of some that husbands who have lost their wives, and wives who have lost their husbands, should continue in that state.[266] By others, however, it is maintained that a second marriage is free from all objection.

"Some again say, that for just cause a man may put away his wife, and a wife leave her husband, and marry again. They insist, for instance, that if a husband be converted, and the wife remain an infidel, he may put her away, or if a wife be converted, and the husband remain an infidel, she may leave him.[267]

"But the great question is, as to marriage in the case of bachelors and maidens, whether they may or not as good Christians marry at all; for some say that the saints ought to live only to God, and that they can do so more effectually as single than as married. This point concerns not only the parties themselves, but also parents who are perplexed what course to pursue as to their daughters, whether to betroth them or not. To some it appears hard to lay any restraint upon the natural inclinations of their children, and they doubt whether, what is insisted upon for their good, may not in practice produce an evil.[268]

"We now pass to another matter of difference—how believers ought to demean themselves as regards idol sacrifices.

---

[262] 1 Cor. xvi. 15, 17.
[263] 1 Cor. v. 2, 6.
[264] 1 Cor. iv. 19; 2 Cor. i. 17, &c.
[265] 1 Cor. vii. 1.
[266] 1 Cor. vii. 8.
[267] 1 Cor. vii. 11, 12.
[268] 1 Cor. vii. 25.

"You know that aforetime we Gentiles were wont on the festival of any idol to attend the temple, and sitting down at the table to partake of the feast. Now many amongst us think that there is still no unlawfulness in this; for as touching things offered unto idols, say they, we are persuaded that we all have knowledge, and therefore the partaking of the meats with that conviction cannot work any evil in the mind of the believer.[269] Certainly the disciples having been accustomed to these banquets are desirous of still joining in them if it can be allowed.[270] Nay, they are subject to ridicule and persecution from their fellow-citizens for not attending,[271] and some of the brethren openly murmur at being debarred from what they hold to be an innocent matter."[272] We know, indeed, that such feasts (particularly in the temple of the great goddess of the city) are accompanied with fornication, and other impure rites, but from these the believers would be careful to abstain.[273] However, the more devout amongst us have set their faces against frequenting the temples at all, and say that the saints ought not to place themselves in the way of temptation."[274] We would, therefore, be advised by you what line of conduct the brethren should pursue in this matter.

"Another doubt connected with the same subject is this: it is well known that a great part of the meat sold in the public market is supplied from victims offered to idols. May the believer buy any meats, asking no question, or must he first ascertain how and whence they were obtained?[275]

"Again, the greater proportion of our fellow-citizens are still idolaters, but we have never understood that the saints are forbidden to associate with the unconverted. Now it happens that the disciples are from time to time invited as guests to the houses of unbelievers, and various meats are set upon the table. It is likely that many of such meats are from the victims offered to idols. May the believer eat on such occasions without question the meats set before him, or must he in point of conscience inquire first whether such meats are free from the pollution of idolatry?[276]

"We would also ask your opinion on certain things pertaining to the *discipline* of the Church. Where, indeed, you gave us any express directions, we remember you in all things, and keep the ordinances as you delivered them to us;[277] but there are some points which, not having been then in dispute, remain to be determined by you.

"Ought, then, the man in preaching or praying to have his head covered or uncovered? We, also, would have the same question resolved in the case of the woman.[278]

* * * * * * [279]

"Concerning the *gifts of the Spirit* ($\tau\tilde{\omega}\nu$ $\pi\nu\epsilon\nu\mu\alpha\tau\iota\kappa\tilde{\omega}\nu$) there are also disputes.

---

[269] 1 Cor. viii.
[270] 1 Cor. x. 6.
[271] 1 Cor. x. 13.
[272] 1 Cor. x. 10.
[273] 1 Cor. x. 8.
[274] 1 Cor. x. 9.
[275] 1 Cor. x. 25.
[276] 1 Cor. x. 27.
[277] 1 Cor. xi. 2.
[278] 1 Cor. xi. 12.
[279] The letter submitted doubts upon various other points. 1 Cor. xi. 34.

"Some amongst us speak with tongues; others are expounders of Scripture (προφῆται); others are teachers (διδάσκαλοι); and so forth. Now for preserving order in the church it is necessary that the precedence amongst these parties should be settled. Are such as speak with tongues entitled to a preference over expounders of Scripture, or the latter over the former? Thus it happens that when in the church the time of preaching has arrived one brother would speak in a tongue, while another would expound the Scripture. The latter all understand; the former is intelligible only to a few, or it may be to none. Sometimes an interpreter is present, and sometimes not. Who, in such a case, is to precede? Again, such as speak with tongues, as acting upon inspiration, sometimes rise two or three together, and then no little confusion prevails.[260] It seemed good to us, therefore, to ask you by what rule the church should be guided in these matters.

"There have also lately risen up amongst us certain men[261] called Sophists (σόφοι), who, incredible as it may appear, insist that there neither is, nor can be, any resurrection from the dead, for that in the nature of things it is impossible that bodies when resolved into their original elements can ever again be compounded—that, in fact, the material particles pass successively into other bodies, and that a general resurrection would involve the absurdity that the same matter could at one and the same time exist in distinct bodies; and other objections drawn, they say, from philosophy, are urged by them, and thereby the faith of the common sort of disciples (who cannot answer such subtle reasoning) is not a little shaken.[262] We could not pass over in silence the existence of such doctrines, as, unless they be confuted, we fear they may gain ground.

"Finally, as regards the contribution which some time since you exhorted us to make for the poor saints at Jerusalem, we earnestly desire to further so laudable an object by all the means in our power. We wait only to hear from you in what manner such a collection should be set on foot; whether it should be made at once, or at intervals; whether it should be begun immediately, or not until your arrival amongst us. The church will readily follow whatever directions you may give us in this respect.[263]

"Know that Apollos, while he was with us, was very useful in the ministry; and as you cannot yourself revisit us at present, we would that Apollos, who left us for Ephesus, and is, we hear, still tarrying there, should, if he can conveniently, return to us again.[264]

"Trusting soon to hear from you touching the various matters about which we have written, and also to see you shortly, we bid you, heartily, Farewell."

It will be observed that in this letter no allusion is made to the irregularities which had invaded the Corinthian church; so far from it, that throughout there is

---

[260] 1 Cor. xii., xiii., xiv.   [261] 1 Cor. xv. 12.   [262] 1 Cor. xv. 12, 35.
[263] 1 Cor. xvi.   [264] 1 Cor. xvi. 12.

an air of complacency and self-gratulation. The Apostle, however, during his absence never ceased to keep a watchful eye upon his flock, and having been apprised of the prevailing abuses, he had already dispatched Timothy and Erastus round by Macedonia to arrest the progress of the mischief. The presence of Stephanas, Fortunatus, and Achaicus, who came with the letter, now enabled the Apostle to acquaint himself more in detail with the exact state of the Corinthian church. The result of his inquiries filled him with the deepest sorrow, and he saw that not a moment was to be lost in applying a remedy. Numerous questions had been referred to him for his decision, and this gave him an opportunity in penning a reply to administer a sharp rebuke, and, while he appealed to the better feeling of the church, to threaten them, if they remained hardened, with the rod of punishment. He proposed, at the same time, to forward the Epistle direct to Corinth by the hands of Titus, to be accompanied by another, who was probably Trophimus. Titus was charged to examine into the state of the Corinthian church, and rectify the disgraceful disorders of it. The execution of these commands would, of course, in great measure supersede the office which had been committed to Timothy, who had been sent to Corinth, but, taking the circuitous route, had gone round by Macedonia. The further progress of Timothy towards Corinth was, therefore, countermanded, and he was directed to rejoin the Apostle at Ephesus with all expedition. The message, however, might not overtake him before his arrival at Corinth; and in that case he was to unite his endeavours with Titus, and return with him.

The task assigned to Titus was one of no little difficulty, and would call for the exercise, at the same time, of great firmness and discretion. Titus himself had great misgivings as to the result; but the Apostle would not believe that his labours at Corinth had been expended in vain, and with gentle earnestness removed the doubts of Titus; pointed out the favourable features of the Corinthian character, and bade him expect success in his mission. This confidence was not misplaced, and the reception of Titus was all that the Apostle could have wished, as he afterwards triumphantly declared, "Therefore we were comforted in your comfort; yea, and exceedingly the more joyed we for the joy of Titus, because his spirit was refreshed by you all. For if I have boasted any thing to him of you, I am not ashamed; but as we spake of all things to you in truth, even so our boasting, which I made before Titus, hath been found a truth. And his inward affection is more abundant toward you, whilst he remembereth the obedience of you all, how with fear and trembling ye received him. I rejoice, therefore, that I have confidence in you in all things."[295]

The Apostle now sat down to the painful task of writing his letter. He was under the necessity of severely reproving those who were beloved by him with more than a father's affection; but he gave no expression to the tender feelings by which he was moved, lest haply the reprimand might lose some of its poignancy. It was many

[295] 2 Cor. vii. 13 to 16.

months after, and when the Corinthians had repented, that he made the confession. "Out of much *affliction* and *anguish of heart*, I wrote unto you with *many tears*, not that ye should be grieved, but that ye might know the love which I have more abundantly unto you."[286]

In the address of the letter the Apostle associates with himself Sosthenes. The last time we heard of Sosthenes was at Corinth, when, as a ruler of the synagogue, he had led the attack upon Paul before Gallio, and had been beaten by the indignant Greeks. Since that time Apollos had visited Corinth, and mightily convinced the Jews, and Sosthenes, amongst others, had become a convert. Apollos and Sosthenes had since joined the Apostle at Ephesus, and as the latter had great weight with the Corinthian church, it was thought that the prefixing his name at the head of the Epistle might give additional force to the appeal.

The Epistle was written about the *Passover*, A.D. 57,[287] as is evident from a passage in the letter itself. "Know ye not that a little leaven leaveneth the whole lump. Purge out, therefore, the old leaven that ye may be a new lump; *as ye are unleavened, for even Christ our passover is sacrificed for us Therefore, let us keep the feast*, not with old leaven, neither with the leaven of malice and wickedness, but with the unleavened bread of sincerity and truth."[288] And with this date tallies the subsequent passage: "But I will tarry at Ephesus until *Pentecost*: for a great door and effectual hath been opened unto me, and there are many adversaries."[289]

After the usual salutation from himself and Sosthenes (i. 1), and the expression of thankfulness for the many graces bestowed upon the Corinthian church (i. 4), he opens the *first* part of his Epistle, in which he applies himself to the correction of the abuses by which the church had been lately disgraced. Under this head he first (i. 10) reproves the divisions amongst them, that one was a Paulite, and another a follower of Apollos, and another of Cephas, and he expatiates by way of episode on the nothingness of σοφία, or worldly wisdom, on which the Greeks so much prided themselves, the source of all the schisms which had arisen amongst them: "Let no man deceive himself. If any man among you seemeth to be wise in this world, let him become a fool that he may be wise."[290] With σοφία, he throughout the Epistle contrasts ἀγάπη, or love, which he so finely describes in c. xiii. He then (v. 1) adverts to the notorious sin in the Corinthian church, the flagrant case of fornication between one of the brethren and his father's wife. He at once passes sentence on the male offender, and directs that he may be delivered over unto Satan, the form of expression at that time for excommunication from the church—"I verily, as absent in body, but present in spirit, have judged already, as though I were present, concerning him that hath so done this deed—In the name of our Lord Jesus Christ, when ye are gathered together, and my spirit, with the power of our Lord Jesus Christ, to deliver such an one unto

---

[286] 2 Cor. ii. 4.   [287] See Fasti Sacri, p. 308, No. 1836.   [288] 1 Cor. v. 6-8.
[289] 1 Cor. xvi. 8, 9.   [290] 1 Cor. iii. 18.

Satan for the destruction of the flesh, that the spirit may be saved in the day of the Lord Jesus."[291] As to the woman, it would seem that she was not a believer, and therefore the Apostle assumes no jurisdiction over her: "For what have I to do to judge them also that are without? do not ye judge them that are within? but them that are without God judgeth. Therefore put away from among yourselves that wicked man."[292] In vi. 1, the Apostle adverts to the third irregularity, viz. their litigiousness, and tells them that they ought not, by wronging one another, to give rise to disputes; but that if they had questions one with another, they should submit them to arbitration amongst themselves, and not entail scandal on the church by bringing their quarrels before Pagan tribunals, and he concludes this part of his Epistle (ver. 9–20) by some general reflections, both on fornication, injustice, and the like, the crimes he had been reprobating.

At c. vii. begins the *second* part of the Epistle, in which the Apostle handles, in order, the various subjects which had been propounded in the letter received from the Corinthians; as first (vii.) the questions relating to marriage; then (viii.) the conduct of Christians with respect to the idol-feasts of the heathen; and (xi.) decency of behaviour at church (in the course of which he rebukes the manner in which they received the Eucharist). Then he treats (xii. to end of xiv.) of the nature and value of spiritual gifts (τὰ πνευματικά), and (xv.) of the doctrines which had been broached amongst the Corinthians by the heretics who denied the resurrection from the dead.

In c. xvi. the Apostle advances to the *third* part of his letter, in which he recommends them to make the collection for the poor saints at Jerusalem by laying by something on every first day of the week, that when the Apostle arrived every one might have in readiness what, according to his means, he was able to contribute.

The Apostle, in *conclusion* (xvi. 5), adverts to some personal matters. Thus he tells them (but without, at this time, stating his reasons) the alteration which had been made in his plans—that he now proposed to pass through Macedonia first, and that on reaching Corinth he should make some stay there, or even remain the winter with them, but that he did not propose to leave Ephesus until after Pentecost, as he was now making great progress there. "Now I will come unto you when I shall pass through Macedonia (for I *do* pass through Macedonia), and it may be that I will abide, yea, and winter with you, that ye may bring me on my journey whithersoever I go; for I will not see you now in passing, but I trust to tarry a while with you if the Lord permit."[293] Further, the Apostle (xvi. 10, 11) bids the Corinthians give a cordial reception to Timothy *if* he came, and to send him back with Titus and Trophimus.[294] As to Apollos, the Apostle tells the Corinthians that he had conveyed to him their request, that he should return to Corinth, but that he could not at present con-

---

[291] 1 Cor. v. 3–5.
[292] 1 Cor. v. 12, 13. τὸν πονηρόν.
[293] 1 Cor. xvi. 5–7.
[294] 1 Cor. xvi. 10.

veniently comply with it (xvi. 12). The Apostle then strongly recommends to the Corinthian church Stephanas, Fortunatus, and Achaicus, an exhortation dictated perhaps by the fear lest the Corinthians might suppose that Paul's knowledge of the disorders in the church had been derived through them. The Apostle, however, had before guarded against this inference, by stating that he had received the intelligence through the household of Chloe. The Epistle itself ran as follows:[295]—

[The *italics* indicate the variations from the Authorized Version. The words in brackets, thus [ ], are not expressed, but only implied, in the Greek.]

Ch. I. "PAUL, CALLED [TO BE] AN APOSTLE OF JESUS CHRIST THROUGH THE WILL OF
2 GOD, AND SOSTHENES OUR BROTHER, UNTO THE CHURCH OF GOD WHICH IS AT CORINTH—TO THEM THAT ARE SANCTIFIED IN CHRIST JESUS, CALLED [TO BE] SAINTS, WITH ALL THAT IN EVERY PLACE CALL UPON THE NAME OF JESUS CHRIST
3 OUR LORD, BOTH THEIRS AND OURS—GRACE BE UNTO YOU, AND PEACE, FROM GOD OUR FATHER, AND FROM THE LORD JESUS CHRIST.

4 "I thank my God always on your behalf, for the grace of God which is
5 given you by Jesus Christ; that in every thing ye are enriched by him,
6 in all utterance, and in all knowledge; even as the testimony of Christ *hath*
7 *been* confirmed in you, so that ye come behind in no gift; waiting for the
8 *revelation*[296] of our Lord Jesus Christ, who shall also confirm you unto the end,
9 that ye may be blameless in the day of our Lord Jesus Christ. God is faithful, by whom ye *have been* called unto the fellowship of his Son Jesus Christ our Lord.

10 "Now I beseech you, brethren, by the name of our Lord Jesus Christ, that ye all speak the same thing, and that there be no divisions among you, but that ye be perfectly joined together in the same mind and in the same

---

[295] The date of the Epistle appears from the contents.

1. Paul was in Asia at the time. "The churches of *Asia* salute you." 1 Cor. xvi. 19. And at Ephesus; "I will tarry at *Ephesus* until Pentecost." 1 Cor. xvi. 8.

2. It was written after his *second* visit to Galatia in A.D. 54, when the collection was made for the poor Hebrews. "Concerning the collection for the saints, as I have given order to the churches of *Galatia*, so do ye." 1 Cor. xvi. 1.

3. And after the mission of *Timothy* and Erastus at the beginning of the year A.D. 57. "For this cause have I sent unto you *Timotheus*," &c. 1 Cor. iv. 17.

4. And after he had made a change in his own plans as to his route on leaving Ephesus. "Now I will come unto you when I shall pass through Macedonia (for *I do pass through Mace-*

donia)." 1 Cor. xvi. 5.

5. The Epistle was written at the time of the Passover, for the Apostle pointedly alludes to the celebration of it as in observance at the time. "Purge out, therefore, the old leaven that ye may be a new lump, as *ye are unleavened*, for even *Christ our Passover* is sacrificed for us. Therefore let us *keep the feast* not with the old leaven," &c. 1 Cor. v. 7.

6. And this Passover was, of course, subsequent to the mission of Timothy and Erastus at the beginning of A.D. 57; and was the Passover next before the time fixed for the Apostle's departure. "I will tarry at Ephesus until Pentecost." 1 Cor. xvi. 8.

The Epistle, therefore, was written at the Passover of A.D. 57, which began that year on 7th April.

[296] τὴν ἀποκάλυψιν. In Eng. ver. "the coming."

11 judgment. For it hath been declared unto me, of you, my brethren, by them
12 [which are of the house] of Chloe, that there are contentions among you. Now
    this I say—that every one of you saith, I am of Paul, and I of Apollos, and I
13 of Cephas,²⁹⁵ and I of Christ.²⁹⁶ Is Christ divided? was Paul crucified for you?
14 or were ye baptized in the name of Paul? I thank God that I baptized none
15 of you, but Crispus and Gaius, lest any should say that I had baptized in
16 mine own name—and I baptized also the household of Stephanas; besides, I
17 know not whether I baptized any other.²⁹⁷ For Christ sent me not to baptize,
    but to preach the Gospel; not *in* wisdom of words, lest the cross of Christ
18 should be made of none effect; for the *word*²⁹⁸ of the cross is to them that
19 perish foolishness; but unto us which are saved it is the power of God; for it
    is written, 'I will destroy the wisdom of the wise, and will bring to nothing
20 the *intelligence* of the *intelligent*' (Is. xxix. 14).²⁹⁹ Where is the wise? where
    is the scribe? where is the disputer of this world? Hath not God made
21 foolish the wisdom of this world? for after that in the wisdom of God the
    world by wisdom knew not God, God was *pleased* by the foolishness of preach-
22 ing to save them that believe. For the Jews require a sign,³⁰⁰ and the Greeks

---

²⁹⁵ It does not follow that Peter himself had been at Corinth. For it is also said, "I am of Christ," and no one would contend that Christ therefore had been there. Dionysius, indeed, Bishop of Corinth, asserts that Peter visited Corinth: καὶ γὰρ ἄμφω [Peter and Paul] καὶ εἰς τὴν ἡμετέραν Κόρινθον φυτεύσαντες ἡμᾶς, ὁμοίως ἐδίδαξαν, ὁμοίως δὲ καὶ εἰς τὴν Ἰταλίαν ὁμόσε διδάξαντες ἐμαρτύρησαν κατὰ τὸν αὐτὸν χρόνον. Euseb. ii. 25. But Dionysius had probably no other authority for this than the surmise arising from the above passage in the First Epistle to the Corinthians. If Peter had been at Corinth, how could Paul have said, iii. 6, "I planted, Apollos watered," without making the least reference to Peter? Had Peter either planted or watered at Corinth, his name would surely have been mentioned with Paul and Apollos.

²⁹⁶ It has been much disputed who are the persons here referred to. According to some the party of Christ were those who were the followers of James, Bishop of Jerusalem, the near relative, i.e. the half-brother of Christ. According to others they were the neutrals of the Corinthian church, who took neither Paul, nor Cephas, nor Apollos for their pattern, but professed to hold Christianity as it came from Christ himself. The more probable supposition is, that they were the adherents of the False Teacher so often referred to in the second Epistle to the Corinthians, who claimed to have known Christ personally, and to be the Apostle of Christ, and so to make known his real doctrines. It is against this heretical teacher that the Apostle directs his remarks: "If any man trusteth to himself that he is Christ's, let him of himself think this again, that as he is Christ's, even so we are Christ's," 2 Cor. x. 7; and again, "such are false Apostles, deceitful workers, transforming themselves into the Apostles of Christ," 2 Cor. xi. 13; and again, "though we have known Christ after the flesh, yet now henceforth know we him no more," 2 Cor. v. 16. See a full discussion of the subject in Baur's Paulus der Apost. 262.

²⁹⁷ Paul himself baptized only on special occasions. Thus the household of Stephanas were the first converts of Achaia. See 1 Cor. xvi. 15. Crispus was a ruler of the synagogue, Acts xviii. 8. And Paul, for some reason, had a great regard for Gaius, for on his second visit to Corinth he lodged with him. Rom. xvi. 23. The other converts at Corinth were baptized by Silvanus, or Timothy, or Titus.

²⁹⁸ λόγος. In Eng. ver. "preaching."

²⁹⁹ The quotation agrees with the Septuagint, except that the Apostle substitutes ἀθετήσω for κρύψω.

³⁰⁰ By a *sign* is here meant a miraculous display of earthly power; the Jews expecting the Messiah to be a temporal prince, and stumbling

23 seek after wisdom; but we preach Christ crucified—unto the Jews a stumbling-
24 block, and unto the Greeks foolishness; but unto them which are called, both
25 Jews and Greeks, Christ the power of God, and the wisdom of God; because
the foolishness of God is wiser than men, and the weakness of God is stronger
26 than men. For behold[262] your calling, brethren, how that not many [of you
27 are] wise after the flesh, not many mighty, not many noble;[264] but God hath
chosen the foolish things of the world *that he might shame* the wise; and God
hath chosen the weak things of the world *that he might shame* the things
28 which are mighty; and base things of the world, and things which are
despised, hath God chosen, yea, and things which are not, *that he might* bring
29, 30 to nought things that are;[265] that no flesh should glory in his presence. But
of him are ye in Christ Jesus, who *was* made unto us from God wisdom, and
31 righteousness, and sanctification, and redemption; that, according as it is
written, 'He that glorieth, let him glory in the Lord' (*Jer.* ix. 23, 24).[266]

Ch. II.   "And I, brethren, when I came to you, came not with excellency of speech
2 or of wisdom, declaring unto you the testimony of God; for I determined not
3 to know any thing among you, save Jesus Christ, and him crucified; and
4 I was with you in weakness,[267] and in fear, and in much trembling, and my
speech and my preaching was not with enticing words of man's wisdom, but

---

at the doctrine of the cross. See instances of the Jews asking a sign from our Saviour. Matt. xiii. 38; xvi. 1; Luke xi. 16; John ii. 18; vi. 30.

[262] βλέπετε. In Eng. ver. "ye see."

[264] But Christianity was not confined to the lower class, for many of the converts occupied a prominent position. Amongst the Apostles were Peter and Andrew and James and John, who, though fishermen, had servants at their command, and John was personally acquainted with the High Priest Caiaphas. John xviii. 15. Amongst the converts in our Lord's lifetime were Joanna, the wife of Chuza, who held the high post of steward or procurator to Herod Antipas, Tetrarch of Galilee, Luke viii. 2, and Nicodemus a ruler (ἄρχων), John iii. 1, and master (διδάσκαλος), John iii. 10, and Joseph of Arimathea, who was a member of the Sanhedrim (βουλευτής), Mark xv. 43, Luke xxiii. 50, and was wealthy (πλούσιος), Matt. xxvi 1. 57. And after the crucifixion we meet with Barnabas, who was a landholder, Acts iv. 36; and Cornelius, a centurion, Acts x. 1; and Paul, whose education shows him to have been a man of mark; and Dionysius, a member of the Areopagus, the supreme court of judicature at Athens, Acts xvii. 34; and Erastus, who was chamberlain of the city of Corinth, ὁ οἰκονόμος τῆς πόλεως,

Rom. xvi. 23; and Manaen, the foster-brother of Herod Antipas, Tetrarch of Galilee, the son or grandson of Manaen the Essene, the favourite of Herod the Great, Ἡρώδου τοῦ Τετράρχου σύντροφος, Acts xiii. 1; and Claudia, supposed to be the daughter of Cogidunus, King of the Regni in Britain (see post, 2 Tim. iv. 21, and note there), and the household of Nero, οἱ ἐκ τῆς Καίσαρος οἰκίας, Philipp. iv. 22, amongst whom were probably Tryphoena and Tryphosa and Hermes and Hermas and Junias, all which names appear in the columbarium of the Nero family at Rome. See post, Rom. xvi. 11, note, &c.

[265] So Euripides:

'Ὁρῶ τὰ τῶν θεῶν, ὡς τὰ μὲν πυργοῦσ' ἄνω
τὰ μηδὲν ὄντα, τὰ δὲ δοκοῦντ' ἀπώλεσαν.'

Troad. 608.

[266] ὁ καυχώμενος ἐν Κυρίῳ καυχάσθω. In the LXX. the passage is: μὴ καυχάσθω ὁ σοφὸς ἐν τῇ σοφίᾳ αὐτοῦ ... ἀλλ' ἢ ἐν τούτῳ καυχάσθω ὁ καυχώμενος συνιεῖν καὶ γινώσκειν ὅτι ἐγώ εἰμι Κύριος.

[267] The Apostle was probably suffering from ophthalmia. He appears to have been afflicted with it more particularly during his second circuit, in the course of which he made the visit to Corinth to which he now alludes. See ante, p. 186.

5 in demonstration of the spirit and of power; that your faith should not stand
6 in the wisdom of men, but in the power of God.[300] Howbeit, we speak wisdom among *the* perfect; yet not the wisdom of this world, nor of the *rulers* of this
7 world, that come to nought; but we speak the wisdom of God in a mystery— the hidden wisdom, which God *pre-ordained* before the world unto our glory,
8 which none of the *rulers* of this world knew; for had they known it, they
9 would not have crucified the Lord of glory; but as it is written, 'Eye hath not seen, and ear *hath not* heard, neither have entered into the heart of man, the things which God hath prepared for them that love him' (*Is.* lxiv. 4);[301]
10 but God hath revealed them unto us by his Spirit, for the Spirit searcheth all
11 things, yea, the deep things of God. For what man knoweth the things of a man, save the spirit of *the* man which is in him? Even so the things of God
12 knoweth no *one*, but the Spirit of God. Now we have received, not the spirit of the world, but the spirit which is of God; that we might know the things
13 that are freely given to us of God. Which things also we speak, not in the words *taught of* man's wisdom, but *taught of* the Holy Spirit, *commending*
14 spiritual things *to the* spiritual. But the natural man[302] receiveth not the things of the Spirit of God, for they are foolishness unto him, neither can he
15 know them, because they are spiritually discerned; but he that is spiritual
16 judgeth all things, yet he himself is judged of no man, for 'who hath known the mind of the Lord, that he may instruct him?' (*Is.* xl. 13);[303] but we have the mind of Christ.

Ch. III. "And I, brethren, could not speak unto you as unto spiritual, but as unto
2 carnal, as unto babes in Christ. I have fed you with milk, and not with meat; for hitherto ye were not able [to bear it], *but* neither now are ye able,
3 for ye are yet carnal; for whereas there is among you envying, and strife, and
4 divisions, are ye not carnal, and walk *after the manner of man?* For while one saith, I am of Paul; and another, I am of Apollos, are ye not carnal?
5 Who then is Paul, and who is Apollos, but ministers by whom ye believed,
6 even as the Lord gave to *each?* I planted; Apollos watered;[302] but God gave
7 the increase. So *that* neither is he that planteth any thing, neither he that

---

[300] δυνάμεως, the display of miraculous power.

[301] ἃ ὀφθαλμὸς οὐκ εἶδε, καὶ οὖς οὐκ ἤκουσε, καὶ ἐπὶ καρδίαν ἀνθρώπου οὐκ ἀνέβη, ἃ ἡτοίμασεν ὁ Θεὸς τοῖς ἀγαπῶσιν αὐτόν. It is somewhat doubtful what is the passage of Scripture here referred to, but the nearest is Isaiah lxiv. 1. If so, the Apostle is citing from memory, and gives a free translation. In the LXX. the words are: ἀπὸ τοῦ αἰῶνος οὐκ ἠκούσαμεν, οὐδὲ οἱ ὀφθαλμοὶ ἡμῶν εἶδον Θεὸν, πλὴν σοῦ, καὶ τὰ ἔργα σου ἃ ποιήσεις τοῖς ὑπομένουσιν ἔλεον.

[302] ψυχικὸς δὲ ἄνθρωπος. There are three degrees to be noted: 1. The πνευματικὸς or spiritual man. 2. The ψυχικὸς, the animal or natural man, relying only on human wisdom. 3. The σαρκικὸς, or carnal man.

[303] τίς γὰρ ἔγνω νοῦν Κυρίου, ὃς συμβιβάσει αὐτόν; In the LXX. the passage is Τίς ἔγνω νοῦν Κυρίου; καὶ τίς αὐτοῦ σύμβουλος ἐγένετο ὃς συμβιβάσει αὐτόν;

[304] Peter therefore had not taught at Corinth, though the Judaising party set him up in opposition to Paul.

8 watereth, but God that giveth the increase. Now he that planteth and he
that watereth are one, and every man shall receive his own reward according
9 to his own labour; for we are *fellow-workmen of* God; ye are God's husbandry,
10 ye are God's building. According to the grace of God which *was* given unto
me, I, as a wise master-builder, laid the foundation, and another buildeth
11 thereon. But let every *one* take heed how he buildeth thereupon: for other
12 foundation can no man lay than that is laid, which is Jesus the Christ. *But
if* any man build upon this foundation gold, silver, precious stones[313]—wood,
13 hay, *straw*,[314] every man's work shall be made manifest; for The Day[315] shall
declare it, for it shall be revealed by fire, and the fire shall try every man's
14 work of what sort it is.[316] If any man's work abide which he hath built
15 thereupon, he shall receive a reward—if any man's work shall be burned,
he shall suffer loss; but he himself shall be saved, yet so as *through* fire.[317]
16 Know ye not that ye are the temple of God, and that the Spirit of God
17 dwelleth in you? If any man *marreth* the temple of God, him shall God
18 *mar;* for the temple of God is holy, which [temple] ye are. Let no man
deceive himself; if any *one* among you seemeth to be wise in this world,
19 let him become a fool, that he may be wise; for the wisdom of this world is
foolishness with God. For it is written, 'He taketh the wise in their own
20 craftiness' (*Job* v. 13).[318] And again, 'the Lord knoweth the *reasonings* of the
21 wise, that they are vain' (*Ps.* xciv. 11).[319] Therefore let no man glory in men,
22 For all things are yours, whether Paul, or Apollos, or Cephas, or the world, or
23 life, or death, or things present, or things to come—all are yours; and ye are
Christ's; and Christ is God's.

Ch. IV. "Let a man so account of us, as ministers of Christ, and stewards of the
2 mysteries of God. Moreover it is required in stewards that a man be found
3 faithful; but with me it is a very small thing that I should be judged *by* you,
4 or *by the Day of* man;[320] yea, I judge not mine own self; for [*say*] *I am
conscious of* nothing *to myself;*[321] yet am I not hereby justified, but he that
5 judgeth me is the Lord. Therefore, judge nothing before the time, until the
Lord come, who both will bring to light the hidden things of darkness, and

---

[313] These may be scorched and blackened by the fire, but the substance remains after it.

[314] These are so consumed by the fire that nothing remains of them.

[315] The Day of Judgment. See 2 Thess. i. 10.

[316] The Apostle refers here to Malachi iv. 1.

[317] That is, he shall be saved as a man escapes through the flames from a burning house.

Τούτου δ' ἐντομέροισι καὶ ἐκ πυρὸς αἰθομένοιο
ὄμφω νοστήσαιμεν, ἐπεὶ περίοδοι νόησοι.
Hom. Il. xi. 246.

[318] Ὁ δρασσόμενος τοὺς σοφοὺς ἐν τῇ πανουργίᾳ αὐτῶν. In the LXX. the words are: Ὁ καταλαμβάνων σοφοὺς ἐν τῇ φρονήσει.

[319] The same as in the LXX., except that we find the words τῶν ἀνθρώπων, instead of τῶν σοφῶν.

[320] ὑπὸ ἀνθρωπίνης ἡμέρας. See iii. 3.

[321] οὐδὲν γάρ ἐμαυτῷ σύνοιδα. In Eng. ver. "I know nothing by myself."

CHAP. XIII.]   FIRST EPISTLE TO THE CORINTHIANS.   [A.D. 57]   377

will make manifest the counsels of the hearts, and then shall *praise be to* every
one of God.

6 "*Now* these things, brethren, I have in a figure[322] transferred to myself and
to Apollos for your sakes, that ye *may* learn in us not to think above that
which is written, that no one of you be puffed up *each over each against*
7 *the other.*[323] For who *distinguisheth* thee? and what hast thou that thou didst
not receive? *But* if thou didst receive it, why dost thou glory, as if thou
8 hadst not received it? Now ye are full! now ye are rich! ye reign as kings
without us![324] and I would ye did reign, that we also might reign with
9 you; for I think that God hath set forth us, the Apostles last,[325] as *men doomed*
to death,[326] for we are made a spectacle unto the world, and to angels, and
10 to men. We are fools for Christ's sake, but ye are wise in Christ! we are
11 weak, but ye are strong! ye are honourable, but we are despised![327] Even
unto this present hour we both hunger, and thirst, and are naked, and are
12 buffeted, and have no certain dwelling-place, and labour working with our
own hands; being reviled we bless, being persecuted we suffer it, being
13 defamed we intreat; we are made as the filth of the earth, the offscouring of
all things unto this day.

14 "I write not these things to shame you, but as my beloved *children* I warn
15 you; for though ye have ten thousand instructors[328] in Christ, yet have ye
not many fathers; for in Christ Jesus I have begotten you through the Gospel.
16, 17 "I beseech you, *therefore,* be ye followers of me. For this cause have I sent
unto you *Timothy,* who is my beloved *child,* and faithful in the Lord, who shall
bring *to* your remembrance my ways which be in Christ, as I teach every
18 where in every church. Now some are puffed up, as though I would not come
19 to you.[329] But I will come to you shortly, if the Lord will, and will know, not
20 the *word* of them which are puffed up, but the power; for the kingdom of
21 God is not in word, but in power. What will ye? *That* I come unto you
with a rod, or in love, and in the spirit of meekness?

---

[322] The Apostle alludes to the figurative language he had used, of himself planting and Apollos watering while God only gave the increase, iii. 6.

[323] I.e. that ye be not puffed up as partisans of Paul or Peter or Apollos against the partisans of some other.

[324] All this is spoken ironically.

[325] The Apostle here alludes to the practice amongst the Romans at their shows, of reserving till the last, when the attention flagged, the criminals who had been condemned to death.

[326] ἐπιθανατίους. So Dionysius Hal.: ἔστι δὲ τὸ χωρίον κρημνὸς ἐξαίσιος ὅθεν αὐτοῖς ἔθος βάλλειν τοὺς ἐπιθανατίους. Dionys. Hal. vii. 35.

[327] This again is spoken ironically as regards the Corinthians.

[328] παιδαγωγούς. The Apostle evidently alludes to the excessive number of teachers, who had been a main cause of the religious dissensions amongst them.

[329] The Apostle therefore had already disappointed them once at the date of this Epistle; and he was now about to disappoint them a second time by deferring his visit until he had passed through Macedonia (xvi. 5); and therefore when in Macedonia he writes that it was the *third* time that he was intending to come. See 2 Cor. xiii. 1.

VOL. I.   3 C

Ch V. "It is reported commonly that there is fornication among you, and such fornication as is not so much as named among the Gentiles, that one should
2 have[330] his father's wife.[331] And ye are puffed up, and have not rather mourned,
3 that he that hath done this deed might be *put out* from among you! For I verily, as absent in body, but present in spirit, have judged already, as though
4 I were present, concerning him that hath so done this deed.—In the name of our Lord Jesus Christ, when ye are gathered together, and my spirit, with the
5 power of our Lord Jesus Christ, to deliver such a one unto Satan for the destruction of the flesh, that the spirit may be saved in the day of the Lord Jesus.[332]

6 "Your glorying is not good. Know ye not that 'A little leaven leaveneth
7 the whole lump?'[333] Purge out, therefore, the old leaven,[334] that ye may be a new lump (as ye are unleavened), for Christ our passover is sacrificed for us.
8 Therefore, let us keep the feast,[335] not with old leaven, neither with the leaven of malice and wickedness; but with the unleavened bread of sincerity and
9 truth. I *have written* unto you in *my letter*[336] not to company with fornicators—

---

[330] ἔχειν here signifies 'to have criminal conversation.' See Plut. Anton. 31: ἔχειν μὲν οὐκ ἀρνούμενος Κλεοπάτραν, γάμῳ οὐχ ὁμολογῶν.

[331] See ante, p. 363.

[332] The Apostle here charges the Corinthian church to call its members together to pass sentence of excommunication against the offender. This was done, and he was brought to contrition, as appears from 2 Cor. ii. 5.

(It should not escape notice that "such an one" in the English version has here been changed to "such a one." The rule is to write *a* when the next word begins with a consonant, and *an* when it begins with a vowel; but the question whether it begins with a consonant or vowel is to be determined, not by the way in which the word is *written*, but in which it is *pronounced*. Thus, 'a horse,' as the *h* is pronounced, but 'an hour,' as the *h* is suppressed. So, 'a youth,' as *y*, though often a vowel, is here a consonant; and so even where *y* is not written at all, but appears in pronunciation, as 'a use,' or where *y* is substituted in pronunciation for another letter, as 'a humourist.' Regard is also to be had to the emphasis or accent. Thus, 'a history,' as, the accent being on the first syllable, the *h* is strongly aspirated, but '*an* historical work,' as, the accent being on the second syllable, the *h* is either silent, or so softened that *an* before it is more euphonious than *a*. It appears, therefore, more correct to write 'such a one' than 'such an one,' as the word 'one' begins in pronunciation with *w* as a consonant.)

[333] This was a proverb, and is repeated at Gal. v. 9.

[334] The Apostle alludes to the Jewish custom of removing all leaven before eating the Passover. The house was carefully searched for this purpose, that not a crumb might remain. See the authorities, Schoettgen's Hor. Hebr. i. 593.

[335] Paul addresses his Epistle, we must remember, not to Jews, but to Gentiles, and as he here speaks of keeping the feast, it would seem that the Christians had already begun to observe Easter as a holy festival.

[336] ἔγραψα ὑμῖν ἐν τῇ ἐπιστολῇ. In Eng. ver. "I *wrote* unto you in *an* Epistle," as if he had corresponded previously with the Corinthians. Some indeed have maintained that two at least of St. Paul's Epistles have been lost, viz. an Epistle to the Corinthians, and an Epistle to the Laodiceans. But the hypothesis appears to the author a vain and groundless imagination.

The argument for a lost Epistle to the *Corinthians* rests on the above text: "I *wrote* unto you in *an* epistle." But this is not the true meaning of the Greek. The original is not ἐν ἐπιστολῇ, 'in *an* epistle,' but ἐν τῇ ἐπιστολῇ, 'in *the* or *my* epistle;' for though the expression ἡ ἐπιστολή *may* refer to a former epistle (as in 2 Cor. vii. 8, when Paul had just before led up to it by alluding to the contents and calling

10 yet not altogether with the fornicators of this world, or with the covetous, or extortioners, or with idolaters, for then must ye needs go out of the world. 11 But now I have written unto you not to keep company, if any man that

it in the same breath ἐκείνη ἐπιστολή, 'that epistle,' ib.), yet where ἡ ἐπιστολή stands by itself, it means properly the letter which the writer is penning, as in 2 Thess. iii. 14, 1 Thess. v. 27, Rom. xvi. 22, &c. So again the word ἔγραψα does not usually, like the second aorist, denote a past act without reference to the present time, but a past act continued up to the present time — i.e. not 'I wrote,' but 'I have written.' Thus in a verse immediately after the passage in question the Apostle proceeds: "But now *have I written*—ἔγραψα—unto you," &c., where no one can say that ἔγραψα refers to any letter but the one he was writing. In the same sense the Apostle uses the word προέγραψα in Ephes. iii. 3.

Independently, however, of verbal criticism, the whole context shows that the Apostle has in his mind not any letter to the Corinthians now lost but a previous injunction in the same letter. He had heard through the household of Chloe that a member of the Corinthian church had been guilty of fornication, and Paul in this Epistle, though absent, had charged the Corinthians, as if he were present, to excommunicate him, i.e. to exclude him from all communion with the Christian society. "Know ye not," he continues, "that a little leaven leaveneth the whole lump? purge out therefore the old leaven," 1 Cor. v. 7, or eject the leaven of the sinner from your church, and then proceeds: "*I have written* unto you in *my letter* not to keep company with fornicators," v. 7, but then checking himself by the reflection that this principle, if taken literally, would isolate the church at Corinth, where, under the worship of Venus, every man not a Christian was a fornicator, he qualifies the expression, "yet not altogether with the fornicators of this world . . . for then must ye needs go out of the world," and he then explains his meaning to be that they were to hold no intercourse, no not to eat with a *brother*, i.e. a member of their own body, who was thus guilty.

The surmise of the other lost letter, viz. one to the *Laodiceans*, hangs by a thread equally slender. The only text cited in support of it is the passage in the Epistle to the Colossians: "When this Epistle is read among you cause that it be read also in the church of the Laodiceans, and that ye likewise read the Epistle from Laodicea," Coloss. iv. 16, which shows, they say, that the Epistle to the Colossians was to be read to the Laodicean church, and *vice versa* that the Epistle to the Laodiceans was to be read to the Colossian church. But the language is, "the Epistle," not *to* but *from* Laodicea, and all therefore that is implied is that one Epistle was addressed to the Colossians, and another was to be *found at Laodicea*. But under what circumstances was it to be found there? The Epistle referred to is unquestionably that commonly called the "Ephesians." It has been proved to demonstration by Paley, in his Horae Paulinae, that it was written at the same time with the "Colossians," was identical in the scheme of its composition, and often identical in its language, and was dispatched by the same messenger, Tychicus. How it came to be designated as the Epistle to the Ephesians is easily explained. It was an encyclical or general letter, not like the Colossians, addressed to a single community, but intended for all the churches of Lydian Asia which had been Christianized during the Apostle's three years' residence at Ephesus. It was therefore inscribed, "To the Saints that are and to the faithful in Christ Jesus," and as Ephesus was the city on the coast to which the Epistle was first delivered, the Ephesians arrogated it to themselves. From their copy (more particularly as Ephesus was the capital of Proconsular Asia) other copies were transcribed from the Ephesian copy; and thus the superscription "to the Ephesians" ultimately prevailed. That it was not addressed to the Ephesians exclusively is manifest, as though Paul passed so many years amongst them it does not contain a single salutation or personal allusion. Why the Apostle tells the Colossians to fetch the Epistle *from Laodicea* is this: as Ephesus was the *first* city of Asia in the direction from Rome, so Laodicea was the *last*, with the exception of Colossae itself, and as Laodicea and Colossae were in sight of each other, the Apostle, to save the time and expense of another copy, bids the Colossians to procure one from the Laodiceans.

As I am persuaded that no part of the Evangelical Scripture has been lost, I cannot part from this subject without adverting to the question whether, as some insist, an Epistle of St. John is missing. Those who maintain the affirm-

is called a brother be a fornicator, or covetous, or an idolater, or a railer, or a
12 drunkard, or an extortioner—with such a one, no, not to eat; for what
have I to do to judge them also that are without? do not ye judge them that
13 are within? but them that are without, God judgeth. '*And ye shall put out
from among yourselves that wicked man*' (*Deut.* xvii. 7).[337]

Ch. VI. "Dare any of you, having a matter against another, go to law before the
2 unjust,[338] and not before the saints? Do ye not know that the saints shall
judge the world? and if the world shall be judged by you, are ye unworthy
3 *of the smallest judgments?* Know ye not that we shall judge angels?
4 (*Matt.* xx. 28)[339] how much more things that pertain to this life? If, then, ye

---

ative rely upon the words in the Third Epistle: "*I wrote unto the church*, but Diotrephes who loveth to have the pre-eminence among them receiveth us not." 3 John 9. The Epistle here referred to, it is said, is not forthcoming. We answer that we have it in the Second General Epistle of John. The address of the Second Epistle is, "To the elect Lady" (ἐκλεκτῇ κυρίᾳ). Now the English word "lady" conveys the erroneous impression that it was to a private person. But Christ himself was the Κύριος, or Lord, and the Church his bride was Κυρία, the Lady, Ephes. v. 25. So Peter sends a salutation from the church in Babylon to the churches of Asia Minor. "The co-elect (Lady) in Babylon saluteth you"—ἡ ἐν Βαβυλῶνι συνεκλεκτή (subaudi Κυρία), 1 Pet. v. 13. As all Christians were brethren, the several churches were similarly spoken of as sisters. Thus John closes the second Epistle with the words, "the children of thy *elect sister* [that is, of the church at Ephesus] greet thee," v. 13. How could John, if writing to any individual, have said: "I have found of thy children walking in the truth?"—εὕρηκα ἐκ τῶν τέκνων σου περιπατοῦντας ἐν ἀληθείᾳ, 2 John 4; for he is here evidently speaking of a numerous class, and members of a divided community, some of whom adhered to the truth, and some perversely broke away from it.

The Apostle then in his *Third* Epistle is writing to some church, and we have no difficulty in distinguishing what church. The Second and Third Epistles are closely connected together, and the Third is addressed to the well-beloved Gaius, who had been appointed by John bishop of the church of Pergamus, Constitut. Apostol. vii. 46; and the occasion of John's Second and Third Epistles was this: The Gnostic heresy had crept into the church of Pergamus, and there were in it those "who held the doctrine of the Nicolaitans," Rev. ii. 15, and denied the Incarnation of Jesus Christ. John therefore, as the Patriarch of the churches of Asia, wrote his Second Epistle authoritatively to the church of Pergamus, denouncing the new doctrine. "Many deceivers are entered into the world, who confess not that Jesus Christ is come in the flesh. This is a deceiver and an anti-Christ." 2 John 7. The well-beloved Gaius and the generality of the church submitted at once to the Apostolic declaration of the true Christian verity, but Diotrephes, one of the pastors at Pergamus, still persisted in his error, and thereupon John writes the Third Epistle to Gaius, the Bishop, commending the obedience of the community at large, but threatening the Apostolic rod against Diotrephes. "I wrote unto the church, but Diotrephes, who loveth to have the pre-eminence among them, receiveth us not; wherefore if I come I will remember his deeds." 3 John 9. The words, therefore, "I wrote unto the church," do not at all imply any lost Epistle, but simply refer to the Second Epistle of John, which had been addressed to the church of Pergamus.

[337] καὶ ἐξαρεῖς τὸν πονηρὸν ἐξ ὑμῶν αὐτῶν. The words are those of the LXX.

[338] By this are meant the Gentiles, as opposed to the saints or Christians. The early Christian church adopted the custom of the Jews, who were prohibited from carrying their grievances before a heathen tribunal. See ante, note [224].

[339] The Apostle here reminds the Corinthians of the declaration of our Lord, that his disciples should judge the twelve tribes of Israel. Matt. xx. 28. See ante, p. 282. By angels are meant departed spirits. Thus, when Peter was mira-

CHAP. XIII.]   FIRST EPISTLE TO THE CORINTHIANS.   [A.D. 57]   281

have judgments of things pertaining to this life, set them to judge who are
5 *nothing*-esteemed [339a] in the church.[340] I speak to your shame—Is it so, that
there is not a wise man among you? no, not one that shall be able to judge
6 between his brethren? but brother goeth to law with brother, and that before
7 the unbelievers. Now, therefore, there is utterly a fault among you, because
ye go to law one with another. Why do ye not rather take wrong? why do
8 ye not rather suffer yourselves to be defrauded?[341] Nay, ye do wrong, and
9 defraud, and that your brethren! Or know ye not that the *unjust* shall not
inherit the kingdom of God?

"Be not deceived: neither fornicators, nor idolaters, nor adulterers, nor
10 effeminate, nor abusers of themselves with mankind, nor thieves, nor covetous,
nor drunkards, nor revilers, nor extortioners, shall inherit the kingdom of God.
11 And such were some of you : but ye are washed, but ye are sanctified, but ye
are justified in the name of the Lord Jesus, and by the Spirit of our God.
12 'All things are lawful unto me, but all things are not expedient;'[342] all things
13 are lawful *unto* me, but I will not be brought under the power of any. Meats
for the belly, and the belly for meats; but God shall destroy both it and them.
Now the body is not for fornication, but for the Lord, and the Lord for the
14 body; and God hath both raised up the Lord, and will also raise up us by his
15 own power. Know ye not that your bodies are the members of Christ? Shall
I, then, take the members of Christ, and make them the members of a harlot?
16 *Far be it!*[343] *Or* know ye not that he which is joined to a harlot is one body?
17 for '*the* two,' saith he, 'shall be one flesh' (*Gen.* ii. 24);[344] but he that is
18 joined unto the Lord is one spirit. Flee fornication. Every sin that a man
doeth is without the body ; but he that committeth fornication sinneth against
19 his own body. *Or* know ye not that your body is the temple of the Holy
20 Ghost which is in you, which ye have of God, and ye are not your own? for
ye are bought with a price. Therefore, glorify God in your body."[345]

CH. VII.   "Now concerning the things whereof ye wrote unto me:"[346] It is good for a

---

culously delivered from prison, and knocked at the door of Mary's house, they thought it was his ghost, and said, "It is his angel." Acts xii. 15.

[339a] τοὺς ἐξουθενημένους. In Eng. ver., "who are least esteemed."

[340] 'If ye have not a wise man among you, appoint as judges even those who are of no reputation, rather than go before the heathen tribunals.'

[341] Οὖτος κράτιστός ἐστ' ἀνήρ, ὦ Γοργία,
ὅστις ἀδικεῖσθαι πλεῖστ' ἐπίσταται θνητῶν.
 Fragment of Gorgias of Menander.
 Grotius, Menand. et Philem. Reliq. p. 32.

[342] This seems to be a quotation. It was perhaps a passage in the letter *from* the Corinthians to Paul; or it may have been borrowed from some Greek dramatist;
πάντα μοι
ἔξεστιν, ἀλλ' οὐκ ἐγὼ ἐξουσιασθήσομαι.

[343] Μὴ γένοιτο. In Eng. ver. "God forbid." See note, Galat. ii. 17.

[344] Taken verbatim from the LXX.

[345] The words, "and in your spirit, which are God's," are rejected by Griesbach, Scholtz, Lachmann, Tischendorf, and Alford.

[346] The Apostle refers to the letter from the Corinthians to himself. See ante, p. 366.

2 man not to touch a woman. *But* to avoid fornication, let every man have his
3 own wife, and let every woman have her own husband. Let the husband
render unto the wife *her* due,³⁴⁷ and likewise also the wife unto the husband.
4 The wife hath not power of her own body, but the husband; and likewise also
5 the husband hath not power of his own body, but the wife. Defraud ye not
one the other (except it be with consent for a time, that ye may *have leisure
for*³⁴⁸ prayer and *may* come together again), that Satan tempt you not *by reason
6 of* your incontinency. But I speak this *way of* permission, and not of com-
7 mandment; for I would that all men were even as I myself.³⁴⁹ But every man
hath his proper gift of God, one after this manner, and another after that.
8 "*But* to the unmarried and widows I say, It is good for them if they abide
9 even as I; but if they cannot contain, let them marry, for it is better to marry
than to burn.
10 "*But* unto the married I command, yet not I, but the Lord (*Matt.* xix. 6),³⁵⁰
11 'Let not the wife depart from her husband.' (But and if she depart, let her
remain unmarried, or be reconciled to her husband;) 'and let not the husband
12 put away his wife' (*Matt.* xix. 9). But to the rest speak I, not the Lord.³⁵¹
If any brother hath a wife that believeth not, and she be pleased to dwell with
13 him, let him not put her away. And the woman which hath an husband that
14 believeth not, and he *is* pleased to dwell with her, let her not leave him. For

---

³⁴⁷ τὴν ὀφειλήν. In the text. recept. τὴν ὀφει-λομένην εὔνοιαν. Josephus uses the word εὔνοια in the same peculiar sense. Οὐδὲ τὴν ἑαυτῆς θυγατέρα συνοικοῦσαν Ἀριστοβούλῳ, θατέρῳ τῶν νεανίσκων, εἴα [ἡ Σαλώμη] τῇ τοῦ γάμου πρὸς ἐκεῖνον εὐνοίᾳ χρῆσθαι. Ant. xvi. 7, 3. However, the best critics, as Griesbach, Scholtz, Lachmann, Tischendorf, and Alford, omit ὀφειλομένην εὔνοιαν, and substitute ὀφειλήν—'her due.'

³⁴⁸ The words τῇ νηστείᾳ καὶ—"fasting and"—are rejected by Griesbach, Scholtz, Lachmann, Tischendorf, and Alford.

³⁴⁹ An idle tradition, arising from mistake, was at one time current, that Paul was a married man. Theodoret, Philipp. c. 4. This was a false inference from the passage in the first Epistle to the Corinthians ix. 5; "have we not power to lead about a sister-wife?" for how, it was argued, could any question arise as to his power to lead about a wife if he had no wife? But this line of argument is certainly erroneous, as is evident from the above passage. "I would that all men were even as I myself," 1 Cor. vii. 7, meaning, in a state of singleness. The interpretation, therefore, of the subsequent words, ix 5, must be either, "Have not we (I and Barnabas) power to marry as do the other Apostles, and then to lead about our wives with us in our circuits amongst the churches?"—or, "Have not we (Paul and Barnabas) power to take about with us a believing woman to minister to our necessities?" Another text cited for Paul's married state, and equally groundless, is from the Epistle to the Philippians, where he writes: "and I intreat thee, *true yokefellow*, help these women which laboured with me in the Lord," Philipp. iv. 3. For it is said that he here refers to his own wife. But such an interpretation is monstrous, as the Apostle evidently alludes to one of his fellow-labourers in the Gospel, and probably Lydia, who had been his first convert, and with whom he had lodged. If Paul was not married at the time of his conversion, he would naturally from that time preserve his celibacy, that he might not burden the church, for he could scarcely hope to support a wife and family by the labour of his hands while he was making his circuits.

³⁵⁰ The Apostle here, as elsewhere, refers to St. Matthew's Gospel. See note ante, p. 282.

³⁵¹ 'I cannot, as in the case of marriage, quote any express command from Christ himself.'

the unbelieving husband is sanctified by the wife, and the unbelieving wife is sanctified by the husband: else were your children unclean; but now are they
15 holy.[352] But if the unbelieving depart, let him depart. *The* brother or *the sister*[353] is not under bondage in such cases, but God hath called us to peace.
16 For what knowest thou, O wife, whether thou shalt save thy husband? or
17 *what* knowest thou, O man, whether thou shalt save thy wife? But as God hath distributed to every *one*, as the Lord hath called every one, so let him
18 walk, and so ordain I in all *the* churches. Is any man called being circumcised? let him not become uncircumcised;[354] is any called in uncircumcision?
19 let him not be circumcised. Circumcision is nothing, and uncircumcision is
20 nothing, but the keeping of the commandments of God. Let every *one* abide
21 in the same calling wherein he was called. Art thou called being a *bonds-*
22 *man*?[355] care not for it (but if thou mayest be made free, use it rather[356]): for he that is called in the Lord, being a *bondsman*, is the Lord's freeman; like-
23 wise also he that is called, being free, is Christ's *bondsman*. Ye have been
24 bought with a price; be not ye the *bondsmen* of men. Brethren, let every man, wherein he is called, therein abide with God.
25 "Now concerning virgins[357] I have no commandment of the Lord:[358] but I give my judgment, as one that hath obtained mercy of the Lord to be faith-
26 ful.[359] I suppose therefore that this is good—*by reason of* the present distress[360]

---

[352] The children have all the privileges of children of Christian parents lawfully married. If the child die before baptism can be administered, the baptism of the father or mother ensures to the benefit of the child. Si gravida sit proselyta, non opus est ut baptizetur infans quando natus fuerit, baptismus enim matris ei cedat pro baptismo. Jebamoth, fol. 78, 1, cited by Wetstein. If therefore the children be thus holy, the matrimonial connexion between the parents is as lawful as if both were of the same faith.

[353] I.e. the believing man or believing woman.

[354] μὴ ἐπισπάσθω. A surgical operation was occasionally performed for removing the effect of circumcision, as is evident from Josephus, for Antiochus Epiphanes, the cruel persecutor of the Jews, περιέλυσεν αὐτοῖς ἕνα ἕκαστον τῶν Ἑβραίων ἐπισπᾶσθαι. Jos. Maccab. c. 5; and see 1 Mac. i. 15; Ant. xii. 5, 1, Mark vii. 30; Talm. de Bab. Jebamoth viii 1; Buxtorf, Lexic. Chald. Talm. Rabb. משך (cited Renan's St. Paul, p. 67). The nature of the operation is given by Celsus de Medic. vii. 25. See a dissertation upon this subject, Schoettgen's Horæ Hebr. i. 1159.

[355] δοῦλος. In Eng. ver. "a servant"—literally a slave, for at that day slavery was a condition established by law.

[356] Some would render this, 'Even if thou canst procure thy liberty do not make the attempt, but remain a slave.' This, however, is repugnant to one's natural feelings, and cannot be accepted as the true interpretation. The grounds upon which it is proved are chiefly technical, and the arguments based on them are not convincing. The word ἐλευθερία must, as implied, be understood after the word χρῆσαι. I would render the passage thus: "If thou art a slave, care not for it. But if also thou canst obtain thy freedom, take it.'

[357] The Greek word παρθένος includes both sexes, males as well as females. Chaucer uses the word 'maid' in the same sense. Thus, speaking of St. Paul, he says:

"I wot well that the Apostle was a maid."
Prologue to Wife of Bath's Tale.

In a similar manner the word 'spinster,' though now applied exclusively to females, denoted in Early English a bachelor as well as a maid.

[358] 'I cannot, as in the case of marriage, [see note, verse 10] cite an express commandment from Christ himself.'

[359] 'I pronounce by virtue of my apostleship.' See xiv. 37.

[360] 'The present difficulties with which the

27 —that it is good for a man to be *on this wise*. Art thou bound unto a wife?
28 seek not to be loosed. Art thou loosed from a wife? seek not a wife. But
and if thou marry, thou hast not sinned; and if a virgin marry, she hath not
sinned. Nevertheless such shall have trouble in the flesh. But I spare you.[361]
29 But this I say, brethren—The time is short. It remaineth, that both they
30 that have wives be as though they had none, and they that weep, as though
they wept not, and they that rejoice, as though they rejoiced not, and they
31 that buy, as though they possessed not, and they that use this world, as *though*
32 *they used it not*:[362] for the fashion of this world passeth away.[363] But I would
have you without *anxiousness*.[364] He that is unmarried careth for the things of
33 the Lord, how he *shall* please the Lord; but he that is married careth for the
34 things that are of the world, how he *shall* please his wife. There is difference
between a wife and a virgin: the unmarried woman careth for the things of
the Lord, that she may be holy both in body and in spirit; but she that is
married careth for the things of the world, how she *shall* please her husband.
35 And this I speak for your own profit—not that I may cast a snare upon you,
but for that which is comely, and that ye may attend upon the Lord without
36 distraction. But if any man think that he behaveth himself uncomely toward
his virgin, if she *be of* age,[365] and need so require, let him do what he will, he
37 sinneth not: let them marry. But he that standeth steadfast in his heart,
having no necessity, but hath power over his own will, and hath so decreed in
38 his heart, that he will keep his virgin, doeth well. So then he that giveth
her in marriage doeth well; but he that giveth her not in marriage doeth
better.[366]

39 The wife is bound by the law as long as her husband liveth; but if her
husband be dead, she is at liberty to be married to whom she will, only in the
40 Lord.[367] But she is happier if she so abide, after my judgment: and I think
that I *also* have the Spirit of God.[368]

---

rising church has to struggle.' We can form but a feeble idea at the present time of the persecutions and annoyances to which the first Christians were constantly exposed.

[361] 'But in sanctioning marriage, I do it as sparing you, and by way of indulgence only.' Or, 'I forbear to go further into detail. In a word, the time is short,' &c.

[362] καταχρώμενοι here means 'using' only, and is employed in the same sense post, ix. 18. In Eng. ver. "as not abusing it."

[363] A metaphor from the shifting of a scene at a theatre.

[364] ἀμέριμνος. In Eng. ver. "without carefulness."

[365] ὑπέρακμος—'of the marriageable age and upwards.' In Eng. ver. "if she should pass the flower of her age."

[366] Such was the conduct of Philip the deacon towards his daughters, with their full approval. Acts xxi. 9.

[367] 'Only let her have due regard to her Christian interests, and not marry one who will put a stumbling block in the road that leadeth to heaven.'

[368] Others, as the twelve Apostles, were inspired; and Paul reminds the Corinthians (and a hint only would suffice) that he also was inspired.

Ch. VIII. "'Now as touching things offered unto idols,[369] we *are persuaded*[370] that we
2 all have KNOWLEDGE.'[371] (Knowledge puffeth up, but *love* edifieth; and if any
man think that he knoweth anything, he knoweth nothing yet as he ought to
3, 4 know; but if any man love God, the same is known of him.) As concerning
therefore the eating of those things that are offered in sacrifice unto idols, we
are persuaded that an idol is nothing in the world, and that there is none
5 other God but one; for though there be that are called gods, whether in
6 heaven or in earth (as there *are* gods many, and lords many), but to us there
is one God, the Father, of whom are all things, and we in him, and one Lord
7 Jesus Christ, by whom are all things, and we by him. Howbeit there is not
in every man *the* KNOWLEDGE; for some with conscience of the idol unto this
hour eat it as a thing offered unto an idol, and their conscience being weak is
8 defiled.[372] But meat commendeth us not to God; for neither, if we eat, are we
9 the better; neither, if we eat not, are we the worse. But take heed, lest by
any means this liberty of yours become a stumbling-block to them that are
10 weak; for if any man see thee which hast knowledge *sitting* at meat in the
idol's temple, shall not the conscience of him which is weak be emboldened to
11 eat those things which are offered to idols, and through thy knowledge shall
12 the weak brother perish, for whom Christ died? But when ye sin so against
13 the brethren, and wound their weak conscience, ye sin against Christ. Wherefore, if meat make my brother to offend, I will eat no flesh *to eternity*,[373] lest I
make my brother to offend.
Ch. IX. "Am I not an Apostle? am I not free?[374] Have I not seen Jesus Christ
2 our Lord?[375] Are not ye my work in the Lord? If I be not an Apostle unto

---

[369] To understand what follows it must be borne in mind that according to the usual custom amongst the heathen, the parts of the victims not used for the sacrifice, and not the perquisites of the priests, were either consumed in public banquets, or were sold in the market. Jos. cont. Apion. ii. 13; and see Meyer, Apostg. 276. But by the law of Moses these meats were unclean, and could not be eaten without pollution. Exod. xxxiv. 15; Mischna Aboda Zara, ii. 3.

[370] οἴδαμεν. In Eng. ver. "we know." But οἴδαμεν is not so strong as γνῶσιν ἔχομεν in the same sentence.

[371] The Apostle apparently here quotes a passage from the letter of the Corinthians to himself. See ante, p. 366.

[372] How strong the prejudice was which a Jew had to "eating of those things that were offered in sacrifice unto idols," we may learn from what occurred in the time of Antiochus Epiphanes, when the Jews suffered themselves to die by the most fearful torments rather than defile themselves so far as εἰδωλοθύτων ἀπογεύεσθαι. Jos. Maccab. c. 5.

[373] εἰς τὸν αἰῶνα. In Eng. ver. "while the world standeth."

[374] "Am I not an Apostle? Am I not free?" That is, 'Am I not an Apostle, though I demean myself as if I were not appointed to that office? Am I not free to use the rights of an Apostle, though I make myself a slave?' 1 Cor. ix. 19. The Apostle is here defending himself against some insidious persons in the Corinthian church, who in his absence had been questioning his apostleship, and endeavouring his authority, and in particular had attributed his gratuitous services in the Gospel, not to want of will, but to want of power.

[375] Viz., at his conversion. See ante, p. 51.

others, yet doubtless I am to you;[376] for the seal of mine Apostleship are ye in
3, 4 the Lord. Mine answer to them that do examine me is this—Have we not
5 power to eat and to drink? have we not power to lead about a sister-wife,[377]
6 as well as other Apostles, and as the brethren of the Lord,[378] and Cephas? or
7 I only and Barnabas, have not we power to forbear working? Who *is a
soldier* at any time at his own charges? who planteth a vineyard, and eateth
not of the fruit thereof? or who feedeth a flock, and eateth not of the
8 milk of the flock? Say I these things as a man, or saith not the law the
9 same also? for it is written in the law of Moses, 'Thou shalt not muzzle
the ox that treadeth out the corn' (*Deut.* xxv. 4).[379] Doth God take care for
10 oxen?[380] or saith he it altogether for our sakes? For our sakes, no doubt, this
is written; *for* he that plougheth *ought to* plough in hope; and he that
11 thresheth [*should thresh*] *in hope of partaking.*[381] If we have sown unto you
12 spiritual things, is it a great thing if we shall reap your carnal things? if
others *partake* of this power over you, *shall* not we rather? Nevertheless we
have not used this power, but suffer all things, lest we should *give any hind-*
13 *rance to* the Gospel of Christ. Do ye not know that they which minister
about holy things live[382] *from* the temple? (*Numb.* xviii. 21) they which wait
14 at the altar *partake* with the altar? (*Numb.* xviii. 2). Even so hath the

---

[376] The original Greek falls into an accidental hexameter:

εἰ ἄλλοις οὐκ εἰμὶ ἀπόστολος, ἀλλά γε ὑμῖν.

[377] ἀδελφὴν γυναῖκα—i.e. a wife who is a sister in the faith, for all Christian men were brethren, and all Christian women were sisters. It has been inferred from this text that Paul was married, an assumption contradicted by the Apostle's own words in the previous part of the Epistle: "I would that all men were even as I myself" (viz., single), 1 Cor. vii. 7. Paul means only, 'Have not we (Barnabas and I) power to marry, as do the other Apostles, and take our wives with us?"

Or perhaps the words ἀδελφὴν γυναῖκα may be rendered, not 'a sister-wife,' but 'a sister-woman,' that is, a believing woman or matron to minister to our necessities. It will be remembered that Joanna and other holy women waited upon our Lord himself. Luke xxiii. 49; Mark xv. 41.

[378] The brethren of our Lord are here mentioned, as distinct from the Apostles, and this agrees with the Gospels and the Acts, for not one of them was among the twelve Apostles, though James, the Lord's brother, was bishop of Jerusalem. See Fasti Sacri, p. 181, No. 1198.

The brethren of our Lord were James and Joses and Simon and Judas. Matt. xiii. 55.

[379] Cited verbatim from the LXX. The proverb has reference to the Jewish (which was also the Greek and Roman) mode of treading out the corn by driving oxen round and round over the haulm spread out on a hard floor, and laid in a circle. The Jews had also two other modes of separating the grain from the haulm: viz., 1. By threshing with the flail, as amongst ourselves; and, 2. By employing a machine, which is thus described by the Rabbins: "Est instrumentum ligneum ac ponderosum crebris incisurarum aciebus ad limae similitudinem eminentibus paratum; quod eo usque trahitur super culmos dum extritis frumentis in paleas minutas redigantur." Rasche ad Isai xli. 15, cited Schoettgen's Hor. Heb. i. 617.

[380] 'Was this precept written for the sake of the ox, or for the sake of man that useth the ox?' Doubtless to inculcate what was incumbent on man towards the ministers employed by him.

[381] Instead of the text. recept. ὁ ἀλοῶν τῆς ἐλπίδος αὐτοῦ μετέχειν ἐπ' ἐλπίδι, we adopt the reading admitted by Griesbach, Scholtz, Lachmann, Tischendorf, and Alford, viz., ὁ ἀλοῶν ἐπ' ἐλπίδι τοῦ μετέχειν.

[382] ἐσθίουσιν. Literally, 'eat.'

Lord[383] ordained that they which preach the Gospel should live of the Gospel
15 (*Matt.* x. 19). But I have used none of these things; neither have I written these things, that it should be so done unto me; for it were better for me to

Fig. 173.—*Mode of threshing by oxen in the East.*
With a plan and section of the *moreg*. The form of the *moreg* was of course various, but the above is that used by the Egyptian.

16 die, than that any man should make my glorying void. For *if* I preach the Gospel, I have nothing to glory of, for necessity is laid upon me; yea, woe is

Fig. 174.—*Mode of ploughing in the East.*

17 unto me, if I preach not the Gospel! for if I do this thing willingly, I have a reward; but if against my will, a dispensation *hath been* committed unto me.
18 What is my reward then? [Verily] that, when I preach the Gospel, I may

[383] Viz. Christ.

make the Gospel of Christ without charge, that I *use not*[384] my power in the
19 Gospel. For though I be free from all men, yet have I made myself *a slave*[385]
20 to all, that I might gain the more; and unto the Jews I became as a Jew, that
I might gain the Jews;[386] to them that are under the law, as under the law,[387]
(*not being myself under the law*[388]), that I might gain them that are under the
21 law; to them that are without law, as without law (being not without law to
God, but under the law to Christ), that I might gain them that are without
22 law;[389] to the weak became I as weak, that I might gain the weak;[390] I *have*
23 *become* all things to all men, that I might by all means save some; and this I
24 do for the Gospel's sake, that I *may be a co-contributor to it.*[391] Know ye not
that they which run in a race run all, but one receiveth the prize? So run,

Fig. 175.—*Medallion of Laodicea struck in the time of M. Aurel. Antoninus, as appears from the obverse.*
The above engraving of the reverse represents the crowning of the victor in a basilica or temple. The legend is Λ. Αυρ. Τυραν.
Αρχ. μεγ. ανεθηκεν. Λαοδικεων Νεωκορων. From Pellerin.

25 that ye may obtain.[392] And every man that *wrestleth* is temperate in all things.
Now they do it to obtain a corruptible crown, but we an incorruptible. I

---

[384] εἰς τὸ μὴ καταχρήσασθαι. In Eng. ver. "that I abuse not."

[385] ἐδούλωσα. In Eng. ver. "a servant."

[386] Thus, "I am verily a man which am a Jew," &c. Acts xxii. 1. So "I am a Pharisee," &c. Acts xxiii. 6.

[387] Thus Paul caused Timothy to be circumcised, Acts xvi. 3; took the vow of the Nazarite, Acts xviii. 18; and observed the requisite ceremonies in the Temple, Acts xxi. 26; attended the public festivals at Jerusalem, Acts xx. 16; or kept them wherever he happened to be, Acts xx. 6, &c.

[388] The words μὴ ὢν αὐτὸς ὑπὸ νόμον, though not in the text. recept., are admitted by Griesbach, Scholtz, Lachmann, Tischendorf, and Alford.

[389] Thus he mixed with the heathen as brethren, though unclean by the law of Moses; pronounced circumcision to be nothing; argued before the Athenians from the altar to the unknown God; and cited the heathen poets; &c.

[390] I.e., 'To the weak in faith, I Paul became weak myself,' acting on the principle laid down ante, viii. 13. The words "that I might gain the weak" cannot mean that he might make converts of them, as they were Christians already; but that he might be the means of salvation to them, or, as he says himself, that "he might by all means save some," ix. 22.

[391] συγκοινωνός. In Eng. ver. "that I might be partaker thereof with you."

[392] Any allusion to the games would of course be familiarly known to all Corinthians, as the Isthmia were celebrated in the immediate neighbourhood of their city.

[Chap. XIII.] FIRST EPISTLE TO THE CORINTHIANS. [A.D. 57]

26 therefore so run, not as uncertainly; so fight I, not as one that beateth the
27 air;[393] but I keep under my body,[394] and bring it into subjection; lest that by any means when I have preached to others, I myself should be a cast away.[395]

Ch. X. "For[395b] I would not that ye should be ignorant, brethren, how that all our
2 fathers were under the cloud, and all passed through the sea, and were all
3 baptized unto Moses in the cloud and in the sea, and did all eat the same
4 spiritual meat, and did all drink the same spiritual drink; for they drank of
5 that spiritual Rock that followed them, and that Rock was Christ. But with the more part[397] of them God was not well pleased; for they were overthrown in

Fig. 176.—Wrestlers, from an ancient vase figured in Montfaucon.

6 the wilderness. Now these things were our examples, to the intent we should
7 not lust after evil things, as they also lusted. Neither be ye idolaters, as were some of them; as it is written, 'The people sat down to eat and drink, and
8 rose up to play' (Ex. xxxii. 6).[398] Neither let us commit fornication, as some of them committed, and fell in one day three and twenty thousand (Numb.
9 xxv. 9).[399] Neither let us tempt Christ, as some of them also tempted, and
10 were destroyed of serpents (Numb. xxii. 4). Neither murmur ye, as some of

---

[393] Alternaque jactat
Brachia præcedens, et verberat ictibus auras.
Virg. Æn. v. 376.
So also Lucian: ἦν τινι καὶ τῶν ἀθλητῶν ἤδη ἀσκούμενον πρὸ τοῦ ἀγῶνος, λακτίζοντα εἰς τὸν ἀέρα, ἢ πὺξ κενὴν πληγὴν καταφέροντα, κ.τ.λ. Hermotim. 33.

[394] ὑπωπιάζω—'make it black and blue with bruises.'

[395] ἀδόκιμος—one who is rejected or set aside as not having conformed to the laws of the games. So Philo, ἐκκριμέον γάρ ἐστιν ὥσπερ ἐξ ἀγῶνος ἱεροῦ καὶ ἀποδεδοκισμένον, &c. De Cherub. c. 22, vol. i. p 152.

[395b] Griesbach, Scholtz, Lachmann, Tischendorf, and Alford, read ὅτι δὲ γάρ, and not θέλω δὲ as in text. recept.

[397] ἐν τοῖς πλείοσιν. In Eng. ver. "many of them."

[398] Cited verbatim from the LXX.

[399] But in Numb. xxv. 9, we read twenty-four thousand. Moses and Paul are speaking in round numbers; and if the actual number was 23,500, both would be right.

them also murmured, and were destroyed of the destroyer (*Numb.* xiv. 2).
11 Now all these things happened unto them for ensamples; and they *were* written for our admonition, upon whom the ends of the world are come.
12, 13 Wherefore let him that thinketh he standeth take heed lest he fall. There hath no temptation taken you but such as is common to man; but God *is* faithful, who will not suffer you to be tempted above that ye are able; but will with the temptation also make a way to escape, that ye may be able to bear
14, 15 it. Wherefore, my beloved, flee from idolatry. I speak as to wise men; judge
16 ye what I say.—The cup of blessing which we bless,[400] is it not the communion of the blood of Christ? the bread which we break, is it not the communion of
17 the body of Christ?[401] for we being many are one bread, and one body; for
18 we all *partake* of that one bread. Behold Israel after the flesh: are not they
19 which eat of the sacrifices *communicants* of the altar? What say I, then? that the idol is anything, or that *what* is sacrificed to idols is anything?
20 But [I say], that the things which the Gentiles sacrifice, they 'sacrifice to devils, and not to God' (*Deut.* xxxii. 17),[402] and I would not that ye should *be*
21 *the communicants of* devils; ye cannot drink the cup of the Lord, and the cup of devils; ye cannot partake of the Lord's table, and of the table of devils.
22, 23 Or do we provoke the Lord to jealousy? are we stronger than he? 'All things are lawful for me, but all things are not expedient;'[403] all things are
24 lawful for me, but all things edify not. Let no *one* seek his own, but every
25 one *the other's good*. Whatsoever is sold in the shambles,[404] that eat, asking
26 no question for conscience sake; for 'The earth is the Lord's, and the fulness
27 thereof' (*Ps.* xxiv. 1).[405] *Now* if any of them that believe not bid you to a feast, and ye be disposed to go, whatsoever is set before you, eat, asking no
28 question for conscience sake. But if any man say unto you, 'This *hath been* offered in sacrifice unto idols,' eat not for his sake that shewed it, and for
29 conscience sake[406]—conscience, I say, not thine own, but of the others; for

[400] The cup which Christ consecrated by blessing at the institution of the Eucharist, and which we now consecrate at its celebration.

[401] From this it appears that from the very earliest times the cup at the sacrament was consecrated, and the bread broken. No doubt the forms of the church generally have been handed down from the first in one unbroken custom.

[402] Cited from the LXX.

[403] See note ante, vi. 12.

[404] ἐν μακέλλῳ, the Latin word *macellum* 'a provision market,' can be easily accounted for, when we recollect that Corinth was a Roman colony. The macellum of Augustus appears on a coin of Nero.

Fig. 177.—*Coin of Nero. From the British Museum.*

Obv. A good portrait of Nero, with the legend "Nero Claudius Cæsar Aug. Germ. Tr P. Imp. P. P."—Rev. Facade of the Macellum Augusti, with the legend "Mac. Aug. S. C."

[405] τοῦ γάρ Κυρίου ἡ γῆ, καὶ τὸ πλήρωμα αὐτῆς. The citation is word for word from the LXX.

[406] Here, in Eng. ver., the words "for the earth

30 why is my liberty judged *by* another man's conscience? for if I by grace be a
31 partaker, why am I evil spoken of for that for which I give thanks? Whether,
32 therefore, ye eat, or drink, or do *aught*, do all to the glory of God. *Be void*
33 *of* offence *both* to Jews *and Greeks and* to the church of God, even as I *also*
please all men in all things, not seeking mine own profit, but *that of the* many,
Ch. XI. that they may be saved. Be ye followers of me, even as I also am of
Christ.

2 "Now I praise you, brethren, that ye remember me in all things, and keep
3 the *traditions*,[107] as I delivered them to you."[108] But I would have you know
that the head of every man is Christ, and the head of the woman is the man,
4 and the head of Christ is God. Every man praying or *preaching*[109] having
5 his head covered, dishonoureth his head;[110] but every woman that prayeth or
preacheth[111] with her head uncovered, dishonoureth her head, for that is even
6 all one as if she were shaven; for if the woman be not covered, let her also be
shorn; but if it be a shame for a woman to be shorn[112] or shaven,[113] let her
7 be covered. For a man, indeed, ought not to cover his head, forasmuch as he
is the image (*Gen.* i. 26) and glory of God; but the woman is the glory of the
8, 9 man; for the man is not of the woman, but the woman of the man; *for the man*
10 *is not from* the woman, but the woman *from* the man, for this cause ought the
woman to have *plenty* on her head,[114] because of the [creating] angels.[115]

---

is the Lord's and the fulness thereof," are repeated; but they are not found in the best MSS., and have been rejected by Griesbach, Scholtz, Lachmann, Tischendorf, and Alford.

[108] See infra, v. 23.

[109] This was probably a passage contained in the letter received from the Corinthians. See ante, p. 366.

[110] προφητεύων. In Eng. ver. "prophesying." The προφῆται were those whom the Holy Spirit impelled to propagate Christian truth; but there is no word in the English language which conveys the sense of the original. The word is afterwards (xiv. 32) rendered in Eng. ver. " preacher," and this rendering has been adopted as nearer to the original than "prophet."

[110] The mixed population of Corinth would naturally adopt different customs during divine service. Jews would cover their heads, Jewesses would veil them. Greeks would uncover their heads, Romans would cover them. For the sake of uniformity, Christian women are here commanded to veil themselves, and Christian men to pray bareheaded. Tertullian accordingly writes: " Nudo capite, quia non erubescimus, . . . oramus." Tertull. Apol. c. 30. See Wordsworth.

[111] προφητεύουσα. In Eng. ver. " prophesieth." That the women were employed in spreading Christian truth, and administering to the necessities of the sick and poor, is evident from the case of the four daughters of Philip the deacon, who were προφητεύουσαι, Acts xxi. 9. But women were not allowed to preach in the *church*. 1 Cor. xiv. 34.

[112] κείρασθαι, 'to be shorn,' which is here distinguished from ξυρᾶθαι, 'to be shaven.' In all ages it has been the custom for women to wear the hair long, and not to shear or cut it as men do.

[113] The shaving the head was the utmost disgrace to a woman, and was the punishment of adulteresses. See Tac. Germ. xix.; Philo de Special. Leg. c. 10; Achill. Tat. lib. viii.; Aristoph. Thesmoph. 838; Apuleius, Metam. ii. p. 44 (Delphin. 1688). Amongst the Greeks, the women sheared or shaved their heads for mourning. Plut. Quaest. Rom. p. 267.

[114] ἐξουσίαν. Literally a "power" of hair.

[115] The woman ought to have a profusion of hair on her head as a mark of subjection; and that because of or out of regard to her original creation by the angels (to whom, as God's minis-

11 Nevertheless neither is the man without the woman, neither the woman
12 without the man, in the Lord; for as the woman is *from* the man, even so is
13 the man also by the woman: but all things *are from* God. Judge in your-
14 selves: is it comely that a woman pray unto God uncovered? Doth not even
   nature itself teach you, that if a man have long hair it is a shame unto him?
15 But, if a woman have long hair it is a glory to her, for her hair is given her
16 for a covering. But if any man seem to be contentious, we have no such
   custom, neither the churches of God.[416]

17 "Now in this that I declare unto you I praise you not, that ye come together
18 not for the better, but for the worse. For first of all when ye come together
19 in the church,[417] I hear that there *are* divisions among you, and I partly
   believe it; for there must be also heresies among you, that they which are
20 approved may be made manifest among you. When ye come together, there-
21 fore, into one place, *it* is not to eat the Lord's supper; for in eating every one
   taketh before [another] his own supper, and one is hungry, and another is
22 drunken! What? have ye not houses to eat and to drink in? or despise ye
   the church of God, and shame them that have not? What shall I say to
23 you? shall I praise you in this? I praise you not. For I received of the
   Lord[418] that which also I delivered unto you, That the Lord Jesus the same
24 night in which he was betrayed took bread, and when he had given thanks, he
   brake it, and said,[419] 'This is my body, which is broken for you; this do in
25 remembrance of me.' After the same manner, also, he took the cup when he
   had supped, saying, 'This cup is the new testament in my blood; this do ye,
26 as oft as ye drink it, in remembrance of me.'[420] For as often as ye eat this

---

ters, all the works of the creation were referred by the Jews). The angels, says the Apostle, made the woman from and for the man, and not the man from and for the woman. There is a similar employment by the same Apostle of the word 'angels' as representing the God of the Jews, in Galat. iii. 19, and again in Heb. ii. 2. See note on Galat. iii. 19.

[416] That is, 'If any one still contends for the practice that men should cover the head and women should not cover the head during the celebration of divine service, my short answer is, that such is not the custom of the church.'

[417] See ante, p. 298.

[418] The Apostle here expressly asserts that the *facts* of the Gospel, as well as its *doctrine*, were revealed to him by the Lord.

[419] The words λάβετε, φάγετε are rejected by the best critics, as Griesbach, Scholtz, Lachmann, Tischendorf, and Alford.

[420] The words of Paul are almost identical with those of Luke. The only substantial difference is that Paul uses the word κλώμενον, for which Luke substitutes διδόμενον, and that Paul adds with reference to the cup, "This do as often as ye drink it in remembrance of me," which Luke omits. But the reading of the word κλώμενον in Paul is uncertain, and some MSS. have the word διδόμενον instead of it; and as regards Luke's omission of the words "This do as often as ye shall drink it," &c., it is observable that those words had been previously introduced by Luke with reference to the *bread*, and they may therefore be considered as implied with reference to the *cup*, under the word ὡσαύτως, 'in like manner.' The other slight variations are to be accounted for by the fact that our Lord spoke in Hebrew, and both Paul and Luke are translating. The two passages are subjoined in parallel columns:—

[Chap. XIII.] FIRST EPISTLE TO THE CORINTHIANS. [A.D. 57]

bread, and drink this cup, ye do shew the Lord's death till he come.
27 Wherefore whosoever shall eat this bread, or drink this cup of the Lord
28 unworthily, shall be guilty of the body and blood of the Lord. But let a
man examine himself, and so let him eat of *the* bread, and drink of *the*
29 cup; for he that eateth and drinketh unworthily,[121] eateth and drinketh a
30 *judgment upon*[122] himself, not discerning the Lord's body. For this cause many
31 are weak and sickly among you, and many sleep. For if we *judged* ourselves,
32 we should not be judged; but *being* judged, we are chastened of the Lord,
33 that we should not be condemned with the world. Wherefore, my brethren,
34 when ye come together to eat, tarry one for another; *but* if any man hunger,
let him eat at home, that ye come not together *for a judgment*.[123] But the
rest will I set in order when I come.

Ch. XII. "Now concerning 'spiritual gifts,'[124] brethren, I would not have you
2 ignorant. Ye know that ye were Gentiles, carried away unto dumb idols,
3 even as ye were led. Wherefore I give you to understand, that no man
speaking by the spirit of God calleth Jesus accursed;[125] and no man can say
4 that Jesus is the Lord, but by the Holy Ghost.[126] Now there are diversities
5 of gifts, but the same spirit; and there are differences of *ministrations*, but
6 the same Lord; and there are diversities of operations, but it is the same God

PAUL.	LUKE.
Τοῦτό μου ἐστὶ τὸ σῶμα τὸ ὑπὲρ ὑμῶν κλώμενον· τοῦτο ποιεῖτε εἰς τὴν ἐμὴν ἀνάμνησιν. ὡσαύτως καὶ τὸ ποτήριον, μετὰ τὸ δειπνῆσαι, λέγων, Τοῦτο τὸ ποτήριον ἡ καινὴ διαθήκη ἐστὶν ἐν τῷ ἐμῷ αἵματι· τοῦτο ποιεῖτε, ὁσάκις ἂν πίνητε, εἰς τὴν ἐμὴν ἀνάμνησιν. 1 Cor. xi. 24, 25.	Τοῦτό ἐστι τὸ σῶμά μου τὸ ὑπὲρ ὑμῶν διδόμενον· τοῦτο ποιεῖτε εἰς τὴν ἐμὴν ἀνάμνησιν. ὡσαύτως καὶ τὸ ποτήριον μετὰ τὸ δειπνῆσαι, λέγων, Τοῦτο τὸ ποτήριον, ἡ καινὴ διαθήκη ἐν τῷ αἵματί μου, τὸ ὑπὲρ ὑμῶν ἐκχυνόμενον. Luke xxii. 19, 20.

Did Paul cite this from Luke's Gospel, or did Luke write from Paul's dictation? Not the former, for Paul tells us expressly that he derived it from no human source, but received it by revelation from the Lord: παρέλαβον ἀπὸ τοῦ Κυρίου. 1 Cor. xi. 23. It is also probable that at the date of the First Epistle to the Corinthians, the Gospel of Luke had not been yet published; for up to this time Paul repeatedly refers to St. Matthew's Gospel (see 1 Thess. v. 2; 1 Cor. vi. 3; vii. 10; xiii. 2), but not to St. Luke's. However, the Gospel of Luke was published before the Second Epistle to the Corinthians, A.D. 57, and apparently not long before, for the Apostle speaks of his "praise in the Gospel throughout all the churches," 2 Cor. viii. 18; and in 1 Tim. v. 18, Paul cites Luke's Gospel as Scripture.

[121] The word ἀναξίως, 'unworthily,' is not found in the best MSS., and is rejected by Lachmann, Tischendorf, Griesbach, and Alford.

[122] κρίμα ἑαυτῷ. In Eng. ver. "damnation."

But damnation cannot be meant, but a temporal judgment only, inflicted, says the Apostle, in order "that he may *not* be condemned with the world," v. 32.

[123] κρίμα, the same word as above. In Eng. ver. "condemnation." See preceding note.

[124] τῶν πνευματικῶν, on which the Corinthians had consulted him in their letter. See ante, p. 366. Another opinion, however, and perhaps the better, is that the comment of the Apostle on spiritual gifts arose not from anything contained in the Epistle from the Corinthians to him, but from the intelligence he had received through the household of Chloe of the disorders in the Corinthian church. It countenances this view, that at the close of the preceding chapter, the Apostle had said, "The rest will I set in order when I come," as if he had there concluded his written answer to their Epistle.

[125] In time of persecution, a Christian was called upon to testify the renunciation of his faith by cursing the name of Christ.

[126] The Apostle here ascribes all religious gifts to the Holy Spirit, and takes as his example the very lowest — the mere profession of the Christian faith. He then rises to other higher spiritual gifts, and assigns to them their relative values.

7 which worketh all in all. But the manifestation of the spirit is given to
8 every man to profit withal. For to one is given by the spirit the word of
9 wisdom; to another the word of knowledge[427] by the same spirit; to another
   faith[428] by the same spirit; to another the gifts of healing by the same
10 spirit; to another the working of miracles; to another *preaching*;[429] to
   another discerning of spirits; to another divers kinds of tongues; to another
11 the interpretation of tongues. But all these worketh that one and the self-
12 same spirit, dividing to every man severally as he will; for as the body is
   one, and hath many members, and all the members of that one body, being
13 many, are one body: so also, is Christ. For by one spirit *have* we all *been*
   baptized into one body, whether we be Jews or *Greeks*, whether we be bond or
14 free; and have been all made to drink into one spirit.[430] For the body is not
15 one member, but many.[431] If the foot say, because I am not the hand, I am
16 not of the body, is it therefore not of the body? and if the ear say, because I
17 am not the eye, I am not of the body, is it therefore not of the body? If the
   whole body were an eye, where were the hearing? if the whole were hearing,
18 where were the smelling? But now hath God set the members every one of
19 them in the body, as *he willed*. And if they were all one member, where
20, 21 were the body? But now are *there* many members, yet but one body; and
   the eye cannot say unto the hand, I have no need of thee: nor again, the
22 head to the feet, I have no need of you. Nay, much more those members of
23 the body, which seem to be more feeble, are necessary, and those members of
   the body, which we think to be less honourable, upon these we bestow more
   abundant honour, and our uncomely parts have more abundant comeliness,
24 for our comely parts have no need:[432] but God hath tempered the body
25 together, having given more abundant honour to that which lacked: that

---

[427] It is difficult to distinguish the λόγος σοφίας from the λόγος γνώσεως. By the former perhaps is meant wisdom where subtlety of argument preponderates, and by γνῶσις, wisdom where there is depth of thought without an adequate power of expressing itself. See the Apostle's use of the words σοφία and γνῶσις, ante, i. 17, ii. 1, and viii. 1

[428] i.e. strength of faith, such as successfully to resist the trials of persecution.

[429] προφητεία. In Eng. ver. "prophecy."

[430] As the first part of the verse refers to Baptism, it seems natural to suppose that the Apostle in the latter part alludes to the cup of the Lord's Supper. However, in an earlier chapter the Apostle had spoken of himself as planting or baptizing, and Apollos as watering—ἐπότισεν, iii. 6; and possibly here the meaning may be, 'We have been baptized into one body, and have been watered (ἐποτίσθημεν) into one spirit.'

[431] We have here the familiar fable attributed to Menenius Agrippa of the mutiny of the limbs against the belly, Liv. ii. 32. In the Essay on Man, Pope has reproduced St. Paul's argument and illustration:

> When if the foot, ordained the dust to tread,
> Or hand to toil, aspired to be the head?
> What if the head, the eye, or ear repined
> To serve mere engines to the ruling mind?
> Just as absurd for any part to claim
> To be another in this general frame;
> Just as absurd to mourn the task or pains
> The great directing Mind of all ordains.

[432] The face, which is the most comely part, is left unprotected, while the unseemly parts are set off by gay apparel.

there should be no schism in the body, but that the members should have the
26 same care one for another. And *if so be that* one member *suffereth* all the
members suffer with it; or one member *is* honoured, all the members rejoice
27, 28 with it. Now ye are the body of Christ, and members in particular; and God
hath set some in the church, first apostles, secondly *preachers*,[432] thirdly
teachers, after that miracles, then gifts of healings, helps, governments,[434]
29 diversities of tongues. Are all apostles? are all *preachers*?[435] are all
30 teachers? are all workers of miracles? have all the gifts of healing? do all
31 speak with tongues? do all interpret? But covet earnestly the best gifts.
Ch. XIII. "And yet shew I unto you a more excellent way. Though I speak
with the tongues of men and of angels, and have not *love*, I am become as
2 sounding brass, or a tinkling cymbal. And though I have the gift of *preaching*,[436] and understand all mysteries, and all knowledge, and though I have
all faith, so that I could remove mountains (*Matt*. xvii. 20, xxi. 21),[437] and
3 have not *love*, I am nothing; and though I bestow all my goods to feed the
poor,[438] and though I give my body to be burned,[439a] and have not *love*, it
4 profiteth me nothing. *Love* suffereth long, and is kind; *love* envieth not; *love*
5 vaunteth not itself,[439] is not puffed up, doth not behave itself unseemly,
6 seeketh not her own, is not easily provoked, thinketh no evil, rejoiceth not
7 in iniquity, but rejoiceth in the truth, beareth all things, believeth all things,
8 hopeth all things, endureth all things. *Love* never faileth; but whether there
be *preachings*,[440] they shall *be done away*, whether there be tongues, they shall
9 cease; whether there be knowledge, it shall *be done away*. For we know in
10 part, and we *preach*[441] in part [442] but when that which is perfect is come, then
11 that which is in part shall be done away. When I was a child, I spake as a
12 child, I *thought* as a child, I *reasoned* as a child; but when I became a man, I
did away childish things. For now we see through a glass darkly,[443] but

---

[432] προφήτας. In Eng. ver. "prophets."

[434] The powers of maintaining order in the church.

[435] προφῆται. In Eng. ver. "prophets."

[436] προφητείαν. In Eng. ver. "prophecy."

[437] The Apostle here, as on several other occasions, refers to St. Matthew's Gospel. See ante, p. 282.

[438] As Barnabas, Acts iv. 36, and perhaps Paul himself.

[439a] An allusion to the martyrdom of the disciples by burning, a common mode of punishment. See Jos. Bell. i. 13, 4.

[439] οὐ περπερεύεται. Some derive it from the Latin *perperam*. Whatever be the etymon, it seems to denote personal display, being so used by Cicero: "Ego autem ipse, Dii boni! quod modo ἐνεπερπερευσάμην novo auditori Pompeio." Epist. ad Att. i. 14, 5.

[440] προφητεῖαι. In Eng. ver. "prophecies."

[441] προφητεύομεν. In Eng. ver. "prophesy" 'Whether we know ourselves or make known to preaching to others, it is only in part.'

[442] 'our knowledge is partial, and our preaching ineffective to attain its objects.'

[443] δ. ἐσόπτρου ἐν αἰνίγματι. Some by the ἐσόπτρου understand the lapis specularis used for a window through which a person looked but imperfectly. However, the lapis specularis would in Greek be δίοπτρον and not ἔσοπτρον, which always signifies a mirror, and amongst the ancients was of metal. The meaning therefore is, that now we see only by reflection, and not at first hand; but hereafter we shall see the objects themselves.

then face to face: now I know in part, but then shall I know even as also
13 I am known. And now abide these three, Faith, Hope, *Love*; but the greatest of these is *love*.[444]

Ch. XIV. "Follow after *love*, and *be zealous of* spiritual gifts, but rather that ye
2 may *preach*. For he that speaketh in an unknown tongue speaketh not unto men, but unto God: for no *one* understandeth him; howbeit in the spirit he
3 speaketh mysteries. But he that *preacheth*, speaketh unto men to edification,
4 and exhortation, and comfort. He that speaketh in a tongue edifieth himself;
5 but he that *preacheth* edifieth the church. Now I would that ye all spake with tongues, but rather that ye *preached*; for greater is he that *preacheth* than he that speaketh with tongues, except he interpret, that the church may
6 receive *edification*. But now, brethren, if I come unto you speaking with tongues, what shall I profit you, except I shall speak to you either *in* revela-
7 tion, or *in* knowledge, or *in preaching*, or *in teaching*?[445] And even things without life giving sound, whether pipe or harp, except they give a distinction
8 in the sounds, how shall it be known what is piped or harped? For if the
9 trumpet give an uncertain sound, who shall prepare himself *for war*?[446] So likewise ye, except ye utter by the tongue words easy to be understood, how
10 shall it be known what is spoken? for ye *will be speaking* into the air. There

---

[444] The Corinthians, being mostly Greeks, had prided themselves more particularly on the spiritual gifts of preaching, and tongues, and knowledge, three things which were adapted only to this world and perishable, and the Apostle urges upon them, instead, three things which would save them in the next world, as well as in this. For preaching, and tongues, and knowledge were miraculous endowments bestowed by the Spirit, not as an earnest of salvation to those who received them, but for the benefit of others and as the means of converting others. Judas Iscariot could work miracles like the rest of the Apostles, but he was not the better man for it. Therefore, says the Apostle, "whether there be preachers they shall fail, whether there be tongues they shall cease, whether there be knowledge it shall vanish away." That is, when you stand at the judgment seat of Christ you will plead in vain, "Lord, Lord, have we not prophesied (or preached) in thy name," &c. But, he continues, there are three things which abide for ever, and which will stand you in stead not only in this world but in the next—Faith, Hope, and Love. For if you *believe* in Christ, and rest your *hopes* on the next world, and live in *love* towards all men you will secure your eternal salvation. But the greatest of these three is love, for it comprises the other two, viz. love includes faith, for it '*believeth* all things' (xiii. 7), and includes hope, for it '*hopeth* all things' (xiii. 7).

[445] διδαχῇ. In Eng. ver. "doctrine." The gift of tongues, argues the Apostle, is of no value in itself, but only as an instrument of instructing others, by communicating to them something revealed by God, or acquired by human application, and this, either by public preaching or private teaching.

[446] The σάλπιγξ here mentioned is the *tuba* or straight trumpet, used by the infantry. It sounded one note for the charge and another for the retreat. Unless therefore the sound was distinct, the soldier was perplexed whether to advance or retire. The *lituus* (so called from its being curved at the end like the augur's lituus) was employed by the cavalry for the like purposes as the tuba by the infantry. Horace (Carm. i. 1, 23) joins them as emblems of the two divisions of the army:

Multos castra juvant, et lituo tubæ
Permixtus sonitus.

The Romans had also the buccina or buccinum, and cornu, the clarion and horn. See a paper on the Roman trumpet in Académie des Inscr. i. 104.

are, it may be, so many kinds of voices in the world, and none of them is
11 without signification. Therefore, if I know not the meaning of the voice, I
shall be unto him that speaketh a barbarian, and he that speaketh a barbarian
12 unto me.[447] Even so ye, forasmuch as ye are zealous of spiritual gifts, seek
13 that ye may excel to the edifying of the church. Wherefore let him that
14 speaketh in an unknown tongue pray that he may interpret: for if I pray in a

Fig. 17.—*Trumpeter.* From a fictile vase in Hope's *Costume of the Ancients*.

15 tongue, my spirit prayeth, but my understanding is unfruitful.[448] What is it
then? I will pray in the spirit, and I will pray *to* the understanding also:[449]
16 I will sing *in* the spirit, and I will sing *to* the understanding also. Else
when thou shalt bless[450] *in* the spirit, how shall he that *filleth the place* of the
17 unlearned say 'Amen'[451] at thy giving of thanks,[452] seeing he *knoweth* not
what thou sayest? For thou verily givest thanks well, but the other is not
18, 19 edified. I thank my God, I speak with tongues more than ye all;[453] yet in

[447] Barbarus hic ego sum, quia non intelligor ulli.
Ovid, Trist. v. 10, 37.

[448] 'Yields no fruit to others.'

[449] 'I will not pray only in my own spirit, but
I will address myself also to the understanding
of my hearers.'

[450] By comparing this passage with 2 Cor. xiv.
6, it would seem that the Apostle here alludes to
the consecration of the elements at the Lord's
Supper.

[451] It is satisfactory to find traces here, as elsewhere, of the same form of divine service as that
which is still observed by the church. The
practice of saying 'Amen' was derived from
the Jews, who made it an imperative duty on
the congregation. See the numerous authorities
cited by Schoettgen, Hor. Hebr. i. 654.

[452] The words are, ἐπὶ τῇ σῇ Εὐχαριστίᾳ—'at
thy Eucharist.'

[453] Paul could speak at least five languages.
1. Greek was his native tongue and he wrote in
it. 2. Aramaic was that in which he addressed
his countrymen from the stairs of Fort Antonia.
3. Hebrew he knew as the language in which the
Law and the Prophets were composed. 4. Latin
he must have learned at Antioch, the seat of
Roman government, and must have employed at
Rome in preaching to the Italians. 5. Arabic
must have been familiar to him or he would not
on his conversion have retired into Arabia. It

the church I had rather speak five words *to* the[454] understanding, that I *may*
20 instruct others also, than ten thousand words in a tongue. Brethren, be not
children in understanding: howbeit in malice be ye *babes*, but in understanding
21 be men. In the Law it is written, 'With men of other tongues and other
lips will I speak unto this people, and yet for all that will they not hear me,
22 saith the Lord' (*Is.* xxviii. 11, 12);[455] so *that* tongues are for a sign, not to
them that believe, but to them that believe not; but *preaching* serveth not
23 for them that believe not, but for them *that* believe. If therefore the whole
church be come together into one place, and all speak with tongues, and
there come in those that are unlearned, or unbelievers,[456] will they not say
24 that ye are mad? But if all *preach*, and there come in one that believeth not,
25 or one unlearned,[457] he is convinced *by* all, he is judged *by* all, and thus are
the secrets of his heart made manifest, and so falling down on his face he will
worship God,[458] and report that God is in you of a truth.

26 "How is it then, brethren? When ye come together, *each* of you
hath a psalm, hath a doctrine, hath a tongue, hath a revelation, hath an
27 interpretation. Let all things be done unto edifying. If any speak in a
tongue, let it be by two, or at the most by three, and that by course, and let
28 one interpret. But if there be no interpreter, let him keep silence in the
29 church, and let him speak to himself, and to God. Let the *preachers* speak
30 two or three, and let the rest judge. *But* if anything be revealed to another
31 that sitteth by, let the first hold his peace; for ye *can* all *preach* one by one,
32, 33 that all may learn, and all may be comforted; and the spirits of the *preachers*
are subject to the *preachers*;[459] for God is not [*a God*] of confusion, but of
peace, as in all churches of the saints.

34 "Let your women keep silence in the churches, for it is not permitted unto
them to speak, but to be under obedience, as also saith the law (*Gen.* iii. 16).[460]
35 And if they would learn anything, let them ask their husbands at home; for

---

would seem that Paul did not know Lycaonian. See ante, p. 148.

[454] In Eng. ver. "with *my* understanding," but in Griesbach, Scholtz, Lachmann, and Tischendorf, μου is omitted with a fair show of correctness. If the μου be retained, the meaning is, 'with my understanding,' so that it shall not be unfruitful to others. See v. 15 supra.

[455] ὅτι ἐν ἑτερογλώσσοις, καὶ ἐν χείλεσιν ἑτέροις, λαλήσω τῷ λαῷ τούτῳ, καὶ οὐδ' οὕτως εἰσακούσονταί μου, λέγει Κύριος. But the LXX. version is very different verbally, viz.: διὰ φαυλισμὸν χειλέων, διὰ γλώσσης ἑτέρας, ὅτι λαλήσουσι τῷ λαῷ τούτῳ . . . καὶ οὐκ ἠθέλησαν ἀκούειν.

[456] That is, unbelievers who do not speak any of the tongues used.

[457] And who speaks the same language with the preacher.

[458] One form of adoration therefore amongst the early Christians was not only to bend the knees, but also to bring the head to the ground as do the people of the East at the present day.

[459] The prophets or preachers of the church are not to be like the Sibyls and Pythonesses of the heathen, who utter their oracles in a state of frantic excitement.

[460] Amongst the Jews, silence was rigidly imposed upon the women. See the authorities cited, Schoettgen's Hor. Hebr. i. 658.

36 it is a shame for women to speak in the church. *Or hath* the word of God
37 come out from you? or *hath* it reached unto you only? If any man think
   himself to be a *preacher*, or spiritual, let him acknowledge the things that I
38 write unto you, *that they* are the commandments of the Lord."⁶¹ But if any
39 man be ignorant, let him be ignorant. Wherefore, brethren, covet to *preach*,
40 and forbid not to speak with tongues. Let all things be done decently and in
    order.

Ch. XV. "*Now* I declare unto you, brethren, the Gospel which I preached unto you,
2 which also ye received, and wherein ye stand, by which also ye are saved, if
  ye keep in memory what I preached unto you, unless ye have believed in
3 vain. For I delivered unto you first of all that which I also received"⁶²
4 that Christ died for our sins according to the scriptures (Is. liii. 5, &c.); and
  that he was buried, and that he rose the third day according to the scrip-
5 tures (Ps. xvi. 10, &c.); and that he was seen of Cephas,⁶³ then of the
6 twelve;⁶⁴ after that he was seen of above five hundred brethren at once,⁶⁵
  of whom the greater part remain unto this present, but some *also have* fallen
7,8 asleep. After that he was seen of James;⁶⁶ then of all the Apostles;⁶⁷ and

---

⁶¹ The Apostle here lays claim to inspiration in respect of his writings.

⁶² The Apostle here again asserts that not the doctrines only, but the facts of the Gospel had been divinely communicated to him.

⁶³ So Luke: ἠγέρθη ὁ Κύριος καὶ ὤφθη Σίμωνι. Luke xxiv. 34. But no appearance to Peter singly is recorded in the Gospels. It may have been mentioned, however, in other contemporary accounts (and there were many) of the life of Christ, and Luke may have derived his information from them, or from the mouth of Paul himself.

⁶⁴ The Apostles were called "the Twelve," though at this particular time they were only eleven. The occasions referred to are recorded Luke xxiv. 36, John xx. 19.

⁶⁵ The appearance here referred to was probably that in Galilee, when our Lord showed himself to his disciples there generally. Most of his followers resided in Galilee, where he had principally exercised his ministry, and after his resurrection it was commanded to his disciples to go into Galilee, and that "there they should see him." Matt. xxviii. 10. They saw him accordingly, on the "mountain where Jesus had appointed them." Matt. xxviii. 16. The Eleven Disciples are *particularly* mentioned by Matthew on this occasion, but the very fact that the place appointed was in Galilee, leads us to conclude that the object was to show himself to great numbers.

⁶⁶ This appearance is not recorded in the Gospels at all. The James referred to, is probably James the half-brother of our Lord, and afterwards bishop of Jerusalem, and as such occupying a prominent position. See Fasti Sacri p. 181, No. 1198.

⁶⁷ As St. Paul had before spoken of the Twelve (v. 5), it is likely that he here uses the word in a larger sense. When St. Paul's apostleship was questioned, he asked "Have I not seen Jesus Christ?" 1 Cor. ix. 1, as if no one could claim to be an Apostle who had not seen the Lord after his resurrection. If so, the Apostles here referred to may be those who were specially appointed to spread the Gospel, and had seen the Lord after his resurrection as part of their credentials. Paul has enumerated several of the appearances of our Lord, but they are not the whole. Christ also showed himself to Mary Magdalene (Mark xvi. 9, John xx. 11), and another Mary (Matt. xxviii. 9), and to the two disciples on the way to Emmaus (Mark xvi. 12, Luke xxiv. 13), and to certain disciples at the Sea of Galilee (John xxi. 1), and to the Eleven at his ascension (Luke xxiv. 50, Mark xvi. 19). In fact, our Lord was seen continually during the forty days that intervened between the resurrection and the ascension. Acts i. 3.

9 last of all he was seen of me also,[468] as of one born out of due time; for I
am the least of the Apostles, that am not meet to be called an Apostle,
10 because I persecuted the church of God; but by the grace of God I am what
I am, and his grace which was bestowed upon me was not in vain; but I *have*
laboured more abundantly than they all; yet not I, but the grace of God
11 which was with me. Therefore whether it were I or they, so we preach, and
so ye believed.

12 " Now if Christ be preached that he rose from the dead, how say some
13 among you that there is no resurrection of the dead? But if there be no
14 resurrection of the dead, then is Christ not risen, and if Christ be not risen,
15 then is our preaching vain, and your faith is also vain; yea, and we are
found false witnesses of God, because we have testified of God that he raised
16 up Christ, whom he raised not up, if so be that the dead rise not; for if the
17 dead rise not, then is not Christ *risen;* and if Christ be not *risen,* your faith
18 is vain, ye are yet in your sins; then they also which *have* fallen asleep in
19 Christ are perished. If in this life only we have hope in Christ, we are of all
20 men most miserable. But now is Christ risen from the dead, and become the
21 first fruits of them that slept. For since by man [came] death, by man
22 [came] also the resurrection of the dead; for as in Adam all die, even so in
23 Christ shall all be made alive.[469] But *each* in his own order; Christ the first
24 fruits; afterward they are Christ's at His coming. Then the end, when he
shall deliver up the kingdom to God, even the Father, when he shall have
25 *done away* all rule and all authority and power; for he must reign ' till he
26 hath put all enemies under his feet' (*Ps.* cx. 1).[470] The last enemy that
27 shall be *done away* is death; for ' He'[471] hath put all things under his
feet'[472] (*Ps.* viii. 6).[473] But when he saith all things are put under him,
28 it is manifest that He is excepted, *who* did put all things under him. And
when all things shall be subdued unto him, then shall the Son also himself be
29 subject unto Him that put all things under him, that God may be all in all.

Else what shall they do which are baptized for the dead, if the dead rise not
30 at all? why are they then baptized for the dead?[474] And why stand we in

---

[468] Viz. at the time of his conversion, on the road to Damascus. See ante, p. 51.

[469] As descendants of Adam we all die, but as sons of God and fellow-heirs with Christ we shall all live.

[470] ἄχρις οὗ ἂν θῇ πάντας τοὺς ἐχθροὺς ὑπὸ τοὺς πόδας αὐτοῦ. In the LXX.: ἕως ἂν θῶ τοὺς ἐχθρούς σου ὑποπόδιον τῶν ποδῶν σου.

[471] Viz. God the Father.

[472] Under the feet of Christ.

[473] πάντα γὰρ ὑπέταξεν ὑπὸ τοὺς πόδας αὐτοῦ. In the LXX.: πάντα ὑπέταξας ὑποκάτω τῶν ποδῶν αὐτοῦ. God shall subdue *all* things unto his Son, and therefore death itself shall be subdued at last.

[474] This text has been variously explained, but the only two hypotheses at all admissible appear to be these: 1. Where persons had died unbaptized, it was the custom to substitute a post-mortem vicarious baptism. See Renan's St. Paul, p. 241. 2. In baptism we use *immersion* to signify our death and rising again; but if there be no resurrection, why do we baptize by immersion? The first interpretation has been objected

31 jeopardy every hour? [I protest] by your rejoicing which I have in Christ
32 Jesus our Lord, I die daily. If after the manner of men I have fought with
beasts at Ephesus,[474] what advantageth it to me, if the dead rise not? 'Let
33 us eat and drink; for to-morrow we die' (*Is.* xxii. 13).[476] Be not deceived:
34 'Evil communications corrupt good manners.'[477] Awake to righteousness,
35 and sin not; for some have *an ignorance* of God; I speak this to your
shame.
36 " But some *one* will say, how are the dead raised up? and with what body
37 do they come? Thou fool, that which thou sowest is not quickened, except it
die, and that which thou sowest, thou sowest not that body that shall be, but
38 bare grain, it may chance of wheat, or of some other grain. But God giveth
39 it a body as *he would*,[478] and to every seed *its proper body*.[479] All flesh is not
the same flesh; but there is one flesh of men, another flesh of beasts, another
40 of fishes, and another of birds. There are also celestial bodies, and bodies
terrestrial; but the glory of the celestial is one, and the glory of the
41 terrestrial is another. There is one glory of the sun, and another glory of the
moon, and another glory of the stars, for one star differeth from another star
42 in glory. So also is the resurrection of the dead; it is sown in corruption, it

to us implying the Apostle's approval of a practice that could be of no avail; but the language of the Apostle is merely an argumentum ad homines. "What shall *they* do," i.e. 'How will they justify themselves,' &c. The second interpretation was applicable to the practice throughout the East in that day, though not to the practice in our own country at the present day. Baptism in the East was then by immersion, but now amongst ourselves by sprinkling.

[475] ἐθηριομάχησα ἐν Ἐφέσῳ. There is not the least ground for the hypothesis that Paul had fought with beasts in the literal sense. He tells us himself that he was speaking κατὰ ἄνθρωπον or figuratively. In the same way Ignatius writes, ἀπὸ Συρίας μέχρι Ῥώμης θηριομαχῶ. Ignat. Rom. c. 5. Besides, how, being a Roman citizen, could he have been condemned to the ignominy of fighting with beasts, or how could so remarkable a fact, if it occurred, have been omitted in Luke's narrative? The meaning is, that during the three years that Paul sojourned at Ephesus, the headquarters of idolatry, he had been engaged in continual conflict, on the one hand with the Jews, and on the other with the worshippers of the great goddess Diana. As he states presently " a great door and effectual was opened to him, but there were *many adversaries*." I Cor. xvi. 9. From the bitterness with which his enemies attacked him, it was like fighting with wild beasts; and had he not possessed the greatest tact, and found protection from the respectable and intelligent part of the community, he must long before have succumbed. It was only a few weeks after the date of the Epistle, that the worshippers of Diana broke out into an open riot against Paul, and obliged him to quit the city.

[476] Verbatim from the LXX. So in Herodot. ii. 78: πίνε τε καὶ τέρπευ, ἐσεαι γὰρ ἀποθανὼν τοιοῦτος.

[477] φθείρουσιν ἤθη χρηστὰ ὁμιλίαι κακαί. An iambic verse which Tertullian turns into a loose iambic verse thus:

Bonos corrumpunt mores congressus mali.
Tertull. ad Uxorem i. 8.

Clement of Alexandria calls it ἰαμβεῖον τραγικόν, Strom. i. 14; and Socrates ascribes it to a tragedy of Euripides, Hist. Eccles. iii. 15. But Jerome, Eusebius, Euthalius, and others attribute it to Menander, and refer it to his lost comedy of Thais, and Wetstein cites the following scholium: Μενάνδρου τοῦ κωμικοῦ γνώμη ἐκ Θαΐδι. Versio Syra posterior in margine schol. cod. 10. Possibly it may have been first composed by Euripides and copied from him by Menander.

[478] καθὼς ἠθέλησεν. In Eng. ver. "as it hath pleased him."

[479] ἴδιον σῶμα—not its own identical body, but an appropriate body or a body of the kind that properly belongs to it.

43 is raised in incorruption; it is sown in dishonour, it is raised in glory; it is
44 sown in weakness, it is raised in power; it is sown a natural body; it is
raised a spiritual body. There is a natural body, and there is a spiritual
45 body; and so it is written, 'The first man Adam was made a living soul'
46 (*Gen.* ii. 7);[480] the last Adam[481] was made a quickening spirit. Howbeit
47 that was not first which is spiritual, but that which is natural, and afterward
that which is spiritual. The first man *was* of the earth, earthy; the second
48 man *was* the Lord[482] from heaven. As *was* the earthy, such are they also that
49 are earthy; and as *was* the heavenly, such are they also that are heavenly;
50 and as we have borne the image of the earthy, we shall also bear the image of
the heavenly. *But* this I say, brethren, that flesh and blood cannot inherit
51 the kingdom of God; neither doth corruption inherit incorruption. Behold, I
52 *tell*[483] you a mystery: we shall not all sleep, but we shall all be changed in a
moment, in the twinkling of an eye, at the last trump; for the trumpet shall
53 sound, and the dead shall be raised incorruptible, and we shall be changed;
for this corruptible must put on incorruption, and this mortal must put on
54 immortality. *But* when this corruptible shall have put on incorruption, and
this mortal shall have put on immortality, then shall be brought to pass the
saying that is written, 'Death is swallowed up in victory' (*Is.* xxv. 8).[484]
55 'O death, where is thy sting? O grave, where is thy victory?' (*Hos.* xiii. 14).[485]
56, 57 The sting of death is sin, and the strength of sin is the Law. But thanks be
58 to God, which giveth us the victory through our Lord Jesus Christ. Therefore, my beloved brethren, be ye stedfast, unmoveable, always abounding in
the work of the Lord, *knowing* that your labour is not in vain in the Lord.

Ch. XVI. "Now concerning the collection for the saints, as I *gave* order to the
2 churches of Galatia,[486] even so do ye. Upon the first day of the week[487] let
every one of you lay by him in store, *whatever he* hath prospered, that there
3 be no gatherings when I come. And when I *am present*, whomsoever ye shall
accredit[488] by your letters, them will I send to *carry*[489] your liberality unto
4 Jerusalem; and if it be meet that I go also, they shall go with me.

---

[480] ἐγένετο ὁ πρῶτος ἄνθρωπος Ἀδὰμ εἰς ψυχὴν ζῶσαν. In the LXX. the words are, Ἐγένετο ὁ ἄνθρωπος εἰς ψυχὴν ζῶσαν.

[481] I.e. Christ, the head of the spiritual man, as Adam was of the natural man.

[482] The words ὁ Κύριος are omitted by Griesbach, Lachmann, and Alford.

[483] λέγω. In Eng. ver. "show."

[484] κατεπόθη ὁ θάνατος εἰς νῖκος. In the LXX. the sense only appears: κατέπιεν ὁ θάνατος ἰσχύσας, καὶ πάλιν ἀφεῖλε Κύριος ὁ Θεὸς πᾶν δάκρυον ἀπὸ παντὸς προσώπου, &c. Neither does the citation agree with the present Hebrew text, but it does with the version of Theodotion.

[485] Ποῦ σου, θάνατε, τὸ κέντρον; ποῦ σου, ᾅδη, τὸ νῖκος; In the LXX. the words are, Ποῦ ἡ δίκη σου, θάνατε; ποῦ τὸ κέντρον σου, ᾅδη;

[486] See remarks ante, p. 312.

[487] Why the first day of the week? Because Sunday, as the day of the resurrection, was already kept holy, as it has been ever since. The *Gentiles*, of course, observed the Sunday, but the *Jewish* Christians for some time observed both Saturday and Sunday.

[488] δοκιμάσητε. In Eng. ver. "approve."

[489] ἀπενεγκεῖν. In Eng. ver. "to bring."

5 "Now I will come unto you when I shall *have* passed through Macedonia
6 (for I do pass through Macedonia),[490] and it may be that I will abide, yea, and
7 winter with you, that ye may *forward* me whithersoever I go; for I will not see you now by the way;[491] but I *hope* to tarry a while with you, if the
8, 9 Lord permit; but I *shall* tarry at Ephesus until Pentecost,[492] for a great door and effectual *hath been* opened unto me, and there are many adversaries.

10 "Now if *Timothy* come,[493] see that he be with you without fear, for he
11 worketh the work of the Lord, even as I; let no man, therefore, despise him,[494] but *forward* him in peace, that he may come unto me, for I look for him with the brethren."[495]

12 "*But* as touching our brother Apollos, I greatly *urged*[496] him to come unto you with the brethren, but his will was not at all to come *now*;[497] but he will come when he shall have convenient time.

13, 14 "Watch ye, stand fast in the faith, quit you like men, be strong. Let all your things be done *in love*.

15 "*Now* I beseech you, brethren (ye know the house of Stephanas, that it is the first fruits of Achaia, and that they have *set* themselves to the ministry of
16 the saints), that ye submit yourselves unto such, and to every one that *worketh*
17 with us, and laboureth. But I am glad of the coming of Stephanas and Fortunatus and Achaicus,[498] for they have supplied that which was lacking
18 on your part; for they have refreshed my spirit and yours;[499] therefore acknowledge ye them that are such.

19 "The churches[500] of Asia salute you. Aquila and Priscilla salute you much
20 in the Lord, with the church that is in their house.[501] All the brethren

---

[490] See remarks ante. pp. 362, 371.

[491] ἐν παρόδῳ—i.e. en passant, or en route.

[492] The Apostle was writing at the Passover, or Easter.

[493] See ante, pp. 365, 369, 371.

[494] Timothy at this time was a very young man, and of delicate health. 1 Tim. iv. 12; v. 23.

[495] According to Acts xix. 22, Paul sent "two of those who ministered unto him, viz. Timothy and Erastus;" but though these were the two envoys regularly commissioned, other brethren may have accompanied them.

[496] παρεκάλεσα. In Eng. ver. "desired."

[497] νῦν. In Eng. ver. "at this time."

[498] The names Stephanas, Fortunatus, and Achaicus in ver. 17 seem equivalent to "the house of Stephanas" in ver. 15. We should therefore surmise that Stephanas was the father of Fortunatus and Achaicus. Stephanas had been baptized by Paul himself (1 Cor. i. 16), and was the firstfruits of Achaia (1 Cor. xvi. 15). Fortunatus after the death of Paul was sent by the Corinthian church to the Romans, and brought back with him the letter of Clemens Romanus, which is still extant.

[499] It is not clear what is meant, but as the house of Stephanas was said ver. 15 to have "addicted themselves to the ministry of the saints," i.e. to their relief, and as they are now said to have refreshed Paul's spirit as well as that of the Corinthians, it is probable that Paul, though he would receive no pay from the Corinthian church as such (2 Cor. xi. 9), yet was now assisted by Stephanas and his sons individually.

[500] Paul had been three years at Ephesus, and during that time not only had a church been established in the mother city, but by the instrumentality of the Apostle's followers, though without his personal ministry, various branches had grown up in the neighbouring cities, as at Colosse, Laodicea, Hierapolis, &c.

[501] Divine service, therefore, was performed in the house of Aquila.

21 *salute*[502] you. *Salute ye one another with a holy kiss.*[503] The salutation *by the*
22 *hand* of me, Paul. If any *one* love not the Lord Jesus Christ, let him be
23 Anathema Maran-atha.[504] THE GRACE OF OUR LORD JESUS CHRIST BE WITH
24 YOU. MY LOVE [505] BE WITH YOU ALL IN CHRIST JESUS."[506]

This letter was delivered to Titus with many instructions as to his course of conduct in regulating the Corinthian church, and more particularly with the parting charge both to himself and Trophimus on no account to receive any money at the hands of the Corinthians. The Apostle had many enemies anxiously watching for some handle to impeach his character, and Paul was equally on the alert to guard himself and his followers from the imputation of interested motives. That a Christian minister should so punctiliously refuse any reward or gratuity from the Corinthian church might almost appear harsh and unkind, but it was not want of love towards them, but a necessity laid upon him from the machinations of a malignant faction. Hear what the Apostle afterwards says of himself, and Titus, and Trophimus, in this respect: "For what is it wherein you were inferior to other churches, except it be that I myself *was not burdensome* to you? Forgive me this wrong. Behold, the third time I am ready to come to you, and *I will not be burdensome* to you, for I seek not yours, but you: for the children ought not to lay up for the parents, but the parents for the children; and I will very gladly spend and be spent for you, though the more abundantly I love you, the less I be loved. But granted, that I did not burden you, nevertheless, being crafty, I caught you with guile! Did I *make a gain of you by any of them whom I sent unto you?* I desired *Titus*, and with him I sent a *brother*. Did *Titus make a gain of you?* walk we not in the same spirit, walk we not in the same steps?"[507]

Titus and Trophimus set sail from Ephesus to Corinth about the Passover of A.D. 57, and were accompanied by Stephanas, Fortunatus, and Achaicus.[508] The brethren who still remained with Paul were Apollos,[509] Aquila and Priscilla,[510] Gaius, Aristarchus,[511] and probably Tychicus. With the aid of this faithful band, Paul continued his

---

[502] ἀσπάζονται. In Eng. ver. "greet."

[503] See ante.

[504] 'Anathema' is Greek, and signifies an offering, or victim, or one devoted to destruction. Maranatha is Syriac, and compounded of the words Maran, 'the Lord,' and atha, 'cometh'—מרן אתה As 'anathema' and 'Maranatha' are in different languages, they ought perhaps to be kept separate in the translation; thus, 'If any one love not the Lord Jesus, regard that man as a castaway. The Lord cometh and will judge such.' See Wordsworth.

[505] 'I regard you all with love, though I have spoken to you with severity, and have over threatened the rod.'

[506] As to the authentication of the letter by the closing words in Paul's own hand, see ante, p. 187. The textus receptus closes with the word 'Amen,' but Griesbach inclines to the omission of it. Lachmann regards it as doubtful, Alford brackets it, and Tischendorf positively rejects it. As the same word at the end of the Second Epistle is repudiated by all the critics, it has probably been added without authority at the end of the First Epistle.

[507] 2 Cor. xii. 13-18.

[508] This may be inferred from their not sending any salutation to the Corinthian church, and from the Apostle's directions to treat them with all due respect.

[509] 1 Cor. xvi. 12.

[510] 1 Cor. xvi. 19.

[511] Acts xix. 29.

labours at Ephesus; but such was his anxiety for the welfare of the Corinthian church, that "he had no rest in his spirit," until he knew the result of Titus's mission.[512] The letter which he had written was couched in terms of severity. "What will ye? shall I come unto you with a rod?"[513] and not knowing how it would be received, whether it would bring them into contrition, or would only alienate their affections, he had secret misgivings as to the propriety of the step he had taken, as he afterwards confessed to them, "Though I made you sorry with a letter, I do not repent, though I *was ready to repent*."[514]

One reason assigned by the Apostle to the Corinthians for his intended stay at Ephesus from Passover to Pentecost was, that "a great door and effectual was opened unto him, and there were many enemies."[515] In these words he seems to allude to some extraordinary opportunity of extending the Gospel, and perhaps he had in view the celebration of the famous Ἐφέσια,[516] or Ephesian games, which were now approaching, and would of course bring together a vast concourse of people from all quarters. About the time of the Passover commenced the month Artemisius,[517] or the month of Diana, so called from the annual festival of the goddess observed at that period throughout Greece and Asia.[518] Originally at Ephesus, certain days only of the month had been devoted to the service of the goddess, but eventually a decree was passed that the entire month should be kept sacred. It is remarkable that this decree has descended to modern times. It was found by Chandler, on a slab of white marble, near the aqueduct, having probably been removed from the temple with other materials for the construction of the new work. The preamble of the decree cannot fail to remind the reader of the recorder's speech in the theatre, "Ye men of Ephesus, what man is there that knoweth not how that the city of the Ephesians is a worshipper of the great goddess Diana, and of the image which fell down from Jupiter?"[519] Who can say that the recorder who addressed the populace in the time of Paul did not himself draw the act? The decree ran as follows:[520]—

"To the Ephesian Diana. Forasmuch as it is notorious that not only among the

---

[512] 2 Cor. ii. 12.
[513] 1 Cor. iv. 21.
[514] 2 Cor. vii. 8.
[515] 1 Cor. xvi. 9.
[516] Ἀρτέμιδος Ἀρτεμίσια καὶ Ἐφέσια. Julius Pollux, i. 1. Ἐφέσια ἀγὼν ἐν Ἐφέσῳ ἐπιφανής. Hesych.
[517] Ideler makes Artemisius in the Ephesian calendar correspond to April, Idel. Handb. i. 419; and according to Galen, ix. 80-9 D, Comm. in lib. i. Epim. Hippoc., the month Artemisius commenced at Pergamus at the vernal equinox, and therefore answered to April. But at Antioch it corresponded to *May*. ἐν τῷ Μαίῳ, τῷ καὶ Ἀρτεμισίῳ μηνί. Malala, lib. xii. See Clinton's Fasti Hell. Append. 'Macedonian Months.' And so at Smyrna, for Xanthicus was the month next preceding Artemisius, and the martyrdom of Polycarp, which was in Xanthicus, is placed πρὸ ἑπτὰ Καλανδῶν Μαίων, Martyr. Polycarp. c. 21, which would make Artemisius May. And see note post.

[518] Diana was worshipped in three characters, viz. as Luna in heaven, Diana on earth, and Hecate in Hades.
[519] Acts xix. 35.
[520] The translation is by Chandler, but with corrections. See the original in Boeckh, Corp. Inscrip. No. 2954.

Ephesians, but also everywhere among the Greek nations, temples are consecrated to her, and sacred precincts, and that she hath images and hath altars dedicated to her on account of her plain manifestations of herself, and that, besides, the greatest token of the veneration paid her, a month is called after her name, by us Artemision, by the Macedonians[321] and other Greek nations and their cities, Artemisius, in which month general gatherings and hieromenia are celebrated, and more especially in our own city, the nurse of its own, the Ephesian goddess,—Now the people of Ephesus deeming it proper that the whole month called by her name should be sacred and set apart to the goddess, have resolved by this decree that the observation of it by them be altered. Therefore it is enacted, that the whole month Artemision in all the days of it shall be holy, and that throughout the month there shall be a continued celebration of feasts and the Artemisian festival and the hieromenia, seeing that the entire month is sacred to the goddess; for from this improvement in her worship our city shall receive additional lustre and enjoy perpetual prosperity."

Thus the whole month was one unbroken scene of festivity. There were processions, supplications and sacrifices in the temple, scenic representations in the theatre, athletic exercises and beast-fights in the stadium, and horse-races in the hippodrome without the walls. Besides these varied entertainments, the festival also answered another purpose. Ephesus was the great mart or mercantile resort of Asia, and the annual *fête* of Diana was, in fact, a fair to which buyers and sellers flocked together from all quarters for the interchange of their commodities. Thus religion, business and pleasure all conspired to draw multitudes to the capital, and a strange medley was thus congregated of Jews and Greeks, priests and buffoons, merchants and jockeys, musicians and magicians, conjurors and quacks.[322] The expenses of the games were defrayed either wholly, or nearly so, by the ten Asiarchs, and these superintended the preparations, regulated the order in which the exhibitions should take place, and arranged the other details.

During the revels there appeared upon the scene certain mock personages too curious to be passed over in silence. The gods themselves were represented, and those who personated them received during the festival the honours usually paid to the divinities. In the games at Antioch, in honour of Jupiter (which those at Ephesus, in honour of Diana, no doubt, resembled[323]), there were three characters. First was the Alytarch, the mock Jupiter, or May King, who was appointed by the emperor or his representative; next, the Grammateus, the mock Apollo, recorder or secretary;

---

[321] Observe that the Ephesian month Artemision is here compared with the Macedonian month Artemisius. But according to Ideler, the Macedonian month *Xanthicus*, which preceded Artemisius, began on the 23rd of March (Idel. i. 398), and therefore most nearly corresponded with *April*; and if so, *Artemisius* would correspond most nearly with *May*.

[322] ἦν δὲ τῆς Ἀρτέμιδος ἱερομηνία καὶ μεθυόντων πάντα μεστά, ὥστε καὶ δι' ὅλης νυκτὸς τὴν ἀγορὰν ἄπασαν κατεῖχε πλῆθος ἀνθρώπων. Achill. Tat. lib. vi.

[323] Probably at Ephesus, as at Patræ, a damsel personated the goddess Diana. See Pausan. vii. 18, 7.

and lastly, the Amphithales, the mock Mercury, or minister. An ancient author has given a graphic account of these fooleries, and from this incidental notice is gained a clearer insight into the Pagan doings at their festivals than from many a learned treatise. "At Antioch," says Malala, citing Domninus, "Aphronius was Alytarch, by the appointment of the emperor, an ex-prefect and a citizen of Antioch, who, having put on the dress of the Alytarch, was by day honoured and adored as Jupiter himself, and during the games he did not return home or recline on a bed, but slept upon the ground, in the open air, on the stones and clean rugs and a rush-mat. But he wore a robe glittering with gold, white as snow, and a crown of carbuncles and pearls, and other precious stones, and he held a wand of ivory, and wore white sandals on his feet, &c.

"But the Grammateus, being the first who was elected by the senate and the people, was one Pompeianus Questor by name, of the family of a Roman senator. He also wore a white robe and a crown, all of gold, after the pattern of laurel leaves, whom they honoured and adored as Apollo.

"But the same senate and the people next elected as Amphithales one Casius Illustrius by name, who, in like manner, wore a white robe, all of silk, and a crown woven of laurel leaves, and at his breast a pectoral of gold, which Amphithales they honoured and adored as Mercury."[523]

It has been thought by some that the Grammateus, or recorder, here mentioned, was the same official who harangued in the theatre at Ephesus; and certainly as the Grammateus was the first elected by the senate and people, and was therefore the most popular man of the day, he might very properly, from his influence with the multitude, have stepped forward to appease the tumult; but as at Ephesus, and in other Asiatic cities, the chief magistrate had also the title of recorder, the rebuke in the theatre, accompanied with an authoritative dismissal of the assembly, is with more probability ascribed to the latter personage.[524]

Such were the scenes that were enacted at Ephesus while Titus was on his way to Corinth, in the interval between the Passover and Pentecost, A.D. 57. Such was "the door that was opened" to Paul, and he laboured incessantly to avail himself of the opportunity, by scattering the seeds of the Gospel over the vast field that lay before him. We can picture to ourselves how, night and day, he was either gaining his livelihood by making tents for the assembled multitudes, or was expounding the doctrines of revealed religion in the school of Tyrannus, or the house of Aquila. His zeal at length roused his enemies to action, and brought his life into jeopardy. It must be obvious to all, that no inconsiderable proportion of the Ephesian population was interested, directly or indirectly, in supporting the worship of Diana. Some supplied the sacrifices, some the sacred robes, some "the sounding brass and tinkling cymbal," and some were engaged in the repairs or garniture of the temple. Amongst others, the silversmiths carried on a lucrative trade by the manufacture of silver shrines of Diana,[525] i. e. small models of the temple, containing the image of the goddess.[526] These had hitherto been eagerly purchased—more particularly at the great fair of Ephesus—by some as amulets to protect the wearer from malignant influences, and by others to carry home for the gratification of their families as an exquisitely wrought representation of one of the wonders of the world. Medallions also were struck, exhibiting the temple and image of the goddess, some of which may still be found in the cabinets of the curious. A noted silversmith of the day was one Demetrius, who, by the manufacture of these silver shrines, had made large profits himself and afforded employment to a multitude of workmen. But now that Paul had been nearly three years at Ephesus, the effects of the Gospel were severely felt, not only in the city itself, but throughout all Asia. The worship of the goddess Diana was evidently on the decline, and the sale of the silver shrines was sensibly diminishing. Demetrius had expected an abundant harvest, at least during the *Fair*, but he could scarcely find a purchaser.

It was towards the close of the sacred month that Demetrius, disappointed of his anticipated gains, and stung with rage against Paul as the cause of this injury to his trade, called a meeting of his own workmen, and of others who pursued a similar occupation—all, in short, whose interests, like his own, were at stake, and thus

---

[525] Ἀρτέμιδος, Acts xix. 24, a name of Diana as the Goddess of Health, from ἀρτεμής, 'sanus,' 'incolumis.'

[526] ναοὺς ἀργυροῦς. Acts xix. 24. So, Asclepiades philosophus. . . . deæ cœlestis argenteum breve figmentum quocunque ibat secum solitus efferre. Ammian. Marcell. xxiii. 13. Cf. also the passages following: ἔπεμψαν χρυσοῦς ναοὺς τοῖς Ἀρσινόημασι. Diod. Sic. xx. 14. ναοὺς χρυσοῦς δύο. Diod. Sic. i. 15. ναὸς Ἥρας βραχὺς ἐπὶ τραπέζης τιοῖς πρὸς ἀνατολὰς ἱδρυμένος. Dion Cass. xxxix. 20. These little shrines were carried about by the heathen in their travels, and were set up in their houses, and as Diana of the Ephesians was everywhere worshipped, these shrines were everywhere to be found.

It is scarcely worth while to mention the fanciful theory of some, that Demetrius, described as ἀργυροκόπος, was the moneyer or mint-master, and that by the ναοὺς ἀργυροῦς Ἀρτέμιδος we are to understand pieces of money so called because they were stamped with a representation of the Temple of Diana. See Kuinoel, Acts xix. 24.

addressed them; "Sirs! ye know that by this craft we have our wealth. Moreover ye see and hear, that not alone at Ephesus, but almost throughout all Asia, this Paul hath persuaded and turned away much people, saying, that they are no gods, which are made with hands; so that not only this our craft is in danger to be set at nought, but also that the temple of the great goddess Diana should be despised, and her magnificence should be destroyed, whom all Asia and the world worshippeth."[327] This harangue was responded to by a shout, "Great is Diana of the Ephesians." The illiterate artisans, soured by reduced wages or want of employment, were roused into a state of phrensy, and full of rage they sallied forth into the streets to wreak vengeance on the object of their blind fury. The living mass rolled along, and the thousands of idlers, whom the games had attracted to Ephesus, swelled their numbers at every step, and the whole city was soon in a state of confusion. The rioters at Thessalonica had rushed to the house of Jason to drag forth Paul, who was his inmate, and now the mob of Ephesus made for the house of Aquila, with whom Paul was lodging. They missed their prey; but as Paul tells us that Aquila and Priscilla "had for his life laid down their own necks,"[328] it is likely that these faithful friends, in shielding the Apostle, brought themselves into the most imminent peril. The mob, though baffled of their principal aim, seized on Gaius and Aristarchus, two of Paul's associates, and dragged them away as criminals. A cry was raised, "To the theatre!" and in a moment the torrent poured in that direction.[329] Here was wont to meet the Assembly, before whom were brought charges of impiety,[330] and such was the accusation against the two prisoners, who were to be allowed a mock trial, and then be led to execution. In a few minutes the theatre, vast as it was, was crowded with a dense multitude, and a scene that defies all description followed. Some shouted one thing and some another, for "the more part knew not wherefore they were come together." The Asiarchs, who, during the games exercised high authority, and the recorder of the city who, in a lawful assembly, was president, found their way into the theatre, but the storm was for the present too violent to be controlled.

Where, meanwhile, was Paul? Possessed of courage amounting almost to rashness, and goaded by the reflection that two of his followers were to be martyred in his stead, he was for hastening to the theatre and making his defence; but the disciples took a calmer view, and would not suffer him. Fortunately also the

---

[327] Acts xix. 25–27. That the Ephesian Diana was universally worshipped is remarkably confirmed by Pausanias. Ἐφεσίαν δέ Ἄρτεμιν πόλεις τε νομίζουσιν αἱ πᾶσαι καὶ ἄνδρες ἰδίᾳ θεῶν μάλιστα ἄγουσιν ἐν τιμῇ. αἰτία δέ, ἐμοὶ δοκεῖν, ἐστιν, κ.τ.λ. And he proceeds to assign the causes. Pausan. Messen. iv. 31, 8.

[328] Rom. xvi. 4.

[329] That the theatre was the great rendezvous of large assemblages amongst the Greeks, is evident from numerous passages. Legati a senatu in theatrum, (ut est consuetudo Graeciae,) introducti, legationem, quibus acceperant verbis, peregerunt. Val. Max. ii. 2, 5. See Pausan. vi. 3, 2; Jul. Frontin. iii. 2, 6; Tac. Hist. ii. 80; Jos. Bell. vii. 3, 3. Many other citations to the like effect will be found in Kuinoel, Acts xix. 29.

[330] As in the case of Alcibiades at Athens.

Asiarchs, who, as men of education, and actuated by proper feelings, had learnt to appreciate Paul's character, and were anxious to protect him from popular persecution, sent a messenger to him privately, and strictly charged him not to adventure himself into the theatre.

The Jews, the fellow-countrymen but bitter and constant enemies of Paul, and ever ready to drive home a blow directed by any hand against him, encouraged the outbreak, and thrust themselves into the theatre; but from the cries and imprecations that were heard amid the general din, it was evident that in the opinion of the people, Jews and Christians, who both worshipped one God, were involved in the same criminality. So false an impression, as the Jews deemed it, they would fain remove by an explanation of the real state of the case. There was amongst them one Alexander; the same probably who was afterwards the mischievous antagonist of the Apostle at Rome, and of whom he writes, "Alexander the coppersmith hath laid many evil things to my charge (*the Lord* reward him according to his works), of whom be thou ware also, for he hath greatly withstood our words."[531] As a coppersmith he was connected in trade with Demetrius, and so may have been thought by the Jews to have some influence with the leaders of the multitude, and from his "greatly withstanding the words" of Paul, we may collect that he was a fluent speaker. The Jews, therefore, singled him out as a fit instrument for their purpose, and urged him by persuasion and reproaches to advocate their cause. It was not the most agreeable task, and he was somewhat loth to undertake it, but encouraged by his friends, and bearing a hearty illwill to the Apostle, he at last stood forth, and beckoned with his hand for silence. No sooner, from his physiognomy and accent was he recognized to be a Jew, than the people were thrown into a fresh ferment, and one universal shout rent the air, "Great is Diana of the Ephesians."[532] Those who have witnessed the extraordinary pertinacity of a vast concourse in sustaining a favourite watchword under great political or other excitement, will feel no difficulty in believing the statement, that for the space of two hours the theatre rang only with the cry, "Great is Diana of the Ephesians." Nature at last became exhausted, and after a long day's violence and indulgence of the fiercest passions, their spirits began to flag.

---

[531] 2 Tim. iv. 14, 15. Meyer argues that Alexander was a *Christian*, and that the Jews pushed him forward as a victim to the wrath of the multitude, but the argument used by him, viz. that the words ἤθελεν [Alexander] ἀπολογεῖσθαι show that he was one of those who were accused, does not convince; as the Jews might equally wish to clear themselves from the imputation of being Christians—for the Jews were often confounded with the Christians—and that they had incurred the general odium is evident from the uproar that arose when the people discovered ὅτι Ἰουδαῖός ἐστι. Acts xix. 34. Wieseler also (Chronol. Apost. 55) thinks from the word ἀπολογεῖσθαι (Acts xix. 33) that Alexander as well as Caius and Aristarchus was a *Christian* and intended to plead their apology, and that the Jews were present in the theatre as the enemies of Christianity, the subject of the uproar. But Wieseler's arguments in this case do not carry weight.

[532] So at Smyrna the shout was "Great is Æsculapius!" Aristides cited by F. M. (F. Martin).

CHAP. XIII.] ST. PAUL AT EPHESUS [A.D. 57]

Now was the time for some grave person of acknowledged rank and character, and popular manners and address, to cast oil upon the waters, and tranquillize the storm. Such was the Recorder of Ephesus, the legitimate president of the assembly, and as such entitled to respectful attention. Having somewhat calmed the disorder, he with great adroitness expostulated with them on the day's proceeding—that the honour of the goddess was beyond all question, for were they not at that moment celebrating her festival?—that they ought to "do nothing rashly," that is, not to take the lives of two innocent men as criminals without proof—that their prisoners were neither guilty of sacrilege, nor of blasphemy against the goddess—that if Demetrius and his company had any private complaint to make, the law courts were

---

νεωκόρον οὖσαν. Acts xix. 35. This expression of Luke, that Ephesus was νεωκόρος of Diana, is remarkable. The riot of Demetrius occurred in the reign of Nero, and the term νεωκόρος appears for the first time on the coins of Ephesus under Nero. See Eckhel, ii. 520 (fig. 179).

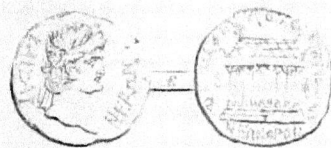

Fig. 179.—Coin of Nero. From J. Y. Akerman.
Obv. Head of Nero, with the legend Νέρων Καῖσαρ (Nero Cæsar).—Rev. Temple of Diana, with the legend Ἐφ. Ἀυικιδ. Ἀσσονία. Ἀιθαινας, Νεωκόρος (Of the Ephesians Neocori. Aichinetes Avola Proconsul).

The word νεωκόρος signifies the person charged with the conduct of worship, and answers in some degree to our 'sacrist' or 'warden.' Ephesus above all other cities claimed the honour of regulating the worship of Diana, and was therefore called the Sacrist or Warden of Diana.

But Ephesus was not only νεωκόρος of Diana, but was often, from this period forward, designated νεωκόρος in quite a different sense, viz. as having been allowed the privilege (which conferred important rights) of erecting a temple to the reigning Emperor as *deus præsens*, and celebrating games in his honour. The use of νεωκόρος in the latter sense originated in the time of Nero, and until the last of the Twelve Cæsars was restricted to Ephesus, but was afterwards extended to other cities. The privilege was granted by a decree of the senate.

In a coin of Caracalla and Geta (fig. 180) we find the νεωκόρος of the Emperors and νεωκόρος Ἀρτέμιδος combined. Thus on the obverse we have Νέοι Ἥλιοι (the new suns, viz. Caracalla and Geta), and on the reverse Ἐφεσίων τρις νεωκόρων καὶ τῆς Ἀρτέμιδος (Of the Ephesians thrice Neocori and of Diana). Eckhel, ii. 520.

Fig. 180.—Reverse of a coin. From Calmet.

Ephesus attained the distinction of being νεωκόρος to the Emperor no less than four times (fig. 181)—the only city that could make this boast.

Fig. 181.—Reverse of a coin. From Calmet. With legend Ἐφεσίων Δ. Νεωκόρων. It appears correct in appearing (?) the Ephesians four times Neocori. In another coin is the legend Ἐφεσίων πρῶτοι Ἀσιας νεωκόροι (Of the Ephesians, the only Neocori of the fourth time). Eckhel, ii. 520. The four temples on the coin of Nero represent apparently the temples erected in honour of the four emperors whose figures are seen within the temples.

It has been much disputed whether the inscriptions νεωκόρος, δίς, τρίς, τετράκις indicate that Ephesus had been honoured by so many different Emperors, or so many times by one

open; but if the public interests were involved, there was the Assembly which sat at stated periods, or might be lawfully convened—that their present doings amounted to a breach of the peace, an offence severely punishable by the Roman law.[534] "Men of Ephesus!" he said, "what man is there that knoweth not how that the city of the Ephesians is a worshipper of the great goddess, Diana,[535] and of the image which fell down from Jupiter?[536] Seeing, then, that these things cannot be spoken against, ye ought to be quiet and to do nothing rashly; for ye have brought thither these men, which are neither guilty of sacrilege, nor yet blasphemers of your goddess. Wherefore, if Demetrius, and the craftsmen which are with him, have a matter against any man, there are assizes[537] and there are proconsuls;[538] let them implead

---

Emperor. There are difficulties in the way of each theory. The reader will find the subject discussed in the Académie des Inscriptions, and more particularly in vol. ii. p. 407 of that work.

[534] Legis Juliae de vi privata crimen committitur, cum coetum aliquis et concursum fecisse dicitur, quo minus quis in jus produceretur, Dig. xlviii. 7, 4. And, Qui coetum et concursum fecerit, capitale sit. Seneca, Controv. iii. 8. Qui coetum et concursum fecerit, capite puniatur. Sulp. Victor. Instit. Orat., cited by Wetstein, Acts xix. 40. And the advice of Maecenas to Augustus was, πρῶτον μὲν οἱ δῆμοι μήτε εἰρωαὶ τινος ἑστωσαν, μήτε ἐς ἐκκλησίαν τοπαράπαν φοιτάωσαν. Dion, lii. 30.

[535] So Ὀμνύω τε τὴν πάτριον ἡμῖν θεὸν τὴν μεγάλην Ἐφεσίαν Ἄρτεμιν, Xenoph. Eph. i.; and Τῆς μεγάλης θεὸς Ἀρτέμιδος πρὸ πόλεως, Inscription at Ephesus, Boeckh, 2963; and ἡ δέ Ἄρτεμις ἡ μεγάλη θεός. Achilles Tat. lib. viii.

[536] τοῦ Διοπετοῦς. Acts xix. 35. It was a common notion among the heathen that their most sacred images had fallen from heaven. φήμη δὲ ἐν αὐτῷ [Minerva at Athens] ἔχει πεσεῖν ἐκ τοῦ οὐρανοῦ. Pausan. Attic. i. 26, 7. αὐτὸ μέν τὰ ἄγαλμα [Cybele of Pessinus] διοπετές, ὡς λέγουσιν. Herodian, i. 11. See other passages cited by Kuinoel, Acts xix. 35; Wetstein, ib.; Appian, Mithrid. liii. According to Pausanias in one place, the Ephesian image was first set up by the Amazons: φήμην τὸ ἄγαλμα ἔχουσιν ἱδρύσασθαι, Pausan. Messen. iv. 31, 6. But afterwards he expresses an opinion that the Ephesian Diana was of greater antiquity. Pausan. Eliac. vii. 2, 4. And see Plin. N. H. xvi. 79.

[537] ἀγοραῖοι [ἡμέραι] ἄγονται. Acts xix. 38. This expression is illustrated by Strabo, who speaking of proconsular Asia, writes that τοὺς Ῥωμαίους μὴ κατὰ φύλα διελεῖν αὐτούς, ἀλλ' ἕτερον τρόπον διατάξαι τὰς διοικήσεις, ἐν αἷς τὰς ἀγοραίους ποιοῦνται καὶ τὰς δικαιοδοσίας. Strabo, xiii. 4 (p. 156, Tauchnitz). See Kuinoel, Acts xix. 38.

[538] ἀνθύπατοί εἰσιν. Acts xix. 38. The expression is very striking, as Asia was ordinarily governed by *one proconsul*; and yet Luke is so exact and accurate, that there must have existed some ground for substituting the plural for the singular number. In A.D. 54, when Paul arrived at Ephesus, Junius Silanus was proconsul, but he was poisoned at the instance of Agrippina, the mother of Nero, by P. Celer, a Roman knight, and Helius, an imperial freedman, the two procurators of Asia (Tac. Ann. xiii. 1), and it would seem that the reward for their villany was the joint proconsulship. It is certain that Celer (and no doubt Helius also) remained at Ephesus during the whole or nearly the whole period of Paul's sojourn there (A.D. 54–57), for on Celer's return he was accused by the provincials, and this was at the close of A.D. 57 (Tac. Ann. xiii. 33), and we do not hear of Helius at Rome until long after, viz. in A.D. 66. Dion, lxiii. 12; Suet. Nero, 23. If Celer and Helius were not proconsuls during Paul's ministry at Ephesus, who could have filled the office? for there is no trace in history of any other proconsul. The only names that can be suggested are Suilius and Aviola, but though Suilius was some time proconsul, yet in A.D. 58 his proconsulship had been almost forgotten, and was raked up as an old story to multiply the charges against him: repertique accusatores 'direptos socios' cum Suilius Asiam regeret. Tac. Ann. xiii. 43. The name of Aviola as proconsul of Asia is found on coins only in connection with the head of Nero or Poppaea or Messalina. Νέρων Καισαρ + Αιχμοκλη Αουιολα Ανθυπατω. Εφ. νεωκορων, and again Μεσσαλινα + Αουιολα Μη . . . Αιχμοκλη Εφε. and again Νερων Ποππαια + Αουιολα Ανθυπατω Αιχμο . . . Εφε. Eckhel, ii. 519. The head of Nero

one another. But if ye enquire any thing concerning other matters, it shall be determined in the regular assembly;[349] for we are in danger to be called in question for this day's uproar, there being no cause whereby we may give an account of this concourse."[340] With these words the Recorder, as if he had presided in a constitutional meeting, and with an air of authority, declared the assembly to be dissolved. The gentle rebuke had its effect. Reason and reflection returned, and gradually the multitude melted away to their homes; and Ephesus was once more in a state of comparative repose.

We have seen that the Recorder and Asiarchs were present; but where were the Proconsuls? Where was the strong arm of the law to put down the riot? It has been mentioned that Ælius and Celer, the imperial Procurators, had recently assassinated Junius Silanus, the Proconsul, and had succeeded to his office. Their crime had not escaped detection,[341] and with this stigma upon them they may not have possessed the hardihood to present themselves in public at the Ephesian games, or perhaps had proceeded on their annual circuit to some distant part of the province, or were absent from other accidental circumstances.[342]

The short narrative by St. Luke of the occurrences at Ephesus has furnished only a few particulars; but enough has been said to show that Paul was exposed to the utmost danger. Aquila and Priscilla had laid down their own necks for him,—the whole city was in confusion—Paul, in the distraction of the moment, would have rushed into the theatre—the disciples laid constraint upon him—the Asiarchs sent him a message. The Apostle escaped with his life; but the scene of violence and the abrupt determination of so successful a career caused him great distress of mind, from which he did not recover for many weeks, not, indeed, till Titus returned to him in Macedonia with the gratifying intelligence of the repentance of the Corinthian church, and their devotion to his cause. When shortly after that event he wrote the Second Epistle to the Corinthians, his thoughts were still full of the tumult at Ephesus; and at the very opening of the letter, he particularly refers to it, and solemnly calls upon the Corinthians to offer a public thanksgiving to God for his

would indicate only some time between A.D. 54–68, but the other names show that he held the proconsulship twice; once when Messalina was empress, and therefore not later than A.D. 48, the date of her death (Fasti Sacri, p. 284, No. 1717), and again when Poppæa was empress, and therefore not before the spring of A.D. 62, when Nero married Poppæa. Fasti Sacri, p. 326, No. 1921.

[339] ἐν τῇ ἐννόμῳ ἐκκλησίᾳ. So Lucian, Deor. Concil. xiv, ἐκκλησίας ἐννόμου ἀγομένης ἐν ὑμῖν ἱσταμένου. So Aristides speaks of the first meeting of a similar assembly at Smyrna on New Year's Day; ἱσταμένου τοῦ ἔτους καὶ γιγνομένης ἐκκλησίας τῆς πρώτης. Arist. Orat. xxvii. The concourse in the theatre of Ephesus was not on one of the stated days, and would be considered a tumult.

[340] Acts xix. 35–40.

[341] Apertius quam ut celarent. Tac. Ann. xiii. 1.

[342] The usual time for holding the assizes at Ephesus was about the middle of February; Ἰδοὺς Φεβρουαρίους διακαθεζόμενοί μοι ἐν Ἐφέσῳ. Jos. Ant. xvi. 6, 7. This probably was the commencement of the legal year, and after dispatching the business at Ephesus, the proconsul proceeded to the other assize towns in order, as Smyrna, &c.

deliverance. "We would not, brethren, have you ignorant of our trouble which came to us in *Asia*, that we were pressed out of measure, above strength, insomuch that we *despaired even of life*; nay, we had the *sentence of death* in ourselves, that we should not trust in ourselves, but in God which raiseth the dead; who delivered us from so great a death, and doth deliver; in whom we trust that he will yet deliver us; ye also helping together by prayer for us, that for the gift bestowed upon us by the means of many persons, thanks may be given by many on our behalf."[343] It was almost matter of course with a Jew of that day upon being rescued from any imminent danger, to take the vow of a Nazarite, namely, for thirty days to let the hair grow, and abstain from wine, and at the expiration of that period to shear the head, and when next at Jerusalem to shave the head and offer the accustomed sacrifices. Paul had taken such a vow at Corinth, and had afterwards completed it at Jerusalem, and he now expressed in the same way his thankfulness to God for so great a deliverance, and we shall see that on reaching Jerusalem the following year he joined with four other Nazarites in paying the usual offerings. His abstinence on this occasion may have contributed somewhat to that depression of the animal spirits which so characterizes the Second Epistle to the Corinthians, written not long after.

[343] 2 Cor. i. 8–11.

Fig. 182.—*An ædicula, or miniature shrine, of Cybele, in illustration of the silver shrines of Diana of Ephesus. The above ædicula was found at Athens, and is of terra-cotta, the more common material. From Dictionnaire des Antiquités.*

END OF VOL. I.

LONDON: PRINTED BY WILLIAM CLOWES AND SONS, STAMFORD STREET AND CHARING CROSS

www.ingramcontent.com/pod-product-compliance
Lightning Source LLC
Chambersburg PA
CBHW050351100426
42734CB00041B/3006